INTRODUCTION TO MIDDLE EASTERN LAW

Introduction to Middle Eastern Law

CHIBLI MALLAT

OXFORD
UNIVERSITY PRESS

OXFORD
UNIVERSITY PRESS

Great Clarendon Street, Oxford OX2 6DP

Oxford University Press is a department of the University of Oxford.
It furthers the University's objective of excellence in research, scholarship,
and education by publishing worldwide in

Oxford New York

Auckland Cape Town Dar es Salaam Hong Kong Karachi
Kuala Lumpur Madrid Melbourne Mexico City Nairobi
New Delhi Shanghai Taipei Toronto

With offices in

Argentina Austria Brazil Chile Czech Republic France Greece
Guatemala Hungary Italy Japan Poland Portugal Singapore
South Korea Switzerland Thailand Turkey Ukraine Vietnam

Oxford is a registered trade mark of Oxford University Press
in the UK and in certain other countries

Published in the United States
by Oxford University Press Inc., New York

British Library Cataloguing in Publication Data

Data available

Library of Congress Cataloging in Publication Data

Mallat, Chibli.
Introduction to Middle Eastern Law / Chibli Mallat.
   p. cm.
Includes bibliographical references and index.
ISBN-13: 978–0–19–923049–5
   1. Law—Middle East—History.   2. Constitutional Law—Middle East.
I. Title.
KMC79.M35 2007
349.56—dc22   2007012837

Typeset by Newgen Imaging Systems (P) Ltd., Chennai, India
Printed in Great Britain
on acid-free paper by
Biddles Ltd., King's Lynn

ISBN 978–0–19–923049–5

1 3 5 7 9 10 8 6 4 2

Preface

The origins of this book lie in a suggestion by the late Albert Hourani almost two decades ago. It is dedicated to his memory.

Acknowledgments

Considering the time needed to complete this volume, even a skimpy acknowledgment of the help of so many friends and colleagues during its slow progress would try the reader's patience. I should at least thank the institutions that have hosted me over the years, the School of Oriental and African Studies (SOAS) at London University, Saint Joseph's University (USJ) in Beirut, and in the last two years Yale Law School and Princeton University. Some outstanding scholars extended unfailing friendship and support through my academic life: at SOAS, the late John Wansbrough, Tony Allan, Andrew Allen (now at the English bar), and Robin Ostle (now at Oxford); at USJ, John Donohue, Sélim Abou, and René Chamussy; at Yale, Owen Fiss, Paul Kahn, and Harold Koh; at Princeton, John Borneman, Kim Lane Scheppele, and Anne-Marie Slaughter. Unnamed reviewers at Oxford University Press offered precious advice, as did the editorial team in the law section of OUP. I am particularly grateful to Gwen Booth, Fiona Stables, and Virginia Williams, and to John Louth, who encouraged me to complete the book. Chimène Philibert, David Leffler, and Misan Okumi helped put the text, bibliography, and footnotes into final shape. To them, as to so many others not mentioned here, all my gratitude. I am of course solely responsible for the book's many shortcomings.

Some chapters in this *Introduction* have been published in various forms, in part or in totality, as articles in journals or chapters in books. I am grateful to the editors for their permission to use the early versions. Chapter 2, on the formation of Middle Eastern Law, originally appeared as 'From Islamic to Middle Eastern law: a restatement of the field', *American Journal of Comparative Law*, 2003:4, Part 1, 699–750, Part 2, 2004:1, 209–86. Chapter 4, on constitutional law, appeared as 'On the specificity of Middle Eastern constitutionalism', *Case Western Journal of International Law*, 38, 2006, 13–57. Parts of Chapter 5, on constitutional review, appeared as 'Constitutional law in the Middle East: the emergence of judicial power', SOAS Law Department Working Paper in February 1993, and in Eugene Cotran and Chibli Mallat, eds, *Yearbook of Islamic and Middle Eastern law*, 1994, 85–108. Parts of Chapter 8, on civil law, were published in French as 'Retour sur un monument législatif: la Majalla ottomane', in *Le Droit en Mouvement- Mélanges en Hommage à Méliné Topakian*, Beirut, PUSJ, 2005, 187–206. Chapter 9 on commercial law appeared as 'Commercial law in the

Middle East between classical transactions and modern business', *American Journal of Comparative Law*, 2000, 81–141. An earlier version of Chapter 10 on family law appeared as 'The search for equality in Middle Eastern family law', *al-Abhath* (American University of Beirut), 48–9, 2000–1, 7–63.

Transliteration, dates, sources

Transliteration. I use the standard transliteration of non-Western words adopted by specialized journals, but the diacritics are omitted, except in the Bibliography. Scholars familiar with Arabic and Persian will recognize the words even without the diacritics, and this work is intended to encourage the interest of non-Middle East specialists, especially jurists, who do not speak its languages. To avoid hampering the flow with too many non-English words, while keeping the original available, I lightened the text by placing as many non-Western words and phrases as possible in the footnotes. The number of the footnote is italicized in that case. Also, the Arabic '*al al-ta'rif*' was sometimes dropped for aural convenience, for example, Sarakhsi instead of al-Sarakhsi, and *Mabsut* instead of *al-Mabsut*.

Dates. Dates are given in the Hijri calendar (AH), which starts in 622 of the so-called Common Era, followed by the corresponding date in the Christian Gregorian/Common Era (CE). When only one unspecified date appears, reference is to the CE.

Sources and bibliography. In addition to ascertaining the source, references have been limited to those articles, books, and journals that either are authoritative in the field, or offer a useful introduction to the reader.

Princeton
November 2006

Summary Contents

Contents

Table of Cases, Legislation, Verses, *and* Hadith

1. *Cases.* For Western decisions, the model of citation common in the country and court concerned is followed. There is no unified mode of citation for Middle Eastern cases, classical or contemporary. Cases are divided here in pre-modern and modern, with the pre-modern cases arranged chronologically, and the modern cases referenced on a national basis.
2. *Legislation.* Includes codes, restatements and 'customary' lawbooks, for which full references can be found in the bibliography. It is also divided into pre-modern and modern texts.
3. *Qur'anic and Biblical verses.* For the Qur'an, citation follows chapter (*sura*) and verse (*aya*). For the Bible, citation refers to the New and Old Testament books, followed by the verse number.
4. *Hadith*, both Sunni and Shi'i (see chapter 2). Many Sunni *hadith*s are accepted by the Shi'is, but Shi'is also have their own *hadith*. The full *hadith* is generally mentioned. In the book, the sources for the *hadith* considerably. For comprehensive compilations of Sunni *hadith*, see in bibliography, A. J. Wensinck, *Concordance et indices de la tradition musulmane.* For Shi'i hadith, al-Hurr al-'Amili, *Wasa'el al-Shi'a.*

Main abbreviations in table and book

CH, Code of Hammurabi, followed by paragraph, Driver and Miles edition
ECC, Egyptian Civil Code
ICC, Iranian Civil Code
JCC, Jordanian Civil Code
Majalla, Ottoman Majalla (*Majallat al-ahkam al-'adliyya*, literally the journal of judicial rules), see chapter 9
Q, Qur'an, standard editions with my translation
SCC, Supreme Constitutional Court of Egypt
SR, *Syrisch-Römisches Rechtsbuch* (Syro-Roman Code), Bruns and Sachau edition, Arabic version, followed by article
TP, *Travaux Préparatoires*
AFLP, Arab Family Law Project, see chapter 10
MAFQ, *al-Majalla al-'arabiyya lil-fiqh wal-qada'* (The Arab journal of jurisprudence and courts)

1. CASES

Pre-modern cases

Mesopotamia

Jerusalem, late Mamluk

Tripoli, early Ottoman

Safad, early Ottoman

Modern cases

Other than Middle East

International courts

3. VERSES

4. HADITH

1

Introduction: The Autonomy of Middle Eastern Law

Al-shar' wal-'aql mutatabiqan.

Mulla Sadra[1]

The present work seeks to define a field of study called 'Middle Eastern law'.

The book consists of eleven chapters, in addition to the preface and tables. I had constantly in mind the remarkable *Introduction to comparative law* by Konrad Zweigert and Hein Kötz,[2] from whom derives one of the central threads running through this book, namely 'that Middle Eastern law is distinct in terms of style'. Unlike the German colleagues' seminal work, the scope of this *Introduction to Middle Eastern law* goes beyond contracts and obligations to include family, constitutional, criminal, and commercial law. But the focus is on style throughout the work, as a leitmotif of the distinctiveness of Middle Eastern law.

In an attempt to render the book more accessible and hopefully more pleasant to read, key theses are tested in each of the eleven chapters. Some legal topics, notably procedure, are not addressed systematically. Procedure as black-letter law and practice is difficult to encompass in any meaningful way for the Middle East at large. Procedure as substantive law (Owen Fiss) is something else. 'Due process' is key to the definition of the rule of law in any country, and suffuses each court decision discussed in this book. 'Substantive procedure' will appear in the course of a systematic attention to the way courts decide cases across the board, but I confess sharing Montesquieu's intellectual distaste for procedure in the restricted sense so essential to daily practice.[3]

---

[1] 'Law conforms with reason', Sadr al-Din al-Shirazi (known as Mulla Sadra, d. 1640), *Al-Hikma al-muta'aliya fil-asfar al-'aqliyya al-arba'a* (The four philosophical voyages), Qum, n.d., 9 vols, i, 12.

[2] Konrad Zweigert and Hein Kötz, *Einführung in die Rechtsvergleichung auf dem Gebiete des Privatrechts*, 1st German edn, vol. 2, *Institutionen*, 1969, vol. 1, *Grundlagen*, 1971. English translation by Tony Weir at Oxford University Press, starting 1977 in 2 vols, then in 3rd rev. edn., 1998, which I use in this book.

[3] 'Quant à mon métier de président, j'avais le coeur très droit; je comprenais assez les questions en elles-mêmes; mais, quant à la procédure, je n'y entendais rien; mais, ce qui m'en dégoûtait le plus, c'est que je voyais à des bêtes ce même talent qui me fuyait, pour ainsi dire.' Montesquieu, *Pensées*, in *Oeuvres complètes* (Paris, 1964) 854.

Some of the conclusions will be taken up again in the epilogue, but it may be useful to present them from the outset as a set of threads through the vast field embraced in the analysis.

The present synopsis covers each of the ten following chapters, then provides a brief note on the nature, philosophy, or 'spirit' of Middle Eastern law, its basic similarity with all other legal families, and its autonomy as a legal system.

The first part of the book, on legal history, follows 'the formation of Middle Eastern law' from earliest times, despite the constraints scholarship faces in the large number of jurisdictions, the difficulty of accessing sources, the multitude of mostly dead languages, and the unique historical depth and variety of Middle Eastern law. It introduces the concepts of *shari'a*, *fiqh*, and *qanun*, which all mean 'law', and dwells on Islamic law as the 'common law' of the Middle East in a long historical perspective. Islamic law is set in history against a wider Middle Eastern legal continuum that starts with Hammurabi and acquires a unique profile in the various manifestations of the law in the classical Islamic age. The chapter analyses contrasting source-material forming the Middle Eastern legal tapestry across the ages, with an imprimatur to be found also in other prominent religious laws, notably those of the Christian and Jewish Near Eastern communities. In its most sophisticated form, Islamic law is primarily developed in *fiqh* books, which are long-winded compendia with a distinct flavour and style, and a comprehensive breadth. Legal literature also includes more limited texts: formulae, deeds, and contracts, fatwas and judgments, manuals for judges and jurisconsults, as well as relevant works of history and *belles-lettres*. After presenting expressive samples from each, the chapter discusses customary law and schools of law, and concludes with a tentative historical periodization of the field. It closes on an advocacy: the study of Islamic/Middle Eastern law in its 'thousand planes' from the early Babylonian records to the present day.

The book is then divided in two parts, on public and private law respectively. Public law opens with a brief introduction to modern Middle Eastern political history (Chapter 3), and includes chapters on constitutional law (Chapter 4), constitutional review (Chapter 5), and criminal and administrative law (Chapter 6). Private law also includes four chapters, starting with an introduction to the age of codification (Chapter 7). The treatment then covers civil (Chapter 8), commercial (Chapter 9), and family law (Chapter 10).

Chapter 4 dwells on constitutional law in the French academic sense of the term, which is akin to political science or government, and discusses constitutions and the organization of state power in modern nation-states of the Middle East. One section investigates the persistent quest for legal and political unity, its overwhelming failure, and its limited successes. The next section discusses constitutionalism, Islamic law, and democracy, in an effort to put some order into a wide-ranging and unruly debate. A third section attempts to explain some of the deeper constitutional Middle East traits through the contrast between personal and territorial law underlying the public law thread of constitutionalism in the region.

Chapter 5 looks at constitutional law from the perspective of judicial review. Constitutional review is a novelty in the Middle East, and the fledgling experiment is a hybrid in comparative terms: broadly speaking, constitutional courts in some countries follow the US model with cases querying legislation whose constitutionality is doubted. Constitutional councils, in contrast, examine the constitutionality of legislation recently passed upon the demand of a limited number of postulants, usually prominent political actors. The latter review, which follows the French model introduced by the 1958 constitution of the Fifth Republic, does not arise in the case of normal litigation. The common thread in both types of review is the constitution understood as canonical text, and/or Islamic law as the superior law of the land in a significant number of jurisdictions.

Only for didactic purposes can constitutional review be separated from judicial review at large. Chapter 6 examines the more traditional adjudication of criminal and administrative cases, and shows the difficulty for an effective judiciary to come of age in protecting the citizen's rights when the state's executive branch is involved.

Following a brief introductory chapter on the importance of codification and case-law for the study of private law (Chapter 7), Chapter 8 discusses civil law, understood as the law of obligations and torts. Civil codes in the Middle East are peculiar in two ways: they have proved more resilient than their public law counterparts, and modern civil codes function as stable institutions offering legal anchors which transcend political changes. Civil codes also stand at the confluence of Islamic law and Western codification. The chapter follows through the two basic model codes which are represented by the Ottoman Majalla and the Egyptian Civil Code, and which have dominated the law of daily transactions from the late nineteenth century to date. These legal 'monuments' are the more significant since they made a formal break with a tradition of Islamic law that did not know any serious codification. Whether the break was only formal is the other question which the chapter pursues, as it tries to frame in legal terms the challenge offered to this codification by those who present local codes as alien to the substance of a deep-rooted tradition. In the dialectic between classical Islamic law and contemporary challenges, some milestones emerge beyond the technical discussion which is carried through the large wealth of statutes and codes available since the Ottoman, Arab, and Persian early prototypes.

'No answer is what the wrong question begets.'[4] Chapter 9, on commercial law, was the hardest to integrate into the book because of the difficulty of finding a distinctive Middle Eastern flavour in the field: witness all the Western lawyers who work in the Gulf with little or no sense of Arabic and/or the local legal system. The thesis in the chapter is that commercial law is the one field where borrowing from the West has taken place most systematically and felicitously. This thesis is illustrated at the outset by a sample of high court decisions across the Middle East.

---

[4] John Hart Ely, *Democracy and distrust* (Cambridge, Mass., 1980) 43, quoting Alexander Bickel.

These decisions will naturally be familiar to any commercial lawyer in the world. The argument proceeds with a historical examination of the classical model and its long-term characteristics, up until the first systematic codification in the Ottoman Empire. It concludes by focusing on the resurgence of the tradition in some controversial areas developing in the 'emerging' markets of the region: agency, company law—including 'Islamic banking'—and commercial arbitration.

Chapter 10 introduces family law from the point of view of legislative reform and the position of women in the legal system. The central thesis sees Alexis de Tocqueville's concept of the 'age of equality' as the dominant paradigm in modern Middle Eastern law. The thrust of the chapter is that contemporary family law in the region is driven by legislative efforts to set increased equality between men and women, against a classical age which was overwhelmingly non-egalitarian. The equality debate in Muslim family law is addressed in the course of an analysis of marriage, divorce, and child custody, and is pursued in the light of legislation and legislative debates, as well as court decisions.

The epilogue addresses the difficulty of lawyering for justice in the contemporary Middle East, some of the happier antecedents in the classical age, and the future of law in the region.

On the Nature of Middle Eastern Law

I mentioned Montesquieu. This *Introduction* covers a wide historical and territorial span, but it does not pretend to distil the 'spirit' of Middle Eastern law like the great French jurist's eighteenth-century masterpiece. It is a book for lawyers rather than for philosophers or political scientists, although hopefully of interest to the latter as well. The book will have achieved its objectives if it helps to identify the specific features of a 'legal family', like the Common law or the Civil law, which can be coherently described as 'Middle Eastern'.

However much one tries to avoid essentialism, a few introductory remarks on the 'nature', 'spirit', or 'philosophy' of Middle Eastern law are in order.

First, what Middle Eastern law is *not*. Middle Eastern law is no different from any other law on earth. Lawyers in the Middle East recognize the language of the law, in the same way as philosophers, physicists, or anthropologists recognize the language of their own disciplines. Law has its own words and turns of phrase, a style that any person recognizes in law's language. Law comes with institutions, central amongst which are the legislator, divine or prophetic law-giver, an elected parliament or a dictatorial government, and the courts, whose judges say how the law applies. Enforcement is key, and is a given. Law is binding. When its rule is not binding through the enforcement power entrusted by state and society to the courts, it becomes something else that intersects with religion, political science, or ethics, but fails in its essential test as discipline. Court decisions are therefore central to this work.

These three traits, style, institutions, enforcement, are the a priori mainstay of this book. I have often emphasized, against lingering perceptions that law in the region is a mysterious and irrational phenomenon, that Middle Eastern law is not different from law anywhere else. This is why the book focuses on legal language as it gets expressed in legal texts by law's privileged agents, mostly courts, but also by its other professional exponents: legislators, lawyers, academic teachers, and notary-publics. I also take as granted that law, in the Middle East as elsewhere, is binding and enforced by the legitimate force of the state if necessary.

Once the normal purview of Middle Eastern law is accepted, one can look into specificities and exceptions. Some of the characteristics of Middle Eastern law come from its history, with a uniquely deep and continuous written record. No other active law on earth has a similar depth of *recorded* history. English law, which offers the best available records in the West, goes back a millennium at most. Roman law, of course, is deeper, but few will argue that, Canon law and the Vatican excepted, it is still central nowadays as a living legal family.

Another characteristic is the dominant *religious* expression one finds in Middle Eastern law, and its main historical component, Islamic law. This religious characteristic, as Joseph Schacht noted half a century ago, results in a ladder of value-judgments which are inherently opposed to a universal divide between law and non-law, or legality and illegality: 'The central feature that makes Islamic religious law what it is, that guarantees its unity in all its diversity, is the assessing of all human acts and relationships, including those which we call legal, from the point of view of the concepts obligatory/ recommended/ indifferent/ reprehensible/ forbidden'.[5]

Too much may have been built on this curious five terms' ladder, which has little to do with the law as lawyers know it. In the great treatises, from time to time such a graded legitimacy can be found, with unclear dispositions considered reprehensible or recommended. This is when the jurist is in doubt. But if one replaces 'recommended' with the word 'preferred', and 'reprehensible' with 'doubtful', there is nothing which is characteristically Islamic, or indeed legal, about this gradation. In the same way that law is by definition binding, it operates in a binary mode: legal or illegal. This postulate is also true for Islamic and Middle Eastern law. Shatibi (d. 1388), one of the great classical theoreticians of the law, saw the profound incoherence of the gradation: 'The prolegomena in the study of this science [jurisprudence], and the arguments adduced, can only be determinate . . . As for the rule being obligatory, or recommended, or indifferent, or reprehensible, or forbidden, it has no place in jurisprudence'. 'Those who introduce it' in our discipline, he concludes, 'have their science mixed up'.[6]

---

[5] Joseph Schacht (d. 1969), *Introduction to Islamic law* (Oxford, 1964) 200. The Arabic terms are *wajeb, mandub, mubah* (indifferent, literally permitted), *makruh, muharram*; see e.g. 'Abd al-Wahhab Khallaf (d. 1956), *'Ilm usul al-fiqh* (Jurisprudence) (7th edn, Cairo, 1956) 118–32, and the definition of *fiqh* by Ibn Khaldun (d. 1406), *al-Muqaddima*, cited in Chapter 2, text accompanying n. 475.

[6] Ibrahim ibn Musa al-Shatibi, *al-Muwafaqat*, 'Abdallah Daraz ed. (Beirut, 1975, 4 vols, vol. 1) 34–5. Determinate, determined, decisive: *qat'iyya*.

If this moral gradation cannot be particularly useful in ascribing some special character to Islamic law as a 'religious' law, the religious dimension remains important to understanding law in the Middle East in two ways: one is historical, with sources being naturally associated with sacred and therefore immutable texts like the Qur'an or the corpus of the Prophet's sayings, and their equivalents in the other Near Eastern religions.[7] The other dimension is ethical. Here the role of religion is no different from the equivalent 'Judaeo-Christian' background of Western laws, except that the dominant historical and sociological background is Muslim in the case of the Middle East.[8] All in all, religion as historical reference and ethical background does not impel reasoning in Islamic or Middle Eastern law which would be different in nature from other legal systems.

Implementation and uniformity present a problem that has little to do with religion, but affects fundamentally the rule of law in the region.

All countries in the present Middle East fail the test of the rule of law, as I conclude in the final chapter. This does not mean that there is no law in the Middle East. Standing at the turn of the twenty-first century, the battle is joined over democracy, human rights, self-determination, rule of law, good governance, public accountability, all in my view variations on the same theme. None of the Middle Eastern jurisdictions has reached the critical mass under which I am comfortable describing it as a state where the rule of law prevails, or as a democratic country. The chapters on public law, the place where the rights of citizens and groups in a democracy are chiefly located, provide more pointed details about this conclusion.

Many citizens in Lebanon, Israel, Turkey, even Iran, will defend the view that their respective states are democratic and observe the rule of law. I hold a different view. This does not mean that law does not play a central part in these countries, or indeed in the dark dictatorships that have governed so many countries over decades, Iraq, Syria, Libya, Tunisia, Egypt . . . The realm of law is crucial to understanding Middle Eastern societies from earliest times, and this historical character may represent a unique feature of the region in a universal perspective. This does not mean that democracy or the rule of law, as I understand them, prevail in any of the Middle East countries.

Failure of democracy and the rule of law, as a *political* reality, does not preclude the shadow of the law from hovering over the region. But I have concluded, over twenty years of human rights and democracy activism, running parallel to legal study and practice, that bringing about democracy and the rule of law in the region is a political, not a legal, task.

---

[7] This is developed in Chapter 2, nn. 77–109 and accompanying text.

[8] More on this comparative aspect and its relative importance in contrast with the territorial-personal dimension in Mallat, 'Comparative law and the Islamic (Middle Eastern) legal culture', in Mathias Reimann and Reinhard Zimmermann eds, *The Oxford handbook of comparative law* (Oxford, 2006) 609–39 at 624–9, and below, Chapter 4. The chapter in the *Oxford handbook* offers a general summary of the present book.

Human rights defenders perform an admirable, courageous, and dangerous role. I have briefly tasted prison on the Iran–Iraq border for the sake of Iraqi democracy in May 1992, as an invited monitor of elections in Kurdish Iraq. The few hours of arbitrary detention were long enough to leave a tragic foretaste of what many friends across the region have endured for merely expressing their opinion. Some have been jailed for over two decades.

In the course of my work as a lawyer, I have defended people whose relatives had been kidnapped or massacred, and people who were tortured. I have myself received direct, personal, threats for taking the side of victims, in the defence of the family of Imam Musa Sadr, who was abducted in Qadhdhafi's Libya in 1978.

I have also been threatened in my academic position as a law teacher, in London no less, when I stood up to the ambassador of Saudi Arabia over the financing of a chair in Islamic studies at the School of Oriental and African Studies. The director of the School at the time failed to respect the minimum conditions I considered necessary for the independence of academic work.

Standing up for one's convictions is a natural part of a lawyer's life, in academia and in practice, but I have come to a bitter conclusion as these fights were taken up time and again: the actual battle for democracy, human rights, the rule of law, good governance, is political and not legal. For our Middle East societies and countries to come of age, believers in democracy, human rights, the rule of law, good governance, call it what you will, must come to power and lead their societies. The work of lawyers, human rights defenders, or judges, is heroic, but it remains marginal. The battle for law in the Middle East is political.

This is what this book is not, a political book. By definition, its subject-matter, law, isn't politics. So long as this distinction is respected, and my personal conviction stated, I hope the reader will not feel misled.

Once we accept that Middle Eastern law is no different from any other law, and that the rule of law in the Middle East is chiefly determined by a political battle, it is possible to dwell on some general characteristics of the field. Attaining a more abstract level, one encounters in Middle Eastern law a number of overall patterns that need to be addressed at the outset of this journey.

A postulate of the present book is that Islamic law is central to Middle Eastern law, in its classical manifestation as well as in its modern reach. Islamic law as a uniquely rich legal tradition carries with it a legal theory, and modern debates over the nature of Islamic law elicit questions on its nature and autonomy as a discrete field.

What theories of law does the Islamic tradition offer from within ? While philosophy tends to be 'the mother of sciences' in the West since Plato put it at this meta-level in the disciplines of the intellect, intellectual primacy in Islam finds in *law* its dominant discipline as the chief exponent of religion and social values and institutions. Within law, the Islamic tradition developed a theoretical reflection on legal categories in a self-contained discipline known as *usul al-fiqh*, literally roots, or principles, of law. The closest Western rendition of the genre would be jurisprudence, in its widest Anglo-American acceptation as a theory of law.[9]

There is nothing closer to legal theory in the Islamic tradition than *usul*. 'Although it would be rash to suppose that *usul al-fiqh* subsumes everything that may be regarded as Muslim legal theory in the broadest possible sense of that term, nonetheless there can be no denying that it constitutes, or came over time to constitute, the mainstream of legal-theoretical thought in Islam.'[10]

The prominence of *usul* is the more striking since classical Islam, despite the prominence of law, never knew a discipline described as 'philosophy of law'. At best, such a field may just be nascent on the contemporary scene, as argued in a recent review of relevant modern writings in the Qum (Iran) seminary by one of its active members.[11] A more detailed historical-legal investigation is unable to identify in the available tradition any coherent discipline that could be considered as 'philosophy of law'. In contrast, a field recognizable as 'philosophy' is undisputable in classical works by such household names as Avicenna and Averroes,[12] through to lesser known luminaries of the later 'Iranian period', most remarkably Mulla Sadra Shirazi, an exact contemporary of Descartes.[13]

While Islamic philosophy never paid sustained attention to law as subject-matter, there were plenty of attempts to develop a theory of law from within the legal tradition of Islam. They cohered in *usul al-fiqh*. But *usul* is not philosophy,

---

[9] The conclusions that follow result from work on *usul* and legal philosophy which appears in three short essays: 'On the philosophy of Islamic law', originally presented at Lund, August 2003, forthcoming in Chibli Mallat and Leslie Tramontini, eds, *From Boston to Beirut via Baghdad, Festschrift for John Donohue* (Beirut, 2007); 'Islamic legal theory: introducing *usul al-fiqh*', entry in Alexander Peczenik et al., eds, *Encyclopaedia of legal theory and philosophy of law*, online since 2005 at <http://www.ivr-enc.info/en/article.php?id=35>, published in a shorter form as a book review in *Islamic Law and Society*, 12, 2005, 422–8; 'Universalité de Michel Troper: du droit musulman', forthcoming in Mallat, ed., 'Dossier—Philosophie du droit', *Travaux et Jours*, 2007.

[10] Bernard G. Weiss, 'Introduction', in Weiss, ed., *Studies in Islamic legal theory*, Leiden, 2002, p. xvii.

[11] Abdel Jabbar al-Rifa'i, ed., *Falsafat al-fiqh wa maqased al-shari'a* (Philosophy of law [*fiqh*] and meanings of law [*shari'a*]) (Beirut, 2001) 33. See also in Rifa'i's book the contributions by leading Iranian scholars in the 'philosophy of law [*fiqh*]' section: Muhammad Mujtahid Shabestari, Mustafa Malikian, Sadeq Larijani, 'Abidi Sharudi, Naser Katuzian (at 39–221), to whom should be added the works of 'Abdel Karim Sorush. In his overview, at 36 n. 12, the editor puts the 'birth' of philosophy of law (*falsafat al-fiqh*) as a project in an interview with Shabestari published in 1994.

[12] Already in Hegel's *Lectures on the history of philosophy* (1817), a section on Arab philosophy features the most important Arab thinkers—including Farabi (d. 966), Avicenna (d. 1064), Averroes (d. 1217), and Maimonides (d. 1204), mostly as commentators on Aristotle's logic, but without offering any 'real progress' in philosophy: 'Wir können von den Arabern sagen: Ihre Philosophie macht nicht eine eigentümliche Stufe in der Ausbildung der Philosophie; sie haben das Prinzip der Philosophie nicht weitergebracht . . . . Aber nach allem, was wir von ihnen kennen, haben sie keinen wahrhaften Fortschritt im Prinzip gemacht; sie haben kein höheres Prinzip der sich bewussten Vernunft aufgestellt.' G. W. F. Hegel, *Vorlesungen über die Geschichte der Philosophie*, ii, *Werke* (Suhrkamp edn in 20 vols, 4th edn, Frankfurt, 2003, vol. xix) 517–18.

[13] Descartes died in 1650, Mulla Sadra in 1640. Mulla Sadra is the author of a philosophical *Summa* in nine large volumes, *al-Asfar al-arba'a* (The four voyages), from which the quote at the beginning of the chapter is taken. This philosophy of the later Islamic period has found its way onto the international scene mostly through the works of Henry Corbin, *En Islam iranien*, 4 vols., (Paris, 1971–2) (on Mulla Sadra and the immediately preceding *ishraqi* school, see especially vol. iv).

since its subject-matter is legal, while philosophy is far more encompassing. *Usul* is not philosophy of law either, whether in the tradition of Plato's *Laws*, or Kant's *Rechtslehre*, or Rawls's *Theory of justice* in the modern period, because the categories that are put to use in the legal derivation are not philosophical categories. Logic, deriving from Aristotle's translations into Arabic in the classical period, is the field closest to *usul*. But even logic as the equivalent to *usul* runs into difficulties. In part, early *usul* texts predate Arabic translations of Aristotle; even after the high period of Greek influence on Islamic thought, the organization and use of the syllogisms in *usul* do not correspond to the Aristotelian *Organon*, or to Aristotle's followers in the genre, from Farabi in the classical age of Islam to the likes of Russell or Wittgenstein in the modern period.

Historically, a founding landmark of the discipline of *usul* is the *Risala* of Muhammad ibn Idris al-Shafi'i (d. 204/820). The eponym of one of the four schools in mainstream Sunni Islam, Shafi'i is the author of both an extensive treatment of positive law known as *al-Umm*, and of a systematic, long treatise in *usul al-fiqh*, which his successive editors through the centuries have considered as the first book in the discipline.[14] Ibn Khaldun (d. 1406), an authoritative reference if any, confirms Shafi'i 'as the first who wrote in the field of *usul*'.[15]

The *Risala* is a mixture of reflections on the relationship between the Qur'an and the Prophetic sayings and deeds as normative texts, interspersed with substantive law questions, and 'jurisprudence' in the sense of rules and categories of legal derivation. Irrespective of chronology,[16] the repetitive fragments of the *Risala* can hardly escape their beginner's status. *Usul al-fiqh*, as the discipline jelled into an autonomous genre in Islamic law, has become over the centuries a far larger and more sophisticated field, and the quintessential locus of a 'theory of Islamic law'. How much does *usul* stand for the autonomy of Islamic law, and define its spirit? How does one make sense of *usul* as legal theory, and what does it say about the nature of Islamic law, or of Middle Eastern law more generally?

To describe the field as it stands at present, I propose to draw a brief historical and comparative sketch of the discipline of *usul* on the basis of a recent textbook by Muhammad Baqer al-Sadr—a leading contemporary jurist, who was executed in his native Iraq in 1980.[17]

---

[14] On the *Risala* as 'the first book in *usul al-fiqh*', see the standard Arabic edition by Ahmad Muhammad Shaker (Cairo, orig. 1939, n.d. repr. 13). The structure of Shafi'i's compendium of law, *al-Umm*, is carefully examined by Joseph Schacht in his *Origins of Muhammadan jurisprudence* (Oxford, 1950). Further on Shafi'i s.v. index.

[15] Ibn Khaldun, *al-Muqaddima* (Beirut edn, 1978) 455.

[16] In *A history of Islamic legal theories: an introduction to Sunni usul al-fiqh* (Cambridge, 1997) Wael Hallaq questions Shafi'i's entitlement to jurisprudential 'masterdom' in the early period, see 18–19, 30–5.

[17] Muhammad Baqer al-Sadr, *Durus fi 'ilm al-usul*, published in three parts and four volumes between 1978 and 1980 in Beirut and Najaf. Translation of vol. i as *Lessons in Islamic jurisprudence*, with an introduction by Roy Parviz Mottahedeh (Oxford, 2003). On Sadr, see my *The renewal of Islamic law, Muhammad Baqer as-Sadr, Najaf, and the Shi'i international* (Cambridge, 1993).

Historically, even a brief comparison between Shafiʿiʾs *Risala* and Sadrʾs *Durus* shows the significant progress made in the abstraction of words and categories, and in the markedly more sophisticated marshalling of arguments. From a reliance on 'sources' of law and their status and arrangement, which appears as the most important contribution of the *Risala*,[18] to the abstractions offered in the twentieth century by writers like Sadr operating with concepts such as rational/substantial/procedural rules and the modes of their contradictions, there is qualitative progress over the same subject-matter, the derivation of a legal rule.

What sort of 'theory of law' does *usul* stand for comparatively? As obtains from a general comparison between Sadrʾs textbook and a Western philosophy of law manual authored by French legal philosopher and constitutional lawyer Michel Troper, many preoccupations appear similar, notably the issue of definition, structure, applicability, and language.[19]

The comparative exercise can be followed through the two legal philosophers' treatment of the injunction: 'it is forbidden to smoke'. Both Troper and Sadr inscribe the injunction within a larger context, which serves also as a reference for any other similar legal norm. For Troper, it operates on two levels: the injunction, for instance in a public building, is distinguished from a statement in a different context, for instance a husband telling his wife that she should not smoke out of concern for her health. Only in the first case does the prohibition carry with it a baggage defined legally, mostly by way of a sanction in case the injunction is violated.[20] That baggage is structurally complex, and always dynamic. It presupposes an authority that enounces it, a mechanism of implementation, including sanctions. The theory, philosophy, or science of the law is a meta-language with its specific vocabulary, and more: the power to enforce its statements viewed as injunctions.[21]

For Sadr, *as a modern rule*, the statement 'it is forbidden to smoke' provides a dual terrain for the *usul* mode of derivation. From the traditional category, of which that legal injunction did not form part, emerges an ensemble of rules which are not dissimilar to Troperʾs structure, except that they rest heavily on linguistic tools from the classical Arabic tradition.[22] When the jurist operates in the absence of a clear ruling, as in the injunction not to smoke, other rules supply the theoretical tools for derivation, including contradictory rules like the need for caution and the principle of freedom. If the principle of caution rules, the injunction stands. If the principle of freedom rules, the injunction fails.[23] In both traditional and modern cases, the outside system of references responds to a self-defined context, which is naturally specific to each legal tradition as a whole.

---

[18] Chapter 2 below nn. 436–44 and accompanying text.
[19] Development in Mallat, 'Universalité de Michel Troper' above n. 9.
[20] Michel Troper, *Philosophie du droit* (Paris, 2003) 29–30.   [21] ibid. 72.
[22] Sadr, *Durus*, above n. 17, vol. i, 80–125.
[23] ibid. 169–94. Caution principle, *ihtyat*; freedom or legality principle, *al-asl al-baraʾa*.

The contextualization is typical of any legal philosophical quest for what law is, and how a rule can be derived from within the system. Once contextualized, the specificity of the injunction within each system becomes dependent on the history and language in which that system has developed to offer a framework for the injunction. The context itself obeys common derivative rules, including the *summa divisio* between literalists and non-literalists, beyond which derivation becomes determined less by a particular philosophical or theoretical bent than by the internal wealth of references provided by the respective legal systems.

This, then, offers another conclusion to be added to the natural similarity between Middle Eastern law and Western laws: the logic of derivation is also the same. What differs is the context, and the corresponding language and style. It is the *context* which marks the difference in the operation of law, in other words the *style* of the Middle Eastern legal family. In turn, context and style open up a whole array of historical and civilisational references, including a stand-alone set of legal works.

To conclude: there is nothing in Middle Eastern law which is, in its essence, different from other traditions of law under the sun. If one insists on differences, then the spirit or philosophy of Middle Eastern law should be sought in two peculiar manifestations: its continuation of legal calques which can be identified as Middle Eastern in a unique tradition and style that extend over four millennia, and the plurality of levels formed in the Islamic legal literature proper. This is a metaphor for multiple, uneven terrains, which Gilles Deleuze and Félix Guattari offered in their major opus *A thousand planes*.[24]

Looking more specifically at the uninterrupted flow of Islamic law since the Muslim revelation in the sixth century, interpreting the discipline as the common law of the region must be approached in ways similar to the study of other major legal systems in the world. This is premised on the universality of legal method. If there are any structural differences with other legal systems, they rest on an openness of the discipline to the wider Middle Eastern historical paradigm in the first place, and to the plurality of Islamic law sources in ways unmatched by other families of law. This is where the thousand planes of Islamic law may offer the more alluring characteristics of its spirit, if not its philosophy. This is what the present book is about: mapping Middle Eastern law as a coherent field of study.

---

[24] Gilles Deleuze and Félix Guattari, *Mille plateaux* (Paris, 1980). Developments and illustration in Chapter 2 *in fine*, below.

PART I
HISTORY

2

The Formation of Middle Eastern Law

So viele Berichte,
so viele Fragen.

Bertolt Brecht[1]

Any approach to law in the region known as the Near or Middle East is doubly selective, as the historical depth of the tradition enhances the diversity of cultures active in the contemporary world. Law is a particular example where the contrasting arrangements which characterize the twenty-five or so modern nation-states are as much a product of a sophisticated and ancient history as they are the result of the onerous requirements imposed by the pace of recent change in the area. Western influence on Middle Eastern law in its contemporary operation is pervasive. But whether in the Bible, the Qur'an, and earlier in Hammurabi's Code, concern with law is a centuries-old phenomenon.[2]

The historical wealth of available legal documents in the Middle East is probably unmatched in the rest of the planet, and many lengthy and complex treatises have yet to be uncovered. The constraints of the historical dimension on an introduction to the Middle East legal systems are considerable. A history of Islamic law, let alone of Middle Eastern law, is yet to be written.[3]

[1] 'So many reports, so many questions', in the poem 'Fragen eines lesenden Arbeiters' (Questions of a reading worker), Bertolt Brecht, *Svendborger Gedichte* (1939), *Werke*, 6 vols. (Frankfurt, 1997) iii, 293.

[2] For a bibliographical overview of Middle Eastern law, see my two essays on 'Islamic law: reflections on the present state in Western research', *al-Abhath* (American University of Beirut), 43, 1995, 3–34 and on 'The state of Islamic law research in the Middle East', *Asian Research Trends* (Tokyo), 8, 1998, 109–36; these essays appear in a slightly different version in French as 'Le droit en Méditerranée musulmane: perspectives de recherches', in R.Ilbert and R. Deguilhem, eds., *Individu et société en Méditerranée musulmane—Questions et sources*, Aix, 1998, 25–47; and 'L'état de la recherche en droit musulman au Moyen-Orient', *Travaux et Jours* (Université Saint Joseph, Beirut), 61, 1998, 231–60.

[3] Noel Coulson, *A history of Islamic law* (Edinburgh, 1964) remains the reference most read in English. It is an elegant work but does not convey the huge lacunae in our knowledge of Islamic and Middle Eastern law at all stages of its development. See also the criticism on substance by Joseph Schacht, 'Modernism and traditionalism in a history of Islamic law', *Middle Eastern Studies*, 1, 1965, 388–400, esp. 396–9. Schacht himself has transformed his *Esquisse d'une histoire du droit musulman* (Paris, 1953) into the first part of his authoritative, but heavy stylistically and historically patchy compendium, *An introduction to Islamic law* (Oxford, 1964). Schacht's bibliography at 214–85, is an indispensible scholarly tool on Islamic law. It can be supplemented by the following references: L. Zwaini and R. Peters, *A bibliography of Islamic law 1980–1993* (Leiden, 1994); John

The horizontal breadth adds to the complexity. The Middle East examined in this book is a large region, stretching from the Atlantic to India, with countries like Spain and Portugal (and islands like Malta, Cyprus, or Sicily) resolutely outside its ambit at present despite their 'Middle Eastern' legal character over several centuries of Arab-Muslim rule.[4]

With all the historical and synchronic diversity in the region, a comprehensive approach to the discipline can depart from a premise which may be useful if taken as a relative guiding point of historical sedimentation: that the common law of the Middle East, in so far as it can be discerned, is Islamic. If there is one shared, dominant, and distinctive historical background to Middle Eastern legal systems, it is in the special historical role taken by Islam in the development of the law. Islamic law—the *shari'a*—constitutes the prevailing common historical legal tradition in the region.

Middle Eastern Legal Calques

Islamic law, however, is a latecomer. If the mere majoritarian fact of present-day populations living in the area is evidence of its centrality, the spread of Islam came last in the history of Middle Eastern civilizations. Its emergence in the early seventh century, a period which is known in Western scholarship as 'late antiquity', appears both as a radical break with previous legal traditions and as the continuity of Middle Eastern patterns that are rooted in the first civilizations of written documents and persist in some forms to the present.

Illustration of this persistence is not necessarily achieved by reducing the pattern to the monotheistic legacy which is evident in any rough comparison between Biblical[5]—both Christian and Jewish[6]—and Qur'anic legal dispositions: if Jewish

---

Makdisi, 'Islamic law bibliography', *Law Library Journal*, 78, 1986, 103–89; and my own essays mentioned in the previous note.

[4] See further on defining the contemporary Middle East Chapter 3 below.

[5] For an introduction to early Jewish law (Hebrew *halakha*), Raymond Westbrook, 'Biblical law', in N. S. Hecht, B.S. Jackson, S. M. Passameneck, Daniela Piattelli, and Alfredo Rabello, eds., *An Introduction to the history and sources of Jewish law* (Oxford, 1996) 1–17, with further references at 15–17. Note Westbrook's mention of the 'wider ancient Near Eastern traditions', and of 'general ancient near practices', 2; these themes are further elaborated in the case of Biblical and Mesopotamian law in his *Studies in Biblical and cuneiform laws* (Paris, 1988). On *halakha* and *shari'a*, the exact equivalent in Islam, studies are fewer than one would expect considering the similarities: see generally Samuel Goitein, 'The interplay of Jewish and Islamic laws', in B. S. Jackson, ed., *Jewish law in legal history and the modern world* (Leiden, 1980) 61–77.

[6] For comparative work on early Christian and Jewish law, leading work has been conducted by Duncan Derrett (also a specialist in classical and modern Indian law) and David Daube. See e.g. J. D. M. Derrett, *Law in the New Testament* (London, 1970); D. Daube, *The New Testament and rabbinic Judaism* (New York, 1973 (repr. of 1959 London edn)). For a bibliography of the two scholars, Gunther-Dietz Sontheimer and Parameswara Kota Aithal, eds., *Indology and the law: studies in honour of Professor M. Derrett* (Wiesbaden, 1982) 413–58; E. Bammel, C. K. Barrett, and W. D. Davies, eds., *Donum gentilicium: New Testament studies in honour of David Daube* (Oxford, 1978).

halakha and Muslim *shari'a* are 'copies conformes', some further distance in history allows the discovery of some striking similarities going back in time as far as early Mesopotamia.[7] In the 282 paragraphs of the Code of Hammurabi (*c.* mid-eighteenth-century BC), 21 are exclusively devoted to criminal dispositions. The 'tooth for a tooth' concept of the Qur'an[8] and the Bible[9] are rendered verbatim in the Code: 'If someone breaks the tooth of a free man, who is his equal, his tooth will be broken' (§ 200); and 'if someone poaches the eye of a free man, his eye will be poached' (§ 196).

In criminal law, the concept of collective responsibility has been the object of some interest in the early history of Islamic law in the discussion of *diyya*, translated as blood-money, and *'aqila*, a concept referring to a group of people who are in their livelihood close to the perpetrator of a crime and become legally implicated upon its commitment. The Code of Hammurabi refers to collective responsibility in two ways: the first is connected with compensation, and §§ 22–4 present the case of the responsibility of the 'state' *vis-à-vis* the group: 'If someone has engaged in highway robbery[10] and is caught, this man will be killed. If the robber is not caught, the robbed person will declare his loss in an official way before God; then the God, and the prefect in the territory and under the jurisdiction of whom the robbery has taken place, will compensate him for his loss; If it is a case of murder, the city and the prefect will grant a measure [equivalent to 500 grams] of silver to his family.'

The second aspect of collective responsibility relates to the law of evidence. The joint responsibility of the larger group is established by a collective testimony which, much like Islamic law, depends on the neighbourhood: 'If someone, whose belonging has not been lost, declares "I have lost a belonging", and if he invokes his neighbourhood, the neighbourhood will declare officially, in presence of the God, that his belonging has not disappeared. He must then restitute to his neighbourhood double the amount he was asking for' (§ 126).

---

[7] For an overview of Mesopotamian law, see Chapter 15 (on law) of the excellent introduction by J. N. Postgate, *Early Mesopotamia: society and economy at the dawn of history* (London, 1992); J. Bottéro, 'Le "Code" de Hammurabi', in *Mésopotamie: L'écriture, la raison et les dieux* (Paris, 1987) 191–223 (suggesting the Code is in fact a collection of cases, a 'véritable traité de jurisprudence', rather than a code of laws, citation at 223); Emile Szlechter, e.g. 'La "loi" dans la Mésopotamie Ancienne', *Revue Internationale des Droits de l'Antiquité*, 12, 1965, 55–78; the most authoritative English study of the Babylonian codes remains G. R. Driver and John Miles, *The Babylonian laws* (Oxford, 1953) 2 vols [hereinafter Driver and Miles]. A French translation, more briefly annotated, was published by André Finet, *Le Code de Hammurapi* (Paris, 1973). Hammurabi himself belongs to a deep-rooted legal tradition, which can be traced back to the 'laws of Eshnunna', elaborated two centuries earlier, Driver and Miles, i, 7: French translation and commentary by E. Szlechter, *Les lois d'Esnuna* (Paris, 1954); English by Reuven Yaron, *The laws of Eshnunna* (Jerusalem-Leiden, 1969, 2nd rev. edn., 1988). The *Revue Historique de Droit Français et Etranger* carries a detailed bibliographical survey of 'droits antiques', including Mesopotamian laws. There are also extensive bibliographical sections in the *Revue Internationale des Droits de l'Antiquité*, which succeeded the *Archives d'Histoire du Droit Oriental*, 1937–51. J. B. Pritchard ed., *Ancient Near Eastern texts*, (Princeton, 3rd edn. 1969), is a classic reference book.   [8] Qur'an v: 45.

[9] Exodus xxi: 23–5; Leviticus xxiv: 18–20; Deuteronomy xix: 21.

[10] On highway robbery, to be punished by death, Qur'an v: 33.

Both in terms of evidence and in terms of the collective responsibility of the neighbourhood for the crime of an individual, these measures are akin to the law of *diyya* (blood-money) and the collective responsibility of the local community in Islam for crimes committed in the neighbourhood.[11] It was recently shown that *diyya* was not associated by necessity with Bedouin 'tribal' law, as the concept and operation of 'neighbourhood responsibility' was also decisive for city dwellers. That it could also cover—and perhaps more typically so—the city is substantiated in early Islamic legal texts with 'primary reference to city life'.[12]

Much in the sense covered by Hammurabi's 'prefect' and 'city', the correlation with Mesopotamian neighbourhood law is further evidenced by the role, in the Islamic operation of compensation witnessed in texts three millennia later, of 'bureaucratic initiative: This is reflected first in the insistence, several times repeated, that all claims for *diya* payments should be taken before a judge, and that payments should not begin till after a judicial decree to that effect'.[13] Conclusions on Islamic criminal law sound similar to those of more ancient systems in the region: 'The social reality behind the juristic rules is at least this, that there was no room in Near-Eastern society of this period for the nuclear family or the isolated individual. People lived in, and owed allegiance to, groups, which, in the case of Muslims, were traditionally demarcated by reference to tribal lineage. Whatever other functions these groups served, they certainly provided mutual support in case of non-deliberate injury.'[14]

Similar traits continue to be in evidence to the present day—where one sees 'collective responsibility' also for deliberate injury—within or outside city life. The collective dimension remains averse to a personalized 'principle of legality', said to have been formally introduced into the Western system by the eighteenth-century Italian jurist Cesare Beccaria.[15] This collective dimension can be summarized

---

[11] Schacht summarizes the issue as follows: 'In most cases it is not the culprit himself but his *'aqila* who must pay the blood-money. The payment is made in three yearly instalments, with the provision that each member of the *'aqila* has to pay not more than 3 or 4 dirhams altogether. If the amount is less than one-twentieth of the blood-money, not the *'aqila* but the culprit himself must pay. The *'aqila* consists of those who, as members of the Muslim army, have their names inscribed in the list (*diwan*) and receive pay, provided the culprit belongs to them; alternatively, of the male members of his tribe (if their names are not sufficient, the nearest related tribes are included); alternatively, of the fellow workers in his craft or his confederates; and the *'aqila* of the client, both in the sense of a manumitted slave and of a convert to Islam, is his patron and the *'aqila* of his patron. The institution has its roots in the pre-Islamic customary law of the Bedouins, where the culprit could be ransomed from retaliation by his tribe, and the inclusion of confederates and of clientship seems to be ancient Arabian too.' Schacht, *Introduction to Islamic law* (n. 3 above) 186. See also the legal restatement of Ibrahim al-Halabi (d. 956/1549), *Multaqa al-abhur*, on which Schacht bases his treatment, with the commentaries of Shaykhzade, known also as Damad Efendi (d. 1087/1676), *Majma' al-anhur*, and Haskafi (d. 1088/1677), *Al-durr al-muntaqa*, in the Beirut 1998 four-volume edition, iv, 397–416. See also the entries on *'aqila* and *diyya* in the *Encyclopaedia of Islam*, first and second editions.

[12] Norman Calder, *Studies in early Muslim jurisprudence*, (Oxford, 1993) 204.

[13] Calder, *Studies*, 207.   [14] ibid., 206. See also on *'aqila*, 202–8.

[15] Cesare Beccaria (1738–94), *Dei delitti e delle pene* (Livourno, 1765, rev. edn., London, 1774, fac-simile Milan, 2001) 7: '§iii. Conseguenze. La prima conseguenza di questi principi è che le sole Leggi possano decretare le pene sù i delitti, e questa autorità, non puó risedere che presso il Legislatore ...

in three central staples of a Middle Eastern criminal law pattern: (1) elements of the *lex talionis*, particularly with regard to murder and deliberate infliction of injury; (2) a collective system of evidence and compensation, particularly for manslaughter and non-deliberate injury; and (3) a formalized role for intermediaries, as both city 'judges' and tribal 'elders'. The logic of criminal law in the Near East is as complex as it is ancient, and has proven remarkably persistent to the present.

The law of talion appears as evident calque in all the monotheistic sacred books.[16] But the Mesopotamian legal pattern is not simply criminal. Some family law institutions of the Qur'an, which have now become rare or obsolete, can be perhaps better understood with reference to their antecedents in old Jewish and Mesopotamian laws.[17]

Other institutions have remained very much alive. The Code of Hammurabi regulates matrimonial issues in some detail: a list of incestuous relationships is forbidden in strong terms for mother and son and for stepmother and son (§§ 157, 158). This is much less detailed than in the Qur'an, which is probably indebted more

---

La seconda conseguenza è, che il Sovrano, che rappresenta la Società medesima, non puó formare che Leggi generali; che obblighino tutti i membri, ma non già guidicare che uno abbia violato il contratto sociale, poichè allora la Nazione si dividirebbe in due parti, una rappresentata dal Sovrano, che asserisce la violazione del contratto, e l'altra dell' accusato, che la nega . . .' For, according to Beccaria, at 5, in '§ii. Diritto di punire: ogni Uomo si fa centro di tutte le combinazioni del Globo.' See on the Beccarian innovation on this score F. Desportes and F. Le Guhénec, *Le nouveau droit pénal*, i, *Droit pénal général* (Paris 1994) 140–8.

[16] The concept of calque was coined by the late John Wansbrough (died 2002) in his *Quranic studies: sources and methods of scriptural interpretation* (Oxford, 1977); and *The sectarian milieu: content and composition of Islamic salvation history* (Oxford, 1978). See also my 'Readings of the Qur'an in Najaf and London: John Wansbrough and Muhammad Baqir al-Sadr', *Bulletin of the School of Oriental and African Studies*, 57:1, 1994, 158–73, and the bibliography of Wansbrough in the same issue of that journal, 4–13. Wansbrough published more recently a book spanning the diplomatic calques of the Mediterranean over a period of three millennia (1500 BCE–1500 CE), *Lingua franca in the Mediterranean* (London 1996), from which much of the attention in the present chapter originally derived.

[17] Now obsolete formula-based divorce categories like *ila'* (Qur'an ii: 226) and *zihar* (Qur'an xxxiii 4; lxiii: 2), which are traditionally considered as pre-Islamic *jahili* 'bad' practice by the commentators and the jurists, have been traced back by Gerald Hawting to Jewish traditions in the Mishna (legal interpretation of the Talmud compiled by the Jewish scholars *c.* 200 CE), '*Ila*' and *zihar* in Muslim law', *Bulletin of the School of Oriental and African Studies*, 57, 1994, 113–25, at 124–5. A clear formula such as the one used for *zihar* (husband to wife: 'you are to me like my mother's back', meaning you are forbidden for me to approach sexually as my mother is) was not found in the Mesopotamian laws available to me, although both *qadhf* and the word *zihar* in connection with some formulaic accusation of the husband appear in the fifth-century Syro-Roman Code (Art. 65 for *qadhf*, Art. 85 for *zihar*, see below nn. 34–73 and accompanying text for an extensive discussion of the Code). Under Islamic criminal law, the penalty of eighty lashes attaching to the crime of *qadhf*, which is the false accusation of unlawful intercourse, finds however a remarkable antecedent in Hammurabi's code: §127: 'If a man has caused a finger to be pointed at . . . a married lady and has then not proved what he has said, they shall flog that man before the judges and shall shave his head'; see also §§131–2, and the procedural similarities with Islamic-Arab law, as well as the question of who is entitled to bring the charges, and the social dimension of the penalty, Driver and Miles, i, 275–84.

directly to the Bible,[18] but incest and *mahr* (dower) are categories which operate as models following which many Middle Eastern variations have taken place. Hammurabi's law anticipates the Islamic dower-*mahr* in the *tirhatum*, and discusses its regulation in some detail. This Akkadian 'bridal gift' (*tirhatum*)[19] has given rise to some controversy on the nature of the marriage contract in Mesopotamian laws: against Koschaker,[20] who identified *tirhatum* as denoting marriage by purchase, with the bride-price constituting the price given to the bride's father for 'selling' his daughter,[21] the legal commentary of Drivers and Miles puts the argument on its head,[22] and adds in support of that alternative theory the fact that in the modern day, 'the Arabs of Palestine emphatically deny that the so-called "bride-price" (Arab. *Mahr*) is paid or given for the purchase of the bride; they explain it as compensation paid by the bridegroom to her father or family for the loss of her services in the home'.[23]

This controversy carries a familiar ring in the assessment of the nature of the marriage contract in Islamic law, with an exact parallel to the Koschaker/Driver and Miles debate on whether this is a price for sexual 'rights' of the husband over the wife, or whether it is an altogether separate institution.[24] Even though the controversy may have been mooted in the modern age, as *mahr* is increasingly associated with the woman receiving it, rather than her guardian, the question has

[18] Compare Qur'an iv: 23 and Bible, for instance Leviticus xviii: 6–24; xx: 8–21, Deuteronomy xxvii: 22–5. S. D. Ricks, 'Kinship bars to marriage in Jewish and Islamic law', in W. M. Brinner and S. D. Ricks, eds., *Studies in Islamic and Judaic traditions*, 2 vols. (Atlanta, 1986–9) i, 123–41.

[19] Also referred to as *nudunnûm*, or *seriktum*, see Driver and Miles, examples at i, 254 and 256 for *nudunnûm* in Babylonian marriage contracts. In Hammurabi's code, §§ 159ff.

[20] Paul Koschaker, early German specialist on Hammurabi's Code, and editor of vols 2–6 of its 6 vol. German edn., *Hammurabis Gesetz* (Leipzig, 1904–23). See also his *Rechtsvergleichende Studien zur Gesetzgebung Hammurabis: Königs von Babylon* (Leipzig, 1917).   [21] German *Brautpreis*.

[22] 'The whole theory of Babylonian marriage as a system of marriage by purchase indeed rests on the identification of the *tirhatum* with the bride-price, and the advocates of this theory seem to have been led astray by the anthropologists who are somewhat inclined to assume that any practice in use amongst primitive people represents a necessary stage in the development of all civilised races. As already shown, however, the *tirhatum* has nothing to do with sale, and it ought to mean something connected with or given in connexion with the sexual act, to which it refers. It is therefore far more probable that its meaning is a marriage-gift or a gift given to secure a marriage with a view to procreation than that it means a price by which a bride is purchased. It is no argument to say that the word must mean 'price' because the father gets something of monetary value when he gives his daughter in marriage, since in a general sense every contract is based on a consideration of such value. Again, it is not an argument to show that if the *tirhatum* is assumed to mean "bride-price", a consistent account can be given of Babylonian marriage, since in fact an equally consistent account is obtained if it means a marriage-gift. It appears then that there was no signification of sale in any of the terms connected with marriage and that there was no such idea in the minds of the Babylonian scribes. The burden of proof that the *tirhatum* was a bride-price must then be on those who advance this theory, and it is submitted that they have so far failed to discharge this requirement. Although in Babylonian marriage the father gets some payment for giving his daughter in marriage, he can be said to sell her only in a figurative sense, just as at this day a father is occasionally said to sell his daughter or a woman is said to sell herself to a man; only to this extent is it normally correct to speak of marriage by purchase at Babylon in the time of Hammurabi.' Driver and Miles, i, 264–5 (footnotes omitted).

[23] ibid., 256 n. 1.

[24] The parallel to the Koschaker/Driver and Miles debate on the nature of the marriage contract, including bride-price, can be found in S. Haeri, 'Divorce in contemporary Iran: a male prerogative in self-will', in C. Mallat and J. Connors, eds., *Islamic family law* (London, 1990) 55–69.

been transposed to a lateral argument over the wife 'selling her body' for the *mahr*. The debate, judging by some recent rebounds in the field of family law, appears as relevant as it may once have been over the Mesopotamian nature of the marriage contract.[25]

Turning to commercial law, the Islamic *commenda* contract[26] can also be found in Hammurabi, who first defines partnership[27] in § U of the Code: 'If a man has given silver to a man for a partnership, they shall divide the profit or the loss which there may be in proportion before a god'. The concept is similar to the one to be found in Islamic law, and is developed at §§ 100–3. 'The Babylonian "partnership" (Bab. *tappûtum*), as it is commonly translated, is not the ordinary partnership of English law where persons become partners in some business for a long term of years. It is a *societas unius rei*, a joint adventure for the carrying out of some particular piece of business, e.g. for a definite "commercial journey" '.[28] Anyone who is familiar with the difficult dissociation, despite the statutes, between personal and corporate liability in the modern Middle East—and most strikingly in the practice of the Arab Gulf States[29]—understands the prevalence of the full liability of the two parties who are partners in the *commenda/mudaraba/tappûtum* 'joint adventure' over the separate juristic person and the limited liability of a Western-style partnership/*société/Gesellschaft*.

Muzaraʿa and *musaqat*, the agricultural contract equivalents to *mudaraba* under Islamic law, could also be expected as calques of Hammurabi's Code, where

---

[25] Thus Haeri, who notes Murtaza Mutahhari's 'vehement objection to the conceptualisation of marriage as a contract of sale, and of women as an object', while she herself reads the classical tradition to carry the 'underlying assumption' that 'as "purchasers" in a contract of marriage, men are "in charge" of their wives because they pay for them'. Ibid. at 58 and nn. 13 and 14. Ayat Allah Mutahhari was one of the foremost theoreticians of the Islamic Revolution in Iran, and the author of *Nizam-i huquq-i zan dar Islam* (Legal rights of women in Islam) (Qum, 1974). He was assassinated in May 1979.   [26] *mudaraba.*

[27] *tappûtum.*

[28] Driver and Miles, i, 187; ii, tr. at 43. The comparison stops however at the recovery by the owner of capital of the sum advanced to his agent. In Mesopotamian law, capital is not repaid by the agent in case 'an enemy causes him to jettison anything that he is carrying' (§ V. 103). Otherwise, 'he shall repay the total amount of the silver [capital] to the merchant' (§ 102). It is interesting to note that the commentators have found the difference between §§ 102 and 103 in Hammurabi's Code difficult to understand: 'In §102 the *bitiqtum* is caused by the perils of the journey, and he must repay only the actual debt; but if the loss is caused by the king's enemies, as in §103, he can exculpate himself by oath and is excused repayment. The reason for the distinction between the penalties in §102 and §103 is not easy to discover; for in both cases the money has been lost through *force majeure.*' Driver and Miles, i, 194. In contrast to the Islamic (and Judaeo-Christian) tradition, 'interest' on transactions seems to be commonly authorized in Mesopotamian laws, see e.g. Piotr Steinkeller, 'The renting of fields in early Mesopotamia and the development of the concept of "interest" in Sumerian', *Journal of the Economic and Social History of the Orient*, 24, 1981, 113–45. However, the concept for interest is related by Piotrkeller (at 145) to an Akkadian word meaning 'to bring an addition, to add ... Accordingly, the approximate translation of *kud-ra* ... would be "to add a portion" (of loan/produce)', which is the exact semantic equivalent to the Qur'an-prohibited *riba*. *Riba* means etymologically 'addition, increase'. Generally on commercial law in Mesopotamia, see W. F. Leeman, *Foreign trade in the Old Babylonian period* (Leiden, 1960).

[29] See the development of this argument in Chapter 9, and the brief comparison of the classical models with the modern 'joint venture' in Mallat, 'Joint ventures', in R. Naser and T. Kashishian, eds., *Lebanon and Europe: forging new partnerships* (Beirut, 1998) 29–37.

the relationship of owner of land and its worker—divided as in Islamic law
between usual crops and orchards—is developed at length in §§ 42–56.[30] Like
Islamic law, distinction between slaves and free men, as well as variations in
degrees of freedom, are also frequently made.[31]

Mutatis mutandis, historical comparisons show repetitions of eminently similar
legal institutions across the centuries: whether in family law, commercial and
crop-sharing contracts, or the law of talion and collective responsibility for crimes,
there is patent continuity to date across Middle Eastern jurisdictions, from Saudi
Arabia to Morocco and Israel.[32] Yet, and for a host of reasons, too little scholarship
stretches over more than one discipline or area. Following pioneering work which
starts where most comparative scholarship involving Islamic law had stopped in
the 1930s, some imagination is needed to help the discipline open up to the
enriching concept of a Middle Eastern legal pattern.[33]

The Syro-Roman book. Among many an episode which have remained unstudied
despite a remarkably close historical calque, stands the fifth-century CE Syro-
Roman Law Book.[34] Since its publication and translation in 1880, this code has

---

[30] § 42. 'If a man has taken up a field for cultivation and then has not raised corn on the field, they
shall convict him of not having done the (necessary) work on the field and he shall give corn corresponding to (the crops raised by) his neighbours to the owner of the field'.

§ 43. 'If he has not cultivated the field but leaves (it) waste, he shall give corn correspondingly to
(the crops raised by) his neighbours to the owner of the field and shall plough the field, which he has
left waste (and) harrow (it), and he shall render (it) to the owner of the field'. The defaulting cultivator will give the owner of the land a share in the produce according to an average defined in common
across the region: 'The subject of §§42–3 is the failure of a cultivator to raise a crop on a field which
"he has taken over" (Bab. *usêsi*) under a contract with its owner "for cultivation" (Bab. *ana irrisutim*),
presumably for one year . . . . It may be added that this method of assessment still survives in the
country [Iraq]'. In the footnote to the concept of *usêsi*, Driver and Miles further add: 'How a verb
meaning "to make to go forth, bring out" (Bab. *sûsû*) can have acquired this special connotation is
obscure; but it may be suggested that the underlying idea is that the farmer takes the property out of
the owner's hands or control for the purpose of carrying out the work which he undertakes to do under
the contract. The relation between them is, then, that of parties to the contract, not that of landlord
and tenant in English law.' i, 136–7. The *muzara'a* model which reproduces § 42 of Hammurabi's
code was until recent years widely used in the Middle East. For an example of a 'method of assessment'
like the one mentioned above, see the example of land legislation in Iran in the 1980s in my *The
renewal of Islamic law* (Cambridge, 1993) 149 ff.

[31] This is common in all slave-based economies, but the recurrence of degrees in an individual's
'freedom-based value' is striking in Islamic and Babylonian law.

[32] Including, in modern Israel, religious-based law in Israel. see Itzhak Englard, *Religious law in
the Israel legal system* (Jerusalem, 1975); *Jewish law in ancient and modern Israel: Selected essays*, with an
introduction by Haim H. Cohn (New York, 1971). See also below nn. 209–13 and accompanying
texts; and Chapters 4 and 6.

[33] The argument for bolder, more 'imaginative' comparative work is made in Patricia Crone,
Roman, provincial and Islamic law: the origins of the Islamic patronate (Cambridge, 1987) 1–18. There is
a famous short note by Joseph Schacht, in 1927, on calques in the law of sale passing from Babylon to
Islam. According to him, they both share, unlike other legal systems, the meeting of offer and acceptance as constitutive of contract. But the rapprochement was never seriously developed or substantiated. English translation by Killian Bälz, 'From Babylonian to Islamic law', in *Yearbook of Islamic and
Middle Eastern Law*, i, 1994, 29–33. (Original in *Orientalistisches Literaturzeitschrift*, 8, 1927, 664–9.)

[34] '*Jami' al-sunan al-hasana wal-hudud al-mahmuda*, collection of all the good laws (*sunan*, plural
of *sunna*) and penalties (*hudud*, plural of *hadd*) of King Constantine, Theodosius and Laon's, in the

lain dormant in the exclusive scholarship of Syriac specialists. Yet the Syro-Roman book points to deep Middle Eastern legal patterns which enlighten several features of Islamic family law. These similarities were generally ignored in the internal Islamic scholarly tradition, which, as with any 'new' religion, is hardly prepared to acknowledge external 'debts': 'Any law other than the law of Islam is obsolete', says one famous compendium of diplomatica in classical Islam.[35] This is echoed by the jurists: 'All laws have been superseded by the law of the Prophet'.[36]

While this resistance comes in the natural order of things when great religions are concerned, it is less understandable why the search for transreligious legal patterns has also been remarkably absent from the analysis of Western authors.[37]

Yet the 130 articles in the Arabic version of the Syro-Roman Code sound so familiar to the modern Arab lawyer that the Code appears as some 'vulgate' for the uninitiated. In comparison with early books on Islamic succession in the tradition of *fiqh*, the layout of that Christian code is clear, and its phraseology in comparison simple.[38] Even from a practitioner's perspective, this is an important book in

introduction to *Syrisch-Römisches Rechtsbuch aus dem fünften Jahrhundert*, edited, translated, and annotated by Karl Georg Bruns and Eduard Sachau (Aalen, 1961 (repr. of Leipzig, 1880)), text in Syriac (three versions), Arabic, and Armenian. (Hereinafter *Syro-Roman Code*). An impressive scholarly edition and translation into German was completed recently by Walter Selb and Hubert Kaufhold, *Das Syrisch-Römische Rechtsbuch*, 3 vols (Vienna, 2002). The third volume offers an article by article commentary.

[35] Ahmad ibn 'Abd Allah al-Qalqashandi (d. 821/1418), *Subh al-a'sha* (Cairo, 14 vols., 1913–18) xiv, 324: '*kullu shari'a siwaha dathira*'. For a more general appreciation of past civilizations by Muslim historians and poets in the classical age, see Roy Mottahedeh, 'Some Islamic views of the pre-Islamic past', *Harvard Middle Eastern and Islamic Review*, 1, 1994, 17–26. On the mysteries of the Pyramids and of the Sphinx in medieval Egypt, a beautiful text of al-Idrisi (d. 649/1251) was published by Ulrich Haarman, also the author of 'Die Sphinx. Synkretistische Volksreligiosität im spätmittelalterlichen islamischen Ägypten', *Saeculum*, 29, 1978, 367–84. The text of Idrisi is not legal, and he hesitates between awe before the pyramids and their civilization ('For all things on earth, save the pyramids, I fear time. For time I fear the pyramids', 85) and the great silence its mute talismans carry: 'On the pyramids are all kinds of writings in the pen of previous nations and defunct kingdoms, and no one knows what the writing is or means . . . The nation that built it lay destroyed, it has no successor to carry the truth of its stories from father to son, as sons of other nations carry from their fathers what they love and cherish among their stories'. 93, 105. Al-Idrisi, *Anwar 'uli al-ajram fil-kashf 'an asrar al-ahram*, in U. Haarman, ed., *Das Pyramidenbuch des Abu Ja'far al-Idrisi* (Beirut, 1991). There is an important but generally inconclusive debate on the debt of Islamic law to other legal systems, see Joseph Schacht, 'Foreign elements in ancient Islamic law', *Journal of Comparative Law*, 3–4, 1950, 9–16; Calder, *Studies*, 208–14.

[36] '*jami' al-shara'e' nusikhat bi-shari'at al-nabi*,' Taqi al-Din al-Subki (d. 756/1355), *Fatawa* (Beirut, 2 vols., 1992) ii, 370, in a long discussion over a dispute on the right of Christians to build churches.

[37] Exceptions include in addition to Patricia Crone, H. Kaufhold, *Syrische Texte zum Islamischen Recht* (Munich, 1971); 'Über die Entstehung der Syrischen Texte zum Islamischen Recht', *Oriens Christianus*, 69, 1985, 54–72. Crone and Kaufhold continue the interrupted tradition of the great Italian scholar C. Nallino, *Raccolta di scritti editi e inediti*, vol. iv: *Diritto musulmano e diritti orientali cristiani* (Rome, 1942). Except for some interface in recent Byzantine studies, works like those of Peter Brown on late antiquity have remained opaque to Islamic studies, and vice versa. The books of Patricia Crone and 'Irfan Shahid offer an exception of sorts.

[38] The earliest extant book on the Islamic law of succession is much less organized and much less comprehensive than the Syro-Roman Code. Text published by Hans-Peter Raddatz, 'Frühislamisches Erbrecht nach dem *Kitab al-Fara'id* des Sufyan at-Thawri, Edition und Kommentar', *Die Welt des Islams*, 13, 1971, 26–78.

terms of the wording and structure of basic rules in such a specialized area as the law of succession.

For the lawyer, most striking in the Arabic version of the Syro-Roman Code is the terminology, starting in the opening words with the use of the Arab-Islamic word *sunna* as law. The code develops then the intestate and testate succession scheme, some of which 'belongs on the whole to Roman law',[39] but some of which is better identified as a mixture of legal patterns.[40]

Several elements in Roman Provincial law appear to be calques for the Islamic law of succession. It is well known to inheritance law practitioners in the Muslim world that the key concept in the system of succession is operated by the principle of the agnatic line—the *'asaba*—complementing distribution to 'Qur'anic heirs' of parts of the deceased's estate. While some shares in the succession are prescribed to a limited number of heirs defined in the Qur'an (including the four closest female relatives: wife, daughter, mother, and sister), the succession is usually not exhausted. The chief characteristic of the system is that once these prescribed Qur'anic shares are distributed, the nearest agnatic male kin receives the remainder of the succession to the exclusion of closer female relatives of the deceased. This male residuary line is known as the *'asaba*.

As a matter of fact, the *'asaba* system dominates succession law principles in the Syro-Roman Code of fifth-century Syria, and the *ab intestat* succession in the Syro-Roman Code can be pointedly compared to Islamic law in that specific and key principle. The following clause, taken from the very first article of the Syro-Roman Code, can equally serve as a good summary of the scheme of succession in Muslim Sunni law: 'If a person dies without a will, . . . and is not survived by his father or his mother or by a child or a brother, then his estate goes to his paternal uncles or the sons of his uncles . . . '.

A few sections later, the word *'asaba* itself appears

Article 19: If a man has sons who all die before him without children of their own, and if he has daughters who are married and who gave birth to sons and then died; if he has a brother and chose to write a will in favour of his brother and to allow his household to inherit this is permissible, he can do as he pleaseth; but if he dies without a will, then his inheritance goes to his brothers and to the sons of his brothers. If he does not have a brother, then his inheritance goes to his paternal uncles and their sons. Only if the family (tribe) of his brother has all been exhausted will the sons of his daughters inherit, and if his

---

[39] Bruns, in *Syro-Roman Code*, 303–16.

[40] 'Im allgemeinen sind es hauptsächlich folgende vier Principien, von denen es behersscht wird:

1. Eine Parentelenordnung von drei Parentelen, wie im Mosaischen Rechte.
2. Ein Vorzug der Agnaten von den Cognaten, wie im römischen Rechte. [Sunni law.]
3. Ein Vorzug der väterlichen Cognaten vor den mütterlichen, wie in keinem der beiden Rechte. [This is actually typically Muslim Sunni.]'
4. Ein Vorzug der Männer vor den Weibern, mit ausnahme der Töchter und Schwestern, wie im römischem Rechte, aber mit subisdiärer Berechtigung der letzteren, die dem Römischem Rechte wieder fremd ist. [Again to be found in Sunni law.]' ibid., 306.

daughters had no sons, the sons of his sisters inherit and in all the *'asaba* men inherit and not women, and if males are exhausted only then will women from his *'asaba* inherit.

Thus Article 19 of the Syro-Roman book lays out *ab intestat* rules which, in form and substance, appear surprisingly familiar to an Islamic lawyer. From a historical perspective, the most striking feature in the system is that the word *'asaba* does not appear in the Qur'an, despite its key importance for the calculation of the succession. Without that pervasive concept, it is simply not possible to understand the mere basics of succession law in Sunni Islam. For example, if a man dies leaving his wife and a distant cousin on the male side of the family, the widow gets a quarter and the cousin the remaining three-quarters. This is because the share of the surviving wife is stipulated in the Qur'an, and the rest goes under the Sunni rules of succession to the nearest agnatic male kin, the *'asaba*.[41] Nor should the system be reduced to extreme instances. In the case of a man (or a woman) who dies leaving one daughter and a paternal uncle, the daughter receives one-half under the scheme laid out in the Qur'an, and the remaining half goes to the distant male relative on the agnatic side. In further illustrations, if the deceased has two daughters and a paternal uncle, the two daughters receive two-thirds of the estate, and the uncle the remaining one-third. The paternal uncle is the *'asaba*, the nearest male kin. A maternal uncle would receive nothing. If a woman dies leaving her husband, a son and a daughter, the husband receives a quarter, the daughter and the son receive the remaining three-quarters, with the son receiving twice the share of his sister (it is said in this case that the presence of the son makes an *'asaba* of his sister, and they receive the remainder as joint *'asaba*, except that the other principle of the son receiving twice the share of the daughter also applies, following Qur'an iv: 11). And finally, if a woman dies leaving her husband, a daughter and no son, then the husband gets a quarter (he is not an *'asaba* as he is not a male blood kin and so receives only his Qur'anic share in the presence of a child, Qur'an iv: 12), the daughter gets one-half (Qur'an iv: 11) and the remainder (a quarter) goes to the closest male kin—the *'asaba*, who may be a paternal uncle, or a paternal cousin.[42]

The scheme is typically Sunni. It is not shared by all Muslims, and the Shi'is, the other most important group in the Islamic world,[43] do not recognize the *'asaba*. In the previous simple example—surviving daughter, paternal uncle—the daughter receives under Shi'i law the whole succession. The paternal uncle is excluded by her closer kinship to the deceased. In the more complicated second case, the two daughters receive everything when they compete with a paternal

---

[41] The widow gets 1/8 if her husband dies and leaves children. Qur'an iv: 12.

[42] Further on succession rules as they continue to be applied in the modern Middle East, see Chapter 10, nn. 10–19 and accompanying text.

[43] Shi'ism commands some 150 to 200 million followers in Iran, Pakistan, India, Iraq, Bahrain, and Lebanon, and represents the most important section of the Muslim population in the world after the Sunnis. The Muslim population in the world is estimated at the turn of the twenty-first century at *c.* 1–1.2 billion people, of whom over 80% are Sunni, and most of the remainder Shi'i.

uncle. And if a woman dies leaving her husband, a son and a daughter, the husband gets one-quarter, and the son and daughter inherit the rest, on the basis of a double share for the son. That rule, double share to the son, is not exclusively Sunni, Shi'is also follow it. In the last case, daughter, husband, no son, the husband gets one-quarter, the rest goes in its entirety to the daughter.

This deep difference in one of the more intimate points of convergence between property law and family law is explained, within the Islamic tradition, as a dispute over Qur'anic interpretation as qualified by the sayings of the Prophet Muhammad, the *hadith*. For the Shi'is, that particular saying is not admitted, and since there is no instance of *'asaba* in the text of the Qur'an, there is no need to extrapolate in the way the Sunnis have done over the centuries.

The dispute as acknowledged within the Islamic tradition is both textual and political.[44] In fact, a possible explanation of this radical difference between Sunni and Shi'i succession may be more alluring for the genealogy of the Islamic law of succession than the one usually received. It is based on a comparison between the Persian Zoroastrian legal tradition, namely the *Matiyan-i hazar dadistan*,[45] and the Shi'i rules of succession. They are similar in many ways. This is how the Sasanian rules are summarized: 'There was no right of primogeniture, every son inherited an equal share, the principal wife the same as a son, and daughters half of this share. There is no evidence of other relatives inheriting',[46] as indeed there was no concept of *'asaba*. From there follows 'the important role' played by women in the succession scheme of ancient Iranian tradition and their continuation as Shi'i law:

The Qur'anic rules about wives' and daughters' right to inherit were on Arabic soil a new phenomenon which gave the women advantages which they had not known hitherto. In Iran, however, it was a matter of course that women inherited, and that succession might be carried on through them; thus the Sunni version of Islamic law meant a step backwards for the Iranian women ... The Sunnites maintained that the successor should be found amongst the agnatic relatives, while the Shi'ites asserted that the succession had to go through Muhammad's daughter Fatimah and her husband to their sons and their descendants. The Sunni point of view reflects the patriarchal, patrilinear system which aimed at keeping the possessions and power within the tribe by its emphasis on the male agnatic heirs. The Shi'ites were not so much concerned with tribes as with families. In their view, the direct descendants of Muhammad through Fatimah were the legitimate successors of the Prophet, and in Sasanian terminology she would have been *ayoken*, daughter, 'Ali *stur*, i.e. intermediary successor. I propose that their viewpoint reflects the traditional succession law which they had followed for centuries.[47]

---

[44] Details below at nn. 106, 107 and accompanying text for textual and political causes of the dispute. Further textual arguments in Chapter 10, below, nn. 16–18 and accompanying text.

[45] This is the main source of Zoroastrian law, 'The Lawbook of 1000 decisions', part 1 edited by J. J. Modi (Poona, 1901); part 2 edited by T. D. Anklesaria (Bombay, 1913). A survey of pre-Islamic Sasanian law in Iran was published by A. Perikhanian, 'Iranian society and law', in the *Cambridge History of Iran*, 3:2, *The Seleucid Parthian and Sasanian periods* (Cambridge, 1970) chapter 18, 627–80. The following was originally inspired by Bodil Hjerrild, 'Islamic law and Sasanian law', in Christopher Toll and Jakob Skovgaard-Petersen, eds., *Law and the Islamic world: past and present* (Copenhagen, 1995) 49–55.   [46] Hjerrild, 'Islamic law and Sasanian law', 52.

[47] ibid. 52–3.

While too tight a comparison might lead to excessive conclusions,[48] it is striking to see the Islamic system of inheritance as a prolongation, on the Sunni side, of the Syro-Roman 'Western' tradition, and for the Shi'is, whose demographic strength remains to date concentrated in the eastern fringe of the Arab world, as a calque deriving without discontinuation from the Persian Zoroastrian legal tradition.

One possible conclusion is that the historical schism between Sunni and Shi'i rules of succession has a much deeper pedigree, hailing, in the Sunni case, from Roman Provincial law as illustrated in the Syro-Roman Code; and, for the Shi'is, from a Persian Zoroastrian tradition. That the divide rests on a specific family structure and social substratum which are peculiar to each of the two large Muslim communities, would be difficult to prove. What is beyond doubt is that the millennia-old differences correspond, in the contemporary Muslim world, to a geographic continuum across the Persian/Arab/Turkish worlds, and one is tempted to ascribe a civilizational depth to such calques on the basis of the available textual evidence.

Dating, however, remains a problem, which can be illustrated in a posthumous note by the Italian legal historian Carlo Nallino. Article 1 of the Christian fifth-century Syro-Roman Code ends in the extant manuscripts, but one, on a statement of equality between male and female in the apportionment of inheritance:

The first words of the first paragraph of the Syro-Roman book are the following: 'If a man dies without writing a will and leaves behind male and female children, they will inherit equally'. But instead of stopping there, like the other Syriac manuscripts and like the Arabic and Armenian versions, the Parisian manuscript *P*, written in 1238–39 by a Syrian Jacobite from 'the province of Syria', continues as follows:... 'From the estate of the deceased, while the male receives two shares, the female only receives one share.'[49]

In other words, the Paris manuscript of the Syro-Roman Code introduces in the later version, some seven centuries after the original pre-Islamic text, the important qualification of a double share of the inheritance for the male against one share for the female. Nallino insists in his commentary that the qualification could *not* have been an oversight of the copyist,[50] and discusses the controversy over the origins of this 'interpolazione del copista' which raged among specialists in Syriac sources at the turn of the twentieth century. 'The conclusions', he writes, 'are not decisive',[51] but the origins of the qualification is according to him Muslim, 'origine che è ormai assoluta certezza'.[52]

---

[48] For instance Hjerrild: 'The Shi'ites did not form their succession law on the basis of the example they set by choosing 'Ali and his sons as successors. On the contrary: they chose 'Ali and his sons as successors and interpreted the Qur'anic inheritance laws according to their former traditions'. ibid. 53.

[49] Nallino, *Raccolta*, iv, above n. 37, 489–500 ('Appendice (inedita): L'interpolazione di *P* 1'), at 489–90: 'Le prime parole del primero paragrafo del Libro siro-romano sono, in tutti i manoscritti, le seguenti: "Si mortuus est vir et non scripsit testamentum et reliquit filios mares et feminas, heridant aequaliter". Invece di fermarsi a questo punto, come gli altri mss. siriaci et come le versioni araba et aramena, il codice parigini *P*, scritto nel 1238–39 da un Siro Giacobita nella "provincia di Siria", così continua: ... "bona eius, cum accipiat mares partes duas, feminae vero unam ex tribus partibus" '. (at 489–90). [50] ibid. 490.

[51] ibid. 499.   [52] ibid. 500. All footnotes omitted.

The consequences of this small addendum are twofold: first the difficulty of dating texts illustrates a more fundamental complexity which arises, as in this case, from the copyist's 'creative editing'. By simply adding one sentence, the 1238 Jacobite copyist may have introduced a central Islamic rule to the Christian law of succession which governs Near East Christians, namely that sons are entitled to double their sisters' share of succession. More significantly, this rule became law in most of the Orient until the twentieth century, and continues to date for significant sections of Christians in the Middle East. But it may simply be that, by the thirteenth century, that rule was so well ensconced in practice that the copyist did not see any problem in 'correcting' the earlier text. From that perspective, Islamic law operates as a 'corrector' of Christian law, while Christian law in the Syro-Roman Code provides a clear model for a dominant Islamic law system of succession in the Middle East. The question of influence becomes a twofold process, in which historical antecedence loses its importance in favour of some form of Middle Eastern 'common law'.

We therefore need to revise our view of Islamic law in the light of the pre- and post-Islamic Christian tradition in the Levant, and seriously consider close resemblances in substance and form across religions and eras in favour of an identifiable, common Middle Eastern legal *koine*. This can be further illustrated in a much later Christian reproduction of the 'Islamic' rule of 'the two shares for the son for one share for the daughter'.[53]

The legal calque occurs in a collection of Christian laws of the Eastern Maronite Church, written by the Bishop of Beirut 'Abdallah Qara'ali (d. 1154/ 1742). Qara'ali's code was entitled *Mukhtasar al-shari'a* (summary of the [Christian Maronite] *shari'a*) and was modelled after the Coptic compendium of Ibn al-'Assal (thirteenth century), 'which Qara'ali summarised some times, and contradicted rarely, in order to follow usage or what has entered into practice from Islamic law'.[54] Ibn al-'Assal is well established as a major point of reference in a continuum of Christian law which extends from Ethiopia's classical texts to the farthest northern tip of Arab Christendom. The *Mukhtasar* of 1720 is a direct successor of Ibn al-'Assal's Nomocanon, which itself incorporates verbatim passages from the Syro-Roman Code.

More than ten centuries after the Syro-Roman Code, and eight centuries after the Qur'anic revelation, Qara'ali's 'code' remains extremely close to the *ab intestat* succession of the Sunni system. 'The wife inherits one-fourth of the estate in the absence of children . . . and one-eighth with children.'[55] The surviving husband's share is respectively one-half and one-quarter. Other calques include the principle of the daughter's half share of her brother[56] and the various *'asaba* as the residuary

[53] The formula appears twice in the Qur'an, iv: 11 and iv: 176: 'To the male twice the share of the female, *wa lidh-dhakar mithlu hazz al-unthayayn*'.

[54] Introduction by Bulos Mas'ad to 'Abdallah Qara'ali, *Mukhtasar al-shari'a* (Beirut, 1959) 11.

[55] Qara'ali, *Mukhtasar al-shari'a*, 131.   [56] ibid. 132.

heirs with the fixed heirs of Islamic law.[57] On the whole, whether for family law or more generally civil and criminal law, Qara'ali's system belongs to common legal patterns of the Middle East.[58] While continuity is hard to prove because of the wide historical gaps between extant texts, parallels in substance, syntax, and terminology are striking.

It is in the context of common legal patterns shared within the Middle East between Islamic and Christian traditions that the Maronite Patriarch Yusuf Hubaysh's remarks in 1826 on his predecessor's *Mukhtasar* are particularly eloquent. There he recommended abandoning the prevailing rules of Islamic succession law since they guarantee a portion of the estate to the daughter: 'It is imperative to return the rules of inheritance of daughters and women to the former usage, meaning that they do not inherit in the presence of males, and are only given their dower... The judges, who presently follow everything in the [Christian Maronite] mountain on the basis of the Islamic laws, [stand against the tradition]...'.[59] In our tradition, the good bishop explains, girls should not inherit anything.

Nor is common legal language limited to the law of succession. In the Syro-Roman Code, frequent are words such as *kharaj* for land tax (Art. 31, 109), *qadhf* for false accusation (Art. 5, 66, 108), *mahr* for dower (e.g. Arts 38, 43, 44, 69 etc.) and the whole matrimonial law panoply of concepts (*talaq, sadaq, nikah*),[60] which appear as calque for an Islamic tradition persisting to the present day, alongside the terminology of abandoned practices relating to slavery, where the classical Islamic lawyer would find the full range of familiar legal concepts and, as demonstrated in the case of the rights of manumission,[61] similar substantive rules and regulations. One can even find such nuances as established in the current laws on guardianship in the Middle East. For the Christian Syro-Roman Code, a young woman is under the tutelage of the guardian (*wasi*) until she is 12, when she passes

---

[57] ibid. 'Qur'anic' heirs, *ashab al-furud*.

[58] These should probably include also the Coptic tradition, whose most famous classical jurist is Ibn al-'Assal, author of *al-Majmu' al-safawi*, a compilation of laws which he completed in Coptic calendar year 955, equivalent to 637/1239. The standard edition of this Nomocanon was published by Jirjis Filothaus 'Awad in Cairo in 1908. The wills and inheritance section can be found at 335–44 and 344–59. The principle of *'asaba* is recognized as 'the precedence of the tribe of the father over that of the mother, *taqdim qabilat al-ab 'ala qabilat al-umm*', at 347. One should also look beyond, to the old Egyptian Pharaonic patterns in the west and the Sasanid empire in the east, and to the Greek and Aramaic laws of the Orient, a vast research if any. The Christian legal tradition itself carries a commonalty of patterns which is easily recognizable in the explicit borrowings made by one Nomocanon to another, for instance those of Qara'ali and Ibn al-'Assal; and the Maronite *Kitab al-huda*, which incorporates two full chapters culled straight from the Syro-Roman book. Antoine Joubair, *Kitab al-huda* (Kaslik (Lebanon), 2nd edn, 1991) 157–9. *Kitab al-huda* is generally dated from the fifth/eleventh century.

[59] Letter of the Patriarch Hubaysh dated 29 September 1826, reproduced in ibid. 25–6. The full text is of great interest to both the sociology and law of the Middle East juridical *koine*. See also Ibrahim Najjar, 'Le droit de la famille au Liban au xviiième et xixème siècles: Contribution à l'étude du droit des non-musulmans sous l'Empire Ottoman', *Proche-Orient Etudes Juridiques* (Beirut, 40, 1987) 9–30.   [60] Respectively repudiation, dower (*sadaq* and *mahr* are equivalent), marriage.

[61] *wala'*, discussed in Crone, *Roman, provincial and Islamic law*, chapters 3 and 7, 35–42, 77–88.

under the control of another guardian defined in the text as *wali*, a word that also connotes guardianship. The upshot is that, in the latter case, she would be entitled to dispose of her property by will. The distinction between guardianship of the *wasi* and the guardianship of the *wali* is a feature of Islamic law to the present, as can be seen in the different legal operations of the two categories in the fields of education and custody.[62]

A final word on the value of comparative exercises in search of Middle Eastern legal patterns—however relative considering the difficulty of assessing genealogies of texts and translations[63]—derives from the emergence, in the text of the Syro-Roman book, of an unexpected feature of the law of marriage.

It was recently pointed out that 'one of the fundamental innovations of the early Church was the abolition of an ancient, venerable institution—divorce, the practice of which was as widespread as marriage itself'.[64] On the basis of documents from the collection of the Dead Sea Scrolls, the rejection of divorce as hitherto 'legal precedent' over millennia is suggested to have been introduced to the early Church by the Essenes—the Qumran or Dead Sea sect. 'It is no coincidence that the basis for a divorce-free Church can be found in the Sectarian literature of the Dead Sea Scrolls, since it suggests that the Essenes or other groups on the fringe of Hellenistic Judaism influenced the early formulation of Christian doctrine'.[65]

Interesting on its own as this finding may be, it is the more valuable in the context of a Syro-Roman Code where divorce initiated by either side is discussed at length, both in terms of unilateral repudiation of the husband 'without harm done' (Art. 51),[66] and in case of harm by the husband to the wife or vice versa: 'If the wife wants to separate from her husband or the husband separate from his

---

[62] See examples under the sections on custody in Chapter 10 below.

[63] The specialists vary in their dating of the Syro-Roman Code between the fourth and the eighth century! Nallino emits the possibility that 'the nucleus of the original Greek'(?) might have gone back as early as 312–37 ('Sul libro siro-romano e sul presunto diritto siriaco', *Raccolta* iv, 513–84, above n. 37, at 525); whilst Bruns and Sachau put the date squarely at 476. A more recent study wonders whether Theodosius, Leon, and Constantine, who are mentioned in the preface of the Code, were not those who reigned between 716 and 775. See Joubair, *Kitab al-huda*, above n. 58, 158 n. 1: 'Toute la question mérite un examen plus approfondi'. The study was carried out by Selb and Kaufhold, *Das Syrisch-Römische Rechtsbuch*, i, 43–46 n. 31, who show the impossibility of fixing a single date for the whole text, but confirm the correctness of Bruns' early conclusion that the texts stood 'nach dem Tod Leos I. im Jahre 474 n. Chr'. (at 46).

[64] M. J. Geller, 'Early Christianity and the Dead Sea Scrolls', *Bulletin of the School of Oriental and African Studies*, 57, 1994, 82–6.

[65] ibid. 85. There is a large literature on the Dead Sea Scrolls. The interested reader can start with Geza Vermes, *The Dead Sea Scrolls in English*, 4th edn. (London, 1995 (originally published in 1962)), which includes, on law, 'the Community rule', 69–94 (rules on joining the community of Essenes, abiding with its Covenant [presumably Biblical], the Master's role and the organization of the sect); 'the Damascus document', 95–119, including fragments of a penal code, 115–16, 'the statutes' on various rituals, Sabbath organization and choice of judges, 106–13; rules of war, 123–50; 'The temple scroll', including various laws on apostasy and rituals, 151–80; commentaries on Biblical law, 357–9. The original scrolls are in Hebrew or Aramaic and are dated between 220 BCE and 70 CE, but the dominant language, like the Bible and the Qur'an, is hardly 'legal'. [66] *min ghayri isa'a*.

wife, let the one who asks for separation send a letter of divorce[67] in which he or she explains his/her wishes. If the harm[68] is dealt by the husband, he must give his wife her dower and dowry.[69] If the woman is responsible for the harm, she only gets her dower and the husband retains her dowry as compensation for the injury.' (Art. 44)[70]

The Christian Syro-Roman book, therefore, does not seem to mind an otherwise banned Christian tradition such as divorce. In historical perspective, it is well known that divorce for followers of the Eastern Churches is much easier than for the adepts of Catholicism, as illustrated by the popular motto likening a glue-like indefectible relationship to a Maronite (Catholic) marriage. To that extent, articles like the one just quoted should not be unexpected. Nor would the various sub-forms of tolerated and regulated extra-marital relations with slave girls mentioned in the Syro-Roman Code come as a surprise.[71]

But it does come as a surprise that the polygamy of the Islamic tradition appears in calque in early Christian Middle Eastern law: 'If a man has two wives,[72] one of whom was wedded to him without *mahr* and the other had *mahr*, and he had children from both, then our law (*sunna*) allows him to bequeath to them equally' (Art. 18). Nor can that explicit mention of polygamy be an exception or the aberration of a copyist, for it is repeated in Art. 93.

Polygamy appears therefore to be an admitted fact which is legally recognized, and accepted, in the Christian Syro-Roman book. If proven true by a more sustained investigation, the consequences of such a conclusion would require a different approach to the marital practice and law of early Christendom. It is true that such instances, as well as those of the acceptable pattern of divorce uncovered by Professor Geller, may be too isolated to draw a Middle Eastern legal pattern running in a continuous thread from Hammurabi to modern Muslim countries, but they constitute one faint example of a phenomenon of legal calques which calls for less bridled 'imagination' by both jurists and historians. In that case, the upshot is significant: for Christians of the early Near East, divorce was legal.

A recapitulation at this stage of the central elements of this proposal of a Middle Eastern legal *koine* may be useful: a comprehensive pre-Islamic legal tradition, which strikes textual root two millennia before the Qur'an; a Muslim scripture

---

[67] *talaq.*   [68] *isa'a.*   [69] *mahraha wa jihazaha.*

[70] Note that both Babylonian and Islamic law allow the wife to leave her husband under special circumstances. Hammurabi's Code, § 131 (in case of false accusation of adultery) and § 142: 'If a woman has hated her husband and states "Thou shalt not have me", the facts of her case shall be determined in her district and, if she has kept herself chaste and has no fault, while her husband is given to going about out and so has greatly belittled her, that woman shall suffer no punishment; she may take her dower and go to her father's house'. However, as Bottéro has noted in a conversation for *grand public*, 'seul le mari avait le pouvoir de répudier sa femme', *Babylone et la Bible* (Paris, 1994) 202. For the equivalent Islamic *khul'*, see nn. 390–402 and accompanying text, and Chapter 10 below.

[71] The Code, like Antiquity codes and medieval Islamic treatises, is replete with references to slaves as commodities (e.g. Arts. 28, 33, 40), slave women (*ama*, e.g. Arts. 38, 41), manumission (*'itq*, e.g. Arts. 21–6) etc.   [72] *In kana li-rajul imra'atayn* (*sic*, instead of *imra'atan*).

which founds in the seventh century a comprehensive system of inheritance on a dominant, non-written system of *'asaba* allowing a central role to the male kin, with that key concept nowhere to be found in the Urtext, the Qur'an; next door (or underneath), a Christian Syro-Roman Code where divorce is permitted and where the system of inheritance follows closely the Sunni law of succession two to three hundred years before Islamic law had emerged; on the other side of the new Muslim empire, a Zoroastrian legal tradition which anticipates the main distinctive features of the Shi'i tradition; Christian judges and clerics in the seventeenth to nineteenth centuries following Islamic law against the hopes and desiderata of the patriarch of the community who deemed it too 'generous' towards women; unresolved questions of chronology and 'influence', including the adoption by Christian Coptic communities in Egypt of a national law which regulates their succession according to 'Islamic law' principles of inheritance, and which continues to apply to them to date.[73]

Against this long and chequered history of little known but recognizable legal patterns, is formed the tidal wave which has dominated the Middle East in the last millennium and a half: Islamic law.

Islamic Law

The fourteen or so centuries which separate us from the first Arab-Muslim conquests are an unwieldy patch with an enormous legal literature. While any linear history in the form of a legal continuum is tentative in the absolute, the denominations under which 'law' appears may be helpful for a general survey of the field.

'Law' gets expressed in the Islamic tradition in one of three words: *fiqh*, generally rendered as jurisprudence; *qanun*, which is used for law as statutes and as positive legal provisions in actual operation in a contemporary Middle Eastern society or state; and *shari'a* (or *shar'*), the generic term for Islamic law. Use of these terms for 'law' offers useful insights into the overall spirit of Middle Eastern legal systems.[74]

Shari'a denotes Islamic law as a whole. Originally 'the place from which one descends to water',[75] *shari'a* in the usuage of Arab lexicographers has developed to mean 'the law of water' and, with time, was extended to cover all issues, like water, which were considered vital to human existence, including 'what God has decreed for the people in terms of fasting, prayer, pilgrimage, marriage, contracts,

---

[73] All Egyptians, including Coptic Christians, follow inheritance Law 77/1943, which is mainly inspired from the Sunni Hanafi tradition.

[74] For a rich perspective on the various Arabic renderings of 'law' in modern Egypt, see Bernard Botiveau, *Loi islamique et droit dans les sociétés arabes: mutations des systèmes juridiques du Moyen-Orient* (Paris, 1993) 24–74.

[75] Lexicographer Ibn Manzur (d. 711/1311), *Lisan al-'arab* (Beirut, 1959) iii, 175. The original meaning of 'path' is common to the etymology of the Islamic *shari'a* and the Jewish *halakha*.

succession, war, . . . '.[76] *Shari'a* has thence become an all-encompassing concept which embraces the entirety of legal disciplines as developed from within the Islamic tradition.

Qur'an and *hadith*

Strictly speaking, the *shari'a* derives from two written sources: the Qur'an, the divine Book revealed to the Prophet Muhammad in the late sixth century CE, and the *sunna*, which is the reported compilation of the conversations (*hadith*) and deeds of the Prophet collected after his death from his companions. Depending on how a legal maxim is defined, the Qur'an encompasses between 80 and 500 verses that deal with 'law'. This has allowed scholars since Goldziher to suggest that the Qur'an's role in early Islamic law was limited.

In Syria, Egypt, and Persia, the Muslims had to contend with ancient local customs, based on ancient civilisations. To some extent they had to smooth over the conflict between inherited rights and newly acquired rights. In a word, Islamic legal practice, religious and civil alike, had to be subjected to regulation. Such guiding principles as the Qur'an itself could supply were not sufficient, for the Qur'anic statutes could not take care of the unforeseen conditions brought about by conquest. The provisions made in the Qur'an were occasional and limited to the primitive conditions of Arabia. They were not adequate for dealing with the new situation.[77]

Yet, the point was also made that Islamic law was first and foremost Qur'anic law. This is argued both textually and historically. Historically, the argument is the 'legal bent' of the Qur'an in an explicit and self-conscious manner, as is illustrated in chapter v: 44. The verse is about the revelation of the Qur'an to Muhammad as a law 'by which standard [the Prophet must] judge' Muslims. The traditional dating of the verse has allowed one authority to put the emergence of Muhammad as law dispenser and interpreter exactly in 627, the fifth year of the Hijra, when the Prophet assumed exclusive jurisdictional competence for Muslims.[78] Textually, it may be true that the Qur'an had 'only' 500 legal verses out of more than 6,000 in total, but this is a significant proportion for a book of this nature, which compares favourably with the Pentateuch, the Bible's legal book *par excellence*. After all, the Qur'an is much shorter than the Bible, and this relatively large number of verses is further enhanced, for the purpose of legal reach, by the unusual length of the legal verses, especially in such areas as marriage and succession.

[76] Al-Zubaydi (or Zabidi) (d. 1205/1790), *Taj al-'arus*, Benghazi, n.d., v, 394. For a comparison with modern water law, see my 'Law and the Nile river: emerging international rules and the *shari'a*', in J. A. Allan and P. Howell, eds., *The Nile: sharing a scarce resource* (Cambridge, 1994) 365–84.

[77] Ignaz Goldziher, *Introduction to Islamic law and theology* (Princeton, 1981) 36. (Original German, *Vorlesungen über den Islam*, 1910.)

[78] Samuel Goitein, 'The birth-hour of Muslim law', *The Muslim World*, 50, 1960, 23–9; also published in Goitein, *Studies in Islamic history and institutions* (Leiden, 1966) 126–34. For a discussion of Qur'an v: 44 in a modern context, see my *Renewal of Islamic law*, 62–7.

For marriage and divorce, the skeleton of the law is readily identifiable in the main distinctive elements which attach to Islamic societies: polygamy,[79] repudiation as a prerogative of the husband,[80] 'men being *qawwamun* over women'—that is, men being more readily 'in the right over women', or in a milder modern translation, men as 'protectors and maintainers' of wife and family,[81] as well as an elaborate but incomplete system of *ab intestat* and testamentary succession.[82] Criminal law is hybrid in the system, and beside the Hammurabi-like *lex talionis*, five particular crimes are mentioned in the Qur'an, to which are attached five penalties circumscribed by the tradition.[83] The text also suggests a parallel collective responsibility, but the resulting picture for criminal law had to be elaborated considerably by later jurists to achieve a coherence which has remained unsatisfactory to date. This incoherence is due to the difference worked out by the jurists on the basis of the Qur'anic text between *ta'zir* on the one hand—that is, for crimes not specified in the text, and therefore incurring penalties which are at the judge's discretion—and, on the other hand, the specific *hadd* crimes attaching to the five categories just mentioned, and which incur a fairly automatic penalty regulated or adumbrated in the Urtext.

As in the case of agnatic priorities in succession, with the agnates appearing in Sunni law as residual heirs, the 'customary' law of crime is also residuary in the concept of *diyya* as collective compensation for both intended and accidental

---

[79] Qur'an iv: 3.   [80] Qur'an iv: 227–32; iv: 35; and Sura lxv, entitled '*talaq*, repudiation'.

[81] Qur'an iv: 34. 'Men as protectors and maintainers of women' is one common translation (in the widely used bilingual text-cum-translation of A. Yusuf Ali, 1st edn., 1934) of the Arabic '*al-rijal qawwamun 'alal-nisa'* '. The formula, together with the mention of 'men having a degree over women (*wa lil-rijal 'alayhunna daraja*)' Qur'an ii: 228, has been the subject of an important controversy over the interpretation of the sacred text in modern 'feminist' literature. See e.g. Mallat, 'Le féminisme islamique de Bint al-Houda', *Maghreb-Machrek*, 116, 1987, 45–58, at 52 and n. 48. The difficulty to project modern gender egalitarian concepts onto the classical age is discussed in Chapter 10. As historical legal calque, compare the *qahriman* of the Syro-Roman book, Art. 72: 'The free woman is empowered to make her husband in charge of her money and her flock, *al-mar'a al-hurra musallata an tusayyira zawjaha qahrumanan 'ala maliha wa mawashiha*'. Like the Muslim tradition, this respects the separate financial legal status of the wife, while allowing her to delegate her financial power to her husband.

[82] The main Qur'anic verses on intestate succession, iv: 11 and 12 are mentioned above, nn. 41, 42, 53, to which should be added iv: 176, establishing *kalala* (traditionally interpreted as the state of the person who dies without children, and without a father). The interpretation of *kalala* (which also appears in Qur'an iv: 12) has been the subject of a radical revision of the early law of succession by David Powers, *Studies in Qur'an and hadith: the formation of the Islamic law of inheritance* (Berkeley 1986) 21–52. For testamentary succession, see Qur'an ii: 181 and v: 109–11, but note that the important qualifications on the right to bequeathe are *hadith*-based.

[83] *zina*, unlawful intercourse, for which the penalty is death by stoning (Qur'an xxiv: 2–3, the Qur'anic text establishes one hundred lashes as penalty for the adulterer or adulteress, but this was modified into stoning by *hadith*); *qadhf*, false accusation of unlawful intercourse, Qur'an xxiv: 4–5, for which the penalty is eighty lashes; wine drinking and gambling, Qur'an ii, 219, v: 93–4, for which no specific penalty is mentioned (on the basis of *hadith*, wine drinking is punished with flogging); theft (Qur'an v: 41), for which the penalty is amputation; and highway robbery, for which the penalty is death by crucifixion, Qur'an v: 33. (Again, note that highway robbery, *qat' al-tariq*, does not appear as such in the Qur'anic text, where the concept is about those who 'create havoc on earth, *fasad fil-ard*' or 'wage war against the Prophet'.)

criminal injuries.[84] As for economic law, the staples are well known, even if particularly skeletal: the necessity to abide by contracts and the prohibition of *riba* (interest, usury) and other distortions of fair markets.[85]

The other formal scriptural source for Islamic law is the *hadith* or *sunna*. The *sunna*, a term encountered for 'law' in the Syro-Roman Code, acquired in Islam the more specific meaning of the acts and words of the Prophet Muhammad. The *sunna* is divided by scholars into Muhammad's sayings,[86] better known as *hadith* (words, conversation), his actions,[87] and his silence.[88] The *hadith* represents the most important part of the *sunna*, and consists of several thousand aphorisms attributed to the Prophet, related by his companions, and collected by scholars over the centuries. As one might expect, there is a vast literature on the subject, resulting from a fully established discipline of *hadith* scholarship. It includes studies of the Prophet's companions, of tradents and relaters, of authenticity and 'strength' of various *hadith* depending on the trustworthiness of reporters and the chains of transmission, and the perusal of the collections of *hadith* and their internal structures. A formally sophisticated taxonomy of *hadith* was elaborated in due course by scholars like Ibn al-Salah (d. 642/1244), and it is generally accepted in the Sunni tradition that the field was unruly 'until Ibn al-Salah came...and elaborated on the arrangements of al-Khatib,[89] put order in its dispersed meanings and added to it some of the best results [of the science of *hadith*], ordering in his book[90] what was disorderly in others. This explains why people used it and followed it so much. Innumerable are the commentaries, manuals, books pro and contra...'.[91] The debate on *hadith* is significant and complex. Like the debate on the Qur'an, it involves problems of canonization and of historical genesis, occupying in the past years a significant number of scholars across East and West.[92]

---

[84] Qur'an iv: 92 (*diyya* for homicide, manslaughter); ii: 178–9 (principle of *qisas*, the law of talion, repeated xvi: 126, developed in v: 45, 'life for life, eye for eye, nose for nose, ear for ear, tooth for tooth').

[85] Abide by your promises and contracts (Qur'an v: 1; xvii: 34); avoid fraud (generally lxxxiii: 1; in weights and measures, xvii: 35), reject *riba* (ii: 275–6; iii: 130). See Chapters 8 and 9 below.

[86] *sunna qawliyya.*

[87] *sunna fi'liyya* (literally the *sunna* of doing, which represents the Prophet's reported acts).

[88] *sunna taqririyya,* which consists of reported silences of the Prophet suggesting either his indifference or acquiescence.

[89] Al-Khatib al-Baghdadi, d. 463/1071, author of *al-Kifaya* and of *al-Jame' li-adab al-shaykh wal-same',* and other books on *hadith.*

[90] Ibn al-Salah, *Muqadimma fi 'ulum al-hadith* (Introduction to the science of *hadith*), M. Dib al-Bagha ed. (Damascus, 1984).

[91] Muhammad Abu Zahu, *Makanat al-sunna fi al-islam* (The place of *sunna* in Islam) (Cairo, 1984 (or 1959)), 490–1, citing the comment on ibn al-Salah by the later *hadith* compiler al-Hafiz ibn Hajar al-'Asqalani (d. 852/1449). See also the more recent M. al-Sabbagh, *Al-hadith al-nabawi* (The Prophetic *hadith*). (Beirut, 1981).

[92] These include the towering figure of John Wansbrough, who joined Qur'an, *hadith*, *maghazi* (literature on the early Islamic conquests) and *sira* (the literature on the life of the Prophet) in an investigation of processes of interpretation which addressed the 'sacred' literature of Islam as a genre. There is now a Wansbroughian school which includes a number of prominent disciples like Gerald Hawting, the late Norman Calder, and Andrew Rippin. Other important scholars in the field include William Graham, *Divine word and prophetic word in early Islam* (The Hague, 1977); John Burton, *The*

First, it is important to underline the fact that *hadith* is more than just a textual font for the *shari'a*. As is the case for the Qur'an, many fields are elicited by the Prophet's *Tischreden*, including for uses internal to *hadith* criticism and the study of the reporters of the *hadith*.[93] The 'science' of *hadith* permeates several fields of scholarship, including history and literature.[94]

Secondly, and this lies in contrast to the Qur'an, there is no definite common Urtext for *hadith*. This means that the two main branches of Islam, the Sunnis and the Shi'is, do not use the same texts as their *hadith*. There is no Shi'i version of the Qur'an, but there are specific Shi'i *hadith* compilations, which came much later in 'official' history than for Sunnis. The process of *hadith*-compiling for the Sunnis is restricted to the sayings of the Prophet Muhammad as related by his companions and eventually recorded by six main compilers: Bukhari (d. 256/870), Muslim (d. 261/875) Ibn Maja (d. 273/887), Abu Dawud (d. 274/888), Tirmidhi (d. 278/892), and Nasa'i (d. 302/915).[95] In addition, one finds other important compilations of varying comprehensiveness,[96] including early books written by the great legal eponyms of the tradition, whose language pertains more closely to

---

collection of the Qur'an (Cambridge, 1979); *The sources of Islamic law: Islamic theories of abrogation* (Edinburgh, 1990); *An introduction to the hadith* (Edinburgh, 1994) ; G. A. Juynboll, *Muslim tradition: studies in chronology, provenance and authorship of early hadith* (Cambridge, 1983). Burton and Juynboll have laid emphasis on the coherence and consistency of the internal *hadith* discipline in classical Islam, against more 'revisionist' schools which started with Ignaz Goldziher and continued with Joseph Schacht, Patricia Crone, and Michael Cook. Cook and Crone have published a controversial essay on the emergence of Islam as a Jewish sect in *Hagarism: the making of the Islamic world* (Cambridge, 1977). (See Wansbrough's criticism in *Bulletin of the School of Oriental and African Studies*, 41, 1978, 155–6). This thesis was toned down in later works of more limited scope, like Cook's *Early Muslim dogma: a source-critical study* (Cambridge, 1981); and his short *Muhammad* (Oxford, 1983). An important discussant of early Islam was the foremost scholar of Islamic law in the twentieth century, Joseph Schacht, who wrote an important book on *The origins of Muhammadan jurisprudence* (Oxford, 1950), eliciting strong reactions from Muslim scholars, notably Muhammad Mustafa Azami, the author of a well-researched criticism of Schacht's findings, M. M. al-Azami, *On Schacht's Origins of Muhammadan Jurisprudence* (Riyadh, *c.* 1985), and in that vein more recently Yasin Dutton, *The origins of Islamic law* (London, 1999). Twentieth-century *hadith* scholars writing in Arabic include the Egyptians Muhammad Abu Zahra and Muhammad Abu Zahu; the Lebanese Subhi al-Saleh and Subhi Mahmasani, and the Syrian Muhammad Sa'id Ramadan al-Buti.

[93] known as *'ilm al-rijal*.

[94] On early history and *hadith*, see Tarif Khalidi, *Arabic historical thought in the classical period* (Cambridge, 1994) 17–82. This includes a serene appreciation of the current state of *hadith* historiography, e.g. at 20 n. 6; and a useful long footnote 20 on *hadith* literature, at 26–7.

[95] See A. J. Wensinck (with, later, J. P. Mensing), *Concordance et indices de la tradition musulmane: les Six Livres, le Musnad d'al-Darimi, le Muwatta' de Malik, le Musnad de Ahmad ibn Hanbal*, 2nd edn., (Leiden, 1992 (8 vols in 4)). The original edition was published between 1936 and 1988. Of common usage is the compilation by the (nominally) Zaydi jurist al-Shawkani (d. 1250/1832), from Yemen, *Nayl al-awtar*, Beirut edn. in 10 vols (orig. Cairo edn. AH 1297), with two volumes of indexes dated 1992.

[96] e.g. the recently published 'Abd al-Razzaq al-San'ani (d. 211/826), *al-Musannaf*, Habib al-A'zami ed., 11 vols (Beirut, 1970–2), used extensively by Harald Motzki, *Die Anfänge des Islamischen Jurisprudenz- Ihre Entwicklung in Mekka bis zur Mitte des 2./8. Jahrhunderts* (Stuttgart, 1991). See the review of Maher Jarrar in *al-Abhath* (American University of Beirut), 40, 1992, 129–42.

hadith than to law. The *Muwatta'* of Malik ibn Anas (d. 179/795) and the *Musnad* of Ibn Hanbal (d. 241/855) are two such examples.[97]

Shi'is share many of these *hadith*, but have developed over time their own books of reference. The four early books of Shi'i *hadith* were compiled by three scholars (Kulayni, d. 328/940; Ibn Babawayh, d. 380/991, and Tusi, d. 460/1068), but there are also vast compilations of Shi'i *hadith* of a later period, notably al-Hurr al-'Amili's *Wasa'el al-Shi'a* (d. 1110/1699). A key difference for the so-called 'Twelver' Shi'is[98] is the use not only of Prophetic *hadith*, but also of the sayings ascribed to the twelve Imams of their tradition, especially, in the case of law, those sayings attributed to the jurist Ja'far al-Sadeq (d. 147/765), the sixth Imam.

In addition to the *hadith* eliciting various types of interpretation which are not always legal, and in addition to different compilations of *hadith* amongst Sunnis and Shi'is, the use of *hadith* as 'law' is a particularly complex one, even if such use is massive and current. One example is the *mut'a*, the temporary marriage permitted by the Shi'is on the strength of a *hadith* qualifying a verse in the Qur'an where the concept appears,[99] whereas Sunnis consider such a legal arrangement absolutely void. 'We must', Goldziher wrote a century ago, 'regard the *mut'a*-marriage as the sharpest legal dispute between Sunni and Shi'i Islam'.[100]

As is the case for the Qur'an in the verse on *mut'a*, the aphoristic nature of the *hadith* has lent itself to a sophisticated body of legal hermeneutics, not least in the dialectic between the two *Ur* sources, the Book and the *sunna*:

The *hadith* collections, by virtue of their size alone, dominated the hermeneutic process, but the relationship between Qur'an and *hadith* was difficult to express. Some jurists accepted that the *sunnah* might 'abrogate' the Qur'an; others preferred to say that the *sunnah* 'passed

---

[97] The *Muwatta'* of Malik, the eponym of the Maliki school of law, was edited by Sahnun (d. 240/854) in a 16 volume collection known as the *Mudawwana*, and by others. See Dutton, above n. 92, at 22–31 and *passim*.

[98] Twelver, *ithna 'ashari*. The majority of Shi'is believe in the special place of the Twelve *imams* of the tradition, from the cousin and son-in-law of the Prophet, 'Ali, to the twelfth *imam*, who disappeared in 329/941. This disappearance started the Great Occultation (*ghayba*) which Twelver Shi'is believe will end when the vanished *imam* returns to redeem the world. The word *imam* is common amongst all Muslims as leader of the prayer, or distinguished scholar, but it is usually reserved for the twelve figures of the tradition by that majoritarian branch of Shi'ism.

[99] Qur'an iv: 24: '*fa ma istamta'tum bihi minhunna fa'tuhunna ujuruhunna faridatan*', literally 'and give them their fees for the pleasure (*mut'a*) you received from them'. Sunnis consider this pre-Islamic practice to have been forbidden by the Prophet, alternatively by Caliph 'Umar (reigned 12–24/634–44). Shi'is rely on a *hadith* by Ibn 'Abbas (d. 68/688) to confirm the standing of the rule. For a clear exposition, see s.v. *mut'a* in the first edition of the *Encyclopaedia of Islam*, Leiden, 1916, by W. Heffening. It is also suggested that the institution of *mut'a*, like the laws of succession, continues for the Persian-Shi'i ambit previous Zoroastrian legal traditions, Hjerrild, 'Islamic law and Sasanian law', above n. 45, 53; M. Macuch, 'Die Zeitehe im Sasanidischen Recht-ein Vorlaufer der Shi'itischen mut'a-Ehe in Iran?', *Archaeologische Mitteilungen aus Iran*, 18 (Berlin, 1985) 187–203; Perikhanian, 'Iranian society and law', above n. 45, 649–50.

[100] Goldziher, *Introduction to Islamic theology and law*, above n. 77, 209. For a comprehensive work on early Shi'i–Sunni differences, S. H. M. Jafri, *The origins and early development of Shi'a Islam* (London, 1979).

judgment' on the Qur'an, or that it 'clarified' and 'explained'. There were variant views within schools. Whatever the preferred wording, none would disagree with the statement attributed to the Syrian jurist Awza'i (d. 157/774) that the Book is in greater need of the *sunnah* than the *sunnah* is of the Book. The vitality, complexity, and exuberance of *fiqh* literature—and many of the fundamental norms of the law—are unthinkable except in relation to the large body of revelation constituted by the *hadith*.[101]

Another example, previously discussed in terms of Zoroastrian/Syro-Roman difference, is the acceptance of the concept of *'asaba* for the Sunnis as key organizer of the whole succession scheme, and its rejection by the Shi'is.

The way this distinction appears within the textual debate shows the importance of the *hadith* as qualifier of central importance in the legal system.

From a textual point of view, the Sunnis rest their case on a key *hadith* which one of the companions, Ibn Tawus, heard from the Prophet: 'Give the shares [of the estate] to those to whom it belongs [under the rules of the Qur'an], and what remains to the closest male'.[102] The formula appears four times in Bukhari's book of succession in his standard compilation of the Prophet's sayings.[103] However, the concept of *'asaba* itself does not appear in that context. Where the word appears— only once—the context relates a rare case of succession in which a woman dies in labour, and her foetus also dies. The *hadith* in this case gives her estate to her sons and husband, but leaves 'reason to her *'asaba*'.[104] The rule is unclear, and seems to relate to the law of blood-money, and not to inheritance. It is also remarkable that the word *'asaba* does not appear in one of the earliest extant treatises on the law of succession, Sufyan al-Thawri's (d. 161/778) *Kitab al-fara'ed*. Still, the *hadith* related by ibn Tawus appears in the following form in Sufyan's treatise: 'Give the money according to the [Qur'anic] shares, but if the shares are left [i.e. exhausted], then to the closest male'.[105]

---

[101] Norman Calder, entry on 'Law', in J. Esposito, ed., *The Oxford encyclopaedia of the modern Islamic world* (New York, 1995) 4 vols, ii, 451. In a long introduction to a standard edition of Bukhari's *Sahih*, the modern Arab editors assert the total equality between Qur'an and *sunna*, but acknowledge that some classical scholars, like Shatibi (d. 790/1388), and some modern scholars like al-Khawli and others, said 'wrongly' otherwise (i.e. that the *hadith* has precedence in law). M. Nawawi, and M. Abu al-Fadl Ibrahim, M. Khafaji, '*Sahih* ibn 'Abdallah al-Bukhari', in Bukhari (d. 256/870), *Sahih*, 9 vols (Cairo, 1376) i, 6–8, and n. 1 at 8. An example of the importance of *hadith* as formal source in Islamic law, as well as a complicating factor in terms of its interaction with the Qur'an, can be found in the famous Prophetic aphorism on *riba*: 'Gold for gold, silver for silver, wheat for wheat, barley for barley, dates for dates, salt for salt, each kind for each kind, in hand; he who increases or asks for increase commits *riba* alike whether he gives or takes; *al-dhahab bil-dhahab wal-fidda bil-fidda wal-burr bil-burr wal-sha'ir bil-sha'ir wal-tamr bil-tamr wal-milh bil-milh mithlan bi-mithlin yadan bi-yadin. Faman zad aw istazad faqad arba al-akhidh wal-mu'ta fihi sawa'.*' Text e.g. in Shawkani (d. 1250/1832), *Nayl al-awtar*, above n. 96, v, 190. See also my 'The debate on *riba* and interest in twentieth century jurisprudence', in C. Mallat, ed., *Islamic law and finance* (London, 1988) 69–88, and Chapter 9 below, section on Islamic banking.

[102] *Alhiqu al-fara'ed bi-ahliha fama baqiya li-awla rajul dhakar.*

[103] Bukhari, *Sahih*, viii, 124–31, once at 126 and 128, twice at 127 (*Kitab al-fara'ed*, book of succession).   [104] *al-'aql 'ala 'asabatiha*, ibid. at 128.

[105] *Alhiqu al-mal bil-farayed, fa-idha turikat al-farayed, fa-awla rajul dhakar*, in Raddatz, 'Frühislamisches Erbrecht', above n. 38, *hadith* at 35.

In contrast, there is no room for the *'asaba*, either as vocable, or as concept, in the Shi'i scheme of succession. This is 'graphically expressed in the dictum of the Shi'i Imam, Ja'far al-Sadeq: "As for the *'asaba* (the agnates), dust in their teeth" '.[106]

There are therefore internal textual explanations for the Shi'i–Sunni differences in the scheme of succession. The textual conflict dovetails with political dissensions over the succession to the Caliphate: for the Shi'is, entitlement to the political succession of the Prophet should have passed through his sole daughter, Fatima, who is both the wife of his cousin 'Ali and the mother of the two grandsons, Hasan and Hussein. The Prophet died in 632, and 'Ali was pre-empted by three other Caliphs until he finally sat at the helm of the young Muslim empire, much later, in 656. But his reign was brief, and he was killed by an assassin in 661, while his arch-rival Mu'awiya took over to found the Umayyad dynasty, cementing the great schism in the Muslim world, still dominant to date, between Shi'is and Sunnis. There is therefore a strong political overtone to the schemes of succession, in which the Prophet's daughter, as his main heir, plays a determining role for the Shi'is as the wife or mother of their three first Imams, and a secondary one for the Sunnis. Sometime in the early classical age, the political, textual, and possibly social traditions fused with a theological approach which was specific to each of the two large Muslim communities. The theological differences are 'unbridgeable', even if attempts at fusion or rapprochement are variously attested to in the present age.[107] In an effort to portray the differences as secondary to a common appreciation of the *shari'a*—a conclusion which depends on the scale and context of comparison[108]—the Ja'fari school of law is sometimes portrayed as the fifth school, alongside the other four 'recognized' Sunni schools: the Hanafi, Maliki, Shafi'i, and Hanbali *madhhab*s. Still, ritual and theological differences between Sunnis and Shi'is are evident in everyday life.[109]

---

[106] Noel Coulson, *Succession in the Muslim family* (Cambridge, 1971) 108.

[107] The presentation of the theological differences as 'unbridgeable' is Hamid Algar's. For another serene appreciation of the differences in historical context, see the chapter by the Iraqi sociologist 'Ali al-Wardi on the rapprochement attempted in 1155/1743 between Sunnis and Shi'is by the Iranian king Nader Shah, in '*Nader Qali wa mashru' al-madhhab al-khames* (Nader Qali and the project of the fifth school)', in Wardi, *Lamahat ijtima'iyya min tarikh al-'iraq al-hadith* (Social approaches to the history of modern Iraq), 8 vols (Baghdad, 1969–79) i, 118–48, esp. 134–6 and 147–8. On this episode of the Congress of 1743, see Algar, 'Shi'ism and Iran in eighteenth-century Islamic history', in T. Naff and R. Owen, eds., *Studies in eighteenth century Islamic history* (Carbondale, 1977) 288–302, and, in the context of modern Iraqi history, my 'Religious militancy in contemporary Iraq: Muhammad Baqer as-Sadr and the Sunni-Shi'a paradigm', *Third World Quarterly*, Spring 1988, 699–729. The main theological difference is about the position and reverence owed to the Twelve Imams in the Shi'i tradition.

[108] For an elaborate argument of 'scale' in comparative law generally, see Hiram Chodhosh, 'Comparing comparisons: in search of methodology', *Iowa Law Review*, 84, 1999, 1025–1131.

[109] Two simple examples: in prayer, a Shi'i person holds his hands alongside his body, whereas a Sunni crosses them. At one point in the recitation, the Sunni will hold up his or her right hand index, the Shi'i won't. These traditions, which are rooted in respective *hadiths* and elucidated in the jurists' works in the relevant sections on rituals, are equally 'unbridgeable' socially, and set the two communities apart, even in common prayer. Nor are these differences less obvious in the way a Near East Orthodox Christian signs her/himself when praying: unlike the Catholic worshipper who does it with

Fiqh

These examples show the importance of interpretation: whatever the exact nature of Qur'anic dominance over the law and the place of the *hadith* in the system, the *shari'a* as discipline was formed over the centuries through arduous and systematic scholarship as developed by jurists of competing schools of law. Whilst formally based on the Qur'an and the *sunna*, the *shari'a* generated a logic of its own as jurists had to articulate their system in conjunction with internal coherence and social interests, needs and customs, even if it is probably impossible to reconstruct with any scientific certainty either 'the Prophet's Arabia' or indeed the scribal and communal 'collection of the Qur'an'.[110] This is echoed in the confusion over the precise definition of the boundary between *shari'a* and *fiqh*. The systematic exercise of developing the law over the centuries has tended to be understood under the umbrella of *fiqh*, with the word *shari'a* being rarely used in this context. In a general simplification, however, the *shari'a* encompasses *fiqh*, whereas *fiqh* as a hybrid of jurists' jurisprudence and substantive 'textbook' law is only one of the several forms taken by Islamic law as a whole, the *shari'a*.[111]

his full hand, the Orthodox Christian will only use three fingers to make the sign of the cross, and the movement is head-chest-right shoulder-left shoulder. Catholics will inverse the last two movements.

[110] In addition to Burton and Wansbrough's recent works, above n. 92, one should mention Henri Lammens' (d. 1937) pioneering books on Mecca and Medina at the time of the Prophet, *La Mecque à la veille de l'hégire* (Beirut, 1924); *L'Arabie occidentale avant l'hégire* (Beirut, 1928) (though heavily criticized by Patricia Crone, *Meccan trade and the rise of Islam* (Oxford, 1987)). There is understandably a vast literature on the early Islamic period, including numerous biographies of the Prophet. They include Montgomery Watt, *Muhammad at Mecca* (Oxford 1953), and *Muhammad at Medina* (Oxford 1956); Maxime Rodinson, *Mahomet* (Paris, 1961, new edn., 1968, English translation New York, 1974); Edmond Rabbath, *Mahomet, prophète arabe et fondateur d'état* (Beirut 1981).

[111] Another way of approaching the field is educational. At the School of Oriental and African Studies in London University, the teaching of what we know as Islamic law started in the 1920s with Professor S. Vesey-Fitzgerald. The course used to be known as Muhammadan law. Two decades later, the course became known as Muslim law, and the word continued to be used until the 1970s. The two main teachers were Norman Anderson, who retired from that branch in the early 1970s and Noel Coulson. The course title had by then turned into 'Islamic law', and remained so entitled after Coulson's death in 1986. The content of the course corresponded generally to the literature published by the three major exponents of the *shari'a* at London University over the century: S. Vesey-Fitzgerald, *Muhammadan law* (London, 1931); N. Anderson, *Law reform in the Muslim world* (London, 1976); and N. Coulson, *A history of Islamic law*, cited above n. 3. The title of Joseph Schacht's two main books moved from 'Muhammadan jurisprudence' (1950) to 'Islamic law' (1964). The terminology Muhammadan-Muslim-Islamic manifests a shift in paradigm in the Kühnian parlance: in the first stage, there was little compunction in reducing the divinely ordained law of Islam to the persona of the Prophet. In a second phase, the use of 'Muslim' allowed a more neutral and more deferential attention to the belief of Muslims, but it expressed a static approach to the discipline, which eventually gave way to a more dynamic third stage. The course was by then known as Islamic law, which corresponded in Arabic to a similar passage from *muslim* to *islami*. The shift has been noted as a sign of the impact of rising religious militancy taking over from the more sedate, Muslim state-of-fact. See Mallat, 'Introduction—Islamic family law; variations on state identity and community rights', in C. Mallat and J. Connors, eds., *Islamic family law* (London, 1990) 1–9 at 3 and n. 20. In my own teaching at London University (1988–96), the course material developed from the traditional coverage of history (part one) and family (part two), to a field encompassing a wide array of legal subjects, including Babylonian and Syriac calques and modern constitutional law and economics.

A serious student of classical Islamic law will find it primarily in *fiqh* books. These are books of law which are renowned for their complex and elaborate phraseology. They are written in a legal language which is difficult to understand even for native educated Arabic speakers. It is only after a long apprenticeship that the law as found in the *fiqh* books starts giving up its secrets.

The span of time covered by *fiqh* literature is unique in the legal history of humanity, and it is difficult to piece together a puzzle which, to say the least, is difficult to reconstruct over almost a millennium and a half. In the present state of scholarship on Islamic law, the Qur'an is considered by most Muslim scholars to mark a decisive beginning for the *shari'a*, and they are supported in this by an established Western authority like Samuel Goitein.[112] Western scholars might not dispute this argument, so long as it does not subsume the *fiqh* genre, the beginning of which has been put by Schacht in the second century AH,[113] while more recent scholarship variously places the beginnings between the first[114] and the third century AH.[115] In the absence of a historical assessment of the interface between orality and law, talk of origins will remain nebulous.[116] Irrespective of Sherlock Holmes-like reconstructions,[117] and the fascination of the field with beginnings,[118] one fact is certain. From the early extant treatises, which go back to the second (or third?) century after the death of the Prophet Muhammad, to the present day, *fiqh* has

---

[112] Goitein, 'The birth-hour of Muslim law', cited above n. 78.

[113] Schacht, *Origins*, 4 (middle of second century for 'considerable body of legal traditions'), 190 (beginning of second century 'when Muhammadan jurisprudence started').

[114] Motzki, *Die Anfänge des Islamischen Jurisprudenz, passim* and 262–4.

[115] Christopher Melchert, *The formation of the Sunni schools of law, 9th–10th centuries C.E.* (Leiden, 1997).

[116] Whilst recognizing the impressive textual work of scholars like Schacht, Calder, Burton, Crone, and other historians, there is an instance which 'outsiders' might miss because of their lack of familiarity with the strength of oral high culture in the Middle East. A remarkable tradition may be just passing, of generations of *lettrés* who committed to memory thousands of verses, for instance much of the extensive poetry of the great Arab poet Mutanabbi (d. 353/965), or the full epic poem of Firdawsi (d. *c.* 410/1020), the *Shahnameh*. One is talking here of thousands of lines. To the extent that orality and oral transmission remain, by definition, beyond the purview of the historian's perusal of texts, assessment of the formation of early Islamic law will never be 'scientific'. Still, one can argue the absence of history when there is no written history. On the discussion of the early 'oral tradition', see preliminary material in R. Stephen Humphreys, *Islamic history* (Princeton, 1991) 85–7.

[117] For example, the bold but excessive conclusions of Calder, *Studies*, at 146 and 180, that passage from oral traditions to systematic writing took the form of the 'notebooks', the *mukhtasar*s; or the brilliant use by David Powers of grammatical inconsistencies to redraw a whole 'proto-Islamic law of succession' which would have preceded the present rules of the Sunni world. Powers, *Studies in Qur'an and hadith*, 211–16.

[118] While that fashion might have passed, historic scholarship of early Islamic law, either in the East or the West, does not seem to ever have been impressed by Michel Foucault and other structuralists' distrust for 'the search of origins'. The Wansbrough school provides new perspectives after its initiator's interest in 'canonical' breaks in Islam, literary genres, and calques, and the consequent avoidance of an obsession with dates, precedence, and other respositories of civilizational and religious debts. It was followed to some extent by Norman Calder, but the fascination with origins has remained dominant in the scholarship despite the contrary direction which I prefer to read in Wansbrough's *Qur'anic studies* and *The sectarian milieu*. See generally my 'Readings of the Qur'an in Najaf and London' cited above at n. 16.

proceeded unabated, with, as a result, thousands of works, some of which extend to twenty or more volumes of commentaries and commentaries on commentaries. Not surprisingly, the staggering wealth of this tradition is viewed with awe and pride by scholars and laity alike in the Muslim world, as both complexity and depth characterize these treatises, most famous among which are *al-Umm* by Shafi'i (d. 204/820),[119] *al-Hawi al-kabir* by Mawardi (d. 450/1058), *al-Muhalla* by Ibn Hazm (d. 456/1064), *al-Mabsut* by Sarakhsi (d. *c.* 490/1097), *Bada'e' al-sana'e'* by Kasani (d. 587/1191), *al-Mughni* by Ibn Qudama (d. 620/1223), *al-Hidaya* by Marghinani (d. 593/1196), *Shara'e' al-Islam* by the Shi'i al-Muhaqqiq al-Hilli (d. 676/1277), *al-Bahr al-ra'eq* by Ibn Nujaym (d. 970/1563), *al-Sharh al-kabir* by Dardir (d. 1201/1786), through to *Radd al-muhtar 'alal-durr al-mukhtar* by Ibn 'Abidin (d. 1252/1836), which is one of the late *fiqh* compendia of the Sunni world.[120] Shi'is continue to produce books in this vein, the latest by scholars such as Muhsin al-Hakim (d. 1389/1970), Ruhollah al-Khumaini (d. 1409/1989) and Abul-Qasem al-Khu'i (d. 1412/ 1992).[121]

The structure of a comprehensive *fiqh* compendium will depend on its length, but it generally consists of a first part on the law of rituals[122] and a second part on transactions,[123] each subdivided into several 'books'.[124] The strictly religious dimension of the first part is obvious, but one may encounter in the works of some authors discussions of more mundane matters such as the payment of tax,[125] or the conditions of a just war,[126] and the appointment of a scholar[127] or a legal

---

[119]   There are several editions of these classic works, many reprinted from earlier editions without acknowledgment. Most serious books on classical Islamic law have a bibliographical list including the main texts, see e.g. Schacht, *Introduction to Islamic law*, 261–9. There is usually no point in providing the translation of classical *fiqh* titles, which are allegorical rather than indicative (e.g. *al-Umm*, The mother [of texts], *al-Bahr al-ra'eq*, The quiet sea).

[120]   Modern compendia of Islamic law by Sunni authors are different, in style much more 'modern', and more accessible to the reader. Among the remarkable authors, the following stand out: Wahbeh al-Zuhayli, *al-Fiqh al-islami wa-adillatuhu: al-shamil lil-adilla al-shar'iyya wa-al-ara' al-madhhabiyya* (Islamic law and its reasons: compendium of legal arguments and school opinions) (Damascus, 1984) in 8 vols; 'Abd al-Razzaq al-Sanhuri, *Masader al-haqq fi al-fiqh al-islami* (Sources of law in Islamic law) Cairo, 1954–59) in 6 vols; Mustafa al-Zarqa, *al-Fiqh al-islami fi thawbihi al-jadid* (Islamic law in its new robe) (Damascus, *c.* 1960) in 3 vols.

[121]   The leading Shi'i scholars usually publish a comprehensive treatise known as *risala 'amaliyya* (practical treatise) to attain the rank of *marja'* (literally reference) in the Shi'i world. The treatise is a compendium of *fiqh* which, in the twentieth century, often took the shape of a commentary/update on the nineteenth-century scholar al-Tabataba'i al-Yazdi's (d. 1329/1911) *al-'Urwa al-wuthqa*, itself modelled on Murtada al-Ansari's (d. 1281/1864) *Makasib*. Khumaini's two-volume 1964 treatise, for instance, is entitled *Tahrir al-wasila*. The Iraqi Muhsin al-Hakim (d. 1970) also wrote an extensive commentary on Yazdi's book, entitled *Mustamsak al-'urwa al-wuthqa*.

[122]   *'ibadat* (or worship).   [123]   *mu'amalat* (transactions, deals, contracts).

[124]   *kitab, kutub*.

[125]   *zakat* (lit. liberality, bounty, calculated usually at 2.5 per cent of annual profits); *khums* (lit. fifth, for the Shi'is).

[126]   *jihad* (literally striving, same root and original meaning as the legal word *ijtihad*), often translated as holy war, but in fact a much wider concept.

[127]   *'alim*, plural *'ulama*; or *faqih* (from *fiqh*), plural *fuqaha'*.

expert[128] to judicial position. [129] In the volume on transactions, there are also several books, with each devoted to a legal category such as marriage, sale, lease, legal penalties, etc. [130] Classical *fiqh* compendia are comprehensive works which deal with worldly matters but also indicate the right ways of worship and individual devotional practice. The two are perceived in theory to belong to the same realm of law, but there is a clear sense, already in early legal treatises, of the distinction between devotional practices and worldly transactions.

An example of classical *fiqh* at work can be seen in aspects of the encyclopaedic work of Shamseddin al-Sarakhsi (d. *c.* 490/1097) known as his *Mabsut*.

A look at earlier extant treatises shows how the treatment of Sarakhsi continues the tradition and improves upon it. This is readily apparent for the lawyer who examines the language and structure of 'the book of sale' [131] in the *Mabsut*,

---

[128] *mujtahid* (from *ijtihad*), plural *mujtahidun*; *mujtahid* is more common nowadays for Shi'i scholars, but the current Shi'i connotation of the word did not hold in the classical age. *Fuqaha*, *'ulama* and *mujtahidun* are words often used interchangeably. The legal expert can also be a *mufti*, plural *muftiun* (who issue a *fatwa*, plural *fatawi* or *fatawa*, equivalent to the Roman and Hebraic *responsa* literature, see below section on fatwa).

[129] *qadi*, judge, plural *qudat*. *Hakem* is also used.

[130] If we take Sarakhsi's *Mabsut* in the standard 1909 Cairo edition as an example, the thirty volumes of the standard edition include: *salat* (prayer, i, 4–253; ii, 2–143), *tarawih* (variations on prayer, ii, 143–9), *zakat* (alms, ii, 149–207; iii, 2–54), *sawm* (fasting, iii, 54–146), *hayd* (women's period, iii, 146–219), *manasek* (pilgrimage, mostly *hajj*, iv, 2–192), *nikah* (marriage, iv, 192–228; v, 2–229), *talaq* (divorce, vi, 2–235; vii, 2–59), *'itaq* (manumission, vii, 60–241), *mukatab* (manumitted slave, viii, 2–80), *wala'* (patronage in slavery, viii, 81–125), *ayman* (oaths, viii, 126–88; ix, 2–35), *hudud* (prescribed criminal penalties, ix, 36–132), *sariqa* (theft, ix, 133–205), *siyar* (conquests, x, 2–144), *istihsan* (preference in legal interpretation, x, 145–85), *taharri* (verification, x, 185–208), *laqit* (foundling, x, 209–21; xi, 2–16), *ibaq* (runaway slaves, xi, 16–34), *mafqud* (missing person, xi, 34–49), *ghasb* (violation, xi, 49–108), *wadi'a* (deposit, xi, 108–33), *'ariya* (free loan, xi, 133–50), *sharika* (partnership, xi, 151–220), *sayd* (hunting, xi, 220–56), *dhibah* (animal slaughtering, xii, 2–27), *waqf* (trusts, xii, 27–47), *hiba* (gift, xii, 47–108), *buyu'* (sales, xii, 108–209, xiii, 2–199), *sarf* (currency, xiv, 2–90), *shuf'a* (pre-emption, xiv, 90–184), *qisma* (division, x, 2–74), *ijarat* (leases, xv, 74–184, xvi, 2–59), *adab al-qadi* (literature of judges, xvi, 59–111), *shahadat* (testimonies, xvi, 111–77), *ruju' 'an al-shahada* (retraction of testimony, xvi, 177–97, xvii, 2–28), *da'wa* (legal action, xvii, 28–184), *iqrar* (admission, xvii, 184–200, xviii, 2–190), *wikala* (power of attorney, xix, 2–160), *kafala* (guarantee, xix, 160–89, xx, 2–133), *sulh* (compromise, xx, 133–83, xxi, 2–63), *rahn* (pledge, xxi, 63–187, xxii, 2–17), *mudaraba* (profit and loss partnership, xxii, 17–187), *muzara'a* (agricultural profit and loss partnership, xxiii, 2–161) *shirb* (water shares, xxiii, 161–204), *ashriba* ([alcoholic] drinks, xxiv, 2–38), *ikrah* (duress, xxiv, 38–156), *hajr* (interdiction, xxiv, 156–84), *al-ma'dhun al-kabir* (slaves allowed to trade, xxv, 2–191, xxvi, 2–58), *diyyat* (blood-money, xxvi, 58–193, xxvii, 2–84), *jinayat* (crimes, xxvii, 84–124), *ma'aqel* (plural of *'aqila*, the group collectively responsible for an individual's tort or crime, xxvii, 124–42), *wasaya* (wills, xxvii, 142–91, xxviii, 2–110), *al-'ayn wal-dayn* (property and debt [in wills], xxviii, 110–213, xxix, 2–22), *al-'itq fil-marad* (manumission during illness, xxix, 22–91), *al-dawr* (adjustment [in the calculation of compensation], xxix, 91–136), *al-fara'ed* (prescribed inheritance, xxix, 136–212, xxx, 2–91), *fara'ed al-khantha* (prescribed inheritance for the hermaphrodite, xxx, 91–103), *al-khantha* (hermaphrodite, xxx, 103–14), *hisab al-wasaya* (calculation of legacies, xxx, 114–28), *ikhtilaf abi hanifa wa ibn abi Laila* (differences between Abi Hanifa and Ibn Abi Laila xxx, 128–67), *shurut* (formularies, xxx, 167–209), *hiyal* (legal evasion, xxx, 209–44), *kasb* (earning, xxx, 244–87), *rida'* (suckling, xxx, 287–310). Compare Kasani's divisions, below n. 206, and modern codes, Chapter 8, sections on Majalla and on the Egyptian Civil Code.

[131] *kitab al-bay'* (singular) or *kitab al-buyu'* (sales in plural).

in contrast with such earlier compilers, like San'ani (d. 211/826), whose own book of sales occupies a good part of the eighth volume of his *Musannaf*.[132] While both texts are extensive and devote dozens of pages to the law of sales, the treatment of Sarakhsi is qualitatively different in terms of the reasoned discussion of various points of law. San'ani's work is generally classified as one of *hadith*. But one could also so describe Malik's *Muwatta'*, a hybrid *hadith-fiqh* treatise which offers the source material for later Maliki law works, an indication of the quality shift of genres underlying the passage from the formative period to that which, certainly by Sarakhsi's time, had become 'classical': more law as we understand it, less Qur'an and *hadith*.

In an attempt at periodization of early *fiqh*, Norman Calder suggested that the formative period extends until the middle of the third century after the Prophet's death, when a new phase starts with the production of *Mukhtasars*, summaries which have a clearly identifiable author—in contrast to the accretions of many an author in previous texts. This emergence, the elegant thesis goes, heralds a normalization of the process of legal teaching—'the world of the academic trainee'[133]—and generations of commentaries.[134]

Because the texts and chronology are fuzzy, the early period elicits various theories which are enhanced by fragmented sources and uncertain links, in addition to a natural propensity for 'new' religions to reject any formal acknowledgment of previous or neighbouring ones with which they are often in competition.

Be the formation of classical Islamic law as it may, there is little doubt that the production of a work like Sarakhsi's *Mabsut* offers a display of legal skills which heralds a different mastery of reasoning and language than the earlier—and rather frustrating—collocation of fragmentary legal segments.

Before devoting more particular attention to the book of sale as an example, within the corpus of a *Mabsut*, of the classical age of *fiqh*, it is useful to say a word about Sarakhsi and, in contrast to his imposing written legacy, the little one knows about his life and times. Such scant material on authors and editors is characteristic of classical law. Legal lore has it that the thirty volumes (in modern print more like the equivalent of a hundred volumes) of the *Mabsut* were shouted by Sarakhsi to his disciples out of a well in which his erstwhile mentor had imprisoned him.[135]

---

[132] San'ani, *al-Musannaf*, above n. 96, viii, 3–318.   [133] Calder, *Studies*, 246.
[134] ibid. 244–7.
[135] The opening of the *Mabsut* (vol. i, 2) refers to Sarakhsi 'dictating' (*imla*) the *Mabsut* from his prison in Uzjand, Transoxania (Central Asia). Sarakhsi is reported to have written the *Mabsut* as a commentary on Marwazi's '*mukhtasar*'. Sarakhsi, *al-Mabsut*, i, 1–3. Khalil al-Mays mentions Sarakhsi's 'dictation without reading to his friends at the top of the well; and he completed it in 477 AH [1084 CE]' (*kana yumli min khatirih min ghayr mutala'a wa ashabuhu fi a'la al-jubb wa anhahu sanat 477 AH*), *Faharis kitab al-mabsut* (Beirut, 1978) 7, and puts the date of Sarakhsi's death at 482/1089, while Calder mentions several dates. See Calder, 'Exploring God's law: Muhammad ibn Ahmad ibn Abi Sahl al-Sarakhsi on *zakat*', in Toll and Skovgaard-Petersen, *Law and the Islamic world*, above n. 45, 57–73, at 58 n. 4, and the entries 'Sarakhsi' in the two editions of the *Encyclopaedia of Islam*. In vol. xxvii of the *Mabsut*, 124, the book on *ma'aqel* (plural of *'aqila*, see above n. 11, the neighbourhood or tribal group that shares collective responsibility with the tortfeasor) starts with the

Shamseddin al-Sarakhsi, who died *c.* 490/1097, wrote his long treatise as a commentary on the *Kafi* of al-Marwazi (d. 332/943), also known as al-Hakem al-Shahid. Sarakhsi refers systematically to *al-Kafi*, although there is much discussion of reports ascribed to the two disciples of Abu Hanifa (d. 150/767), Muhammad al-Shaybani (d. 189/804) and Abu Yusuf (d. 182/798), and, in the book of sale, to Ibn Abi Laila (d. 148/765), often also to Shafi'i (d. 204/820), and more rarely to Malik (d. 179/795), as well as other authorities who are less well-known in the field, like Zufar (d. 158/775). A systematic indexing of Qur'anic verses in the *Mabsut* shows how much sparser references to the Qur'an are in the book of sale, as opposed to other sections of the work.[136]

It is not always clear whether Sarakhsi's disciples, who physically committed the *Mabsut* to paper, are referring to their master's comments on Marwazi (d. 332/943), or referring directly to Marwazi. Only a patient reconstruction of Marwazi's *Kafi*—which to my knowledge has not been published yet—can give the answer. My work on the Hanafi books of sale suggests that the influence of Shaybani's (d. 189/804) *Asl* is very strong in terms of structure, but the full unravelling of the logic in the *Mabsut* has yet to be undertaken. As in all classical glosses, the polyphonic text's clarity is dimmed by the various layers of commentary.

Sarakhsi's treatment remained constrained by its nature as a commentary on his acknowledged predecessor Marwazi, himself following Shaybani and others, and the legal logic which develops in the book of sales is to be found more in the treatment of his predecessors' 'principles' than in a *sui generis* new structure of the subject-matter. Only when one comes to Kasani in Hanafi law,[137] a hundred years later, does the full skill of a lawyer as a re-organizer of material in a coherent legal construction appear fulfilled. Like most scholars, Sarakhsi is a commentator, and his creativity is constrained by the internal structure of the earlier text he writes his comments upon. This is certainly true of his book of sales, where the imprint of Shaybani's *Asl* can be documented in terms of both structure and content.

---

following reference: 'The respected, detached shaykh imam Shams al-a'imma Abu Bakr Muhammad ibn Sahl al-Sarakhsi, peace on his soul, dictated the following on Wednesday 14 Rabi' ii in the year 466 [16 December 1073] … *qal al-shaykh al-imam al-ajall al-zahed Abu Bakr Muhammad ibn Sahl al-Sarakhsi rahimahu allah imla'an yawm al-urba'a' al-rabi' 'ashar min shahr rabi' al-akhir sanat sitt was sittin wa arba'ma'at …*' Another date appears in the very last book, on suckling, xxx, 287, as 12 Jumada ii 477 [17 October 1084]. It is doubtful that it took Sarakhsi over ten years to complete the last two books only. This suggests that the books of the *Mabsut* may not have been arranged by their editor or editors in the order originally chosen or even dictated by the author.

136 From the Lebanese scholar Khalil al-Mays' useful indexes to the thirty volumes in *Faharis kitab al-mabsut*, cited in the previous note. There is unfortunately no thematic index in this important work. The indexes are those of the subdivisions of the *Mabsut*, volume by volume (11–355), Qur'anic verses cited (356–410), Prophetic *hadith* (411–82), names (483–578), sons ('*ibn* …' 679), nick-names (*alqab*, 580–2), women (583–7), and books (588–90). It appears that the two volumes and a half of the *Mabsut* (vols 12–14) relating mostly to the law of sale include 34 Qur'anic verses, compared for instance with 79 verses for the sole *Kitab al-siyar* (law of conquest), which occupies about half of volume 10. In contrast, al-Mays relates 119 *hadith* in *kitab al-siyar*, which compares well with over 200 *hadith* he relates in the law of sale.

137 And Maimonides in Jewish law, see below nn. 209–12.

Still, the sheer scale of the *Mabsut* and the quality of Sarakhsi's legal reasoning should reserve for the Transoxanian scholar a prime place in legal history. Sarakhsi deserves a book-length monograph as the classical age full-blown lawyer *par excellence*. My treatment here will be limited to a few characteristics typical of the *Mabsut*.

The first characteristic appears in the pell-mell treatment of law by Sarakhsi, as indeed by most great commentators in the tradition. Roy Mottahedeh once observed that the reader will find in *fiqh* books unexpected gems in unexpected places. Before I examine the logic of Sarakhsi in the field of obligations, let me consider one such gem in the twenty-third volume, in a discussion by Sarakhsi in the 'book of water shares'.[138]

The passage appears in the section of the *Mabsut* dealing with water, where one suddenly hears Sarakhsi complaining about the impairment of a person's right.

The question put to the Transoxanian jurist is about 'the validity of the granting of the emir of Khurasan to an individual of a right of irrigation from the waters of a great river, when that right was not [so established] before, or when the individual has irrigation for two *kuwwa*s [a measure of flow] and the Emir increases this measure and grants him that right [i.e. extends it] over a land which may or may not be the land of a third party'.

This is the occasion for Sarakhsi to explain the limits of the ruler's powers:

If this decision of the Emir harms the public, it is prohibited, and it is permissible if it doesn't, that is if [the operation] did not take place on the land of a third party, for the *sultan*/ruler has a right of supervision[139] without harming the public. So in case there is no such harm, the grant is valid for the grantee, but if harm occurs, the grant would be harmful to the public and the *sultan* is not allowed to carry it out.

'It is not permissible', Sarakhsi continued, 'for the Emir of Khurasan to empty (*asfa*) a man's right of irrigation over his land for the benefit of another, and the right must be given back to the original beneficiary and his heirs.'

This is followed by a most candid account of the limits of law in real life, as Sarakhsi explained that

what is meant by the word *isfa'* [from *asfa*] is usurpation (*ghasb*) but he [Sarakhsi, or Marwazi?] kept his tongue and did not use the word usurpation, *ghasb*, for the actions of rulers because of its rough connotations, and he chose instead the word *isfa'* out of caution [towards the ruler].

Abu Hanifa, God be merciful to his memory, used to advise his friends in this manner, for man should be attentive to his own interest, keep his tongue and respect the ruler even if in such an action the ruler is equal to others before the law. Didn't the Prophet say: the hand is responsible for what it takes until it gives it back? The granting of ownership to anyone other than the right owner is void, and the good which is wrongfully appropriated must be

---

[138] Sarakhsi, *Mabsut*, xxiii, 161–204, *kitab al-shirb* (*shirb* is the water share, as opposed to *shurb*, which is drinking).   [139] Supervision, *wilayat nazar*.

returned to his owner if alive and to his heirs after his death, and so for the ruler's appropriation of what belongs to the people.[140]

This excerpt expresses the limits of law which Sarakhsi, as a jurist prisoner, will have experienced first hand. It is eminently practical and realistic. In other texts relating to the classical law of partnership which Abraham Udovitch has thoroughly explored, one realizes the close connection between our author and the realities of commerce, against the received idea of a legal exercise disconnected from real life.[141] Contrary to the erroneous concept about the 'theoretical' and impractical legal considerations of *fiqh* works, *fiqh* treatments therefore deserve a closer analysis for their reflection of legal practice.

This can be further illustrated in a more attentive analysis of that part of the *Mabsut* which is devoted to sales. The patterns of continuity and distinctiveness offered by the Hanafi Transoxanian scholar in the specific instance of the book of sale can also shed some light on the historical evolution of Islamic law.

Fiqh is case-law and its products are, to a variable extent, the result of the jurist's intellectual construct. With English common law it shares the inductive method by adducing a number of examples out of which some more general principles can be drawn. It does not posit, as in the continental European system of civil law (or Roman law in its late codified form), an overall principle or set of principles from which application derives. But *fiqh* is different from both in that it is eminently casuistic, and the cases it discusses are not necessarily based on precedents in real life.

This last proposition remains a hypothesis, in so far as the exact interaction between law and reality in the classical age has not been tested in any significant manner. But irrespective of work yet to be done in this important field, casuistry in the negative sense of the term can certainly be widely found in *fiqh* books, and Sarakhsi, who can rise with ease to arguing for mere arguing's sake, is no exception.

A typical example of casuistry appears in the latter part of the book of sale, where the treatment of the risk for the buyer and the seller is extensive.[142] The chapter starts with the case of the buyer of a slave who comes into possession of the commodity only after the seller has cut off the hand of the slave. The buyer has a right of option. He can pay half the price for the slave, 'since the hand of a person is half of him',[143] or he could rescind the contract as the object of sale has changed in nature under the seller's responsibility. The concept of risk is rendered by one of

---

[140] 'The ruler is equal to others before the law: *al-sultan ka-ghayrihi shar'an*', al-Mabsut, xxiii, 183.

[141] 'This identity between the theoretical formulations of the late eighth century and the actual commercial practice of the eleventh through thirteenth centuries corroborates the thesis that the earliest Hanafi law treating partnership and commenda contracts is to be viewed, with minor qualifications, as a veritable Law Merchant', Abraham Udovitch, *Partnership and profit in medieval Islam* (Princeton, 1970) 259. Also, for the definitive work based on the Cairo Geniza, S. Goitein, *A Mediterranean society: the Jewish communities of the Arab world as portrayed in the documents of the Cairo Geniza*, 5 vols (Berkeley, 1967–88) vol. 1, 1967, 148–272: 'the world of commerce and finance'.

[142] *bab jinayat al-ba'e' wal-mushtari 'alal-mabi'*, al-Mabsut, xiii, 170. The citations which follow refer to the *Mabsut*, 170–81.   [143] *fa-inna al-yad min al-adami nisfuh.*

contributory liability, which is combined here with an option for the buyer: 'If he [the buyer] chooses to rescind the contract, the whole price is foregone, and if he chooses to take the [diminished] slave, he must pay half the price'.[144]

The figure is relatively simple so far, but it rapidly becomes more complex, as Sarakhsi introduces a difference between his view and that of Shafi'i. The result in practice may be the same, as Shafi'i requires the buyer to pay the whole sum, and then to turn to the seller in order to recoup the seller's contributory share for the diminished value of the commodity. In both cases, regardless of the reasoning of the two scholars, the buyer pays half the value of the slave. For Shafi'i, Sarakhsi explains, the buyer remains responsible for the value of the slave even if the slave dies, that is even if the commodity perishes.[145] *Caveat emptor stricto sensu.* If the seller chooses to exercise his option to see the contract to the end, then the buyer is bound by the contract. He must first pay the price stipulated, even if the object of the contract has by then disappeared upon the slave's death. The buyer must therefore pay the price, Shafi'i holds, and then recoup the full amount from the seller.

Here, recourse against the buyer leads to the same end result for both Sarakhsi and Shafi'i, even if it is somewhat laboured in the latter's case. But the argument of Sarakhsi makes a practical difference in the case of a slave who loses the use of his hand through no fault of the seller. For Sarakhsi, the buyer can exercise his option to have the contract fully executed. If he decides to carry on with the contract and keep the slave, he must pay the whole price. Not so for Shafi'i, explains Sarakhsi: 'Shafi'i considers both cases equal [that is whether the buyer rejects the contract or decides to go ahead with it], and considers that risk falls on the seller for half the value in both cases'.[146] The seller remains liable for half the value because the object of sale is still his responsibility. It makes no difference for Shafi'i that the commodity is defective because of the buyer or not. Under the Shafi'i position as interpreted by Sarakhsi, 'there is no difference if part of the commodity perishes because of the person who is still liable or for no action of hers'.[147] The example adduced is the sale of two slaves, one of whom perishes before reception by the buyer: unlike for Sarakhsi, 'the answer would be the same' for Shafi'i whether or not it is the buyer who is responsible for that death and responsible therefore for the decrease in the value of the overall value of the commodity constituted by the two slaves as the one object of the sale. The seller remains liable because he assumes the risk of the commodity perishing or diminishing in value while still under his control.

Sarakhsi then explains why his solution is different in that case. The key consideration is 'intention'.[148] If loss is through no fault on anyone's part,[149] then the loss is accessory and not intended, and no compensation is required from the

---

[144] liability, *daman*; the diminished slave, *al-aqta'*.   [145] value, *qima*.

[146] Shafi'i considers them equal, *Shafi'i yusawwi baynahuma*; the risk falls on the seller, *al-mabi' fi damanih [daman al-ba'e]*.   [147] liable, *damin*.

[148] intention, *qasd*.   [149] '*fa-in fat bi-ghayr sun' ahad ... la mahala*', *al-Mabsut*, xiii, 171.

seller. Only if loss occurs because of a tortious act of the seller, he explains, can compensation be requested from him.

Sarakhsi goes on with an elaborate legal argument, and his solution is further supported by the contrasting case of a third party cutting the hand off the sold slave: 'The buyer has an option: [he could reject the sale altogether or,] if he still wants the performance of the contract, he must pay the seller the full price and then exercise a recourse against the third party for half the price, as the tort of that third party has affected [what is now] his property'.[150]

As is manifest in these quotes, the examples increase in complexity with variations on cases with regard to the commodity and the way it is affected—for example, if it is the foot against the hand, or the 'other' foot, or two slaves, or a slave woman who is pregnant and loses the child, or a slave girl who loses her virginity. The solution varies with the type of intermediation (distinction between direct or indirect causation),[151] with the persona of the intervener (seller, buyer, third party), or with intention. All these figures and variations of case-law are pursued by a similar process of reasoning, sometimes involving a comparison with Shafi'i, or comparisons within other Hanafi lawyers, to which is added the complexity of the computation of the 'shares'[152] in the ultimate liability or debt.

The imprint of Shaybani's earlier treatise is evident throughout. One figure appeared in the original work of Shaybani's text, *al-Asl*, as follows:

[Case:] A slave is sold to a buyer who does not take delivery and does not pay the price until after the seller has cut the slave's hand. In addition, the buyer, together with a third party, are also responsible for the loss of the 'opposite' foot. Then the slave dies. [Solution:] Because of the cut hand, the buyer is exonerated for 1/2 of the price. He is liable for 1/4 of the price for his tort and the third party's tort in cutting the foot. Then the buyer can exercise a recourse against the third party for 1/2 of the penalty, which is in fact 1/8 of the slave. Since the slave eventually dies, a share of 1/3 left in the value of the slave is spared the buyer, which represents therefore 2/3 of the total price. He then owes 1/8 plus 1/3 of 1/8 of the price because of his tort and the tort of the third party on what is left of the slave. The buyer exercises then his recourse against the third party for 2/3 of the 1/8 of the value for that party's tort. The third party owes therefore 1/8 of the slave's value for cutting his foot, and 2/3 of 1/8 of the value for what he wasted from the slave's soul [i.e. his integrity as a commodity]. The buyer will then owe 3/8 of the price and 1/3 of 1/8 for his tort and that of the third party.

The buyer does not have to give away any part of the compensation he takes from the third party, even if what he receives from him exceeds his share of the value, because the third party is liable in tort to the buyer who has been delivered the commodity.[153]

---

[150] property, *milk* (or *mulk*), ibid. 172.

[151] *siraya* and *jinaya*, loosely translatable as direct or indirect criminal tort.

[152] share, *sahm*, plural *ashum*.

[153] The passage appears at 300–1 of Shaybani, *Kitab al-Asl*, Shafiq Shihata [= Chafic Chehata] ed., (Cairo, 1954) (which includes only the book of sale, with a useful brief annotation); and, in the larger 5 vols. edn. of *al-Asl*, Abul Wafa' al-Afghani ed. (Beirut, 1990 (orig. edn Haydarabad, 1386/1966)) v,

The same hypothetical case runs as follows in the *Mabsut*:

[Case:] A slave is sold to a buyer who does not take immediate delivery and does not pay the price until after the seller has cut the slave's hand. In addition, the buyer, together with a third party, are also responsible for the loss of the 'opposite' foot.

[Solution:] The buyer is liable for 3/8 of the price as well as 1/3 of 1/8 of the price, which is the share of his tort and that of the third party. By cutting one hand, the seller has destroyed half of the commodity and the buyer, together with the third party, have destroyed 1/2 of what has remained. What is left, which is 1/4, is destroyed by tort to the extent of 1/3, so 1/3 of that 1/4 is destroyed by the tort of every one of them all. The equation of eighths has been further cut by thirds so one multiplies 8 by 3, which makes 24, then this is divided in halves since the destruction of the buyer together with the third party is shared equally between the two, so one multiplies 24 by two for these half shares, and the sum total is 48. Liability for the [commodity] destroyed because of the seller's action is 24 and for the subsequent effects 4, that makes 28, which amounts to 4/8 of the [value] of the slave added to 2/8, bringing [the lowest common denominator] for the shares of the slave to 48, with 6 equalling 1/8, 24 equalling 4/8 and 4 two-thirds of 1/8. Because of his [the seller's] tort, 1/8 must be deducted; this is why 4/8 of the price plus 2/3 of 1/8 are deducted. As for the buyer, he owes 3/8 of the price in addition to 1/3 of the 1/8 as share of what was lost by his fault and as share of what was lost by the fault of the third party. The third party is [also] liable for the value [of the diminished commodity]. To the extent of the loss due to the third party's tort, the value of the sale follows: here the loss is both [the buyer's and the third party's] fault and their tort is in the end [computed under a factor of] 20: 3/8 of the slave value and 1/3 of the 1/8. The buyer claims back from the third party 1/8 of the value and 2/3 of 1/8, because of the third party's fault, and loss is 1/2 of 20 i.e. 10, which is 1/8 of the slave plus 2/3 of 1/8. The buyer can then exercise a recourse against the third party for 1/8 of the value plus 2/3 1/8 and does not need to give away any of it even if there remains a surplus, because the buyer has, following his tort, come into possession [of the commodity] and the fault of the third party has now become associated with the fault of the buyer...[154]

The matter is different, continues Sarakhsi, if the buyer and the third party have committed their tort *after* the slave was delivered. There follows an ever more complicated commentary.

These discussions appear almost intractable: But if one looks closely at the case and its solutions in the original Shaybani and the commentators, Marwazi and Sarakhsi, there is no significant difference either in the hypotheticals adduced or in the result reached. The difference is mostly one of Sarakhsi explaining away the figures he finds in *al-Asl*. Sarakhsi's text sounds like a mathematics professor explaining to his students the logic of a formula they are reading to him from a textbook. To make the formula clearer(!) the total is reduced to the lowest common denominator, which is 48, and the shares calculated accordingly.

276–7. Note that Shaybani's *Asl* is also known as *al-Mabsut*. Penalty, *arsh*; 1/8 of the slave's value, *thumn al-'abd sahihan*; tort, *jinaya*.

[154] destroyed, *al-talef*; death consequent to *siraya*; *al-Mabsut*, xiii, 180–1.

A set of temporary conclusions on the method and logic of classical *fiqh* can be attempted on the basis of this brief discussion.

There is no doubt that later jurists have at heart the earlier texts which are authoritative, as in the case of Shaybani for Sarakhsi. Developments occur on a mechanistic level of refinement and explanation, without any apparent addendum beyond the ever more complex figures of seemingly absurd hypothetical cases. Here, *fiqh* does not change.

From a semantic point of view, Sarakhsi uses in his explanations the word *damin*, as well as the concept of *siraya*, neither of which appears in the discussion by Shaybani. Shaybani, however, uses *arsh*, and already has a clear concept of what *siraya* represents. In terms of legal vocabulary progress is limited.

What of structure? The general arrangement of the book of sale is difficult to ascertain in the absence of Marwazi's *Kafi*, and it is necessary to speculate on the exact structural debt which the *Mabsut* owes it.[155] The influence of Shaybani's *Asl*, in contrast, is evident in terms of structure: the insertion of some chapters will appear odd to modern eyes, for instance 'The sale of date trees if they bear fruit', which forms chapter 16 of *al-Asl*, and can be found tucked away in the latter part of Sarakhsi's book, also fitting uneasily into the treatment.

Overall, the format followed in the *Mabsut* hardly departs from that chosen by Sarakhsi's predecessor in *al-Asl*. Both authors start with a long treatment of deferred sale, or sale on credit,[156] then deal with agency in such sales, followed by imperfect sales, conditions,[157] options,[158] mark-up partnership contracts,[159] defective sales,[160] the sale to and from non-Muslim monotheists,[161] then other special circumstances which confirm that, even in terms of the internal structure of each chapter,[162] Sarakhsi does not willingly depart from Shaybani.

Constraints derived from sticking to the predecessor's plan also explain the marshalling of other issues in the law of sale which do not readily belong to the book of sales proper. These issues are included in such chapters as currency sale,[163] which is dealt with separately as a special type of sale, the regulation of land sale, preemption,[164] sale in the contracts of *commenda* partnerships,[165] and so forth. Despite these constraints of form imposed by the previous model which he comments upon, a distinguishing feature of Sarakhsi's treatment of like hypotheses and figures appears in the consistent and logical exposition which is unique to the *Mabsut*.

---

[155] I have been able to examine a manuscript of Marwazi's *Kafi* from the Chester Beatty library in Dublin (ms. 4263), which indeed follows the *Mabsut* of Sarakhsi in its general structure. Unfortunately, the ms. is not complete, and stops at *bab al-rida'*, (chapter on suckling) well before the corresponding section on the book of sales in Sarakhsi's *Mabsut*. *Bab al-rida'* appears in Sarakhsi at vol 5 (out of 30). This suggests the full *Kafi* is a large book. [156] *salam.*

[157] *shurut.*   [158] *khiyar*, plural *khiyarat*. On options in the law of contract, see Chapter 8.
[159] *murabaha.*   [160] *'uyub.*   [161] *dhimma.*   [162] *bab.*   [163] *sarf.*
[164] *shuf'a.*

[165] *mudaraba.* On *murabaha* and *mudaraba*, which is the equivalent of the Roman *commenda* and the Babylonian 'joint adventure'/*tappputum*, see above nn. 28–9 and accompanying text, and Chapter 9, sections on company law and on Islamic banking.

So we find in Sarakhsi's *Mabsut*, despite the commentary faithfully respecting the order and solutions of predecessors such as Shaybani and Marwazi, a conscious and sophisticated development in style and reasoning, resulting in a sensible improvement in the overall logic and exposition of the law. In the case of the book of sale, as treated by Sarakhsi in contrast to his predecessors, the structure improves significantly within the limits of the texts with which the commentator is dealing.

This can be illustrated by pursuing such apparently absurd hypotheticals, like the casuistic passage quoted above, and by making sense of how the treatment differs from that offered by the predecessor. It would take some time and effort to see how the risk on the seller and the buyer gets assessed in law, but the exposition is not beyond the reach of a sophisticated contracts lawyer. Much as the example of the hand of the slave being lost 'in transit' through the fault of either party appears far-fetched, one could take the trouble to delve into the logic of such fractions. For logic there is, and the modern reader would feel less lost or alienated if the subject of the example were, say, a large oil tanker. The discussion would, in the oil tanker hypothetical, examine the exact moment in time when the ship was lost, the terms of the contract or charter party, the contributory negligence of the parties, the Act of God dimension in the loss, the moment when risk passes, and the like. Even such tiny fractional details as the one adduced in the case of the lost slave would appear meaningful if the object of the dispute were a valuable commodity in a non-slave economy.

Still, there is a significant amount of sheer casuistry, which appears even more bewildering in the case, dear to our classical jurists, of the hermaphrodite's inheritance. While the discussion, page after page, of the hermaphrodite's succession appears ludicrous to modern eyes, both the pleasure of the arithmetic application of the Islamic rules of succession and the potential transposition of the hermaphrodite discussion to large successions appear more alluring to the reasoning of a modern jurist.[166]

Casuistry should therefore be taken into account when one reads the *fiqh* books for their pedagogic value. Sophistication in the computation of compensation ratios is not the sole locus of Sarakhsi's legal skills. Legal logic in its most positive sense is also pervasive in the *Mabsut*: less empathy is required for the twentieth-century reader of the following taxonomic rearrangement by Sarakhsi of the law of sale, adumbrated in the very first lines of his book-long chapter on the subject.

Sarakhsi starts with a broad brush: 'God has made money the reason to establish the benefits of the people in the world';[167] commerce was regulated 'because what each person needs is not allowed in all circumstances'. *Riba* follows, as 'commerce is of two kinds: what is allowed[168] is known in the law[169] as sale.[170] What is

---

[166] Examples of the literature on hermaphrodite (*al-khantha*) can be found in Sarakhsi's *Mabsut*, xxx, 91–103, and Kasani's *Bada'e'*, vii, 327–30.   [167] reason, *sabab*, *al-Mabsut*, xii, 108.
[168] *halal*.   [169] *shar'*.   [170] *bay'*.

forbidden is called *riba*. Both *riba* and sale are commerce'. The relevant verse in the Qur'an on the distinction between *riba* and sale is then quoted,[171] and Sarakhsi goes on to the definition of sale and *riba*.

'The conclusion of the contract takes place with two expressions which are formulated in the past tense, "I sold and I bought", over two objects, each of which is of fungible value and can be acquired'.[172] This definition of a contract reveals the combination of formalism, as expressed in the need to use the past tense for verbs, and of substantive appreciation, which appears in the concept of fungible value.[173] To explain the importance of the formal use of the past tense, Sarakhsi introduces his difference with Shafi'i, who allows the use of the present tense in both the contract of sale and the contract of marriage. Why does Sarakhsi, unlike Shafi'i, permit the use of the present tense to contract a marriage, while rejecting it for the parties in the contract of sale? The rationale is twofold: first, Sarakhsi explains, use of the present tense is unnecessary for the contract of sale because there are no preliminaries in sale which find their root in the distinction between preparation and conclusion, as is the case of betrothal in contradistinction to proper marriage. Secondly, use of the present tense is possible in marriage, in contrast to sale, because the parties are always separate and distinct in a sale, whereas use of an agent is common in marriage by proxy. Whereas the father or brother usually contract marriage for the daughter or sister, agency is not the usual format for the contract of sale, and only the use of the past tense makes the sale transaction secure.[174]

Sarakhsi then compares sale contract and lease: 'The contract changes in nature not because of the [parties' outward] expression', for 'we know that what matters is what is intended'.[175] By referring to examples which contradict formalism in practice and give way to intention, and by insisting on general use in order to contradict 'rare cases' which conform in principle more strictly with a rule, Sarakhsi appears at considerable variance with Shafi'i as well as with Shaybani's treatment of the sale contract.

One can see in these examples how the logic of the academic lawyer develops: the sale contract, in Sarakhsi's view, is the standard contract. It operates *sui generis*, and other important contracts, like marriage, are modelled after it. While each retains its own characteristics, the contract of sale is the model contract, and must be entered into in a determined/past form to avoid uncertainty as a matter of

---

[171] 'God has allowed sale, and forbidden *riba*', Qur'an ii: 275.

[172] two objects, *mahallayn*; fungible value, *mal mutaqawwim*. ibid. 109.

[173] By further refining the analysis, Sarakhsi distinguishes between a contract which is a sale, and the donation for a consideration other than a financial reward, *al-hiba bi-shart al-'awad*. ibid. 109.

[174] It was drawn to my attention by John Donohue that the translation of the Arab verb mode *fa'ala* as 'past' is inaccurate, even if contemporary schoolchildren are taught that the mode is *madi*, literally 'past'. In fact *madi* should be translated as 'determined', as opposed to the 'present', *mudare'*, which is 'undetermined'. The nuance makes particular sense in a juridical setting like the issue discussed by Sarakhsi. The past tense is actually the 'determined' (or determinate, or even terminated to use an equivalent legal jargon) form of the verb.

[175] *fa-'arafna anna al-mu'tabar ma huwa al-maqsud, ... wa-bihi yakhtalif al-'aqd la bi'tibar al-lafz*, *al-Mabsut*, xii, 140.

guidance for other contracts. As the standard contract, it allows many inferences of a general type, most remarkably the intention of the parties. Less current contracts, such as leases, must follow that model.[176]

Against the formalistic image of the law of contracts, the rest of the book is studded with references to intention, as mentioned incidentally by Sarakhsi with regard to intervening factors in the sale of a slave in the example quoted at length earlier. In another anti-formalistic example, the six genres of the *hadith* on *riba* are considered not to be exclusive, meaning for Sarakhsi that the list could be extended if the appropriate analogy is drawn. Except for some jurists like Dawud al-Zahiri (d. 270/884), the eponym of the literalist Zahiri school, and 'Uthman al-Batti (d. 143/760), Sarakhsi explains, the jurists of the land have agreed 'that the rule of *riba* is not meant in the six commodities [of the *hadith*][177] and that it includes a meaning which goes beyond them to other commodities'.[178] In another instance also related to *riba*, Sarakhsi refuses to acknowledge that 'meaning be restricted to what it entails in the language'. If *riba* means excess or increase, then 'it is an increase in itself because [the example] of what is being eaten, if compared to other such things that could also be eaten, will not be equivalent in taste except rarely. The rule however cannot rest on rare cases, and even though this increase stands in itself, its importance was dropped in law to facilitate matters on people.'[179]

One can see the constraints faced by the legal commentary, however extensive. On the one hand, it must be based on the template offered by earlier distinguished authors like Shaybani and Marwazi. Their stature, and the naturally conservative nature of law, constrains the later author. On the other hand, a master commentator like Sarakhsi must remain attentive to prevailing trade practice. Respect for trade practice as it evolves requires him to provide a more practical basis than previous masters' handbooks might allow.

Even in terms of structure, there is no doubt that Sarakhsi's contribution offers a more developed and convincing legal treatment than his predecessors and masters, Shaybani and Marwazi, through the elaborate arguments which Sarakhsi develops at key junctures as effective transitions within a chapter. In the first section of the book of sales, which follows Shaybani's *Asl*, Sarakhsi introduces the contract of sale after a brief word on the philosophy of commerce. Next are discussed the void contract of sale upon the advent of *riba*, and after an extensive discussion of the various figures of *riba* invalidating sale contracts, the valid sale of future things, which is known as deferred sale, or sale on credit.[180] Within this type of sale, the discussion is extensive. In part, this follows Shaybani, who has a

[176] Such an insistence on the use of proper verbal tense was probably the reason why some twentieth-century authors, like the Egyptian scholar Sanhuri, insist on the formalistic dimension in contracts, against a number of *hadith*—and to some extent Qur'anic verses—which imply a stronger role for intention, and which require a different emphasis in the understanding of the Islamic law of obligations, see Chapter 8.

[177] Reference to the six commodities *hadith* can be found in n. 101 above.

[178] Jurists, *fuqaha*; meant, *maqsud*, *al-Mabsut*, xii, 112.

[179] To facilite matters on people, *taysiran 'ala al-nas*, ibid. xii, 115.   [180] *salam*.

long chapter on the subject;[181] but Sarakhsi's distinctive coherence replaces his predecessor's haphazard juxtaposition of legal aphorisms with a consistent analysis of several facets of the credit contracts. This starts with the definition, which is ascribed to Marwazi: '*Salam* means taking possession of a commodity against future payment. It is a type of sale to exchange money against money'. Sarakhsi explains that *salam* is synonymous with deferral,[182] and shows why *salam* is different from *riba*:

The sale occurs in time after the object of the contract comes into the ownership of the [seller]. *Salam* is accepted in usage because it does not come into the [buyer's immediate] property. The contract anticipates in time, and was therefore called *salam* or *salaf*. By way of analogy, *salam* should not be accepted because it is the sale of the non-existent commodity... The sale of a non-existent commodity should be void, but we set analogy aside on the basis of the Qur'an and the *sunna*.[183]

A tight legal argument on the conditions of *salam* is then presented, and seven conditions attributed to Abu Hanifa (d. 150/767, the eponym of the Hanafi school to which Sarakhsi belongs) are discussed in terms of the need for certainty in a valid contract and 'the avoidance of ambiguity conducive to dispute'.[184] Here again, there are extensive developments relating to each of Abu Hanifa's seven conditions,[185] which provide Sarakhsi with an occasion to elaborate on '*salam* [as] a commercial contract',[186] three days as the minimal time period for *salam*, the distribution of risk in case of loss, the contractual session in the event of *salam*,[187] the types of commodity which can be the object of *salam*, and the consequences of death on *salam*. Sarakhsi is then drawn onto the terrain of *istisna*', a type of manufacturing contract which clearly lies for him within the financially problematic terrain of contracting future things, a practice which should also be prohibited because of uncertainty. To explain the prohibition away, he offers an elaborate solution which can be summarized as the need to accept this type of contract by law as a matter of usage and practicality.[188]

One can see the progression of an argument in a style which a lawyer will find enticing despite the relative strait-jacket imposed by the earlier commentaries of Shaybani or Marwazi. Sarakhsi's ability as a lawyer appears throughout in two ways: he operates transitions which are convincing and logical, and he tries to transform the commentary into a coherent textbook. Where no apparent legal

---

181 Shaybani, *al-Asl*, 1–70 in the edn. of Chehata, 5–69 in the Afghani edn.

182 '*salam* is synonymous with deferral, *al-salam wal-salaf bi-ma'na wahed*', *al-Mabsut*, xii, 124.

183 ibid. 124. *Salaf* is credit, also downpayment, advance.

184 *kull jahala tufdi ilal-munaza'a al-mani'a 'an al-taslim wal-tasallum yajib izalatuha bil-i'lam*, xii, 124.

185 The seven conditions of Abu Hanifa are, according to Sarakhsi: '*i'lam al-jins fi al-musallam fih, wa i'lam al-naw', wa i'lam al-qadr, wa i'lam al-sifa wa i'lam al-ajal wa i'lam al-makan alladhi yufihi fih wa i'lam qadr ra's al-mal fima yata'allaq al-'aqd 'ala qadrih*: so 'category', *jins*; type, *naw'*; quantity, *qadr*; quality, *sifa*; term of delivery, *ajal*; place of delivery, *makan*, 'in addition to capital as quantity might require' *al-Mabsut*, xii, 124.   186 *al-Mabsut*, xii, 126.

187 the contractual session, *majlis al-'aqd*, on which see Chapter 8. Sarakhsi, *al-Mabsut*, xii, 126 ff.

188 This centrality and prevalence of custom in *fiqh* is developed below in the section on custom, in Chapter 8 on the law of obligations, and in Chapter 9 on commercial law.

outline was followed by his predecessors, he is consciously and painstakingly constructing one, whence the progression in the book of sale from the overall logic of commerce, to the contract of sale and its impediments, to formalism and intention, to the pitfalls of *riba*, to the sale on credit[189] and/or future things, and finally to the specific case of manufacturing.[190] This does not mean that Sarakhsi will not, from time to time, fall prey to casuistry in the negative sense of the word, but the legal logic of the *Mabsut* is compelling overall. Hence also its popularity with Islamic law specialists to date.

If a generalization on the basis of Sarakhsi, surely, cannot be conclusive, a brief glance at the next great Hanafi work will show the new level of legal abstraction and rigour reached by the jurists in the classical age. Kasani (d. 587/1191), who died about a hundred years after Sarakhsi, starts his equally extensive book of sale with the following sentence: 'The treatment in this book deals with the basis of sale, the conditions relating to that basis, the categories of sales, unacceptable sales and related issues, the effectiveness of sale and [lastly] the suspension of the effectiveness of a sale'.[191]

What follows is systematic and orderly, and the reader is able to fathom the reasoning for each chapter in the manner announced in the outline, and within each chapter, in the form of subdivisions which are presented from the start, and thoroughly discussed in the order of their announcement.

Following his outline, Kasani addresses the nature of the offer and acceptance in sale contracts. That nature is determined by the complementarity of the two constitutive parts in the sale contract—offer and acceptance—and the necessity for them to be simultaneous. Hence the corollary of the contractual session concept (the 'unity of the contractual session' is suggested but not spelled out by Kasani here[192]), which introduces the possibility of a change of mind before the meeting is over on the basis of various *hadiths*.

Thirdly, Kasani deals with the conclusion of the contract by behaviour, in contrast to the contract by verbal commitment. Sale may be 'an exchange in fact, which is a deal, and is called sale by *murawada*'. Here, he explains the difference he has with Shafi'i, who rejects the validity of such a contract, since Shafi'i does not allow this type of sale under 'custom of law'.[193] The Hanafi Quduri (d. 428/1037) is also said to have made a further distinction between precious and ordinary commodities, rejecting non-verbal sale for precious commodities, though not for ordinary ones. Kasani, using elaborate parallels from Qur'anic verses, differs both from Shafi'i and from his illustrious Hanafi predecessor, and concludes that there is nothing which should prevent the conclusion of a sale in this way: 'Validity is in principle free from such distinction'.[194]

---

189 *salam.*   190 *istisna'.*
191 'Ala' al-Din al-Kasani, *Bada'e' al-sana'e' fi tartib al-shara'e'*, 7 vols. in 5 (Beirut, n.d., copy of the Cairo edn, 1328/1910). This and the following quotations start at v, 133.
192 *majlis al-'aqd.* Discussion of *majlis* in Kasani, *Bada'e'*, v, 137 middle and 193 bottom. Basis, *rukn.*
193 *'urf al-shar'.*
194 Kasani, *Bada'e'*, v, 134 middle: *'Al-jawaz fil-asl mutlaq min hadha al-tafsil'.*

This is clearly an elaborate juristic argument which betrays a well-structured, mature, legal mind. The rest of the book of sale is equally consistent, and a close examination of each division shows the effort of a systematic exposition in accordance with a clear outline announced from the outset.

The whole book can be followed through six main subdivisions which Kasani presents at the opening of the book, starting with the definition of sale through to its dissolution.[195] This structure, which Kasani follows systematically, is adapted from his master Samarqandi (d. 540/1145). It may not be totally comforting to modern eyes, but it contains much of what one needs to know for a comprehensive understanding of the law of sale. After what corresponds to a general definition,[196] Kasani devotes two long chapters to the conditions and types of sale,[197] then a chapter on 'the unacceptable sale',[198] followed by the various consequences of imperfection in the sale contract.[199] The fifth chapter analyses the dissolution of the contract. In the sixth and last chapter, he discusses the suspension of the effectiveness of a sale.[200] To the end, divisions and subdivisions follow rigorously as announced. In the last chapter, for instance, Kasani explains once more that there are two ways to terminate the contract (or 'end its effectiveness', which is the same thing): by dissolution,[201] and by 'novation'.[202] Termination of the contract by dissolution is distinguished from its termination by novation in that the first affects invalid or imperfect contracts, whereas novation terminates the perfectly valid contract by mutual agreement between the parties. Having just discussed dissolution, he proceeds with the analysis of the second type, novation.[203]

Kasani's systematic mind is particularly well illustrated in this last chapter of the book of sale, which is divided into four subsections.

The first subsection explains the basis of novation, and the various verbal tenses to be used in order to ascertain the meeting of minds between the offer of one party and the acceptance of the other party. The second subsection discusses the differences between various Hanafi jurists over the nature of novation, with some considering it a variation on sale, while others look at it more as a *sui generis* contract, as *riba* does not really affect it. The third subsection explains the conditions of validity of the novation, which include agreement between the parties, the unity of the contractual session, the transfer of whatever compensation may have been agreed in the novation, and, for some Hanafis, the continued existence of the original object of sale. This is discussed at some length.[204] Kasani concludes with a

---

[195] Kasani, *Bada'e'*, v, 133–310.

[196] Section entitled *rukn al-bay'*, literally the cornerstone of sale, v, 133–4.

[197] Mixed together, with Kasani clearly preferring to talk first about types of sale, then about the conditions, rather than the reverse which appears to be favoured by Samarqandi. Kasani, *Bada'e'*, v, 134–201 (types, *aqsam*); 201–28 (conditions, *shara'et*).

[198] *ma yukrah min al-baya'at*, 228–33.

[199] The regime of the sale contract, *hukm al-bay'*, with a gradation including *sahih* (valid), *fased* (voidable), *batel* (void), *mawquf* (conditional), 233–306.

[200] ibid. 306: *bayan ma yarfa' hukm al-bay'*.   [201] *faskh*.   [202] *iqala*.

[203] Kasani, *Bada'e'*, v, 306–10.   [204] Kasani, *Bada'e'*, v, 309.

fourth subsection about the effectiveness of novation, with various examples flow-
ing from the buyer and seller's possession of the original object of sale.[205]

Kasani did not seem encumbered in his summa, *al-Bada'e'*, by a previous commentator, and his outline in each chapter, as well as the transitions within it, belong
to the finest textbook tradition,[206] if somewhat verbose given the sheer length of
the material.[207] Whether for Hanafi *fiqh* compendia or for other schools, a case can
be made in favour of an ever increasing refinement of style along two main lines:
overall exposition, and internal coherence including transitional clauses within a
chapter or a section.[208] Style, of course, is difficult to compare.

---

[205] ibid. 309–10 bottom.

[206] In the opening of his *Bada'e'* (i, 2–3), Kasani acknowledges his debt to his master Samarqandi
(d. 540/1145), 'the only one who gave attention to the arrangement, *tartib*, of legal rules', and
explains the need for a new method of presenting and explaining these rules so that students can
understand them and follow the law better. Kasani's seven published volumes are divided into books
(*kitab*, plural *kutub*) as follows: *tahara* (purity, i, 3–88), *salat* (prayer, i, 89–325), *zakat* (alms, ii,
1–75), *sawm* (fasting, ii, 75–107), *i'tikaf* ([spiritual] retreat, ii, 108–17), *hajj* (pilgrimage, ii,
118–227), *nikah* (marriage, ii, 228–340), *ayman* (oaths, iii, 1–87), *talaq* (divorce, iii, 88–228), *zihar*
(special Qur'anic instance of *talaq*, iii, 229–36), *li'an* (another special instance of *talaq*, iii, 237–49),
rida' (suckling, iv, 1–14), *nafaqa* (maintenance, iv, 15–40), *hadana* (custody, iv, 40–4), *i'taq* (manumission, iv, 45–111), *tadbir* (post-mortem manumission, iv, 112–23), *istilad* (parenting the child of
a woman slave, iv, 123–33), *mukatab* (manumitted slave, iv, 133–59), *wala'* (patronage in slavery,
iv, 159–73), *ijara* (lease, iv, 173–224), *istisna'* (manufacturing contract, v, 1–4), *shuf'a* (pre-emption,
v, 4–35), *dhaba'eh wa suyud* (animal slaughter and hunting, v, 35–61), *tadhiya* (sacrificial offering, v,
61–81), *nidhr* (religious pledge, v, 81–94), *kaffarat* (atonement, 95–111), *ashriba* ([alcoholic] drinks,
v, 112–17), *istihsan* (preference in legal interpretation, v, 118–32), *buyu'* (sales, v, 133–310), *kafala*
(guarantee, vi, 1–15), *hawala* (transfer, vi, 15–19), *wikala* (power of attorney, vi, 19–39), *sulh* (compromise, vi, 39–56), *sharika* (partnership, vi, 56–78), *mudaraba* (profit and loss partnership, vi,
79–114), *hiba* (gift, vi, 115–34), *rahn* (pledge, vi, 135–75), *muzara'a* (agricultural profit and loss
partnership, vi, 175–85), *mu'amala* (transaction, vi, 185–8), *shirb* (water share, vi, 188–92), *aradi*
(land, vi, 192–6), *mafqud* (missing person, vi, 196–7), *laqit and laqta* (foundling, male and female,
vi, 197–203), *abaq* (runaway slave, vi, 203–6), *sibaq* (races, vi, 206–7), *wadi'a* (deposit, vi, 207–13),
'ariya (free loan, vi, 214–18), *waqf wa sadaqa* (trusts and alms, vi, 218–21), *da'wa* (legal action, vi,
221–66), *shahada* (testimony, vi, 266–82), *ruju''an al-shahada* (retraction of testimony, vi, 283–90),
adab al-qadi (literature of judges, vii, 2–16), *qisma* (division, vii, 17–32), *hudud* (prescribed criminal
penalties, vii, 33–65), *sariqa* (theft, vii, 65–90), *qutta''al-tariq* (highway robbers, vii, 90–141), *ghasb*
(violation, vii, 142–69), *hikr wa habs* (attachment and retention, vii, 169–75), *ikrah* (duress, vii,
175–91), *ma'dhun* (slave allowed to conduct business, vii, 191–207), *iqrar* (admission, vii, 207–33),
jinayat (crimes, vii, 233–327), *khantha* (hermaphrodite, vii, 327–30), *wasaya* (wills, vii, 394), *qard*
(loan, vii, 394–6). It is clear from the last chapter that the book is not complete in its present standard
edition. A few important chapters are also missing, such as the book of intestate succession (*fara'ed*).
Compare the list with the structure of the *Mabsut*, above n. 130.

[207] For an appreciation of the treatment of each of these chapters, it is useful to keep in mind that
an average page in the current edition of Sarakhsi's *Mabsut* includes some 400 words, against 700
words for an average page in Kasani's *Bada'e'*. There are over 6,000 pages in Sarakhsi's *Mabsut* (i.e.
c. 2,500,000 words), and 2,100 pages (i.e. c. 1,500,000 words) in Kasani's *Bada'e'*. This makes
Kasani's work about 60 per cent the length of Sarakhsi's *summa*. In comparison, the present chapter is
some 65,000 words long.

[208] One should also compare this structure with classical law books by Shi'i jurists, who make a
general separation between acts of devotion and transactions, with nuances such as a quadripartite
distinction in al-Muhaqqiq al-Hilli's (d. 676/1277) *Shara'e' al-Islam*, 4 vols (Najaf, 1969); see Hossein
Modarressi, *An introduction to Shi'i law* (London, 1984) 18–22. One should also note the importance
of some books and passages for Shi'is which one will not find discussed extensively among Sunnis,
generally on matters involving the Shi'i *imams*, specific taxes, or the role of the jurist. Among the

As a word of supplementary caution, a comparison of legal structures may be as attractive as it may be deceiving. To pursue Middle Eastern legal calques of the Jewish-Islamic mode, it is alluring to note that the great Arab-Jewish scholar Ibn Maimun (d. 600/1204), better known as Maimonides, was a contemporary of Kasani. Ibn Maimun's celebrated philosophical work, *The guide to the perplexed*, was written in Arabic in 586/1190,[209] a year before the great Hanafi jurist died. Even more alluring is the fact that Maimonides was, like Kasani for Islamic law, the first scholar who put some order[210] into the dishevelled layers of the legal tradition he inherited, in the form of the famous *summa* known as *Mishneh Torah* ('the second Torah'), the construction of which was the basis of the authoritative structure, to the present day, of his great Spanish-Ottoman successor Rabbi Yosef ibn Ephraim Karo (d. 982/1575), *Shulhan Arukh* ('The prepared or set table').[211]

Less compelling, however, is a closer comparison between the structure of the great works of all these scholars in the proposed Middle Eastern legal *koine*. Maimonides' works may be said to resemble, in many ways, the structure of Kasani's *summa*, but the chapters or books do not correspond on a one-to-one basis.[212] Somewhat more appealing from a comparative perspective is the structure of four books adopted by Karo after the *Tur* (row) tradition (*c*. 1340) of his Spanish predecessor Jacob ibn Asher. The first book covers liturgy, the second rituals, the third

modern scholars, Muhammad Baqer al-Sadr (d. 1980) has suggested a novel, more reasoned typology, but it has not been yet adopted by other jurists. See my *Renewal of Islamic law*, 13–14. The extensive treatment of any one topic in the large books makes the issue slightly redundant, and a good thematic index will do the trick, such as in the model alphabetical six-volume rearrangement by Khaled al-'Atiyya, *Mu'jam fiqh al-jawaher* (Beirut, 1996), of the large nineteenth-century compendium of Muhammad Hasan Najafi (d. 1266/1850), *Jawaher al-kalam*, 15 vols (Beirut, 1992). Najafi's *Jawaher* is a super-commentary on Hilli's *Shara'e'*.

[209] Ibn Maimun, *Dalalat al-ha'irin*, Muhammad Zahed al-Kawthari ed. (Cairo, 1369/1949). The full title of the *Dalalat* is *al-Muqaddimat al-khams wal-'ishrun fi ithbat wujud Allah wa wahdaniyyatih wa tanazzuhih min an yakun jisman aw quwwatan fi jism min dalalat al-ha'irin*: The twenty-five prolegomena in the proof of the existence of God, his uniqueness, his not being a body or a potentiality of a body, a guide to the perplexed. The argument of the *Dalalat* is one clearly reminiscent of the dispute over the creation of the Qur'an, see below nn. 468 and 469 and accompanying text.

[210] The title of Kasani's work is *tartib al-shara'e'*, a conscious choice by the author of the need 'to put order in the knowledge of the law'.

[211] Ibn Maimun fled Spain, which the Almohads conquered in the twelfth century, forcing conversion to Islam, and settled in Fustat-Cairo, where he died in 600/1204. Karo was also a Spanish refugee, fleeing this time the intolerance of the Catholic Reconquista, and settling in Ottoman-ruled Greece, then Palestine. On these central legal scholars of Judaism, see Hecht et al, *An introduction to Jewish law*, above n. 5 especially at 277–9 (chapter by Eliav Schochetman) and 339–43 (chapter by Stephen Passamaneck), respectively. Great jurists were never free from the rulers' ire, even if they shared their religion. Kasani fled his native Farghana, near Tashkent, to Aleppo, and Sarakhsi spent, as we saw, a long time in prison.

[212] Maimonides' *Mishneh Torah* is also known as 'the fourteen books', in Hebrew *yad hahazakah*, divided as follows: 1. (*sefr* in Hebrew and Arabic, but the Islamic scholars use *kitab*) Knowledge (theology), 2. Adoration (prayer, worship), 3. Seasons (sabbath, festivals), 4. Women (family law, marriage, divorce), 5. Holiness (ritual prohibitions, incest, dietary restrictions), 6. Asseverations (oaths and vows), 7. Agriculture, 8. Service (at the temple), 9. Offerings, 10. Purity (ritual purity), 11. Torts, 12. Acquisition (sales etc.), 13. Civil laws,14. Judges (administration of justice). A scholarly English edition of most of the *Mishneh Torah* was published at Yale in the Judaica series, starting in 1949.

family law, and the fourth transactions and the judiciary.[213] One can identify in both Kasani's and Sarakhsi's summas clusters of books which share a similar quadripartite logic. As in all legal comparisons, however, limitations are inherent in the exercise, and depend on the measures and criteria chosen in the scholarly use of large compilations. Good thematic indexes serve their purpose better than a search for sophisticated architectonics which are too general, and not always meaningful.[214]

The brief remarks on the structure and development of *fiqh* literature can help us re-assess a number of theses strongly connected with the perception of Islamic law, in the West as well as in the East, and show the need to be more cautious in the assessment of the field. In short, one should abandon the belief that Islamic law does not or did not develop because of the authors' attachment to precedents established either during the Prophet's time, or during the formative stages of jurisprudence in the second and the third centuries after the Islamic revelation. The structure and terminology, and consequently substantive rules themselves, get refined and changed through the centuries. This is clear in the different treatment of the law of sales by Sarakhsi in comparison to the earlier Shaybani. It is also clear, within a shorter period of time, in the much more systematic treatment of the contract of sale by Kasani in comparison to Sarakhsi.

While difficult to document because of the sheer weight and complexity of the material, and the persistence of both structural and substantive legal calques, there have been other examples of demonstrably substantive change in at least three important legal areas: one is the passage to 'intention', in a determined way, in the texts of the later period.[215] Another is the acceptance, amidst strong resistance by 'conservative' jurists, of movables as the subject of a trust.[216] A third appears in the changes introduced to the Hanafi doctrine of land ownership in order to accommodate the taxation of private property in the tenth/sixteenth century.[217] All these can be found in the arguments of the jurists in 'classical' treatises, and they may include structural, stylistic, and substantive matters.[218]

---

[213] *Shulhan Arukh* consists of four parts: (1) *orah hayyim* ('parts of life')—daily, sabbath, and festival laws; (2) *yoreh de'ah* ('the one who imparts knowledge')—dietary laws; relations with non-Jews; usury; menstruation; vows and oaths; charity; circumcision; proselytes and slaves; offerings; the ban; illness, death, burial, and mourning regulations; (3) *even ha'ezer* ('the rock of help')—procreation, marriage, divorce; (4) *hoshen hamishpat* ('breastplate of justice')—Laws about judges and witnesses; loans and claims; agencies and partnerships and neighbours; pecuniary transactions, loans, sales, bailment; legacies and inheritance; theft, robbery, homicide, battery, damage and injury.

[214] 'Atiyya's *Mu'jam*, cited above n. 208, is a powerful tool with no equivalent to my knowledge for Sunni treatises, although the indexes available in some new editions of Ibn Qudama's *Mughni*, Mawardi's *Hawi*, Ibn Hazm's *Muhalla*, are extremely helpful.

[215] See vol. 2 in Chafik Chehata, *Etudes de droit musulman*, 2 vols (Paris, 1973).

[216] Jon Mandaville, 'Usurious piety: the cash *waqf* controversy in the Ottoman empire', *International Journal of Middle Eastern Studies*, 10, 1979, 289–308.

[217] Baber Johansen, *The Islamic law on land tax and rent* (London 1988), and my review in *Bulletin of the School of Oriental and African Studies*, 54, 1991, 155–6.

[218] Change can be documented differently: in the law of divorce, documents show the strong trend, in Moroccan notary-public documents, towards enhanced powers for the wife in the formularies of the nineteenth century in contrast to those found in Maliki texts from Granada in the twelfth century. See the section on formulae below.

Like all laws, the change operates on the basis of precedent and analogy, whilst remaining consonant with the Qur'an and the *hadith* as canonical references. As time went by, some texts acquired more importance and authority than others, chief among them the *fiqh* treatises of the better legal scholars.

Courts, judges, case-law

Central to understanding the classical and the modern legal world are the rulings of courts. Law reporting as understood nowadays is unknown in a systematic and pervasive Middle Eastern form during the classical age, or before, although some cases have survived from Babylonian times, such as a famous report known as the Nippur homicide trial.[219] Even in the present day, nowhere in an Arab country is precedent an established rule, following a fiction which is common to both the French legal tradition and the classical *shari'a*. Neither admits of formal judicial precedents which are binding.

Nevertheless, there are attempts from courts and judges to offer consistency in their judgments, and most Middle Eastern jurisdictions have established a hierarchical system of courts with a supreme tribunal which helps the integration and consistency of points of law within a legal discipline. One may safely assume that judges belonging to a great tradition of the past were no different in their attachment to consistency and logic than their modern counterparts.

Judges in the Islamic classical legal tradition have suffered from the oft-quoted image of a simple mind dispensing justice under the tree. The image is derived from the Weberian derogatory remark on the *qadi* as the wielder of raw and irrational justice.[220]

Colourful studies have shown how the pomp and attire of the *qadi* in the classical age belies the received image of a simple ceremony-less rendering of justice.[221] Scholarship has also established the position of the chief judge[222] in the classical age, a theory of judgeship in which the judge was considered the agent of the caliph or sultan, the prevalence of a single-judge court in the absence of a structured system of appeal, the presence of parallel courts or law officers with a special

[219] Decision in Postgate, *Early Mesopotamia*, 278 (wife of a murdered person considered guilty of complicity in homicide for covering up her husband's murder, and sentenced to death).
[220] Max Weber, *Economy and society* (Berkeley 1968) 3 vols, ii, 895, 806; iii, 976–8, e.g. at 976: 'Kadi-justice knows no rational "rules of decision" whatsoever'. For a nuanced view of Max Weber and Islam, see Wolfgang Schluchter, ed., *Max Webers Sicht des Islams: Interpretation und Kritik* (Frankfurt, 1987), and my review in *MESA Bulletin*, 25, 1991, 200–2. See Chapter 11.
[221] Emile Tyan, *Histoire de l'organisation judiciaire en pays d'Islam* (Paris, 1938–43), 2 vols, i, 288–312, later collected in one volume at Brill (Leiden, 1960). Also Norman Calder, in a communication on Islamic law in Copenhagen, March 1993. In the Islamic manuals for judges, which will be examined below in the section on literature, and in Chapter 11, the judge's composure and dignity (*ubbaha*) are recurrent themes. Illustrations of the judge and his court can be found in some thirteenth and fourteenth century miniatures reproduced in microfilms included in the appendix to Oleg Grabar, *The illustrations of the maqamat* (Chicago, 1984).   [222] *qadi al-qudat*.

competence,[223] the lack of professional legal representation and of a body of lawyers representing the parties.[224] More recent scholarship has questioned these views,[225] but that structure, as described in Emile Tyan's classic two-volume *Histoire de l'organisation judiciaire en pays d'Islam* (1938–43),[226] remains on the whole true to the texts examined: these are essentially *fiqh* books, but also include the great classics of *adab*, literature in a large sense, the *tabaqat*, which are biographies with a relatively short analytic span, and historical chronicles. What one misses in the analysis is mainly what the courts produce best: judgments. There are, however, no verbatim records of judgments rendered in the classical age. Only when the period gets much nearer, starting generally with the Ottomans, can one find significant series of cases retained in the archives of major capitals.

Work on court records from classical Islam is notoriously difficult. Sometimes, as in some records from sixteenth-century Egypt, the script itself is special.[227] Handwriting may also be a problem, in addition to the conditions of work which may face the researcher, with the usual bureaucratic problems of access to understandably protected archives, indexing, and photocopying. Court archives are usually a pell-mell collection of various legal records, including deeds and acknowledgements, occasionally of full-fledged decisions. The case of the trove in

[223] E.g. the *qadi 'askar*, or military judge, and the *muhtasib*, the market inspector and generally an 'administrative' judge.

[224] Tyan, *Histoire de l'organisation judiciaire*, i, 182 ff. Joseph Escovitz, *The office of qadi al-qudat in Cairo under the Bahri Mamluks* (Berlin, 1984). Also 'Isam Shbaru's two books on *al-qada' wal-qudat fil-islam* (The judiciary and judges in Islam) (Beirut, 1982); and *qadi al-qudat* (The chief justice) (Beirut, 1986). The position has naturally experienced ebbs and flows over the long period of classical Islam. For an early example of 'the decline of the Chief *Qadi*' in e.g. the period of Caliph al-Mu'tadid (269/883–289/902), Irit Bligh-Abramski, 'The judiciary (*qadis*) as a governmental-administrative tool in early Islam', *Journal of the Economic and Social History of the Orient*, 35, 1992, 40–71, at 69–70. For the continuing uncertain place of the equivalent chief justices and supreme court presidents in the contemporary Middle East, see Chapter 5.

[225] This has taken different forms in the scholarship. In 'Appellate review and judicial independence in Islamic law' (in C. Mallat, ed., *Islam and public law* (London, 1993), 49–83), M. H. Kamali detects forms of appeal in the possibility for judges to revise their judgment because 'a decision rendered yesterday, if you come to your senses, should not prevent you from reviewing the right, for truth is old [i.e. established] and a review of the case is better than persistence in the wrong', Sarakhsi, *al-Mabsut*, xvi, 62. Contra, see in the same 'book of judge' (*kitab adab al-qadi, Mabsut*, xvi, 59–111) the arguments of Sarakhsi on the possibility of the judge changing his opinion 'only for the future', at 84–5. For the possibility of another judge reviewing the 'wrong' decision, see Kamali, 73–4, citing Ibn Qudama, *al-Mughni*, ix, 56. David Powers discusses several cases of judicial review in Cordoba (Arab Spain) and Salé (Morocco), and one should note the continuation of disputes over several generations: see Powers, 'A court case from fourteenth-century North Africa', *Journal of the American Oriental Society*, 110, 1990, 229–54; 'On judicial review in Islamic law', *Law and Society Review*, 26, 1992, 315–41; '*Futya* in medieval Spain and North Africa', in Mallat, ed., *Islam and public law*, 85–106, esp. 104–5. This conjures up a different problem relative to the closing of files, and of *res judicata*.

[226] Martin Shapiro provides an interesting comparative account based on Tyan's conclusions in 'Islam and appeal', *California Law Review*, 68, 1980, 350–81.

[227] André Raymond mentions that some of the very early Cairo court documents were written in the ancient stenography type called *qirma*. But the bulk of the texts he deciphered in the period 1550–798 were written in Arabic. André Raymond, *Artisans et commerçants au Caire au xviiième siècle*, 2 vols (Damascus, 1973) vol. 1, at xxi.

the Islamic Museum in Jerusalem, which is part of the 'haram al-sharif' esplanade, is illustrative of the problem: while some 600 documents were included in the documents discovered, the *haram* material was scant on reasoned court decisions which a jurist could examine more closely. One significant case available within the twenty 'court records of cases and actions initiated by individuals who appeared in court before a judge' involves a decision rendered in 797/1394 in which the judge rejects the action of four plaintiff-slaves who claimed that their owner manumitted them before he died. The judge ruled against manumission on the grounds that the owner was under age when he freed the slaves. Together with another three cases dating from 793/1390 to 797/1394, this manumission case is to my knowledge the earliest extant legal report from the Islamic period. It belongs to the late Mamluk age in the Levant, before the region yielded to the long Ottoman rule, which, despite some long interruptions, stretched from 1516 to the First World War.[228]

Whatever the state of pre-Ottoman archives, the regions ruled by Istanbul since the sixteenth century have started opening up their immense potential. The field is young, but the literature is growing fast, especially among historians.[229] In addition to the increasing material available, and the 'global history' focus prevailing in the field,[230] in a spirit reminiscent of Goitein and Raymond's exceptional scope of work, one should expect other treasure troves of documents in some hidden Geniza.[231] This might happen in the vast and little studied Yemen, or in recently

[228] D.H. Little, *A Catalogue of the Islamic documents from al-Haram al-Sharif in Jerusalem* (Beirut, 1984) 261–3 (*Al-Muqaddam at-Tawashi 'Anbar et al. v. estate of Muhibb ad-Din Ahmad ibn Qadi al-Qudat Burhan ad-Din Ibrahim ibn Jama'a*, Case 31, dated 19 Muharram 797/14 December 1394). The case is published in full in Kamel al-'Asali ed., *Watha'eq maqdisiyya tarikhiyya* (Historical Jerusalemite documents), vol. 1 ('Amman, 1983, 221–3). The documents collected by 'Asali in three volumes (vol. 2, 'Amman, 1985; vol.3, 'Amman, 1989) offer a wealth of information to historians like Little and Huda Lutfi, e.g. her remarkable 'A study of six fourteenth century *iqrars* from al-Quds relating to Muslim women', *Journal of the Economic and Social History of the Orient*, 26, 1983, 246–94. The three cases from 793/1393 to 797/1394 are reproduced and transcribed in 'Asali, vol. 2, 18–29. Earlier texts, including papyri (researched by A. Grohmann and A. Dietrich) and epigraphic inscriptions, yield little in terms of legal rationale, except possibly for the development of the terminology.

[229] With Raymond, another pioneering work is Galal Nahal, *The judicial administration of Ottoman Egypt in the seventeenth century* (Minneapolis, 1979). Specialists have increased several fold since, including work by Rafeq, Bakhit, Ziadeh, Jennings, Doumani, Marcus, Tucker, Qattan, and many others. I discovered recently a most interesting little book, *Some Arabic legal documents of the Ottoman period*, edited and translated by R. Y. Ebied and M. J. L. Young (Leiden, 1975). It consists of two main manuscripts, the first a formulary (probably Christian, as it makes reference to the Maronite community and uses Peter and Paul as hypothetical parties), probably dating from the mid-nineteenth century. This is further evidence of the same Mideast legal world across the main religious sects. The second manuscript in Ebied and Young comes from a collection of court records from the city of Safad at the end of the seventeenth century, which turned out to be very similar, with a few nuances, to the register from the city of Tripoli that provides the main basis for my discussion of judicial decisions in this chapter.

[230] See my introductory remarks in 'Islamic law: reflections on the present state in Western research', and in 'Le droit en Méditerranée musulmane: perspectives de recherches', cited above n. 2.

[231] This refers to the famous Geniza of Cairo. The Geniza is a room near or above the synagogue where superseded documents are kept in deference to their possible inclusion of sacred words which should not be physically done away with. The Cairo Geniza was discovered in the second half of the

more accessible loci of Islamic glory like Bukhara and Samarkand, and in the archives of Cairo or Istanbul when they are better organized and easier to access. Research in court records will also allow for a more legal focus, addressing procedure, judicial reasoning, and substantive law, in addition to the more general 'traditional image of urban society' examined by Raymond and Ziadeh.[232] In the present survey of the multi-layered legacy of Middle Eastern law, I can offer a brief overview of one such treasure trove, made partly accessible with a facsimile publication by three Lebanese historians of a full one-year register of Tripoli's court in the seventeenth century.[233]

The court as notary-public. The extant collection of the Tripoli court comprises seventy large registers, covering a long period, from 1667 to 1883. The series is almost continuous with some interruptions of a few years at various junctures, and a significant interruption between register 3 (1096–8/1684–6) and register 4 (1127–36/1715–23). Not all the documents available are judgments. The court also served as a repository of various legal texts, collected and kept for the evidence they offer, whether to ascertain a succession deed, confirm a lease, or establish a *waqf* (trust).

The registers reveal dozens of sale contracts,[234] which generally include the object of the sale, its specifications—for instance a house and its borders on the four cardinal points—the conclusion of the sale by offer and acceptance, delivery, the price with the note 'fully paid', and legal confirmation of the operation by the two parties, in addition to outside witnesses and court witnesses. Documents may also include the confirmation of a position, for instance arising upon the death of one sheikh, with another sheikh appointed to oversee the hospital in Tripoli and to receive the money which it yields.[235] Formal litigation is even introduced to

nineteenth century, and has now been relocated mainly in the library of the University of Cambridge. Work on the Geniza is mostly associated with the late Samuel Goitein, and his five-volume encyclopaedic work is based primarily on these documents. S. D. Goitein, *A Mediterranean society: the Jewish communities of the Arab world as portrayed in the documents of the Cairo Geniza*, 5 vols (Berkeley, 1967–88). Goitein mentions a potentially essential court register in vol. 2, 343, dated 1156: 'It consists of 28 consecutive folios comprising 66 items, all but one written by the judge Mevorakh b. Nathan'. This may be an exceptional trove from a much earlier period than the Jerusalem Haram even, and deserves to be investigated thoroughly.

[232] Khaled Ziadeh's books on seventeenth-century Tripoli, *Al-sura al-taqlidiyya lil-mujtama' al-madini* (The traditional image of urban society) (Tripoli, 1983) and *Arkeologia al-mustalah al-watha'iqi* (The archeology of documentary terminology) (Tripoli, 1986), are little-known works of great excellence.

[233] 'Umar Tadmuri, Frederic Ma'tuq, and Khaled Ziadeh, eds., *Watha'eq al-mahkama al-shar'iyya bi-Tarablus* (Documents of the shar'i court of Tripoli) (Tripoli, 1982), cited here as 'Tripoli', followed by the page number in *Watha'eq* and the names of the parties when there is litigation. If, as sometimes happens, the large facsimile page includes two or three documents, they are designated as a, b, and c.

[234] Heading of the documents: *bay' wa shiri* (sale and puchase), e.g. two sales at Tripoli, 64, and two at p. 76.

[235] Tripoli, 2b and c, heading: *taqrir wazifa* (confirmation of position). Other headings include the occasional *iqrar* (legal admittal, or affidavit), 40a; *wikalat ila dhimmi* (agency to a non-Muslim), Tripoli register 2, 158, cited in Tripoli i, *jim*.

get official approval by the court of an undisputed transaction.[236] Proof of transactions without any litigation is common, as in a typical formula attesting to the agreement of the parties and their full confirmation of a settlement reached before action:

[1] *A case of settlement*

[2] In the court of law and good judgment in Tripoli-Syria—may God protect it

[3] appeared each of Hajj Mansur Ibn al-Hajj 'Ali al-Misri and his brother Hajj Ahmad

[4] and they confirmed their legal, valid, binding settlement to the effect that

[5] there were previously between them give and take, and transactions, and that each of the two parties to this settlement has nothing left due to him by his companion and no claim whatsoever, either in law or in debt or in property or in gold or in silver or in [unclear] or in fabric or in copper or in lead, whether little or a lot, and no right whatsoever from the past to this date, except for the three houses located in the Rashid entry in the 'Abbas market, which belong to the aforementioned Ahmad on his own, without his brother the aforementioned Hajj Mansur

[6] and they mutually settled on the above in the legal form of settlement

[7] and this took place and was written in the late days of the month of Muharram 1078 [mid-July 1667].

[8] witnesses of the act [signed fives names, including the registrar]

[9] and others who were present.[237]

How judgments themselves are used for evidence appears in the following two cases. In a dispute over succession, which confirms the *ab intestat* rules under the Sunni scheme, a mother claimed her share in the succession of her deceased daughter against the daughter's husband, who had allegedly deprived her of her right to one-sixth of the legacy. The defendant husband denied that the division of the estate between the heirs had been carried out unlawfully. His wife had died leaving a father, a mother, him as husband, and a son, he explained, and both the mother and the father of the deceased had received their full share (one-sixth). Upon denial by the plaintiff mother, D asked for time to prove his case. He came back with a

---

[236] Below n. 267 and accompanying text.

[237] Settlement, *musadaqa* (literally confirmation), 31b, with a typical formula: '[1] *qadiyyat musadaqa*. [2] *Bi-majlis al-shar' al-sharif wa mahfal al-hukm al-munif bi-tarablus al-sham al-mahmiyya ajallahu allah ta'ala* [3] *hadara kullun min al-hajj mansur ibn al-hajj 'ali al-misri wa shaqiquh al-hajj ahmad* [4] *wa tasadaqa tasaduqan shar'iyyan mu'tabaran mar'iyyan* [5] *'ala annahuma kana baynahuma akhdh wa 'ata' wa mu'amalat wa anna kullan min al-mutasadiqayn lam yabqa yastahiqq wa la yastawjib qibla sahibihi haqqan wa la istihqaqan wa la da'wa wa la daynan wa la 'aynan wa la dhahaban wa la fiddatan wa la qanran[?] wa la qimashan wa la nuhasan wa la rasasan wa la qalilan wa la kathiran wa la haqqan mutlaqan li-ma mada min al-zaman fi yawmi tarikhihi ma 'ada al-thalath dur al-ka'ina bi-thaghr rashid bi-suwayqat[?] 'abbas fa-innahuma mulk al-hajj ahmad al-mazbur bi-mufradih duna shaqiqihi al-hajj mansur al-mazbur* [6] *hasbama tasadaqa 'ala ma fihi al-tasaduq al-shar'i* [7] *wa jara dhalik wa hurrira fi awakhir muharram al-haram li-sanat thaman wa sab'in wa alf.* [8] *shuhud al-hal* [five names follow] [9] *wa ghayruhum min al-hadirin'.* The same formula is also used in a slightly more complex situation involving a lawsuit in which D accepts the debt claimed by P and settles it in court, with the formula of *musadaqa* clearing him from any claim or debt in full settlement of all rights and duties on either part. See Tripoli, 34a, heading: *musadaqa wa da'wa* (attestation and action).

probate letter from the Saida judge confirming his claim. Judgment for D after the
judge checked the proper witnessing of the Saida court document.[238]

Similarly, in a dispute over a deposit entrusted by P to D four years earlier,
D admitted that he had received some money which he duly returned in Saida at a
given date, but rejected the plaintiff's claim for a more important debt. While P
was unable to provide evidence supporting his claim, the defendant produced a
letter from a court official in Saida confirming what he said in his testimony.
Judgment for D.[239]

The judicial process. While the notarization process was clearly important, including for judgments issued elsewhere, litigation is the more alluring object of analysis. In the facsimile edition of the first register of 1077–8/1667–8 examined here,
the 154 large pages of photographic reproductions include some fifty-five judgments, which give the lawyer a precise idea of the pattern followed by the court
beyond individual cases, most of which involved civil disputes.

Here is the translation of the last case reported in that register:

[1] *A case of action and injunction*

[2] In the court of law and good judgment in the presence of our master the fair judge in
     Tripoli-Syria—may God recompense him—, bearer of the above handwriting—long
     life to his virtues, may his days and nights be ever better,

[3] appeared the Christian woman called Franjiyyeh, daughter of the Christian Jirjis, and
     she brought legal action against the Christian man Ibrahim, son of Jirjis, known as Ibn
     al-'Ukaika,

[4] claiming in her action against him that he had, ten months earlier, come to her house
     in the neighbourhood of Tibbaneh, one of Tripoli's neighbourhoods, that he entered
     her house and said to her that the governor of Tripoli-Syria previously, the late Ahmad
     Basha, had told him of his wish to [kill/kiss?][240] her or else that he would drown her in
     the salted sea, and that he scared her and threatened her with sundry threatening
     words; and that, out of fear for herself, she bribed him with an amount of 170 piastres,
     that she paid them to him, that he took them from her in her house unjustly and under
     duress, without legal right, and she asked him [presently] to return the money;

[5] requesting [the court] to put the question to him,

[6] so [the judge] put his question [to the defendant], who denied [the allegation],

[7] and the plaintiff was asked to prove her claims legally, and she demanded some time,
     then more time, until three days passed and she was unable to produce evidence prov-
     ing her claim, and was unable to do so legally,

[8] so when the plaintiff appeared unable to prove her allegations,

---

[238] Tripoli, 15, *Zahida bint Ibrahim v. Sulaiman ibn al-Hajj Shihab al-Din ibn Sasun al-Saydawi*,
mid-Dhi al-Qi'da 1077, mid-May 1667. Asked for time, *fa talaba al-mihla fa-umhila*; a probate letter
from the Saida judge, *kitab naql shar'i sader min . . . al-qadi bi-madinat saida.*

[239] Tripoli, 2–3, *Muhammad ibn Bilal al-Saydawi v. Merhej walad Bayif* [?], mid-Shawwal 1077,
mid-April 1667. Note the defendant who won the case is a Christian, *dhimmi*. The case misses a few
lines at the end.   [240] It is not clear whether it is *yuqabbiluki*, kiss you, or *yaqtuluki*, kill you.

[9] and the defendant swore after he was put to the oath in the name of God almighty the revealer of the Gospels to our lord Jesus, upon him and upon our Prophet best prayers and perfect salutations be rendered, and repeated that he had neither entered her aforementioned house nor taken any of the money which is cause for the action, and that he was totally free from all that,

[10] and when [the defendant] took the legal oath for all what he said, our aforementioned master and judge issued an injunction to the plaintiff to desist from addressing the defendant further with this action,

[11] such injunction being issued in accordance with due legal process,

[12] and this took place in the early days of the month of Jumada II, 1078 [mid-November 1667].

[13] witnesses of the act [signed eight names]

[14] and others who were present.[241]

This is a typical pattern, divided here into fourteen sections which correspond in the main to all other reported legal decisions in the register. The report is structured along a tight model which closely resembles modern *arrêts* of the French Court of Cassation in the formal way they are organized. Following an indented title/classification of the case—simply 'action', often 'action and injunction', or more specifically 'action over dower' or 'action against a testament...'—[1], a typical formula follows, starting with 'in the court of law', a reference to the judge's 'writing above'—but without the judge's name—and a few words on his judgeship's greatness [2]. In a third section, the plaintiff/claimant's (or claimants') name appears, then the defendant or defendants. Sometimes, an attorney for the party is mentioned, and his power ascertained by witness [3]. This is followed by a longer section stating the particulars of the claim [4]. Once the particulars have

---

241 Tripoli, 153, *Franjiyyeh bint Jirjis v. Ibrahim ibn Jirjis alias Ibn al-ʿUkaika*, early Jumada II, 1078, mid-November 1667: '[1] *qadiyyat daʿwa wa manʿ*. [2] *bi-majlis al-sharʿ wa mahfal al-hukm al-munif bi-tarablus al-sham al-mahmiyya ajallahu allah taʿala lada mutawallih mawlana wa sayyiduna al-muli al-hakem al-sharʿi al-muwaqqaʿ khattuh al-karim bi-aʿalih damat fadayiluh wa maʿalih wa hasunat ayyamuh wa layalih* [3] *hadarat al-dhimmiyya al-madʿuwwa franjiyya bint al-dhimmi jirjis wa-iddaʿat ʿala al-dhimmi ibrahim walad jirjis al-shahir bi-ibn al-ʿukaika* [4] *muqarriratan fi daʿwaha ʿalayh bi-annahu min madi ʿashrat ashhur taqaddamat tarikh bi-dhailihi jaʿa ila baytiha al-kayen bi-mahallat al-tibbaneh min mahallat tarablus wa-dakhala ila ʿindiha wa qala laha bi-anna wali wilayat tarablus al-sham sabiqan al-marhum ahmad basha akhbarani bi-anna muradahu yaqtuluki [yuqabbiluki?] aw yughriquki fil-bahr al-malih wa khawwafaha wa haddadaha fi mithli hadha al-kalam min anwaʿ al-tahdid fa-min khawfiha min sharrih ʿala nafsiha arshathu bi-mablagh qadruhu mayat wa sabʿun ghirshan asadiyyan dafaʿatha lahu wa-huwa qabadaha minha fi baytiha al-mazbur wa la akhadha minha al-mablagh al-muddaʿa bihi sharʿi wa talabathu bi-dhalik* [5] *wa saʿalathu suʿalahu* [6] *fa suʿila fa-ajab bil-inkar* [7] *fa talaba min al-muddaʿiya ithbat ma iddaʿathu bil-tariq al-sharʿi fa talabat al-muhla baʿda al-muhla fa-madat thalathat ayyam wa lam taʿti bi-bayyina tashhadu laha bi-dhalik wa ʿajizat ʿan dhalik al-ʿajz al-sharʿi* [8] *falamma ʿajizat al-muddaʿiya ʿan ithbat muddaʿaha* [9] *wa halafa al-muddaʿa ʿalayh ghubba an istuhlifa billah al-ʿazim munazzil al-injil ʿala sayyidina ʿisa ʿala nabiyyina wa ʿalayh afdal al-salat wa atamm al-taslim annahu ma dakhala ila baytiha al-mazbur wa la akhadha minha al-mablagh al-muddaʿa bihi wa la baʿdahu wa anna dhimmatahu bariʿa min dhalika* [10] *al-yamin al-sharʿi al-jamiʿ li-maʿani al-half sharʿan manaʿa mawlana wa sayyiduna al-muli al-hakem al-sharʿi al-mushar ilayh al-muddaʿiya min al-taʿarrud lil-muddaʿa ʿalayh bi-khusus hadhih al-daʿwa* [11] *manʿan sharʿiyyan awqaʿahu bil-tariq al-sharʿi bil-iltimas al-marʿi* [12] *wa jara dhalik wa-hurrira fi ghurrat shahr jumada al-akhira min shuhur sanat thaman wa sabʿin wa alf* [13] *shuhud al-hal* [signed eight names] [14] *wa ghayruhum min al-hadirin.*'

been stated, another formula appears in which 'question is put to the defendant' [5] and the defendant denies or accepts the plaintiff's claim in part or in full [6].

Then the pattern develops depending on the defendant's acceptance or denial of the plaintiff's claim. When, as is usual, D denies P's particulars or varies upon them, evidence is sought. Upon the evidence the case hinges.

The burden of proof is on the plaintiff [7], then on the defendant for his counter-claim if the plaintiff succeeds in producing evidence supporting his or her claim. Oath may be administered in addition to, or in lieu of, the evidence [8, 9], and is expected to be sworn in support of the parties' respective claims, although there is one case in the 1667 register when a party was unwilling to take the oath, and duly lost.[242] The judge then takes note and disposes of the action [10]. This is followed by a formula confirming that the judgment was made in accordance with law [11]. The final section mentions the date of the case [12]. This is sometimes an exact date, sometimes a reference to the beginning, middle, or end of the month, which suggests the report might not have been written immediately when issued. Finally there are the signatures under the decision, often seven or eight persons called *'shurut al-hal'*, witnesses to the act [13], usually followed by mention of 'others who are present' [14], assuring the full publicity of the trial.

Evidence. In the report reproduced here in full, the plaintiff Franjiyyeh was unable to prove her case 'in accordance with law', and she lost. On such a model of the search for 'legally valid evidence' most of the cases turn, and the issue of fact as presented in the evidence is decisive.

Simple examples include a dispute over a bequest, in which P claimed a house which the deceased had wilfully, and in full control of his mental faculties, bequeathed to him. D was the heir of the deceased and had kept the property for himself. P was asked for evidence for his claim, which he produced in the form of the testimony in court of two apparently venerable sheikhs who confirmed their witnessing the oral bequest. Judgment for P.[243]

In a restitution case, P claimed he had entrusted D, a woman, with a necklace of gold of 22 carats. D denied the necklace was that valuable, claiming it weighed only 16 carats. She further explained that she went that day to the house of a potential buyer, where she stayed the night after hanging the necklace on a pillar in the house. The second day she went home and sent her daughter in the evening to get the necklace back. It was gone. P produced two witnesses who confirmed the 22-carat value of the necklace, and the judge held for P, 'because the defendant was negligent and betrayed her trust [over the property] by hanging the necklace on the said pillar'. This took place in the 'middle of the month of dhu al-qi'da 1077 [early May 1667]'.[244]

---

[242] Tripoli, 23, *Tijan bint Yusuf v. al-Hajj Muhammad ibn Wiya al-Hallaq.* Case discussed below n. 265 and accompanying text.

[243] Tripoli, 7, *Sheikh Mustafa ibn Abi Al-lutf al-Karami v. Hajj Muhammad Halabi ibn Kamal al-Din*, mid-Shawwal 1077/mid-April 1667.

[244] Tripoli, 13, *Hajj Zayn ibn 'Ala' al-Din v. Fakhri bint al-Dalala*, early Shawwal 1077, late March 1667: *likawniha qassarat wa farratat fi hifzih bi-wad'iha lahu 'ala al-watad al-mazbur.* Necklace,

The story did not end there. A few days later, the losing party appeared as plaintiff. She explained again that she had spent the night at friends, and hung her necklace on the pillar. This time she sued a Christian servant in the house, and claimed that he had covered the necklace with some cloth. This is why she forgot it when she woke up. The second day, she left the house, and then came back for the necklace, which had meanwhile disappeared. She was then asked for evidence, which she could not produce, so the oath was put to the D, who took it. P's case was dismissed.[245]

Other simple cases involved the immediate acknowledgment by an estranged husband, D, of his wife's deferred dower. P, the repudiated wife, was successful in getting paid the remainder of her dower in court. There was a small twist in the proceedings when 'the mediators intervened', and the two parties agreed that only 22 out of the acknowledged 30 piastres would be paid. Payment was made immediately, and full release was registered.[246]

Also straightforward was a case in which P sued D over a piece of land which P said he had inherited from his father, and which he now claimed was part of a *waqf*. However, P 'did not produce the deed of the *waqf* or any evidence to that effect', so the judge confirmed D's title.[247]

Absence of evidence was also cause for P losing a case where, acting as attorney for his wife, he brought action against two beneficiaries from a *waqf*, whom he accused of appropriating for themselves eleven out of fourteen shares which the wife was entitled to by virtue of the *waqf*. The defendants answered that they were the exclusive heirs of the founder of the *waqf*. P was asked to prove entitlement of his wife on the basis of her kinship with the *waqf* founder. In the absence of proof, the case was thrown out.[248]

A more elaborate decision was issued over a succession dispute. The plaintiff claimed he and his father were the closest male relatives of the deceased. They asked for the estate, which had been taken over by other relatives, to be returned to them. Evidence was requested and P produced the testimony of several notables

---

baghmaq (probably the phonetic rendering for the word '*baghma*'); carat is a lose translation of *mithqal*, which is a monetary unit corresponding, according to Ziadeh, *Arkeologia*, 65, to 3/17 of a dirham. The dirham is the traditional silver coin, while the dinar is the gold coin.

[245] Tripoli, 16a, *Fakhri bint al-Dalala v. Allas ibn Ya'qub*, 20 Dhu al-Qi'da 1077/14 May 1667. Note that P said she came herself to get it, as against her claim in the earlier proceedings that she had sent her daughter to fetch the necklace. The second case is dated a few weeks after the first one. The first signature is that of the clerk, *kateb*, perhaps because more important court witnesses had simply lost patience with her.

[246] Tripoli, 136, *Fakhri bint Muhammad ibn Nushuk v. Murad ibn Fakhr al-Din*, early Rabi' al-Awwal 1078/late August 1667. *Mu'akhkhar al-sadaq*, deferred dower; *wa dakhala al-muslihun baynahuma bil-sulh*, mediators intervened between them with a compromise.

[247] Tripoli, 14, *Ahmad ibn Beik ibn 'Umar alias ibn al-Qila al-Timari v. Hasan ibn Muhammad*, mid-Dhi al-Qi'da 1077/mid-May 1667. *Falam ya' ti bi-kitab waqf wa la bayyina tashhadu lahu bi-dhalik.*

[248] Tripoli, 143, *Abu Bakr ibn al-Hajj 'Umar al-Khabbaz al-Shami (attorney of 'A'isha bin Ramadan al-Khabbaz) v. Umm Husain Salha and 'Abd al-Rahim ibn al-Shaykh Zein ibn Mubarak*, early Jumada I 1078/mid-October 1667.

who confirmed 'that they had heard about that kinship from their fathers and the old folk with knowledge of family trees'. The rules of succession were therefore applied by the court in the light of the evidence, and P's share vindicated.[249]

In contrast, lack of evidence was key to the Christian caretakers of an orchard defeating the Muslim plaintiff, who was unable to produce proof of the debt he claimed they owed him;[250] evidence was also key to the defendant husband winning the case against his estranged wife who claimed that he had taken money away from her and from her children from a previous marriage,[251] and to the restitution of a sum of money brought into partnership between two brothers for operations of trade in fabric. The formula in the last case is typical: 'Since the plaintiff was unable to prove his allegation and the defendant took the oath, the judge issued a legal injunction preventing the plaintiff from further addressing the defendant on that issue'.[252]

A more complex set appears in a dispute in which the plaintiff demanded his share in a common building in the historic city of Jbeil (Byblos), which he claimed should have gone to him in succession of his deceased father. D's attorney—her son—denied the claim on her behalf. Plaintiff was asked for evidence, so he produced two witnesses, who testified that the defendant had confirmed in their presence the fact that the house was originally owned in common between two ascendants. But the witnesses added that the plaintiff's deceased father had sold his share. As evidence turned against him, the plaintiff denied that his father had sold his share, and he was asked in court to disprove the sale. In a development which is not too clear, but which might have resulted from the fact that witnesses called up on behalf of the plaintiff ended up testifying against him, P was asked to take the oath, swearing he did not know of any such sale. Judgment was entered in his favour.[253]

Another dispute over the ownership of a house arose between claimants who exhibited written proofs of their respective title. Judgment was entered in favour of the holder of the earlier document: 'The right sale is the earlier sale', the judge decided, but he also held that the second buyer, who was clearly harmed by buying

---

[249] Tripoli, 131, *Sheikh Mustafa ibn Abi Al-lutf v. Hajj Muhammad ibn al-Qadi Kamal al-Din*, Rabi' I 1078/September 1667.

[250] Tripoli, 132, *Husain ibn Naser al-Bawwab v. Farah and Elias sons of Lahham*, early Rabi' I 1078, late August 1667. Note Christian defendants winning the case against Muslim plaintiff. In the register, the son of a Christian (*dhimmi*, also possibly a Jew) is mentioned as *walad*, as opposed to *ibn* for Muslims. To keep the distinction clear, I have translated *walad* as son and kept *ibn* without change. For females *bint* is used in both cases.

[251] Tripoli, 90, *Karima bint 'Ali alias Abi Tizan v. Muhammad ibn al-Sayyed 'Abd al-Qader alias ibn al-'Ajmiyya*, 8 Jumada II 1078/25 November 1667. Note defendant husband was also put to the oath.

[252] Tripoli, 86–7, *Taj son of Abu al-Ha v. Salem son of Abu al-Ha*, early Jumada II 1078/mid-November 1667.

[253] Tripoli, 83, *'Abdallah ibn Salim v. Ahmad ibn Raslan (Attorney for Dalal bint Muhammad)*, Jumada I 1078/October 1667. Note terminology on power of attorney: *wakil shar'i 'an walidatih, wikalatan 'anha fi sama' hadhih al-da'wa*, legal attorney for his mother, by a power of attorney to hear this case in her stead.

a property which had already been sold, 'could claim back the price paid at the time of sale from the original owner'.[254]

The efficiency of court proceedings appears in a case brought by the attorney of the two sole heirs of a woman who had died 'over five years ago', and who claimed the return of a flat 'occupied illegally', in addition to 'the rent for the aforementioned period'. The defendant admitted that he was not entitled to ownership of the property, but claimed that he had agreed with the deceased woman that he would look after her in return for staying in the flat after her death, and produced a written document confirming the alleged agreement and his payment of some expenses upon her death. The court admitted the document after it was witnessed by two people, and proceeded with the calculation of the set-off between expenses and the value of the rent. This resulted in credit for P. Whereupon D paid his outstanding debt to P in court, and vacated the property against full release.[255]

Another clear pattern for the way evidence is used in court appears in a case where plaintiffs requested that D return the belongings of a deceased relative from a succession which D was not entitled to. When queried, D admitted he had taken a few items, but denied taking the rest. Plaintiffs were then asked to prove their allegation as to the other items to be restituted. As they were unable to provide evidence, oath was put to the defendant, who took it. He was therefore asked to return only the items he had acknowledged taking unlawfully.[256]

In the absence of witnesses or other evidence to prove payment twice for the acquisition of a 'draught animal' which was not delivered immediately, oath was administered to the defendant, who took it, and the plaintiff buyer lost.[257] Similarly, a plaintiff won who was able to produce witnesses to the effect that he had paid 100 piastres to the father of a minor daughter in advance of marriage, then changed his mind. The defendant was simply unable to rebut the evidence.[258]

In an inheritance-related dispute where P claimed that he had sold to the defendant's now deceased brother, four years earlier, a horse for which only part of the price had been paid, two witnesses confirmed the transaction, and P swore on oath that he had not received anything since that first payment. D, who was the sole heir to the buyer's succession, was asked to pay the balance.[259]

---

[254] Tripoli, 73, *Dhaiba bint Husain and Fatima bint 'Amr v. Sharafeddin ibn 'Ali Qanbar*, 29 Rabi' I 1078/18 September 1667. Written proof, *hujja shar'iyya*, the right sale is the earlier sale, *al-bay' al-sahih li-sabiq al-tarikh*.

[255] Tripoli, 68–9, *Hasan ibn 'Ala' al-Din (attorney for Ahmad ibn al-Hajj and al-Hurma Fakhri) v. Yusuf ibn Sulaiman al-Jabi*, end Rabi' I 1078/ mid-September 1667. Occupied illegally, *wadi' yadah bi-ghayr wajh shar'i*. Note admittance (*i'tiraf*) of D, note also efficiency in proceedings and full release in court.

[256] Tripoli, 111, *Kamal ibn 'Ali al-Najjar (attorney or Fatima bint al-Hajj and Khadija bint Ibrahim) v. Hajj 'Abd al-Rahman*, early Jumada II 1078/mid-November 1667.

[257] Tripoli, 68, *Rizq ibn al-Halabi v. al-Hajj Ibrahim ibn al-Hajj 'Abdallah*, end Rabi' I 1078, mid-September 1667. The draught animal is an *ikdish*, a mule.

[258] Tripoli, 74c, *Shaikh 'Abd al-Jawad ibn al-Shaikh Kamal-Din al-Misri v. Shaikh Kamal al-Din ibn al-Shaikh Rajab ibn Sharaba*, 10 Muharram 1078/2 July 1667.

[259] Tripoli, 58, *Shahin ibn al-Hajj Ahmad v. Muhammad ibn Naser al-Din*, early Rabi' I 1078, late August 1667.

In all these cases, the dominant dimension is factual. In one instance, several plaintiffs had brought a case against D, the widow of a deceased man who, they claimed, owed them money. D denied all the claims, upon which the plaintiffs were asked to provide evidence. They couldn't, but asked for D to be sworn legally. She took the oath, confirming her denial. 'Since plaintiffs were unable to provide legal evidence, and since D was sworn accordingly', the judge ordered plaintiffs to desist.[260]

The use of evidence is here at its simplest. Claim by P. Denial by D. If P is unable to produce the evidence, oath may be put to D. As often appears in these cases, and true to the received tradition, evidence does not need to be produced in writing, and must be supported by witnesses even if it is provided in writing.[261]

Straightforward evidence is often decisive in disputes over debts. In a case in which a debt was allegedly contracted by the deceased and claimed from D by the heirs to the succession, the defendant was able to win the case by providing witnesses who testified that he had paid the deceased what he owed him prior to his death.[262]

In a dispute over a partnership which had incurred a large debt, one of the partners had gone away. The remaining partner sued third party D, claiming that the absent partner owned an orchard which D exploited and for which he owed him money. Since there was a mutual guarantee between the partners, P claimed that he was entitled to recover the land and its revenues, hence the suit brought before the court. D retorted that he had actually bought the orchard, that he had paid part of the price and set off the remainder against a debt of the orchard's owner (the absent partner). Witnesses to that effect were produced, and P lost.[263]

Occasionally, a more complicated situation is elicited, for instance in a case of compensation between two debts, which was the object of contention between parties to the sale of an orchard. Only part of the orchard price had been paid, because of a pre-existing debt between the buyer and the seller. Plaintiffs in this case were 'a man and his divorced wife', and the defendant produced 'a legal set-off' note attesting equivalence between the value of the plot and the debt owed to him. Plaintiffs attacked 'the content of the note', so D produced witnesses who confirmed it, and judgment was entered in his favour.[264]

---

[260] Tripoli, 58–9, *Zainab bint al-Hajj Habib and Hajj 'Uthman ibn Abi Bakr (Attorney for Zlikha and others) v. Safa bint al-Hajj Naser*, 10 Rabi' I 1078/30 August 1667, incidentally an interesting case on *hajj* and various payments in the pilgrimage journey.

[261] Classic exposition by Emile Tyan, 'Le notariat et le régime de la preuve par écrit dans la pratique du droit musulman', *Annales de la Faculté de Droit de Beyrouth*, 2, 1945, 3–99. For modern law see Chapter 8.

[262] Tripoli, 60, *Yusuf ibn 'Abd al-Rahman (Attorney for Mu'mina wife of Hajj Shitaiwi al-Misri and their daughter Hafiza) and 'Awad ibn Muhammad v. 'Abd al-Qader ibn al-Hajj Khalil (as principal and attorney)*, end Safar 1078/mid-August 1667.

[263] Tripoli, 56, *Al-Hajj Mustafa ibn al-Hajj Salem al-Atmakji v. Shaikh Nureddin ibn al-Hajj Muhammad*, late Safar 1078/mid-August 1667. *Mufawada* partnership.

[264] Tripoli, 73–4, *Husain Khair al-Din and Fakhri bint al-Hajj 'Uthman v. Muhammad ibn Shehadeh al-Khabbaz*, early Rabi' I 1078/mid-August 1667. Legal set-off, *al-muqasasa al-shar'iyya*; content of the note, *madmun al-hujja*.

In another more complex case, P, a woman, appeared in court to ask her tenant for payment of four years of rent, amounting to 28 piastres. The defendant alleged he had been living in that place for only eighteen months, and that he had rented it for six piastres per year from an 'Abd al-Rahman ibn al-Hajj Mansur, who had rented it, in turn, from the plaintiff's husband. The plaintiff rejected the allegation that her husband owned the house, which she had bought from him, she said, four years earlier. Testimony to this effect was produced in the person of two witnesses, but then 'Abd al-Rahman ibn al-Hajj Mansur showed up in court claiming that P's husband had contracted a debt towards him of 32 piastres. A partial set-off was arranged with the rent of the D for 12 piastres, leaving the debt of the husband at 20 piastres, for which a one-year grace period was accorded to the plaintiff against a guarantee. The judge asked 'Abd al-Rahman to prove his case, which he was unable to do. He then directed the oath, 'time and again', to P, who refused to swear it. She was ordered to pay the 20 piastres.

The convoluted case reveals some of the technicalities in the set-off operation, the interventionism of the judge to cut through complexities, as in the arrangement of a guarantee. Most remarkable, however, is the operation of testimony and oath, as P was not capable of lying under oath, even though she did lie about conniving with her husband.[265]

Also complicated was a dispute over the proceeds of the property entrusted by a man who left Tripoli for Istanbul, and who appointed the defendant as his attorney. The defendant argued that he had indeed acted as the plaintiff's attorney in his absence, that the mandate he held was absolute, and that the proceeds had been either used up for his expenses, or confiscated by some administrative official—with two witnesses testifying to the latter—so that he was left 'penniless as a result'.

The plaintiff then shifted the argument, alleging that, contrary to D's claim, the power of attorney which was given was not 'absolute'. Whereupon D produced witnesses confirming the absolute nature of the power of attorney—'except over his *halal* and that meant his wife'. In addition, he exhibited a fatwa from the *mufti* of Tripoli 'in which the answer to the question is that the attorney is a fiduciary and that the fiduciary is believed upon his word, with an oath on all his allegations' when necessary. The fatwa was acknowledged by the judge, who ruled for D.[266]

As in 'the set-off note', several decisions confirm the importance of written evidence. In one case, a person appeared in court so that written act be noted of a sum of money which was transferred from one place to another, here 'thirty-three

---

[265] Tripoli, 23, *Tijan bint Yusuf v. al-Hajj Muhammad ibn Wiya al-Hallaq*, 8 Muharram 1978/ 30 June 1667. Partial set-off, *qasasahu bi-naziriha*.

[266] Tripoli, 75, *'Umar Agha ibn Sha'ban v. 'Umar ibn 'Abdallah al-Rajil*, late Rabi' I 1078, mid-September 1667. On fatwas and their use in court, see below section on fatwas, *in fine*. Penniless, *wa la al-dirham al-fard*; absolute power of attorney except over his *halal* meaning his wife, *wikala mutlaqa fi ma lahu wa 'alayhi, ma 'ada halalahu wa 'ana bi-dhalika zawjatahu*; the attorney is a fiduciary and the fiduciary is believed upon his word, with an oath [on all his allegations], *al-wakil amin wal-wakil musaddaq bi-qawlihi ma'a yaminihi*.

Egyptian pounds... The aforementioned *fondé* Hasan has requested from the aforementioned judge a legal acknowledgment in the matter, so that he has a witness at hand, in case of contest, and his request was accepted'.[267]

On the availability of written evidence hinged a dispute between two brothers. P's attorney lodged a suit to get his share in the inheritance—including a house, gardens, and a buffalo—which he alleged his brother had deprived him of. Upon which the brother responded that all of the above had been paid for, including to relieve P from debts contracted with third parties. D produced written evidence which was ascertained by witnesses, 'and which confirmed what was said'. The judge took notice and ruled for D.[268]

Written documents are, therefore, important, although they still require to be confirmed orally in court. Their importance features in a short case in which P had gone to Istanbul for two years, leaving D in charge of looking after his property. In court, the defendant produced accounts in a register, showing the revenues from the property in kind and in cash. He was ordered by the court to pay them to P. It is clear that there was no active dispute in that case, but accounts were produced in court to allow for an official acknowledgment of full settlement between cautious parties.[269]

Naturally, elaborate arrangements like trusts generally require that the trust be made in writing, and written evidence worked to the advantage of the defendant who was capable of producing the trust deed. In one case, the plaintiff was acting through an attorney (her son) to assert her right, coming through her grandmother, for revenues of a *waqf* she said was established in her favour. When asked for evidence, P was unable to produce any, but D requested that the deed be read in court. The text did not contain any disposition in favour of P's ascendant. Judgment for D.[270]

Admittance of evidence could be flexible. In a case over deferred dower, a woman plaintiff brought a suit against her former husband, but she had lost her marriage contract and was unable to prove the compensation she claimed. The judge ordered

---

[267] This is a case from the second register, quoted in full in the introduction of Tripoli, jim, as 'qadiyyat ikhbar... 'alayhi thalatha wa thalathun ratlan misriyyan: kadhalika iltamasa al-qayyim hasan al-mazbur min al-hakem al-shar'i, al-mushar ilayh, an yusattira lahu bidhalika sakkan shar'iyyan, li-yakuna bi-yadihi shahidan fil-hal, 'ind al-ihtiyaj lada al-ihtijaj, fasuttira bil-talab' (qadiyyat ikhbar: case of notification/acknowledgment, Tripoli register 2, 1079/1669, at 158). According to Ziadeh, *Arkeologia*, 65, a *ratl* (here loosely translated as pound) 'is a unit of weight equivalent to 12 ounces. In turn the ounce (*awqiya*) is equivalent to one *estar*. Two-thirds of one *estar* equals 4 *mathaqil*, [plural of] *mithqal*, which equals [as noted earlier] 3/17 of a dirham'. Weight denominations will vary considerably over the centuries following debasing of a coinage. In seventeenth-century Tripoli, the register indicates the central role of the *asadi* piastre, a few of which are sufficient to rent a house for a year. With 200 piastres, as will be discussed below n. 273, parties taken away by the pirates were able to reclaim a ship (and their freedom).

[268] Tripoli, 20, *Hasan Jawish (Attorney for Mustafa Jalabi) v. Fakhr Amthalih Ahmad Agha*, late Sha'ban 1077/ late February 1667. Written evidence, *hujja*.

[269] Tripoli, 46b, *'Umar Agha ibn Rajab v. 'Umran ibn 'Abdallah al-Rajil*, 15 Safar 1078/6 August 1667. *daftar*, notebook, private register.

[270] Tripoli, 53, *Ahmad ibn Muhammad (Attorney for Ruqayya bint Ahmad) v. Fakhr al-Kiram al-Hajj Muhammad*, mid-Safar 1078/early August 1667.

that she be paid the equivalent dower for women of her status and requested further enquiries, which showed that the minimum dower in that case was less than what she claimed. She was therefore granted her demand in full.[271]

Such judicial activism develops more fully in other cases. One amusing example appears in a dispute in which P, who shared a property with D 'on a fifty-fifty basis', complained to the court about his partner building a wall over his half share of the property. D denied the wall had been built on P's share, so P asked the judge to ascertain the situation. The judge delegated one of his trusted scribes, who went to the property 'with a large group of Muslims', measured it, and confirmed that the wall had eaten up some 'two feet' of P's share. Upon which the judge ordered the destruction of the wall, the registration of his decision, and the acquiescence of the parties to it, as well as an end to all pending disputes between them.[272]

A court for all seasons. The structure and exact workings of the Tripoli court are difficult to assess on the basis of a one-year register, but one thing is certain. Its jurisdiction was wide and varied, and covered several civil law cases arising in debt, title over land, landlord-tenant, succession, marital and property disputes. A court for all seasons with a wide jurisdiction, it also ruled in the administrative and criminal field, which I shall turn to after mentioning some general cases which are particularly colourful.

One such case arose in early Safar 1078/mid-July 1667. Plaintiff, a Christian, brought a suit against D, another Christian, to pay him back his share in the ownership of a ship. P had boarded that ship in Egypt, but 'Western—*Franj*—pirates' had taken her forcibly to the island of Castros(?). P bought the ship back from her Western abductors, on 'a half and half basis' with another Christian, who was the captain of the ship. Of the total paid, 210 piastres, the captain had produced 100, and P 110. They then sailed to Cyprus, where the captain informed P that the ship was actually the property of D, and that 'our buying her from the *Franj* was not valid'. The captain then dismissed P from the ship and refused to pay him the 110 piastres which P was now claiming from D in the Tripoli court. D responded that the ship was indeed his property, 'but that since the *Franj* had forcefully taken her and sailed with her to their land, which is abode of war, the ship had gone outside his ownership to that extent, and that if plaintiff had bought half of the ship then his purchase was valid and he can dispose of his share in her'. There is at this point a curious legal twist, because the judge decided that 'since the *Franj* had taken

---

[271] Tripoli, 89, *Shaikh Ahmad ibn Shaikh Badr al-Din (Attorney for Khadija bint Ibrahim alias Ibn Malha) v. Kamal ibn 'Ali al-Najjar (Attorney for Fatima bint al-Hajj 'Abd al-Rahman)*, early Jumada I 1078/ mid-November 1667. Dower, *sadaq*.

[272] Tripoli, 16b, Al-*Hajj 'Ali ibn al-Hajj 'Abdallah al-Mawlawi v. Shihab al-Din ibn al-Hajj Yusuf al-Bahri*, 28 Dhi al-Qi'da 1077/9 May 1667. Two feet, *dhira 'ayn*. 'On a 50–50 basis', '*ala tariq al-ishtirak, likullin minhuma nisfuhu*, literally 'in participation, for each one half of it'. One finds often also the term *munasafatan* for joint ownership.

the ship forcefully . . . the sale was valid', concluding that P had nothing against D and that P should desist.[273]

There is no evident explanation for the court reasoning, as one would expect P to be compensated half the price paid since the transaction was considered 'valid'. Possibly, the argument was that D should be considered a third party to the transaction, that the confiscation of the ship was a *force majeure* in which he bore no responsibility, and that consequently P could not bring a suit against him. Still, the phrasing of the argument is unexpected, as it suggests that neither P nor D questioned the right of P in a share of the ship. It may be that the judge was persuaded by some clever legal argument on the part of the defendant which did not make its way to the written record.

The cunning litigator fully appears in a case where plaintiffs sued D over the rent of a property which was subject to *waqf*. When all the terms of the rent were agreed, D asked the plaintiffs to write in court the lease contract, 'and the fact that he paid them'. He promised he would pay the plaintiffs 'outside' what he owed them under the terms of the lease. They wrote up the agreement, and once he was in possession of the release, he refused to pay them 'outside'. Asked about it in court, he explained a long history of transactions between them, and claimed a set-off arrangement whereby the sum of money which remained in dispute would be written off in compensation for previous debts owed to him by the plaintiffs. At this point, D produced another written document, a commitment confirming his version of transactions precedent. He further produced two witnesses who also confirmed the plaintiffs' effective commitment, upon which the judge ruled in his favour, as the obligation arising under that promise had been confirmed 'under the law'.[274]

One of the longest reports that year illustrates a number of common issues before the Tripoli court. Plaintiff was the head of the corporation of weavers. A year earlier, he claimed, he had lent the defendant, by instalments, the total sum of 42 piastres, of which the last loan was for 7 piastres. Defendant denied the loan except for the 7 piastres, and said that the rest of the loan had been the subject of litigation between them, and that the matter was settled with a legal document drafted to this effect. The document was produced, in which P was acknowledged as husband of D's deceased sister. Also acknowledged was the full distribution of the estate amongst the deceased woman's three heirs, husband P, brother D, and her mother. The document was entered in full settlement of the correct and final division of the estate, and P acknowledged in it that he was owed nothing by the

---

[273] Tripoli, 32b, *René al-Saqizi v. Habib son of Ilias*, early Safar 1078, late July 1667. Ship first boarded in Damietta, Egypt, *thaghr* Dumyat. Western Frank pirates, *qursan al-ifranj*; our buying her from the French was not valid, *ishtira'ana laha min al-franj laysa bi-sahih*; dismissed him from the ship, *akhrajahu minha*; abode of war, enemy territory, *dar al-harb*.

[274] Tripoli, 41–2, *Yunis ibn 'Izz al-Din (Legal guardian for his under-age children Nasr, 'Ali and Mustafa, and attorney for his daughter Fatima) and al-Hajj Muhammad ibn 'Ali al-Mahdar (Attorney for Mu'mina bint al-Thabit) v. Yusuf ibn Muhammad al-Ghazzal*, 9 Safar 1078/31 July 1667. Legal guardian, *wali shar'i*, written commitment, *tamassuk*.

other heirs. However, he argued in court that the settlement concerned the estate only, and that the debt which was the cause of the current suit remained outstanding. He was then asked to prove it, and he produced several witnesses to the various loans. Defendant was then required to come up with evidence about his exoneration from those claims, but he was unable to rebut the evidence. Nor was he able to deny the loan of 7 piastres, which he did not dispute in any case. In addition, the plaintiff produced a fatwa from the *mufti* of Tripoli supporting his case, and D was ordered by the judge to pay the full debt of 42 piastres.[275]

Unusual on facts was the case brought by the owner of a runaway slave against D, with whom the slave was staying. D acknowledged that the man was indeed staying with him, but argued that he did not believe he was the slave of P, who was asked for evidence. This was produced in the form of a written document signed by an official from the Palestinian city of Nablus. Of note procedurally is the fact that an attorney, and not the plaintiff himself, had appeared in court, and that the power of attorney was restricted to the case and duly witnessed by two people from Nablus, who were also asked to confirm the authenticity of the document. Judgment for P on the basis of the written evidence.[276]

In a long decision, the judge had to assess a case brought by two plaintiffs—actually one plaintiff acting also for his brother—against the legal attorney of a (wealthy) woman who lived in Istanbul, asking for their share of the proceeds in a property yielding silk, which the brothers owned with the lady and which the defendant was looking after. D explained relatively complicated arrangements which were agreed with the absent mistress, who had sent a man, with an order from the Sultan, to collect her share from him. In the report there follows what seems to be a conversation between the defendant and the plaintiff on the nature of the arrangements between D and the Istanbul lady, which was documented in a letter she wrote to him about how the proceeds should be disbursed, and his share in the proceeds. It appears that P was not aware of that exchange. He then produced witnesses supporting his claim to part of the proceeds, which was a third of the money sent to the lady by D. The judge took notice of the various documents and ruled for P to the extent of the 300 or so piastres which seem to have been confirmed by 'a group of Muslims' in the evidence produced by P.[277]

Administrative cases. Along with its general jurisdiction over what we would regard as civil disputes, the court's work included tax and administrative cases.

---

[275] Tripoli, 44, *Murghib ibn Ahmad v. 'Abdallah ibn Muhammad*, late Dhi al-Qi'da 1077/late August 1667, fatwa discussed, below n. 349 and accompanying text. Head of the corporation of weavers, *shaykh ta 'ifat al-khayyatin*; litigation between them, *tarafa 'a*.

[276] Tripoli, 47b, *Rasul Balukabashi (Attorney for Khawaja Ahmad ibn Sulaiman) v. Hasan Agha*, 19 Safar 1078, 10 August 1667. Fleeing slave, *abiqa lahu*, from *abiqa*, which is running away without legal ground (such as mistreatment); written document, *hujja shar'iyya*.

[277] Tripoli, 65–6, *Ahmad Agha ibn Muhammad Agha alias ibn al-Kihiaji v. Bushr ibn 'Abdallah (Attorney for 'Ayesha Khatun bint Muslih al-Din Agha)*, mid-Rabi' I 1078/early September 1667. The case is not too clear, probably because of suspicion over 'collusion' between the Istanbul lady and D. Written commitment, *tamassuk*; collusion, *muwata'a*; a group of Muslims, *jama'a min al-muslimin*.

Most administrative cases revolve around accusations brought by some low-level officials against residents who did not pay their taxes.

An administrative case not related to tax was a complaint in court by a plaintiff who alleged that the defendant 'had denounced him to the political rulers', who fined him 70 piastres. The defendant denied the allegation, which went unproven. Judgment for D.[278]

In the more usual field of tax dispute, plaintiffs were village sheikhs from the vicinity of Tripoli, who were asking the court to force the two defendants, as 'village citizens', to pay their residency tax. The defendants demurred, explaining that they were simple soldiers and had no property or land in the village. The 'new Sultanic register' was produced, and it did not contain the defendants' names. Judgment in their favour.[279]

In another similar case, several plaintiffs came to court to sue an official in charge in the area they were working in. They claimed that D, a local governor, had taken from them taxes, apparently charging each one of them for what they should have owed him collectively, and they produced a document which included payment by each to him as claimed. D denied the charge, and the plaintiffs were asked to prove their allegation. They produced two witnesses. Judgment against D.[280]

A similar 'class action', also involving several residents, was brought before the Tripoli court in a case which is illuminating on the relationship between Sultanic orders/statutes and the application of the law. The plaintiffs were asking the two defendants, who were monks from the order of the Franks (Franciscans), 'Padre 'Awn and Samuel', to pay the residence tax. Upon which the defendants produced a 'sultanic rescript' to the effect of their exemption, and all monks of the Franciscan order, from all legal dues. The judge acknowledged the rescript, and the plaintiffs were ordered to further desist from requesting the monks in Tripoli to pay taxes.[281]

Another poll-tax case, which will be of interest to economic historians, involved a suit brought by an official in charge of taxation in a village near Tripoli, in the name of the official in charge in the area, claiming that D was a resident of the village, that D's father had also been a resident, and that he owned property in

[278] Tripoli, 121, *Husain ibn 'Abdallah v. Ahmad ibn Yusuf*, early Jumada II 1078/mid-November 1667. Denounced him to the political rulers, *ghamaza 'alayhi li-hukkam al-siyasa*.

[279] Tripoli, 129, *'Ali ibn Ahmad and Trad ibn Yusuf v. Muhammad ibn Ahmad Kanun and his brother Hajj Sharaf*, early Rabi' II 1078/late September 1667. Citizens, *ra'aya*; new register, *daftar al-tahrir al-jadid al-sultani*.

[280] Tripoli, 26, *Shaykh Ibrahim Hajj Muhammad and fifteen others v. Hasan Agha ibn al-Husami*, mid-Muharram 1078/early July 1667. Official, *dizdar*. According to Ziadeh, *Arkeologia al-mustalah al-watha 'iqi*, 64, the *dizdar* (or *disdar*) is a word of Persian origin used for the governor of a citadel. Note here that the document, *daftar*, albeit an official document, needed to be supplemented as evidence by witnesses.

[281] Tripoli, 47a, *Shaykh Ibrahim ibn al-Sari 'Ali and several others [five named] v. Padre 'Awn and Padre Samuel*, mid-Safar 1078/early August 1667. *Amr sharif sultani*, high sultanic rescript or order. Note here that there was no need to witness the rescript, it being an emanation of the Sultan.

the village and had not paid his taxes. D denied he was a resident, and claimed he was born in the city of Tripoli, where he had always lived and where 'he was equal with its other residents in all they had to pay in terms of taxes'. When D denied his residency, P was asked to provide evidence of his claim. Upon his failure to come up with the evidence, judgment was rendered in D's favour.[282]

A similar case arose a few days later, this time with two sheikhs from a nearby village, one of whom represented the 'official in charge in the area'. They asked two D brothers to pay the tax they owed. The brothers denied they were residents, and said that their father was from Aleppo, that their name did not appear 'in the new register', that they had no property in the village of the plaintiffs, and that they lived in Tripoli and paid their dues, like others, in the village of Mina. Upon the failure of plaintiffs to produce evidence, the judge ruled for the defendants.[283]

For lawyers, these administrative cases are interesting both in terms of evidence and in terms of justice generally. Clearly, the judge was not bothered by the official character of the plaintiffs, and applied rules of evidence as usual in the first case, thereby avoiding a harsh double taxation on the citizens. Nor would the cases brought in court against local officials be so numerous if justice was not seen to be done.

Finally, I should mention a rare administrative-criminal case, in which P was the head of one of the Tripoli neighbourhoods asking D, who owned a house in the area, to share in the collective compensation for a man who had drowned in the river, such share standing at 1 piastre. D responded that he had taken over an abandoned ruin in the neighbourhood by legal deed from the trustee of the local school, but that he did not complete the building—so he was not yet living there. P dismissed.[284]

Criminal cases. Notwithstanding this last case involving unnatural death and possibly manslaughter, the only 'criminal' case mentioned in the records of that year concerned the minor theft in the necklace case.[285] Where a more serious crime appeared, it had long been adjudicated before the civil consequences arose in court. This was the case of two partners owning in common a herd of 120 goats.

---

[282] Tripoli, 31a, *Muhammad ibn Jamal al-Din v. Abi Bakr ibn Mustafa*, end Muharram 1078/end July 1667. Representing the official, *min taraf dabit*; resident, *min ra'aya*. Tax, *miri*; he was equal to other residents in what they had to pay in terms of taxes to the rulers, *yusawi ahali al-mahalla al-mazbura bi jami' ma yutlab minhum min al-jawanih wal-takalif li-jihat al-hukkam*. In other tax cases, the denomination of capitation is *kharaj*.

[283] Tripoli, 37–8, *Mansur ibn 'Abd al-'Aziz and Midlij al-Hamadi v. Hasan ibn Yusuf and his brother Muhammad*, early Safar 1078/late July 1667. Official in charge in the area, *min taraf dabit al-nahiya al-mazbura*. Tax, *miri*. The new register, *daftar al-tahrir al-jadid al-khaqani*. There is a 'typo', with *tawasaya* instead of *tasawaya*.

[284] Tripoli, 66b, *Hasan ibn Mustafa v. Mahmud ibn Abi Bakr alias ibn Lakhmi*, 19 Rabi' I 1078/8 September 1667. Note this is a blood-money, *diyya* case; one of Tripoli's neighbourhoods, *ihda mahallat Trablus*; asking for the share in the blood-money of a man drowned in the river, *mutalibun by shay' min diyyat al-ghariq fil-nahr*; taken over, *istahkara*; school, *madrasa*.

[285] Above nn. 244 and 245 and accompanying text.

P was suing his partner for the dissolution of the partnership. D claimed in response that the keeper of the goats, a Christian, had accused none other than Tripoli's governor of engaging in pederasty with a minor, and then fled. D also explained that he was arrested, jailed, and fined 130 piastres, on grounds that the herdsman was working for him, so he asked in court his partner P to share with him the fine 'on a half-half basis' because they both owned the herd. P was put that request by the court, and answered that the governor had charged D, not him, and that he should not be responsible for D's fine. The judge ruled that P was not involved in the crime for which D was fined. Therefore, 'upon the legal rule that the victim cannot victimise another', P could not be made responsible 'even if the governor had been unjust towards the defendant'. D could not implicate his partner, and the dissolution of the partnership went ahead.[286]

We do not have enough records in the first register to make a full assessment of the criminal jurisdiction of the court. The judge certainly had some criminal competence, as in the next case, which is criminal in nature, although P went for civil redress. She appeared herself in court claiming that D had entered her house and taken various goods 'without legal right'. D denied, but P produced two witnesses, upon which judgment was entered in her favour. No penalty was decided, but D had to return the goods.[287]

However, the criminal jurisdiction of the court was sometimes more important, as appears in a capital punishment case reported in the second register.[288] Plaintiffs were a large group of people including the head of the tanners' corporation, bringing action against one Shehadeh ibn al-Hajj, also a tanner by profession and known as 'Antar, for 'denouncing them, trying to destroy their property by setting up aides of injustice against them ... and repeating his bad acts time and again'. They asked the judge 'to implement the rules of the pure *shari'a*'. The judge put the question to 'Antar, who denied all the accusations, whereupon witnesses were brought confirming his mischief, 'in his presence'. They also confirmed 'that his harm was relentless, and that ending his mischief was a duty on the people of Islam, and that his killing would rid [the city] from his public nuisance'. The judge then formally 'informed' the *mufti* and a number of high dignitaries from

---

[286] Tripoli, 24a, *Mansur ibn al-Hajj Muhammad Qarqur al-Labban v. Muhammad ibn 'Ali ibn Kanun*, 12 Muharram 1078/4 July 1667. Pederasty, *liwata*; upon the legal rule that the victim cannot victimize another, *al-qa 'ida al-fiqhiyya wa hiya laysa lil-mazlum an yazluma ghayrahu*; because the governor had been unjust towards him, *li-anna wali al-wilaya zalamahu bi-ghayri haqq*. Two words seem to have been crossed out in the text.

[287] Tripoli, 24b, *Hajja Khadija bint al-Hajj Muhammad v. Hasan Agha*, mid-Muharram 1078/early July 1667. Without legal right, *bi-ghayr haqq shar'i*. This is the same official (*dizdar*) Hasan Agha mentioned already in case cited above n. 280 but perhaps not the same Hasan Agha mentioned in case at n. 276 as a former official in the district of Hums (*dabet sanjaq hums*). Hasan Agha appears again as plaintiff in the Antartus case at n. 349 below, Tripoli, 27, *Hasan Agha ibn Naser Agha alias ibn al-Husami v. Hajj Ibrahim Bitar and other inhabitants from Antartus*, and shows himself capable of many a political intrigue, so he might also have been operating in some official role in the nearby city of Hums.

[288] The 'Antar case appears in full in Ziadeh, *Al-sura al-taqlidiyya*, at 88–90, referring to the report of the second register, at 5. The case is dated end of Safar 1079/July 1668. The second register covers twelve years, from 1078/1667 to 1090/1679, see Tripoli, *jim*.

Tripoli, as well as the large public. 'He was convinced in his heart of the need to kill him, and he ruled that said 'Antar be killed and buried in the Muslims' cemetery so as to bring peace from his mischief to Muslim believers, and order for this to be taken act of'. The witnesses-signatories include the *mufti* of Tripoli, the head of the Tripoli notables, and a number of professors and prayer leaders.[289]

This was evidently an important case in the city. While the evidence was no different from that used in normal civil cases, it was clearly overwhelming. The judge, albeit ultimate decision-maker, seemed keen to involve in the capital punishment sentence a large number of notables.

Nor was the criminal jurisdiction restricted to these *hadd* measures. Though rare, Ziadeh reports in other registers decisions to relieve a religious official convicted of bribery of his job, in addition to a heavy fine, his beating and jailing, and his banishment from the city. Such discretionary (*ta'zir*) criminal powers were also recognized by the court, and several instances are reported.[290] Ebied and Young report a case of blood-money from the city of Safad in Palestine dated mid-Jumada I 1098/end March 1687, in which the brother of a slain man received compensation from those whom he accused of having killed his brother a year earlier. They denied the accusation in court, which P was unable to prove, but a compromise was reached nonetheless over a sum of money to be paid in three instalments. A large number of court witnesses, as in the other criminal cases, are mentioned in the report.[291]

But it is clear from the registers that criminal law was also conducted elsewhere, and that it had precedence over civil law. A fictional story in Hariri's (d. 1122) famous *Maqamat* illustrates that time-honoured procedural divide:

While an impoverished al-Harith [the narrator] is traveling, he comes across a tent filled with many servants and beautiful furnishings. The old man who lives in it turns out to be

---

[289] All quotes at Ziadeh, *Al-sura al-taqlidiyya,* '*Antar* case, 89. Denouncing them, trying to destroy their property by setting up tools/aides of injustice against them … and repeating his bad acts time and again, *wa qad ghamaza 'alayhim wa sa'a bi-itlaf amwalihim wa-idmihlal ahwalihim wa huwa yusallit 'alayhim a'wan al-zulma, wa qad ta'addadat minhu hadhih al-af'al al-dhamima miraran*; to implement the rules of the pure *shari'a, ijra' ahkam al-shari'a al-mutahhara 'alayhi fi dhalik*; in the presence of the defendant, *bi-muwajaha min al-mudda'a 'alayh*; his harm was relentless, ending his mischief was a duty on the people of Islam, and his killing would rid [the city] from his public nuisance, *inna al-mudda'a 'alayh dararuh 'amm muttasil wa inna izalatahu wajiba 'ala ahl al-islam wa qatlahu fihi rahatun min sharrihi al-'amm*; informed, *ikhbar*; and ruled the killing of said 'Antar and his burial in the Muslims' cemetery to bring peace from his mischief to Muslim believers, and order for this to be taken act of, *wa itma'anna qalbuhu al-sharif bi-qatlih, hakama ayyada Allah ahkamah bi-qatl 'antar al-mazbur haddan wa dafnihi fi maqabir al-muslimin lima fi dhalik min al-rahat min sharrihi li-'ammat al-muslimin al-mu'minin, wa amara bi-tastir dhalik fa suttira*. The compulsory penalty (*hadd*) relates to the accusation of 'highway crime', *al-fasad fil-ard*, mentioned above nn. 10, 83.

[290] Ziadeh, *Al-sura al-taqlidiyya,* 90–3, citing registers 2 to 9. Criminal law judgments include *ta'zir* in the form of jailing and beating for bribery; imprisonment of a woman convicted of theft; fines for sheltering foreigners without permit, in addition to an interesting illustration of collective responsibility for 'the people of the neighbourhood, *ahali al-mahalla*'.

[291] *'Ali ibn Sulaiman known as ibn Mishal (as ward of his orphaned nephew) v. Husain ibn Shalabi and his cousins Farrukh and Sa'd,* 15 Jumada I 1108/29 March 1987, Ebied and Young, cited above n. 229, 31–3, translation at 67–9 (with a misinterpretation: the compromise took place in court on the occasion of the lawsuit, and not as in the translation 'when the act occurred', i.e. a year earlier

Abu Zayd [the funny rogue of the *Maqama*], now happy and rich. Al-Harith follows him for a while and soon finds out the reason for his good fortune. Once in Tus, relates Abu Zayd, he had troubles with a creditor who wanted to take him to the qadi. That particular qadi was notorious for his severity, so to avoid his court Abu Zayd beat up his creditor so that he had to appear before the higher court of the governor. When brought before the governor, he composed a magnificent epistle with alternating pointed and unpointed letters. Impressed, the governor paid his debt for him and kept him in his service.[292]

Beating up one's creditor as a forum shopping device is a fictional device of some originality. On the institutional set-up, Hariri's formulation is alluring, adorned as the *Maqama* genre is with literary artifice: 'When I saw that I could not escape my creditor, I sought quarrel with him and aggressed him so that he takes me to the governor, and not to the judge because of what had reached me about the goodness of the governor, and the harshness and pettiness of the judge'.[293] The unusual forum shopping underlines the perceived difference between civil jurisdiction which deals with ordinary debts before the judge, and criminal jurisdiction which is adjudicated by the governor. Such concurrent jurisdiction, with graver crimes going to the head of the executive for adjudication and punishment, seems also to have characterized the Tripoli legal scene.[294]

Substance and procedure. It should be clear from the workload of the court, and the way it disposed of issues it handled, how the general operation of justice went. Evidence, as already emphasized, is key. By order of importance, that is of power of persuasion effected on the judge, the cases in the 1667 register show, alongside the prevailing oral testimony, three types of written evidence: contracts, inferred standard obligations, and customary arrangements, all of which are eventually confirmed by witnesses. Only when evidence supported by witnesses fails, does the judge turn to administering the oath, which the plaintiff is first asked to swear, then the defendant.[295]

The single judge is at the centre of the action, and directs the questions and the administration of evidence according to a systematic pattern which ensures that

when the alleged murder took place. But the case is curious. Notable is the importance of the blood-money, 450 Asadi piastres. Unless there was a significant inflation in the Levant between the Tripoli record and the Safad record (20 years separate the reports, and the cities are 200 kilometres apart), the sum is significant. See n. 267 above.

[292] Oleg Grabar, *The illustrations of the maqamat*, above n. 221, 71. On the genre of *Maqamat* and their usefulness for discovering the life of the law, see below n. 403 and accompanying text.

[293] '*falamma ra'ayt ihtidad ladadih, wa anna la manassa li min yadih, shaghabtuhu thumma wathabtuhu, li-yurafi'ani ila wali al-jara'em, la ila hakim al-mazalim, lima kana balaghani min ifdal al-wali wa fadlih, wa tashaddud al-qadi wa bukhlih.*' *Maqamat* al-Hariri, Beirut 1978, 208 (twenty-sixth *maqama* or session entitled 'the dotted *maqama*, *al-maqama al-raqta*'', in which the hero escapes his debt by going to the governor and praising him with a long panegyric using in every word alternate letters, with and without dots). Governor, lit. the overseer of crimes, *wali al-jara'em*, judge, *al-hakim fil-mazalem*; judge, *qadi*.

[294] This confirms Emile Tyan's conclusions half a century ago on the special place of the *shurta*, police, as the repressive and jurisdictional agent of the state in classical Islam. Tyan, *Histoire de l'organisation judiciaire en pays d'Islam*, chapter on *shurta*, 567–616 (in the consolidated Leiden edn.).

[295] As in Tripoli, 86–7, *Taj son of Abu al-Ha v. Salem son of Abu al-Ha*, above n. 252.

both parties are fully heard. The 'discovery' of evidence is straightforward, and the parties may exceptionally introduce new evidence, which will also be disposed of quickly. The party which does not produce evidence may be accorded a few days to buttress his or her arguments with further proof. The effectiveness of the sentencing becomes remarkable in these conditions, as is the publicity of the proceedings. We know from other sources that the 'professional witnesses' were important in the daily work of the court, but the register at hand does not indicate their dominant presence, except that 'the witnesses to the act' operate very much like professional fixtures of the system.

The flexibility, predictability, and consistency of the trial are notable for the modern reader. The legal background is assumed without being too technical. When a legal rule appears in doubt, the judge allows an outside expert reference to the *mufti*, as will be detailed in a moment. There are also passing references to lawbooks and classical scholars, but the decisions are rendered generally without reference to any legal authority, Qur'anic verse, or *hadith*. Nor is there, in our seventeenth-century register, trace of professional counsel. Powers of attorney are common, and tend to be used when women have to appear as parties, even if the register shows several cases of women coming in person to defend their rights. The judge can be sympathetic to their pleas, as in the case of the assessment of 'the equivalent dower' despite the woman's loss of her marriage contract.

The rapid judicial rhythm, together with the respect for legal procedure by way of an established format for the judicial report, is remarkable in the register, and is no doubt assisted by the absence of appeal. By the late nineteenth century, the courts in the Ottoman ambit had lost their earlier autonomy, with their decisions 'open to cassation' in Istanbul.[296] It is clear in the seventeenth-century registers that the judge had a final say, and that appeal was not entertained. The wide publicity in the court session suggests forms of consensual decision-making, with the judge as the holder of the last say in the matter at hand.

It may be useful to close this section with reference to the rare appearance of a series of cases in the Tripoli court register of 1667 'in the matter of *Laila's Estate*', which offers some insights into the effective daily working of the judicial system in the eleventh/seventeenth century.

The register records a string of decisions over the same dispute, all concerning two plaintiff brothers claiming five-sixths of the estate of a deceased relative, Laila bint al-Hajj Abi Bakr. The defendant was the deceased's uterine brother, who had taken over the whole of her estate. Upon evidence produced by the plaintiffs on their agnatic kinship with the deceased, D was ordered to surrender five-sixths of the estate, 'in accordance with the legal rules of inheritance'.

Nothing so far appears out of order, except that there are two decisions on the issue. The first decision is crossed several times with the word 'altered' across the

[296] Tamer Mallat (d. 1914), *Ahkam* (judgments) (Beirut, 1999) (C. Mallat, ed., facsimile edn. of the 1899 court register of Kisrawan, Mount Lebanon), *passim*.

text, but it is readable.[297] The second decision bears the same date, and the same judge seems to have presided over both decisions, with some of the witnesses-signatories remaining the same, and others different. This suggests that the session in the first decision might have taken place earlier in the same day, and the latter session, with the corrections, perhaps in the afternoon of that day, with another case decided in-between.[298]

On substance, the question was about hearsay and the quality of the witnesses. In the first decision, the judge seemed originally satisfied with the two witnesses produced by the plaintiffs, who said that they had heard the deceased say several times in their presence, when she was 'alive and in full health', that the father of the plaintiffs was her full brother. In the second decision, the witnesses called by the plaintiffs were different, this time a man and two women, who said that they had 'heard many trusted Muslims' mention that the plaintiff's father was the full brother of the late Laila. So far, and apart from the change in witnesses, the same argument was made in both the first and second decisions. This was apparently not sufficient, however, and a question over that testimony clearly arose, with pre-sumably the defendant arguing that the produced testimony was hearsay which could not be accepted. Then the plaintiffs produced a fatwa from the *mufti* of Tripoli 'that day', in which the question was whether hearsay was acceptable for ascertaining family kinship, and specifically the kinship of a full brother. The *mufti* answered in the affirmative 'for all the Hanafis', citing well-known author-ities. In the face of the evidence and the supportive fatwa, the judge ruled for the plaintiffs.[299]

It appears therefore that the plaintiffs were allowed to change tack that day, hurrying to other witnesses and to the *mufti* in the course of a few hours to get their support in the testimony over their kinship with the deceased. The *mufti*, who is the author of three reports in Turkish found in the register,[300] was surely close to the courtroom, and he is the same *mufti* whom we encountered in the capital punishment case discussed earlier.

Nor was that the end of the legal story for *Laila's Estate* in the records of the Tripoli court. On the next page there appears a long decision arising from a claim of

---

[297] Tripoli, 28a, 29, *Mustafa ibn al-Hajj Ibrahim and his brothers Badri and Murad v. al-Hajj 'Abd al-Nabi Ibrahim*, 18 Muharram 1078/10 July 1667 (Hereinafter the case of *Laila's Estate*). Agnatic relationship, *'usuba nasabiyya*; in accordance with the legal rules of inheritance, *bi-hasab al-farida al-shar'iyya* (under Sunni law, the uterine brother would be likened to a sister and receive one-sixth of the estate in the presence of an agnatic relation, such as a son, father, or paternal uncle.); *'uddilat*, altered, corrected.

[298] Tripoli, 28b, *Mansur ibn Muhammad (Attorney for Fatima bint Muhammad and her brothers Muhammad and 'Ali) v. Ahmad ibn al-Hajj Muhi al-Din and Husain al-'Alabi and Murad ibn Qais and 'Ala' al-Din ibn Shihab*, mid-Muharram 1078/early July 1667, a simple dispute over the payment for the purchase of a house.

[299] Tripoli, 29, *Laila's Estate* ii, above n. 297. They heard many trusted Muslims, *sami'u min kathirin min al-muslimin al-thiqat*, hearsay, *tasamu'*, that day, *yawma'idhin*. Both al-Nasafi's (d. 710/1310) *Kanz al-daqa'iq* and Ibn Nujaym's (d. 970/1563) *al-Ashbah wal-naza'er* are cited in support of the conclusion, full text below n. 354.   [300] Tripoli, at 17–18.

a plaintiff suing his father and his cousin Mustafa the son of al-Hajj Ibrahim (one of the two plaintiff brothers in the earlier case) over part of the property they inherited from Laila. The plaintiff claimed that the property inherited had been partly bought by him and paid for in full by instalments. He produced witnesses to the downpayment, and other witnesses to his settling the balance. Judgment for P on 21 Muharram 1078, 13 July 1667, three days after the earlier two decisions.[301]

Most remarkable in *Laila's Estate* cases is the speed of the court proceedings. In a matter of three days, a complicated inheritance case involving several parties and multiple transactions was settled. While we cannot be certain why the first decision had to be superseded by the one which followed it that day, the marshalling of the evidence was evidently key, and the judge must have felt it more compelling to rule in the matter in the light of further evidence supported by a fatwa and by scholarly authorities. This should be an indication of the high legal standards expected from the court.[302] To the modern lawyer, numbed as she gets with the procedural hurdles in Middle Eastern jurisdictions, the swift and prima-facie fair disposal of cases is simply astonishing.

Still, there remain questions to which there are no easy answers to be found within the registers. What we do not have is either the name of the judge,[303] or the internal mechanisms of the court: from outside well-documented sources, we know that judges in the Ottoman empire were appointed for a limited number of years, except in the highest positions in Istanbul and possibly in the great centres.[304] We do

---

[301] Tripoli, 31–2, *'Abdallah ibn Hajj 'Abd al-Nabi v. 'Abd al-Nabi and Mustafa ibn Ibrahim*, 21 Muharram 1078/13 July 1667.

[302] Although a cynical view could also be put forward: was pressure exercised that day on the judge, notably with the intervention of the *mufti*, in order to reconsider? While it is impossible to rule out such a possibility altogether, the fact that the judge actually held in the same way, with more solid evidence, would suggest otherwise.

[303] 'Umar Tadmuri offers in a recent book on the Tripoli court a partial list of judges in Tripoli, including Nuh Efendi for 1078/1667, *Watha'eq nadira min sijillat al-mahkama al-shar'iya bi-tarablus* (Rare documents from the records of the shar'i court in Tripoli, Tadmuri ed.) (Beirut, 2002) 532. As we have seen in the Tripoli decisions, the name of the judge does not appear in the judgment itself, unlike decisions from the late Ottoman period. The judge was obviously well known to the litigants. In the record from the Safad court, however, both the names of the sitting judge (*bil-asala*) and his replacement (*al-muwalla*, or *al-mula*, *bi safad khilafatan*) are mentioned. Ebied and Young, *Some Arabic legal documents of the Ottoman period*, cited above n. 229, 31 (main judge Rajab Efendi, case mentioned above n. 291), 33–41 (associate judge Mahmud ibn Mustafa, but maybe registrar, as the seven documents where his name appears are simply registered in the court).

[304] We now have two solid monographs on the top *mufti*s at the centre of the Ottoman empire, R. C Repp, *The Mufti of Istanbul* (London, 1986) and Colin Imber, *Ebu's-su'ud, the Islamic legal tradition* (Edinburgh, 1997), in addition to the remarkable work of Jennings on court records in various Ottoman-speaking parts of the early Empire: 'Kadi, court and legal procedure in 17th-century Ottoman Kayseri', *Studia Islamica*, 48, 1978, 133–72, 'Limitations of the judicial powers of the Kadi in 17th-century Ottoman Kayseri', *Studia Islamica*, 50, 1979, 151–84, 'Divorce in the Ottoman shari'a court of Cyprus, 1580–1640', *Studia Islamica*, 78, 1993, 155–67. Jennings' pioneering articles were collected in *Studies on Ottoman social history in the sixteenth and seventeenth centuries* (Istanbul, 1999). The reports in the 1077–8 AH Tripoli register do not tell us how the judge earns a living, and how fees are paid and by whom. Ziadeh, who has examined the series for a relatively extensive period over the first ten registers, was unable to ascertain the remuneration system, but work on the Ottoman *mufti*s gives a clear indication of the strict hierarchy in judges' positions and salaries. This is

not know either how much litigation costs, and whether judges and *mufti*s receive salaries from the authorities that appoint them, and whether a proportion of the court expenses is paid for by litigation fees, or by endowment revenues.

These are all important issues bearing on the autonomy of the judiciary, the leeway and independence judges have towards the society they regulate, and towards the 'executive' branch. For this, court records need to be supplemented by other source-documents. What is certain is that the court is a point of convergence for matters in dispute in the city, and the judge is the repository of regulated life, and 'a metaphor' for normative conviviality.[305] On the strength of the court registers, one feels confident of the need to study Middle Eastern civilizations, especially in periods of peace and stability reconstructed in and around the courtroom, for their obsession with, if not domination by, pervasive forms of the rule of law.

Qadi literature

So with formal judgments. There exists in addition a body of specialized literature known as the literature of the judge, of which Waki' (d. 330/941) has left one of the earliest samples.[306]

The problem with this literature on 'the stories of judges' of the early period is that it is less informative than one would expect. Waki', as narrator/compiler, juxtaposes segments of narratives associated with famous judges from the Prophet in Mecca to remote district judges in Ahwaz (Western Iran), Palestine, Andalus, the Iraqi city of Musil, closing the lists with judges from areas in the vicinity of

discussed at length in Repp, *The Müfti*, 33–6 and *passim*, and 'Appendix 1—on the pay of the learned profession', at 305–6, and briefly confirmed by Imber, *Ebu's-su'ud*, 5–8. Together with the documents produced by Ziadeh on the appointment of some ten aides to the judge in Tripoli and their confirmation from Istanbul (*Al-sura al-taqlidiyyya*, 87, citing register 10 of 1161/1748), it is unlikely that the judge, as head of the court apparatus, would not have been remunerated even in the outer provinces, where his tenure seems to have been much shorter than at the centre. On judges' salaries and retribution in classical Islam, the concept is that the judge is entitled to a salary if he cannot afford the job, see Ibn Abi al-Dam (on which, below, section on *qadi* literature and Chapter 11), *Kitab adab al-qada'* (The book of the ways of judgeship), Muhammad 'Ata ed. (Beirut, 1987) 57–8; in fact, the judge was traditionally allocated financial support from the state treasury, Tyan, *Histoire de l'organisation judiciaire*, i, 501–13; Adam Mez, *The Renaissance of Islam* (London, 1937 (orig. German 1922)) 220–2, and 227 for a list of salaries of the court staff. It is more difficult to assess the compensation which goes to the judge as overseer of charitable endowments. On 'hierarchy of judges, and importance of the chief judge in Baghdad, *maratib al-qudat, kaqadi qudat baghdad*', see Ibn Abi al-Dam at 353. While Tripoli was not an important city, Damascus undoubtedly was, and an extensive discussion of the hierarchy of top law officers, including its chief judge (*qadi al-qudat*, usually an Ottoman appointee), the *mufti* and the *'ulama* of the city, can be found, on the basis of archival work, in Muhammad Adnan Bakhit's chapter on 'the office of the chief judge, the *mufti* and administration of religious offices', *The Ottoman province of Damascus in the sixteenth century* (Beirut, 1982) 119–42. Corruption seems to have been rampant at the time, see at 127–30.

[305] 'The judge as metaphor', concept suggested by Anthony Kronman, Yale Law School Middle East Legal Studies Seminar, Fes, 9–11 May 1999.

[306] Waki', *Akhbar al-qudat* (stories of judges), ed. 'Abdel 'Aziz Mustafa al-Maraghi, 3 vols (Cairo, 1366–9/1947–50).

Baghdad.[307] In other sections, he devotes one or two pages on average to each 'famous' judge, and the narration is interspersed with long *hadith*-type sentences[308] and repetitions. As a result, it is only in the longer accounts devoted to exceptional judges in that first period that the reader finds less arid news on judgeship in Islam. An example is 'Abdallah Ibn Shubruma, an early judge (d. 145/762)[309] who was appointed in Kufa then was replaced by another well-known judge, Ibn Abi Laila (d. 142/759), and transferred to Sijistan.[310]

The pattern in Waki''s report on Ibn Shubruma is similar to those on other judges in his account, albeit more extensive.[311] After a brief description of his appointment,[312] Waki' cites various reports where Ibn Shubruma is mentioned as a link in a chain of Prophetic *hadith* tradents, as well as in reports from other early companions of the Prophet. The report often takes the form of variations on an aphorism, as in the example of wine:

Hamza ibn 'Abd al-'Abbas told us that Yahya ibn Nasr ibn Hajeb said that 'Abdallah ibn Shubruma told us on account of Muhammad ibn 'Amr, on account of Abi Salma, on account of Abi Harira who said: 'what inebriates is forbidden'.

'Abdallah ibn Ahmad ibn Hanbal told me that his father said that Mus'ab ibn Salam said that 'Abdallah ibn Shubruma said, on account of Salem who said on account of his father: whatever inebriates is forbidden and whatever inebriates is wine.[313]

It is true that not all the accounts in the book are *hadith* going back to the Prophet's companions, and Waki' also relates reports which stop at Ibn Shubruma and deal more directly with the judge's own original contribution to the literature. But the treatment of Ibn Shubruma remains restricted to aphorisms or short stories, occasionally verses. There is no discernible logical structure for the whole beyond the juxtaposition of brief narratives which start with Ibn Shubruma crying over his appointment and lamenting his bad luck.[314] This fear and distaste for the position because of the difficult choices it entails was presented in the first book of Waki' extensively, as an introduction to the judges starting with the Prophet, and is common in all *qadi* literature.[315] Many of Waki''s judges conform to this pattern. Then appear the Prophetic and similar *hadith* with Ibn Shubruma as tradent. Finally, the part on Waki' as judge is reported.

Repetition is rife in these accounts, and one will find a story appearing, with little variations, in several places in the hundred-page account on Ibn Shubruma. Some historical pointers emerge, such as the early possibility for the woman to retain a right to exercise divorce (although the text is unclear), for which Ibn Shubruma is asked by Hammad ibn Zaid: 'A man gives his wife a right to divorce.

---

[307] Waki', *Akhbar al-qudat*, iii, 322–6.
[308] '*haddathana fulan 'an fulan*, x said that y said etc.'
[309] Mistake in Waki' mentioning death at 45 AH, iii, 107.
[310] Waki', *Akhbar al-qudat*, iii, 37.   [311] ibid. iii, 36–129.   [312] ibid. iii, 36–7.
[313] What inebriates is forbidden, *ma askara haram*; whatever inebriates is forbidden and whatever inebriates is wine, *kullu muskirin haram wa kullu muskirin khamr*, Waki ', *Akhbar al-qudat*, iii, 43.
[314] ibid. iii, 37.   [315] Waki', *Akhbar al-qudat*, i, 30.

[The judge] replied: if she chooses herself, then she can operate the divorce in one irrevocable time.'[316]

Another account includes a section on the disagreements of three contemporaneous jurists from Iraq over the inclusion of a condition in the contract of sale. For Abu Hanifa, both the sale and the condition are void. For Ibn Shubruma, both the sale and the condition are valid. For Ibn Abi Laila, the sale is valid and the condition void. The contemporary narrator, whom Waki' refers to, is astonished by the discrepancy, goes back to each jurist and mentions to him the opinions of the other two. Whereupon all three merely repeat their conclusions with supportive *hadith* from the Prophet.[317]

Many of the reports do not make sense to the modern reader, and some refer to curious institutions such as the marriage 'per day'[318] where the husband stays with his wife only during the day. This, according to Maraghi, Waki''s twentieth-century editor, is accepted in Hanafi law. It seemingly stops operating in the case of formal polygamy, as the law requires an equality of nights for each of the wives, thus requesting the husband's presence notwithstanding a 'per day' clause. Waki' himself ascribes to Ibn Shubruma the rejection of this type of arrangement in the absolute: 'This is not a marriage in Islam, Ibn Shubruma dislikes it, that is he dislikes the marriage per day'.[319]

And so on for many aspects of generalities or detail.[320] For the purpose of assessing judges and the law, the four-part work of Waki'[321] is therefore disappointing, especially since it comes as the most significant early account on judges in the literature. It is not particularly different from literature at large, where similar table-talk accounts are numerous. Whether in Qalqashandi's *Subh al-a'sha*,[322] Abu al-Faraj al-Asfahani's *al-Aghani*,[323] or al-Tannukhi's *Nishwar al-muhadara*,[324]

---

[316] ibid. iii, 87 top, and a similar account repeated at the bottom. The passage continues in a less clear manner: '[Hammad] said, I asked, if you entrust the matter to the husband, [the judge] replied: nothing [ensues]'. This might mean that the right for the wife to initiate the divorce must be expressly given by the husband, typically in practice as a 'clause' in the marriage contract. If this is left open (i.e. 'entrusted to the husband'), 'nothing happens' and she is left with no right to initiate the divorce.

[317] Waki', *Akhbar al-qudat*, iii, 46–7.

[318] per day, *zawaj al-nahariyyat*. An equivalent of the Shi'i *mut'a* marriage?

[319] Waki', *Akhbar al-qudat*, iii, 85 and n. 1.

[320] Among the most alluring accounts, the veiling of the wife being disliked (presumably at home), iii, 69; verses on judgeship, iii, 97; the story of Prophet Sulaiman and the bird, iii, 117; the legitimacy of *ta'zir* in the Qur'an, iii, 122.   [321] Published in 3 vols in the edn. of Maraghi.

[322] Qalqashandi (d. 821/1418), *Subh al-a'sha*, cited above n. 35 with reference to the 'abrogation' by Islamic law of previous laws. Qalqashandi's monumental work is used extensively by such different scholars as Emile Tyan for his works on judges and notary-public, above nn. 226 and 261 and John Wansbrough, *Lingua franca*, above n. 16 for his work on diplomatic-legal calques in the history of the Mediterranean.

[323] Abu al-Faraj al-Asfahani (or Isfahani, or Asbahani, d. 356/967), *al-Aghani* (Beirut edn., 1955), in 25 vols. including 2 vols. of indexes. An example is the two sections devoted to another famous early judge mentioned earlier, Shurayh, *al-Aghani*, xvii, 145–53. Al-Asfahani relies heavily on Waki' in his account of Shurayh, but the passage is delightful in literary terms, and scant on law. The only reference in the *Aghani* passage to law proper is about the judge who is so upright that he refused the testimony of 'Ali ibn Abi Taleb's two sons (i.e. the grandsons of the Prophet) in favour of their father, at 148–9.

[324] Muhassin ibn 'Ali al-Tannukhi (d. 384/994), *Nishwar al-muhadarah*, well edited by 'Abbud al-Shaliji, 8 vols. (Beirut, 1971–3). The *Nishwar* is a mine of information on the city of Baghdad in the

segments of court stories are adduced for their literary quality and their illustration of some *hadith*, but there is little to glean in terms of legal reasoning or actual application of the law. In most cases, the parties are not relevant, and any actual dispute immaterial.

Much more interesting for the lawyer are later books of *qadi* literature, which can be illustrated here in the Syrian jurist Ibn Abi al-Dam's (d. 642/1244) manual entitled, as are many in the same genre, *Kitab adab al-qada'*.[325] As a reminder of the high quality and self-consciousness of an epoch where Islamic jurists knew that their lawmaking was the most sophisticated in the world, the book deserves a fuller presentation which I take up against modern lawyering in the conclusion to the present work.

It is actually possible to revise one's view of the whole field of Islamic law from the perspective of the practitioner as appears in the *qadi* literature. While this may not be purposeful in a historical restatement of the field, it is important to keep in mind the natural intermingling of sources, as well as the delightful evidence which can be adduced on social mores on the occasion of discussing the proper practice which judges should follow. We have in Ibn Abi al-Dam evidence of widespread lying in court,[326] taking of oaths by all kinds of people with various religious backgrounds, including those whom one would portray nowadays as agnostics or atheists,[327] and abuse by paper merchants of the propensity of court officials to write a lot unnecessarily.[328]

'Abbasid preriod, as portrayed by Tannukhi, sometime judge in Iraq, whose *al-Faraj ba'd al-shidda*, also edited by Shaliji in 5 vols (Beirut, 1978), is another compilation of literary stories. The importance of the *Nishwar* was underlined by D. S. Margoliouth; see his *The table-talk of a Mesopotamian judge: being the first part of the Nishwar al-muhadarah or Jami' al-tawarikh*, partly edited [vol. 1 and] translated [vol. 2] by Margoliouth (London, 2 vols, 1921–22). It is used to good effect in 'Isam Shbaru's two books on the judicial system mentioned above n. 224. Little new is added in these treatments on *qadi* literature to Tyan's contributions, as the information on the 'judge' is more literary than legal. In none of these books can one find serious legal motivations for the judges' 'opinions'. There is, however, a wealth of historical detail if one can, in John Donohue's words, 'ferret them out'. See the patient illustration in his masterpiece on 'The development of political and social institutions in Iraq under the Buwayhids, 334–403 H.: the fall and rise of the caliphate', Harvard Ph.D., 1966, especially the section on the judiciary, 557–601. This work was published as *The Buwayhid dynasty in Iraq 334 H./945 to 403 H./1012: shaping institutions for the future* (Leiden, 2003). The section on the judiciary is at 288–303.

[325] Shihab al-Din Ibn Abi al-Dam, *Kitab adab al-qada'* (the book of the ways of judgeship), cited above n. 304. Other books in the genre include another famous Shafi'i, al-Mawardi (d. 450/1058), *Adab al-qadi*, M. Sirhan ed., 2 vols. (Baghdad, 1971). Comprehensive *fiqh* treatises invariably include long books on *adab al-qadi*, for instance in vol. 16 of Sarakhsi's (d. *c.* 1090) *Mabsut* for the Hanafis, and vol. 14 of Muhammad Hasan al-Najafi (d. 1266/1849), *Jawahir al-kalam* (Beirut edn., 1992) for the Shi'i Ja'faris. (*Jawahir al-kalam* published in 15 vols.) See a more detailed analysis of Ibn Abi al-Dam's book in Chapter 11.   [326] And how to deal with it, Ibn Abi al-Dam, 212–13.

[327] ibid. at 198–9: 'If the person who takes the oath is agnostic, and does not believe in creator or worship, he is asked to swear by God the creator and benefactor. If one protests that such a person would not be deterred by the formula, what's the use . . . ', the good judge has two answers: we rule over him by our law, whether he likes it or not, and his guilt might increase, his luck may turn, eliciting quicker divine vengeance. '*Wa-in kana al-halif dahriyyan, la ya'taqidu khaliqan, wa la ma'budan, uhlifa billah al-khaliq al-raziq. Fa-in qil: fahuwa la-yanzajir biha, ma al-fa'ida, qulna fiha fa'idatan, ijra' hukmina 'alayhi . . . wal-thaniya, an yuzad bihi ithman, wa yudrikahu shu'maha, fa-rubbama yata'ajjal biha intiqam*'.   [328] ibid. at 415.

Fatwas and *mufti*s

The reader can now appreciate the multi-layered nature of Islamic law 'sources' over the immense span of time covered by the literature. Caution against narrowing the field to Qur'anic or *hadith* texts is further warranted by the necessity to expand the ambit of Middle Eastern law in several directions: in addition to judges and their judgments, one cannot omit the peculiar role of the *mufti*s. The notorious pronouncement of the late *Ayat Allah* Khumaini against the novelist Salman Rushdie has suddenly turned the term fatwa into a household expression.[329] In addition to the absence of due process in a capital punishment matter, one of the problems in the formulation of that edict is that it does not correspond to the usual format of a fatwa, which is a legally competent scholar's (the *mufti*) response to a specific point of law put to him, generally privately, by a lay person. In that particular case, there is no trace of an original question formally addressed to the Iranian leader. Furthermore, there is no doubt that Khumaini had in mind a ruling which is as tightly binding as a judgment issued in a court of law, whereas the fatwa's binding dimension is limited by its nature as an answer to a specific questioner. It is therefore authoritative, but not normally binding in the sense that the executive power's threat of force ensures its application. As in all matters of authority, its power of 'persuasion' depends on who the *mufti* is.

Although *mufti*s acquired with the Ottoman Empire an increasingly official function,[330] the *mufti*'s role has traditionally been confined to an advisory dimension. In the modern Middle East, important individual *mufti*s or collective bodies like the Egyptian house of *ifta'* (*dar al-ifta*) have tended to become government appointees, and the state has made certain that they do not compete overtly with the courts.[331] Binding decisions remain a prerogative of the courts and must be implemented, if need be, by public force. This is certainly not the

---

[329] 'Fatwa' is now an entry in the *Oxford English Dictionary*, so there is no need for italics any longer. This is how the 'message' of Khumaini was broadcast on 14 February 1989: 'In the name of God Almighty. There is only one God, to whom we shall all return. I would like to inform all the intrepid Muslims in the world that the author of the book entitled *The Satanic Verses* which has been compiled, printed and published in opposition to Islam, the Prophet and the Koran, as well as those publishers who were aware of its contents, have been sentenced to death. I call on all zealous Muslims to execute them quickly, wherever they find them, so that no one will dare to insult the Islamic sanctions. Whoever is killed on this path will be regarded as a martyr, God willing. In addition, anyone who has access to the author of the book, but does not possess the power to execute him, should refer him to the people so that he may be punished for his actions. May God's blessing be on you all. Ruhollah Musavi Khomeyni'. *Summary of World Broadcasts* (Britain), 15 February 1989, ME/A2.

[330] Now documented by Repp, *The Müfti of Istanbul* (how the *muftilik* gradually grew in the fifteenth and sixteenth centuries as a pre-eminent institution in the Empire), and Imber, *Ebu's-su'ud*, the most famous Ottoman *mufti*, cited above n. 304.

[331] Discussion in Mallat, 'Tantawi on banking', in Muhammad Khalil Masud, Brinkley Messick, and David Powers, eds., *Islamic legal interpretation: muftis and their fatwas* (Cambridge, Mass., 1996) 286–96, at 294–5. Also J. Skovgaard-Petersen, *Defining Islam for the Egyptian state: muftis and fatwas of the dar al-ifta'* (Leiden, 1997).

case with fatwas: 'To the fatwa coercion does not attach, unlike [the decision of] the judge'.[332]

Be the fatwa binding or merely persuasive, there is little doubt that 'the fatwa collection [is] a discrete literary genre'.[333] In these collections some of the most famous are, under the Mamluks, the fatwas of Taqi al-Din al-Subki (756/1355); in North Africa, the multi-volume work compiled by Wansharisi (913/1508);[334] in the Ottoman world the pronouncements of the official grand *Mufti* of the early empire Ebu-Su'ud (981/1574) and the works of the Levantine Khayr al-Din al-Ramli (1081/1671);[335] and in Muslim India various collections named after the Mogul Emperors who commandeered them (*Fatawa Ghiyathiyya, Fatawa Qarakhani, Fatawa Tatarkhaniyya, Fatawa Babari*).[336] The system of fatwa pronouncement is particularly interesting in view of the absence of surviving original court documents in the early period, as fatwa collections offer a long series of 'cases' which can be used for both comparative and historical purposes. A recent article sums up the direction in which the study of fatwas should be taken: 'The juridical genre of the fatwa was chiefly responsible for the growth and change of legal doctrine in the schools, and ... our current perception of Islamic law as a jurists' law must now be further defined as a *muftis*' law'.[337] As a practical indicator of legal change, it is argued, fatwas have affected law in practice, though not perhaps *fiqh* treatises.

Hallaq's conclusion, of course, is premised on the idea that the main legal books of *fiqh* did not change over time, a contention which I have cast some doubt upon through exempla drawn from some of our classical authors' style and methodological approach. Whether in the literature of fatwas, the *fiqh* books, or stories of judges, the impression of history in the following famous aphorism of the nineteenth-century Ottoman civil code known as the Majalla must now be a point of departure for the understanding of the larger picture of Islamic law. In a

---

[332] *Wa fatwahu la yartabitu biha ilzam bi-khilaf al-qadi*, Ibn al Salah (d. 643/1245), *Adab al-mufti wal-mustafti*, edited by Muwaffaq 'Abd al-Qader (Beirut, 1986) 106.

[333] Muhammad Khalil Masud, Brinkley Messick, and David Powers, '*Muftis*, fatwas and Islamic legal interpretation', in Masud, Messick, and Powers, eds., *Islamic legal interpretation*, above n. 331, 10. This is a remarkable collective work including several classic and modern fatwas studied in historical context.

[334] Ahmad ibn Yahya al-Wansharisi, *al-Mi'yar al-mughrib wal-jami' al-mu'rib 'an fatawa ahl ifriqiya wal-andalus wal-maghrib*, M. Hajji ed., 13 vols (Beirut, 1981–3). The North African H. R. Idris, the French Emile Amar and Robert Brunschvig, and the American David Powers have written extensively on the world of Wansharisi.

[335] On Ebu-Su'ud, above n. 304. Ramli is the author of *al-Fatawa al-khayriyya li naf' al-bariyya* (Beirut, 1974) (1st edn. printed in Egypt in 1858).

[336] See Masud, Messick, and Powers, '*Muftis*, fatwas and Islamic legal interpretation', above n. 333, 14–15. Book titles might be misleading. The Indian *Fatawa 'Alamgiriyya* (or *Fatawa Hindiyya*), which was collected under the Mughal emperor Awrangzeb in the seventeenth century, is actually a *fiqh* book. As in the case of Subki, cited n. 36, the fatwa, even in the classical period, could be the subject of an extensive treatise. Fatwa is also known as *nazila*, plural *nawazil*.

[337] Wael Hallaq, 'From *fatwas* to *furu'*: growth and change in Islamic substantive law', *Islamic Law and Society*, 1, 1994, 17–56, at 33.

fiqh aphorism turned Majalla article, is stated 'the impossibility to deny the change in legal rulings with the change of time'.[338] The idea is constant and recurs in *fiqh* books, such as Ibn Nujaym's (d. 970/1563) *Ashbah* from which many of the Majalla principles are taken,[339] and even in judges' manuals: 'To each time its wording', one reads in Ibn Abi al-Dam's manual, 'and to each people their habits'.[340]

Some of these modifications can be readily observed in fatwa collections, whether as responses to pressing questions of the time, individual or collective, or as 'expert opinion' in court. There is in addition, as in the case of the *qadi*, a specific literary genre known as *adab al-mufti*, which explains the qualifications and modus operandi of *ifta*, sometimes with practical examples on a variety of circumstances in which the *mufti* might find himself. An example in the literature is a book by Ibn al-Salah, author of one of the best manuals for *mufti*s, *Adab al-mufti wal-mustafti*.[341]

Here we find, as expected, a repetition of how difficult it is to reach the position of *mufti*, the traditional fear of getting it wrong, the qualifications needed to fulfil the position.[342] Again, this is not so different from the case of a judge, including a few remarks on *ifta* as a social need which must be fulfilled,[343] and the distinction between the 'absolute and independent *mufti*' and the *mufti* 'who is not independent'.[344] The absolute *mufti* will be able to answer all the questions put to him without extensive recourse to 'researching' the issue,[345] whereas there is no harm in requesting the help of a 'non-independent *mufti*', for example on a case of inheritance if that *mufti* is specialized in inheritance. He need not know about every single legal issue to solve the case put to him, since his inheritance law expertise would be sufficient to answer questions on the issue at hand.

The treatise on the art of the *mufti* lists informative, sometimes entertaining questions: (i) Must the *mufti* be male? (ii) Can a *mufti* be a *qadi*? (iii) If there are two *mufti*s in some region, who prevails? (iv) What happens if the *mufti* discovers that his opinion was wrong? (v) Is there any liability on the *mufti*? (vi) How long should the *mufti* wait to issue his opinion? (vii) Does the *mufti* get paid? (viii) What books of law should the *mufti* adopt for his opinions? (ix) Are

---

[338] *la yunkar taghayyur al-ahkam bi-taghayyur al-azman*, Art. 39 of the Majalla.

[339] *Al-ashbah wal-naza'er* is a famous restatement of law by Ibn Nujaym, published e.g. by Zakariyyya 'Umairat ed. (Beirut, 1999) 79–89. See Chapter 8.

[340] *wa li-kulli zaman istilah, wa li-kulli qawmin marasem*, Ibn abi al-Dam, *Kitab adab al-qada'*, 353.

[341] Ibn al Salah, *Adab al-mufti*, cited above n. 332.

[342] Ibn al Salah, *Adab al-mufti*, 71–85. This is the same Ibn al-Salah (d. 643/1245) who developed the methodology of *hadith*, see above n. 90.

[343] This is the famous *fard kifaya* (sufficient duty), which means that at least one person in society should discharge the duty, thereby absolving the others from it. The concept may be rendered by the difference between 'sufficient' and 'necessary'. It is sufficient for one person to perform *ifta*, it is not necessary that each person in society does so. The contrastive duty to *ifta* appears for instance in prayer. The duty to pray is necessary. It is not sufficient for one person to pray for other Muslims to be absolved from the duty. Prayer is a *fard wajib*, a necessary duty that every person must perform.

[344] Ibn al-Salah, *Adab al-mufti*, 85–106. 'al-mufti al mutlaq al-mustaqill' and 'al-mufti alladhi laysa bi-mustaqill'.   [345] ibid. *min ghayri mu'anat ta'allum*, 88; *min ghayri ta'ab kathir*, 89.

there precedents for a *mufti*? (x) Can a *mufti* from one school issue an opinion according to another school? (xi) If there is a difference of opinion within one school, which should the *mufti* follow?

These are all eminently practical questions, which Ibn al-Salah duly discusses, answering when he can, and showing the pros and cons when he cannot.[346] Accordingly, (i) the *mufti* should not necessarily be a male; (ii) it is preferable for a *mufti* not to be a *qadi* at the same time; (iii) if two *muftis* in the same region are asked simultaneously, at least one should answer(!); (iv) if a *mufti* discovers his opinion was wrong, then whether the questioner should follow the new response depends on a number of factors. These include whether the act which was the reason for seeking the *mufti* is reversible, or whether the *mufti* was able to reach the questioner to tell him that he had erred; (v) a *mufti* who harms a person because of his wrong opinion is liable; (vi) the *mufti* should take time for consideration, but his knowledge of law should be sufficient to issue his opinions reasonably quickly; (vii) the mufti should volunteer his fatwa without being remunerated, although he could be paid by the treasury or by the locals who assign him to be *mufti* of their area. He should beware compensation akin to bribes, but ways round the prohibition are also mentioned; (viii) the *mufti* should follow the works within the school he belongs to; (ix) sticking to precedent is preferable, if the *mufti* remembers the opinion issued in like matters. Ibn al-Salah suggests that the *mufti* should always provide a rationale for his opinions;[347] (x) despite (viii) above, the *mufti* might want to exercise some eclecticism, and Ibn al-Salah discusses at length the use of opinions by scholars from different schools; (xi) if the *mufti* is faced with several opinions within his own school, he should move cautiously.

In this brief account of a relatively detailed discussion, with citations, precedents, and arguments to boot, perhaps the most remarkable feature is the closeness of the fatwa theoretician to real life and to the constraints which a *mufti* will be faced with. While one could dwell also on other sections of the book, for instance, on the art of the fatwa,[348] let me briefly consider 'fatwas in context', namely in their use in judgments.

Among the fifty-five or so cases reported in the 1667 Tripoli court record, five explicitly mention a fatwa.[349] All the fatwas originate from the *mufti* of Tripoli, and the series of *Laila's Estate* described earlier offers clear evidence on the proximity of the *mufti* and the rapid recourse to his expertise in the litigation over the estate.

---

[346] Ibn al-Salah, *Adab al-mufti*, 106–34.

[347] *wa balaghana ... 'an ahad a'immat al-madhhab annahu kana la yufti fi shay' min al-masa'el hatta yaqul hatha al-dalil*, it was reported that one of the schoolmasters refused to issue a fatwa without noting the rationale, Ibn al-Salah, *Adab al-mufti*, 117. We know also, from fatwa collections, that answers were not usually reasoned.

[348] *kayfiyyat al-fatwa wa adabuha*, the formulation and arts of the fatwa, Ibn al-Salah, *Adab al-mufti*, 134–57, including 'nineteen common practical issues'.

[349] Tripoli, 27, *Hasan Agha ibn Naser Agha alias ibn al-Husami v. Hajj Ibrahim Bitar and other inhabitants from Antartus*, early Muharram 1078/late June 1667; Tripoli, 29, above n. 297, *Laila's*

The other interesting element in the court use of fatwa relates to its format and argumentation. Typically, the person who seeks the fatwa has a clear objective in mind, and the *mufti* offers her the fatwa which meets her interest. In addition, the *mufti* may provide supportive *fiqh* evidence, in the shape of reference to recognized Hanafi authors, who were the dominant school in seventeenth-century Tripoli and in the Ottoman world at large.

In the course of litigation in the matter of *Laila's Estate*, the issue was about hearsay in kinship, that is whether hearsay evidence about family kinship stood in court:

The defendants produced in hand a fatwa from the great scholar, our teacher 'Ali Efendi, the *mufti* at the time in Tripoli, the content of which was the answer of the Hanafi masters about

[Start question] whether the testimony over hearsay evidence is acceptable, and if so [unclear?] does it need to concern evidence about a brother or else?, please give us a fatwa for which God will recompense you. Answer: yes, it is preferably acceptable,[350] and they must show that he is the uterine or consanguine brother according to the *Durar* and *Ghurar*,[351] in which it so stated: 'testimony by hearsay is possible in matters of kinship when professed by two men, or one man and two fair women' End [of fatwa].

A similar conclusion appears in the *Kanz*[352] and in *al-Ashbah*,[353] where it is stated that 'if they testify in his favour that he is [his] brother or uncle or cousin, they must show that [the relative] is related through his father or his mother, or through his father.'[354]

The same 'Ali Efendi had produced, a few days earlier, another fatwa running as follows:

Content [of the fatwa]: what is the answer of the Hanafi masters about people who give X a general power of attorney to receive and spend money, and X disburses by virtue of the power of attorney money which they did not thereafter accept? Is X's statement [to that effect] accepted if supported by his oath? Please give us a fatwa for which God will recompense you.

Answer: the agent[355] is a fiduciary,[356] and the statement of the fiduciary supported by oath is accepted. In the *Ashbah wal-Naza'er*,[357] the statement of the agent who claims to have delivered the object entrusted with him to the beneficiary is accepted, like the depositor who claims the return of the deposit, and the trustee who claims a disbursement [in accordance with the trust]. Their statement supported by oath is accepted.[358]

Estate ii; Tripoli, 44, *Murghib ibn Ahmad v. 'Abdallah ibn Muhammad,* above n. 275; 75, *'Umar Agha ibn Sha'ban v. 'Umar ibn 'Abdallah al-Rajil,* above n. 266; Tripoli, 147, *Fatima bint al-Hajj Muhammad and her sister Amina v. Muhammad ibn 'Ali,* mid-Jumada I 1078/late October 1667.

[350] *istihsanan.*

[351] The *Durar al-ahkam fi sharh Ghurar al-ahkam* is a commentary by the Hanafi author Mulla Khusraw (d. 885/1480) on his own *Ghurar al-Ahkam.*

[352] This is the Hanafi jurist al-Nasafi's (d. 710/1310) *Kanz al-daqa'iq*, a manual of law which elicited several commentaries, including Ibn Nujaym's (d. 970/1563) extensive al-*Bahr al-ra'iq.*

[353] *Al-Ashbah wal-naza'er,* the restatement of law by Ibn Nujaym, cited above n. 339.

[354] Tripoli, 29, *Laila's Estate* ii, above n. 297. Fair, *'udul.*   [355] Agent, *wakil.*

[356] Fiduciary, *amin.*   [357] by Ibn Nujaym.

[358] Tripoli, 27, *Hasan Agha ibn Naser Agha alias ibn al-Husami v. Hajj Ibrahim Bitar and other inhabitants from Antartus,* above n. 349.

The judge in that case decided in favour of the plaintiff, who had claimed to have acted as agent for the residents of Antartus to get rid of a difficult official in the person of the governor of the city,[359] and who was not paid for his efforts. P was a notable from the city who had been approached six months earlier by a number of local residents. 'The residents had been harmed by the newly appointed official in the citadel of Antartus', and they 'mandated P to work his best for the revocation of the official', adding that they would reimburse him for any costs, 'whatever they may be'. P was apparently successful in getting rid of the governor, but they refused to honour their obligations, and he produced a record of the expenses incurred, which amounted to the important sum of 2,008 piastres, as well as two witnesses who confirmed that he was indeed asked by the people of Antartus to help dismiss the official and that they would reimburse him for 'any expenses, small or large'. It is at this point in the proceedings that P produced the fatwa likening the attorney to a depositor or a trustee. On the strength of the evidence and the fatwa, the judge held that he should be reimbursed.[360]

Another agent who was sued for breach of trust would use this same ruling of the *mufti* a few months later, and argue that he had spent all the revenues which accrued from the principal's property, and that the judge should take his word for it. This time, however, there was no need for verbatim illustration of the proposition that the agent was to be trusted prima facie. This is remarkable evidence of the memory of the court, and a rare proof of an explicit adoption of precedent, this time in the form of the judgment confirming a fatwa.[361]

Similarly, in the long decision in favour of the head of the corporation of weavers,[362] the evidence he produced as plaintiff, in addition to witnesses to the loan claimed from D, was a fatwa by the Tripoli *mufti* concerning a point of law: would a settlement over immovables, such settlement having been agreed to requite a debt, stand in law? D was arguing that the whole debt had been settled because of an agreement which involved the estate in which both he and P were party, but the plaintiff produced a fatwa from the *mufti* of Tripoli, answering the question in the negative. D's argument that the debt should be considered as a

---

[359] On Antartus, an early Phoenician island-city, Arados to the Greeks, now known as Arwad, opposite the northern Syrian littoral, see the nicely illustrated little book by Françoise Briquel-Chatonnet and Eric Gubel, *Les Phéniciens, aux origines du Liban* (Paris, 1998) 58–9.

[360] Tripoli, 27, *Hasan Agha ibn Naser Agha alias ibn al-Husami v. Hajj Ibrahim Bitar and other inhabitants from Antartus*, above n. 349. *Nazer al-waqf*, trustee; residents had been harmed by the newly appointed official in the citadel of Antartus, *tadarraru min su' af 'al al-dizdar al-mu'ayyen 'alay-him bi-qal'at antartus*; they instructed P to do his best to bring about the revocation of the official, *wa wakkaluhu an yajtahida li-'azlihi*; any costs, whatever they may be, *wa an-yasrufa mahma lazima dhalika min al-darahim*; record, *daftar*; any expenses, small or large, *qalilan kana aw kathiran*.

[361] Tripoli, 75, *'Umar Agha ibn Sha'ban v. 'Umar ibn 'Abdallah al-Rajil*, above n. 266: *wa abraza fi yadih fatwa sharifa sadira min 'umdat al-'ulama' al-a'lam mawlana 'ali efendi al-mufti bi-tarablus damat fadayiluh madmunu jawabiha ba'da bast al-su'al anna al-wakil amin wal-amin musaddaq bi-qawlih ma'a yaminihi fi jami' ma yadda'ih*, and he showed a fatwa in hand, issued by the great jurist the *mufti* of Tripoli—may his virtues endure—the content of which after the question was posed was that the agent is a fiduciary and that the fiduciary is trusted upon his word, together with the oath in all that he says.   [362] Tripoli, 44, *Murghib ibn Ahmad v. 'Abdallah ibn Muhammad*, above, n. 275.

whole did not curry favour with the judge in the light of the fatwa and its supporting authorities, and he duly lost the case.

The last use in the register of the fatwas of 'Ali Efendi appears in the longish
decision over the reported statement of a dying wife to the effect that all matters
had been settled with her husband. In that case, plaintiffs were the daughters of a
deceased woman, suing their mother's second husband for payment of their share
in her inheritance, including the deferred dower. The second husband rejected the
claim, and

produced a fatwa in his hand, by the leading scholar 'Ali Efendi, *mufti* of Tripoli.

Content: what do the Hanafi masters say about the dying wife who is conscious and in full
mind, and who says I have no claim and no case and no demand whatsoever against my
husband? Would this clear the husband and would he be protected against other heirs'
legal actions? Please give us a fatwa for which God will recompense you in heaven.

Answer: It is stated in *al-Ashbah wal-Naza'er* that if the dying patient acknowledges that he
has no claim on one heir, then no legal action of another heir will be entertained, End [of
fatwa].

In it [*al-Ashbah*] also, and in *al-Bazzaziyya*,[363] following Khassaf's book of legal fictions,[364]
if she states that the husband owes her no dower, or if she says, I have nothing against X,
then that person [the husband, or X] is cleared. End [of scholars' quote].[365]

The judge used the fatwa to clarify the legal point, and to reject the claim of the
daughters against the second husband of their mother for their share in her inheritance, including the deferred dower. Of note is 'the scholarship' of the text, which
is relatively rare in the register, with recourse to a *mufti* on a fine point of law, and
the *mufti* himself arguing his conclusions on the basis of known authorities.

Most striking about the fatwas as used in court is their authoritativeness as
'expert opinion'. In all five instances mentioned, the party who produced the
fatwa won his or her case. The judge defers to the *mufti*, and does not question the
matter further. No doubt the *mufti* was physically close to the court, as appears in
the 'errata' series in *re Laila's Estate*, and that factor must have weighed heavily in
the judge's decisions. But it is also true that the party who seeks the *mufti's* scholarly support will have shown more diligence in bolstering his case. It would be
interesting to see, on a longer span of registers, whether any fatwas are turned
down or disregarded by the court.

So fatwas in court practice. Whatever the chain of authority between judge as
decision-maker and *mufti* as expert-advisor, the room afforded by scholarship for
fatwas is real in daily practice, as is the attention of the *mufti* to consistency.

[363] This is probably a collection of fatwas known as *al-Jami' al-wajiz*, by Muhammad ibn
Muhammad al-Bazzazi (d. 827/1474).
[364] This is the collection of legal fictions (*hiyal*) attributed to Abu Bakr al-Khassaf (d. 261/875),
edited by J. Schacht in Hanover, 1923.
[365] Tripoli, 147, *Fatima bint al-Hajj Muhammad and her sister Amina v. Muhammad ibn 'Ali*, above
n. 349.

Formularies, deeds, and contracts

For a fuller appreciation of the available legal material in classical Islamic law, one cannot forget the major genre represented by the legal forms used in court and in private life, known in Arabic as *shurut* (lit. conditions, clauses) or *watha'eq* (lit. documents, acts). The history of Middle Eastern and Islamic law is equally one of formalized acts, in which the role of writing and reporting—however patchy it may seem to the modern eye—has allowed the preservation of a sophisticated and complex legal culture.[366] The *shari'a* encompasses important forms of legal material such as deeds, contracts, and formulae, which recent scholarship has drawn attention to. These have tended to be legal acknowledgments of various types of transactions, personal as well as commercial.

The wealth of such documentation can be illustrated in recent scholarly editing and translation of some of the Arabic documents of the Geniza.[367] While one does not find in the collection any court archives like the ones available in the eleventh/seventeenth century collection examined earlier, documentation concerns varied notarial and judicial exercises like sale, lease, endowments (*waqf*), marriage contracts, powers of attorney, as well as fatwas. The collection also includes various administrative documents, including petitions to various officials, accounts, and receipts for taxes.

Works of this kind are few and far between, with one of the best treatments going back to 1972.[368] Despite a renewed interest in formulae by German and Spanish scholars,[369] the field remains little studied. This is understandable, as

---

[366] For a remarkable analysis of documents in the context of pre-Islamic/Islamic continuity, see Gladys Frantz-Murphy, 'A comparison of Arabic and earlier Egyptian contract formularies', in 4 parts, *Journal of Near Eastern Studies*, 40, 1981, 203–25, 355–6; 44, 1985, 99–114; 47, 1988, 105–12; 47, 1988, 269–80. Some quittance formulae are traced back to the Aramaic, Egyptian Demotic, and Akkadian periods, in the fourth article at 279, 274. Early sale contracts are presented and discussed in 'Abd al-Rahman Fahmi Muhammad, '*Watha'eq lil-ta'aqud min fajr al-islam* (contractual documents from early Islam)', *Bulletin de l'Institut d'Egypte*, 53 and 54, 1971–2, 1972–3, Arabic section, 1–58; Yusuf Raghib, *Marchands d'étoffes au Fayyoum au iii/ix siècle d'après leurs archives (actes et lettres). I, les actes des Banu Abd al-Mu'min* (Cairo, 1982).

[367] Geoffrey Khan, *Arabic legal and administrative documents in the Cambridge Genizah collections* (Cambridge, 1993). See my review in *Yearbook of Islamic and Middle Eastern Law*, 1995, ii, 638–40.

[368] Jeannette Wakin, *The function of documents in Islamic law* (Albany, N.Y., 1972). See also the classic collections of documents and studies published by Nabia Abbott, *Studies in Arabic literary papyri*, 3 vols. (Chicago, 1957–67) (albeit more historical than legal); Alfred Grohmann, *Arabic papyri in the Egyptian museum*, 6 vols. (Cairo, 1934–62) and Emile Tyan, 'Le notariat et la preuve par écrit', cited above n. 261. Comprehensive *fiqh* books, like Sarakhsi's *Mabsut*, in vol. xxx, 167–209, often include books of *shurut*.

[369] e.g. F.J. Aguirre Sádaba, 'Un documento de compraventa árabico-granadino', *Andalucía Islámica*, 1, 1980, 163–72; P. Chalmeta-Gendrón, 'Un formulaire notarial hispano-arabe du iv/x siècle: glanes économiques', *Revista del Instituto Egipcio de Estudios Islámicos en Madrid*, 23, 1985–6, 181–202. Monica Gronke, *Arabische und persische Privaturkunden des 12. Und 13. Jahrhunderts aus Ardabil (Aserbaidschan)* (Berlin, 1982), Gabriela Linda Guellil, *Damaszener Akten des 8/14. Jahrhunderts nach at-Tarsusis Kitab al-I'lam, Eine Studie zum Arabischen Justizwesen* (Bamberg, 1985).

deeds are by nature dry texts, and their interpretation requires a combination of specialities hard to find, in law, in history, and in the difficult scripts and languages of the classical age.

For a legal historian, there is a mine of information in these books. They are limited for the lawyer by the fact that such documents do not record an active dispute and its adjudication. The texts show the dexterity of draftsmen in contracts of sale,[370] or *waqf*,[371] but the place or reasoning of the judge cannot be appreciated on the strength of the documents provided. Nor can the position and arguments really be appreciated, as the deed comes to register a fact which has either never been disputed, or one where the dispute in question has now been settled. Nevertheless, the imaginative (and well-versed) historian may be able to use such work to reconstruct a legal world that is particularly elusive.

For a modern lawyer, these documents hold a special flavour, as they underline the care over legal wording that has preoccupied contract draftsmen from early on in the Middle East: 'Lawyers have changed little over the centuries'.[372] The language is strikingly similar to that presently used by drafters of similar subject-matter, although the syntax, and the details, of course, will naturally differ. There is here a vast resource which is available for comparative historical work, and the work is still in its infancy.

To illustrate these proposals, I examine next two recently published formularies of North African and Spanish law which give a sense of the wealth of Islamic law material for research, and show the possible historical and comparative routes which can be followed.

One finds in the Granadan judge Abu Ishaq al-Gharnati's (d. 579/1183) *al-Watha'eq al-mukhtasara* a compendium of documents in use in Muslim Spain where the judge lived for most of his life.[373] The text starts by stressing the importance of written documentation for the ascertaining of the law, as enjoined in various Qur'anic verses. This is developed in three areas.

First, there is 'the requirement to write down obligations', as in verse 282 of the second chapter of the Qur'an, from which Gharnati derives that 'there must be as many copies as there are witnesses'.[374]

---

[370] Khan, *Arabic legal and administrative documents*, above n. 367, 5–140.

[371] ibid. 181–90. There is a large literature on *waqf*, with recent work ranging far and wide in history and geography, e.g. from Randi Deguilhem and J. P. Pascual in the pre-modern and modern period on Syria and McChesney's monograph on the development of a shrine in Central Asia over four centuries, to Michael Dumper on the current situation of Muslim foundations in Jerusalem. A list of some of the best works can be found in Humphreys, *Islamic history*, 220–1.

[372] 'Whatever historical value these legal texts may or may not possess, they are hardly transparent. They can only be used by those acquainted with their peculiar technical language (lawyers have changed little over the centuries)', ibid. 213.

[373] Abu Ishaq al-Gharnati, *al-Watha'eq al-mukhtasara* (Summary of forms), Mustafa Naji ed. (Rabat, 1988). (Hereinafter *WM*.)

[374] *wujub katb al-watha'eq li-daf' al-da'awi wa hifz al-amwal wal-ansab wa tahsin al-furuj*, Gharnati, *WM*, 8.

Secondly, a notary is necessary in the city. This need, which one finds expressed also in relation to judges, *muftis*, and leaders of the prayer, is expressed as a legal duty which must be performed by the community as a whole at any one time, without the duty necessarily falling on each Muslim individually. It is enough if one person in the community carries it out, and here one notary suffices for the duty, which shall be remunerated.[375]

Thirdly, the Granadan judge explains the general operation of deposing and using witnesses, including variations on oral testimony *vis-à-vis* written evidence;[376] the restriction of the testimony of women to three areas: money, acts which lead to pecuniary consequences (manslaughter, wills, theft), and issues closely associated with women which 'men are not generally cognizant in';[377] and the rejection as witnesses of some categories like children and 'the enemy'.[378] The conclusion reached is the necessity to put evidence in writing despite the wide place given to oral testimony in the tradition.[379]

These basic facts are also an occasion for the Granadan jurist to note 'six issues' in which the people of Spain depart from received Maliki law, some legally trivial, like allowing trees to be planted in mosques,[380] others not very clear, with regard to the value of oral testimony against written evidence.[381] Perhaps of importance is the fact that lawyers in the classical age appear, once more, much less constrained by allegedly immutable regulations than they are perceived to be in the modern age: 'This is why', Gharnati explains in one of his cases, 'the apparent [interpretation] of Islam is not followed, and this goes against the opinion of Sahnun [d. 240/854]', himself a major figure of the dominant Maliki law in Islamic Spain.[382]

The qualifications needed for the position of notary are then explained. Among the eight compulsory qualifications, he must be Muslim, honest, competent in the knowledge of documents,[383] deploy easily readable handwriting as well as use clear and unambiguous expressions.[384] Technical advice follows on the public notary's assessment of the parties' capacity to contract, on dates and post-dating of documents, including the precise computation of months and dates in a number of contracts, and the dating of affidavits.[385]

---

[375] As noted above, n. 343, the legal term for this duty is *fard kifaya*. Examples of *fard kifaya* for judges in Ibn Abi al-Dam, *Kitab adab al-qada'*, 31; for *muftis* in Ibn al-Salah, *Adab al-mufti*, 87, for notary-publics Gharnati, *WM*, 8.

[376] *al-shahada 'alal-khatt la tajuz*, testimony about writing is not allowed, ibid.

[377] *ma la yattali' 'alayh al-rijal 'adatan kal-wilada, wal-saqt wal-istihlal*. Gharnati, *WM*, 9.

[378] *al-sabi wal-'aduww*, ibid. 9.   [379] Gharnati, *WM*, 11–13.

[380] *ajazu ghars al-shajar fil-masajid, wa huwa madhhab al-Uza'i*, they [our Andalus scholars] allowed the planting of trees in mosques, which is the school of the Syrian Uza'i (or Awza'i, d. 157/774), Gharnati, *WM*, 9. What may be legally trivial is not so architecturally, and the distinct beauty of Cordoba's mosque lies also in the charm of its orange orchard.   [381] Gharnati, *WM*, 8–9.

[382] *la yura'a zaher al-islam, khilafan li-Sahnun*, Gharnati, *WM*, 9, further also 9–10. Sahnun (d. 240/854) is the author of *al-Mudawwana*, the early reference book of the Maliki school.

[383] *'alim bi-fiqh wal-watha'eq*, Gharnati, *WM*, 10.   [384] Gharnati, *WM*, 13.

[385] ibid. 13–15.

After this general introduction, the bulk of the *Forms* is divided into three books: formulas which are related to marriage and divorce, formulas which are related to sales and other monetary transactions, and court registers.[386]

Unlike *fiqh* books, these texts are easy to read, and they tend to be eminently practical, though dry. They therefore deserve particular attention for research into the application of law in everyday life, as they allow a direct view of both the development of Islamic law generally, and the cultural and economic practices of a society at a given time from the perspective of the most common documents which the compiler—judge or notary—might have collected.

An example of Abu Ishaq al-Gharnati's treatment of the notary's job can be found in his book on marriage. The book includes a long section on *sadaq*, which is the word used in North Africa and Spain for the Near Eastern *mahr* (dower), and lists impediments to marriage and other relevant aspects for the conclusion of the marriage contract.[387] The section on divorce starts with a description of what the document of divorce must include: 'the name of the two parties, the quality [profession] of the husband and wife, ... the number of pronouncements of *talaq* and type of *talaq*, whether it is *raj'i* or *mumallik* or *khul'i* or *batat* [all variations on *talaq*] ... The contract must be drawn in two copies and include the opinion of the guardian [of the wife] and the terms of guardianship, and some add that compensation in the release of the guardian of his duties towards the orphan[ed divorced wife]'.[388] The section is followed by some explanations in *fiqh*. Then appears another formula relating to the wife initiating the divorce. Here, the Granadan judge mentions two documents: the first dwells on the absent husband and the discontinuation of maintenance. It lists details such as the time of disappearance, the likely place the husband went to, the absence of payment to maintain the wife, what she is usually entitled to etc. The text is then dated. The second model form focuses on the non-payment by the husband of maintenance, although the effect of marital abandonment seems also to be present, and regulates the divorce on the wife's behest:

Contract of divorce for absence and non-payment of maintenance. [Must be mentioned the name of the judge, his position, the two spouses, the absent husband and the non-payment of maintenance], the fact that he is not sending her maintenance, the oath of the wife to that effect in the relevant mosque, her divorcing herself for non-payment in one pronouncement; the husband's right to her return to him if he comes back with financial ease during her *'idda* [the three month 'waiting' period during which she cannot remarry], unless the pronouncement [of repudiation] is the third pronouncement, and after the judge allows her returning to him upon evidence to the judge that her return is needed, leaving the possibility of further evidence to the absent husband and the production of witnesses. The oath of the wife requires her physical presence, in the said place, by order of the judge; the judge must hear her pronouncement of the divorce, the judge then hears witnesses, and the document is dated.[389]

---

[386] registers, *sijillat*.   [387] Gharnati, *WM*, 17–21.
[388] Gharnati, *WM*, 22. On the substantive dimension of marriage and divorce, see Chapter 10.
[389] Maintenance, *nafaqa*; her divorcing herself, *tatliquha nafsaha*; in one pronouncement, *talqa wahida*; further evidence to the absent husband, *irja' al-hujja lil-gha'eb*, ibid. 23.

Let me turn now to the thirteenth/nineteenth century Moroccan author, Muhammad Ibn Muhammad Bannani, known as Fir'awn (pharaoh), whose collection of formulae under the title *The Fes forms* is dated 1262/1846:[390] here there is no introduction, but the formulae cover similar ground, namely family and economic transactions. Corresponding sections on divorce in Fes, seven centuries after the Granadan collection, feature formulae for the revocable divorce, divorce before consummation of the marriage—which entails, in contrast to consumed marriage, the payment of only half of the dower— divorce pursuant to conditions introduced in the marriage contract. An example of a formula of the rights and duties when the divorce is initiated by the woman against forms of compensation to the husband (*khul'*) is also given. The *khul'* contractual formula is comprehensive and reads as follows:

Talaq al-khul'. Praise be to God, the wife X daughter of W has divorced her husband Y son of Z, against the forfeiting of all the rights which she may have had, [including] the dower and other money[391] in her full knowledge of all details, and in the observance of the 'waiting' period[392] till the end, her acknowledgement of no pregnancy and his acquiescent supposition of the same, and, if she is pregnant, until birth, and the termination thereafter of her maintenance under the law, and the rent of the household, the fees of a guardian [here a list of consequences on guardianship follows], and the fact that they have jointly renounced all possible legal actions and consequences deriving from marriage in a full total and complete renunciation;[393] following which the husband has pronounced one divorce *khul'i* after having known her,[394] and in accordance with which they have separated in front of witnesses and in their full knowledge ...[395]

The model *khul'i* divorce is followed in the notary's collection by other types of divorce, including the formulae for the irrevocable three-time repudiation,[396] and the conditional divorce which the wife can stipulate in her marriage contract. In that case, the marriage would be terminated upon her demand if, under the contract's initial terms, the husband forces her to live outside an agreed area 'like the city of Fes', or if he commits himself not to live far from her for a given period of time and forfeits his promise. In these contracts, which are described as contracts

---

[390] Muhammad ibn Muhammad al-Bannani (d. 1261/1845), known as Fir'awn, *al-Watha'eq al-Fasiyya* (The Fes formulae), 'Abd al-Karim Masrur ed. (Rabat, 1988). (Hereinafter *WF.*)

[391] This translation is guesswork, as the original, *'wa ghayrih naqduh wukalayh'*, is unclear to me.

[392] *'idda* again, which is the period of three months before the divorced wife can remarry.

[393] Here Fir'awn includes a variation: 'her tutor A was present and he guaranteed the husband against any detriment which may affect the said husband because of her, so that if payment is due, he the tutor will be liable in a mandatory fashion on his own property'.

[394] The text reads awkwardly: *ba'd bina'ahu biha*, where the word *bina'* is written wrongly (*hamza 'ala al-satr* instead of *hamza bi-kursi al-ya*). Does that mean that the husband acknowledged he had sexual intercourse with her, perhaps to avoid paying more dower, as some schools stipulate the payment of half the dower in case there is a separation between spouses before sexual intercourse?

[395] has divorced, *ikhtala'at*; under the law, *shar'an*; a guardian, *hadina*; her tutor, *wali*; after taking cognizance of her, *ba'da bina'ih biha*, Fir'awn, *WF*, 13.   [396] ibid. 14–15.

of engagement or commitment,[397] it is possible for the wife to be freed from her obligations 'without consulting the judge and without the solemnization by oath or by witnesses'.[398] The wife must only pronounce the requisite formula in the mosque, in front of two witnesses.[399] This seems to offer the wife significant leeway to decide herself upon the separation.

Another example of apparently increased control by the unhappily wedded woman over her affidavit, and over her fate, appears in a formula which the earlier Granadan judge did not mention, and which is included in *The Fes forms*. This is the demand for divorce by the wife in the event of her husband's mistreatment, which is entitled 'The demand by the wife to get her *khul* back after separation because of her husband's mistreatment'. This title indicates that the wife is entitled to receive the money she forfeited to obtain a divorce where marriage has been discontinued because of ill-treatment by her husband:

Demand by the wife to get her khul' back after separation because of her husband's mistreatment. God be praised, the witnesses whose names appear after the date [of the document] name the two spouses, X son of Y and W daughter of Z, and confirm their full knowledge of them under the law, and testify that they have heard ample talk from the people who know and others,[400] to the effect that the aforementioned husband was mistreating his aforementioned wife by beating her and cursing her, and variously violated his relationship with her as he would abandon her and injure her with all types of harmful behaviour, and he continued in this fashion and did not stop until she freed herself from him with the money forfeited for her divorce,[401] all the above in the [witnesses'] full knowledge and certainty from ample talk, and their testimony, for which they stand responsible, is recorded in the present document: [signed] A, B, C, D, E, F, G, H, I, J, K, L, sons of M have testified to the above, which now stands [confirmed].

God be praised, this is certified by the respected jurist and virtuous scholar, the judge of the city of N, by the name of . . . , God protect him, with the payment of the above fee and in full authenticity of the debt, God protect him, for what is owed to him for the above for the date aforementioned.

These examples offer a convenient reference for the development of Islamic law from the source-material of the notarial documents' genre, since it is possible to compare some aspects of the Maliki law in its practice as portrayed by notaries seven centuries apart. In family law, the text of the earlier Spanish judge on the woman's right to initiate divorce yields interesting differences in substance and in style over the later Moroccan jurist, suggesting that the late Malikis have firmly incorporated what is more generally associated with Hanbali stipulations giving

---

[397] *'uqud al-tatawwu'at*, ibid. 15 ff.
[398] *duna bayyina wa la yamin yalzamuha fi dhalik wa la mashurat qadin.* ibid. 15.
[399] Fir'awn, *WF*, 16.
[400] Variation: from a large number of women and servants and neighbours.
[401] Literally bought him off, *iftadat minhu.*

the wife more authority,[402] and (perhaps) expanded the sway of divorce on the wife's request in case of mistreatment to the extent of her receiving back the price paid to get the divorce if the husband renders the marriage intolerable.

But it is mostly in terms of style, that is, the clarity of the documents and their practical usefulness for the parties, that the development of the law is manifest. This will not prevent the retention of specific legal formulae which the non-initiate might well understand but would not be able to reproduce. The protection of the jargon, as for any other legal system, remains to date a staple of Middle Eastern law. Whether for acts and contracts with the notary-public, or for judgments by courts, or even for private documents drafted by lawyers, the legal trade protects its expertise in the Middle East no differently from the profession elsewhere in the world. But change in style there is, and, as in the example of divorce for mistreatment in the two Maliki notaries from Arab Spain and nineteenth-century Morocco, also in substance.

One thing is certain: writing is crucial and widely used in evidence, even if it needs to be supplemented by witnesses when the material is not entrusted to the court directly. On the importance of writing in urban society, one can find evidence in other sources, such as in one delightful story in the novellas of Badiʿ al-Zaman al-Hamadhani (d. 398/1007), master of the genre of short rhymed stories—known as *Maqamat*—in classical Islam. The episode features the *Maqamat* hero, Abu al-Fath al-Iskandarani, who is the victim of a pretentious, wealthy man inviting him to a sophisticated meal. The invitation turns into a nightmare, and our hero is so sick of his host's bombast that he ends up running away without having lunch, and hates the promised dish forever. Here is the rich host's insufferable soliloquy:

We ended up at his house door. 'This is my home', he said, 'how much do you think I spent on the door? Well I spent a lot, how do you see its make and style? Have you by God ever seen anything like it?' ... Then he knocked and we went in the corridor. He said: 'God make you thrive, o house, and o wall may you never be shaken ... Now look at these beautiful staircases, imagine all the house entries and exits, and ask me: how did you get it and what ingenuity did you manage to contract [its purchase]?

Well, I had a neighbour nicknamed Abu Sulaiman living in this place, who had more money than he could store, and more gold and silver than could be weighed. He died, peace on him, and left an heir who squandered the wealth on wine and songs, and destroyed it in gambling and game, so I got worried that necessity drive him to sell the house to a stranger in a moment of weakness, or put it under threat, such as I might see it escape me and I would wail over its loss until I die. So I resorted to buying some valuable clothes, which I took and presented to him, and enticed him to buy them on credit, which the miserable thinks is blessing and the retarded believes is gift. And I asked him for a deed attesting the debt, which he executed and contracted to me. But I avoided asking him to settle his debt, until I could see that his clothes were getting thinner, whereupon I went and requested payment. He asked for some time,

---

[402] See Chapter 10, nn. 7–10 and accompanying text.

which I gave. He asked for more clothes, which I brought, and I asked him for his house in guarantee, and requested a deed to attest it, which he executed, then I gradually induced him into further transactions until he sold me the house . . .[403]

The written contract, clearly, is the determining legal clue in the story. This should be expected in a Baghdad of such sophistication as the *Maqamat* genre. But it does not mean that orality is superior to writing, and we have seen the complex interplay at work in some of the passages in the *mufti* and *qadi* literature. What needs to be acknowledged, against the received picture, is that writing offers an important anchor point for evidence. Nor should it be surprising that custom is also widely recognized as a determining element in the law, even if the received methodology of Islamic lawyers in the *usul al-fiqh* genre rejects custom as a formal legal 'source'.

Custom

Custom, which is technically not considered as a 'source' of Islamic law by the jurists,[404] needs to be revisited for an appreciation of the operation of law in the classical age and the modern period alike. In the absence of consistent law reporting, rules cannot be understood outside customary practice.

To correct both the generally received idea of a pure intellectual exercise—if not sheer casuistry—as the essence of the books of *fiqh*, and the formal rejection of custom as 'source' by Islamic law,[405] let me turn again to the great fifth/eleventh century jurist Sarakhsi. The *Mabsut*'s book of sale is replete with references to custom.

I have mentioned how, after defining sale, Sarakhsi had proceeded to discuss the law of sale's nemesis, *riba*, and offered ways to avoid the constraints of formalism in such important contracts on 'future things' as *salam* (sale with deferred delivery) and *istisna'* (manufacture).

In another example where formalism is consciously contradicted, I can refer again to Sarakhsi's discussion of the contract of manufacturing, this time in the context of deferred delivery. This is a comment on Marwazi's enunciation that 'if a person asks another to manufacture two gloves, or a hat or a recipient or vessel in copper, by analogy, this is not allowed'.[406] Sarakhsi explains first the reasoning of his predecessor. What is being manufactured does not exist and the Prophet forbids

[403] Badiʿ al-Zaman al-Hamadhani, *Maqamat*, 5th edn. (Beirut, 1965) (1st edn. with the commentaries of Muhammad ʿAbduh in 1898), 107–8: deed, *wathiqa*; on credit, *nasiyya*; contracted it, *ʿaqadaha*; requested payment from him, *iqtadaytuhu*; guarantee, *rahina*; transactions, *muʿamalat*.

[404] It never appears among the 'four principles, *usul*', see below n. 436 and accompanying sections on sources and *ijtihad*, and my criticism of the traditional approach to the discipline.

[405] A useful treatment of the subject of custom can be found in Issam Chanbour, *La coutume et l'usage conventionnel en droit musulman* (Beirut, 1981) esp. 61–109 (custom not formally a source of law), and 111–69 (several examples in various legal areas in which it operates in as such practice). Conclusion, at 172: 'Mais les controverses soulevées ne revêtent pas un caractère assez général pour qu'il soit permis, selon la doctrine, d'attribuer au *ʿurf* la valeur d'une règle légale (*asl*)'.

[406] Sarakhsi, *al-Mabsut*, xii, 138.

the sale of what doesn't exist. This is the rule. 'But we say that we have abandoned analogy because of the use of the people, [as] they have been dealing in this fashion from the time of the Prophet to this day without contradictor. The use by the people without contradictor is one of the fundamental principles.'[407]

Custom or usage, *'urf*, is a recurring reference for Sarakhsi. On a question of criteria for measuring and weighing commodities, Abu Yusuf (d. 182/798), one of the two most famous students of Abu Hanifa, is quoted in a typical formula: 'What matters in all things is *'urf* '.[408]

In these remarks, Sarakhsi's distinctive imprint operates in terms of language with such key concepts as intention, tradition, or usage, and the way people deal with each another. This is set against formalism, and against hallowed rules and received 'source methodology'. Nor should it be particularly surprising in the law merchant, which has been the principal area everywhere in the world where development arises from professional practice.[409]

But customary law is pervasive in the Middle East, and not only in the practice and law of merchants. Other illustrations are as varied as the urbanism of the old city of Tunis, which constitutes the recipient of a millennium of building practices defined by customary law,[410] the writing down in 1359/1939 of 'customs and conventions governing relations among the pearl-fishing crews' of pre-oil Kuwait,[411] or the *amin*, a figure from the Jewish Moroccan world of jewellers, who, as a practitioner with some knowledge of Biblical law, presides over an informal process of arbitration within the trade.[412] The importance of local uses will obviously vary from one country to another, and will depend within each country on various factors premised on professional, geographical, and other social settings. Many local uses will find an explanation in customary law, such as the process of succession and power-sharing in Saudi Arabia, which takes place as a compromise between the two branches of power in the State—the Sa'ud family and the religious jurists descended from the family of Muhammad 'Abd al-Wahhab, the twelfth/eighteenth century-legal scholar and eponym of the Wahhabi school.[413] Similarly, there is documented analysis on Bedouin law in matters of crime. This is another instance of a

---

[407] analogy, *qiyas*; without contradictor, *nakir munkir*; use, *ta'amul*; one of the fundamental principles, *asl min al-usul kabir*. ibid. [408] *al-Mabsut*, xii, 142.

[409] For a remarkable treatment on the basis of a close reading of Sarakhsi's *Mabsut* and other classics, see generally Abraham Udovitch, *Partnership and profit in medieval Islam*, above n. 141. The point is developed in Chapters 8 and 9.

[410] Originally adumbrated in Robert Brunschvig, 'Urbanisme médiéval et droit musulman', *Etudes d'islamologie*, 2 vols (Paris, 1976) ii, 7–35, it was developed by Basem Hakim on the basis of a manuscript on the regulation of the city of Tunis, *Arabic-Islamic cities: building and planning principles* (London, 1986).

[411] Herbert Liebesny, 'Administration and legal development in Arabia: the Persian Gulf principalities', *Middle East Journal*, 10, 1956, 33–42, citation at 39.

[412] Information kindly provided by an anthropologist colleague from field work in Morocco.

[413] The central issue in Middle Eastern monarchies is whether sons are entitled to the succession, or whether brothers could be first in line. This is essentially determined by custom. In Saudi Arabia and Jordan, succession used to go to the brothers of the King, although the late King Hussein did appoint his son at the last moment instead of his brother, who was until then the constitutional

pervasive Middle Eastern pattern which was identified as early as Hammurabi, persisted in the dichotomous division in the penal law of the Qur'anic verses between tribal and 'normative' justice,[414] and has remained to date in Jordan and in Saudi Arabia a source of law parallel to the state legal structure.[415] Nor has the relevance of customary law as it interacts with modern legislation subsided. It extends to several social areas, not least the regulation of water and water rights in many contemporary Arab and Middle Eastern societies.[416]

The pervasive use of custom cannot be understated: it appears in the *fiqh* books extensively, in the manual of judges, in collections of fatwas and formulas, and it also appears in judgments, as in the ready reference by the judge 'to the usual dower' when the plaintiff's original contract of marriage was lost.[417] The famous legal aphorism of the Ottoman Majalla, 'what is known as custom is as binding as a condition in a contract',[418] feeds on an age-old tradition which is obvious in the standard contracts which the jurists always encouraged practitioners to follow. Ibn Abi al-Dam's book is replete with reference to custom, for instance when the price is omitted in a sale.[419] In that case, a disagreement between buyer and seller will lead to rescission of the sale only if there is a significant discrepancy between the price paid and the average market price.[420] The importance of the discrepancy is appreciated according to usage: a differential fraction of one-tenth would not lead to the failure of the contract for most scholars because of '*lésion*',[421] but even then there is no hard-and-fast rule: 'This will only be decided by custom ... Anything which custom and the people of the trade do not consider *lésion* will not be so considered'.[422]

Crown Prince. In Saudi Arabia, the system weighs in favour of brothers, in a tradition which was also Ottoman, and which was incorporated in the 1876 Ottoman Constitution, Art. 3: 'The Ottoman Sunni sultanate, and the great Caliphate, goes to the eldest sons of the family of Othman in accordance with established rule'. In Morocco, King Hasan was succeeded by his eldest son.

[414] Above, texts accompanying nn. 10–16 (Hammurabi, Islamic law), n. 284 (case-law in the seventeenth century.)

[415] For a good overview of the literature, F. H. Stewart, 'Tribal law in the Arab world: a review of the literature', *International Journal of Middle East Studies*, 19, 1987, 473–90.

[416] On water rights and the *shari'a*, my 'The quest for water use principles: reflections on *shari'a* and custom in the Middle East', in J. A. Allan and C. Mallat, eds., *Water in the Middle East: legal, political and commercial implications* (London, 1995) 127–37 and references cited.

[417] Tripoli, 89, *Shaikh Ahmad ibn Shaikh Badr al-Din (Attorney for Khadija bint Ibrahim alias Ibn Malha) v. Kamal ibn 'Ali al-Najjar (Attorney for Fatima bint al-Hajj 'Abd al-Rahman)*, above n. 271 and accompanying text: *sadaqat amthal al-muwakkila*.

[418] Art. 43 of the Majalla, *Al-ma'ruf 'urfan kal-mashrut shartan*, is a formula one finds in the classical *fiqh* books. See e.g. the reference to the *Durar* of Mulla Khusraw (d. 885/1480) and to the *Fatawa Hindiyya* in one commentary of the Majalla, Salim Baz, *Sharh al-Majalla* (Beirut edn., 1923 (orig. edn. 1887)), 37–8. A very close formulation can already be found in Kasani, *Bada'e'*, v, 167: *al-ma'ruf bil-'urf kal-mashrut bil-shart*. See further details in section on custom in civil law in Chapter 8, and section on custom in the law merchant, Chapter 9.   [419] Ibn Abi al-Dam, *Kitab adab al-qada'*, 493–4.

[420] ibid. at 494: market price, *thaman al-mithl*.

[421] Sarakhsi has an alluring expression: *al-yasir min al-tafawut ghayr mu'tabar*, a slight difference is not considered, *Mabsut*, xii, 133.

[422] Ibn Abi al-Dam, *Kitab adab al-qada'*, 494: usage, *'ada*; French *lésion*, *ghubn*; custom, *'urf*; people of the trade, *ahl al-'urf*.

We even have a full-fledged treatise on custom by one of the late jurists of the Hanafi school, Muhammad Amin ibn 'Abidin (d. 1252/1836).

The treatise of Ibn 'Abidin is divided into three major parts, which follow a telling introduction: I have written it, says the thirteenth/nineteenth-century jurist, 'because I did not see anyone who has given the subject its due, or explained it as it deserved . . . '.

The first and second parts of the treatise try to put some order into the concept of custom by distinguishing 'custom in contradiction with a legal disposition' (Part 1),[423] and 'custom in contradiction with the apparent text' (Part 2).[424] The third and last part discusses various derivations and applications.[425]

It is true, says Ibn 'Abidin in the first part, that when custom contradicts an established textual rule, the latter prevails. There may be exceptions, however, notably when the customary exception to the rule is general and does not fly in the face of a Prophetic *hadith*, or when the custom is specific to one field or one region. The well-known example of manufacturing,[426] which allows the sale of an object which has yet to be produced, is an instance of the first type. Customs which may be specific to one particular city are an example of the second type. They will prevail in that city though not elsewhere. While some might be tempted to see custom prevailing over a *hadith*, this is hardly acceptable. However, it is clear that custom may prevail over analogy.[427] In this first part of the treatise recurs the notion of the importance of custom in facilitating people's lives. The jurists call it the 'determination' of custom amongst people of the trade, notably merchants.[428]

In the second part, the arguments of Ibn 'Abidin veer radically. When custom is at loggerheads with an established legal rule, he solves the contradiction by insisting that the good jurist cannot be unaware of the customs of his age. It is not sufficient for him to know the law in the book, so custom should be made to prevail. The well-known adage on 'the changes in the rules in accordance with the times' is illustrated in several ways. For instance the need to remunerate teachers of the Qur'an and *hadith*, or mosque leaders and orators, even if previous texts had refused payment to such apparently charitable religious activities. Otherwise, says Ibn 'Abidin, we would lose all our preachers and religious teachers.

Other examples include, contrary to the distinction made in some classical texts between immediate and indirect causation, the strict liability of the entrepreneur,[429] of the custodian for the money of the orphan, and of other tortfeasors previously beyond the pale in the law of compensation because of that distinction.[430] 'Therefore the *mufti* cannot be stopped by the inertia of reports in the

---

[423] Ibn 'Abidin, *Majmu'at rasa'el*, (collected treaties), 2 vols., Beirut, n.d., ii, 116–25, '*idha khalafa al-'urf al-dalil al-shar'i*'.   [424] ibid. 125–34, '*idha khalafa al-'urf zahir al-riwaya*'.
[425] ibid. 134–47, '*fi dhikr ba'd furu' muhimma mabniyya 'alal-'urf*'.
[426] Again *istisna'*. See above n. 190 and section preceding n. 406.
[427] *Al-'urf qadin 'ala al-qiyas (wa laysa) 'alal-hadith*. Ibn 'Abidin, *Majmu'at rasa'el*, 121.
[428] *mukhassas*, determinate or specific, *al-muta'araf bayn al-tujjar*, what is usual amongst merchants, Ibn 'Abidin, *Majmu'at rasa'el*, 124.   [429] Entrepreneur, *sa'i*.
[430] Ibn 'Abidin, *Majmu'at rasa'el*, 126–8.

established texts, and ignore the times and the people of his time. Otherwise, many rights would be lost ... '.[431]

Summing up:

Since the *mufti* must follow custom even if it contradicts the written text in the established reports, is there a difference between general custom and special custom, as in the first part [of the treatise], that is when custom contradicts the textual rule? I say: there is no difference between them except that general custom establishes general rules and special custom establishes a special rule. In conclusion, the rule of custom applies to all people, whether custom is general or special, with general custom in all countries applying to people in all countries, whereas a custom special to one area applies only to this area.[432]

The last part of the treatise also includes several illustrations adduced from the experience of Ibn 'Abidin as practitioner. One example is a fatwa on the need to consider water sources running through a large mansion in Damascus as part of the house, even if not technically a fixture under established law. Otherwise, he explains, the house would not be worth half its value, and the people in town have always considered water sources as part of that mansion and its large orchard, where they have taken to walks. It does not matter that the law would not have included those sources as part of the sale.[433]

Other examples of the prevalence of custom are the validity of writing as evidence, especially in merchants' books,[434] and the equality of women and men in receiving their benefit under *waqf*s despite the rules of inheritance apportioning the division in a two-to-one ratio in favour of the male. These two examples are significant in appreciating the shifting social relations in the Levant of the early nineteenth century.[435] This must have been true, *mutatis mutandis*, at other times in history.

'Sources' revisited

This sampling of the various manifestations of the *shari'a*—*fiqh* compendia, custom, judgments, manuals for judges and *mufti*s, fatwas, contracts and formularies, custom, and literary and historical texts as a whole—against a wider setting which draws upon a multi-layered Middle Eastern legal pattern—should allow us now to consider the so-called 'sources' of Islamic law in a different light.

The argument over the sources is generally construed, following a passage of Shafi'i (d. 204/820) in his *Risala*,[436] as the existence of 'four major sources or roots

---

[431] *kulluhu wa amthaluhu dala'el wadiha 'ala anna al-mufti laysa lahu al-jumud 'ala al-manqul fi kutub zahir al-riwaya min ghayr mura'at al-zaman wa ahlihi wa-illa yudayyi' huquqan kathiratan.* ibid. 131.   [432] ibid. 132.

[433] ibid. 136.   [434] ibid. 144.   [435] ibid. 145–6.

[436] The text of the *Risala* was edited in Arabic by Ahmad Shaker (Cairo, 1940) passage at 498–508. See also Shafi'i, *al-Umm*, 7 vols. (Cairo, 1903–8) vii, 274. The *Risala* is available in English in a translation by Majid Khadduri, *al-Risala fi usul al-fiqh: treatise on the foundations of Islamic jurisprudence* (Baltimore, 1961, repr. Cambridge, 1987). See for state-of-the-art discussion on the *Risala*, Wael Hallaq, *A history of Islamic legal theories* (Cambridge, 1997) 21–35, and Radwan al-Sayyed, 'Al-Shafi'i wal-risala', *al-Ijtihad*, 8, 1990, 65–74.

(*usul*) of law. The first of these is naturally the Qur'an'. The other three are the *sunna* (the traditions of the Prophets), *ijma'* (consensus of the community or of legal scholars), and *qiyas* (analogy).[437] Although his *Introduction to Islamic law* repeats this argument several times,[438] Joseph Schacht was more discerning when he observed that intellectual developments in legal theory in the Islamic tradition retained a logic of their own, which rarely corresponded to the practice of Islamic law. In fact, he wrote elsewhere in his *Introduction*, there are 'two material sources', the Qur'an and the *sunna*, 'a method' (analogy) and 'a declaratory authority. It follows that this last, *ijma'*, is the decisive instance; it guarantees the authenticity of the two material sources and determines their correct interpretation'.[439]

Schacht's afterthought is deservedly given prominence by an authoritative book on comparative law: 'It will be obvious that this classical system of the four "roots" of Islamic law comprises very different things, namely two sources—the Koran and the *sunna* —a method—the use of analogy—and a judgement—that of *igma*'.[440]

If sources mean textual origins, then there is little doubt that a concept like *qiyas* is out of place. As 'analogy', *qiyas* is an analytical or methodological tool which is hardly characteristic of Islamic, in contrast to English or French, law. 'Sources' should be understood in a less formalistic sense, so that the approach to law in Middle Eastern history takes into account a wealth of primarily written documents which, all together, form the rich and complex culture of Middle Eastern law.

In the same vein, consensus, *ijma'*, is hardly a source. Whether one deals with hair-splitting and inconclusive arguments in the Islamic tradition over consensus being one among scholars as opposed to a consensus shared by the full community of Muslims, or whether 'consensus' is put in plain legal language as a result in the form of a 'judgement', the word 'source' is misleading in the case of *ijma'*. As with the other nebulous 'sources' which often find their way into textbooks, such complicated phraseology should not be introduced to students of Islamic law under the pretext that the discipline is a special and distinct legal animal on account of a separate set of sources, namely *qiyas, ijma', ra'i, istihsan, siyasa shar'iyya, masaleh mursala*, and the like: all these Arabic words either become hollow when translated into simple English terms, respectively analogy, consensus, opinion, preference, legal policy, overarching social considerations; alternatively, they could be understood as categories belonging to the specific, sophisticated, and peculiarly complex field within Islamic law of *usul al-fiqh* (again the roots, sources, or fundaments of *fiqh*), which operates at the confluence of law, logic, and philosophy.[441]

---

[437] Coulson, *History of Islamic law*, 55, 55–61.

[438] Schacht, *Introduction to Islamic law*, 60, 72, 114.   [439] ibid. 114.

[440] Konrad Zweigert and Hein Kötz, *An introduction to comparative law*, 3rd edn. (Oxford, 1998) 308.

[441] See the discussion of *usul* above Chapter 1 n. 9 and my short contributions to the field therein listed. On Sunni *usul*, a good introduction in Arabic is by 'Abd al-Wahhab al-Khallaf, *'ilm usul al-fiqh*, 7th edn. (Cairo, 1956) cited above Chapter 1 n. 5; in English, Hallaq, *A history of Islamic legal theories*, cited above n. 436; Muhammad Hashim Kamali, *Principles of Islamic jurisprudence* (Malaysia, 1989, repr. Cambridge, 1991); On Shi'i *usul*, Muhammad Baqer al-Sadr, *Al-ma'alim al-jadida fil-usul*

Usul al-fiqh is a discipline which still awaits a better appreciation of its distinctiveness in comparative jurisprudence, or perhaps more appropriately, in comparative logic.[442] The lawyer should therefore proceed carefully with words which are either simple and non-distinct, or concepts which belong in the category of methodological instruments of thinking proper to comparative logic. A fresh reading of Shafiʿiʾs *Risala* would easily find supportive evidence for various conclusions, not all consistent with one another. '*Istihsan* (preference)', the *Risala* says for instance, 'is pleasure, art for art'.[443] There is even one passage where Shafiʿi sounds resolutely at odds with the sophisticated construction associated with the 'four sources'. Legal interpretation, he writes, is the same as analogy: *ijtihad* and *qiyas* 'are two words for a same meaning'.[444] Law is precedent.

Rather than interminable discussions on specific Islamic legal-logical categories, it is the variety of legal layers in the Islamic and pre-Islamic tradition, and the compelling stylistic ensemble which should appear as the distinctive feature, if any, of the system. An insistence on formal sources in disregard of the immense wealth of the tradition is a recipe for impoverishment, as is the widespread use of the famous cliché of 'the closure of the gate of *ijtihad*', so often brandished as 'proof' of the 'medieval backwardness' and 'immobilism' of Muslim societies, a concept to which I now turn.

Ijtihad and schools

Contrary to earlier twentieth century scholarship, recent studies have suggested that the phenomenon known as the 'closing of the door of interpretation',[445] which was ascribed to the *shariʿa* towards the tenth or eleventh century CE, is unfounded.[446] One easy rebuttal of such a strange theory is the simple fact that a 'legal closure' in any society or civilisation, since silence itself is interpretation, cannot be sustained. Within the Islamic legal tradition proper, some changes in style and form have been already illustrated, even if the textual original sources are naturally resistant to alteration once they become canonized in collective memory and fixed in specialists' books:

> Much has been said of the 'closing of the gate of *ijtihad*'. The phrase, however, has never been documented. I have not come across any statement to this effect in any document of the Middle Ages when such 'closing' was supposed to have taken effect. To my mind, this

(The new configuration of *usul*) (Beirut, 1964), and a more elaborate 'comparative' treatment by Muhammad Taqi al-Hakim, *Al-usul al-ʿamma lil-fiqh al-muqaran* (General principles in comparative jurisprudence) (Beirut, 1963). See also Robert Brunschvig, 'Les *usul al-fiqh* imamites à leur stade ancien', in *Le Shiʿisme imamite* (Paris, 1970).

[442] This argument is developed in my 'On the philosophy of Islamic law', forthcoming in Chibli Mallat and Leslie Tramontini, eds., *From Boston to Beirut via Baghdad, Festschrift for John Donohue* (Beirut).   [443] *innama al-istihsan taladhdhudh*, Shafiʿi, *Risala*, Shaker ed., 507.

[444] *al-ijtihad wal-qiyas isman li-maʿna wahed*, ibid. 477.   [445] *ighlaq bab al-ijtihad*.

[446] An encapsulation of the debate can be read, together with a rich chapter on 'Islamic law and Islamic society', in Humphreys, *Islamic history*, 209–27 at 212: 'By the late fifth/eleventh century, the

phrase would make sense in two ways: first, as putting an end to the formation of add-itional *madhhabs*, the 'personal' schools of law; and second, as putting an end to the free play of *ijtihad* in the regular disputations [of jurisconsults] . . . The 'closing of the gate' to the formation of new *madhhabs* could only be the result of refusal by the jurisconsults themselves to form them . . . This 'closing' may be said to have occurred in the fourth/tenth century with the formation of the last of the four *madhhabs* . . . The fourth/tenth century put an end to new *madhhabs*, but not to *ijtihad*, since the method of disputation, the scholastic method, which could not exist without *ijtihad*, did not reach the peak of its development until the fifth/eleventh century.[447]

There is no point in going over, yet again, the tortured discussions about *ijtihad*. In recent years, such discussions have filled many a volume, both in the Middle East[448] and in Western scholarship.[449] Suffice it to say that the passage just quoted brings together, in a particularly felicitous and novel way, two central themes in Islamic law, those of '*ijtihad*, interpretation' and '*madhhab*, school'.

The significance of the schools of law is not well understood by historians of the *shariʿa*. The early rise of the schools in the second/eighth century has now been documented with some precision in their legal ordering and classification of the original textual fonts of Islamic law, the Qurʾan and the *sunna*;[450] but the reasons why the several hundred schools which were extant in the early centuries have vanished to give way to only four recognized schools in Sunnism are still unclear. The received 'official' history suggests that the process of maturity had reached such sophistication that it was considered superfluous to allow more schools to emerge. There may be some validity in this assessment, since recognition by the

idea had begun to spread that the "gate of *ijtihad*" was closed—that is, that future jurists were not entitled to evolve new theories of jurisprudence, or even (in more rigid formulations) to depart from the established rulings of their *madhhab* [school] where these were applicable to the case before them. This was no simple and rapid process, however, nor does it mean that *fiqh* became more and more a purely scholastic enterprise devoid of flexibility and realism. In the first place, many jurists contested the new doctrine for several centuries; it was not universally accepted until the tenth/sixteenth century. *Second, ijtihad (the application of reason to the solution of the legal issues) is a very complex concept which comprises many different levels of inquiry*' (emphasis added).

[447] George Makdisi, *The rise of colleges* (Edinburgh, 1981) 290.

[448] The journal *al-Ijtihad* dedicated four full issues to the subject of *al-ijtihad wal tajaddud* (legal interpretation and renewal) in 1990–1; see also the closing assessment by Khaled Ziadeh, 'Hal al-ijtihad amr mumkin, qiraʾa fi malaff al-ijtihad wal-tajaddud (Is *ijtihad* possible? A reading in the dossier on legal interpretation and renewal)', *Al-Ijtihad*, 11–12, 1991, 375–82.

[449] Classical presentation in Schacht, *Introduction*, 69–73, 209–10 and Coulson, *History*, 81–2. This view was challenged by Wael Hallaq in a Ph.D. thesis with Farhat Ziadeh at the University of Washington, The gate of ijtihad: a study in Islamic legal history, 1983, published as 'Was the gate of *ijtihad* closed?', *International Journal of Middle East Studies*, 16, 1984, 3–41; see also Bernard Weiss, 'Interpretation in Islamic law: the theory of *ijtihad*', *American Journal of Comparative Law*, 26, 1978, 199–212; Rudolph Peters, '*Idjtihad* and *taqlid* in 18th and 19th century Islam', *Die Welt des Islams*, 20, 1980, 131–45. The anchoring of the image of 'gate closure' in Western literature seems to go back to the colourful but simplistic rendering of Mustafa Ataturk's legal reforms, in which he jettisoned the whole Islamic legal tradition, by 'Count' L. Ostrorog, *The Angora* [Ankara] *reform* (London, 1927). See also S. Ali-Karamali and F. Dunne, 'The *ijtihad* controversy', *Arab Law Quarterly*, 9, 1994, 238–57.

[450] Schacht, *Origins of Muhammadan jurisprudence*, above n. 92; Melchert, *The formation of the Sunni schools of law*, above n. 115; Calder, *Studies in early Muslim jurisprudence*, above n. 12; Motzki, *Die Anfänge des islamischen Jurisprudenz*, above n. 96.

Prince bestowed on any school official legitimacy and allowed its judgments to be enforced by the Prince's coercive authority. The Prince would therefore allow only a limited number of recognized schools which he could control. But it is also suggested that the geographical expansion of the schools and their dependence on trade routes explain the dwindling and eventual disappearance of once important *madhhab*s such as the Syrian Uza'i's (d. 157/774), although the apparent economic marginalization of the Syrian economic sphere after the establishment of the 'Abbasid empire in Baghdad in the middle of the second/eighth century might more readily explain the collapse of the Uza'i school than any 'economic' explanation could account for the disappearance of the school of the Iraqi Tabari (d. 310/921).

In another possible theory, the phenomenon of the schools must be understood in the light of philosophical-theological controversies in the 'Abbasid period (the period in the middle of the third/ninth century known as the *Mihna*, or Inquisition) which allowed traditionalism, in the form of the Hanbali school, to take root and open the way to a retrospective legitimization of the other three Sunni schools.[451] But this will remain conjectural without a more detailed study of classic Hanbalism, which is a puzzling school in the history of Islamic law.

From the beginning Hanbalism appears more as a theological current than a proper legal school, even if Hanbali *madrasas* can be found in various parts of the classical Muslim world: a classical Hanafi jurist like Sarakhsi cites Ahmad ibn Hanbal only three times, according to the indexation of his extensive treatise by Khalil al-Mays, whereas other Sunni schools' eponyms, including Malik and Shafi'i, are often quoted and discussed.[452] Over a longer historic span, Hanbalism seems to have been 'legitimized' at the level of the state retrospectively with the victory of Wahhabism in the Arabian desert in the twelfth/eighteenth century and the stabilization of Saudi rule in the larger part of the Arabian peninsula in the twentieth century.[453]

The history of Hanbalism is also puzzling because it is not associated with any geographical area in the vast Muslim world save the Kingdom of Saudi Arabia. Only there and in some adjoining states in the United Arab Emirates federation does one find Hanbalis in any significant number, whereas the other Sunni schools are coextensive with larger territories and straddle several states. Even for Saudi Arabia, Hanbalism came only in the eighteenth century on the wings of 'the Wahhabi call', and how much Wahhabism can be equated with Hanbalism is yet to be researched.

Could Hanbalism, as a maverick historical phenomenon compared to the three other Sunni schools, help in a reassessment of 'the significance of the schools of

---

[451] G. Makdisi, 'The significance of the Sunni schools of law in Islamic religious history', *International Journal of Middle East Studies*, 11, 1979, 1–8.

[452] Al-Mays, *Faharis kitab al-mabsut*, above n. 135, 513.

[453] George Makdisi has written extensively on classical Hanbalism, see most recently his *Ibn 'Aqil* (Edinburgh, 1997), about a leading Hanbali jurist (d. 513/1119) whose work on *usul al-fiqh* was also edited by Makdisi: Ibn 'Aqil, *al-Wadih*, 2 vols. (Beirut, 1996).

law' in the complex system? The answer is not conclusive, for there is no evident difference, in legal style or substantive result, to be found in the Hanbali books of *fiqh*. Hanbalism, because of the association with present-day Saudi Arabia, is often equated with a rigid, conservative literalism. In the face of impressionistic research, the equation of classic Hanbalism with arid conservatism does not hold true. *Al-Mughni*, the great compendium of the leading Hanbali jurist Ibn Qudama (620/1223), does not differ in its treatment of various subjects in any 'qualitative' manner from other classical texts.[454] In the case of family law, the exemplum of the wife's legal position *vis-à-vis* marriage actually yields a totally opposite conclusion to the received idea that Hanbalism is strict and conservative.[455] The Hanbali jurists are, for example, well known for viewing favourably and legitimizing special conditions in the marriage contract that exclusively benefit the woman.[456]

The Zahiris are perhaps more easily contrasted with 'the four orthodox schools'.[457] They, at least, can be judged by an apparently simple criterion which sets them apart from the rest: they are strict literalists, whereas the other schools allow a measure of interpretation. Literalism and interpretivism, in comparative legal jurisprudence, are difficult and unyielding concepts, but they offer a workable division that shows schools of law on the two sides of exegesis. The Zahiris (and allegedly the Hanbalis) appear as literalists who are strictly faithful to the original texts. The other schools (Malikis, Hanafis, and Shafi'is) have historically been better disposed towards the accommodation of a larger room for interpretation. This distinction further allows a description of jurisprudence separating those literalist readers of texts who refuse to be tempted by any reference outside a document's four corners, and the interpretivists who go beyond. Thence a distinction which can be carried into the wider sociological sphere, in which literalism is politically conservative as a principle, as opposed to the 'liberal' and 'progressive' bent of the interpretivists.

This literalist-interpretivist divide appears to be supported if one goes beyond the Sunni schools. Nor is it possible to envisage the schools of law solely on the basis of Sunnism. Twelver Shi'i Islam is said to constitute the fifth *madhhab* known as the Ja'fari school (in reference to the sect's foremost classical jurist-cum-Imam, second/eighth century Ja'far al-Sadeq).[458] The Ja'fari tradition itself

---

[454] These remarks are made on the basis of an examination of sections of Ibn Qudama's great opus, *al-Mughni*, on partnership, water, and family, 'Abd Allah ibn Ahmad Ibn Qudama, *al-Mughni* (Beirut, 14 vols., 1984). There is a useful 2 vol. index to that edn.

[455] Apud e.g. Ibn Khaldun: 'As for Ahmad ibn Hanbal, his followers are rare because of the distance in his school to *ijtihad* and his insistence on keeping to the tradition and reports to explain each another ... They are most attached to the Sunna and the transmission of the *hadith*.' Ibn Khaldun, *al-Muqaddima* (introduction [to his more traditional history known as *Kitab al-'ibar*]) (Cairo edn., n.d.) 448. The full *Muqaddima* was translated by Franz Rosenthal in 3 vols. (New York, 1958) iii, 9; my translation here includes slight amendments.   [456] Details in Chapter 10.

[457] Ignaz Goldziher, *Die Zahiriten: ihr Lehrsystem und ihre Geschichte* (Leipzig, 1884) translated and edited by by Wolfgang Behn as *The Zahiris: their doctrine and their history* (Leiden, 1971).

[458] Zahiris are considered Sunni. Twentieth-century advocates of '*taqrib*, rapprochement' between Sunnis and Shi'is have revived the 'agreement' reached by Nader Shah in the Najaf Congress

has been historically divided between two strongly opposed *madhhab*s, the Usulis and Akhbaris, with the former favouring an interventionist role for the jurists, and the latter strictly narrowing this role to one of 'relaters', as opposed to 'interpreters'. Since the twelfth/eighteenth century, Usulism has been dominant in the Shi'i tradition, with only pockets of Akhbaris in such places as Bahrain, but the debate has carried on well into the twentieth century in Usuli literature.[459]

But things are never so simple, as is substantiated by the American example of Supreme Court Justice Hugo Black, for it is Black's literalism which has resulted in some of the most 'progressive' or 'liberal' decisions of the US Supreme Court.[460] A well-known example in modern Middle Eastern law will show that the analogy is perhaps not so far fetched. The Tunisian legislator was the quintessential literalist when it introduced in the family law of Tunisia the monogamy requirement, based on a literal and strict interpretation of the following Qur'anic verse: 'Marry women as you desire, two, three or four, but if you fear not being fair, then one'.[461] For some literalists, the injunction requesting fairness must be understood strictly, and marriage is consequently allowed with only one woman. In addition, they argue, the sacred text itself explains in the same chapter that 'you will not be able to be fair among women, even if you so wish'.[462] How can you have more than one wife if you can't be fair to all even if you so wish? *Quod erat demonstrandum* for the literalist Tunisian legislator.[463]

Another example of the difficulty of reading conservatism *versus* liberalism into the literalist/interpretivist divide between the schools can be drawn from the classical law tradition. The Zahiris are famed for an instance in which their literalism leads to what one might see retrospectively as a 'non-conservative, liberal' position: by interpreting the *hadith* on the six commodities of *riba* literally,[464] they prevent the prohibition from being extended to any other commodity, and therefore restrict the limitations on transactions accepted on the basis of analogy by the

---

of 1743 to include the Shi'i Twelver school of law as the fifth, Ja'fari *madhhab*, see above n. 107. There exist also important Shi'i non-Ja'fari traditions in the Yemen and in Oman, and various small Muslim sects and offshoots across the world that are neither Shi'i nor Sunni.

[459] On Usulism-Akhbarism, see Mallat, *the Renewal of Islamic law*, 28–35, and the literature cited therein.

[460] Literalism is called interpretivism by John Hart Ely in his celebrated *Democracy and distrust*, whereas looking for norms beyond 'the four corners of the documents' (Ely, *Democracy and distrust* (Cambridge, Mass., 1980) 1) is called non-interpretivism. 'Black is recognized, correctly, as the quintessential interpretivist . . . It happened that in enforcing the principles stated in the constitution, Black was generally in a position of enforcing liberal principles . . . [T]he clauses [of the Bill of Rights] incorporated principles expressed elsewhere in the Constitution, *and that was it*'. (ibid. 2, emphasis in original). See also on Black as consummate literalist, Owen Fiss, *Liberalism divided* (Boulder, Colo., 1996) 112–13: 'The First Amendment provides, "Congress shall make no law abridging the freedom of speech", and, laying the foundation for a certain kind of absolutism, Justice Black insisted again and again that "no law" means "no law"'.   [461] Qur'an iv: 3.

[462] Qur'an iv: 129.

[463] Y. Linant de Bellefonds, *Traité de droit musulman comparé*, 3 vols. (Paris, 1965–73) ii, 135, traces this interpretation to the Egyptian reformist *mufti* Muhammad 'Abduh (d. 1322/1905). Art. 18 of the 1956 Tunisian code of personal status prohibits polygamy explicitly.

[464] Above n. 101 and accompanying text.

remainder of the schools. Literalism in this case introduces a more permissive commercial practice for the Zahiris, which is not shared by the other schools.[465]

The difficulty in finding a satisfactory key to the phenomenon of the schools along political or exegetical lines has been noted:

> To appreciate the position [of Hanbalism], we must abandon an erroneous conception which mixes theological movements and legal schools, and according to which we would allegedly have, on the extreme left of the schools of law, the Hanafi school, and, on the extreme right, the Zahiri school. Next to the Hanafis the Malikis would stand, whilst the Hanbalis would stand next to the Zahiris, and that would leave the Shafi'is in the middle... Such a conception might appear reasonable, but it has nothing to do with historic truth. Theological rationalism and traditionalism pursued their struggle within each of the schools of law.[466]

Nor is the question of the *madhhab*s to be resolved without appreciating the general historical and intellectual set-up, including the division along strict quadripartite lines of the judiciary, ascribed to the Egyptian sultan Baybars (r. 658–75/1260–77), who appointed *qadi*s in Fustat and Cairo exclusively from the four schools:

> The situation continued in this way as of the year 665 H. [1267 CE] until there remained in all the cities of Islam no other school of law of the schools known in Islam except these four... Those who followed any other schools were shunned, disavowed. No *qadi* was appointed, no testimony was accepted of any notary, no one was appointed as a preacher of the Friday sermon or as the leader of the Friday prayers, or as professor of law, unless he was a follower of one of these schools of law.[467]

As Makdisi also points out, the theological factors played a role in the formation and continuation of schools, especially at key junctures of Islamic history such as during the *Mihna* (known as 'the Muslim inquisition'), with the debate on the createdness or uncreatedness of the Qur'an being also played out by the schools.[468] In the great historians' account, like Ibn al-Athir's *Kamil*, the dispute started with

---

[465] This was already noted by Sarakhsi, *Mabsut*, xii, 112: 'Most jurists, except Dawud [al-Zahiri, the eponym of the Zahiri school, d. 270/ 884] have agreed that the rule of *riba* is not restricted to the six commodities, and that it involves a meaning which goes beyond a limited rule to involve other goods ... Dawud says that the rule of *riba* is limited to these six objects, because it is not possible to compare what is not written with what is written, *ittafaqa fuqaha' al-amsar rahimahum Allah 'ala anna hukm al-riba ghayr maqsud 'ala al-ashya' al-sitta wa anna fiha ma'na yata'adda al-hukm bi-dhalik al-ma'na ila ghayriha min al-amwal, illa dawud ... fa inna dawud yaqul hukm al-riba maqsur 'ala hadhih al-ashya' al-sitta li-annahu la yajuz qiyas ghayr al-mansus 'alal-mansus.'*

[466] Makdisi, 'L'islam hanbalisant', originally published in *Revue des Etudes Islamiques*, xlii/2–1974; xliii/1–1975; cited here in the offprint published at Geuthner, Paris, 1983, 38.

[467] Maqrizi (d. 845/1442), historian of Cairo, *Khitat*, 3 vols. (Beirut, 1959) ii, 344, as quoted Makdisi, *The rise of colleges*, 6. See also Ibn Taghribirdi (d. 874/1469), *al-Nujum al-zahira fi muluk misr wal-qahira*, in 16 vols. (Cairo, 1963–71), vii, 122–37; Ibn Shaddad (d. 632/1235), *Tarikh al-malik al-zahir*, Ahmad Hutait ed. (Beirut, 1983) 274. Notary, *shahid*; preacher of the Friday sermon, *khatib*; leader of the Friday prayers, *imam*; professor of law, *mudarris*.

[468] Early scholarship in Walter Patton, *Ahmed ibn Hanbal and the Mihna: a biography of the Imam including an account of the Mohammedan inquisition called the Mihna, 218–234 A.H.* (Leiden, 1897). See also above n. 209.

a letter from Caliph al-Ma'mun requesting the admission by all judges and jurists that the Qur'an was created by God. The letter, written in early 218/833, suggests that the Caliph insisted on the createdness of the Qur'an for fear that the opposite view would undermine the belief in God's unity. 'Muslims would be like the Christians in the latters' pretence that Jesus the son of Mary was not created and that he was the word of God'. Not wanting the Qur'an to be coterminous with God, judges and jurists were put to the test, Ibn al-Athir continues. They all recanted, except Ahmad ibn Hanbal, who was taken away in chains.[469]

Thus the theological account turned legal because of the position of ibn Hanbal as the eponym of a major school. In the end, lbn Hanbal had the upper hand, as he was set free upon Ma'mun's death two months later, and eventually returned to great favour once the *Mihna* was over. Nor would the intrigues of politics ever be far from the struggle between the schools, as illustrated for instance in Iraq under the Buwayhids.[470] History books even record violent fights between adherents of different schools.[471] Several centuries later, the restriction by the Ottoman sultans of judgeships to the four Sunni schools, under the aegis of the Hanafi chief judge, must again be appreciated in the light of their championing Sunni orthodoxy against the Persian Shi'i empire in a lingering conflict that lasted from the sixteenth to the twentieth century.[472] Last but not least, one should constantly bear in mind the close connection between the schools as *madhhab*s in the classical age and the schools as *madrasa*s, equally divided along the quadripartite historical cluster.[473]

Whatever the relation between state and school, the full significance of the schools of law remains to be more carefully investigated, and research might yield clues about a more precise relationship, at one or other juncture in the history of Islamic law, between political struggle, theological debate, educational competition,

---

[469] Ibn al-Athir (d. 630/1232), *al-Kamil fil-tarikh*, 9 vols. (Cairo edn., 1348/1929) v, 222–6, citation and text of the letter at 223n.: ' . . . and they resembled the Christians in their contention that Jesus son of Mary is not created since he is the word of God, *wa dahu bihi qawla al-nasara fi iddi'a'i-him fi 'isa ibn mariam annahu laysa bi-makhluq idh kana kalimat allah*'.

[470] John Donohue, *The Buwayhid dynasty in Iraq*, above n. 324, features an in-depth section on the 'law' schools, including the Shi'is, 317–38.

[471] In an early work, C. Snouck-Hurgronje mentioned examples of 'fights in the streets' following disputes between the schools, for instance the Hanbalites and the Shafi'ites in Baghdad in the fifth century AH/eleventh century CE and the Hanafites and Shafi'ites in Isfahan in the sixth/twelfth century, in 'Le droit musulman' (1898), collected also in *Selected works*, J. Schacht and G. Bousquet, eds. (Leiden, 1957) at 235. Other instances mention that 'in 323/935 the Malikites assaulted Shafi'ite pedestrians in the streets but they reserved their fury for the Shi'ahs and their theological foes. Even, according to Muqaddasi, the Shafi'ites were decidedly the most quarrelsome among the jurists.' Mez, *The Renaissance of Islam*, above n. 304, here quoted in the Beirut, 1973 repr., at 215. For a recent example of a political struggle involving the Zahiri school, see Lutz Wiederhold, 'Legal-religious elite, temporal authority, and the caliphate in Mamluk society: conclusions drawn from the examination of a "Zahiri revolt" in Damascus in 1386', *International Journal of Middle East Studies*, 31, 1999, 203–35.

[472] The literature on the two great Empires is important. A good starting point is the multi-volume *Cambridge History of Iran*.

[473] Extensive discussions in Makdisi, *The rise of colleges*, Louis Pouzet, *Damas au VII/XIIIème siècle. Vie et structures religieuses dans une métropole islamique* (Beirut, 1988).

economic stakes, and one or more schools vying for supremacy and recognition. This is a Titanic task considering the fragmentary state of our knowledge and the interplay of numerous factors against a documentation which is never explicit, let alone comprehensive. What is established is that the four schools which survived the classical period—the Hanafi, Hanbali, Shafi'i, and Maliki *madhhabs*—have remained in Sunni history exclusive of any other *madhhab*. This qualification, together with the general geographical spread of the schools, may be the only historical certainty attaching to the schools of law in the Sunni world. It also determines the structure of change in Islamic law, which was constantly enriched by interpretative theories and innovations, albeit *within* the formal ambit of the respective four schools.

To telescope a still embryonic debate, one may venture the conclusion that the competition between and coexistence of the schools, which mark their differences over the centuries, have predominantly been educational-statist.

Educational: this is dictated by a structure of learning which, for obvious reasons, would attach primarily to established law colleges hailing from the various schools. This explains how the Hanbali school, which seems to have been uncertainly rooted in society at large, would still be well represented in colleges in a city like Damascus in the seventh/thirteenth century, as described by Pouzet.

Statist: this conjures up the relationship between the state and the implementation of law. In a typical Weberian formulation, the *madhhab*s were effective in terms of the application of Islamic rules only in so far as the exclusive power of state coercion was lent to them. The dominance of Hanafism in the Ottoman Empire is directly derived, in this context, from the higher recognition of that particular school by the Porte over any other Sunni school. Such a legitimizing investment also explains the scope for the application of law left to the three other Sunni schools, in a continuation by the Ottomans of a policy ascribed to the Mamluk Baybars four or five centuries earlier. It also explains why Shi'i law, in its 'Ja'fari' variety, remained truncated in matters of application in classical Islamic history until the advent of the Safavids in Persia at the beginning of the sixteenth century and their establishment of Shi'ism as the state 'official rite'. It is doubtful whether any Shi'i court record would emerge from the Ottoman empire. By contrast, research on court records under the Safavids would yield important conclusions on whether and how Ja'fari law was applied in Persia over the three centuries preceding the advent of modern Iran.

After these preliminary remarks on the schools of law in Islam one can turn to the debate over 'the closure of the gate of *ijtihad*'. A further digression on the works of the great sociologist Ibn Khaldun (d. 808/1406) is not amiss. In the larger scheme of his formidable book, the *Muqaddima*, Ibn Khaldun was clearly not impressed by the jurists. He describes them severely. In their interpretation of the real world, he writes, 'they fall often into error and cannot be trusted'.[474] While this view

---

[474] Ibn Khaldun, *Muqaddima*, Arabic edn., 542. Rosenthal, iii, 308–10.

should be qualified—he was himself a legal scholar and a judge—the paradigm that attaches to date to the dominant scholarly view of Islamic law has hardly moved from the pointed analysis the celebrated Arab historian makes of the jurists' methods and schools. The paradigm, as will be developed presently, includes the dominant views to this day on the history of Islamic law.

The first dominant idea concerns the question of method, or interpretation, or *ijtihad*. Here is where the concept of 'the closure of the gate' appears forcefully. In his chapter on *fiqh*, defined as the 'knowledge of the rules of God in the works of those responsible in what is obligatory, forbidden, recommendable, disliked and permitted', Ibn Khaldun points out 'the inevitable disagreement' amongst the interpreters of law with regard to sources,[475] 'the contradictions in most rules in the Sunna', let alone 'new facts which are not covered by the texts'. 'All of this is indicative of inevitable disagreements'. Ibn Khaldun goes on to sketch out the development of *fiqh* and the various lawyers and their followers in the 'schools'. When he reaches Ahmad ibn Hanbal, and the establishment by his followers of a 'fourth school', Ibn Khaldun writes:

Studying stopped in the cities at those four [schools] and the students studied others, and *the people closed the gate of disagreement* and its ways because of the complexity of the lexicon of science and the difficulty of reaching the degree of *ijtihad* and the fear of acknowledging it to people either incapable of exercising it or to people who cannot be trusted in their opinion or in their religion. So they declared their impotence and shortcomings and pushed people to follow those who specialised in a school. Following others was prohibited for fear of playing havoc with the rules. The only way left was for them to keep transmitting their doctrines and each jurist kept to the school of the person he followed after correcting the rules and its proper transmission from the traditions ... There is no result in *fiqh* today but this.[476]

The key word in this text is 'the closure of the gate of disagreement'.[477] The occurrence of the metaphor of 'the closure of the gate' has determined, at least since Ibn Khaldun, the approach to Islamic law, qua *fiqh*, as one which stopped developing by a self-imposed contrivance.

---

[475] *adilla.*
[476] The text of the *Muqaddima* in Arabic, at 448, reads as follows: '*wa waqafa al-taqlid fil-amsar 'inda ha'ula' al-arba'a waqad darasa al-muqallidun liman siwahum wa* sadda al-nas bab al-khilaf *wa turuqahu lamma kathura tasha' 'ub al-istlilahat fil-'ulum wa lima 'aqa 'an al-wusul ila rutbat al-ijtihad wa-lima khushiya min isnad dhalik ila ghayr ahlihi wa-man la yuthaq bi-ra'yihi wa la bi-dinihi fa-sar-rahu bil-'ajz wal-i'waz wa raddu al-nas ila taqlidi ha'ula' kulla man ikhtussa bihi min al-muqallidin wa hazaru an yutadawala taqliduhum lima fihi min al-tala'ub wa lam yabqa illa naqlu madhahibihim wa 'amila kullu muqallidin bi-madhhab man qalladahu minhum ... la mahsula al-yawma lil-fiqh ghayru hadha*' (emphasis added). The language is particularly elusive, note *taqlid* for what we would nowadays depict as *ijtihad*. The closure relates to *ikhtilaf*, difference, disagreement, rather than *ijtihad*, interpretation (note that there is a full *ikhtilaf* genre in classical Islamic law). In another illustration of the difficulty of translating legal terms of art from the classical age, I use studying, students, for *taqlid*, *muqallidun*, in the first sentence, but for the same derivations from *taqlid*, the words 'following others' and 'jurist' later in the same paragraph. 'Students studied others' should be understood in the sense that students stopped following any new master, because there was no one capable of taking on the mantle of the great jurists, or as Ibn Khaldun writes, 'reach that degree.'   [477] *sadd bab al-khilaf.*

Ibn Khaldun was also behind other important paradigms defining our view of Islamic law.

One major paradigm concerns the development of Islamic law doctrine in the early years, and the geographical and doctrinal division between so-called interpretivists,[478] and literalists.[479] From readings of the Qur'an carried out by those few Muslims who were not totally illiterate, Ibn Khaldun explains, the field developed into the discipline of *fiqh*, as the early generations of readers were transformed with time into 'interpreters, so *fiqh* perfected itself and became a craft and a science making readers to be known as jurists…[480] Then *fiqh* divided in two, and the jurists developed two different ways, that of supporters of interpretivism and analogy,[481] who are the people of Iraq, and the others, the literalists,[482] who are the people of the Hijaz'.[483]

Hence the second received idea about the development of Islamic law, which is the early difference between the legal hermeneutics of the people of Iraq and those of Western Arabia. As time went by, again according to Ibn Khaldun, opinion crystallized into 'schools', eventually eliciting the concept of closure.

The distinction between literalists and interpretivists, a geographical division of the schools, and the absence of legal development beyond the confines of the recognized schools: the three brilliant insights in this chapter of the *Muqaddima* still form our overarching appreciation of Islamic law.

Ultimately, the development of the law poses daunting questions with elusive, and at best, fragmentary answers. Regardless of what future research may show on the 'significance' of the schools—within the appropriate methodological framework—the *madhhab*s remain attached to specific geographic areas. With the exception of Saudi Arabia and regions in Africa and South East Asia which embraced Islam after the death of Ibn Khaldun, the spread of the schools closely mirrors the description of their dominance in the *Muqaddima*.[484] Hanafism, which covers the largest part of the Sunni population of the world, can be found in the Near and Far East. In those areas as well, and in parts of Eastern and Western Africa, Shafi'ism is also strongly present. In North Africa, Malikism seems to have been dominant at least since the seventh-eighth/thirteenth-fourteenth century, and Hanbalism, which is more generally associated with a theological, in contrast to legal, tradition, is limited to parts of Saudi Arabia and the Gulf.

Whatever the historical dimension of the schools of law, the actual relevance of the differences among them in the contemporary Middle East is limited. It is true that the dominant school of law in each country informs the prevailing *shari'a* rules which may still be in force, mostly in the field of family law. In Saudi Arabia, Hanbalism is the law of the land, which was super-imposed over the traditionally Hanafi and Shafi'i systems of pre-twentieth century Western Arabia—the Hijaz,

---

[478] *ahl al-ra'i*, interpretivists, literally the people of opinion.
[479] *ahl al-hadith*, literalists, the people of *hadith*.   [480] jurists, *fuqaha* and *'ulama*.
[481] supporters of interpretivism and analogy, *ahl al-ra'i wal-qiyas*.   [482] *ahl al-hadith*.
[483] *Muqaddima*, Arabic edn., 446, Rosenthal, iii, 4–5.
[484] *Muqaddima*, Arabic, 448–51, English, Rosenthal, iii, 9–20.

where Mecca and Medina lay. Shi'i Ja'farism is the law of the land in Iran. But in most other countries, several schools coexist, and the integration efforts attempted by the state through unified courts and legislation were carried out through the process of *takhayyur* (choice, eclecticism), and not through the imposition of any one school. Modern family law statutes, for instance in Iraq, Syria, Egypt, Morocco, show how the legislator preferred to choose, from among various schools, the one most appropriate to twentieth-century conditions, with perhaps a specific concern in each country to preserve its own historically dominant school. This is particularly true in the law of divorce and succession, with a view to extending more legal protection to the wife and daughter.

Outside the sphere of family law, the contemporary importance of the Sunni schools of law is even more limited. In each country, the civil law of the land is unified in legislation as well as in the court system. The judge is generally a layperson who has received a 'modern' legal education. His or her training in civil law tends to be inattentive to strict *shari'a* concerns. This limitation can be coupled with a classic dictum according to which 'there is no school for the people',[485] which means that the specific school is indifferent to a lay person, in so far as he or she does not have the required education and legal sophistication to delve into the subtleties and variations as between the four schools.

For want of an easy explanation, schools therefore remain a puzzling historical phenomenon, which awaits difficult investigations in areas where data will probably remain insufficient. One is left, in a historical perspective, with various hypotheses concerned with trade routes, with the theory of the Prince's favouritism, with the quest for the lineage of teachers and schools, against a span of time which cannot be encompassed in a single theory. It may also be worth wondering whether the 'significance' of the schools of law is a correct question at all, if we pursue style and language as a matrix of investigation: it was noted by a contemporary Shi'i scholar, in a passing remark, how even a perfunctory comparison between nineteenth-century texts and works from the tenth or eleventh century CE shows the chasm in style and language, and the great renovation and progress since.[486] In Sunni Islam, this is more true, as the first great compendia go back further in history, and as research into the post-classical scholars—the *muta'akhkhirin*—is still pointedly scarce: there, it may be useful to note that a comparison between a self-styled Hanafi jurist of the thirteenth/nineteenth century with a Hanafi of the sixth/twelfth century will probably yield more differences in style and in substance than a comparison between two jurists who belong formally to a different school, but who lived in neighbouring areas in the nineteenth century.

---

[485] *la madhhab lil-'ammi*, a common reference which can be documented for instance in Ibn al-Salah, *Adab al-mufti wal-mustafti*, 161, together with the antithesis that the people follow a school because they 'believe so'. There is both in *adab al-qadi* and *adab al-mufti* an extensive treatment of 'conflict' between judges and *muftis* from various schools.

[486] Muhammad Bahr al-'Ulum, '*al-dirasa wa tarikhuha fil-najaf* (Studies and the history of education in Najaf)', in Ja'far al-Khalili, ed., *Mawsu'at al-'atabat al-muqaddasa, qism al-najaf* (Encyclopaedia of the Shi'i holy places, section on Najaf), 3 vols. (Beirut, 1964) ii, 98.

From a contemporary comparative perspective, the question has lost relevance to the extent that the process of eclecticism [487] has been key to legislation, and that we might even have reached in some areas, like codified civil and family law, [488] a process of eclecticism at one remove, where the original *fiqh* books are less important than precedents established in the legislation of other Muslim countries.

This brings us in the appreciation of comparative and historical research to the third important word, which next to *shari'a* and *fiqh*, also stands for 'law': *qanun*.

The Age of qanun. Qanun, plural *qawanin*, from the Greek *kanon*, rod, bar, is more strictly reserved for what is generally known as statute law, or in French 'droit positif'. These are laws as laid down by legislative authorities, parliaments, or the executive. Originally unknown in the tradition of Islamic law, statute books in the form of decrees (*qanunnameh*) became common in the Ottoman Empire in the tenth/sixteenth century. [489] By extension, *qanun* has come to mean the modern law as laid down and practised in contemporary societies. With statutes becoming increasingly dominant in the modern world of the law, *qanun* has also acquired a dimension which operates in contradistinction to the less organized and more diffuse classical system dominated by the *fiqh* books.

However uncertain a phenomenon 'codification' might have been, in contrast to a classical age which did not know statutes even in a primal form, [490] the laying down of *qanun* in the Ottoman period operated as a precursor to a phenomenon which would crystallize in the Middle East in the middle of the nineteenth century with late Ottoman decrees and codes known as the *Tanzimat*. The most important *Tanzimat* were of a constitutional, real property, and commercial nature, [491] but this was, unmistakably, a process of comprehensive codification which became the norm for the whole region thereafter. The process of codification was also tied closely to the phenomenon of the 'reception' of European laws. It was a process directly associated with colonization, and the Middle East was no different from other parts of the non-Western world in this respect, except that its legal tradition, as developed in this chapter, was particularly rich and deep-rooted. The resurgence of Islamic law in the late twentieth century should also be seen as an indigenous reaction to that aspect of colonization which took the form of codes. With the

---

[487] *takhayyur.*   [488] Developments in Chapters 8 and 10.

[489] An extensive review of the literature available on early Ottoman *qanuns* was contributed at a workshop in Vienna, 26–7 September 1997, within the 'Individual and society in the Mediterranean Muslim world' programme, by the Turkish scholar Yunus Koç, 'Le droit coutumier du sultan et la cheri'a dans les premiers codes de lois ottomans'. The article includes references to the main scholars in the field (Ömer Lütfi Barkan, Halil Inalcık, Heath Lowry) and to the most important general and provincial codes of the fifteenth and sixteenth centuries. Pioneering work in the field was started by Uriel Heyd, and posthumously collected by V. L. Ménage as *Studies in old Ottoman criminal law* (Oxford, 1973). See also Haim Gerber, *Islamic law and culture 1600–1840* (Leiden, 1999) and his *State, society, and law in Islam: Ottoman law in comparative perspective* (Albany, NY, 1994).

[490] Abortive story of ibn al-Muqaffa' (d. 139/756) and Caliph al-Mansur (reigned 754–75) related below Chapter 7, at n. 1.

[491] A list can be found under the entry 'Tanzimat' in the 1st edn. of *the Encyclopaedia of Islam*, by J. H. Kramers.

advent of the age of *qanun*, the nineteenth century becomes intrinsically inter-woven with the 'modern' age. It forms the obligatory departure point for the study of law in the contemporary Middle East.[492]

Coda: Periodization and *Mille Plateaux*[493]

There exists a distinguished and extensive body of law in the history of Middle Eastern societies. Tablets, papyri, and books comprise the deepest documented history of law on the planet, and, since the emergence of Islamic law in the seventh or eighth century, the legal tradition offers a varied and sustained body of sources including the Urtexts—Qur'an and *hadith*—fatwas and court documents, con-tracts and formulae, legal biographies and stories of judges, judgments proper, custom, and doctrinal treatment in the *fiqh* books. The history of this tradition, like the present study, is patchy, but it is hoped that an analysis of Middle Eastern law will gain more from an appreciation of its complexity than from a hasty reduc-tion which supports superficial or dogmatic assertions about the 'immutable nature of Islamic law', its simplistic equating with the Qur'an, its pristine readi-ness for all times and all seasons, the *qadi* dispensing rough justice under the tree, 'the closing of the gate of *ijtihad*', or the virtue or maleficence of Western-style imposition.

Nor is a serious periodization of Islamic, let alone Middle Eastern, law possible at this stage of our knowledge of the field. On a continuum consisting of millennia, rather than centuries, one might be tempted by the identification of three bodies of law which correspond to three linguistic blocs over a period of four or five thousand years: the first 2,000 years, *c.* 3000 BCE to 1000 BCE, is the Akkadian-Sumerian, or Babylonian period, of which the most significant text is Hammurabi's Code *c.* 1750 BCE, with Akkadian as *lingua franca*. The second period is the passage from Babylonian to Assyrian-Syriac (1000 BCE to 500 CE), crowned in the fifth century by the Syro-Roman Code, with Syriac-Aramaic as *lingua franca*. The third period, which starts at about the time of the advent of Islam in the late sixth century and continues to date, witnesses Arabic as the *lingua franca* of Middle Eastern law, at its most sophisticated with jurists like Sarakhsi and Kasani. One might even find support for such a sweeping approach among leading historians of the twentieth century like Fernand Braudel and John Wansbrough, with Braudel's concept of *longue durée* and Wansbroughian calques exemplified in the development of law and language.[494]

---

[492] Further in Part III, Chapter 7.

[493] With reference to the masterpiece of French philosophers Gilles Deleuze and Félix Guattari, *Mille plateaux* (A thousand planes) (Paris, 1980).

[494] A forgotten masterpiece of Fernand Braudel, starting with pre-history and ending in the late Roman empire, was recently published as *Les Mémoires de la Méditerranée* (Paris, 1998), and underlines such a continuity, see especially at 174–5. For Wansbrough, see *Lingua franca in the Mediterranean*,

Neat as such a periodization might sound, it could easily be disputed: in the first period, what about the Hebrew dimension, and why emphasize Hammurabi's Code over the Bible's Deuteronomy? What about the long duration of ancient Egypt and its laws? Similarly, in the second period, was the Syro-Roman Code that important? And even if the gospels were written in Syriac originally, they were extant in Greek. What about the early Greek legal tradition in Egypt and elsewhere,[495] let alone the Graeco-Roman legal world, with its formidable legacy, which has certainly held sway in parts of the Levant at significant moments, stretching well into the Byzantine empire?[496] Arabic as legal *lingua franca* from the eighth to the twentieth century is a less controversial proposal, with perhaps some reservations about its dominance in current legal scholarship in Iran, and until recently in Turkey and Israel. Arabic as *lingua franca* is obviously not as true if one wishes to incorporate the Persian and Ottoman traditions, let alone a deep Byzantine tradition of which we know very little in our research on Islamic law.

There is another possible, shorter, periodization, which looks at the body of Islamic law exclusively, and makes a distinction between the first phase of *fiqh*, a second phase in the 'classical high age',[497] and a third stage with the post-classical 'latecomers'.[498] Joseph Schacht has made an undisputable mark on the origins of *fiqh* and its consolidation under Shafi'i—despite some recent scholarly reservations, such as the questioning of Shafi'i's *Risala* as the founding treatise in *usul al-fiqh*, or the exact time when the passage to *fiqh* took place, as recently argued in relation to the emergence of summaries.[499] Regardless of the nuances—the texts are too fragmentary and imprecise in the early period to draw sharp lines—the dated testimony of the great Sunni jurists of the third/tenth and fourth/eleventh centuries offers arguments of sufficient sophistication and coherence to make the legal discipline enter an incontrovertibly mature period then. The suggestion that it froze thereafter in its classic legal splendour, despite the later jurists, from Ibn Nujaym (d. 970/1563) to Ibn 'Abidin (d. 1252/1836) and the Majalla drafters, is now a dubious proposal. My own eclectic readings suggest that the theory of

above n. 16 on the Aramaic papyri at 111–13, also citing the Aramaic-Hebrew papyri of Elephantine. See in addition to calques identified in scholars cited above n. 366, the impressive linguistic scholarship in Yochanan Muffs, *Studies in the Aramaic legal papyri from Elephantine* (Leiden, 2003).

[495] As in the many works of Joseph Mélèze Modrzejewski; see e.g. a remarkable series of Middle Eastern legal calques in *Les juifs d'Egypte de Ramsès II à Hadrien* (Paris, 1997 (1st edn., 1991)): 'pluralisme juridique', at 151–3; repudiation of wife in a seemingly Greek-Jewish marriage and compensation sought by her in 218 BCE, at 157–9; prohibition and tolerance of interest, 160–70.

[496] The school of law in Beirut is a well-known example; see the classic work on Berytus by Paul Collinet, *Histoire de l'école de droit de Beyrouth* (Paris 1925). The school, where teaching was carried out in Latin then in Greek (Collinet at 211–18), was destroyed by a massive earthquake in 551 CE.

[497] Following a multi-volume encyclopaedic work by Ahmad Amin (d. 1954) on the classical high age (*sadr al-Islam*) of Arab-Islamic civilization, published in Egypt between 1930 and 1952. The ten-volume collection is divided into *Fajr al-Islam*, *Duha al-Islam*, and *Zuhr al-Islam*, Islam's dawn, early morning, and noon.   [498] Latecomers, *muta'akhkhirun*.

[499] See discussion, above n. 117 and accompanying text, on the new theories proposed by Calder, and Hallaq, 'Was Shafi'i the master architect of Islamic jurisprudence?', *International Journal of Middle East Studies*, 25, 1993, 587–605.

Islamic law freezing at some date in the fourth/tenth or fifth/eleventh centuries, or even with Ibn Khaldun in the eighth/fourteenth century, is unsustainable. There are too many riches in the Ottoman, Safavid, and Moghul periods, whether strictly in terms of coherent and comprehensive *fiqh* books, or in attempts to codify the rules sectorally or comprehensively, with *qanunnameh*s that resemble in style the English habit of obscure statutory drafting, or with the more literary restatements of the Ottoman Majalla and its predecessors, the *Ashbah wal-Naza'er* genre. No doubt, the great *mufti*s always had something 'new' to say, as had the authors of individual *fiqh* treatises, such as Ibn 'Abidin himself, who wrote vibrant legal opinions on inflation and depreciating coins, custom, or insurance.[500] The all too brief references to the massive *fiqh* books in the present study do not give enough credit to those subject areas of systematic innovation in the Middle Eastern legal tradition, from the treatise on the difference in the legal views of the early masters of Hanafi law,[501] to the legality of smoking or coffee-drinking in the Ottoman and Persian empires.

One could also follow an exposition which some Muslim jurists have advocated. In this approach, the periods of Islamic law get divided into tranches of one century each, following the poetical aphorism of the Prophet on how 'God sends to his people, at the head of every one hundred years, someone to renew their faith'.[502] Accordingly, the fourteen centuries which separate us from the Islamic revelation feature one leading jurist each. This is the argument which Suyuti, himself a formidable scholar of the tenth/sixteenth century, develops in a treatise addressed to 'those who forget that *ijtihad* is a duty at all times'.[503] Such an approach

---

[500] Ibn 'Abidin, *Majmu'at rasa'el*, ii, above n. 423, 57–67 for the treatise on the effect on contracts of depreciating coins, see Chapter 9 n. 150; Ibn 'Abidin, ii, 114–47 on custom, discussed, above at nn. 423–35; and on insurance, Ibn 'Abidin, *Radd al-muhtar 'alal-durr al-mukhtar*, 5 vols. (Cairo, 1327/1909) iii, 273–4, discussed in a classic article by Carlo Nallino, 'Delle assicurazioni in diritto musulmano hanafita', *Raccolta*, iv, above n. 37, 62–84 (orig. 1927). Systematic works on individual jurists, such as Martin McDermott on al-Shaikh al-Mufid (d. 413/1044), Sherman Jackson on Shihab al-Din al-Qarafi (d. 683/1285), George Makdisi on ibn 'Aqil (d. 513/1119), Bernard Weiss on Sayf al-Din al-Amidi (d. 631/1234), Bernard Haykel on Shawkani (d. 1250/1832), Baber Johansen on late Mamluk and early Ottoman jurists, Imber and Repp on Ebu-Su'ud (981/1574) and his *mufti* colleagues, all yield original insights into great legal figures in various political, theological, and historical contexts.

[501] *Ikhtilaf Abu Hanifa (d.767) wa ibn Abi Laila (d.765)*, as related by their student Abu Yusuf (d. 798) and edited by Sarakhsi (d. 1095) in *al-Mabsut*, vol. 30, 128–67.

[502] *inna Allah yab'ath li-hadhih al-umma 'ala ra's kull mi'at sana man yujaddid laha dinaha*, which can be found in Ibn Dawud's *Sunan*, section 72 of the book of *tahara* (purity).

[503] Jalal al-Din al-Suyuti (d. 911/1505), *Kitab al-radd 'ala man ukhlida ilal-ard wa jahila anna al-ijtihad fi kulli 'asrin fard*, Khalil al-Mays ed. (Beirut, n.d). Suyuti, in another work, hoped he would serve as the renovator of his own age (*Al-tahadduth bi-ni'mat Allah*, cited in *Kitab al-radd*, 11). He even has a poem listing each century's leading scholar, and himself hopefully as the renovator of the ninth-century Hijri: '*wa hadhih tasi'atu al-mi'in qad/atat wa la yakhlufu ma al-hadi wa'ad; wa qad rajawtu annani al-mujaddid/fiha fafadlu Allahi laysa yujhad* (and here comes the ninth of the hundreds and the Promisor never fails; I hope to be its renovator, and God's bounty will never be neglected)', poem in 'Abd al-Mit'al al-Sa'idi, *al-Mujaddidun fil-Islam, min al-qarn al-awwal ilal-rabi' 'ashar* (The reformers in Islam, from the first to the fourteenth centuries) (Cairo, n.d (mid-1950s)) 11–13. There are reports of similar hopes by Ghazali (d. 505/1111) and Shawkani (d. 1250/1832). For a long list of

has clear advantages, at least in stressing the continuity of legal excellence across the ages, and rightly blurs the differences among the schools. It also fits well into 'educational periods', with leading jurists, as in modern discussions amongst Shiʻi scholars, heading their own schools of thought in a break with, or qualitative progress over, previous scholarship.[504]

The weaknesses in this approach are no less obvious. Suyuti himself could not always restrict the arbitrary choice of one century to a single leading jurist, let alone find the criteria to classify a jurist as 'absolute', that is, deserving of the immense recognition needed, as opposed to 'partial'. The consequences of the impossibility of agreeing on a leader-*faqih* continue to reverberate to date in 'the Shiʻi international',[505] in Iran and elsewhere. Would there be a scholar at the forefront of Sunni law, as opposed to Shiʻi law, let alone a leading scholar within each of the 'five' schools? How about other schools: those which disappeared like Awzaʻi's and Tabari's, and those considered 'minor', like the Zaydism of the great Shawkani? Or those other currents, which may deserve, once the scholarship of Islamic law matures beyond its current impressionism, to be recognized as identifiable 'schools', the Transoxanians, or Marawiza (from Merv/Meru, Sarakhsi's home town), as Ibn abi al-Dam refers to them in the twelfth century?[506] And what is the nature of progress in law, in any case, that marks the transition from one scholar or school to another?

Maybe the more alluring periodization scheme for the shorter Arabic *lingua franca* period could espouse the shape of this chapter's tripartite exposition of the terms for law: *shariʻa, fiqh, qanun*. The first phase—'the age of the *shariʻa*'—would cover the fragmentary search for coherence in the first two centuries, with the passage to *fiqh* as the second stage with the crystallization of the epigones such as Shafiʻi and the two companions of Abu Hanifa, and, why not 'the passage to the summaries' as suggested by Calder, through to the pinnacles of legal reasoning with Sarakhsi, Kasani and the other encyclopaedic jurists of the fourth/tenth to the ninth/fifteenth centuries? This second stage is 'the age of *fiqh*'. A third age would be introduced by the hesitant statutory restatement genre of *Ashbah wa Nazaʻer*, together with the first Ottoman statutes around the tenth/sixteenth century, as the antecedent of the systematic codification of law by modern legal codes in a prefiguration of modern nation-states. In pursuit of this architectonic, one should appreciate the new genre which may just have started, actually representing

centenary Sunni candidates, see also Suyuti, *Kitab al-radd*, 185–98, for Shiʻis, Zayn al-Din al-ʻAmili (d. 966/1599), known as al-Shahid al-Thani (the second martyr), *al-Rawda al-bahiyya*, i, 55, with comments by Muhammad Kelantar.

[504] For the Shiʻi leading scholars, see the syntheses of Muhammad Baqer al-Sadr, *al-Maʻalim al-jadida fil-usul*, cited above n. 441, 46–89, esp. 88–9 (*usul* scholars), and Hossein Modarressi, *An introduction to Shiʻi law*, above n. 208, 23–59 ('the periods of Shiʻi law', generally).

[505] Discussed in detail in *The Renewal of Islamic law*, part 1, 'Islamic law and the constitution,' and my *The Middle East in the 21st Century*, 127–72.

[506] Ibn abi al-Dam, *Kitab adab al-qadaʻ*, 421: *madhhab al-marawiza*, the school of the Marawiza, in contrast to the Iraqis, 461.

an altogether new treatment of the tradition, classical and modern, with a focus on *ijtihad* in its present sense in Middle Eastern law schools as courts' decisions, forming precedent—'jurisprudence' in French terminology.[507] Whatever the allure, or suspicion, of such generalizations, there is little doubt that Middle Eastern law is formed of all of the above, with solid texts in each genre. Cumulation, rather than separation, becomes key to effective legal scholarship, in a *Mille Plateaux* tradition which, on the vertical plane, is a superposition of the three ages within the Islamic tradition proper, itself opening up to pre-Islamic traditions; and, on the horizontal plane, is open to other, non-legal fields, in an ever enriching interdisciplinary mode.

As in the use of the Arabic word 'Allah' to artificially set apart the Muslims' God from 'God' in any great religious tradition, all instances of an allegedly specific methodology for Islamic law should be treated with circumspection. Instead, it is far more useful to describe Islamic law sources, if short-cuts are needed, as a multi-layered composition of texts. Such a composition must include parts of the Qur'an and of the collected sayings of the Prophet (and the seven or twelve Imams for the Shi'i traditions); their interpretation, rejection, or silence within larger legal structures in *fiqh* compendia; social and legal interaction with customary rules; the world of notarial acts and formulae literature; judgments proper; fatwas; 'stories of judges'; and legal literature *lato sensu* in various historiographic and literary books. For the Middle East, the picture, complex as it may already be when restricted to the Islamic tradition, would benefit from being open to ancient and new worlds of comparative law on a 'thousand planes'.

Sarakhsi deserves the last word on law in the classical age:

The best that has been said about the lawyer is that he should assimilate the dispositions and meanings of the Book and the *sunna* in its diverse forms and texts, and that he must be good in analogy and knowledgeable about the ways of the people; and with all that, he could still have a case for which he has no reference in the Book or in the *sunna*. Texts are finite and cases infinite. Then he has no other means but to consider, and the way of his consideration has been alluded to in the *hadith*: know the examples as well as doubts, and measure matters with them, this is the method of the jurists, which is that precedent is argument, and all events are not to be found, unlike what the literalists say, in the Book and the *sunna*. So turn to the closest to God and to justice, this is the way of precedent, in order to bring the ruling in a matter to the closest in meaning...[508]

[507] Argument developed in Chapter 7 for private law.

[508] *Al-Mabsut*, the book of the judge (*adab al-qadi*), xvi, 62–3: *mujtahid*, the lawyer generically, actually in this book meant as judge; analogy, *qiyas*, which we can now safely translate as precedent; the ways or custom of the people, *'urf al-nas*; Texts and finite and cases infinite, *al-nusus ma'duda wal-hawadeth mamduda*; method, *dalil*, of the jurists, *fuqaha'*; analogy is argument, *al-qiyas hujja*; literalists, *ashab al-zawahir*.

PART II
PUBLIC LAW

3

The Contemporary Middle East: A Historical Primer

At the turn of the twenty-first century a motley collection of democratic, republican, monarchical, and tribal countries, including occasionally or persistently 'failed' states like Somalia, Iraq, Afghanistan, Palestine-Israel, and Lebanon, provides the student of Middle Eastern law with a series of challenges.

A first challenge is linguistic. In addition to Arabic, the mother tongue of some 300 million people, the Middle East officially speaks Persian (Dari in Afghanistan), Pashto, Turkish, Kurdish (official language in Iraq only), Urdu, and Hebrew. It also speaks Armenian, French and English, and other non-official local languages, with native speakers ranging from a few hundreds in the case of Syriac (or Aramaic, the language spoken by Christ, still the mother tongue of small communities in Iraq, Syria, Lebanon), or Circassian in Jordan, to thousands who speak African languages like Nuer and Peul in the Sudan, to millions who speak Azeri in Iran, Tamazight (Berber) in Western North Africa, or Kurdish in Syria, Iran, and Turkey.

A second challenge is geographic. Middle East is meant here as the area extending from Morocco and Mauritania on the Atlantic, to Afghanistan and Pakistan in Asia, including the twenty-two Arab countries which are formally members of the Arab League in Asia and Africa, in addition to Palestine-Israel, Turkey, and Iran.[1] Although this study is primarily concerned with the core of the states which form the present-day Middle East—the loose domain known as the Arab-Muslim world—non-Arab legal systems also need to be included.[2]

---

[1] The map at pp. 460–1 of Albert Hourani, *A history of the Arab peoples* (London, 1991) illustrates the 'Middle East' area covered in the present book. Countries included are Mauritania,* Western Sahara, Morocco,* Algeria,* Tunisia,* Libya,* Egypt,* Sudan,* Djibouti,* Somalia,* Israel, Lebanon,* Jordan,* Syria,* Turkey, Iraq,* Kuwait,* Bahrain,* Qatar,* the United Arab Emirates,* Saudi Arabia,* Oman,* Yemen,* Iran, of which 20 are official members of the Arab League (here with an asterisk, plus Palestine and, much further south, the Comoros), where the majority of the population speaks Arabic. Pakistan and Afghanistan are also covered in the book when legally relevant. The main political problems of the area are discussed in my *The Middle East into the 21st century* (Reading, 1996 (paperback edn., 1997)), which includes a bibliographical essay on the modern Middle East at pp. 236–47.

[2] A regular update on the area from a legal perspective is offered in E. Cotran and C. Mallat, eds., *Yearbook of Islamic and Middle Eastern law*, 1994–9, then under the editorship of Eugene Cotran and Martin Lau. Individual entries are usually available for: Egypt, Syria, Iraq, Jordan, Palestine, Lebanon, Libya, Sudan, Kuwait, Saudi Arabia, United Arab Emirates, Bahrain, Qatar, Oman, Yemen, Iran, Algeria, Morocco, Tunisia, Turkey, Pakistan.

With some twenty-five states in the Middle East, including small and large countries where the people or their government would not readily accept they 'belong', the area covered is large and fluid. Turkey is both European and Asian. It played a major role throughout Middle East history, but it chose after the collapse of the Ottoman Empire at the end of the First World War an autarky which it has been slowly shedding only to join the European Union.

Iran under the Shahs (mid-1920s to 1979) always liked to see itself as Middle Eastern, and was dubbed the region's 'policeman', though more Aryan than Muslim in the way its Western-supported rulers presented themselves. Pakistan and Afghanistan are generally perceived to be outside the region, on account of tighter historical and geographical ties to the so-called Indian subcontinent. The two countries' trajectories are very different, but both have gravitated Westwards increasingly over the past quarter of a century.

After its occupation by the Soviet Union in 1989, and the emergence of the phenomenon of 'Afghan Arabs', Afghanistan became increasingly part and parcel of the geopolitics of the Middle East. Afghanistan has a unique history of independence, even during the century-long domination of India by the British Empire. Its recent constitution and politics show how much more attuned to Middle Eastern issues it has become, a trend which was consolidated during the Taliban domination from the mid-1990s to October 2001.

Pakistan ('Land of the pure', in Urdu) remains more preoccupied with India to the east than with the Middle East to the west, but this inclination has been slowly mitigated on account of the Islamic identity that Pakistan has identified with since the break with India in 1947–8. This identity developed politically and legally into a 'Middle Eastern' trait in the early 1980s.

If their large Muslim population and location warrant the inclusion of Pakistan and Afghanistan, this book should also cover the Central Asian Republics which seceded in the 1990s from the Soviet Union, and Bangladesh after its secession from Pakistan in 1972. But even if Pakistan, Afghanistan, and Iran are included in this book as Middle Eastern states, Bangladesh and the five Central Asian countries (Kazakhstan, Uzbekistan, Kyrgyzstan, Tajikistan, and Turkmenistan) are not. Few would describe these countries as Middle Eastern, even though Islamic law is destined to play an important role in their domestic debate owing to the majority Muslim component of their populations. Armenia, Georgia, and Azerbaijan, which have also emerged as independent states after the collapse of the Soviet Union, are closer geographically to the Middle East. They also are not included in this book. Like the five Central Asian Republics, they have little historical, political, or legal affinity with the Middle East. Because of the special history of the Armenians under Ottoman rule, including an important emigration to a number of Middle Eastern countries in the wake of large-scale massacres during the First World War, the Middle Eastern Armenian community surfaces occasionally as part of a mosaic typical of the Arab Levant.

Problems of defining the modern Middle East are not solely geographic or linguistic. There is no discernible *Middle Eastern* identity with which any individual living in the region would readily associate. As a concept of geographical convenience, 'Middle East' sounds neutral enough, but extreme politicization and world tensions have made the term highly controversial at times. Some critics fear it is purposefully played up by Western interests to stand against 'Arabism' and 'Islamism', with which it intersects and inevitably competes. An intense debate raged during the early negotiations between Israelis and Palestinians in the 1990s, when ruling circles in Israel were accused of flaunting the concept of 'a new Middle East' with the malevolent design of wrenching Palestine away from the Arab world, or worse, as a tool to destroy Arab identity and subject the Arab world to Israeli domination. That debate is bound to ebb and flow, especially since the US administration has advocated a democratization programme called 'the broader Middle East' (or MENA, Middle East and North Africa region). Political vocabulary remains extremely sensitive, even in apparently neutral terms. This is not unique to the region; any country or cluster of countries with outstanding identity and boundary problems knows similar controversies over names and appellations. As a concept, like Europe or America, the Middle East is a human construct. It is always subject to the challenge of outer limits and internal divisions, but there is one, unfortunate, Middle Eastern trait in modern history: the persistent violence that characterizes the region, exacerbating the tension of appellations and vocabulary.

Despite such lasting controversies, the concept of Middle East remains useful for an Arab native speaker who believes, like I do, that there is an Arab world worth bringing closer together. The contradiction is easily solved by favouring multiple identities and concepts rather than vying for an exclusive, dominant, single term of reference. On a sheer practical level, the Middle East encompasses countries like Iran, Israel, or Turkey, which it would be wrong to keep outside the pale of legal analysis. Considering the pervasive influence of non-Arab legal systems on many Arab countries, whether Israel over Palestinians, or Iran over countries with large Shi'i communities like Iraq, Pakistan, or Lebanon, major blind spots would weaken the study if it were restricted to Arab-speaking countries.

Matter-of-fact practicality is not the sole factor, and the coherence of the legal family proposed in this book as 'Middle Eastern law' is a more important consideration. Whether in its constitutional personal law specificity or in the civil codes which developed from a deep and rich tradition, Middle Eastern *legal* affinities are too strong to be ignored on account of linguistic, territorial, or ethnic divisions.

Divisions are real: language, territory, and identity are paramount in the understanding of Middle Eastern law, and mark it with a set of specificities that are not found in the same form elsewhere in the world. Modern history adds a key variable to the uniqueness of public law in the region. As a broad-brush introduction to the next chapters on public law, modern Middle Eastern history can be summarized as a succession of defining eras over the past two centuries, in an extension of the deeper periodization of the formation of Middle Eastern law adumbrated in the previous chapter. There I called this large, modern historical period 'the age of codification', which followed the age of *fiqh* and the age of *shari'a* in the classical period. For public law since the onset of the age of codification, a periodization of the last two centuries will help us appreciate the 'spirit' with which modern history has infused Middle Eastern law. These eras need to be perceived cumulatively. As broad brushes, they should be taken in their generality and are meant to provide an overall framework that facilitates the more specific detailed legal treatment that follows.

1798. End of self-rule. Era of Western (colonial) law.[3] The modern Middle East starts, in received historiography, when the troops of Napoleon occupied Egypt in 1798. For the soon-to-become Emperor this was just the beginning of a campaign of conquests which took place in Europe, and his military forays in Egypt and Palestine were a mere prelude to his European policy of military self-aggrandizement. In the Middle East, the effect turned out to be far more momentous: the break occasioned by the occupation of Egypt marked the beginning of Western colonialism, which slowly spread European domination through the nineteenth century, a domination which was far from over at the turn of the twenty-first century.

Domination brought Western law in its wake, and the Napoleonic metaphor is particularly apt to mark the beginning of the age of codification in the Middle East, against the background of a millennium-plus era of the *fiqh* age. A tidal wave brought European law to the Middle East, a law which the locals knew little or nothing about. Had Martians disembarked on the coasts of Egypt, any law they conveyed would have had no more dramatic impact on the region.

What Westerners brought to the Middle East in 1798 was not only military domination, but more lastingly dominant tools to read and understand the region. These tools were alien to Middle Easterners, not least the normative framework with which Western laws had infused their societies, and which they brought, by force or by persuasion, as the new normative framework for local societies. In the process, which lasted throughout that era and continues to date, the Middle Eastern legal tradition was shunted aside or asked to conform to the new legal spirit of the colonial masters. 1798 marks the symbolic beginning of the era of European, for which read colonial, law.

---

[3] For each era, I suggest one or two books which illustrate its 'spirit'. The spirit of the colonial era was magisterially conveyed in Edward Said, *Orientalism* (London, 1978). I have noted in 'The state of Islamic law research in the Middle East', *Asian Research Trends* (Tokyo), 8, 1998, 109–36, at 109–12, the inadequacy of the legal research conveyed by Said's book, but also the extraordinary paradigm shift it has brought to the study of Middle Eastern law, among disciplines focusing on the region in the field and collectively known as 'Orientalism'.

1920. End of empire. Era of oil law and nation-states.[4] The reader will find little about oil in this book, and less about empire. Not much remains in the living memory of Middle Easterners when it comes to the smouldering ashes of the last local empire, which had established Ottoman domination over the previous four to eight hundred years. Talk of artificial nation-states is common, in contrast, together with many a failed scheme to redraw the map away from the boundaries created by British and French colonizers on the ashes of the Ottoman Empire.

What happened at the end of the First World War that brought a peace full of wars to come? As the Ottoman Empire collapsed into a Turkish isolationist state and a constellation of countries with roughly defined boundaries, formal colonization became dominant. Its two main agents were Britain and France, but Italy and Spain had their own smaller colonies as well. The new contours of public law followed, marked by the sudden emergence of nation-states and their slow but inexorable solidification.

Less apparent at the outset, the oil factor was equally dominant in the shaping of public law. Oil was sheer luck, increasingly seen as bad luck by the more perceptive politicians and analysts, as it subjected the region to an artificial link which became vital to the rest of the world. Early in the twentieth century, the discovery of oil as a strategic reserve for the world economy mostly located in the Middle East transformed a natural search for stability within societies and states, into a chaotic process in which the international dimension was dominant. What mattered was not the balance which societies would find, through law, within each of the jurisdictions carved out of the Ottoman Empire. Such balance became secondary to the demand for free and unimpeded cheap oil that fuelled the Western-dominated world economy. This ensured that oil defined production and the distribution of wealth within Middle Eastern producer countries at the expense of the checks and balances which fiscal and commercial channels would have created more slowly and far more steadily. One early tragic example is Iraq. Britain was pondering the heavy burden on its finances of the colonization of Iraq in the early 1920s, when the discovery of oil tipped the balance in favour of continued dominance by Whitehall against those who considered the country too burdensome to retain. Another example is Saudi Arabia. The famous meeting of the Saudi King 'Abdelaziz ibn Sa'ud and the American president Franklin Delano Roosevelt aboard the USS Quincy on 14 February 1945 marks the formal establishment of a policy that continues to date. It can be summarized as an exchange of American military and diplomatic protection against the secure Saudi flow of oil, through Aramco and other American oil companies. For law, this

---

[4] Spirit of the era in Daniel Yergin, *The Prize, the epic quest for oil, money, and power* (New York, 1991) (oil as the dominant factor in international politics, including the Middle East); David Fromkin, *A Peace to end all peace: the fall of the Ottoman empire and the creation of the modern Middle East 1914–1922* (New York, 1989) (artificial nation-states under colonial rule in the wake of the First World War).

was a policy of no questions asked about what happens inside Saudi Arabia, however abhorrent to democratic values. A third example is Iran. When the United States toppled the government of Muhammad Musaddiq in Iran in 1953, his nationalization of the oil industry was a major factor in galvanizing American support for the deposed Shah, leading in turn to the Islamic revolution riding two decades later on a strongly anti-Western backlash. The dominance of oil in Middle Eastern history is a trite observation. Less obvious is the imbalance oil wreaked on the region by preventing a normal taxation system to obtain, and with it a healthier relation between governors and governed. Those who governed did not require the consent of their societies as would have been expressed naturally in the people's fiscal contribution to their state budgets. 'No taxation without representation' was replaced by 'no taxation because of oil'. This also meant that popular representation lost any financial leverage it might have had on the normal relationship between state and citizens. Oil turned into the bane of the democratic balance of societies. New Middle Eastern nation-states have lived since the 1930s in an era of oil law dictated by the imbalance wrought by oil revenues. Oil replaced the fiscal responsibility of citizens and governments and undermined representation and the development of democracy.

1948, 1956, 1967, 1973, 1982, 2006 . . . Era of the law of force.[5] The Hizbullah–Israel war initiated on 12 July 2006 was the latest in a series of Arab-Israeli wars. Full-fledged Arab-Israeli wars had taken place upon the establishment of the State of Israel in 1948, in 1956 during the Suez crisis, in 1967 when Israel occupied the West Bank and Gaza, the Syrian Golan and the Egyptian Sinai, in 1973, when Syria and Egypt launched a war to try to get these territories back, and in 1982, when Israel occupied Beirut to try to impose a new order on the Eastern Mediterranean.

Tragic as they were, those wars were not the most devastating in terms of human losses. Over a million casualties resulted from the Iran–Iraq War, started by the Iraqi dictator on 22 September 1980 to 'busy giddy minds with foreign quarrels' (Shakespeare). The ceasefire came eight devastating years later, with Iraq plunging again into adventurism when it invaded Kuwait on 2 August 1990. Despite a resounding defeat within six months, the regime of fear established in Iraq came to an end only thirteen years later, when US troops and their allies occupied Baghdad on 9 April 2003.

What have these wars done to law in the region? Two major traits resulted from that long era of wars: acquisition of territory by force as *fait accompli*, and military regimes. In retrospect, it is clear that the Arab-Israeli wars have wrecked the rule of both international and domestic law, and that the violence unleashed across the

---

[5] Spirit of the law of force era illustrated in Benny Morris, *The Birth of the Palestinian refugee problem revisited*, 2nd enlarged edn. (Cambridge, 2004 (orig. 1988)), and my review, 'La Nausée and Al-Nakba: rewriting 1948', *The Daily Star* (Beirut), 4 September 2004.

region forced might upon right. Forty years after Israel's takeover of the West Bank and Gaza, sixty years since 90 per cent of its native inhabitants were prevented from returning to Palestine, the military strength of the Israeli state has ensured that law is allowed minimal impact on conflict, and that force governs the two issues central to the contending peoples, land ownership and refugee status. There are several narratives and counter-narratives for Israel-Palestine; here is not the place to assess them. What cannot be disputed is the absence of law as central arbiter of the conflict, a fact epitomized in the mooting of the advisory opinion of the International Court of Justice against the wall of separation erected by the Israeli government inside the West Bank, which was simply ignored by Israel and the international community.[6]

Overpowering the other being the rule, might as right has translated domestic-ally in the Arab world as the dominance of crude power, typically by the army or a self-perpetuating narrow group representing a party or a sect. The paragon of this group is the Revolutionary Command Council, which was introduced as a model of central governance by the coup waged by Egypt's 'Free Officers' in 1952, and honed into extremes in Iraq and other self-styled republican regimes, includ-ing off-on variations in Pakistan and Turkey. 29 March 1954 marks the most sym-bolic date for that long trend, which started in the 1940s. On that day, 'Abdelrazzaq al-Sanhuri, the most respected jurist in the Arab world, was beaten inside his court by a small group of revolutionaries who could not accept any legal constraints on their bosses' takeover of the country.[7]

One may question the causal link between the emergence of Israel and brutality against an Egyptian judge. I submit that the causal link is far stronger than appears at first. When a large sense of injustice is meted out to a people, in the heart of a region, societies all around look for violent remedies which take the shape of short-cuts by narrow-based, law-averse, dictatorship-prone military, single-party or sectarian leaders. The law is left hanging, like Sanhuri at the door of his court, while states and societies slowly descend into lawlessness.

1948, Israel, Pakistan. 1978, Iran. Era of sectarian-religious law.[8] Mention of sect is particularly appropriate for the public law of the modern Middle East. Against the liberal age dominant in the first half of the twentieth century among leaders and people advocating self-determination and democracy to break colonization, a sub-type of legal logic emerged on the basis of religious affiliation: that was the

---

[6] International Court of Justice, *Advisory Opinion on the Legal Consequences of the Construction of a Wall in Occupied Palestinian Territory*, 9 July 2004 (Wall in the West Bank violates international law, should be dismantled and harmed landowners compensated).

[7] On Sanhuri see index, s.v. On the episode, and the picture of Sanhuri at the court's door after he was beaten up, Mona Anis, 'The state we're in', *Al-Ahram weekly* (Cairo), 16–22 June 2005.

[8] On the spirit of the religious law era, see my *The renewal of Islamic law: Muhammad Baqer as-Sadr, Najaf and the Shi'i international* (Cambridge, 1993). On its effects on the international rela-tions' paradigm, Samuel Huntington, *The clash of civilizations and the remaking of the world order* (New York, 1996).

logic of sectarian-based states, of which in 1948 Israel and Pakistan were typical. Jews in Israel-Palestine, Muslims in India-Pakistan, considered it necessary to carve out a territory where the Jewish and Muslim communities respectively govern, in open espousal of their sectarian-religious identity. That legal logic is not new in the Middle East, and I develop it as a deep and specific constitutional pattern in the next chapters. What matters is not its age, but its pervasive impact, which precludes as a matter of law the attachment of a person to her country without the mediation of her sectarian belonging. Both in Pakistan and Israel, that logic proved tragic for those communities which the definition did not embrace, within the country and around it: non-Jews ejected from Palestine in 1948–9, Jews fleeing Arab countries in the following decade, Muslims and Hindus fleeing India and Pakistan respectively upon the 1947 partition. The problem of religion-based exclusion remains acute to date. Sectarianism rules the constitutional day, as equality before the law gets mediated by religion or sect.

Because any society is a mosaic of identities, and the Middle East is particularly rich in competing identities, national, ethnic, religious, sectarian, and linguistic, the dominance of the sectarian state as a mode of legal structuring has far-reaching consequences on law. The phenomenon is not all negative. In some important ways, it should be perceived positively. After all, who is to say to an individual that his religious identity should be less important than territorial affiliation? The failure of the law as the arbiter of conflicts between individuals was not so much about the equality of the citizen before the law, but about the constitutional arrangements that regulate communities defined religiously. Although difficult to regulate, a Jewish or Muslim state is conceivable as a valid legal abstraction. The question is how to deal with people who are not ready to consider that their primary identity is religious or sectarian in a state so defined. Legal arrangements may have failed due to the absence of constitutional innovation, rather than because sectarian identity is in itself unacceptable.

To solve the problem, the Western model creates a legal distance between state and religion, and posits as principle that government is religion-neutral. Maybe there is another type of accommodation that allows non-Jews in Israel, or non-Muslims in Pakistan, to be equal citizens with fellow Jews or Muslims. It has yet to be worked out in constitutional theory and practice.

In a fundamental constitutional debate that is only starting to be addressed seriously, the era of sectarian law adumbrated in the birth of Israel and Pakistan has won the day. The logic of sectarian law has been upon the Middle East ever since, competing with, reinforcing, and complicating the dominant law of force.

The Islamic revolution in Iran came as a powerful variation in the era of sectarian-religious law. If 'Arabism', primarily defined by language, competes with 'the Middle East', which is primarily defined by geography, then a third competing concept, primarily defined by religion, is 'Islamism'. Islamic law, Shi'i law in the case of Iran, has come of age upon the access of the Islamic jurists to power in Tehran in 1978–9.

For modern Middle Eastern states, Islamic law as a major component of civilization is significant on two levels. Politically, and because of its thirteen centuries-old tradition, the *shari'a* is associated with the quintessence of Islam, and the projected Islamic state invariably defined as 'a state ruled by the *shari'a*'. Since the triumph of the Islamic revolution in Iran in 1979, the *shari'a* has served as the rallying point for the Islamic agenda across the Muslim world, including for more conservative states whose application of Islamic law, as an important element of the rulers' legitimacy, was being stretched defensively. Saudi Arabia is a case in point. Since the conquest of the Hijaz in 1926, the Kingdom's founding reference is Islamic law, but it remained limited to the domestic realm. Saudi Arabia's militant dimension developed slowly against Egyptian leader Jamal 'Abdel-Naser's secular Arabism, but the Iranian Revolution accelerated Saudi rulers' identification with puritanical Wahhabism. This became particularly marked both as a domestic Sunni counterpoint to Shi'i Iran, and as an active agency abroad, most pointedly in Soviet-occupied Afghanistan, where the US alliance dating from the oil era led to a chiefly Saudi-organized support for the Afghan militants. The Saudi and other Arab nationals who led that effort turned eventually against the rulers of Riyadh and their American supporters.

Legally, the content described in the Islamic project is more difficult to articulate, but significant efforts were exerted with a view to expand the application of the *shari'a* away from restricted areas, family law typically, into wider legal subjects. Chief among these subjects are constitutional and economic law. In the first case, the model of the Iranian Constitution became important for a government viewed from the *shari'a* prism. In economic law, the two most urgent areas for the adaptation of the *shari'a* were the regulation of production and the distribution of goods in the light of a reconstruction of legal precedents taken from the Islamic tradition; and the establishment of an Islamic financial system in which interest would be banned. The various works and models in these two fields have met with mixed results, but the sway of the *shari'a* was significantly extended in the process of investigation.

The revival of the *shari'a* in the wake of the Islamic revolution in Iran and the subsequent rise of Islamic political militancy across the Middle East is difficult to assess in terms of lasting impact. Whether the Islamic wave has peaked or not in political terms, there is little doubt that the renewed interest in Islamic law has struck intellectual root.

On the level of the positive application of law defined as a total break with the legal 'secular' past, the picture is more difficult to ascertain. Even if Iran prides itself as the mother-country of revolutionary Islam in power—as opposed to smothered attempts in several other Middle East countries such as Syria, Iraq, and Egypt—reference to Islamic law, even in the Iranian experience, has failed to overhaul the system known to the *ancien régime*. A typical illustration is the Iranian Civil Code, which was promulgated in the 1930s, and which was only marginally amended by the Islamic revolution. Apart from limited restructuring of the family court system and the introduction of a few provisions destined to reverse legislation passed by the Shah, the Civil Code of Iran was in the main left intact.

Most countries in the Middle East are self-styled 'Muslim' countries, with many either officially known in their constitutional appellation as 'Islamic states'—for example, Mauritania, Pakistan—or closely associated with Islam—Saudi Arabia, Sudan, Egypt—in the standing they accord to the operation of Islamic law in their constitutions and in their codes. In practice, every country, including Israel, recognizes some application of Islamic law. The ongoing debate concerns the exact ambit of the *shari'a*. 'Back to the *shari'a*' slogans should not mask the forest for the few trees of passing fashion, and it is important to assess the positive dimension of a Middle Eastern legal tradition in which Islamic law has played the dominant role for the past 1,400 years. Such is the paradox of the religious era that it does not allow the many nuances so badly needed to assess the complexity of deep religious-legal traditions.

September 2001. Era of Middle Eastern and global law. Western (colonial) law, oil law, law of force, sectarian law, these are all metaphors for non-law. Legal deformity as a cumulative metaphor exploded on the world scene when some 3,000 people were killed in spectacular suicide attacks in New York, Washington, and Pennsylvania on the morning of 11 September 2001.

Not until the end of the twenty-first century will it be clear whether that date represents a turning point in world history or a mere footnote in the larger scheme of things. Less than a decade after the conscious targeting by Islamic militants of the two symbols of America's world power—finance and trade, and the military—I will risk a long-term projection. The date is here to last as a defining historical moment, because it marks the irruption of the Middle East into the daily lives of Western citizens. On that day the history of the Middle East became part and parcel of the *domestic* history of the United States of America. America and the rest of the Western world have lived the Middle East ever since as an internal issue.

Violence has always been a midwife to history, and massacres are not new to the contemporary Middle East, nor of course to the rest of the world. Soon after the New York massacre, Robert Fossaert, the great French polymath,[9] reminded

---

[9] Historian, banker, sociologist, from outside traditional academic circles, Robert Fossaert is the author of an eight-volume Summa entitled *La Société*, 6 vols. published between 1977 and 1983 at Le Seuil, Paris, followed by 2 vols. on *Le Monde au 21ème siècle: une théorie des systèmes mondiaux*, at Fayard, Paris, 1991, and *L'Avenir du socialisme*, at Stock, Paris, 1996. I have often benefited from his encyclopaedic thought, including his incisive remarks on the present chapter. For the relativity of Septembers in modern history: 'Quand on évoque le 11 septembre, rares sont ceux qui pensent à l'année 1973 où, ce jour-là, le coup d'État de Pinochet contre le gouvernement Allende secoua le Chili, avec l'aide de la CIA américaine. Le vrai 11 septembre est celui de 2001 où des "terroristes"—naguère entraînés par cette même CIA et ses alliés pakistanais, pour chasser d'Afghanistan les envahisseurs soviétiques—détruisirent une aile du Pentagone et les deux tours du *World Trade Center* new-yorkais. Aucun bouclier anti-missiles n'aurait pu entraver l'action de ces "terroristes" qui s'armèrent de Boeing piratés en vol. Et bientôt, toute la planète retentit des rugissements médiatiques du lion américain dont l'orgueil venait d'être blessé. De 1973 à 2001, la différence des 11 septembre résulte

people of those other infamous days of September 1973 in Chile, when the democratic government of Salvador Allende was overthrown and thousands of Chilean civilians taken to their death, with the complicity of the United States government of the time. For Middle Easterners, September is a cruel month associated with the Sabra and Shatila massacres of 1982. While the response to violence is dominantly couched in violence, an alternative is slowly emerging. Like Pinochet before the British judiciary, then before Chilean courts, a response to wide-scale killings is also being sought in law. That was the choice made by the Sabra and Shatila survivors. In June 2001, they brought a case in the Brussels criminal court on the basis that the crime against humanity which defines in law the Sabra and Shatila massacres should be tried under the universal competence law passed by the Belgian legislator in 1993, a statute reinforced and enlarged in 1999. Against strong resistance from the main accused, then Prime Minister of Israel, the case succeeded in a landmark decision of the Belgian Supreme Court on 12 February 2003, subsequent to which the Israeli government withdrew its ambassador from Belgium.[10] In law, another defining moment was emerging: a judicial response to large-scale violence defined as crime against humanity. The fact that the case ultimately failed to put the accused behind bars should not obscure the titanic fight, both real and symbolic. Within the Middle East, and on the world scene, the battle is joined between the rule of law and the rule of violence.

The conflation of Septembers puts the legal question as follows: will violence continue to rule the Middle East, and by extension the world in so far as Middle Eastern violence is no longer confined to the region? Since the sole alternative to violence is law, what are the chances of the rule of law replacing the law of the jungle inside the region, and in its projections onto a planetary scale?

This book tries to provide some answers, as the emergent era's defining features suggest a far more intricate common destiny between the Middle East and the rest of the world. A Middle East-defined state of war has become enmeshed in the domestic life of the Western world on account of the new era's birth in immense violence. As a consequence of the extremist drive which is inevitable in war, the dominant political message has been revenge in both East and West. The expression of political and economic frustration in the Middle East takes a religious form which Islamic militants have imposed on the world agenda, however much of a fringe group initially. The dominant Western response is equally defined in violence, with a heavy military response including the occupation of two Middle

---

du rôle que les États-Unis s'assignent dans le monde actuel et, plus encore, de la place qu'ils y occupent.' Robert Fossaert, *Civiliser les Etats-Unis* (Paris, 2003) opening sentence. This and other works by Fossaert are easily accessible on the site managed at the Université du Québec à Chicoutimi, <http://classiques.uqac.ca/> (last consulted October 2006).

[10] English translation of the decision of the Belgian Cour de Cassation of 12 February 2003, *Samiha Abbas Hijazi and 28 others v. Ariel Sharon, Amos Yaron et al.*, in appendix to John Borneman, ed., *The case of Ariel Sharon and the fate of universal jurisdiction* (Princeton, 2004).

Eastern countries within two years of the New York massacre. Revenge and war are the *de facto* dominant trends emerging from the planetary earthquake caused on 11 September. There is little meaning for law in such a polarized picture.

This, on the negative side, but the demand is equally high for an alternative to revenge and the cycle of death. Life must prevail. The common destiny now steeped in blood forces a renewed search for a common language. Much of that language will be defined legally, against an ongoing chasm between legal models that are alien to each another in historical and eschatological terms.[11]

The legal challenge is clear: how much can global law, understood in its cosmo-politan Kantian sense as adumbrated in the German philosopher's *Treaty on perpetual peace* (1795), accommodate the local legal tradition? So far, a dialogue of the deaf persists between the language of democracy, understood as a universal calling in the Western tradition best described by Kant two centuries ago, and the description by Muslim militants of their own calling as one defined by Islamic law. A passage to Middle Eastern law may offer that common platform. The ques-tion is whether Middle Eastern and Western law can find a common language in the midst of a violence that has been uninterrupted in the region for some 200 years, and has now extended to the heart of Western capitals after engulfing the daily lives of Middle Easterners for so long. The next chapters provide legal elements that help in understanding that battle for the soul of the Middle East, and of the rest of the planet.

---

[11] The fight also takes place within the United States, where a 2006 bi-partisan report has chosen to put forward an alternative national security strategy under the title 'Liberty under law'. See Anne-Marie Slaughter and John Ikenberry, eds., *Forging a world of liberty under law: US national security in the 21st Century* (Princeton, 2006), and my brief comment 'From Princeton, a new power paradigm', *The Daily Star*, 10 October 2006.

4

Constitutional Law: The Specificity of Middle Eastern Constitutionalism

Religion as such is not our subject, but in the spheres reflected in our documents Mesopotomian religion *is* politics.[1]

René Maunier, a prolific French ethnologist and jurist (1887–1951), summed up in 1935 the radical transformation of Middle Eastern law since the nineteenth century. In a brief report entitled 'Outline of the progress of law in Muslim land', he noted the centrality of law in the immense change affecting the societies of North Africa he knew:

Amongst the *social* changes which can take place, one should put first *legal changes*. In Islamic countries, there have been sometimes, over more than one hundred and fifty years already, a transformation of *legislation*, and a transformation of *jurisdiction*: new laws, new judges. This transformation (which was at times evolution, at times revolution) is an important occurrence, which can busy an investigator who is at once a jurist and a sociologist. *Rara avis*.[2]

The sociologist, of course, is not the only social researcher concerned with the irruption of new laws and new judges in 'the age of codification',[3] replete as it is with statutes and codes. Political scientists and students of 'government' have been naturally concerned with the emergence of founding charters and constitutions in the new nation-states in the region. If taught in the Middle East, an introductory course on these founding texts would generally take the shape of a discussion of current constitutions and constitutional models in the world, with an emphasis on the local or regional constitutions, much in the way 'droit constitutionnel'

---

[1] J. N. Postgate, *Early Mesopotamia* (London, 1992) 260. Emphasis in original.

[2] 'Parmi les changements *sociaux* qui peuvent avoir lieu, il faut placer, au premier rang, les *changements légaux*. Dans les pays d'Islam, il y a eu parfois, depuis déjà cent cinquante ans, transformation de la *législation*, transformation de la *juridiction*: des statuts nouveaux, des juges nouveaux. Cette transformation (qui fut tantôt évolution, tantôt révolution) est un grand fait, qui pourrait occuper un enquêteur qui fût juriste et sociologue en même temps. *Rara avis*' (emphasis in original). The text, which was originally published in 1942, is reproduced in M. Flory and J. R. Henry, *L'enseignement du droit musulman* (Marseille, 1989) 168–9, in an appendix to the article by Henry on 'Approches ethnologiques du droit musulman: l'apport de René Maunier', at 133–69.

[3] Argument on 'the age of *qanun* (or codification)' in Chapter 2 *in fine*, and Chapter 7.

would, until recently, have been taught in France. This will be my approach in the
present chapter. In an American setting, such a presentation would qualify under
the rubric of 'government' or 'political science'. A course on constitutional law
taught in an American law school entails a very different type of discussion, centred on case-law as developed over two centuries of constitutional review by the
US Supreme Court. The discrepancy between the two modes of constitutional
law study is qualitative. It also underlines the passage to an American style of constitutional review in the Middle East in a slow but perceptible move away from the
European tradition, at a time when many European countries have themselves
been affected by the 'Americanization of the law'.[4]

The long ignorance by Middle Eastern countries of constitutional review is
rooted in the process of colonization. Neither Britain, nor France until the emergence of the Fifth Republic in 1958, was ready to accept judicial fetters on
Parliament's sovereignty. The Middle Eastern colonies didn't know any better. In a
region where French legal education had prevailed in universities, and continues to
dominate as far as the teaching method is concerned, the model of the US Supreme
Court was a remote and alien phenomenon. Curricula and courts followed suit.[5]

The absence until recently of constitutional councils and courts means that
there has been scant judicial review in the US mode in any Middle Eastern jurisdiction. Even in a common law country like Israel, where the English legal model
was influential and remains central to date,[6] judicial review always fell short of the
judges' constitutional review of parliamentary statutes. In the absence of a constitution, there is in Israel no 'superior' text which can serve as the yardstick for ordinary laws, although piecemeal 'Basic Laws' with so-called 'entrenched rights' have
been introduced since the foundation of the state in 1948 to enlarge that writ.
Still, the legacy of the British concept of absolute parliamentarian sovereignty
remains a marked feature of the Israeli system. This applies, *mutatis mutandis* until
the 1980s, across the region. Only in Pakistan is it different, following the example
of the neighbouring Indian constitutional court, but the turmoil of the Pakistani
political system since independence in August 1947 has rendered that experiment
relative and inconsistent.[7]

---

[4] See e.g. Bruce Ackerman, 'The rise of world constitutionalism', *Virginia Law Review*, 83, 1997,
771–97; François Terré, ed., *L'américanisation du droit* (Paris, 2001).

[5] A cursory reading of the curricula of law schools in the Middle East shows the domination, with
few exceptions such as in Saudi Arabia, of Western-style courses. Even in Saudi Arabia, the teaching
of law with an insistence on *fiqh* does not really count as *droit positif*. There are few monographs and
articles on the subject of law schools. See Enid Hill, *Al-Sanhuri and Islamic law*, Cairo Papers in Social
Science, 10, 1987, 18–20 (early law schools in modern Egypt); J. Ducruet, *Livre d'or (1913–1993) de
la Faculté de droit, de sciences politiques et économiques* (Beirut, 1995) 7–64 (law schools in the modern
Lebanese state); Donald Malcolm Reid, *Cairo University and the making of modern Egypt* (Cambridge,
1990); Bernard Botiveau, *Loi islamique et droit dans les sociétés arabes* (Paris, 1993) Chapter 5, 'La
réforme à l'oeuvre: l'enseignement du droit', 167–89. Also Chapter 7 n. 6.

[6] English decisions are quoted extensively by Israeli courts, and the Israeli bar continues to recognize UK law degrees. See for an introduction in English, Shimon Shetreet, *Justice in Israel: a study of
the Israeli judiciary* (Dordrecht, 1994).

[7] On Pakistan, see Martin Lau, 'Introduction to the Pakistani legal system, with special reference
to the law of contract', in E. Cotran and C. Mallat, eds., *Yearbook of Islamic and Middle Eastern Law*,

Against this weak tradition, the trend towards judicial constitutional review is strong across the Middle East, with the introduction of various models of constitutional review in the last decades in Egypt, Iran, and the United Arab Emirates, and more recently in Yemen, Lebanon, Jordan, Algeria, and Morocco.[8]

An analysis of Middle Eastern constitutional law is therefore possible on two levels. Following the French model, the analysis examines the political institutions of various states, the way elections are carried out, the separation of powers if any, and the division of responsibilities between executive and legislative powers in constitutional texts and in practice. The system is studied from a top-bottom perspective, the way constitutional law is usually taught in France (*'gouvernants* and *gouvernés'*). This is the analytical course pursued in the present chapter.

The other type of analysis follows a US mode of exposition. There, decisions of the courts are the focus of the analysis, in so far as they shed cumulative light on the rule of law getting fleshed out in the practice of judicial review understood broadly, and in constitutional adjudication in more recent experiments. This is the focus of the next chapter.

The same subject-matter, constitutions and constitutional law, can be appreciated therefore from these two different perspectives, which also correspond to a top-down as opposed to a bottom-up process.

In addition to the distinction between classical French constitutional law in its descriptive exposition on the one hand, and, on the other hand, the US discussion of the Supreme Court's constitutional decisions (the US law schools' 'Socratic method'), a further distinction, this time between English law and US law, helps identify the two different ways in which judicial review may get carried out. When, as in the UK, a constitution does not nominally exist—as is the case in Israel and in Saudi Arabia until 1992—Middle Eastern judges must resort to 'ordinary' laws or to general principles of the law of the land. More often a constitution does exist, but the courts have no constitutional jurisdiction. This is the most common situation, which prevails in the Maghreb, in the Levant, Iraq, and the Gulf. When they examine a case which involves a 'human right', judges cannot turn to the constitution which usually enunciates it. In effect, the situation becomes close to that of countries without a constitution. Courts are limited to applying ordinary law. Administrative law as known in France or in the United Kingdom has traditionally been the main place for judicial review of state acts, especially state violation of citizens' rights.[9]

Overall, Middle Eastern constitutional law has predominantly followed the French 'political science/government' model, and ignored constitutional scrutiny in its American—and since 1949, German—form. But recent years have witnessed the timid but increasing allure of constitutional review. This rise deserves a full, separate chapter, together with the shape of 'constitutional law' in Middle

---

vol. 1, 1994 (Leiden, 1995) 3–28, and Lau's subsequent annual entries in the *Yearbook of Islamic and Middle Eastern Law.*

[8] Discussed next chapter.   [9] Chapter 6 below.

Eastern countries under the English model of 'judicial review' in their sub- or pre-constitutional nature, specifically in criminal and administrative law.

One follows constitutional law in the Middle East in a traditional French-style manner by examining executive, legislative, and judicial powers, their respective attributions and interaction, and the way rulers get chosen (or not) to govern a country. While some of this traditional description is inevitable, it is more useful to underline specific Middle Eastern themes. Accordingly, this chapter examines contemporary constitutionalism under three headings, which define a broad concept of constitutional law from the point of view of *gouvernants*: (1) the shadow of trans-jurisdictional unity and its failure; (2) the dominant ideological and legal debate on the key concepts of constitutionalism, democracy, and Islam, often presented under the wide rubric 'democracy and Islam (or sometimes other local religions and sects)'; and (3) the suggested *summa divisio* between personal and territorial law. All of this is law—or political, institutional power—as exercised from the top.

The Failure of Transnational Institutions

However hazy, a Middle Eastern pattern exists which, for particular historical reasons connected with colonialism and the fragmentation of the area, needs some attention: the craving of people for a unity built on a real or imagined Arab or Islamic commonwealth.

Article 52 of the Charter of the United Nations favours the emergence of sub-regional groupings as a matter of principle.[10] Yearning for such a regional grouping is hardly an exclusively Middle Eastern phenomenon. Many countries which appear less prone to integration have managed to create working regional subsystems the world over. Europe is the most successful example. In the one area which prides itself on a centuries-old legacy of Arab-Muslim empires and offers in its rhetoric a deep obsession with 'unity' against the fragmentation forced upon the region by modern colonialism, it is ironic that nearly all transnational endeavours have ended in failure. Still, the ebb and flow between nation-states' exclusive sovereignty and transnational models have considerably affected the structure of the rule of law in the Middle East.

Through the historical domestic formation of each state, as well as with regard to regional processes, constitutions in twentieth-century Middle East offer the spectre of a tug-of-war between transnational integration and the independent

---

[10] UN Charter, Chapter viii, Regional arrangements: 'Article 52: 1. Nothing in the present Charter precludes the existence of regional arrangements or agencies for dealing with such matters relating to the maintenance of international peace and security as are appropriate for regional action, provided that such arrangements or agencies and their activities are consistent with the Purposes and Principles of the United Nations ... 3. The Security Council shall encourage the development of pacific settlement of local disputes through such regional arrangements or by such regional agencies either on the initiative of the states concerned or by reference from the Security Council.'

development of national institutions. Constitutional development of the region's legal systems can be followed along these two lines: the separate growth of the twenty-five or so independent countries in the Middle East, and the complex and uncertain process of their integration and/or dismemberment.

The political disenfranchisement of nation-states in the region has generally unfolded in a battle for self-determination followed by independence, but the constitutional development of the Middle Eastern system has lain primarily in the specific and discrete legal and institutional construction within each state. Owing to individual countries' separate national development, the region is more accurately approached jurisdiction by jurisdiction. This is also consistent with history. The mode of colonization is different for every single jurisdiction. Algeria's colonization by France for 130 years means that the constitutional setting of independent Algeria was profoundly different from the process which took place in neighbouring Morocco, where the French protectorate (1906–56) did not seek to uproot the local ruler altogether. Across Western North Africa, French legal influence is evident. This is not the case in the Gulf states, especially Saudi Arabia and Iran, the only two countries that were never formal colonies.

In parallel with developments prevalent in each individual jurisdiction, suprastate unity was pursued at various moments on the basis of geographic or national-religious commonalty. This effort was pervasive in twentieth-century Middle East, where the search for transnational unification operates on linguistic-ethnic (Arabic, Kurdish, Turkish-Turanian . . .) and religious (Muslim, Shi'i, Sunni . . .) bases, together with, on the opposite side, the rejection of the nation-state boundaries in favour of sometimes smaller and allegedly more homogenous entities (Christian Maronites in Lebanon, Berbers/Amazighs in Algeria, Kurds in Iraq, Syria, Turkey, Kurds and Azeris in Iran . . .).

In most instances, the institutional development within unchallenged boundaries has carried the day. Such is the situation of Morocco, Algeria, Libya, Tunisia, Egypt, Mauritania, Syria, Jordan, Saudi Arabia, and so far also of Turkey and Iran. In some cases in contrast, the nation-state is problematic, and the regional overtone dominant. This is evident in Lebanon and Palestine-Israel, where fragmentation did (or does) threaten the unity of a given territory. Protracted civil strife tends to lead to *de facto*, if not *de jure*, distinct entities, for instance in the endemic civil wars in Afghanistan and Sudan, in the Kurdish 'safe haven' established in June 1991, which lasted until the reunification of Iraq in April 2003 when Baghdad fell to American power, or in Somaliland as a break-away state from war-ridden Somalia: all are cases in point of failed states resulting in self-ruling, unstable subnational entities. But regional considerations and transnational yearnings also regularly push Middle Eastern governments to attempt mergers on the basis of larger entities—with various degrees of failure or success.

The interconnection between state development and regional integration is clearest in the case of the Arab-Israeli conflict. In September 1993, when the Israeli Prime Minister and the leader of the Palestine Liberation Organization—as the umbrella organization of Palestinian nationalism—initialled a first agreement in Washington, there already existed in theory a Palestinian state which had been proclaimed in November 1988 and officially recognized by over 100 governments in the world. But the state of Palestine did not receive a recognition strong enough to allow it to figure as such in the United Nations, nor did it have any territorial control over the part of Palestine in which it purported to be located, and to which, in any case, the founders of the new state had not ascribed any defined boundaries.

The Palestinian 'entity' lacked the formal attributes of a normal state until it achieved some 'territorial' being. As a consequence, even though the Chairman of the PLO had put himself forward as the President of the State of Palestine, there was no Palestinian government, and the rest of the PLO institutions had retained a non-statal character, with only shades of diplomatic 'embassy-status' in some friendly countries. This meant in terms of constitutional law a complex picture of a state-in-formation with the hallmarks of a transitory and frail authority where institutions cannot be recognised as similar to those of any other normal state. The Oslo Accords altered the picture, transforming the 1988 Palestine state into a more real hope, but its reality in the first decade of the twenty-first century was still elusive.[11]

This is not to say there was no 'constitutional' law for Palestine, or for Palestinians, even before the Oslo Agreement and subsequent texts came into being. One could distinguish a clear institutional Palestinian format under the umbrella of the Palestine Liberation Organization (PLO), a 'Basic Law' of sorts under the name of the National Charter,[12] and a 'legislative' body constituted by the Palestinian National Council (PNC). The PNC regrouped, from both the Palestinian diaspora and the Territories occupied by Israel in 1967, Palestinian notables who met and debated regularly. The PNC also elected an Executive Committee, headed by a Chairman.[13]

Despite the formal Palestinian recurrent get-together, the split representation between Palestinians of the interior and Palestinians in exile expressed the limited legislative role of the Palestinian National Council. For the PNC, it was never a question of issuing statutes for a homeland over which Palestinians have no legal control. Yet, because of the in-built consensual process and a relatively meaningful representation among the Palestinian constituencies that the PLO had forged, the decisions of the Executive Committee of the PLO were not tantamount to dead letter. There was significant financial power—although not strictly a budget—tightly controlled by the Executive Committee's Chairman, as

---

[11] Out of an extensive literature, see the collective work I edited with Eugene Cotran, *The Arab-Israeli accords: legal perspectives* (Leiden, 1996). See also next section below.

[12] Palestinian National Charter(s) discussed in my *The Middle East into the 21st century* (Reading, 1996) 61–6.

[13] Good overview of the institutions of the PLO in Helena Cobban, *The Palestinian Liberation Organization* (Cambridge, 1984) chart at 13. Yazid Sayigh, *Armed struggle and the search for state: the Palestinian national movement, 1949–1993* (Oxford, 1997).

well as an important social and military infrastructure, which was regulated by the semi-institutionalized consultations of the PLO organs, including 'revolutionary courts' with a dubious track record and varying degrees of autonomy in and around the Palestinian camps of the diaspora.

This is the 'domestic' side of the Palestinian state. But the internal structure paled into insignificance constitutionally in comparison with the dominant regional process. The regional process, in turn, is only legal to a limited extent. It has been determined, in the twentieth century, by a violent struggle involving communities and armies whose technological and disciplinary cohesion allowed the Jewish colonies and, after 1948, the Israeli state, to have the upper hand. On the legal level, the agreements and treaties in the area, mainly the Camp David Accords of 1978 and the Oslo Accords in 1993 and 1995,[14] offer a sense of the importance of law for states and peoples involved. The implications are evident for any Palestinian state, entity, homeland, or regional formation which may emerge from the peace process, with its roller-coaster hopes and failures. Meanwhile, the law for the majority of Palestinians in exile has been refugee law as administered by the United Nations through a special agency called UNRWA, adding to a motley of laws in areas like the West Bank, where Israeli military decrees were superimposed on Jordanian and Ottoman law. West Bank residues of Jordanian law are themselves composed of articles of the Ottoman nineteenth-century Majalla, classical Islamic law regulations,[15] and state-of-emergency decrees dating from English domination, adapted and updated by Israeli military decrees. Hence the importance of the regional framework for a definition of Palestinian 'constitutional' law.[16]

The supra-state dimension may be glaring in the case of Palestine, but it is also significant in almost all the Arab countries after independence. Examples can be listed of the regional conflicts which have plagued the area since the Second World War, the last and most spectacular occurring upon the invasion of Kuwait and its annexation for seven months by Iraq between August 1990 and March 1991.

The vanishing and re-emergence of the state in the case of Palestine and Kuwait show the prevalence of regional considerations over internal state formation. Another instance of the problem of the nation-state in the Middle East, in contrast,

---

[14] The official title of the agreement between Egypt and Israel is The Egyptian-Israeli Treaty. It was signed in Camp David in 1978. The so-called Oslo Accords stand for The Declaration of Principles on Interim Self-Government Arrangements, signed in Washington on 13 September 1993 (known as Oslo 1) and the Israeli-Palestinian Agreement on the West Bank and the Gaza Strip, signed in Washington on 28 September 1995 (Oslo 2). There were no further formal agreements in the following decade, despite various tentative accords, including two 'Taba agreements' soon after the so-called Second Intifada broke out on 28 September 2000, but a number of Security Council Resolutions 1397 (12 March 2002) and 1515 (19 November 2003), and international plans (by 'the Quartet', especially) established, or promised to establish, a Palestinian state.

[15] For instance for *waqf*, see Michael Dumper, *Islam and Israel: Muslim religious endowments and the Jewish state* (Beirut, 1993).

[16] For the legal dimension, a major source of scholarship and reference is *The Palestinian Yearbook of International Law*, edited since 1984 by Anis F. Kassim, then by Camille Mansour.

suggests that the regional factor may act in a constructive way. In 1990, for the
first time since early colonization two centuries before, the two parts of South
West Arabia known as the Yemen were united. With the foundation of the Yemen
Arab Republic in 1962 and the independence of South Yemen in 1967, two different legal systems had ruled the southern Popular Democratic Republic of
Yemen and the northern Arab Republic of Yemen. Their union in 1990 triggered
a number of transitional steps, starting with the formation of a unified government under a new constitution. From the inception of the politically united
Yemen, difficulties in streamlining legal institutions were apparent, not only in
commercial, civil, land, and criminal matters, with South Yemen coming out of a
socialist and collectivist system of laws, but also in other sensitive matters such as
family law and the structure of the judiciary. As the populations merged, the family law of South Yemen, one of the more egalitarian Arab statutes in terms of
women's rights, and the more traditional family law of North Yemen, passed in
1984, needed to be unified both procedurally and in substance.[17] Unification of
the judiciary into a single court system also meant that the looser, more informal
Northern system had to accommodate a British-inspired hierarchical structure
which prevailed in Southern courts until the Union. While operational for three
years, unified Yemen fell prey to what proved to be a trying merger of institutions.
With the country in the throes of civil war from 27 April 1994 to the fall of Aden
into the hands of the Northern-based army in June of that year, the collapse and
reunification of the Yemen illustrated, once again, the hazards of dreams of unity.[18]
The initially voluntary merger was consolidated by sheer force, and the question
of the long-term stability of the merged Yemen remains open, but unity has survived
into the new century.

On the western side of the Arab world, the Grand Maghreb was declared
in 1989, at the meeting in Marrakesh on 17 February of five heads of state—
Mauritania, Morocco, Algeria, Libya, and Tunisia. Unlike several previous
attempts between various countries to move towards integration, the Treaty on
the Arab Maghreb Union (AMU) created formal institutions, including a
Presidential Council with a six-month rotating head of state, a Council of
Foreign Affairs Ministers, a Consultative Council formed of members of the
respective Parliaments, as well as a committee of judges drawn from each country
to adjudicate potential litigation. This institutional shell remains to date, but the
domestic uncertainties plaguing the government of each country, and the tendency for the leaderships to act outside the framework of the AMU have not
made the prospects for integration any closer two decades into the AMU Treaty.
With less than a fraction of the overall economic exchange taking place in the

---

[17] Full section on Yemen family law in Chapter 10.

[18] An elaborate work on law in the Yemen is Brinkley Messick, *The calligraphic state* (Berkeley,
1993). On Yemeni law generally, and other Middle Eastern and Arab jurisdictions, the annual entries
in *The Yearbook of Islamic and Middle Eastern Law* usually offer most helpful points of legal entry in
jurisdictions some of which have very little legal scholarship available for study.

Grand Maghreb despite the geographic contiguity of the five states, and the auto-cratic traditions prevailing at the helm, the grand design and ideals of the heads of government have hardly stood the test of time.[19]

A similar attempt can be found in the Gulf Cooperation Council (GCC), and in the Arab Cooperation Council. The first of these two regional formations, con-stituted in 1981 between Saudi Arabia, Kuwait, the United Arab Emirates, Bahrain, Oman, and Qatar, was a response to the Iran–Iraq War, which had dis-rupted the stability of the Gulf region from September 1980. Despite the com-mon institutions—a Supreme Council, a Ministerial Council, and a Secretariat, the fragility of the group was evident in the inability of the GCC to defend Kuwait, one of its member states, against its legal obliteration by Iraq in August 1990. The second regional group, created on 16 January 1989, from Iraq, Egypt, Jordan, and North Yemen, also fell victim to the quick pace of regional changes in the form of the unity between North and South Yemen and the hiatus between Egypt and Iraq after the invasion of Kuwait.

This striving for unity on a regional basis persists as a lasting magnet in the Middle East. Although this drive had more often than not been defeated before the ink had dried on 'the acts of unity', there are some significant instances where unity developed into real constitutional integration. The first case occurred when Syria and Egypt merged in 1958 in the United Arab Republic. The experience lasted two years and ended in total disarray, but the two years saw significant, if not lasting, changes in the constitutional set-up of the two countries, including the merger of Parliaments and the entrusting of executive leadership to one president.[20]

A more enduring enterprise of unity is that of the former Trucial States of the Eastern Arab Peninsula. The United Arab Emirates is a federation of the Emirates of Dubai, Sharjah, 'Ajman, Umm al-Quwayna, Fujaira, Ras al-Khaima, and Abu Dhabi.[21] It was formed in 1971 and operates under a constitution which was

---

[19] Together with the *Yearbook* mentioned in the previous note, see the useful surveys, with a strong public law content, conducted by the French *Annuaire de l'Afrique du Nord*, published since 1962. A plethora of semi-official publications in French and Arabic accompanied the declaration of the Grand Maghreb.

[20] Text of the Provisional Constitution of the United Arab Republic in Yusif Quzma Khuri ed., *Al-dasatir fil-'alam al-'arabi 1839–1987* (Constitutions in the Arab world 1839–1987) (Beirut, 1988) 567–70. This is a good reference book, hereinafter *Al-dasatir*, to be supplemented by the bilingual French-Arabic *Constitutions des pays arabes* (Beirut, 2000) edited by Eric Canal-Forgues and compris-ing useful introductions to each constitution. English texts of constitutions can generally be found in the collection of Albert Blaustein and Gilbert Flanz, eds., *Constitutions of the countries of the world* (New York, 1971–(looseleaf, updated)). Unless otherwise specified, references hereinafter to articles in Middle East constitutions can be found in these collections.

[21] For a good history of the coming together of the Emirates, see Rosemarie Said Zahlan, *The making of the modern Gulf states: Kuwait, Bahrain, Qatar, the United Arab Emirates and Oman* (London, rev. edn., 1999, orig. 1978). Political and historical studies on the UAE are few and far between, but the importance of business in the UAE has generated the rare publication of a collection of decisions of the UAE appellate courts in Richard Price and Essam Al Tamimi, eds., *United Arab Emirates Court of Cassation judgments 1998–2003* (Leiden, 2005). For earlier decisions see the same editors, *United Arab Emirates Court of Cassation judgments, 1989–1997* (The Hague, 1998).

designed originally for a period of five years, and which has since been extended periodically. The greatest difficulty in the federal experience of the UAE consists in finding the right balance between federal power and the power of individual Emirates; it was agreed that the major issues were to be decided by the federation, but that each Emirate could legislate until the matter was covered by UAE federal law. In this way, the Emirates retained a significant residual legislative role not specifically granted to the federation by the constitution.

The deciding body of last resort in the UAE is the Supreme Council, which comprises the Rulers of each Emirate and their deputies. It establishes UAE policy, decrees laws, and is entrusted with ultimate decision-making for the Federation on the basis of majority vote, but Abu Dhabi and Dubai retain a veto power because of their greater importance as the richest and most populated Emirates in the Federation. The Supreme Council appoints, from amongst its own members, the President and the Vice-President of the UAE, who are in charge of issuing union laws after consultation with the Council of Ministers, in turn appointed by the President. The President is also the Chairman of the Supreme Council.

Alongside the President, the Supreme Council, and the Council of Ministers, a National Federal Council is in theory responsible for passing laws. In fact, the forty members of the Council are not elected, and their role as appointees of the Rulers is predominantly consultative. The legislative process is therefore in the hands of the Rulers and, by delegation, the Council of Ministers. Article 110 of the Constitution stipulates that a bill becomes law after 'preparation' by the Council of Ministers, which submits it to the approval of the Supreme Council and the President.[22] In theory the bill should also receive the agreement of the National Federal Council. The agreement can be dispensed with if the bill is ratified by the President after approval by the Supreme Council.[23]

The Federation allows for a distinctive limitation of powers by the individual Emirates, including control over their natural resources, taxation, and police. In 1981, Article 142 of the Constitution was amended by the Supreme Council in order to strengthen federal power by restricting the right to levy an army to the federal authorities. The leeway left to local Rulers for the regulation of their own affairs tends to slowly give way to federal power, with part of the oil revenues going into the federal budget, which is drafted by the Council of Ministers and approved by the Supreme Council.

Although it is clear from the constitutional set-up of the state that the main separation of powers derives from the traditional autonomy of the local rulers, the UAE represents the only working federation in the Middle East. It depends in practice on the achievement of consensus amongst the individual rulers, rather than on the democratic interplay between institutions, and renders the federal

---

[22] Art. 110 of the Provisional Constitution of the State of the United Arab Emirates (1971), *Al-dustur al-mu'aqqat li-dawlat al-imarat al-'arabiyya al-muttahida*, text in *Al-dasatir*, 83–95.
[23] Art. 110.3 and 110.4, UAE Constitution.

arrangements fragile. The UAE experiment is exceptional, since other regional integration attempts have all ended in failure.

The most telling example of the failed attempts at Arab integration is the Arab League,[24] founded in Cairo in the wake of the Second World War.

The Arab League is neither a unitary nor a federal system. As a loose confederation, it lacks central political authority, and the decisions it takes are reached on the basis of unanimity. The treaty establishing the Arab League was signed by Egypt, Iraq, Lebanon, Syria, Saudi Arabia, and Jordan, on 22 March 1945. It defined its objectives generally as better cooperation among the Arab countries and the defence of their common interests. With many more Arab countries acquiring independence, the League grew in size and importance, and it has often acted as a mediating body in conflicts between Member States. It occasionally plays a role in the relations between Member States and the outside world—such as the European Union—but in the main it has tended to be active in the confrontation between the Arab world and Israel. Badly bruised after the expulsion of Egypt from its midst in the wake of the Camp David Accords (1979), the League took ten years to re-erect a new façade of Arab unity, only for the 1990 invasion of Kuwait by Iraq to signal the swan-song of its efficiency.

Yet the Arab League did play a role as the cultural and social focus enhancing regional exchange, including in the field of law. This was done in two ways: in the first place, the League's Secretary-General retains a role not dissimilar to the United Nations Secretary-General in the world system. He is chosen for a renewable period of five years by two-thirds of the League's Member States' representatives. Although his functions are not specified with any precision, he has acted as the Arab League spokesman in times of consensus, as well as a mediator between states in conflict. Through him and the Arab League offices are implemented the decisions of the League's Council; the Council itself is made up of representatives of the Member States who meet irregularly, sometimes at summit level. The second regional focus of the Arab League lay in the various treaties and sub-organizations that it has spawned since its establishment. In 1950, a 'common defence and economic cooperation' treaty was entered into as a way to institutionalize military and economic councils. It has remained a dead letter. Many other Arab organizations emerged, such as the Arab Postal Union (1954), the Arab Bank for Development (1959), the Arab Financial Institute (1961), the Arab Common Market (1964), the Arab Federation for Tourism (1965), all equally ineffective. There are specialized offices which tend to be more useful than the 'organizations', like the Institute of Arab Manuscripts, which has managed to coordinate efforts in a marginal area, and the Anti-Israel Boycott Office, which issues guidelines for legislation that bear some of the hallmarks of 'federal' legislation. For example, standard international business contracts in Arab countries included until the peace treaties with Israel a clause which renders the contract void if the non-Arab

---

[24] Jami'at al-duwal al-'arabiyya. Founding Charter (*mithaq*) of 1945 in *Al-dasatir*, 125–7.

party has a manufacturing branch in Israel. In the absence of a controlling body, which never materialized despite the repeated talk about an Arab Court of Justice, it was left to each state to issue regulations and to implement commonly agreed boycott policies. In practice, legal integration at the level of such Arab institutions has been haphazard, poor, and inefficient.

Less official but in practice more significant inter-Arab organizations were professionally based. To date, such bodies as the Union of Arab Writers and the Union of Arab Lawyers can be viewed as lasting, if not particularly successful, region-wide professional organizations. Although the world of politics has dominated their irregular meetings, joint work was possible on a professional basis, occasionally resulting in comparative legislative drafts. A case in point is the Draft Personal Status Law issued in 1986 by the common endeavour of the Arab Ministers of Justice.[25] While it is not likely to be implemented in the near future, it offers a meaningful example of the continuing search for regional legislative convergence.

On the whole, the Arab League has been unable to transcend its image as an inefficient parleying forum to become a real federative unit. At the economic level in particular, where some progress was expected *pace* the European model, the Arab Common Market has proved a failure.

Although there is significant labour and business traffic between Arab states due to deep family and cultural ties, the bulk of the exchange has taken place between each Arab country and the industrialized world, and it is notable that a visa to visit, or work in, other Arab countries, is much harder to obtain for Arabs than a similar permission for European or Asian citizens. On a wider level, after the Camp David Accords and the isolation of Egypt, the headquarters of the Arab League was transferred from Cairo to Tunis. Only after Egypt went back to the Arab fold in the late 1980s was pressure re-initiated to bring the headquarters back to Cairo. The move was completed in late 1990. But the occupation of Kuwait in August 1990 showed in dramatic fashion the limitations of the Arab League's power, with the Secretary-General tendering his resignation in the face of the incapacity of the organization to solve the problems it was set up to address. Despite talk about amending Article 7 of the Charter of 1945 to change decision-taking from consensus to qualified majority as in recent treaty developments in Europe, the mere opposition of a single state remains sufficient to cripple the Arab League institutions.

What about federation efforts through Islamic, in contrast to Arab, common values? Inefficient as the Arab League may have been in making the legal systems of the Middle East more cohesive, the parallel efforts introduced at the level of

---

[25] The Project for a Unified Arab Code of Personal Status, *Mashru' qanun 'arabi muwahhad lil-ahwal al-shakhsiyya*, 'agreed' in final form in 1986, was some ten years in the making. It appears, together with a detailed commentary in the form of preparatory works, in *al-Majalla al-'arabiyya lil-fiqh wal-qada'*, 2, 1985, 11–43 (for the text), 43–263 (for the preparatory works). The Code is presented and discussed in Chapter 10 on family law.

Islamic integration have faltered even more patently. In the first place, integration through Islam is a much wider enterprise, and is more difficult to fathom in a practical manner than integration under the label of Arabism. Arab countries tend to be more cohesive and better defined than 'Muslim' or 'Islamic' countries, and offer a geographical and linguistic continuum: the Arab world stretches, in the formula of the advocates of Arab unity, 'from the Atlantic Ocean to the Gulf'. In contrast, Muslim countries are more numerous—the Muslim population in the world is about 1–1.2 billion, against some 300 million Arabs—and they are geographically far apart. Unity of the Muslim world would have to include Indonesia, Nigeria, Iran, and Albania, since all these countries number more than 80 per cent Muslim citizens, but Islam has not yet proved able to offer sufficient economic and legal common ground for privileged cooperation between them. Furthermore there are sizeable Muslim minorities in Europe, Africa, Asia, including the former states of the Soviet Union, China, and South Africa, and increasingly articulate Muslim communities in Europe demanding that aspects of Islamic law be taken more seriously into account by the national legislatures.[26] The unity of the Muslim world seems even harder to achieve than the elusive search for Arab integration.

Notwithstanding these disparities between Muslim countries, the rise of Islam as a political phenomenon in the 1980s has been matched by an increase in the demand for the application of the *shari'a* worldwide. Yet the aspiration towards greater Islamic unity has been organizationally poor. The Islamic Conference, which included fifty-two states at the Casablanca Summit in December 1994, fifty-five states at the Tehran Summit of December 1997, and fifty-six states in the first decade of the twenty-first century,[27] meets irregularly, and its decisions are taken even less seriously than the Arab League's.

This does not mean that the Islamic legacy is an insignificant feature of the legal process of Middle East countries. But its international dimension has been mooted at the legal level since the heyday of the Islamic Revolution in Iran, in contrast with its political prominence. True, the Constitution of Iran itself stipulates in its preamble that Islamic solidarity should be pursued worldwide, and one can find in the operation of the Saudi state the desire to organize Islamically at the world level—for example, in the works of the Islamic World League, based in Jeddah,[28] not to mention long-standing pan-Islamic claims of leaders such as

---

[26] Extensive literature and case-law on the subject since Jean-Yves Carlier and Michel Verwilgen, eds., *Le statut personnel des musulmans: Droit comparé et droit international privé* (Brussels, 1992); see also the section on 'Europe' in C. Mallat and J. Connors, eds., *Islamic family law* (London, 1990) 119–201 (chapters by Bernard Berkovits, Sebastian Poulter, Riva Kastoryano, Dima Abdulrahim, and references mentioned therein).

[27] Website at <http.www.oic-oci.org>. The Organization of the Islamic Conference (*Munazzamat al-mu'tamar al-islami*) was established in Morocco in 1969, and its Charter adopted in 1972. See Saad Khan, *Reasserting international Islam: a focus on the organization of the Islamic Conference and other Islamic institutions* (Oxford, 2001). See also M. Baderin, *International Human Rights and Islamic Law*, (Oxford, 2003).

[28] Rheinhardt Schulze, *Islamischer Internationalismus im 20. Jahrhundert: Untersuchungen zur Geschichte der Islamischen Weltliga (Mekka)* (Leiden, 1990).

Egypt's Naser or Libya's Qadhdhafi. Still, the *legal* impact of Islam has been restricted to the domestic level.

Since 11 September 2001, the confrontation has taken a global course, but this operates mostly on a political rather than legal level. I have argued elsewhere that there are forms of legal internationalism in Islam based on the classical Shi'i system of the *marja'iyya*, whereby a lay Shi'i freely chooses his or her leader (the *marja'*) irrespective of nationality or boundaries.[29] Selected amongst a number of prominent legal authorities by every Shi'i individual, the *marja'* becomes in effect a binding legal reference for Shi'is across the world, if his followers are significant enough for him to become the 'exclusive' supreme leader. On the Sunni side of the divide, there is little doubt that an 'international Sunni' has developed around al-Qa'eda, but the organization is secretive and lacks state support since the rapid collapse of Taliban rule in Afghanistan in October 2001. Unlike the structured institutions of the Shi'i *marja'iyya*, there is little 'law' in the Sunni international, but the Sunni nebula and the planetary scope of Qa'eda-related violence raise pressing questions about the international dimension of Islamic law in its Sunni expression. Here, explicit references in modern constitutions discussed in the next section may be less telling than the deeper constitutional structure which we examine in the final section. But explicit references, which operate in an uneasy matrix grouping the *shari'a*, constitutionalism and democracy, are also important.

Islamic Law, Constitutionalism, Democracy

Muslim advocates of democracy often quote those verses in the Qur'an in which God requires the believers to decide their affairs by a process of consultation—*shura*.[30] Supportive examples are adduced from the first Caliphs' process of selection—the *bay'a*[31]—and various aphorisms on the intrinsic freedoms of the individual, notably Caliph 'Umar admonishing 'the unacceptability of putting fetters on people whose mothers created free'.[32] Handy as the aphorisms may be, they can be countered by other sayings and realities of 'Oriental despotism',[33] as in the image of the sword-wielder standing behind *The Thousand and One Nights*

---

[29] See discussion in Mallat, *The renewal of Islamic law* (Cambridge, 1993) part one ('Islamic law and the constitution'), 21–107, and *The Middle East into the 21st century*, Chapter 5 ('Iran, Shi 'ism and the Arab world'), 127–72.

[30] Qur'an 42: 36 and 3: 53 enjoining 'politics by consultation' (*al-amr shura baynakum*). On *shura* in early historical context, see Roy Mottahedeh, 'Consultation and the political process in the Islamic Middle East of the 9th, 10th, and 11th Centuries', in Mallat, ed., *Islam and public law* (London, 1993) 19–27; Patricia Crone, 'Shura as an elective institution', *Quaderni di Studi Arabi*, 19, 2001, 3–39.

[31] On *bay'a* in an early historical context, see Mallat, 'Introduction: on Islam and democracy', in Mallat, ed., *Islam and public law*, 1–15, at 7–8. The concept does not appear in the Qur'an.

[32] For this and other such references, see Wajdi Mallat, *Mawaqef—Positions* (Beirut, 2005) 23–5.

[33] Karl Wittfogel, *Oriental Despotism: a comparative study of total power* (New Haven, 1957).

sultan to execute his master's 'off-with-their-head' commands.[34] On balance, the textual tradition is probably more supportive of the values of justice and freedom—as would be expected in any world religion. A lawyer can and will make the point, however, on whatever evidence he or she can find, blowing an aphorism out of its original proportion and away from context to fit the case at hand. In a less cynical rendering of lawyerly opportunism, it is a healthy and normal feature of societies to keep rediscovering their tradition, and adapting it to their preferred vision of contingent realities. The process of discovery is never neutral. As value-bound by the present, the modern interpreter will consciously or unconsciously operate surgical interventions in the past to feed on immediate and pressing demands.

From the professional historian's more detached perspective, anachronisms for or against 'the compatibility between Islam and democracy', or 'between constitutionalism and Islam' cannot be too useful. The original *shura* and *bay'a* are only vague cousins of the corresponding consultation and election processes of the modern age. Slavery is a universal feature of the Middle Ages, which in some Middle East countries continued well into the twentieth century, and talk of freedom in such a context is perforce vitiated. Yet freedom is a strongly rooted concept,[35] and there is a palpable civil society at work in classical Islam, if by civil society one understands organizations and people whose activity is not directed by the state.[36] In classical Islam, professions, a merchant bourgeoisie, and an active judiciary in various forms—judges, *mufti*s, and law scholars—offer a reality which is clearly autonomous from the state, and qualifies naturally as civil society. Equal justice before the law and the presence of individual rights suffuse the Islamic legal tradition. To that extent, the modern Middle East may have ignored precious forms of proto-democratic balance to the state's raw and arbitrary power.

As for the problem of Islamic law being prevented from change because it is God's law—as the political expression of the 'closing of the gate of *ijtihad*'—the issue has been for all societies, including those professing allegiance to Islam, a

---

[34] Despite the received notion, the image of the *sayyaf*, the sword-wielder standing behind the ruler to execute his orders on the unfortunate soul who might have antagonized him, is not dominant in the *Thousand and one nights*. Mas'ud ('the happy one'), Caliph Harun al-Rashid's aide/executioner eunuch, appears only in a few stories.

[35] See critical treatment in Franz Rosenthal, *The Muslim concept of freedom prior to the nineteenth century* (Leiden, 1960).

[36] On civil society in the Arab world, see John Donohue, 'Individualisme, corporatisme et Etat: où se trouve la civilité dans la société civile au Moyen Orient?', *Travaux et Jours*, 65, 2000, 161–79, and the many references he cites for classical and modern times. I have often used the works of Robert Fossaert as the clearest and most remarkable definers of 'civil society' within society at large, see e.g. '*Madkhal ilal-adab al-saghir: al-mujtama' al-madani, Huquq al-aqalliyyat wath-thaqafa fil-mashriq* (Introduction to littérature mineure: Civil society, minority rights and culture in the Mashreq)', in A. al-Na'im, ed., *Al-ab'ad ath-thaqafiyya li-huquq al-insan fil-watan al-'arabi* (Cultural perspectives on human rights in the Arab world) (Cairo, 1993) 453–89; 'Renforcer la Société Civile contre l'Etat: Horizons du travail international au Proche et Moyen Orient', commentaire sur le Rapport de la Banque Mondiale sur la Gouvernance au Proche et Moyen Orient (Etats PMO, MENA countries), Paris 2003, 21 November 2003, <http.www.worldbank.org/europe>.

matter of 'the ultimate interpreter'. In this context present crises surrounding democracy tend to get befuddled. The problem is not so much the issue of whether man or God makes the law, but which of the many competing men, and more rarely women, are empowered to interpret it.

On a modern historical timeline,[37] developments towards a democratic polity did not come much later to the core of the Islamic world—the Middle East—than to most European countries. The three major blocs which had some room for manoeuvre, the Ottoman Empire, Iran, and Egypt, featured prominent reformist ideas throughout the nineteenth century. The movement known as constitutionalism had so matured by the beginning of the twentieth century that radical changes were attempted in each of these three blocs to bring about a founding charter for a social contract of sorts. Room for manoeuvre is critical here, and it is no surprise that the process did not develop in that direction in North Africa, where colonization was keen to prevent any form of indigenous political representation threatening the French-ness of Algeria and neighbouring countries and that it was scuppered in Lord Cromer's Egypt. Where some democratization went ahead in practice, in 1908 in the Ottoman Empire, and from 1905 to 1909 in Iran, Islam was used by reformists to great effect. Na'ini (d. 1936), an Iraqi classical jurist of Iranian descent, wrote a solid treatise on the virtues of constitutionalism as the 1905–9 constitutional revolution was unfolding,[38] and the Constantinople Majlis-e Mab'uthan (Parliament of the emissaries) featured between 1908 and the First World War the first elected proto-federal Parliament in the Middle East, which included Ottoman subjects from present-day Turkey, Syria, Iraq, Israel-Palestine, and Saudi Arabia.[39] On a comparative timeline, federal and democratic developments came only a few years after the establishment of the Third Republic in France and are contemporaneous with brief interwar Parliamentary experiments in Germany and Italy. They precede similar constitutional developments in Spain.

Then came all-out war in Palestine. War is a great distorter. Democracy and human rights in times of war tend to remain frozen, as in the case of the US citizens of Japanese descent who were interned during the Second World War, with the blessing of the US Supreme Court, or more recently, as in internments with little due legal process of 'Arab suspects' in the UK in the early run-up to the Gulf War, anticipating in turn the 'black legal hole' of Guantanamo Bay prison.[40] Interfering wars have been endemic in the twentieth-century Muslim world. First

---

[37] For a tentative periodization in terms of legal eras, see Chapter 3 above.

[38] Muhammad Husain Na'ini, *Tanbih al-umma wa tanzih al-milla*, was published in Persian in Najaf *c.* 1906 and reprinted in 1957 by Mahmud Taleghani (d. 1979), one of the leaders of the Islamic revolution; see the extensive (pre-revolutionary) treatment of Na'ini's treatise by Abdul Hadi Hairi, *Shi'ism and constitutionalism in Iran* (Leiden, 1977).

[39] The minutes of that Parliament are available, and the present debate on federalism in the Middle East will gain a lot from scholars looking at them seriously. See now Khaled Barazi, The Majlis Mebusan (Meclis-i Mebusan): The Ottoman Parliament (London Ph.D., 2002).

[40] Early literature in Peter Rowe, ed., *The Gulf War 1990–91 in international and English law* (London, 1993) (articles by Gordon Risius and Bernadette Walsh). 'One of the most important cases

came colonialism, which will remain a troubling episode of raw domination in humanity's modern course, dovetailing with a First World War which was itself very colonial. When the killing frenzy stopped, the call for parliaments and freedom was loud and clear, without an exception, across the region.[41] Again, such calls for independent representation did not curry much favour with Britain and France, the main winners of the spoils, for whom the rule of law was only worth pursuing if defined within the scope of their own unchallenged dominance; and in the case of Britain, one should always remember that a whole people was permitted to be uprooted from their land in Palestine hitherto under British control.

For indigenous liberal movements, of which the Egyptian al-Wafd party offered in-between the two world wars the paragon of an outspoken and well-structured liberal-democratic party for the whole Middle East, as well as being the most attentive to the necessity of fair and free representation, distaste for violence meant a long and drawn-out conflict. British stonewalling prevented it from yielding decisive fruit in time before the onset of the Second World War and the subsequent emergence of the Palestine conflicts. The self-determination transition to democracy, unlike in India, was scuppered, and the Palestinian-Israeli wars acted, in turn, to radicalize extremism and heralded in authoritarian regimes, many of which were still in place several decades after the coups that brought them to power.

Within these historical constraints, a synchronic perspective of the sundry forms of 'constitutional law' in the Middle East can be presented in a brief typology of the constitutional-political systems as they function at the turn of the twenty-first century in the area, with the focus on the role of Islamic law, or democracy, or both, as the background to an increasingly central debate. This is typically an exercise in constitutional law in its French traditional form.

Several studies have appeared in recent years, offering an overview of the political-constitutional systems of Arab and Middle Eastern countries.[42] Whilst

which the House has had to decide in recent years' [speech of Lord Hofmman] is *A (FC) and others (FC) (Appellants) v. Secretary of State for the Home Department (Respondent); X (FC) and another (FC) (Appellants) v. Secretary of State for the Home Department (Respondent)* [2004] UKHL 56 (House of Lords), lowering the standard of proof for the accused in 'terrorism' acts but rejecting any 'legal black hole' that the terrorism phenomenon may create, that is one where no proper judicial review is possible. See also *Secretary of State for the Home Department (Respondent) v. Rehman*, [2001] UKHL 47 (House of Lords). In the US, a similar ruling can be found in *Rasul v. Bush*, 542 US 446 (2004). For leading reflection on the subject, see, in England, Johan Steyn, 'Guantanamo Bay: the legal black hole', *International and Comparative Law Quarterly*, 53, 2004, 1–15; in the US, Owen Fiss, 'The war against terrorism and the rule of law', *Oxford Journal of Legal Studies*, 26, 2006, 235–56, Some of the most proficient material was put together in Paul Gewirtz, ed., *Global constitutionalism: nationhood, same-sex marriage*, Yale Law School Global Constitutionalism Seminar, 21–4 September 2005, Part iii. A nagging problem remains the legal definition of terrorism; see my 'The original sin: "terrorism" or "crime against humanity"?', *Case Western Journal of International Law*, 34, 2002, 245–48.

41 For the best depiction of the intellectual atmosphere in the period, see Albert Hourani, *Arabic thought in the liberal age 1789–1939* (Cambridge, 1983 (orig. edn, Oxford, 1962)), Hamed Enayat, *Modern Islamic political thought* (Austin, Tex., 1982).

42 For two classic compendia in English and French respectively, see Michael Hudson, *Arab politics—search for legitimacy* (New Haven, 1993, orig. 1977). Maurice Flory and Robert Mantran, eds., *Les régimes politiques arabes* (Paris, 1991).

political studies inevitably devote some attention to wider historical processes, historians have also developed syntheses on political and constitutional developments, and the two approaches converge significantly.[43]

Rather than repeat or summarize this French-style constitutional exercise with a description of the various institutions in each state and their respective operations and competence, I propose to look more closely at the incorporation of 'Islam' as a differentiating factor into the constitutional framework of the Middle East.

Islam figures in the majority of the constitutions and founding texts of Middle Eastern states, and most Arab countries have included in their constitutions a reference to Islam. The Islamic Republic of Mauritania and the Islamic Republic of Iran carry the reference in their official appellation as states. In other countries, Islam is consecrated as the official religion. In yet others, the Muslim affiliation of the head of state is required.[44]

Although cosmetic in some cases, the Islamic reference is clear overall. Its reassertion in constitutional law was encouraged by the rise of revolutionary Islam in Iran and elsewhere. A famous amendment to Egypt's constitution in 1980 stipulated, for example, that the *'shari'a* would be "the"—as opposed to the previous "a"—sole source of legislation in the country'. (Art. 2)[45] This opened up the debate over the exclusive or pervasive role of the *shari'a* in the system. The controversy over Article 2 remains, especially over such significant issues as *riba* and interest in the financial and civil system. In countries like Egypt or Pakistan, executive and judicial efforts to prevent the supremacy of Islamic law from overtaking the totality of the financial system have not been decisive, despite a 1992 decision of the Federal Shariat Court of Pakistan that deemed the whole banking system to stand in contradiction to the requirement, under Article 227 of the Pakistani Constitution, to conform with the *shari'a*.[46]

In the Sudan, the *shari'a* is the single most divisive constitutional issue in a country where the southern population is in its majority not Muslim. The introduction and implementation of strict *shari'a* criminal legislation in 1983, with the cutting of the thief's hand and executions for 'apostasy',[47] led to the deposition of

---

[43] Among the best works, Malcolm Yapp, *The Near East since the First World War: a history to 1995* (London, 1996) Albert Hourani, *A history of the Arab peoples* (London, 1991); for the deeper historical period covering the whole world of Islam, Ira Lapidus, *A history of Islamic societies* (Cambridge, 1988) Bernard Lewis, *The Middle East: a brief history of the last 2000 years* (New York, 1995). See also, for the contemporary Middle East, the works of Nathan Brown that straddle political science and law, *Rule of law in the Arab world: courts in Egypt and the Gulf* (Cambridge, 1997); *Constitutions in a nonconstitutional world* (New York, 1991).

[44] United States Commission on International Religious Freedom, *The Religion-state relationship and the right to freedom of religion or belief: a comparative textual analysis of the constitutions of predominantly Muslim countries*, released 8 March 2005, available on the commission's website, <http://www.uscirf.gov/countries/global/comparative_constitutions> (last visited April 2005).

[45] Art. 2, Egyptian Constitution, as amended in 1980. Original text in *Al-dasatir*, at 591.

[46] On the decision on *riba* in Pakistan, and the debate over it, see Chapter 8, section on Islamic banking.

[47] For the execution of Mahmud Muhammad Taha by Nimeiry in 1985, see Abdullahi Ahmad an-Na'im, *Toward an Islamic reformation: civil liberties, human rights and international law* (Syracuse,

the country's autocratic leader, but the subsequent governments continue to face a deadlock which has persisted for decades.

It is perhaps in Iran that the greatest juristic effort was exerted towards introducing Islamic law in its allegedly pristine form at all levels of the state. The constitutional experience of post-revolutionary Iran is mitigated, and the system was not running so smoothly as to avoid the numerous Amendments introduced to the text only ten years after the Constitution was adopted in 1979. Still, partly because of the relative openness of the domestic debate in contrast to Arab countries, the constitutional experiment of Iran remains one of the most alluring in the region.

The Iranian Constitution was elaborated under the concept of *wilayat al-faqih* (*velayat-e faqih* in Persian), or the governance of the jurist(s). This theory was adumbrated by Ruhullah al-Khumaini back in 1970 and developed in the 1979 writings of the Iraqi scholar Muhammad Baqer al-Sadr, who was executed by the Ba'th regime a year later. It appears in the Iranian Constitution that year as the adaptation of the deep-rooted Shi'i institution of the *marja'iyya*: we have seen that the *marja'iyya* vests the elaboration of the law in the most knowledgeable jurists in the Shi'i world, who in the tradition are known as *marja'* (plural *maraje'*, reference) and act as a source of emulation.[48] As the best experts in the law, the jurists are, in the system, entrusted with protecting the Islamic nature of the state. This is reflected in Articles 5 and 107 of the Iranian Constitution, which vest the ultimate constitutional decision in the 'supreme' jurist, the leader or guide,[49] a position held by Khumaini until his death in 1989, and taken on after him by a man he effectively appointed to the job after dismissing another 'leader' who turned out to be averse to Khumaini's version of what the Islamic revolution should be.[50]

In another form, the dominance of the jurist is manifest in the Council of Guardians, which examines the conformity of each law passed by Parliament with the *shari'a* and with the Constitution. In effect, the Council of Guardians has turned out to be such a powerful organ in the first decade of the Constitution that its role was curtailed in the 1989 Amendments by the creation of a political body overarching the Council—the *Majma'-e Tashkhis-e Maslahat-e Nezam*, the Council for the determination of the nation's interest, whose role is to solve the recurrent conflicts between the Council of Guardians and Parliament.[51]

NY, 1990). On the early forced islamization of the Sudan, Carolyn Fluehr-Lobban, *Islamic law and society in the Sudan* (London, 1987).

[48] Chapter 3, section on 'Era of sectarian-religious law'. Emulation, *taqlid*. The *maraje'* are known nowadays in Iran as Ayatollahs (Arabic and Persian *Ayat Allah*, lit. sign or verse of God). In English, see on the Iranian revolution two works which have stood the test of time: Roy Mottahedeh, *The mantle of the prophet* (London, 1986); Shaul Bakhash, *The reign of the Ayatollahs* (New York, 1984). In the Persian tradition, clerics of all categories are derogatorily known as *mullahs*.   [49] *rahbar* in Persian.

[50] Mallat, *The renewal of Islamic law*, 89–91, 104–7, *The Middle East into the 21st century*, 129–32 (on the leadership dispute between Khumaini, Muntaziri, and Khamene'i).

[51] Mallat, *The renewal*, 89–107 and 146–57, and *The Middle East*, 143–7 (on the constitutional crisis leading to the emergence of the *Majma'*).

But the dominance of the jurist as expert in Islamic law is not total in the system, for there are a number of other institutions which are similar to Western constitutional models. Mention was made of the Iranian Parliament, but there is also a President who is voted in by universal direct suffrage. Neither presidential nor parliamentary elections are free. To prevent free representation, the supreme jurist—the 'leader'—as well as the jurists of the Council of Guardians, exercise a right of veto over all candidates. This is typical of a country in search of safeguards and self-perpetuation for its ruling group of clerics. The problem with the Council vetting candidates to both Parliament and the Presidency is fundamental, leading in a succession of elections to an increasingly meaningless contest between 'conservative' and 'progressive' supporters of the *mullahs'* leadership. The Iranian set-up pretends to offer a concrete Islamic challenge to classical constitutionalism, but the jurists of the Shi'i tradition become vested in the key role of guardians of the Constitution, in effect preventing any contender from getting to power, or exercising it, outside the bounds they have designed as the exclusively righteous interpreters and exponents of a self-labelled Islamic constitution.

On the other side of the spectrum of explicit Islamic constitutionalism stands the Kingdom of Saudi Arabia. A monarchy that has systematically rejected the principle of representative elections,[52] Saudi Arabia offers a marked contrast to its Persian neighbour across the Gulf. The antagonism between the two countries shows the wide variety allowed under the concept of an Islamic state. Saudi Arabia so prides itself on being an unadulterated Islamic system in following the theses of Wahhabi Hanbalism that it refuses to formally adopt a constitution. For Saudi rulers, 'the Qur'an is the constitution', and the whole institutional set-up is but a derivative of the Qur'an. This is confirmed in the first article of the Basic Law of 1992: 'The state's constitution is the Book of God and the *sunna*' of the Prophet.[53]

Beyond the overall reference to the Qur'an, how is Islamic Saudi Arabia governed, and what is the role of Islamic law?

The most significant legislative and executive powers in the Kingdom are concentrated on the King and the immediate Sa'ud family, while lip-service is paid to Islamic law. Already under the 1926 Fundamental Law of the Hijaz, the western part of Saudi Arabia, which was joined by conquest to the Najd central area in the 1920s, Article 5 stated that 'His Majesty was bound by the rules of the *shari'a*'. No separation of powers was recognized in government until the basic laws

---

[52] King Fahd: 'The system of free elections is not suitable to our country, the Kingdom of Saudi Arabia', quoted in Abdulaziz Al-Fahad, 'Ornamental constitutionalism: the Saudi Basic Law of governance', *The Yale Journal of International Law*, 2005, 30, 376–96, 376. Limited elections were conducted in 2005 at the municipal level. No democratic breakthrough resulted. There are also recurrent elections to the Jeddah chamber of commerce elections, where women were allowed to run in 2005 for the first time.

[53] *Nazam al-hukm*, Law of governance (hereinafter Basic law of governance), was decreed by King Fahd on 28 March 1992, together with two other laws, the Law on the consultative assembly (*Nazam majlis al-shura*), and the Law of provinces (*Nazam al-manatiq*). The texts are available as separate booklets. They are also available on <http://www.saudiembassy.net>, last accessed in 2005.

introduced in March 1992. An explicit recognition was then acknowledged for the first time, resulting in the establishment of a 'consultative assembly, *Majlis al-shura*'.[54] 'The *Majlis* is composed of a president and 60 members whom the King chooses among persons of knowledge and experience.'[55] Article 44 offers potentially the most significant change in the system with a limited set of reforms: it acknowledges the principle of the separation of powers. 'The powers in the state are composed of judicial power, executive power, and legislative power'.[56]

Even this 'revolutionary' acknowledgment is undermined by a qualification introduced in the same breath. Article 3 continues: 'the King is the *marja'* of these powers'. [57] The word *marja'* (literally reference) is unexpected for Hanbalis, as it is steeped in the Shi'i tradition of the *marja'iyya*, but the neologism carries enough respectability across the modern Arab world to make its use alluring to the Saudi rulers. Notwithstanding the haziness of the concept in a Saudi context and the ambiguity in the relationship of the King to these three powers because of the difficulty of defining what a *marja'* is, any uncertainty is soon removed. The *Majlis* may, if requested by ten or more members, initiate bills or propose amendments to existing ones. This proposal is transmitted to the President of the *Majlis*, who may pass it on to the King. The King decides what to do with it, and there is no recourse against his decision.[58] Legislation remains clearly the prerogative of the Council of Ministers under the presidency of the King. Should any doubt about the absoluteness of the monarch's power persist, the *Majlis*'s legislative competence is limited to 'the voicing by the *Majlis al-shura* of its opinion in the general policies of the state which are passed onto him by the President of the council of ministers',[59] who stands for the King. According to the first President of the *Majlis*, Muhammad Ibn Jubayr, these powers entail 'the examination of the laws[60] which the *wali al-amr*—literally the person in charge, i.e., again, the King—will issue, before these laws are promulgated'.[61] In effect, the power of the Council of Ministers is discretionary. The government chooses the laws it may submit to the opinion of the *Majlis al-shura*, and all the necessary safety valves to avoid any significant power of the *Majlis* at the expense of the King can be found in the key areas of basic laws: discretionary appointment by the King of all the members of the *Majlis*, no financial power for the *Majlis*, no right for the deputies to deliberate in public, and a residual right to initiate legislation, but not to approve or vet it.

As a result, legislative and executive powers operate in terms of a division of labour that confers on the King and his family dominant legislative fiat, through decrees, and sole executive power. Forms of supervision and consultation are

---

[54] hereinafter *Majlis*.   [55] Art. 3, *Nazam majlis al-shura*.
[56] Basic law of governance, Art. 44. The Arabic term for legislative here is *tanzimi*, which is unusual. In other Arab countries, the word used is *tashri'i*.   [57] Idem.
[58] Art. 23, *Nazam majlis al-shura*.   [59] Art. 15, *Nazam majlis al-shura*.
[60] Arabic *anzima*, the word usually used in Saudi for decrees and laws alike, including codes.
[61] Interview, *al-Majalla al-'arabiyya* (Saudi Arabian magazine published in London), 24 February 1993, 2.

retained to accommodate a first tier of religious jurists, notably the descendants of Wahhabis, and, increasingly, the prominent merchant and business families and the growing tier of educated technocrats.

This larger process of consultation was formalized in 1992 with the establishment of the *Majlis*, which gives some public prominence and recognition to the larger Saudi public, but no executive power. The veneer of 'constitutional reform' notwithstanding, the King, who has now shed all other titles to don the more simple and evocative 'Protector of the Two Holy Places (Mecca and Madina)', [62] rules much in the way of absolute monarchs in the medieval period. The text openly acknowledges that 'the system of governance in the Kingdom of Saudi Arabia is a monarchy'. [63] In so far as there are no constraining constitutional texts outside his allegiance to the Qur'an, the monarch is absolute and the system self-perpetuating. The King appoints during his life a successor from amongst the 'sons of the founding King 'Abd al-'Aziz', [64] who, in turn, is confirmed in power by the 'citizens' [65] when the King dies, under the process of *bay'a*. Since there is no formal mechanism for the *bay'a*, any popular confirmation or rejection remains theoretical. Over a decade after the 1992 basic laws, the pressure of an increasingly large royal family is moving the leadership to put some order even into the *bay'a* process.

Regardless of the succession quandary, the King in effect embodies all executive, legislative, and judicial prerogatives in Saudi Arabia. Any autonomous power operates on the basis of the monarch's right to delegate. In 1953, a royal decree instituted for the first time a Council of Ministers directed by the Crown Prince. It responds exclusively to the King, who remains its official head. Of note is the fact that the concentration of formal powers in the hands of the King has been reinforced under the 1992 'constitutional' arrangements. Delegation operates vertically, through the Council of Ministers, the various ministries, and the bureaucracy. Delegation also operates horizontally, with the King appointing a number of representatives from amongst the ruling family to head the various administrative regions in the vast Kingdom. [66] Here again, the new law on the regions introduced in 1992 did not present any tangible break with the previous regime, and members of the Sa'ud family directly man the direction of regions as Emirs.

In this constellation of predominantly authoritarian texts, the riches of Islamic law do not appear as a source of inspiration for the system in any noticeable way. But the *shari'a* resurfaces on a number of levels other than the personal devotion of the King and his appointees. In part, conformity with the tradition derives from conservative puritanism rooted in Wahhabism, both a legal and theological tradition. It is within the tribal system that the protection of the Islamic values *lato sensu* operates. Alongside the increasingly powerful bureaucracy, and sometimes

---

[62] Arabic *hami al-haramayn al-sharitayn*.   [63] Art. 5a, Basic law of governance.

[64] Art. 5b. The heir apparent is not necessarily a descendant. Note that the precedent appears in the 1876 Ottoman Constitution, where brothers succeed the ruler rather than sons.

[65] Arabic *muwatinun*, Art. 6, *Nazam majlis al-shura*.

[66] Now under the second 'basic law' enacted in March 1992 on provinces, *manatiq*.

despite it, the Saudi tribes follow their own traditions, which are arguably Islamic, with at the head of each tribe a shaykh whose connection with, and influence on, the ruling family depends on a number of factors including historical allegiance and size and centrality of the tribe.[67] In criminal law for instance, the old system of blood-money (*diyya*), which is typical of tribal justice, and whose roots go back in time at least until the Prophet,[68] has remained a manifestation of the continuing blending of tribal customs and Islamic law, as well as a further example of the persistence of an ancient Middle Eastern legal pattern.

More formally, Islamic law is protected by the presence of the *'ulama* (the jurists) in sensitive ministries such as education and justice, as well as in the judiciary. Even where, as in commercial law, massive Western inroads have taken place, lip-service allegiance to the *shari'a* remains evident, and is encountered at all tiers of the system.

For Islamic law in Saudi Arabia, the problem is that there may not be as much of it as would be desirable. The Islamic legal tradition offers a great wealth of layers which, together, constitute a deep and sophisticated legal system. Because of a tradition of secrecy in public affairs, which has been reinforced for a long time by the financial compensations which the state uses to soothe its citizens and secure their silence, Saudi law is an elusive world: notwithstanding some recent efforts to regulate the profession, there is no acknowledgment by the government of lawyering as profession, and no bar association.[69] Saudi lawyers, who number no more than a few hundred in a population of 15 million, are mainly dedicated to disputes over wealthy state procurement contracts, generally with foreign companies that find it difficult to operate without a specific set of legal rules and enlist the support of legal counsel to navigate the bureaucratic maze. Counsel is essentially restricted to matters of commercial law and foreign investment. In family law disputes, which are adjudicated by loosely regulated tribunals, and even in criminal law, where the writ of courts is limited as the prosecution has a wide and purposefully imprecise competence which includes sentencing, lawyers are not welcome.

The most important court in the Kingdom is Diwan al-Mazalim, which is also exceptional in so far as some of its decisions have been published.[70] Since 1989, the

---

[67] On this little studied aspect of Saudi Arabian tribes and *'ulama*, for early literature see A. Bligh, 'The Saudi religious elite (*ulama*) as participant in the political system of the Kingdom', *International Journal of Middle East Studies*, 1985, 37–50, H. Eilts, 'Traditionalism v. Modernism—a royal dilemma?', in P. Chelkowski and R. Pranger, eds, *Ideology and power in the Middle East.* (Durham, NC, 1988); recent good books on Saudi Arabia include Natana Delong-Bas, *Wahhabi Islam: from revival and reform to global jihad* (London, 2004), Mai Yamani, *The Hijaz and the quest for an Islamic identity* (London, 2004), Madawi al-Rasheed, *A history of Saudi Arabia* (Cambridge, 2002).

[68] See discussion in Chapters 2 and 6.

[69] Despite efforts to put some order into the legal profession, see Hussam Salah Hejailan, 'Saudi Arabia', in Eugene Cotran, ed., *Yearbook of Islamic and Middle Eastern law*, 7, 2000–1, 271–81, at 275, 'The law of legal practice'.

[70] The collection available to me on the decisions of Diwan al-Mazalem consists of seven volumes, all published by the secretariat of the Diwan. It includes *Majmu'at al-mabade' al-shar'iyya wal-nizamiyya* (collection of legal and statutory principles), 4 vols. covering 1397–9 (1977–9) , 1400

Diwan has also been competent to hear commercial cases, and there is a strange right of appeal to the Diwan al-Mazalim from within the Diwan al-Mazalim. In the absence of reports, little can be known about the work of other courts, and even Diwan al-Mazalim has stopped publishing its decisions.

This problem of secrecy *vis-à-vis* the law can be seen in the poor quality of the official journal, *Umm al-Qura*, in which are brought together laws and statutes, news bulletins on the most trivial activities of the main dignitaries, as well as announcements of tenders and of religious conversions. Still, a skeletal official journal and skimpy law reporting do not allow much leeway for justice to be seen to be done. A telling example of the constraints of law as can be fathomed in the secretive Kingdom appears in the constraints put on the deliberations of the sixty-strong members of the new *Majlis* (enlarged—or watered down—since to 150). The members are 'forbidden, under any condition whatsoever, from carrying with them outside the Majlis any papers or laws or documents which relate to their work'.[71]

Across the Arabian Gulf, one therefore witnesses two conspicuously different Islamic constitutional traditions, both proud of their respect for Islamic law and its pervasive application. In Saudi Arabia, the dominance of a rigid monarchical system allows for various forms of informal consultation, but, unlike Republican Iran, a representational process in the shape of elections is all but absent. Despite this significant difference, the self-portrayal of government as Islamic is dominant in both countries.

On the other side of the Middle Eastern constitutional world, in countries like Turkey, Israel, and Lebanon, the main reference in the system is to democracy. This is also the case in the slow move away from absolutism in Jordan and in Morocco, operating in fits and starts under the pressure of society and the patronizing whims of haphazardly enlightened monarchs.

In Turkey, the democratic process has been respected for half the period that separates us from the end of the Second World War, but the past two decades offer

---

(2 vols), and 1401. This series includes miscellaneous disputes, mainly administrative, and features full decisions. The second series is criminal and includes three volumes. It is entitled *Majmu'at al-qararat al-jaza'iyya* (collection of criminal decisions), part one on *qadaya al-tazwir* (cases of forgery) in 1400, part two on *qadaya al-rashwa wa muqata'at isra'il* (bribery cases and cases of boycott of Israel) also in 1400 (1980). A third volume covers also *qadaya al-rashwa wal-tazwir* (bribery and forgery cases) for 1401. These are hefty compendia which yield much information on the rule of law in Saudi Arabia in that short period. It is the more remarkable since the Diwan discontinued publication of its decisions after that period. No published decisions are available on usual criminal law, or from family courts. Even death sentences are not published.

[71] Art. 14 of the *la'iha dakhiliyya* (internal organization) of the *Majlis*; the 1992 basic laws have generated much interest, but the studies, including mine here, tend to remain more descriptive than analytical. I have had occasion in the past decade to discuss the Council with some of its prominent members: our conversations confirmed my sceptical assessment. This should not be surprising considering the secretive nature of the Kingdom's politics. Two useful introductions to the changes can be found in A. M. Tarazi, 'Saudi Arabia's new Basic Laws: the struggle for participatory Islamic government', *Harvard International Law Journal*, 34, 1993, 258–75, and Al-Fahad, 'Ornamental constitutionalism', above n. 52, arguing that empty as they may be, those limited changes are at least 'frank'.

a consistent attempt to protect constitutional normalcy after a long spate of military coups, including a remarkable Muslim-Democratic experience since the accession to power of the Refah-style Islamic party in the early twenty-first century.[72] In Israel, where freedom of expression generally goes unchallenged, the democratic process has been vitiated by the domination over a large, unrepresented Arab population in the 1967 Occupied Territories, coming on the heels of a pattern of ethnic cleansing now firmly documented in archival research.[73] Within Israel proper, a two-tier structure of citizenship segregating Arab Israelis from their Jewish counterparts also undermines the democratic character of the system, both in terms of law—segregation against Arabs in naturalization, land ownership, and military service—and in effective governmental participation.[74] All these negative elements are in a constant state of flux against free elections and an independent judiciary which marks a significant repository of basic individual freedoms and rights for the Jewish part of the population.

If formal democracy as understood in Western legal literature can be defined as the combination, over a period of time, of freedom of expression and association and the recurrence of representative elections for the whole population, it was also upheld with some consistency in Lebanon between 1943 and the outbreak of the civil war in 1975.

The Lebanese Constitution was elaborated in 1926 when the country was under French mandate. Much of the original text did not survive independence in 1943, but the overall presidential and parliamentarian structures and the separation of powers were retained. Until the 1975 breakdown into civil and regional wars, the Lebanese institutional configuration was a combination of the 1926 Constitution and an oral, customary agreement between leaders of the Christian and Muslim communities in the so-called 'National Pact' of 1943.

[72] There is a large literature of political science/history on both Turkey and Israel. The classic work on the passage from the Ottoman Empire to the modern republic of Turkey remains Bernard Lewis, *The emergence of modern Turkey*, 1st edn. (Oxford, 1961). The works of Halil Inalcik, especially *The Ottoman empire: The classical age, 1300–1600* (London, 1973) and Stanford Shaw, *History of the Ottoman empire and modern Turkey* (Cambridge, vol. 1, 1976; vol. 2 (with Ezel Kural Shaq), 1977) offer comprehensive introductions to the Ottoman period. For overviews of recent Turkish history, see Andrew Mango, *The Turks today* (London, 2004); Soli Özel, 'Turkey at the polls: after the tsunami', *Journal of Democracy*, 14:2, April 2003, 82–94 (on the strenuous efforts towards electoral stability). The role of the military in modern Turkey is thoroughly analysed by William Hale, *Turkish politics and the military* (London, 1994).

[73] In Israel, within exensive literature, a pioneering study of the role of the military is Yoram Peri, *Between battles and ballots: Israeli military in politics* (Cambridge, 1983). I have found the most inspiring studies of modern Israel to be Baruch Kimmerling's, a sociologist. An early book is *Zionism and territory* (Berkeley, 1983). More recently, see *The invention and decline of Israeliness* (Berkeley, 2001).

[74] Legal critique in two books by David Kretzmer, *The legal status of the Arabs in Israel* (Boulder, Colo., 1990); *The occupation of justice: the Supreme Court of Israel and the Occupied Territories* (New York, 2002). More on Israel below in the next section, and in the next two chapters. The authoritative exponent of Israeli law as applied by the courts is Israel's chief justice, Aharon Barak, 'Foreword: a judge on judging; the role of a supreme court in a democracy', *Harvard Law Review*, 116, 2002, 16–162.

The essential features of this combination can be summed up in the way Article 95 of the original Lebanese Constitution has been interpreted from 1943 until its amendment in 1990. Article 95 stated: 'As a temporary measure, and for the sake of justice and concord, the communities shall be equitably represented in public employment and in the composition of the Cabinet, such measure, however, not causing prejudice to the general welfare of the State'.[75] The various euphemisms in this 'provisional' text mean that the representation of the religious communities at all levels of public employment, from the President down to the lowest echelons, must follow a specific communitarian power-sharing formula. At the top of the state structure, this formula is exemplified in the requirement that the three most important positions in the country, those of President, Prime Minister, and Speaker, be respectively allotted to the exclusive appointment of a Christian Maronite, a Muslim Sunni, and a Muslim Shi'i. Following a similar formula, the number of deputies in Parliament was calculated on the basis of a multiple of a 6:5 ratio of Christians to Muslims. Accordingly, out of 99 Members of Parliament, 54 were Christian and 45 Muslim. Within the Christian group, 30 were Maronites, with the remainder 24 MPs divided across several smaller Christian communities. On the Muslim side, electoral law assigned 20 Sunni, 19 Shi'i, and 6 Druze posts.

The combination of regional turmoil, internal demographic changes, and political leaders' incompetence destroyed the delicate democratic experience in 1975. After a protracted civil war marked by regional and international interference, the constitutional balance was altered in 1989 in the Accords known after the Saudi city of Ta'ef, where they were first agreed. In September 1990, the Ta'ef Accords were implemented in various amendments to the original Lebanese Constitution.

In essence, the religious-based 'consociational' democracy prevailing until 1975 remains typical of Lebanese 'democracy'. In the post-Ta'ef system, a slight decrease in Presidential powers in favour of a collective Cabinet role and an equal balance in a now 128-strong Parliament between Christian and Muslim deputies constitute the most important alterations, but the main hallmarks of pre-war Lebanon have been retained. A crucial test of the re-establishment of democracy appeared in the planned conduct of new elections under the Accords, but the occasion for the country to be back on firm democratic track was scuppered in the summer of 1992, which saw poor Christian participation and the rise of Syrian power, with thousands of Syrian troops remaining in the country despite an explicit clause in Ta'ef requesting their withdrawal from Beirut and most Lebanese coastal cities. There was more participation in the elections of 1996, but the process was marred by irregularities, leading to the resignation of the President of the newly established Constitutional Council in April 1997.[76] The 2000 elections

---

[75] Text in *Al-dasatir*, under 'Lebanon', at 438–44.

[76] I have briefly described the course of the 1997 crisis in the Lebanon entry in the *Yearbook of Islamic and Middle Eastern Law*, 3, 1996, 221–41 at 221–7 and references therein. See also next chapter.

saw a surprise victory for a loose opposition coalition, but it was only after the shockwave occasioned by the brutal assassination of the former Prime Minister on 14 February 2005 that the so-called Cedar Revolution succeeded, together with international pressure, to force the Syrian troops out.

Between the 'Islamic' systems in Saudi Arabia and Iran, and the incomplete democratic experiments in Lebanon, Morocco, Jordan, Turkey, and Israel, range a number of authoritarian regimes typical of which is the system of Iraq until the fall of its three-decade dictator in April 2003.

The Constitution in Iraq during the long dictatorship is a good example of the way fundamental laws can be shaped to accommodate the authoritarianism of a regime. At the heart of the system is the Revolutionary Command Council, and the head of the RCC is the effective highest power in the Republic. From 1979 until his downfall, Saddam Hussein held that position, as well as that of president, army commander-in-chief, and leader of the Ba'th party—adding in a 1994 reshuffle that of prime minister. Of all the Middle Eastern countries, Iraq proba-bly held the most negative record in human rights violations and the centraliza-tion of all authority under a single ruler. *Mutatis mutandis*, the same is true of Libya and Syria, and, to lesser degrees all the Arab countries that followed the Naser 'constitutional RCC model'. This model, established in Egypt informally with the 1952 'free officers' coup, was constitutionalized in a combination of military faction and single-party leadership (the Revolutionary Command Council) across the self-labelled parliamentary regimes in the region, with vari-ations from Mauritania to Pakistan, including Algeria, Tunisia, Sudan, the 'PLO state', and Eritrea. All these countries followed the core model established in Egypt in 1952 and adopted by Iraq in increasingly authoritarian fashion since 1958, by Libya wholeheartedly in 1969, and by Syria determinedly since 1970.[77]

The picture is not uniformly dark. Significant though inconclusive pressure has resulted in some democratic openings. In the elections of Northern Iraq in May 1992, which were made possible by the so-called 'safe haven' imposed on Baghdad in the wake of its defeat in the second Gulf War, seven parties were competing for a Kurdish assembly under a new electoral law.[78] In unified Yemen, the elections

[77] In an extensive literature, mostly of history and political science, stand out the works of Roger Owen, *State, power and politics in the making of the modern Middle East*, 3rd edn. (London, 2004) (comprehensive essay on Middle East politics); Alan Richards and John Waterbury, *A political econ-omy of the Middle East: state, class, and economic development* (Boulder, Colo., 1990, 2nd edn., 1996) (on the economic aspect of rentier-bureaucratic states); Gilles Kepel, *Muslim extremism in Egypt: the Prophet and Pharaoh* (Berkeley, 2003) (orig. French, Paris, 1984, on Islamism in Egypt); and Hanna Batatu, *The old social classes and the revolutionary movements of Iraq* (Princeton, 1978); *Syria's peasantry, the descendants of its lesser rural notables, and their politics* (Princeton, 1999) (best works on twentieth-century Iraq and Syria).

[78] Upon the invitation of the Kurdish leadership to the International Committee for a Free Iraq, which I animated in part, members of the ICFI helped organize the monitoring of the elections. Some of this mixed experience appears in the preface to the Arabic translation of *The renewal of Islamic law* (*tajdid al-fiqh al-islami*) (Beirut, 1998).

of April 1993 were held in a remarkable atmosphere for a country whose rate of illiteracy is staggering, but the Revolutionary Command Council/president-for-life system continued its quasi-exclusive domination. More significantly, experiments in Turkey and Israel have reaffirmed, respectively, a rooted if intermittent practice, and an unblemished regularity. In the case of Israel, this regularity has been marred by the long-term occupation of the West Bank, the Golan and Gaza, and by too slow an enfranchisement of the Arab citizens of Israel proper. In Turkey, several military coups have disrupted democratic life, together with a pattern of brutal treatment for Turkey's minorities, especially the Kurds in the southeast of the country.

Part of this openness has come from a general drive towards democracy in the world as a whole, compared to which the Middle East has trailed behind. On balance, constitutionalism as embodied in free and regular political consultations has taken the pattern of a see-saw, as in Egypt, Tunisia, and Jordan, with authoritarianism eventually regaining the upper hand in more brutal manner. In some cases like Algeria, democratization was boldly introduced in 1990–1, only to produce a backlash which has brought violence in a fashion unprecedented since the war of independence between 1956 and 1961. Other systems have failed to offer more than cosmetic reforms, and all share the dwarfing of constitutional attempts by the rulers' adroit combination of Western fear of extreme Islamic militant groups, who tend to snub democracy as a Western ploy which is incompatible with Islam, and the persistence of regional crises which offer easy excuses to the regimes in place not to move further towards democracy. But electoral democracy remains conspicuously high on the Middle Eastern agenda, with real success in some instances, like the Kurdish elections in Northern Iraq in May 1992, the Yemeni elections of April 1993, and the January 2005 elections in Iraq. Peaceful street movements in Lebanon and elsewhere started in 2005, combining the yearning for free elections and presidential change, but these experiments have not yet been decisive for the countries involved.

Democracy, of course, cannot be limited to a one-time electoral consultation, and in the fragile systems across the region, elections are meaningless if they are not recurrent. The civil wars which raged inside the Kurdish safe haven and in the Yemen in 1994 are powerful reminders of the difficult nature of the search for the rule of law and earnest political representation across the Middle East.

If war and the colonial West distorted the nascent liberal movements between the First and the Second World Wars, a period when Islamic ideology was generally on board the process of liberation/self-representation, there were also strong voices within the Islamic movement against democracy as a Western, and hence 'bad', product. But even then, attention to detail is needed. When the dissenting Islamic voices came forcefully to the fore in the shape of the Khumainist revolution in 1978–9 Iran, they had been adumbrated in his lectures in Najaf in 1970 in a political, not in a constitutional, garb. There, Khumaini's hatred for the West was rooted in the bitterness of many Iranians towards United States policy, which supported the Shah's despotism in return for cheap oil and extraterritorial jurisdiction for its citizens. In a pamphlet essentially directed at frustration in the face of what he perceived as the hypocritical onslaught of US power, Khumaini's 'Islamic' argument was never against parliaments, or elections. The Iranian *Majlis* flourished after the Revolution, even if any public debate remained heavily constrained by the principle of the *marja'*'s constitutional dominance and the vetting power massively used by the Council of Guardians in both parliamentary and presidential elections.[79]

This should leave us with the acknowledgment that the zero-sum debate on incompatibility or compatibility between Islam and democracy—often interchangeable with 'the West'—will remain active and unanswered for some time, until at least some of the political dust settles and a stable political and economic course is reached in one or more Middle Eastern countries. Meanwhile, the real questions on both sides of the Islam–West divide need to be defined with more precision.

First, the argument must steer clear of any quintessential compatibility. More sophisticated indices of the political-constitutional process are required to assess Middle Eastern constitutionalism in its relation to Islam. These indicators could be grouped in three core areas: electoral processes and alternation in power, civil society, and the courts. Since politics develop primarily on a national basis, each Middle Eastern country must be examined against those three prisms.

The first indicator concerns the existence and effectiveness of parliaments, and the recurrence of free elections to determine alternation in the leadership: thanks to parliamentarian life, Turkey and Yemen have shown themselves in the past quarter of a century to be more democratic than Ba'thist Iraq, and Iran a far more lively place of public debate than Saudi Arabia or the United Arab Emirates.

Whether elections allow for a stable democracy hinges on the fact of their recurrence. The case of Algeria is the most dramatic in recent years, as the point was not so much to have elections, but how to create the conditions for them to recur as a matter of course. Any assessment of the 'best conditions' for recurrence of elections involves an array of international and domestic legal considerations which have developed around the elusive concept of 'a new international order' in the wake of the 1990 Gulf War. Since the Middle East is a natural candidate for realignments of potential significance, the analysis requires attention, at both domestic and regional level, to the complex picture which is slowly emerging in Iraq, in Palestine, the neighbouring Levant countries, and in North Africa. This question will no doubt see significant developments for mechanisms which may

---

[79] On Khumaini's Najaf lectures of 1970, considered the central ideological source of 'Islamic government' in Iran, see e.g. my treatment in *Shi'i thought from the South of Lebanon*, Centre for Lebanese Studies (Oxford, 1988) *passim*; *The renewal of Islamic law*, 69; *The Middle East into the 21st century*, 129–31. Khumaini's lectures were published in Arabic and Persian alternatively as *Al-hukuma al-islamiyya* (Islamic government) and *wilayat al-faqih* (*velayat-e faqih* in Persian, the rule of the jurist). They were translated into English and annotated by Hamid Algar, *Islam and revolution* (Berkeley, 1981) 27–151.

ensure that a group coming to power is constrained enough to think that democracy equals not free elections, but free recurrent elections.

A related central element for stability emerging from the electoral processes revolves around what should be the natural result of the voting exercise: the right to choose one's ruler, which entails the right to end the ruler's mandate. Trite as this consideration may be, it is particularly dramatic in the Middle East where countries whose supreme ruler changes in the electoral process are the exception rather than the rule. In the past decades, this was the case for only a handful of systems, which included Israel (for its Jewish population), Turkey and Pakistan (with several military coup interludes, the latest being the Parviz Musharraf dictatorship), and Lebanon (with one short and one long civil war, in addition to the constitutional order being interrupted with the prorogation of the mandate of an incumbent president in October 1995, and again in September 2004). In all other countries, the supreme ruler dies in office, is killed, or flees into exile. A peaceful, orderly change at the top following a model defined by the rule of law is an exception which is for the moment limited to Israel, and to a lesser extent to Algeria and Turkey. Across the rest of the region, there is not one example of orderly alternation at the helm.

Secondly, there is civil society at large: the parties, the press, the trade unions, the associations. Again, the quality of democratic life depends on the variety and strength of these organizations.

Saudi Arabia offers an example on one extreme side of the spectrum of 'civil society' organizations. In the tribal Kingdom, where secrecy is of the essence, television dishes appeared in the mid-1990s as a formidable opening up to uncensored information.[80] In addition to systematic purchase of controlling shares in any Arabic-speaking cable or satellite station, and ownership of major international Arab newspapers published in London, the Saudi government followed in March 1994 the Iranian example by forbidding dishes and satellite television. These measures are largely ineffective, and the law inapplicable and ignored.

This is a faint example of government and civil society being at odds, and it is difficult to see how sustainable such intellectual impoverishment can be. A state cannot allow people good education and expect them not to be ambitious or want to learn more, and governments are always a fax or an electronic mail message behind in terms of control. In Iran itself, the story of the dissemination of Ayatollah Khumaini's speeches and sermons in 1977 and 1978 on audio cassettes is well known, and London-based Saudi and Bahraini oppositional groups have made systematic use of the internet (after heavy use of faxes) to introduce their messages at home.

One might venture that civil society will eventually take care of censorship and constraints on various freedoms, as the people tend to be, in the long term, more

---

[80] On the break-up of the state monopoly over information, see early work by Jon Alterman, *New media new politics: from satellite television to the internet in the Arab world*, The Washington Institute for Near East Policy (Washington, 1998).

inventive than the governments that strait-jacket them as a matter of principle, more often than not in the name of religion. But governments can also be remarkably dogged in preventing the growth of civil society, and will pursue the muzzling of the press, imposing censorship, jailing dissidents, and preventing political and trade union groups from making an impact on the public scene. As a matter of course, human rights reports tend to feature a long catalogue of governmental abuses against constantly re-emerging voices of dissent. The widespread turmoil affecting at the turn of the twenty-first century the domestic scene in all countries—without exception—suggests that the battle between governments and civil societies has been joined.[81]

One last indicator concerns the courts: is there an independent judiciary? Does this judiciary have a constitutional writ? How effective is it? The effective protection of human rights depends on the answer to these questions. The historical tradition of a respected judiciary in classical Islam should have triggered some concern for reviving and strengthening the judiciary, but too little attention has been paid to courts in the modern Middle East. In the military dictatorships which prevailed in Syria, Tunisia, Sudan, Iraq, and Libya, the writ of the courts does not go beyond the judge's desk. In Saudi Arabia, sections of the judiciary have triggered some respect when they were allowed public coverage, but the banning of law-reporting for the highest court is expressive of the absoluteness sought by the monarch. In Egypt, the system depends on an ongoing battle between the executive branch and a judiciary which survived both Naser and Sadat. The effectiveness of courts—the subject of the present book—is at the heart of the rule of law: the Middle East provides no exception to this universal requirement.

A Deeper Constitutional Structure? Personal versus Territorial Law

Whatever the transnational appeal to Arab, Muslim, or other ethnically or religiously defined constituent groups, all countries in the modern Muslim world have adopted constitutions or basic laws, including the Kingdom of Saudi Arabia in 1992. For comparative public law, more telling than a discussion of the explicit 'reference to Islam in the constitutional text' is the Westphalian model of nation-states. This is a 'territorial model' set against a Middle Eastern 'personal model'. Under the personal model, law adheres to the person as member of a given religion or sect rather than to her belonging, as citizen, to a nationally defined territory.

The system of nation-states is well entrenched in all Muslim countries with sizeable Muslim populations. This is a fact of the twentieth century, the era of

---

[81] For rapid developments, see coverage on <http.www.mallat.com> (under *issues*), especially on the 'Forum for the future', spearheaded by the US government as 'new' policy of democratization in the larger Middle East. Texts also available in *Awraq ri'asiyya* (Presidential papers) (Beirut, 2005) part 3.

nation-states. Also fact is that the nation-state strait-jacket does not operate well. In his *Summa* on Mediterranean society as seen from the Cairo Geniza documents of the tenth–thirteenth centuries, Samuel Goitein provides archival evidence on the historical depth of a dysfunctional structure: 'At the root of all this was the concept that law was personal and not territorial. An individual was judged according to the law of his religious community, or even religious "school" or sect, rather than that of the territory in which he happened to be.'[82]

Compare René Maunier, in a passage from his 1935 report quoted at the beginning of this chapter, on the 'effects of the transformation of law'. After noting 'the gains of written law over customary law, with the emergence of *Codes* in Muslim land', Maunier describes the second most important characteristic to be 'the gains made by *territorial* law over personal law'.[83]

Confronted by the failure of democratic constitutionalism in terms of both working transnational institutions and domestic arrangements, one may wonder whether the persistent governance crisis is not rooted in the deeper historical structures outlined, in the same society a thousand years apart, in the quotes of Goitein and Maunier. In the early twenty-first century, this outline remained palpable across the region.

While fashionable after Samuel Huntington's *Clash of civilizations*,[84] in which the fault line between Islamic and Western civilizations emerges as the defining paradigm of the international scene, any grand approach requires an initial caveat: the comparison between the West and Islam is uneven by nature, especially for lawyers. A depiction of a clash between two world patterns may have its merits, but the image breaks down in the many nuances and precisions needed for a comprehensive and accurate picture. 'Civilization' is a fleeting concept. Islam is a religion, and several countries with a Muslim majority seem to have little in common despite sharing the same religion. Tunisia, Nigeria, and Indonesia hardly appear as a common legal bloc. Similarly, 'Western civilization' is rarely defined in terms of religion, however one stretches the concept of 'a Judaeo-Christian culture' to become Muslim-Judaeao-Christian. Nietzsche's devastating critique in *Beyond good and evil* (1886) and *Genealogy of morals* (1887) is also true for the rather crude, extended concept. On the world scene, the dominant legal subject remains the nation-state.

True, the modern nation-state is eminently territorial, in the Middle East as elsewhere: within its borders there operates a legal system which is by definition exclusive of any other. All citizens in the state are bound by that system, and they become bound by the next-door system as soon as they cross the international

---

[82] S. D. Goitein, *A Mediterranean society: the Jewish communities of the Arab world as portrayed in the documents of the Cairo Geniza*, 5 vols., 1967–85, vol. 1, *Economic foundations*, 1967, 66.

[83] Maunier, 'Plan d'enquête sur le progrès du droit en pays musulman (1935)', above n. 2, 168 (emphasis in original).

[84] Samuel Huntington, *The clash of civilizations and the remaking of the world order* (New York, 1996).

boundary. And yet the historical fault line already identified in Goitein's works on Egypt in the tenth to thirteenth centuries persists. In the received world of Islamic law, this is illustrated in the divide made by classical lawyers between *dar al-harb* and *dar al-silm* or *dar al-islam*, the war territory as opposed to the peace *(silm)*-Islam territory.[85] The distinction forces a relation to the law which tends to be far more personal than it is territorial. The citizen carries under the divide her or his *religious* attachment to the law wherever he/she goes: while this is not completely unknown to an American or a French national, who may be bound for instance by the fiscal laws of her country irrespective of territory, personal law is not the dominant relation outside one's country in a Westphalian system. It is the dominant relation in an Islamic one.

This sort of generalization may be facile, with examples or counter-examples strengthening or weakening assumptions that the theory may render unnecessarily rigid. Still, one component is decisive, which grounds the issue of personality versus territoriality of laws in the special mould of a typical Middle Eastern constitutional system—and arguably beyond, in Pakistan, India, Malaysia, and now Europe because of emerging, self-defining Muslim communities.

The Westphalian dimension of the debate can be brought into a more philosophical perspective. John Rawls addressed precisely the issue of democracy and religion in one of his last works by giving the example 'of Catholics and Protestants in the sixteenth and seventeenth centuries when the principle of toleration was honored only as a *modus vivendi*. This meant that should either party fully gain its way it would impose its own religious doctrine as the sole admissible faith.' In this case, which Rawls finds in 'a constitution resembling that of the United States . . . honored as a pact to maintain civil peace', one does 'not have stability for the right reasons, that is, as secured by a firm allegiance to a democratic society's political (moral) ideals and values'.[86] Tolerance as *modus vivendi* is not a sufficient ground rule for the conviviality of citizens.

Democracy is not ensured either in the second example offered by Rawls, which is based on majoritarianism:

> Nor again do we have stability for the right reasons in the second example—a democratic society where citizens accept as political (moral) principles the substantive constitutional clauses that ensure religious, political and civil liberties, when their allegiance to these constitutional principles is so limited that none is willing to see his or her religious or non-religious doctrine losing ground in influence and numbers, and such citizens are prepared to resist or to disobey laws that they think undermine their positions.[87]

---

[85] For some of these classical works, see my 'The need for a paradigm shift in American thinking: Middle Eastern responses to "what we are fighting for"', in John Borneman, ed., *The case of Ariel Sharon and the fate of universal jurisdiction* (Princeton, 2004) 150–75, and literature cited therein. See also Khaled Abou El Fadl, *Rebellion and violence in Islamic law* (Cambridge, 2001) and Noah Feldman, *After Jihad: America and the struggle for Islamic democracy* (New York, 2003).

[86] John Rawls, 'The idea of public reason revisited', in *The law of peoples* (Cambridge, Mass., 1999) 149–50. Footnotes omitted.　　　　　　　　　　　　　　　　[87] ibid. 150.

Rarely has the 'demographic threat' in Israeli, Iraqi, or Lebanese societies been more clearly depicted in philosophical terms. The demographic argument, which attaches to communities fearing the loss of their numerical majority, is deafening in the Middle East. 'Here again, democracy is accepted conditionally and not for the right reasons', which is the equality of individuals coming together as transcendental citizens, that is as citizens moved by a moral law which is superior to their communitarian belonging, and even to the morality that may derive from their religion. Rawls again:

What these examples have in common is that society is divided into separate groups, each of which has its own fundamental interest distinct from or opposed to the interests of the other groups and for which it is prepared to resist or to violate legitimate democratic law. In the first example, it is the interest of a religion in establishing its hegemony, while in the second, it is the doctrine's fundamental interest in maintaining a certain degree of success and influence for its own view, either religious or nonreligious. While a constitutional regime can fully ensure rights and liberties for all permissible doctrines, and therefore protect our freedom and security, a democracy necessarily requires that, as one equal citizen among others, each of us accept the obligations of legitimate law.

The conclusion is a damning verdict for any Middle East-style democracy based on religious/sectarian rights, as against the individual's:

While no one is expected to put his or her religious or nonreligious doctrine in danger, we must each give up forever the hope of changing the constitution so as to ensure its influence and success. To retain such hopes and aims would be inconsistent with the idea of equal basic liberties for all free and equal citizens.[88]

Powerful as the conclusion may be, it does not offer a decisive indictment if the religious belonging of the individual, which forms in much of the Middle East a defining bond to his and her community, is perceived in a different mould: one that includes a multiplicity of identities rather than the one national/constitutional bond which is premised on a Kantian vision which Rawls develops to its ultimate legal logic. Rather than considering any bond to the state other than the ethical-constitutional one to be negative because of irrationality or arbitrariness, the view is cumulative of a dual bond: one is Rawlsian, eminently individualistic and territorial, the other is communitarian, eminently personal and non-territorial.

In constitutional terms, the Middle Eastern model finds some comfort in the way majoritarianism gets trumped in democracies by the federal principle, and by the role of courts and government when they defend the individual as part of a 'discrete and insular minority'. The upshot is that some constitutional arrangement must be sought to accommodate that pervasive communitarian trait of Middle East societies.

The issue described as personal versus territorial may be prospectively put in terms of communitarian versus territorial federalism. Three pressing constitutional

---

[88] ibid. 150.

examples at the beginning of the twenty-first century illustrate the difficulties that obtain.

Lebanon, whose population is divided more or less evenly between its Christian and Muslim components, is a useful place to start. I have described the Lebanese constitution in the previous section. Let me now examine more closely its structural characteristic, derogatorily known as sectarianism or communitarianism, *confessionalisme* in French, *ta'ifiyya* in Arabic.[89] Lebanese constitutionalism recognizes that the relationship between the citizen and the state is not an immediate, direct one. The relation—or allegiance—is filtered by his or her community, in the case of Lebanon one of the eighteen or so sects that make up the country, resulting in a complicated realm of combinations simplified by an overarching line separating, in law, Muslims and Christians, and by the sometimes no less powerful separation between Muslim Sunnis, Muslim Shi'is, and Christian Maronites, the three largest communities in the country. While shocking to the equality of citizens as individuals, this complex sociological-constitutional situation is better approached positively, albeit approximately, as 'communitarian' (or personal) federalism. Communitarian privilege derives from the personal approach of looking upon the *shari'a* as a millennium-guiding model, such a pattern no doubt an old Middle Eastern characteristic harking back to whenever religion became the nexus of the individual's relation to the community: a person is Muslim, or Christian, or Jewish, before she is Lebanese, French, or Saudi. In his great work on tenth- to thirteenth-Century Egypt, Goitein describes that model 'as medieval religious democracy'.[90]

However frustrating to the Western constitutionalist, one should approach that feature *positively*: like Egypt or Morocco in the classical age, the Lebanese system is not an all-bad system, and people who sneer at it may see in the worldwide debate over the post-Ba'th Iraqi Constitution why they should reconsider their assessment. It is a correct assumption, widely held and full of merit, that matters of governance in Iraq cannot be stable or fair, if the Sunni community, composing less than 20 per cent of the population, is not represented in the decision-making process. This, actually, is the Lebanese constitutional litmus test: however 'low' a community may rank, it will retain, under the Lebanese Constitution, representation in government. Nor is this trait exclusively Lebanese. Its Middle East roots are deep, and were elegantly recognized by Karl Marx, for whom the puzzling nature of Middle Eastern history is that 'it always takes the *appearance* of religion'.[91]

[89] It appears in political science literature under the denomination 'consociationalism', a word coined by Arendt Lijphart in the late 1970s. See e.g. Arendt Lijphart, 'Consociational democracy', in Gurpreet Mahajan, ed., *Democracy, difference and social justice* (Delhi, 1988) 128–37. In the Lebanese context, most prominent are the works of Theodor Hanf, *Co-existence in wartime Lebanon—death of a state and birth of a nation* (Oxford, 1993), Antoine Messarra, *Théorie générale du système politique libanais* (Paris, 2004), and Elisabeth Picard, *Lebanon, a shattered country* (London, 1996).

[90] Goitein, *A Mediterranean society*, vol. 2, *The Community*, 1971, 5.

[91] Letter from Marx to Friedrich Engels, 2 June 1855, in Karl Marx and Friedrich Engels, *Sur la religion* (Paris, 1980) 123 (emphasis in original).

The persistent Lebanese constitutional model offers a wide archetype which replicates the personal as opposed to the territorial model in the rest of the region. It may not be out of place to conjure up Palestine-Israel as a *negative* counter-example, namely that a discrete and insular, historically victimized minority of Israeli Arabs, representing over a fifth of the population, has never had serious executive representation in Israel's government. Under a Lebanese-like model, non-Jewish Israelis would be entitled to a fifth or a quarter of cabinet posts. The legal protection and representation of the indigenous Palestinian community (defined as Christian or Muslim by the Jewish majority), which stands at the root of a conflict over a century old, is no different from the primary constitutional definition of Lebanese citizens as Christian or Muslim, of Iraqis as Shi'is or Sunnis—except that the definition in Israel is about who is a Jew and who isn't. In the legal and sociological study of Israel, Jewishness is granted to be the exclusive characteristic of the country, in the same way as 'Muslim-ness' would be emphasized in Iran or Pakistan. Because of the historic legacy of the Holocaust, this is an issue which is overwhelmingly seen as be-all and end-all of Israel as a state.

Over a period of fifty years, with remnants of the debate still current for the latest waves of immigration, Ethiopian and Russian, the central question for law in Israel was about 'who is a Jew?' Christians and Muslims directly affected by the emergence of Israel are by definition outside the legal order of a state defined by its Jewishness. This structural discrimination obtains in the three strands of victimization of non-Jews since 1948: those who were evicted from their homes and never allowed to return simply do not exist in the eyes of Israeli law. These are the refugees of 1948, defined by Israeli law as perpetual and irrevocable 'absentees'. For those who came in 1967 under occupation, a four-decade long domination coupled with slow and relentless expropriation of land hemmed them into an ever narrowing territory. For the one-tenth of the native population that was not evicted in 1948, and which grew to become about a million souls at the turn of the twenty-first century, the Israeli Arabs as they are called—the Palestinian Israelis as they could more scientifically be depicted—the Jewishness of the State of Israel has meant that their constitutional participation, at bottom, was made available by an absolute right to vote, but that executive representation at the top remained tightly constrained by a combination of harsh legal rules and by overt discrimination against their participation in government and in the judiciary.

One can now better understand Lebanon's deeper constitutional structures as defining a counter-constitutional model to the one dominant in the West since Montesquieu and the *Federalist papers*. In the spring of 2001, drafts of the 1926 Lebanese Constitution were released, and they are sobering.[92] Two texts stand in

---

[92] These are facsimile texts of an important exhibit in Beirut in May 2001, which coincided with a conference held at the American University of Beirut on Michel Chiha, a prominent figure of twentieth-century Lebanon who authored the first drafts of the Constitution. See Mallat, 'Constitutionalism in Lebanon: continuities and discrepancies', not yet published. Paper contributed

open contradiction: Article 7 of the would-be constitution, and its Article 95. In Article 7, as in any other country, all citizens are declared equal. In Article 95, the communities must be respected as legal agents or intermediaries for those very citizens. As we saw in the previous section, this has not changed almost a century later, except that the present Article 95 has established parity between Christians and Muslims in Parliament, away from a multiple of the original formula (six Christians to five Muslim MPs) that prevailed until the so-called Ta'ef Agreement in 1989.

It would be wrong to think the retrospective view stops at 1926. The earliest extant prototype of Lebanese constitutionalism, a text that goes back to 1834, established municipal councils, that is, representation plus executive power, in the major cities (then Sidon and less prominently Beirut), on the basis of parity between the number of Christian and Muslim councillors.[93] By any historical measure, parity in representation between Muslims and Christians from 1834 to the twenty-first century is a deep structure, but that model is further entrenched in the so-called Ottoman *Millet* system, itself rooted in the medieval religious democracy so learnedly documented by Goitein, and possibly by legal calques of public law that go back much further in time. To simply jettison it under the name of individual equality, whatever the merit of the approach, is unwarranted, if at all feasible.

On this complex and difficult legacy a new debate has taken place, with the concept of federalism in its midst. Federalism, among the constitutional concepts available to human thought, stands ahead of the traditionally centralized nation-state, and Middle East national systems are increasingly challenged by the example of such diverse countries as the United States, Germany, Nigeria, or Malaysia where the federal model is common constitutional ground.[94]

The problem is that federalism, in any system that constitutionalist lawyers recognize on the planet, is inevitably territorial. With federalism following territory (and history), one has Rhode Island's and California's representatives coexisting happily as equals in the US Senate.

California takes the revenge of numbers over Rhode Island in other ways, but the territorial model remains the rule. When it comes to the executive branch, majority votes tend to bring the person chosen by the majority of people to the

to 'The lebanese system: a critical reassessment', conference organized by the Center for Behavioral Research (AVB) and the Chiha Foundation, 18–19 May 2001. The Chiha drafts are reproduced in full in Claude Doumet-Serhal and Michèle Hélou-Nahas, eds., *Michel Chiha 1891–1954* (Beirut, 2001).

[93] Discussed in my 'Du fait religieux dans les institutions', in Mallat ed., *L'Union Européenne et le Moyen-Orient: Etat des lieux* (Beirut, 2004) 83.

[94] Generally on the US and federalism as a major contribution to world political theory (and practice), see Mallat, *Al-dimuqratiyya fi Amirka* (Democracy in America) (Beirut, 2001) Chapters 12 ('Federal values for the world'), 107–14 and 1 ('A passing summer cloud: the presidential contest in Florida'), 15–20. On federalism in the Middle East compared: 'Federalism in the Middle East and Europe', *Case Western Journal of International Law*, 35, 2003, 1–15.

presidency, with Californians and Rhode Islanders counting almost equally at the polls.

Here appear the many difficulties of constitutionalism beyond the sociological set-up in Lebanon, Iraq, Israel, and the Middle East and North Africa generally, where the principle of full equality between two citizens within the country is at stake. Federalism, to be meaningful, is forced to give way to corrective representation of communities standing in lieu of states or regions, and this is a non-territorial scheme by and large.

Nor is the scheme easy to implement. Populations are interwoven, people move about, and while there may be majorities, often dominant, in a given territory, cities and the urban trend which had become a universal sociological trait by the end of the twentieth century blur that alleged racial, religious, or national cohesion. Rarely if ever is there territorial 'purity', and the absence of real or imagined cohesion entrenches the problem: communitarian federalism requires territories which are homogenous. They are not readily available in most of the Muslim world, and when they are, result from forms of ethnic cleansing which no one wishes to consecrate in law. Even when such territories appear to be homogenous, the problem gets translated on their borders, as one can see at the turn of the twenty-first century in Kirkuk between Arab and Kurdish Iraqis, in Baghdad between Sunnis and Shi'is, in Jerusalem between Jews and non-Jews (or Israelis and Palestinians), or in Beirut and its suburbs between Shi'i and non-Shi'i Lebanese.

The central problem for federalism, in Iraq, Lebanon, or Israel, is also thornier than elsewhere in the world, since the issue tends not to be separation of powers in the three executive branches of government, but the fight in the centre over executive power. Executive power is a difficult puzzle by nature, as Robespierre saw 200 years ago: one cannot have executive power if one has only part of it. Yet any democratic system is premised on the exercise by the individual citizen of his or her free choice, by casting a vote for an executive chief chosen by the majority.

There is no readily available answer to that conundrum, and various future arrangements are being examined and tested, as in the presidential triumvirate of Iraq that emerged in 2004.[95] Such schemes tend to become bewildering and unduly complex due to the pervasive quotas they encourage, and multi-religious and multi-ethnic mosaics cloud one's moral principles on the basic equality amongst citizens. The problem remains: to put the issue in simple words, the individual's allegiance in the Middle East, including Israel and Lebanon, is dual in law. He or she operates nationally, as constitutional citizen in a Habermasian way. But he or she also relates to public affairs through his or her religious/sectarian affiliation, which makes the community a constitutional agent recognized in law. That fault line is hard to bridge, and new constitutional formulae may be needed that

---

[95] Transitional Administrative Law (2004) in Iraq discussed in Mallat, 'Constitutions for the 21st century: emerging patterns—the EU, Iraq, Afghanistan ...', Herbert L. Bernstein Memorial Lecture in International and Comparative Law, Duke Law School, 28 September 2004, confirmed in the 'permanent' Constitution of 2005.

bring together not only the dilemma identified in this section, between the personal and the territorial, but also the two other constitutional difficulties that follow: (a) how does a federal system acknowledge communities on the other side of the border—for instance for Kurdish Iraqis their folk in Syria, Iran, or Turkey, and even communities who do not live in adjacent states, for instance Lebanese Shiʻis *vis-à-vis* their sister communities in Iraq or Iran; and (b) how will the classic pillars of constitutional democracy, popular and competitive choice of leaders, separation of powers, and judicial/constitutional review, operate in such a system of competing personal and national allegiances?

For the Middle East, bringing citizenship and community allegiances together in one working framework is the challenge of constitutionalism for the twenty-first century. Meanwhile, the clash between the two legal logics of personality and territoriality remains daunting, and it is against the pulls and pushes that they force onto the world system that constitutional law must be assessed inside each Middle Eastern jurisdiction.

Conclusion: Persisting Puzzles

No doubt the search for transnational accommodation continues in the Middle East, but the nation-state remains the essential framework for constitutional law. With the possible exceptions of Yemen and the United Arab Emirates, formal transnational unions have failed. It may be that the planet-wide economic and informational networks have started to undermine the dominance of the nation-state, but it will be some time before Middle Eastern legal and judicial institutions accommodate the international process hazily adumbrated as 'globalization'. Meanwhile, the example of neighbours keeps weighing heavily on the domestic developments in each country, for better and for worse. In 1992, the halt to constitutional democratization in Algeria froze a similar process in the whole of Arab Africa, whilst successful elections and the assertion of judicial independence and effectiveness anywhere in the Middle East are envied by neighbouring populations and feared by the ruling potentates, who are naturally concerned about any exemplary impact on their own overbearing powers.

At the same time, the debate on the Islamic tradition accommodating democratic mechanisms persists, with two alternative poles: the collapse into chaos if the accommodation is blunted or prevented at one end of the spectrum—as in Algeria during a decade of civil war in the 1990s, or Afghanistan under the Taliban; at the other end, the slow emergence of movements having at heart the recurrence of free elections in their societies to choose their leader and, as importantly, to change him. The prevalence of one trend over the other is not easy to predict, but the battle is joined, with factors of density of civil society, domestic, regional, and international power politics, and neighbourhood exempla pulling constitutionalism in several directions at once.

The challenge of personal, as against territorial law, which affects the Middle East in arguably the most significant challenge to constitutional law since Montesquieu, remains unanswered. With the constitutional entrenchment of communities defined on the basis of religion, and even sect, the communitarian model openly espoused in the Lebanese constitutional system appears increasingly as a dominant calque for countries in which minorities seek representation over and above basic majority rule. The conflict between personal and territorial models of constitutional conviviality is intense. If history is to be any guide, it will not be resolved soon.

Within this larger challenge, the question of the compatibility or incompatibility between a world civilization—Islam, and a political system—democracy, is best avoided. Emergence of Muslim-democrat movements across the Islamic world, as in Turkey in the 1990s, helps bring a calming perspective to the red herring argument of Islam's intrinsic incompatibility with democracy. Islamic or Muslim political movements need to be appraised in each country, in the same way as other nationalist or otherwise based political groupings, against the activities of governments when in opposition and, when in power, for their own activities with respect to recurrent and meaningful elections; the texture of civil society; and the protection of the individual's basic rights.[96]

Constitutional law plays itself out also in the judicial 'mirror' of civil society, with courts being constantly curtailed by executive power, and judges, lawyers, and society at large fighting to enhance an independent and meaningful judiciary as the main factor of civilized stability. In the absence of the realization of the independence and integrity of the judicial process as the neutral terrain for the resolution of social problems, the whole constitutional process is left to 'civil society' in sheer opposition to the state. In that case, the state finds itself in a situation where legality precludes legitimacy.[97] In that case indeed, where the protection of human rights is left to 'civil society', constitutions are emptied of any significance. Judges are part of the state as a matter of course. As the third branch of government, including for their normally exclusive access to the Weberian 'monopoly of violence', they should first and foremost be approached for the proper appreciation of constitutional law as the constitution's chief guardians. The slow emergence of judicial constitutional review is a novelty in the Middle East, which now needs to be examined in far more detail.

[96] See my *The Middle East into the 21st* century, Chapter 6.
[97] Point argued in the case of Iraq in my 'Obstacles to democratization in Iraq: a reading of post-revolutionary Iraqi history through the Gulf War', in E. Goldberg, R. Kasaba, and J. Migdal, eds., *Rules and rights in the Middle East: democracy, law and society* (Seattle, 1993) 224–47.

5

Constitutional Review: The Spread of Constitutional Councils and Courts

When they exist, bills of rights are a dead letter in the Middle East. Unless and until watchdogs are established to protect effectively the rights of citizens in accordance with the typically generous array of constitutional entitlements in the supreme texts, the rule of constitutional law remains confined to what best fits the decision-maker of the day.

The absence of constitutional protection is a combined legacy of the circumstances in the twentieth century which undermined the liberal experience, and the noted absence of a legal tradition which is historically American. Whether in the British tradition of parliamentary sovereignty or in the bicentenarial supremacy of the French Civil Code, the colonial experiment in the Middle East has left behind it a judiciary which was not entitled to measure a statute against the supreme law of the land.

Constitutions, when they exist, are therefore left to regulate the establishment of non-judicial institutions. They may be important to the extent that they provide a general framework for executive and legislative power, and they offer legitimacy rods often advocated in times of crisis. A usual indicator of the difficulty faced by a Middle East government is the threatened potentate's revival or amendment of a dormant constitution. One can see in that exception turned rule how irrelevant basic texts remain when it comes to the normative protection of the citizen. Even when a constitution 'functions', a person's fundamental rights tend to be the last item on the government's list of constitutional priorities.

Over the last quarter of a century, disparate and seemingly unconnected factors have converged to remove the constitutional texts from their ivory towers of ineffectiveness in various countries of the Middle East, at least formally. Rights mentioned in the constitution started being entrusted to independent bodies whose chief task was to protect and implement the previously innocuous fundamental texts. The formal spread of 'constitutional review' is striking in modern Middle Eastern law, within a similarly identifiable global trend.

Although the phenomenon is recent, in that its clear emergence does not go further back than the early 1980s, there have been attempts to introduce the mechanisms of such fundamental review at various moments through the twentieth century.

Antecedents and Fringe Experiments

The origins of a constitutional review model cannot be fully ascertained in the Middle East, but the concept of a constitutional council can be found in the 'dean of Middle Eastern constitutions', the Iranian *mashruteh* of 1906.[1] The concept may have come too early for its time, for no such council ever saw the light of day, but it did set the stage for its determined espousal by the Iranian Revolution, seventy years later, in the Council of Guardians (*Shura-ye negahban*), which survived the vicissitudes which beset the system through the stormy two decades that followed. One can also detect an early move towards constitutional review in Egypt, where 'Abd al-Razzaq al-Sanhuri developed his brief tenure as an administrative judge to transform *Majlis al-Dawla* into a proto-constitutional court, anticipating developments in France which saw the equivalent Conseil d'Etat agreeing to review administrative excesses in the light of the higher *principes généraux du droit*. In 'its famous decision of 20 February 1948', the Egyptian Conseil d'Etat stated: 'There is nothing in Egyptian law which prevents Egyptian courts from addressing the constitutionality of laws whether issued as decrees or legislation or from the point of view of form and substance'.[2] After rejecting the government's argument that such review would contradict the principle of the separation of powers, the Conseil d'Etat concluded that 'if one of the powers is using the principle of separation of powers as a pretext to undermine the Constitution, then matters would result in endless chaos'.[3]

Chaos by way of the marginalization of the legal process did eventually come in the form of the 'Free Officers' revolution, which destroyed in 1952 the fledgling experiment of constitutional review, and, more seriously, the formidable example of a functioning judiciary which had been painstakingly constructed in the country.[4] Despite a continuous interest in constitutional review through successive courts, Egypt had to wait for three decades before the Supreme Constitutional Court started to review legislation on the basis of the constitution in a systematic manner.

Research into proto-constitutional review is scant. The more attention is given to the phenomenon, the more forgotten experiments emerge, which generally date from the early days of a country's independence. There even appears to be a

---

[1] Significant literature on the *mashruteh*, including classics by E. G. Browne in English and Ahmad Kasravi in Persian. Further literature in Mallat, *The Middle East into the 21st century* (London, 1996) 244.

[2] Decision in *Majmu'at ahkam majlis al-dawla* (Collection of decisions by the Conseil d'Etat), Cairo, ii, 3150, quoted in Ahmad Hiba, '*Ta'liq 'ala ijtihad hawla wilayat al-mahkama al-dusturiyya al-'ulya* (Comment on a case on the competence of the Supreme Constitutional Court)', *Al-Majalla al-'arabiyya lil-fiqh wal-qada*', (MAFQ) 12, 1992, 239–62, at 254.

[3] ibid. See also Nathan Brown, 'Arab administrative courts and judicial control of the bureaucracy', February 1997 (available online at <http.www.geocities.com/nathanbrown1/SOGpaper.html>, consulted 2004); Enid Hill, 'Majlis al-Dawla: the administrative courts of Egypt and administrative law', in Mallat, ed., *Islam and public law* (London, 1993) 207–27.

[4] Above, Chapter 3, 'era of the law of force'.

recurrent pattern of constitutional review as part of institution-building in the nascent Middle Eastern nation-states, a pattern which was invariably frustrated as the power of the executive developed. This is the case in Iran, where the review body set up by Article 2 in the Iranian Constitution of 1906 never got off the ground. Another little known example is the Sudan:

In 1965, the Constituent Assembly (Parliament) passed a law banning the Communist party on 'the basis of its atheist principles.' The decision led to the expulsion of the communist deputies from parliament, and they brought a case to the Supreme Court against the Assembly and the government. Two years later, a judgment condemned the violation by these measures of Art.5 of the Constitution, which establishes the freedom of assembly, but neither the executive nor the legislative power honoured the judgment. This led the head of the judiciary to tender his resignation. Some analysts consider this event as one of the causes of the collapse of the Parliamentary experiment in 1969.[5]

Another Sudanese key constitutional development occurred in 1975,

when a number of lawyers brought a case against the government for issuing the 'law on state security' permitting arrests without judicial warrant, on the basis that such a law contradicted the permanent Constitution of 1973. Before the Supreme Court looked into the matter, a constitutional amendment was carried out and the President of the Republic given power to suspend part or all of the public liberties embodied in the Constitution. At the same time, legislative texts which punish 'the encouragement to sedition and state hatred' were expanded. The case on the anti-constitutionality of the law on state security was naturally mooted.

Early models of a fully-fledged constitutional court include Libya before the coup d'état of Colonel Mu'ammar Qadhdhafi in September 1969: 'The jurisdiction of the Supreme Court according to the provisions of the Act by which it was established in 1953, included judicial review of legislation'.[6] This did not survive the political turbulence of the country started by the coup. Whatever the texts, it is difficult to see how a system like the one in place in the Jamahiriyya can take seriously any law, let alone constitutional law.

One should note a number of countries where some constitutional review appears on the books, but where the required institutions are not established. Sometimes, they even get formally established and staffed, but are simply prevented from working.

To take the example of Libya again: one witnessed the revival on the statute books of constitutional 'supervision' in 1994, but the undermining of the rule of law by 'revolutionary measures' and the establishment of 'popular committees'

---

[5] This and the following quote come from a note of Dr 'Abd al-Salam Sayyed Ahmad, at the meeting in London of the Arab Organization of Human Rights in summer 1992. See also Ibrahim Hajj Musa, *Al-tajriba al-dimuqratiyya wa tatawwur nazam al-hukm fil-Sudan* (The democratic experiment and the development of the system of government in Sudan) (Cairo, 1970); Mansur Khaled, *Nimeiry and the revolution of dismay* (London, 1985).

[6] Mustafa El-Alem, 'Libya', in Eugene Cotran and Chibli Mallat, eds., *Yearbook of Islamic and Middle Eastern law*, 1, 1994, 225–36, at 227.

continued, regardless of good intentions proffered by the leadership on various occasions.[7]

In Syria, a full section of the 1973 Constitution is devoted to a Supreme Constitutional Court,[8] but no such court ever meant much. In neighbouring Jordan, the constitutional experience is more akin to advising than to judging. A High Council for the Interpretation of the Constitution[9] is entrusted by Article 57 of the Constitution with the task of 'explaining constitutional provisions' if Parliament or the Cabinet requests it, and another Special Council for the Clarification of Legislation[10] explains laws and decrees upon the request of the Prime Minister.[11] Within this limited role, there are some small side benefits, such as the publication of the full dissent of members of the High Council alongside the opinion of the majority. In a case where the majority considered unconstitutional a law requiring the assent of Parliament to confirm the dismissal of a public servant, two members of the Council dissented on the basis that constitutional practice allows Parliament to specify which official positions benefit from enhanced protection as represented in the law under consideration.[12] Still, Jordanian constitutionalism cannot be deemed to be properly judicial. Like many other countries where a department in the Ministry of Justice advises the government and governmental bodies on the meaning of a given statute, its role is mainly advisory.

In Kuwait, a Constitutional Court was mentioned in Article 173 of the 1962 Constitution. It was established much later by Law 14, 1973, which allows Parliament and the Council of Ministers to directly ask the Court about the constitutionality of legislation. In addition, Article 4 of that law allows private parties to benefit from constitutional review by exception, that is if a case in a lower court raises a matter of constitutionality and the lower court decides to stay the proceedings until the issue is ruled upon by the Constitutional Court. But the Court was reluctant to admit these cases. Any 'direct' appeal against the constitutionality of a law or decree was not entertained. This was the case with two decisions in which

[7] 'On 29 January 1994 Act 17/1423 was issued to amend some articles of the [previous Libyan law], including Article 23 which defines the jurisdiction of the [Supreme] court. Amended Article 23 extended the jurisdiction of the Supreme Court to the control "or supervision" of the constitutionality of legislation. This means that the Supreme Court is empowered again to declare legislation invalid on the ground that it is "unconstitutional".' ibid.

[8] *al-Mahkama al-dusturiyya al-'ulya*, Arts 139–48 of the Syrian Constitution.

[9] *al-Majles al-'ali li tafsir al-dustur.*   [10] *al-Diwan al-khass fi tafsir al-qawanin.*

[11] See decisions of the two bodies (five decisions of *al-Majles al-'ali* on constitutional interpretation between 1976 and 1992, and 239 decisions of *al-Diwan al-khass* in Jawdat Musa'ida, ed., *Al-qararat al-sadira 'an al-diwan al-khass fi tafsir al-qawanin wal-majlis al-'ali li-tafsir al-dustur min 1/1/1976 ila 31/12/1991* (Decisions rendered by the Special Council for the Clarification of Legislation, and by the High Council for the Clarification of the Constitution from 1/1/1976 to 31/12/1991), 'Amman, 1992.

[12] *Qarar raqm 1 sader 'an al-majlis al-'ali li-tafsir al-dustur li-sanat 1991* (Case 1 of the High Council for the Clarification of the Constitution in 1991), Majority opinion of nine members decided 6/4/1991, in Musa'ida, ed., *Al-qararat al-sadira*, 921–3; dissent (*mukhalafa*) of two members, 924–5; see also three separate dissents in case 2/1991, 926–34; and opinion of three dissenters in case 3/1993, 935–7.

a challenge to laws allowing the executive to prevent the publication of news-papers or journals was considered a 'direct' attack for which the Court denied its competence.[13]

The Spread of Constitutional Review: The Two Models

These early or fringe experiments notwithstanding, two basic types of constitu-tional review emerged in the Middle East, which generally correspond to the differ-ence in constitutional adjudication between the French Conseil Constitutionnel and the US Supreme Court.[14]

The difference between the two systems can be presented in the shape of the operation of the Council of Guardians[15] in Iran on the one hand, and of the Supreme Constitutional Court of Egypt (SCC) on the other.[16] In both cases, a statute is tested against the constitution by an independent body of judges, but the crucial distinction is that only specifically circumscribed authorities can peti-tion the Iranian Council for a law within a few days of its passing by Parliament, while the constitutional review of the Egyptian Court, in the second model, arises on the occasion of a case in which the litigant is an ordinary citizen arguing that the application of a particular law violates his or her constitutional right, regard-less of how long ago that particular legislation was passed.

Thus Middle Eastern courts exercise constitutional review in one of two ways. Under the top-heavy style introduced in 1958 France, a Conseil Constitutionnel reviews legislation immediately after it is passed by Parliament. Such Constitutional Councils can be asked by a limited number of senior political figures, typically the presidents of the executive and legislative branches or a group of deputies, who ask the Court to review the constitutionality of a given statute recently promulgated. The model is typical of states where French jurisprudence remains influential, and is found in Algeria, Lebanon, and Morocco, but its first effective prototype is the Iranian Council of Guardians, which was established by the 1979 Constitution following the success of the Islamic revolutionaries under the leadership of Ruhollah al-Khumaini.

---

[13] Excerpts of the two decisions in A. Tabataba'i, '*Al-Athar al-qanuniyya al-mutarattiba 'ala hukm al-mahkama al-dusturiyya 1/1994* (Legal consequences deriving from the Constitutional Court's decision 1/1994)', *al-Muhami* (Kuwait), 18, August–September 1994, 9–55, at 21–3 (Decision 1/1993, issued 26/3/1994) and 24–5 (Decision 1/1992, issued 27/6/1992). See also Nathan Brown, *The rule of law in the Arab world* (Cambridge, 1997) 157–79 for a good treatment of Kuwait's 'judi-cial timidity' (at 173), especially the Constitutional Court.

[14] On comparative constitutional law, a classic book is by Mauro Cappelletti, *The judicial process in comparative perspective* (Oxford, 1989).

[15] *shura-ye negahban*, Council of Guardians, Art. 94 of the Iranian Constitution.

[16] *al-mahkama al-dusturiyya al-'ulya*, Arts. 174–8 of the Egyptian Constitution.

The other model allows constitutional review to be exercised by any court, subject to ultimate review by a Supreme Court American-style. Here the constitutionality of a statute is decided by the Constitutional Court on the occasion of its application in a litigated case. Judicial review of this second type can be found in Yemen, Kuwait, and the United Arab Emirates, but its most remarkable exponent is the Supreme Constitutional Court of Egypt.

Neither type of constitutional review was known to a significant extent in the Middle East before the 1980s, and both models have been particularly enriched since by a large body of decisions, especially in Iran and Egypt. I have had occasion to discuss at length the rise and fall of the Council of Guardians in Iran through its case-law and judicial tribulations.[17] The reader is referred to that discussion to which little can be added since the constitutional demise, in 1989, of the Council of Guardians in favour of the *Majma'-e tashkhis-e maslahat-e nezam* (lit. Council for the discernment of the interest of the regime), an eminently political body.[18]

Two pioneering experiments involving constitutional councils in the region took place in Algeria and Lebanon in the 1990s. Like Iran, they ended in failure, but they deserve some attention. One should also add the case of Morocco, where a Constitutional Council was established along similar lines. The experience has yielded little constitutional jurisprudence of worth, despite Moroccan jurists' high hopes for the Council.[19]

Conseils constitutionnels: the Algerian interlude

In Algeria, democratization gathered pace in the late 1980s and resulted in a new Constitution being promulgated on 1 March 1989. The text established a presidential system with both Parliament and the President elected by universal suffrage. The democratic process which ensued was brought to a brutal halt by the military take over in the wake of the first round of parliamentary elections in December 1991, which saw the relative electoral success of the opposition Front Islamique du Salut. The abrupt halt to the democratic process resulted in a collapse in public order pitting the army against the Islamists in a whirlwind of violence and atrocities, and a drawn-out civil war plagued the country in the following decade.

---

[17] Mallat, *The renewal of Islamic law* (Cambridge 1993) 79–107 and 146–57.

[18] Recent introduction by 'Ali Ahmadi, *Majma'-e tashkhis-e maslahat-e nezam* (Tehran, 2005). One should note that the Council of Guardians remains extremely powerful under a very different competence, as it vets the candidates to Parliament and to the Presidency, preventing any serious reformist candidate from getting through its net. Out of several hundred candidates, only a handful is allowed to go forward to the Presidential election. For a useful review of the system, see Asghar Schirazi, *The Constitution of Iran* (London 1997) and the thorough chronicles on Radio Free Europe (rferl.org) by Bill Samii.

[19] 'Abdal-'Aziz al-Nuwaidi, *Al-Majlis al-dusturi bil-Maghreb* (The Moroccan constitutional court) (Casablanca, 2001) (see at 66 table of decisions of the Court since its establishment in 1992, with a handful of decisions concerning constitutionality of laws and over 300 adjudicating electoral disputes); Nadia Bernoussi, 'Les méthodes constitutionnelles du juge marocain', in *Les aspects récents du droit constitutionnel* (Tunis, 2005) 279–89, at 289: 'grande attente de la part des juristes, mais aussi et surtout de la part de la classe politique et de la société civile'.

The role of courts and constitutional councils in such an atmosphere, as in the Yemen after the brief civil war between former South Yemen and the North in 1994, could only be seriously curtailed.

Prior to the interruption of the elections in early 1992, the Algerian Constitutional Council had been operating in a French-style model. Articles 153 to 159 of the 1989 Algerian Constitution and later decrees specify its competence and work. It is composed of seven members chosen for six years, and can be asked by the President and the Speaker to review alleged unconstitutionality of legislation. The Council is also in charge of ensuring the regularity of parliamentary and presidential elections.[20]

The Council's first decision was rendered when the President of the Republic asked the Council whether dispositions under the electoral code specifying the conditions for candidacy to public office were legal. Several details of the law were analysed by the Council, and it left some standing while voiding others. The decision held 'that the requirements regarding the nationality of origin of the candidate [to the Presidency] and his wife in Article 86 of the Electoral Law' were unconstitutional, and established the necessity not to discriminate between candidates to public office by requesting some to gather more signatures supporting their candidacy than others.[21]

Two other decisions were also rendered in 1989. The first invalidated a distinction in the law allowing deputies to teach at university while requesting their exclusive dedication to their job. This distinction discriminated between deputies unnecessarily, the Council held. It also examined a number of stipulations concerning the deputy's right to sit on local bodies and to exercise an executive role, and held unconstitutional those parts of the law which contradicted a strict separation of powers, whether national as opposed to local, or whether of an executive, rather than legislative, nature.[22]

The second decision also allowed a strict scrutiny of the internal regulation of Parliament, in which the Council struck out a provision of the law which was in its view unduly vague. That portion of the article in the law, the Council held, could enlarge the power of legislative committees and make them investigative bodies. The provision was invalidated for violation of the separation of powers between legislators and judges.

All three cases were brought by the President in the early days of the new Constitution. They were the last before the civil war started. It was not until the summer of 1995 that the Algerian Constitutional Council had the occasion to

---

[20] See the Algerian Constitution of 1989, which was approved by referendum on 23 February and published in the Algerian Official Journal (OJ) on 1 March. See also the presidential decree of 7 August 1989, regulating the functioning of the Council, OJ 7 August 1989 and the documents published in the two pamphlets published in Algiers in 1990 in Arabic and in French, entitled *al-majlis al-dusturi* and *Le Conseil constitutionnel*, respectively.

[21] Decision 1 of the Algerian CC dated 20 August 1989, OJ, 30 August 1989 (Arabic and French, quote at 1051 and 874 respectively).

[22] Decision 2 of the Algerian CC dated 30 August 1989, OJ, 4 September 1989 (Arabic and French, 1054–61 and 879–81 respectively).

examine again the constitutionality of legislation. There was not much substance in the new decision either, which confirmed the first decision of the Council and reaffirmed it to the extent of the unconstitutionality of conditions for a candidate to the Presidency as to the nationality of his wife.[23] The ruling indicated a new impetus under a new President of the Council, despite the continuing political deadlock in Algeria, to move towards a new lease of life for the rule of law, but the general tragic circumstances in the country kept the Conseil Constitutionnel, the judiciary in general, indeed the whole institutional system, at bay. The military rules Algeria with an iron fist, and the Council's decisions are kept deliberately 'modest':[24] It took ten months to find a successor to the Council's President in 2001. This stalled phenomenon of judicial appointments appears increasingly as a common, additional complication across the region.

Conseils constitutionnels: the Lebanese failure[25]

Like its Algerian cousin, the Lebanese Constitutional Council was modelled after its French equivalent, the Conseil Constitutionnel. The Council was established in the wake of the constitutional enactments following the so-called Ta'ef Accords of 1989. As amended by the Constitutional law of 21 September 1990, Article 19 of the Lebanese Constitution established the Constitutional Council 'to control the constitutionality of laws and examine the conflicts arising from petitions questioning presidential and parliamentary elections'. Article 19 of the Constitution and Law 250 of 15 July 1993, which regulate the Constitutional Council, show the duality in the character of the Constitutional Council, as both an arbiter of problems connected with electoral disputes and a court of constitutional review.[26]

The Council is composed of ten senior legal figures chosen for a period of six years from the legal professions and from academia. Five members are elected by Parliament and five are appointed by the government. In turn, the members of the Council elect their president and vice-president.[27]

[23] OJ, 8 August 1995 (Arabic and French, at 11–12 and 15 respectively).

[24] Romain Graëffly, 'Le conseil constitutionnel algérien. De la greffe institutionnelle à l'avènement d'un contentieux constitutionnel?', *Revue de Droit Public*, 5, 2005, 1381–404, at 1401, 1403 ('le nombre de décisions contraignantes en quinze années est très modeste: elles sont au nombre de sept (quatre de 1989 à 1991 et deux de 1995 à 2004) et ne portent aucunement sur les droits et les libertés des citoyens').

[25] On Lebanon, see my '*Al-majlis al-dusturi al-lubnani: min ajl dirasa naqdiyya muqarana* (The Lebanese constitutional council: for a comparative critique)*', al-Hayat* (London), 12 August 1993, criticizing the absence of recourse before the Council by the citizen; and my annual 'Lebanon' entries in the *Yearbook of Islamic and Middle Eastern law* from 1994 to 1998.

[26] Under the competence of the Council falls the examination of election results and of complaints resulting from parliamentary and presidential elections, including the invalidation of one or more such electoral consultations. This resulted also in the change of the internal statute of Parliament, which acknowledges the role of the Council in this respect and the necessity for the Speaker to inform Parliament of the Council's decision on a disputed election (OJ 44, 3 November 1994, 1177).

[27] The Council's first president, Wajdi Mallat, received the highest number of parliamentary votes, and was in turn chosen by the majority of his peers to preside over the Council in July 1994.

The Council reviews legislation within two weeks of its approval by Parliament, and the invalidation of the law requires a majority of seven out of the ten members. Legislation becomes final otherwise. Only a limited number of officials can request the Council to review the non-constitutionality of legislation: the President, the Prime Minister, and the Speaker, or at least ten deputies—in addition to the heads of the religious communities for matters of religious law.

The first decision of the Constitutional Council was issued on 21 February 1995. The case concerned a petition brought by twelve deputies challenging a law that consisted of a single article: 'Exceptionally for this one time, and contrary to any other text, it is possible for the Prime Minister to transfer the President of the High Ja'fari [Shi'i] court [a religious, *shar'i*, as opposed to lay, jurisdiction] or dismiss him'. The case was complicated by a procedural issue, when some of the petitioners tried to retract their earlier demands for the Court intervention. This was brushed aside by a preliminary decision of the Court,[28] in which it suspended the law prima facie, and rejected the retractions on the basis that the exercise by deputies of their right to petition the Constitutional Council was a public right, and not a private grievance which could later be withdrawn. In its final decision, the Court held that the law was unconstitutional on substance: clearly a bill of attainder, it stood in manifest violation of Article 20 of the Constitution, which speaks of judicial guarantees and judicial independence: 'Whereas the law undermines the independence of the judiciary and the guarantees which the Constitution grants to judges and parties in Article 20, ... and whereas the law which is under consideration stands, in that case, in contradiction with Article 20 of the Constitution and the general constitutional principles which are established to protect the independence of the judiciary and to provide the necessary guarantees for judges and parties, ... it is invalidated'.[29]

Parliament went back to the drawing board, and passed a more sophisticated piece of legislation allowing a full review of the position of *shar'i* judges in addition to the appointment of a judicial inspector delegated to that effect by a number of judges under the supervision of the higher *shar'i* council. The Council found no constitutional problem with such arrangements, and noted that 'the two-thirds majority needed for the impeachment of any of the heads of the three *shar'i* tribunals ... increases the guarantee accorded to those officials in comparison with the rest of the *shar'i* judges'. A further procedural consideration for the transfer or dismissal of a *shar'i* judge after the approval of the two-thirds of the higher *shar'i* council was also considered constitutional, but the Council voided the disposition, in the same paragraph, that such decision for dismissal or transfer 'be carried out in the absence of the judge concerned'. This sentence was found to stand in violation of the constitutional principles of the right of the accused—let alone a judge—to defend herself. Only that portion of the law was considered

---

[28] OJ 7, 16 February 1995, decision of 11 February 1995, 145–46.
[29] Undermines, undermining, *intiqas*. OJ 9, 1995, 183–5, at 184.

unconstitutional and struck out, while the rest of the statute was left standing.[30] The case was finally closed at the end of the year with the decision of the Prime Minister, after agreement of the higher *shar'i* council, to replace the president of the Ja'fari (Shi'i) court at the root of the controversy.

The Constitutional Council handed down its first decision of 1996—its second year in action—on the matter of the budget.[31] The challenge, again brought by ten deputies, was rejected on procedural grounds, but the decision exposed some of the problems of lawmaking in the country and their scrutiny by the Council. Law 490 on the Annual Budget and its Annexes bears the date of 15 February, and was published in a Special Addendum to issue 7 of the Official Journal, also dated 15 February. The law was challenged on various grounds, but the demand was brought to the register of the Council on 15 March, well after the statutory time limitation had run out—fifteen days from the date of publication of the challenged law. The deputies had explained in their demand that although the Addendum did bear the date of 15 February, 'the law had effectively been published on 1 March', thus bringing their challenge within the maximum term allowed. The Council rejected the argument, after a preparatory decision in which it asked two of its members to ascertain the real date of publication of the relevant issue of the Official Journal, which was clearly not the one which the Journal bore. Additionally, the deputies' demand had mentioned two different dates for the law's effective publication: 28 February and 1 March. The contradiction was noted by the Council, which proceeded to reject the challenge on the basis of the investigation it asked the two Council members to carry out. The investigation showed that the parliamentary official in charge of retrieving the issues of the Official Journal from the governmental offices where it was produced had signed a receipt to that effect on 26 February. The Council concluded that 26 February was the latest possible date for the publication of the law. The fifteen days permitted by law to lodge the challenge had clearly passed by the time the deputies brought their request to the Council. On that basis, the Council concluded that it could not exercise its review of the law.

While the conclusion may not seem important, the decision by the Council to conduct its own investigation was noteworthy. With the procedural decision of the Court in its first decision of 1995, and now its readiness to carry out active field enquiries, expectations rose in the country. Here had emerged a court which was ready to stand up to Parliament and the government, forcing them to redraft the law, and deciding, to make its writ effective, that it could strike a section of the law and avoid unnecessary to-ing and fro-ing in the legislative process. The Council was even ready to conduct its own investigation into the manoeuvres of the administration to tamper with constitutionally mandated deadlines.

---

[30] Decision 3/1995, 18 September 1995, OJ 39, 1995, 1047–50.
[31] Decision 2/96 of 3 April 1996, OJ 15, 1996, 699–701.

In a pattern one encounters across the region, the Lebanese Constitutional Council would soon be faced by pressures it could not resist. In the case of Lebanon, they resulted from the second task it was asked to perform by the Constitution: adjudicating electoral issues. In the summer of 1996, elections to the Lebanese Parliament were carried out, and the Council was first solicited to examine the constitutionality of the law regulating the electoral consultation. As Parliament had been slow to draft the required legislation, the rhythm of the challenge to the law and its examination by the Council transformed the process into a particularly heated episode. For reasons he never fully explained, except to say on one public occasion that the Council came a quarter of a century too early for the country, its first president resigned suddenly in April 1997. While the Lebanese Constitutional Council continued its work with the remainder of the members, and soon with another president, it never recovered. Ten years later, it was still paralysed by judges hanging on beyond their legally mandated terms and the incapacity of the body politic, for months on end, to replace them.

US-style review: the Yemen Supreme Court and the UAE

Despite the heavy legacy of wars and the general economic backwardness in the country, the Yemeni union of 1990 gave way to an innovative constitution which formally espoused the principles of an independent judiciary and the guardianship of a Supreme Constitutional Court. The writ of the Supreme Court is embodied in Article 124/151 of the Constitution,[32] which stipulates the following headings for its competence:

1-The control of the constitutionality of laws, regulations, decrees and decisions.
2-Conflicts of competence within the judiciary.
3-Claims arising from elections.
4-Final appeal in civil, criminal and personal status decisions.
5-Final appeals in administrative conflicts and disciplinary cases.

This is a wide and far-reaching competence for a court by any standard, and is clearly drawn from the US Supreme Court model.

On 21 September 1992 the Yemeni Supreme Court issued the first constitutional review decision in the history of Yemen. The facts were simple and of limited importance, and concerned an action brought against the Speaker of Parliament by two members of the parliamentary constitutional committee. It was argued that the Speaker had put forward, in the field of education, legislative projects which were unconstitutional.

The Court held against the plaintiffs on procedural grounds by refusing to assert its jurisdiction over bills or legislative projects. In the reported decision, the

[32] The Constitution of unified Yemen was changed after the 1994 civil war, and several articles amended, hence the renumbering of the articles.

Court appeared conscious of the important role it would be called on to play, but refused to be drawn into internecine parliamentary disagreements. The full argumentation of the plaintiffs was reproduced and then rebutted: 'Since this case is the first constitutional case before the judiciary in the Yemeni Republic, the Court must explain what is meant by judicial constitutional review', mentioned in Article 124/151 of the Constitution and in Articles 12 and 19 of the Law on Judicial Power 1/1991. These articles, the Court explained, entrust the review of the constitutionality of legislation to the Supreme Court. They do not extend to legislation which is in preparation and which has not yet completed the full process leading to its enactment into law. This protective role which the Court was being asked by the plaintiffs to perform was not within the purview of the constitutional tasks entrusted to the Supreme Court. 'Does not fall under the jurisdiction of the Court the power to examine projects of law or the review of their constitutionality or the constitutionality of measures taken in relation to them'.[33] The Court could not examine a text before it became enforceable law.

The second constitutional case was of a more directly political nature, as it concerned the elections which were to be held in Yemen on 27 April 1993. The Prime Minister and others brought before the Supreme Court an action which arose from the implementation of the electoral law by the High Committee in charge of the elections. The arguments of the plaintiffs were based on the legality of cumulating the offices of minister and parliamentarian under Articles 60 and 76 of the Constitution. There is a specific exception in Article 83, they argued further, which states that 'cumulating public office and membership in Parliament is forbidden—except in the case of the Prime Minister and the members of Cabinet'.

The Supreme Court dismissed the action, explaining that constraints imposed by the Electoral Committee on the candidacy of the Prime Minister were unwarranted and unconstitutional. In a slightly confused argument, it held that 'the constitutional order in our country allows for a member of parliament to be appointed Prime Minister or Minister', and that the declaration of the Electoral Committee, which 'includes the Prime Minister and his deputies among those [prevented from holding joint office by the electoral law] is a departure from the text of the law which stops at ministers and their deputies and does not include the Prime Minister and his deputies. To request the latter to resign before presenting their candidacy is a mere intellectual exercise which burdens the text with a meaning that it cannot support.'[34] The electoral law was therefore upheld, and the explanatory decree of the Electoral Committee restricted.

In the two constitutional decisions available, it is clear that the Supreme Court of the Yemen has taken its task to heart. While it ultimately refused to consider

[33] Case 1/1992, Supreme Court of the Yemen, Constitutional Division, decided 21 September 1992, reported in Mallat, 'Three recent decisions from the Yemen Supreme Court', *Islamic Law and Society*, 2, 1995, 71–90, at 76–80, citation at 80.

[34] Case 1/1993, Supreme Court of the Yemen, Constitutional Division, 28 March 1993, reported in ibid. 81–6, citation at 85.

unconstitutional any of the measures attacked, on a convincing argument in the first instance (no scrutiny of bills and projects of law), and in a more befuddled argument in the second instance (no resignation needed by ministers before they are candidates for Parliament), the difficulty of the Court in handling hot political issues was evident. Its careful and perhaps voluntarily confused wording underlines the fear of being drawn into what is clearly political terrain—preventing the Prime Minister and other ministers from being candidates for Parliament.

As for basic human rights and the possibility for the citizen to resort to the Court in order to solicit its constitutional protection, it is remarkable that the issue which came up in such a delicate matter was one of apostasy.[35] It was handled by the criminal section of the Supreme Court and not by the Constitutional Chamber. The reversal of the apostasy charge was made by the Criminal Chamber on the grounds of facts ('the accused was a true Muslim'), rather than on Book 2 of the Constitution listing the 'basic rights and duties of the citizen: ... The state guarantees the freedom of thought and the freedom to express one's opinion in speech, writing or photography [i.e. television] *within the limits of law*'.[36]

The formula 'within the limits of law' is typical of the shortcomings of Arab constitutionalism, and is consistently used to blunt the basic freedoms listed in constitutions. The constraining formula is used across the Middle East, and 'limits' are included in special legislation or in criminal or media codes to undermine the constitutional protection of basic rights.

In the specific case of Yemen, it is also true that the odds were overwhelming. When the civil war started in early 1994, the whole judicial process came to a standstill. Since the guns fell silent in the summer of that year, the Supreme Court has been slowly emerging again as a court of last resort, but its constitutional writ remains feeble. Years after the civil war came to an end, there is no evidence of important cases being been brought before the Court despite the relative ease of constitutional adjudication. This interruption of constitutional review is also true of the more dramatic experience of Algeria and Lebanon.

Before leaving Yemen, a positive element ought to be mentioned in its judicial system, which offers some hopeful guidance to other Middle Eastern jurisdictions. Whether in Egypt, Iran, Lebanon, or Algeria, a major unspoken hurdle for the development of the highest judicial scrutiny—constitutional review—is the proliferation of courts. The division inherited from the French system between Conseil d'Etat (administrative courts) and Cour de Cassation (the other courts, including civil and criminal chambers which deal with police matters) is a first complication in the system. When a separate constitutional judicial body is added, courts develop a jealous or guarded attitude towards one another, especially since constitutional judges tend to be in the public limelight, and their aura consequently increased. In the Yemen, as noted by a member of the Supreme Court,[37]

---

[35] *Al-'Udi* case, discussed next chapter.
[36] Art. 26, which opens Book 2 of the Constitution (emphasis added).
[37] Judge Nagib Shammiri, in conversation with author, London, 1994.

the fact that a single body stands at the apex of the system, including for commercial, criminal, and civil matters, avoids unnecessary bickering between judges. Such matters, of course, are not written or documented. But any knowledge of the practical work in court shows the destructive power of judicial fragmentation.

A last point ought to be made in the search for so-called 'decentralization' problems, which are acute in some countries like Yemen or Iraq because of the specific regional, communitarian, or ethnic tensions in society. From the ineffectiveness of the American Supreme Court to prevent the Civil War in 1861 can be drawn a further theme of reflection on the constitutional failings in the Yemen in which the judiciary can only be partly to blame. I refer here to the federal problem.

As in all momentous actions on this scale, the unification of the Yemen in 1990 appears retrospectively flawed by the haste with which institutions of two independent countries were made to fuse together: one diplomatic corps, one presidential council, one parliament, one judiciary, one set of personal status laws, one commercial code. With the onset of economic problems and political conflicts, the unifying mould fell prey to grand ambitions: the pace of unity was too rapid and too rigid, and the law did not take into account the country's diverse constituencies and economic and human riches. Regardless of the wide writ granted to the Supreme Court, a major prerogative was missing: the arbitration of region-based conflicts.

This does not come as a surprise, considering that the Constitution itself did not want to recognize any of these variations: unity meant oblivion to particularism, with 'sulking' by the former South Yemen leadership as the only way of protest, and the civil war as the only way to end the sulking.

One can elaborate on the way these particularisms should be handled. One conclusion is easy: the first Yemeni Constitution failed to address this problem, and the absence of a federal (in Arabic unitary, *ittihadi*) agenda, with a judiciary as ultimate arbitrator of regional and central dysfunctions, cost the unity its dream. There is little room in such daunting circumstances for the patient and fragile workings of the judiciary, let alone of a Supreme Court. From that derives the difficulty for a court, particularly a constitutional one, to mediate and ultimately decide on regional or federal constitutional issues. While the attraction of a 'neutral' judicial body is persuasive, it continues to be the case that any form of federalism, let alone of judicially regulated federalism, has so far remained outside the general legal ambit of most Middle Eastern societies.

An exception is the UAE. Unlike so many frustrated experiments, a little known but alluring instance of federal constitutional review has surfaced in the United Arab Emirates.[38] Information on the subject is scant, but a documented UAE case addresses several issues of central relevance to the exercise of constitutional review in the Middle East, including the federal-regional issue.

---

[38] Institutional structure described in Chapter 4.

This was 'an explanatory decision' rendered on 25 November 1983 by the Federal Supreme Court in answer to a query of the Federal Court of Appeal in Abu Dhabi concerning the application of the penalties established by various laws dealing with the drinking of wine.[39] The petitioner had been caught drinking in public and sentenced in the city of Abu Dhabi, and various cross-appeals lodged. One of the relevant laws was Law 8 of 1976 of the Emirate of Abu Dhabi, which sets a jail penalty of a minimum of two months and a maximum of a year, together with a fine of 500 dirhams, for being apprehended in a public place in a state of drunkenness (Art. 17). At the same time, Art. 75 of Federal Law 10 of 1973 had determined that 'the Supreme Court must apply the rules of the Islamic *shari'a* and federal and other legislation in force—in the Emirates which are members of the Federation—in conformity with the rules of the Islamic *shari'a*. The Supreme Court [must also] apply the principles of custom and the principles of natural law and comparative laws which do not conflict with the *shari'a*.'[40]

Several issues lay before the UAE Federal Supreme Court in that case: the first concerned the extent of the application of Islamic law in the Emirates and its constitutional status. Another issue concerned the specific federal problem, which is a rare case in the region, as the United Arab Emirates offers the only working federal system of government in the Middle East. Which of the two laws would apply, the federal law or the Abu Dhabi local law? Finally, and from a substantive point of view, the question was whether the judge should apply the penalty stipulated by the Abu Dhabi law, or whether he was bound by the strict regulations of classical law in the matter.

On the federal issue, the Court circumvented the problem by ruling that both the federal law and the local law should be taken into account simultaneously, and that the jail penalty was not exclusive of the more severe *hadd* (prescribed) penalty of classical law, which calls for the offender's flogging: 'Even though the principle in the *hadd* penalties is that the *hadd* allows disregarding *ta'zir* [discretionary power of the criminal judge in the absence of a *hadd*], ... there is no contradiction between the application of the penalty of *hadd* on wine drinking and the penalty of *ta'zir* specified in [the Abu Dhabi] law'.[41]

As for defining the penalty of *hadd*, the Court found that there is no dissent in the various schools of law over the matter, and that the penalty of flogging was well established by the *sunna* and by the consensus of the classical schools. It also suggested that a minimum of eighty lashes should be the basis of punishment according to federal law, which had accepted the principle of Islamic law as the overarching reference of the system.

On the central place of Islamic law in the Constitution, the Court was most emphatic. It considered the law of the Abu Dhabi Emirate which establishes the

---

[39] Decision secured from the National Library in Abu Dhabi (on file with author).
[40] ibid. at 3.   [41] This and following quotes at ibid. 5–6.

penalty of *ta'zir* to conform to the *shari'a* as required by the Constitution. Neither did the law stand in conflict with the federal law which, in the Court's argument, requested the *hadd* penalty:

Article 7 of the Provisional Constitution of the Federation has provided that Islam was the official religion of the Federation and that the Islamic *shari'a* is a principal source for legislation. This Constitution, as specified in its preamble, is the meeting over rules and objectives between the will of the Rulers of the Emirates and that of its people, amongst which the move forward in the union towards a democratic parliamentarian government with complete pillars in an Arab and Islamic society.

Together with this wide declaration *obiter*, the Court concluded that the expression

'a principal source' does not elicit a debate like the one in another country [reference here is to the Egyptian constitution].[42] This controversy was solved when the legislator expressed his wish that the Islamic *shari'a* be the unique and principal source for all legislation emanating from the powers of the state.

The Court left no doubt that it considered the *shari'a* as the supreme and dominant reference in the country, concluding that 'it is a divine law which stands above all legislation'.

It is not clear how much of a standing that precedent holds in the system. The fact that the decision was issued 'by the majority' of the Court, together with the absence of consistent law reporting since the late 1980s in the Emirates, suggests that the constitutional writ of the Supreme Court remains limited. Much as in the case of *Diwan al-Mazalim* in Saudi Arabia, which, in the absence of a constitution, cannot but issue its decisions 'in consonance with Islamic law', law reports may have proved too unnerving for the executive to allow the continued systematic publication of the decent reports which were for a brief while available in the Arab Peninsula.

US-style review: the difficult assertion of the Egyptian Supreme Court

The Egyptian experiment best represents the US-style model of constitutional review in the region, despite some important differences in procedure. The Supreme Constitutional Court (SSC) looks into a dispute only when another court stays its decision pending the SCC's constitutional review of the statute relevant to the dispute.

By the summer of 1991, when its presidency was entrusted to 'Awad al-Murr, the Supreme Constitutional Court of Egypt was already well established.[43] The

---

[42] See below nn. 58–60 and accompanying text. See also Chapter 4.

[43] This section owes a lot to long discussions with the late Chief Justice Dr 'Awad al-Murr (d. 2004), in several meetings in Cairo, London, and Washington over the years, about his work and vision of the Egyptian Supreme Constitutional Court. See my brief comment in 'The man who

decision for which the SCC had gained fame beyond the confines of legal experts was its voidance of parliamentary elections on 19 May 1990, which followed other landmark decisions the previous year with regard to local elections as well as to elections to the Egyptian council of notables known as *Majlis al-shura*.[44] But it was the now steady competence of the Court in both separation of powers questions and the protection of the electoral processes, and more generally basic rights in accordance with the Egyptian Constitution, that offered it as the most advanced model for a Middle East in search of the rule of law.

The first decision of the Murr Court, rendered on 6 July 1991,[45] shows the progress made over the previous decade. In a brief opinion, a by then usual paragraph tersely reaffirmed the Court's law:

The decisions expressed in constitutional cases—which are by nature specific decisions in which the constitutionality of legislative texts is challenged—have, according to the [previous] judgments of the present Court, universal effect[46] and are not limited to the parties in the case. Rather, this evidence applies to all and is binding on all the powers of the state, whether these decisions end up in affirming the unconstitutionality of the challenged legislation or not. The present [governmental] decree is therefore rejected.[47]

In the circumstances, the challenged text was a decision of the governor of Suez to punish a fisherman who fished without a proper licence as required by a decree the Governor had issued in 1985. In 1989, the decree was challenged by the lawyers of the accused before the lower courts, who transferred the case to the SCC. The Court, then under the Presidency of Mamduh Hasan, declared the decree unconstitutional, because it contravened several articles of the Constitution, 'for establishing penalties outside [the power to pass] legislation which is of the competence of the People's Assembly or the President of the Republic'.[48]

The Murr Court was standing by the verbatim record of the judgment which the SCC had pronounced on a similar case raised before it earlier. The first judgment

---

took on the system and won', *The Daily Star*, 12 December 1996. Under Art. 178 of the Constitution, the decisions of the Court must be published in the Egyptian Official Journal, which was the primary source for these decisions until the late 1980s, when the Court took over publication of its decisions. Since then, ten large and comprehensive volumes have appeared as *Majmu'at qararat al-mahkama al-dusturiyya al-'ulya* (Collection of the SCC decisions). I refer to cases which I studied in the Official Journal as OJ, and to the cases in the Collection as SCC, followed by the volume number and the page. A fuller description of the Court's work on human rights, written in English by Dr Murr, can be found in 'The Supreme Constitutional Court of Egypt and the protection of human and political rights', in Mallat, ed., *Islam and public law*, above n. 3, 229–60. The SCC also deals with 'requests for constitutional interpretation' and 'conflicts in judicial competence', which are not analysed here as they are relatively insignificant. There is increasing literature on the Court. Of note is Kevin Boyle and Adel Omar Sherif (a prominent justice on the SCC, and its vice-president in the mid-2000s), *Human rights and democracy: the role of the Supreme Constitutional Court of Egypt* (London, 1996). The reader can find a good English digest of the SCC cases at 229–80. At one point in the 1990s, the SCC convened an annual conference, see Eugene Cotran and Adel Omar Sherif, eds., *The role of the judiciary in the protection of human rights* (London, 1997).

[44] Decisions of 15 April 1989.   [45] OJ, 1 August 1991, 1701.
[46] Carry universal evidence, *hujjiyya mutlaqa*.   [47] ibid. 1703.   [48] ibid. 1702.

invalidating the Governor's decree was more detailed, and the subsequent decision merely restated the conclusions reached a few months earlier, adding the now familiar *erga omnes* paragraph just quoted. The original decision had ruled a governmental decree unconstitutional on two grounds: the protection of private property, and the exclusive powers of the Presidency and Parliament to pass criminal legislation.

On the first principle—protection of private property—the Court cited Article 36 of the Constitution, explaining that

> the Article had categorically forbidden general expropriation,[49] and had specified the mechanisms for specific expropriation,[50] requesting that it take place by judicial decision and not by administrative decree, thus protecting private property from expropriation outside a judicial decision which grants the possessor of the right [due] process and its guarantees.

As will appear to be a hallmark of the SCC style, it went on to explain the philosophy under which it operates:

> [Only] through this process are doubts over the abuse and violation of this right set aside, and is reaffirmed the principle of separation between judicial power and executive or legislative powers; for judicial power is the original power established by the Constitution over matters of justice and has been vested with [the SCC] exercising it to the exclusion of the other [two powers] to the extent of its competence, including for decrees of expropriation.[51]

As for the violation of the other principle—exclusive powers of the Presidency and Parliament to pass criminal legislation—the Court established that the Governor's decree, which included both a criminal penalty in the form of a fine and the excision of 50 per cent of the proceeds of the unauthorized sale of the fish for the officers in charge of applying the decree, violated Articles 36 and 66 of the Constitution. These articles 'erase all the consequences of the act [taken in violation], including the gratification of the [fish] seizure and its disbursement under the attacked decree's stipulations to the officers in charge of its application'. Furthermore, the actions of the Governor were taken in violation of the general rule of legislative delegation established by the Constitution in a series of articles. Here, the task of the Court was more difficult, since the Constitution had clearly granted some 'legislative' powers to the executive branch. Why, if the President and the Ministers were able to legislate, including in criminal matters, would an executive-appointed governor in the provinces not be entitled to do the same?

The answer of the SCC was based on a confluence of articles which, together, did not warrant in the opinion of the Court a decree such as the one decided by the Governor. This decree could not, the Court explained, be considered part of the executive orders allowed under Article 144, nor could it stand as a delegated order under Article 108. The latter article vests the executive power with a right to

---

[49] General, public, *'amma.*   [50] Specific, *khassa.*
[51] Decision of 6 April 1991, OJ, 27 April 1991, 815; see also the two other decisions taken on the same day to invalidate other similar parts of the same decree, reported ibid., at 821 and 831.

legislate under special circumstances, following a limited and specific delegation by Parliament, and the former article allows 'the President to issue the necessary orders to apply laws'.

In the case at hand, the SCC did not find the decree taken by the Governor, which included a penalty contrary to the text of Article 66 ('There will be no crime or penalty without law'), to come under the umbrella of legislative delegation allowed by the Constitution. Delegation contradicts in this particular instance the separation of powers scheme as understood by the Egyptian Constitution. The President, under Article 112, and Parliament, under Article 86, are allowed to issue laws. The Governor of Suez is not. If derivative delegation may be possible, according to the Court, the law in which such delegation was couched specified that only the Minister of Equipment was entitled to impose such penalties.

Although some of the fine print indicates the limitations that the Court respects, primarily with regard to the higher echelons of executive power, it remains true that the decision boldly brings together various constitutional rules, including separation of powers, independence of the judiciary, and the SCC's own role as the ultimate arbiter that protects private property and ensures that no crime or penalty is established without a law to define it and due process to apply it.

The assurance in the style of the first judgment of the Murr Court did not result solely from the precedent decided a few months earlier under the presidency of Mamduh Hasan. By the beginning of the tenure of its fourth president, it was clear that the SCC had accumulated a string of consistent judgments which had turned it into a power not to be disregarded. The decisions were not all unfavourable to the executive. Other judgments of the Mamduh Hasan era show many examples of the failure of bids for unconstitutionality and established the neutrality and the balance of the SCC.

One instance is that of fiscal decrees by the Ministry of Finance, which established customs on the basis of the 'supportive price' of foreign currency. The supportive price is different from the 'official price' in Egypt owing to the special assessment by the government of some imports, which increases the rate of tax levied on the merchandise. The plaintiff had argued that the decrees violated the constitutional basis needed, as a matter of budgetary procedure, in all fiscal matters, but the Court ruled that none of the decrees establishing different pricing for tax purposes was unconstitutional. Unlike the previous case, there was ample evidence of laws which had given the Ministry of Finance the power to determine the value of foreign currencies in such international transactions, and nothing in the Constitution warranted that such fiscal distinctions be deemed unconstitutional. The SCC upheld the contested decrees.

A case on zoning ordinances, decided on 4 May 1991, brought the Court onto the more controversial terrain of Islamic law and property rights under the Constitution.[52] The case arose in conjunction with governmental determination

---

[52] OJ, 16 May 1991.

of what constitutes agricultural land and its consequent fining of the plaintiff, who contravened the interdiction of building on such land without a permit.

There, a decision of the criminal court to jail and fine the plaintiff was brought before the SCC for alleged unconstitutionality of the law on which the decision rested. Agricultural legislation passed in 1966 and amended in 1983 prohibited the building without permit on 'land within a village "urban" domain' and on 'land adjoining such villages'. The plaintiff argued that the prohibition contradicted the sanctity of private property established by Article 34 of the Constitution, as well as its sanctity under Islamic law. One recalls that Article 2 of the Egyptian Constitution was amended in 1980 to read that 'the *shari'a* is *the* principal source of legislation', as opposed to the previous formulation, which considered the *shari'a* to be '*a* principal source of law' (emphasis added).

The SCC rejected both challenges:

Private property, which is protected by Art.34 of the Constitution, is not an absolute right. The Constitution established it because of a social function which the law organizes, and Art.32 of the Constitution has delimited the elements of this function by demanding that private property operate ... with a view to the benefits accruing to the national economy ... The social function of property requires taking into consideration public welfare.[53]

Similarly, zoning ordinances did not contradict the principle of the *shari'a*, the Court held, 'because [under the *shari'a*] the ruler may intervene to regulate property'.[54]

With regard to property and its protection in the Constitution, the SCC was avoiding, in the words of 'Awad al-Murr after American fashion, a 'strict scrutiny' test. This was also valid for other areas which the Court addressed, but it may be that one—seemingly isolated—decision in 1989 in landlord-tenant relations points to a more stringent test. In that case, the Court held unconstitutional a law which distinguished, for taxation purposes, between two types of buildings on the basis that the first type was 'rented for living purposes' and the second type 'rented for reason other than living purposes'.[55]

We should note in passing the divergent views on Islamic law in relation to property as held by the higher constitutional authorities in Iran and in Egypt—the Council of Guardians supporting absolute private property, while the SCC considers property as the object of a relative right.[56] It is also significant that Islamic law was being brought into the constitutional field by both systems at the beginning of the 1980s, and that the *shari'a*, in contrast to more 'secular' legislation, would also be an important constitutional consideration in the two countries. Unlike the Iranian Council of Guardians, the Egyptian Court was careful not to ascribe absolute sanctity to private property, trying instead to prevent the cruder types

---

[53] OJ, 16 May 1991, 968, 971. Public welfare, *maslaha 'amma*.
[54] Ruler, *wali al-amr*, ibid., at 972.   [55] Decision of 29 April 1989, in OJ, 18 May 1989.
[56] Mallat, *Renewal of Islamic law*, 146–57. Schirazi, *The Constitution of Iran*, above n. 18, 227–31.

of governmental expropriation without compensation.[57] This allowed the court to remain on a more even keel with both government and society at large. But the question of the *shari'a* in other areas was more delicate to handle than in the case of state and private ownership, where articulate advocates on both sides could be found supporting views in defence of the state's right to intervene, or, conversely, in defence of the citizen's absolute entitlement to enjoy the benefits of ownership.

A famous instance of the SCC's approach to Islamic law is the *riba* case of 1985.[58] In a key decision which introduced its guarded policy on the place of the *shari'a* in the constitutional system, the SCC made a clear distinction between laws passed before Article 2 of the Constitution was amended (the *shari'a* as *the* principal legal reference in Egypt) and new laws introduced after the Amendment of 1980. Following this distinction, the bulk of Egyptian legislation passed constitutional muster under the *shari'a*'s constitutional test. This included the whole of the Egyptian Civil Code, which goes back to 1949, and which is the centre-piece of Egypt's daily transactions.[59] The SCC held on scrupulously to this procedural distinction as long as it could, but more delicate issues regarding conformity with the *shari'a* arose, as time passed, in relation to legislation passed after 1980. Two important cases fall in that category.

Both cases arose from Law 100 of 1985, which had introduced some significant reforms in family law. Law 100 included dispositions increasing the mother's right to custody of her children after divorce; provisions protecting the wife from a second marriage by requesting at least her being informed by her husband that he would take another wife; as well as some radical dispositions for the compensation of a divorced wife and her right to the marital home for as long as she remained in charge of the children.[60]

These dispositions had been subject to attack since the early airing of the reform. The statute was introduced by executive fiat in 1979—it was known as the Jihan law through its association with President Sadat's wife who had sponsored it. The SCC was called upon a first time, and declared it unconstitutional because the normal legislative process had been bypassed in favour of an executive decree which was unnecessary, since the passing of the law did not carry any danger or emergency requiring it to be handled by the executive branch. The law was frozen, then reintroduced with little change before Parliament, which passed it in 1985. Since the legislative procedure had now been respected, the SCC had to deal with

[57] Various decisions of the court, e.g. Decision of 28 July 1990, in OJ, 16 August 1990 (procedure: unconstitutionality of a law that considers final the estimate by an administrative committee of the value of health institutions).

[58] Decided 4 May 1985, translated in full in English, 'Supreme Constitutional Court (Egypt)—Shari'a and Riba', *Arab Law Quarterly*, 1, 1985, 100–7.

[59] See also two decisions of 3 February 1990, OJ, 22 February 1990, rejecting the challenge to the constitutionality of Arts. 226, 227, and 228 of the Civil Code, which cover all cases of 'interest' on the basis of the *dicta* of the 1985 decision. On the Civil Code, see Chapter 8.

[60] See Chapter 10 for the family law context.

the substantive dimension of the law, which arose on the occasion of marital disputes tried first before the lower courts.

Both decisions were occasions for the court to carefully weigh Islamic law and its role in the Egyptian system. In both cases, Law 100 was upheld by the SCC. But the Court took the occasion of highly controversial reforms favouring women to explain its position *vis-à-vis* the *shari'a* and its constitutional place in the Egyptian legal system.

In the first, long, judgment,[61] a number of articles in Law 100, 1985 had been brought before the Court on the occasion of a dispute before the family court of the Cairo neighbourhood of Gizeh. The SCC refused, on the basis of standing, to examine them all. It declared, following a now established precedent, that it would not adjudicate the constitutionality of laws in theory. A dispute and a personal interest for the parties in litigation, the Court held, must first be clearly established.

The Court also went on at length about the legislative process in what looked like a complete side-track of the issue by discussing the importance of *Majlis al-shura*, which in Egypt is a consultative body of advisors appointed by the executive, and its relation to Parliament.[62]

Whilst this was a side-track, it seems to have been introduced for two reasons. One possible motive might have been that the SCC was looking for a less activist role on the always controversial Islamic conformity of laws passed by the Egyptian legislator. The SCC reserved the right to act as a protector of the role of Parliament and of *Majlis al-shura* as delineated by the Constitution, expressing in a long passage a view that both bodies are able, competent, and complementary institutions which have at heart the welfare of the country, including its attachment to Islam and what Islam requires. In this way, the SCC was preparing the ground for a more passive role as ultimate interpreter of the *shari'a*, which, as new legislation gets passed and the cut-off date of 1980 recedes further in time, it would want to trust the normal legislative process to address.

A more immediate reason for the long *obiter* of the SCC in the decision appears in its comments on the 'laws that complement the constitution' and the consequences of such laws for compatibility with the *shari'a* as the principal source of legislation in Egypt.[63] One of the plaintiff's arguments was the necessity for Law 100 to 'complement the constitution', that is to conform specifically to Article 2. In response, the SCC made a distinction between definitive Islamic rules, which are not subject to change, and those secondary regulations which the legislator must pass on matters of detail. Those rules which the *shari'a* regulates 'in a decisive manner' are definitive and general, and the SCC is called upon to protect them against any deformation by the legislator. In contrast, the legislator must step in to regulate details of implementation so long as the 'decisive' principle is respected.

---

[61] SCC 5:2, 15 May 1993, 260–90.
[62] SCC 5:2, 275–7. The Egyptian *Majlis al-shura* is a consultative political body. The *Majlis al-dawla* is the high administrative court.   [63] ibid. 278–9.

This was the case with 'the best interests of the child', which, the Court said, is the general and decisive rule that the *shari'a* establishes with regard to guardianship. Law 100 did not violate any Islamic principle related to this decisive, general category, 'since it was inspired by the general objects of the *shari'a*, and does not contradict its main pillars ... The violation by this law of Art.2 of the Constitution does not hold true.'[64]

Thus there were three qualifications by the SCC with regard to the Islamic scrutiny of legislation: (a) the importance of a personal interest and the limitation of the scrutiny to the portion of the law violating that interest; (b) the principled respect for the choice of the bodies involved in the legislative process and the SCC's presumption that all deal with Islamic law in a way that advances the welfare of the nation in accordance with present-day needs; and (c) the distinction between laws complementing the Constitution and laws that are not required to complement the Constitution, with possibly a lesser scrutiny for the latter.

The decision was not only procedural, and the SCC did address, despite all these narrowing qualifications, the substantive dimension of Islamic law in the case at hand. This regarded principally the new law's increase of the automatic mother's right to custody to the age of 10 for the boy and 12 for the girl, coupled with her retaining the marital home so long as custody continues.[65]

Here the Court dealt with the issue head on, by using the argument of the Explanatory Memorandum of Law 100, to the effect that these reforms has been advocated by the Maliki school, and that the legislator could choose, as it had in the past, the opinion of any of the four official Sunni schools: 'The Malikis have said in an emphatic way that custody of the minor boy can go on, without a date limit, until he comes of age; and that the minor girl remains in [the mother's] custody and can extend until her marriage is consummated'.[66] There was therefore no reason to attack that provision under Article 2 of the Constitution on the *shari'a* as the main source of Egyptian law. The law was in perfect conformity with the Maliki school.

The Court also mentioned in the course of the discussion other scholars, like Shafi'i, making a more general argument about '*ijtihad* which the ruler can exercise in uncertain areas by looking into the real interest which derives from legal argumentation'.[67] It is in this context of derivative legal areas that the legislator is entitled, nay required according to the SCC, to exercise its power for the benefit of the country. In the particular case of custody, the legislator was rightly looking after the interest of the child, which is the legal objective of the reform, including the issue at hand, where the son was left by decision of the judge with his mother beyond the legal age of 10.[68] However, and this is in the judgment the only area where the SCC appears to put some reins on the reform, the provision in the law granting the family flat (whether owned or rented) to the children of the wife repudiated without cause, limits the divorced wife's right to stay in the flat until

---

[64] ibid. 285. [65] Art. 20 and Art. 18 bis of Law 100, 1985. [66] SCC 5:2, 285.
[67] ibid. [68] ibid. 286.

the boy reaches the age of 10, and the girl the age of 12. If the judge chooses to extend custody beyond this, the automatic occupation of the flat does not follow.[69]

The second case under consideration came a year later on the occasion of another challenge to Law 100 of 1985.[70] Procedurally, the case was treated in the same way by the SCC, which reduced the request to the strict interest of the plaintiff. This was a father who had challenged the fourth paragraph of Article 18 bis of the statute. Under Article 18 bis, the principle was that the father had to pay for the maintenance of children, but paragraph 4 specified that maintenance was a debt owed from the time he had stopped paying it. The challenge was based on a rule ascribed to the Hanafi school, namely that the debt for maintenance would be owed from the time of judgment. The court rejected the argument on several grounds: Hanafi writings should not be treated as an exclusive source of Egyptian Islamic law, since legal details were for the legislator to decide. In addition, a delay in payment is common and the innocent mother would often have to wait for quite some time before a court passed judgment in her favour. The law would be defeated if payment ran from the day of judgment; and, generally, the rationale of the provision was, again, 'in the best interest of the child'.

The SCC has therefore had several occasions to examine the compatibility of legislation with the *shari'a*, despite the fact that most of the challenges were undermined by the procedural device established by the Court since 1985, according to which it would not look into legislation passed before the 1980 Amendment to Article 2.[71] As time passed and new legislation was introduced, the SCC could no longer leave Article 2 on one side. The considered and learned way Islamic law was being reviewed should be noted. The quality of the arguments presented by the Murr Court is probably the most sophisticated instance of a serious adaptation of Islamic law in the modern Middle East.

This revival of the classical tradition might in the long run constitute the most important contribution of the Egyptian SCC. As in the rest of the world, however, the most famous decisions of the SCC are at heart political. In Egypt, they were directly related to the electoral process, and came in 1989 and 1990 to try to cleanse with constitutional review a political process which was vitiated by widespread constraints and corruption. The results of the SCC efforts have been chequered.

Corruption was not addressed by the SCC. It lies within the power of the normal judiciary (the civil and administrative courts), which has seen several actions begun against corrupt politicians in recent years. The most spectacular instance of corruption was the expulsion of deputies from the National Assembly in November–December 1991 on charges of drug trafficking. As in previous years,

[69] ibid.   [70] SCC 6: 231–59, 26 March 1994.
[71] For the period 1987–91, see the long index of decisions rejecting the demand for unconstitutionality on this basis in SCC, 4, 644–7. This includes land reform, criminal procedure, wine drinking, wills, and various articles of the civil and criminal codes.

when the Speaker had coined a famous sentence in defence of parliamentary protection against the intervention of the courts on the occasion of the suspension by the administrative tribunal (*Majlis al-dawla*) of the election of seventy-eight deputies,[72] the courts—this time in their civil sections—looked into the charges which had been made in the press against half a dozen deputies who were accused of drug dealing. Unlike the 1988 precedent, when Parliament had its way against the courts, the result was the resignation—or expulsion—of some of the deputies under pressure. The constitutional text itself prevented in both cases a more radical outcome, as the Constitution specifies that the courts may indeed hear the charges, but that it was ultimately up to Parliament to decide all matters arising from the election and any irregularities by its members.[73]

The cases brought before the SCC were more central to the electoral process, because the Constitution had entrusted the Court with protecting the right to vote and to be elected, and it was not possible for Parliament to question this authority as in the case of charges brought against its members.

Decision 37 of the ninth year, issued on 19 May 1990, was the most far-reaching of three such decisions rendered by the SCC. On that occasion, the Court clearly saw the occasion as a landmark opportunity to dwell on the constitutional philosophy underlying its work.

The Constitution is the highest fundamental law which establishes principles and rules on which the system of government is based; the Constitution defines public authorities, delineates their duties, puts limits and constraints over their activities, and organizes the basic guarantees to protect them;

The Constitution consequently enjoys a special quality which bestows upon it superiority and sovereignty as the guarantor and anchor of freedoms, the pillar of constitutional life and the basis of the system; its rules must therefore operate at the top of the legal construct of the state, and take priority within the rules of public law, because these [constitutional] rules are the highest commanding principles which the state must respect in its legislation and its judgments as well as in executive practice, without separating in this regard between the three public powers—the executive, the legislature and the judiciary.

The text is deliberately didactic, with a clear *Marbury v. Madison* tone.[74] The next passage was more subdued, expressing the SCC's respect for the other two branches of government.

All three [branches] are founding powers established by the Constitution, and derive its existence and being from the Constitution, which is the reference[75] in defining their duties. All three powers are therefore equal before the Constitution, each with the same standing as the other, and exercising its constitutional duty in collaboration within the limits prescribed, respectful of the rules of the Constitution which has, exclusively, the last word and to the rules of which all public authority bows.

---

72 Rif'at al-Mahjub: '*al-majlis sayyid qararih*', Parliament is master of its decisions, i.e. fully sovereign.
73 Art. 93 of the Egyptian Constitution.   74 *Marbury v. Madison*, 5 US 137 (1803).
75 *marja*', reference, see Chapter 4 nn. 29, 48–50, 57, and accompanying texts.

Back to *Marbury v. Madison* language:

In that, the state follows an axiom of democratic rule, which is respect for the rule of law, a principle which the Constitution was careful to reaffirm in Art.64, 'the rule of law is the basis of government in the state', and in Art.65, which stipulates that 'the state must bow to the law . . .'; there is no doubt that law means here the law in its most general and object-ive acceptation, which includes any abstract public principle regardless of its origin, pri-marily and most centrally the Constitution itself as the highest and most distinguished law. Since the respect by the state in all its powers for the rule of law is an established principle and a binding rule for any healthy democratic system, it is the duty for all public authority, whatever its work and regardless of its competence and the nature of the duties it is entrusted with, to abide by the rules and principles of the Constitution; if [public author-ity] contradicts these rules or trespasses on them, its work is vitiated by a constitutional infringement. This violation is subject—when the infringement derives from a law or a bill—to judicial review which is entrusted by the Constitution to the SCC as the highest judicial body which is exclusively vested with judging the constitutionality of laws and bills with a view to conserve, protect, and defend the Constitution from these measures operat-ing outside it.[76]

This long passage, with its touch of epic repetition, expresses well the sense of historic mission which the SCC felt vested with. The Court was facing a serious challenge. The challenged law was an electoral law distinguishing between 'inde-pendent candidates' to Parliament, and those who were members of recognized political parties—with the lion's share of seats for the latter. In that opinion, which drew clear inspiration from the US Supreme Court *Gomillion v. Lightfoot* deci-sion,[77] the Court considered this distinction to so weaken candidates as to stand in clear violation of both the electors' constitutional right to vote and the citizens' constitutional right to be elected.

The consequence was that the Parliament which resulted from the 1987 con-sultation was deemed unconstitutional. Conscious of the danger of the ruling for the stability of the state as a whole, the Court tried to put some fetters on the con-sequences of its judgment: 'The abovementioned Parliament is considered void since its election, but this annulment does not result, as claimed by the [govern-ment], in the collapse of the constitutional order'. The legislation and activities of the annulled Parliament stood until they were formally repealed by the subse-quent Parliament.[78] But Parliament was considered illegal, and a new national consultation had to take place that conformed with the Court's ruling.

Despite this stunning record, and with all the boldness of the Egyptian SCC deci-sions in elections and the annulment of various executive decisions, the judicial system in Egypt remained subject to many humiliations. Recurrent reports on human rights mention widespread torture in Egyptian prisons, compared to

---

[76] special quality, *tabi'a khassa*; superiority and sovereignty, *siyada wa sumuww*. Decision of 19 May 1990, quoted here from the original typed text provided by Chief Justice al-Murr, 11–13. The decision can be found in OJ 3 June 1990, and in vol. 4 of the court decisions, SCC 4: 256–93.
[77] 364 US 339 (1960).   [78] Decision of 19 May 1990, above n. 76 at 31.

which the mistreatment of the fishermen of Port Said does not stand serious comparison. The judiciary itself is upset by the flouting of basic rights and the inability to address them through the normal court procedure. In March 1989, a group of senior judges presented the Court of Cassation (which is the court of last resort for criminal cases) with a report 'on the attack of security authorities on the competence of the Egyptian judiciary by arresting people whom the courts had set free, imprisoning them again, collective punishments in neighbourhoods and villages, the forcing of confessions upon innocents ...'[79] Two decades later, hardly a word needs to be altered to describe the state of the judiciary, slowly drawn into open conflict on the streets with the President of the Republic.

The 1989 report went on to identify the struggle between the judiciary and executive power, essentially in the security police: 'Police exactions are now flouting the message of the judiciary and of the judges in their protection of the rights and properties of citizens. They undermine public trust and create a general feeling that the executive branch usurps the competence of judicial power and uses it for repression and the pursuit of political goals.' The message is unambiguous. In the indictment of the Egyptian executive appears the belief of senior judges in the insufficiency of judicial independence, and, more significantly, in the strait-jacket imposed by the police on judicial decisions.

No doubt the SCC offers a beacon of law in an otherwise worrying set-up, where martial law established three decades ago continues to be used for massive violations of basic human rights by the state security apparatus. At the same time, violations of human rights have become a staple of extremist groups in Egypt, which target the police systematically, and have widened their reach to innocent and helpless citizens. The case of the celebrated octogenarian writer Nagib Mahfuz, who was knifed in the street and miraculously survived, and that of the outspoken intellectual Faraj Fodah, who was assassinated for his defence of basic rights against Islamic extremists, are examples of a spiral of violence which has done much to undermine the patient construction of the rule of constitutional law in Egypt. Whilst the SCC has acquired over time an exceptional reputation inside and outside the most populated Arab country, the odds against the rule of law remain heavy, for which an increasingly dictatorial rule has much to answer. But the track record of the court is impressive, and its well-designed case reporter will remain for a long time a major reference for constitutional review in the Middle East, and in the wider world of comparative constitutional law.

The Future of Constitutional Review

At the end of this journey into constitutional review, the record is disheartening. Naturally, situations vary depending on each jurisdiction, but there is not one clearly decisive successful story of the rule of constitutional law in any one country.

[79] Al-Ahram, *Al-taqrir al-istratiji 1989* (Strategic report 1989) (Cairo, 1990) 401.

The impossibility of meaningful constitutional review in the context of civil war as in the case of Algeria is evident, and it is hard to see how constitutional judges can jump-start a process where the political odds are stacked against the judiciary. In the rest of North Africa, there is either little place for judicial review, as in Libya or Tunisia, or little impact by impressive-sounding yet empty institutions like the Moroccan Conseil Constitutionnel.

In Iran and Lebanon, the crises of 1989 and 1997, respectively, resulted in much weakened constitutional courts. In the Gulf countries, judges of supreme courts have adopted a low profile resulting in marginal institutions of which few citizens are aware. In the case of Yemen, the decisions discussed above constitute an alluring sample of the Yemeni Supreme Court's work, but the Court never reached the decisive critical mass required to impact society at large. It is keen on its independence, it has been given a crowning constitutional role which it has put to good effect, and it is aware of its political limitations so as not to allow itself to be drawn into a constitutional dispute between all too powerful actors. But the operation of the judiciary in the Yemen did not prevent the descent into civil war in 1994. There has been little worth reporting since.

On this failure across the region several answers come to mind. One is evident. However remarkable a judicial system may be, including when it assumes a high-brow constitutional role, there are in the history of nations moments at which the political tide of disarray is simply too strong for courts to withhold or reverse, namely, the American Civil War or the collapse of the Weimar Republic.

It has been argued that the American Supreme Court did not rise to its historic task as the repository of human equality when it left the abolition of slavery to be decided by the force of arms. It could also be argued that the greatest shortcoming in the Weimar Republic may have been the smothering of the judiciary and its silence and ineffectiveness before the rising spate of Nazi political murders, from the timid condemnation of Hitler in the early Munich Putsch through to the burning of the Reichstag and Crystal Night.

Such events will sound familiar to the observer of recent Middle Eastern constitutional history. There is an immediate parallel in the Yemen: the spate of unpunished assassinations in the two years preceding the civil war of 1994, especially those directed at cadres of the opposition Yemeni Socialist Party, were a focal point of the collapse of trust in the new united republic. The ineffectiveness of the judiciary in this respect is obvious. The same is true for the rest of the Middle East, and assassinations have since become transnational. They have been carried out by states like Israel, Syria, Iraq under Saddam Hussein, or groups like al-Qa'eda and its sister organizations.

From a technical point of view, two fundamental questions recur at the domestic level, as legislation and constitution-framers are required to make a choice.

The first question concerns the models available: French constitutional council or US supreme court? The second issue is about the meaning of the constitution as fundamental law, including the place of the *shari'a* in the system.

French constitutional council or US supreme court? Constitutional adjudication in the absence of litigation, and the restriction of constitutional standing to specific political officials (typically a number of deputies) set apart the Lebanese, Iranian, Algerian, and French models from their American, UAE, Yemeni, and Egyptian counterparts. Which is better?

One possible response concerns the effectiveness of adjudication. The main difference between the two constitutional institutions is the plaintiff's standing: in US-style adjudication, an individual claimant can bring his or her constitutional right to the court by way of action or exception. In the French system, the council examines the constitutionality of laws, usually upon the demand of a limited number of authorities in the state, generally the President of the Republic, the Prime Minister, the Speaker of the House, or a number of deputies or senators. Constitutional action is thus withheld from the citizen. Standing is unimportant for these courts and the review operates automatically, regardless of the practical application of a statute. In that lies probably the least satisfactory feature of the French model, which deprives citizens of the right to a constitutional hearing. On another significant register, this type of constitutional review ignores the value of the passage of time as revelatory of the effective impact of legislation, and as an important factor in defusing acute political crises.

The best illustrations of the constraints brought about by the time factor are found in the Iranian and Lebanese experiments. In Iran, Article 94 of the Constitution requires an automatic constitutional review of all enacted legislation. The exercise of this prerogative has polarized the system in such a way that the constitutional role of the Council of Guardians was seriously undermined. A higher institution, with a majority of members from outside the Council, was allowed to overrule the Council. This was done through a semi-constitutional coup in 1988, later incorporated in major changes to the Constitution through the establishment of a new body, *Majma'-e tashkhis-e maslahat-e Nezam*. The least that could be said is that its political composition dominates any judicial pretensions it may have.

In Lebanon, the entrusting of challenges to electoral law to the Constitutional Council, and the difficulty the Council has had in rising to this challenge, have been major factors in the crisis of spring 1997. Nor is it possible to surmise how many years are needed for the Council to survive the crisis, if at all.

The stability of the American-style courts in the Middle East suggests that this separation of powers has a better chance of success. The example of Egypt supports, to some extent, this conclusion. The ten large tomes of SCC decisions stand as eloquent testimony to its achievements. This experience of a constitutional court, as opposed to constitutional councils, allows the voice of a citizen to be heard more readily. This is a major novelty in the Middle East, even if the citizen's grievance is not decisively remedied yet. Because of the turbulent political atmosphere in the region, the gap in the judicial protection of basic rights remains wide across the region. Within the constraints of that background, the US model has a relative advantage, as it takes into account the time factor in the constitutional process, and allows the rule of law a breathing space—away from pure politics—which a constitutional council cannot generally afford.

Still, there have been shortcomings in the Egyptian experience which may be addressed in the overall Middle Eastern context in two ways.

First, the SCC had occasion to intervene in major political exercises, including the annulment of the legislative elections of 1987 on the basis of their unconstitutionality. Considering the wobbly electoral system in Egypt, and the control by the leading presidential party of a good half of the Assembly through the requirement, dating back to the Naser era, of having a disproportionate number of 'workers and peasants' in Parliament, let alone new devices honed by the deepening dictatorship, the investment of judicial capital to cancel the elections was stunning when effected in May 1990. As time passed, it was clearly not decisive for the conduct of fair elections in the country.

Secondly, as the late President of the Supreme Constitutional Court once explained to me, there are violations of the Constitution which do not take place by law or by decree. These constitute the run-of-the-mill authoritarian bent which allows the President of the Republic to bypass the SCC. Since these violations develop without a textual ground, there is no tangible legislative tool on which action could be taken before the SCC. More egregious violations emerge when cases are referred to parallel courts like the State Security Court. These parallel courts offer the government a major tool for repression, and illustrate the worst forms of rule by law in the Middle East.

6

Judicial Review: Criminal and Administrative Law

Humans fight for their rights with whatever legal means are available to them. This is a universal law. From time immemorial, these fights have been recorded in a wide array of sources, ranging from specialists' textbooks to anecdotes and stories in the literature at large. The Nippur homicide trial may have been the first instance of a criminal case report in history.[1] Considerable scholarship on the trial, and on similar 'law reports' that survived for four millennia as clay tablets, suggests their conscious writing down by the scribe-reporters of the time as 'model court cases'.[2]

In the contemporary Middle East, the natural recourse of the individual to the courts has been increasingly based on codified statutes. In civil, commercial, and family matters, the typical case gets adjudicated between two private parties over what each considers his right, with the court arbitrating: lest one is confused by late twentieth-century terminology, 'human rights' get decided upon in each and every such case. Rights are by nature human, and even the emerging category of animal rights is centered on the increased sense of justice some humans have developed towards animals, much in the way that the protection of the environment is human rather than environmental *stricto sensu*. 'Human rights' is a redundant concept, since all rights are by definition human. Human beings decide what

---

[1] Decision reproduced in Nicholas Postgate, *Early Mesopotamia* (London, 1992) 278, cited above Chapter 2 n. 219 (wife of a murdered person considered guilty of complicity in homicide for covering up her husband's murder, and sentenced to death). The decision was originally published and discussed by Thorkild Jakobsen, 'An ancient Mesopotamian trial for homicide', in *Studia Biblica et Orientalia III: Oriens Antiquus* (Rome, 1959) 130–50.

[2] William Hallo, 'A model court case concerning inheritance', in Tzvi Abusch, *Riches hidden in secret places, ancient Near Eastern studies in memory of Thorkild Jacobsen* (Winona Lake, Ind. 2002) 141–54, at 142–3; see also Martha Roth, 'The slave and the scoundrel CBS 10467, a Sumerian morality tale ?', *Journal of the American Oriental Society*, 103, 1983, 279–82, at 282, discussing five instances of such court records as legal genre, including the Nippur homicide trial: 'The single unifying factor in these records is the puhrum of Nippur [Roth at 279 translates *puhrum* as Assembly, but it sounds like an appeals court, 'which King Ur-Ninurta referred the trial to.']. The cases recorded were doubtless actual cases, which were adapted and incorporated into the law curriculum of the Nippur eduba [scribal school]. It is not surprising to find that cases adjudicated by the local assembly might be used in the schools for didactic purposes, in order to teach the student scribes the forms of a court record.'

rights are and how they apply, whether they ultimately hail from divine statutes, correspond to environmental needs, or punish cruelty towards animals. This is best understood in the American legal tradition, where individual rights have been anchored in 200 years of judicial review ultimately decided by the Supreme Court. Henry Steiner, who long taught the subject of international human rights at Harvard Law School, once observed that an academic chair in US law schools which is expressly dedicated to 'human rights' is hard to find. For a lawyer, 'human rights' is a tautology.

True, some rights tend to be considered more 'fundamental' or 'basic' than others, and they get entrenched in bills of rights that accompany constitutions and 'basic laws'. Any jurist familiar with the British legal system knows that such rights may equally be protected without a written constitution. Regardless of the debate over the value of engraved charters, as opposed to the cumulative tradition of cases in the 'common law' tradition, there is no denying that rule of law is well served in Britain and similarly Westminster-style governed countries, even in the absence of constitutions. The confusion is reflected in the terminology. Following the British nineteenth-century jurist A. V. Dicey, constitutional law has become coextensive with 'rule of law', itself equivalent in French to the expression *Etat de droit* and in German to *Rechtsstaat*. There is an extensive literature on *Etat de droit* and *Rechtsstaat*, and on its rough 'rule of law' equivalent. In a Middle Eastern context, the Lebanese leader Kamal Jumblatt, who was assassinated in March 1977, offered a prescient treatment of the subject in a lecture on 18 November 1946. Inaugurating his membership of Parliament, he cited Dicey to underline the importance of the rule of law as the central message of what an elected official should stand for.[3]

While constitutional rights are more readily associated with courts with a constitutional writ, there is always an artificial element in setting ordinary judicial review apart. Basic rights are what courts are supposed to protect in each and every case, be that case civil, commercial, criminal, or related to family law. The present book looks at judicial expressions of the rule of law in civil, commercial, and family cases,[4] after having examined constitutional cases in the recent history of the Middle East.[5] Even when there is no constitutional judge to provide a narrowly defined constitutional review, a right which one would label basic or constitutional may still be protected under the wide umbrella of judicial review.

In the previous two public law chapters, I first discussed constitutional law in the Middle East from the perspective of transnational and national institutions. I then examined constitutional review by courts and councils formally entrusted with the protection of rights enumerated in the constitution. This chapter looks at 'ordinary' judicial review, especially in administrative and criminal cases. Judicial

---

[3] Kamal Junblat (Jumblatt), '*Risalati ka-na'eb* (My calling as parliamentarian)', published e.g. in *Les Années Cénacle* (Beirut, 1997) 91–9 (quoting Dicey's rule of law, which he translates as *hukm al-qanun*, at 94).   [4] Chapters 8, 9, 10.
[5] Above, Chapter 5.

review is to be understood here in its widest possible meaning, rather than under the rubric generally associated with it in English or American law.

If the rule of law is to be considered outside the formal framework of strict constitutional review, its various manifestations are expressed in the operation of normal courts.

Courts and *qadi*s have a deep and persistent importance in the history of Islamic law, but modern judges operate at significant variance from the traditional system. Three hallmarks of *qadi* justice have all but disappeared.

First, whereas the classical Islamic court was limited to a single *qadi*, modern courts operate, in most countries, as benches comprising three or more judges.[6] Secondly, the *shari'a* knew no formal right of appeal. Unless reviewed by the ultimate dispenser of justice—the Caliph or Sultan—the decision of the *qadi* was considered final. In modern systems, appeal is the rule and not the exception. Thirdly, the refusal in the classical age to treat previous cases as precedents has slowly given way to more formal consistency among the courts, as law reporting developed, and as the hierarchy of the courts allowed a central unified bench at the system's apex. Such 'supreme' courts in the pyramid are tasked with securing consistency and order in judicial decision-making.

At a general level, judicial upholding of the rule of law has been marred by two phenomena: the first, which is endemic in the Arab world, is the lack of systematic and reliable reporting. Alongside the rejection in theory of precedent in both the Islamic and in the civil law system,[7] the lack of reporting has prevented lawyers from drawing persuasive arguments from decided cases. Except for hearsay and personal experience, there is no public yardstick by which one can assess the consistency of the courts.[8]

In so far as it depends on the way it is fleshed out by the judiciary, the rule of law is coterminous with the sound operation of courts. So much is acknowledged universally. In the Middle East, the judiciary has been undermined in its effectiveness and independence by two additional factors.

The first factor is financial, as a snapshot from the mid-1990s will show. The salaries of the judges sitting in the highest court in Egypt, the Supreme Constitutional court (SCC), were defined by law when the court was established in 1979.

---

[6] Details on judicial organization in Chapter 2. The Islamic single-*qadi* characterististic was not shared by the Jewish judges (*dayyan*) in the classical period, and Samuel Goitein documents the traditional three-judge bench through the Geniza period in tenth–thirteenth century Egypt, *A Mediterranean society: the Jewish communities of the Arab world as portrayed in the documents of the Cairo Geniza*, 5 vols. (Berkeley, 1967–88) vol. 2, *The Community*, 1972, 319.

[7] This difference has become less important due to the increasing convergence between the common and civil law systems. See Konrad Zweigert and Hein Kötz, *Introduction to comparative law* (Oxford, 3rd edn. 1998) 267, 270. But it is important in practice because of the expressed belief, in Middle Eastern common law jurisdictions like Pakistan and Israel, that law is judge-made. Reporting then becomes more naturally comprehensive and reliable.

[8] A number of studies, often tied to programmes of the World Bank, have tried to 'quantify' the operation of the courts in the Middle East. They have to my knowledge generally yielded few scientific results beyond common-sense notions of a slow and unreliable court system.

The salary of a member of the Court ranged between 3,700 and 4,400 Egyptian pounds.[9] This was equivalent then to an average of US$1000. Only this salary, as the President of the SCC explained to a bemused non-Egyptian questioner, was annual and not monthly. In Lebanon in 1993, the monthly salary of the members of the highest civil court, the Court of Cassation, did not exceed US$600. It has improved significantly since, but judges earn far less than successful lawyers in private business. This is true also in the West, but the difference is less marked. In Saudi Arabia, for instance, great prominence was given in the Kingdom's Official Journal to the decision of the King to increase the salary of the judges in December 1993 by some 35 per cent. The starting salary of a judge varied then between 8,490 rials and 15,070 rials monthly. For a senior judge, it varied between 18,530 and 28,320 rials (1 US$ = 3.7 rials in October 1995).[10] These are much better judgeship salaries than for their counterparts in the Levant or the Maghreb, but they remain unusually low in comparison with private legal practice at equivalent seniority in an oil country. Whilst the salaries of judges reflect the low pay of public officers generally, they are in comparative as well as in absolute terms derisory for any hope of real financial comfort or independence.[11] Even in the United Arab Emirates, salaries of judges are disappointingly low.[12]

The second factor weakening the courts results from the suspicion of the executive towards any public role for judges, let alone their independence. This has led to the systematic undermining and marginalization of courts and judges. The most sensitive top positions, especially of a prosecutorial nature, are carefully chosen by the presidents and kings. Even in countries that boast some independence for their judiciary, politicians do not hesitate to call up judges on the phone to influence their decisions. When they threaten to be effective against executive power, courts are either stacked, or their power undermined by a multiplication of various 'supreme' institutions with conflicting or conflating powers. The pride which distinguished jurists find in their job is undermined by proliferation of numbers and degradation of financial compensation. The derelict situation of administrative jurisdictions in Egypt is not surprising, when branches of the Council of State had multiplied to over 700 in the country by the late 1990s. Streamlining the rule of law becomes an impossible task, as does reporting their decisions in a professional way.

To make even harder on the rule of law as expressed in court, finding judicial decisions is strikingly cumbersome. With few exceptions, it is difficult to find good law reporters in Arab jurisdictions. They either do not exist (Saudi Arabia),

---

[9] *Majmu'at qararat al-mahkama al-dusturiyya al-'ulya* (Collection of the SCC decisions), hereinafter SCC (Cairo 1986) vol. 1, 92.

[10] *Umm al-Qura* (Saudi Official Journal), 17 December 1993.

[11] Measure of comparison in the mid-1990s: UK, House of Lords, £120,000 per annum; US Supreme Court, US$150,000; European Court of Human Rights, US$180,000.

[12] A telling anecdote: a Jordanian judge who had been seconded to the inexperienced Emirates' courts in the early 1970s soon felt he had to leave the bench for a legal consultancy job, as he could not afford to pay his rent on his judge's salary.

their access is made difficult (the United Arab Emirates, Algeria), their distribution gets hampered (Libya, Iraq, where even some governmental decrees were secret under the three-decade long dictatorship), their publication is late: published decisions of the Egyptian Court of Cassation, historically one of the most distinguished courts in the Middle East, were running six years behind schedule in the 1990s, with large law offices in Cairo establishing direct contact with clerks in the Court to get photocopies of judgments that they can then use as precedents. It is true that the reporting tradition in some countries is much better: in Pakistan and Israel, great care is given to law reporting. In Morocco, Tunisia, Iran, reporting is decent. In Lebanon and Jordan, thanks to efficient private publishers or the bar, and sometimes to the services of the courts themselves, judgments of the higher courts are more easily available. On the whole, however, the difficulty of access to decisions and the sorry state of law reporting hamper the effectiveness of the judiciary and constitute a factor of discouragement for hard-working, poorly paid judges and lawyers alike. In the absence of systematic law reporting, the judge's effort cannot even begin to be acknowledged.

And yet some courts try hard to uphold their role of independent, serious, and stabilizing power. The pattern varies considerably depending on each country's specific conditions, but the judicial experience of Egypt offers a telling example of a legal system at odds with its independence and with its social effectiveness.

For over a century, Egypt has known a well-structured appeal system, making the principle of several judges sitting on benches and the concept of appeal the norm in the Middle East.[13] For all practical purposes, absence in the *shari'a* of formal appeal and the dominance of the single *qadi* have given way to a more centralized and elaborate system across the Arab world, generally inspired by the Egyptian model.

Besides the acceptance of appeal and of benches that include several judges, in a pattern which is the norm in the whole Middle East, the Egyptian court system has also heralded two parallel jurisdictions, known under the French model as 'administrative' and 'judicial' courts.[14] At their helm sits *Majlis al-dawla* (*Conseil d'Etat*), which handles disputes involving the state, and *Mahkamat al-naqd* (Court of Cassation), which stands at the top of the civil and criminal legal hierarchy.

Like its French counterpart, the Egyptian *Majlis al-dawla* looks into disputes involving governmental institutions in their relation to each another and in their relation to private individuals. The *Majlis* was for a while in the early 1950s a major protector of the citizen against state exactions. It was then matched by a respected

[13] See the development of the system in Byron Cannon, *Politics of law and the courts in nineteenth-century Egypt* (Salt Lake City, 1988).

[14] *Ordre administratif* and *ordre judiciaire*. In Egypt, the court sitting at the head of the administrative jurisdictions is called *Majlis al-dawla*, in other countries it is called *Majlis al-shura*. Note that the *Majlis al-shura* in Egypt is a consultative political body, not a court, see above Chapter 5 n. 62 and accompanying text. The highest 'judicial' court in Egypt is *Mahkamat al-naqd*, which is called in other countries *Mahkamat al-tamyiz*. In Tunisia it is called *Mahkamat al-ta'qib*.

Court of Cassation which exercised final appeal jurisdiction in criminal, commercial, and family matters. The *Majlis al-dawla* collapsed during the Naser era (1952–70) and never recovered from the physical humiliation of its chairman 'Abd al-Razzaq al-Sanhuri on one infamous occasion in March 1954.[15] In turn, the power of the Court of Cassation was slowly and systematically eroded.

The model of separation between administrative courts and civil courts is directly inspired by the French judicial tradition and can be found in most jurisdictions of the Middle East. Sometimes the separation between civil, administrative, and constitutional jurisdictions is blurred. This is the case in Pakistan, where, following the English model, a jurisdictional separation between administrative and civil courts does not exist. This is also the case in Israel where administrative decisions are decided by the Supreme Court sitting as High Court of Justice; and in Saudi Arabia, which knew neither English nor French domination, and where the judiciary is in a state of flux. A significant number of autonomous courts were created in Saudi Arabia to adjudicate specialized labour and administration litigation. The Saudi *Diwan al-Mazalim*, which developed from the classical Islamic court bearing the same name to look into the legality of administrative or governmental acts, constitutes an administrative court of special importance in a country where business has massively involved contracts with the state during the oil boom. The extension of *Diwan al-Mazalim*'s jurisdiction to all commercial law disputes in 1989 was a natural development of the proto-administrative function of its namesake in the classical age.[16]

Mention of Saudi Arabia is useful here to gain some perspective on a phenomenon which has remained marginal across the region, even if its resurgence depends on developments which are difficult to predict. This is the rare application of classical criminal law in the contemporary Middle East. The traditional exception was Saudi Arabia and some neighbouring Gulf States, where the tug-of-war in criminal law between 'private' vengeance and state rights has endured since Hammurabi. A recent *cause célèbre* is the case of the murder of an Australian nurse in Saudi Arabia in December 1996, and the question whether the acceptance by the family of the British victim (Yvonne Gilford) of financial compensation paid to her brother was sufficient for the crime to be absolved by the state, or whether the state as party has a case independent of the right to compensation by the victims' family.[17]

The recent revival by some excessive governments of classical law practices like the cutting off of a thief's hand or the stoning for adultery is intolerable as well as untenable in the twenty-first century in any society. Such application could be found in Afghanistan under the Taliban, Sudan under the military Islamist junta,

---

[15] See Chapter 3 n. 8 and accompanying text.

[16] On the importance of *Diwan al-Mazalim*, see above Chapter 4 n. 70 and accompanying text.

[17] The full decision, as usual in Saudi Arabia, was not made available, but see 'Defence submission by Salah Ibrahim al-Hejailan in the case of *Lucille McLauchlan and Deborah Kim Parry*', *Yearbook of Islamic and Middle Eastern Law*, iii, 1996, 491–505.

Somalia's 'Islamic courts' government, Iran occasionally under the Ayatollahs, Pakistan in some of the provinces, even Egypt in a particularly shocking manner, leading to the forceful separation of a leading scholar from his wife on account of his 'abandoning Islam'.[18] In all these countries, use of classical criminal law has tended to be opportunistic, as far as the skimpy reporting, even in journalistic accounts, can be assessed. The more spectacular penalties, like the cutting off of a thief's hand and the stoning of an adulteress, are generally conceived as sending a political message with a provocative content, and there are few constructive comments one can make about it. The study of that aspect of criminal law is more alluring in a historical perspective, as well as in countries where it continues to apply as a residue of penal continuity often directly connected with tribal or communal set-ups. Considering the poor state of law reporting in the field, sociological and anthropological work may evince better results than a purely legal approach. All in all, there is too little by way of a 'Middle Eastern style' in contemporary criminal law to warrant a fuller treatment.

Of more concern for criminal and administrative law is the systematic flouting of basic rights of the citizen in the ordinary mode of judicial review. In extreme cases like Iraq under Ba'th rule, a court would as a matter of course be disqualified from the review of any violation of human rights. In others, like Israel, judicial review is well entrenched, even if its application depends on the status of the individual whose case the court is reviewing. Between these two poles falls an illustrative sample of the rule of law in the judicial practice of various Middle Eastern jurisdictions.

Rule of Law, Rule by Law: Jews and Non-Jews in Israel/Palestine

The various expressions of the rule of law in Israel can be appraised in a series of decisions by the Israeli Supreme Court, a jurisdiction which is highly attentive to its projected image as key upholder of democracy and the rule of law in the country.

The 'deportations case' of 1993 offers a convenient point of departure. On 17 December 1992, 415 residents of the West Bank were arrested and expelled to Lebanon on suspicion of their activities in the Islamic movement Hamas. Various individuals and associations filed a petition with the Supreme Court sitting as High Court of Justice. The government of Israel in various capacities—Ministry of Defence, Attorney-General—supported by a number of individual respondents, defended the deportation order. The Court held for the government and set the order nisi aside.[19] While the issue was mooted by the return of all the deportees a

---

[18] This is the infamous case of leading Egyptian philosopher Nasr Hamid Abu Zayd, see Kilian Bälz, 'Submitting faith to judicial scrutiny through the family trial: the Abu Zayd case', *Die Welt des Islams*, 37, 1997, 134–55.

[19] HCJ 5973/92, *Association for Civil Rights in Israel v. Minister of Defence*, available in English on the Israeli Supreme Court website, <http://elyon1.court.gov.il/eng>. Following English common law

year later, the case is significant as a telling illustration of judicial review in Israel. Its indecisive result also shows the uneasy role of courts in the system.

After presenting in 'the facts of the case' the argument that Hamas was a terrorist organization bent on the annihilation of the state of Israel by violent means, the Court explained the nature of the expulsion orders, which were based on British Mandate Regulation 112 of the Defence (Emergency Provisions) Regulations, 1945. In the main, these orders were made for a maximum deportation period of two years. They were considered immediately effective. The petitioners contended that expulsion was prohibited by Article 49 of the Fourth Geneva Convention on the Protection of Civilians during War, to which Israel is a party, and that denial of a hearing prior to the expulsion was contrary to Israeli law as understood by the High Court.

The Court rejected both arguments, on the oft-repeated basis that 'principles of necessity or constraints of time can deny the application of the rules of natural justice' (including *a fortiori* the Geneva Convention or Israeli administrative law),[20] but introduced a nuance, namely 'that there was no *collective* order but a set of *personal* orders, each of which exists independently'.[21] The main requirement was that 'the evidence relating to each deportee should be clear, unequivocal and persuasive'.[22] On the basis of a precedent involving the expulsion of Palestinian mayors from the West Bank in 1980—the *Kawasma* case[23]—the Court held that even though the right to a hearing before the expulsion was deemed a natural right, it '*did not* see fit to set aside the deportation order ... The correct remedy for the wrong is reinstatement, namely placing the petitioners in the situation in which they would have been had they not been deprived of the right to apply to the committee [in charge of reviewing each case]'.[24] It concluded 'that as regards the personal expulsion orders, the absence of the right of prior hearing does not invalidate them. We order that the right of hearing should now be given as detailed above',[25] that is, by allowing each petitioner to make his plea to the review board in which is vested the right to assess his individual case, *subsequent* to his deportation and while remaining under the impact of the deportation order.

The deportees refused to exercise the qualified right granted to them by the courts, and the problem was eventually solved politically by the government rescinding the order under international pressure.

In terms of judicial review, the deportees' case shows one pole of the Israeli spectrum, in which 'necessity' allows setting aside an acknowledged right of hearing for non-Israeli citizens. Even then, judicial review is not barred: it is allowed by the Court in the form of an individual hearing *post facto*.

terminology, an order nisi is a conditional court injunction compelling the relevant authority to answer a petitioner's application or comply with the injunction by a specified date. Setting it aside means rejecting the petitioner's request.

[20] *Association for Civil Rights in Israel v. Minister of Defence*, para. 12a, 39.
[21] ibid., para. 8, 21 (emphasis in original).   [22] ibid., para. 9, 21.
[23] HCJ 320/80 *Kawasma v. Minister of Defence*, 35(3) Piskei Din [PD] 113.
[24] *Association for Civil Rights in Israel v. Minister of Defence*, para. 10c, 25 (emphasis in original).
[25] ibid., para. 17, 36.

The deportations case of 1993 is a typical manifestation of the Court systematically avoiding to question the substantive power of the military governor who issues the deportation order,[26] or of the military review board where petitions usually stop, while exercising its formal right to review each and every case. Recourse to the Supreme Court is essentially procedural, and its review revolves around the right to a hearing. Considering the state of Palestinians in all walks of life, this is not particularly useful for the petitioner: the deportations' case illustrates how curtailment of a basic right can coexist with procedural rules which should protect an individual but end up being meaningless to him. The court deemed the hearing necessary *after* the deportation, resulting in a *fait accompli* particularly hard to reverse for the person already deported.

Many other such procedural safeguards were imagined by the Israeli courts to project the appearance of trials while the right sought was denied in substance. It is hard to gainsay the claim that the exercise by the Israeli Supreme Court in the Occupied Territories of its power of judicial review has been of little comfort to the Palestinians residing in them.

Absence of judicial protection is manifest in the case of Palestinian collective and individual rights over land, the central issue of contention in the Israeli-Palestinian conflict over more than a hundred years. Only 7 per cent of Israel's land in the 1948 territory is private. The remaining 93 per cent are either directly state owned, or owned by a semi-public institution called the Jewish National Fund (JNF), which remains dedicated by law to Jewish ownership and lease. Seventy per cent of the Jewish population of Israel lives on JNF-owned land.

Such ineffectiveness of the court was not pre-ordained. In the case of land expropriation in the West Bank, hope for effective judicial review against discriminatory expropriation had surfaced in the 1979 *Elon Moreh* case,[27] when the Court forced the government to destroy a settlement established on private Palestinian land after requiring stringent 'security' arguments to justify the expropriation. The settlers simply moved a few hundred yards away. *Elon Moreh* remained a solitary decision which the government emptied of significance in a spate of expropriation measures which led to the de-Palestinization (or Judaization) of over 60 per cent of the land in the West Bank. The pattern was repeated some twenty years later in another test case, *Katzir*, where non-Jewish petitioners were granted the right to lease an apartment in a property owned by the state within the 1967 boundaries.[28] The decision was not implemented, nor was the discriminatory pattern reduced on the basis of it.

For the Israeli citizen of Jewish denomination, in contrast, Israel offers standards similar to most democracies, if not sometimes more exacting, as typified by

---

[26] For instance, also in 2005, the conclusion that expropriation of land and establishment of a special route for Jewish pilgrims to a site called 'Rachel's Tomb' on the West Bank (Judea and Samaria for the Court) were reasonable for ensuring the pilgrims' 'freedom of movement'. HCJ 1890/03, *Bethlehem Municipality & 21 others v. The State of Israel—Ministry of Defense and others.*

[27] HCJ 390/79, *Dweikat et al. v. Government of Israel et al.*, 34(1) PD 1 *(Elon Moreh).*

[28] HCJ 6698/95 *Qaadan v. Minhal Mekarkai Israel*, HCJ 6 54(1) PD 258 (2000) *(Katzir).*

the doctrine of 'public fiduciary duty', which was uniquely developed in Israeli administrative law. There, the genius of some Israeli judges operates at its best, notably in the case of Supreme Court Justice—and since 1995, President— Aharon Barak, who expanded the concept of the 'public fiduciary duty' to regulate gross mismanagement of elected or appointed officials. Under the doctrine, judicial review is made to encompass not only the action in good faith of officials in specific areas (notably, in 'the Derri affair', the appointment of a Minister who had flouted the trust of the public by accepting bribes), but also the exercise of any type of statutory duty by a public official: in the 'Pinchasi affair', there was no question of bribery by the minister concerned, but suspicion of him conspiring with others to produce false accounts to the State Comptroller. This led to a stringent concept of judicial review for public servants and officials, including politicians. The doctrine can be summarized in the wake of these landmark decisions of the 1990s as one in which 'public officials owe a public fiduciary duty which imposes strict norms of conduct, and may form the basis of a Mandamus order'.[29]

This doctrine comes in the wake of a similar review by the judiciary of what it considers governmental excesses, by way of an extension of standing in court to persons only marginally affected by a governmental decision. In that case, a lay Jew was allowed to challenge the right of Jewish seminary students to avoid military service.[30] The enlargement of *locus standi*, the strict scrutiny of appointment and conduct of officials (political appointees as well as civil servants), and the introduction of a test of institutional 'justiciability' for the review of 'political' decisions,[31] all these judge-made doctrines have significantly increased judicial control over the legality of governmental activities, and expanded the domain of the civil rights of the Jewish citizens of Israel in the process.

In between the Palestinians in the Occupied Territories who are governed under 'rule by law', and the Israeli Jews who are protected by a sometimes exacting 'rule of law', stands the case of the Israeli Arab.[32]

An Israeli Arab is defined in law by his or her non-Jewishness. Historically and ethnically, Israeli Arabs are the Muslims and Christians who stayed in Palestine in the wake of the establishment of the Jewish state on 14 May 1948, and who hold Israeli citizenship. They should technically be known as Palestinian Israelis.

---

[29] These cases are discussed thoroughly in Shai Wade, Ll B thesis, SOAS, University of London, 1993 (on file with author). Quote here at 76. Mandamus is an injunction ordering a person to perform a public or statutory duty.

[30] HCJ 910/86 *Major (Res.) Yehuda Ressler v. Minister of Defence*. The Court held that the plaintiff had standing, but did not reject the government's distinction between seminary students and lay Jews.

[31] On the expansion of standing, and generally on the philosophy of the Israeli Supreme Court, Aharon Barak, 'Foreword: a judge on judging: the role of a supreme court in a democracy', *Harvard Law Review*, 116, 2002, 16–162. Complementing too rosily the picture of the judiciary in Barak's article are the works of David Kretzmer, cited above Chapter 4 n. 74; Raja Shehadeh, *From occupation to interim accords: Israel and the Palestinian Territories* (London, 1997), Emma Playfair, ed., *International law and the administration of Occupied Territories* (Oxford, 1992).

[32] For an approach to the same problem from a constitutional law-political science perspective, see above Chapter 4 nn. 72–3 nn. 90–1 and accompanying text.

Consequent to the self-defining by Israel of its Jewishness, *de jure* discrimination in key areas against the Israeli citizen of non-Jewish Arab descent has long obtained. Most apparent is the application of the right of return of Jews from any country on earth to Israel-Palestine, where the state grants them immediate nationality and offers them a comprehensive set of resources to facilitate their linguistic and social insertion in the country, whereas Palestinians who fled or were expelled in 1948 simply 'do not exist', in a notorious statement by Israeli Prime Minister Golda Meir in 1970. This is not a mere political statement of fact: despite the wide expansion of *locus standi* consciously exercised by the Supreme Court, especially under the leadership of Aharon Barak, Palestinians from the diaspora remain outside the pale for Israeli courts. They are considered by law 'permanent absentees', and denied any legal standing.

For those Palestinians who did not leave, about a tenth of the Palestinian population in 1948, the situation has widely fluctuated historically.[33] Compared to the state of emergency which ruled Palestinian Israelis for twenty years after the establishment of Israel, the three following decades have seen their rights expanded considerably. They were able to organize politically, and secure a significant presence in the Israeli Parliament, if not one which is commensurate with their numbers. But legal discrimination remains dominant, most glaringly in access to land ownership, over 90 per cent of which remains under the control of a state defined by its Jewishness, and in terms of executive power. From 1948 to 2000, there wasn't a single judge of non-Jewish descent as a permanent member of the Supreme Court, and not one Arab minister served in the Israeli Cabinet. Having enshrined the legal exclusion of the non-Jew in the very Declaration of Independence of the State of Israel,[34] the problem remains acute to date. The case for total equality in law between the Palestinian Israeli and the Jewish Israeli is likely to persist and develop alongside the difficulties and discrimination faced by disenfranchised Palestinians on the other side of the 1967 Green Line.

So rule by law rather than rule of law is typical of Palestinian rights in and around Israel. Treatment of citizens' basic rights reveals a hierarchy of human rights

---

[33] I tried to take stock of the literature and controversies surrounding the 'revisionist school' of Israeli historians, especially Benny Morris, in 'La Nausée and al-Nakba: rewriting 1948', *The Daily Star*, 4 September 2004, cited also above Chapter 3 n. 5.

[34] 'Declaration of Israel's Independence 1948', issued in Tel Aviv on 14 May 1948: 'We, members of the People's Council, representatives of the Jewish community of Eretz-Israel and of the Zionist movement, are here assembled on the day of the termination of the British mandate over Eretz-Israel and, by virtue of the natural and historic right and on the strength of the Resolution of the United Nations' General Assembly, hereby declare the establishment of a Jewish State in Eretz-Israel, to be known as the State of Israel'. The Declaration goes on to assert that 'The State of Israel will be open to the immigration of Jews from all countries of their dispersion; will promote the development of the country for the benefit of all its inhabitants; will be based on the precepts of liberty, justice and peace taught by the Hebrew Prophets; will uphold the full social and political equality of all its citizens, without distinction of race, creed or sex; will guarantee full freedom of conscience, worship, education and culture; will safeguard the sanctity and inviolability of the shrines and Holy Places of all religions'. Text available e.g. on the Avalon project at Yale Law School (<http//www.yale.edu/lawweb/avalon/mideast/israel.htm>).

standards which the Israeli Supreme Court has established, at the apex of which sits the most protected type of petitioner, an Israeli Jew—of mild political persuasion. At the bottom stands the exiled Palestinian, who 'does not exist' legally under the system. In between one finds an array of categories with various levels of discrimination, including the Israeli Arab and the non-Jewish citizens of Jerusalem and the Occupied Territories, and an uneven gradation of complex and fluid basic rights.

Arbitrary Arrest and Torture in Kuwait

A hypothetical deriving from a real case which was brought before the English courts in 1991 provides an insight into another model of failed judicial protection.[35] In the Emirate of Kuwait, and for reasons of private vengeance, a citizen is arrested in broad daylight by the police, taken into custody, denied a hearing, beaten up and variously mistreated before he is released from prison several days later. What legal redress is open to him?

A number of regulations and statutes on the books offer a prima-facie route for a case to be brought before the Kuwaiti courts by the victim of police or a shadowy security agency. In a survey of the relevant statutes, the legal headings for redress run as follows:

Administrative and constitutional redress. The Constitution of Kuwait (1962), in addition to mentioning that 'the State safeguards the pillars of Society and ensures security, tranquillity and equal opportunities for citizens' (Art. 8), specifically forbids arbitrary arrest, let alone torture:

No person shall be arrested, detained, searched or compelled to reside in a specified place, nor shall the residence of any person or his liberty to choose his place of residence or his liberty of movement be restricted, except in accordance with the provisions of the law.

No person shall be subjected to torture or to degrading punishment. (Art. 31)

The fundamentals of fair trial are guaranteed under Article 34:

An accused person is presumed innocent until proved guilty in a legal trial at which the necessary guarantees for the exercise of the right of defence are secured.

The infliction of physical or moral injury on an accused person is prohibited.

The Constitution also establishes a number of general mechanisms in the form of judicial review which, if applied, would secure effective legal protection. Two such

---

[35] The case mentioned here has become an important point of reference for international human rights, after it was litigated before the British courts and the European Court of Human Rights. The section which follows derives from an expert opinion I wrote for the lawyers of the victim, Suleiman al-Adsani, in the early 1990s. See also Chapter 11 n. 43.

institutions can be mentioned here: the Council of State (*Conseil d'Etat*) and the Constitutional Court. The first directly concerns the administration, including the police and the security apparatus. 'A council of state may be established by a law to assume the functions of administrative jurisdiction ...' (Art. 171).

In fact, the judicial organization of Kuwait—unlike Morocco, Egypt, or Lebanon—does not have an administrative jurisdiction, and wrongs emanating from the police or from any other security apparatus cannot be challenged on administrative grounds. A writer on Kuwaiti administrative law put it as follows:

Among the three headings which are outside Kuwaiti jurisdictional reach are .... suits which seek to annul or stop and interpret an administrative decision. This is the case even if the administrative decision does not attach to an act of state. This is clearly expressed in Art.2 of the Law on the Organization of the Kuwaiti judiciary. Thus, the judiciary in Kuwait can be considered to have a smaller writ than in other countries, as it is prevented from looking into the most important form of judicial control over the acts of the administration.[36]

This despite another clear constitutional disposition. Under Article 173 of the Constitution,

Law shall specify the judicial body competent to decide upon disputes relating to the constitutionality of laws and regulations and shall determine its jurisdiction and procedure.

Law shall ensure the right of both the Government and the interested parties to challenge the constitutionality of laws and regulations before the said body.

The formation of a constitutional court in Kuwait took a long time. It was eventually established by law in 1973, but in such a way as to curtail constitutional review significantly. Soon after the law was passed, Parliament, which, along with the Council of Ministers, was the only body allowed to bring a case before the Court, was suspended for a long period. It was only in the wake of the liberation from Iraqi occupation in 1991, three decades after the Constitution had required its establishment, that the Court started a timid life of its own.[37]

Criminal and civil redress. Let us pursue the hypothetical, and examine whether the victim can seek redress through two other avenues which are also open to him in principle: a criminal suit for wrongful imprisonment, and an action for damages under civil law.

Breach of substantive law can be found in criminal legislation, as well as in the civil laws of Kuwait. The General Penal Code punishes assault as follows: 'Whoever assaults a person or wounds him or injures him physically ... is punishable by (either or both) a maximum prison term of two years and by a fine of no more than 2,000 rupees or its equivalent' (Art. 160). The prison term can be increased to ten years and the fine to 10,000 rupees if 'the injury is serious'.[38]

---

[36] Fathi Wali, *Qanun al-qada' al-madani al-kuwaiti* (The law of Kuwaiti civil judiciary) (Kuwait, 1977) 106–7, footnotes omitted.   [37] See overview in Chapter 5 above.
[38] *adha baligh*, Art. 161.

More specific legislation, passed in 1970, is also relevant to the case. Under the heading 'mistreatment by civil servants of individuals', Article 53 of Law 31, 1970 stipulates:

Is punished by a maximum prison term of five years and by a fine of no more than 500 dinars, or by either, any public servant or employee who tortured, himself, or through another person, an accused or a witness or an expert to force him to confess to a crime or to proffer statements to that effect. If torture leads to an injury which is punished more severely under another law, the more severe punishment applies.

Under Article 56, the prison term is set at 'three years maximum . . . if the public servant or employee uses coercion with people on the basis of his function . . .'.

How about civil redress, granted that the public prosecutor will hardly budge on a case involving high-ranking Kuwaiti officials? Together with criminal action, a civil action for damage is in theory possible. Detailed provisions are provided under the civil laws of Kuwait as enacted in the 1980 Civil Code. Of particular relevance are the following tort dispositions.[39] On injury generally, Article 227 states:

(1) Every person who by his faulty act has caused harm to another person shall be liable to reparation regardless of whether he was perpetrator or inciter and abettor.

(2) A person even if he is prudent is liable for reparation of the harm resulting from his faulty act.

The measure of reparation is indicated in Articles 230, 231, and 245ff:

Art. 230 (1) Compensation for the harm caused by the unlawful act for which a person is responsible shall be determined by the loss caused and the lost profit, so long as it was a natural result of the unlawful act . . .

Art.231 (1) Reparation of the unlawful act covers the injury, even if it is moral.

(2) Moral harm comprises in particular the harm—corporal or moral—suffered by a person as a result of undermining his life, body, freedom, purity, honour, reputation or his social or moral standing or financial credibility; it furthermore covers the sorrow and anguish felt by the person as well as the emotional loss of love and tenderness resulting from the death of a dear one.

On the measure of reparation, Article 245 further stipulates:

Where an agreement is not reached to determine reparation for the injury caused by an unlawful act the judge shall do so without prejudice to the provision of Article 248 [which deals with reparation in the event of death].

Articles 246 and 247 establish the way the court assesses damage:

Art.246 (1) The judge shall assess compensation in currency.

(2) The judge may according to circumstances and upon application by the victim return the case to the situation which existed prior to the damage or order monetary payment as reparation.

---

[39] The articles which follow are cited after the English translation of the Code by Nicolas Karam, *Business laws of Kuwait* (Leiden, 1992).

Art.247 (1) The judge shall fix the reparation at such an amount which he considers will remedy the injury in accordance with the provisions of Articles 230 and 231, with due consideration to the victim's personal circumstances.

(2) Where it is not possible for the judge, at the time of passing judgment, to determine clearly the amount of damages, he may reserve a right for the victim to claim, within a time limit set by the judge, a revision of the assessment.

The law, therefore, clearly defines the right to compensation for unlawful harm, but it is rendered inoperative in our case by Article 237 of the Civil Code:

A public official shall not be held responsible for an act committed by him which caused injury to another person if he had implemented the provisions of a law or complied with an order given by a superior if he had or believed on acceptable grounds he had to obey, and if he proves he had reasonable grounds which made him believe that the act committed by him to be legitimate and that, in carrying out his action he exercised due care.

There are therefore four categories under which the laws of Kuwait were violated in the case at hand: under the constitution, under principles of administrative law, under the general as well as specific criminal laws, and finally under the civil code.

And yet judicial remedy remains unavailable. Existing rights are rendered ineffective by substantial and procedural means. In part, redress is undermined by special limitations introduced within the legislative texts. These come under a variety of headings. Any constitutional redress is made impossible, despite the apparently fine bill of rights included in the Kuwaiti Constitution and a full Article 173 about the Court, by the formation, alongside the Court, of a Committee which sifts through constitutional challenges before they come before the Court.[40] Martial law (Art. 69 of the Constitution in Kuwait) is another device to empty constitutional rights, and is often used in Middle Eastern jurisdictions to blunt human rights dispositions. As for judicial control of administrative acts, it is made hollow by the absence of an administrative court, and by the difficulty of challenging administrative acts and regulations in the first place.

More commonly, rights are undermined by procedural devices which prevent a case from reaching the courts, and by the absence of control over the police and repressive agencies. Criminal law is difficult to apply against the police or a security apparatus, and public prosecution, which is in charge of indictment, is reluctant to challenge the authority of the Minister of Interior and its agencies, let alone the ruling family. There are no documented actions in Kuwait against a public official under Law 21, 1970.

This leaves civil law and civil jurisdictions as a possible recourse for the wronged citizen. A combined suit on the basis of criminal, administrative and civil breach could succeed in theory, but there is a panoply of 'acts of state' considerations that strengthen the immunity of wrongdoers, such as the protection offered to public officials under Article 237 of the Civil Code, even if it contradicts criminal dispositions stipulated by the 1970 statute.

---

[40] See Nathan Brown, *The rule of law in the Arab world* (Cambridge, 1997) 173.

One should not be surprised at the poor application of the rule of law in Kuwait being reproduced in similar patterns across the Middle East. In fact, Kuwait is one of the less repressive countries in the region. Since its beginnings on independence in the early 1960s, Kuwaiti parliamentary democracy has been the object of unease for Gulf monarchies and for Arab rulers generally, leading to heavy regional pressure to freeze normal constitutional life for long stretches of time. Courts are unable to perform their role as defenders of basic rights in such an atmosphere, and it is no surprise to find judicial remedies constantly curtailed in Kuwait and elsewhere. Across the Middle East, the courts see their power of judicial review hemmed in as soon as the constitution and parliament are suspended, and it takes a long time to restore their authority even after parliament and the constitution become active again. Courts in the Middle East do not exist in a vacuum, and when the political heat is on, they are unable to withhold the pressure and eventual wrath of executive power. Nor would it be surprising that the above case in Kuwait—briefly a *cause célèbre*—would not even have been heard of before the restoration of constitutional rule in the aftermath of the liberation from Iraqi occupation in 1991.

Since then, the establishment at last of the constitutional court, as well as a clearly more active parliament, has offered a new model, that of 'two-steps forward one-step backward' for the rule of law. At one point in the mid-1990s, newspapers reported that judicial action was even taken, for the first time, against a former minister who belongs to the Emir's family. But the authority of the criminal court was diverted to a special court where the issue was eventually shelved.[41]

Administrative Law: Right to Passport in Morocco

Administrative jurisdictions are not available in Kuwait for the protection of individual rights, but this is not uniformly the case in the Middle East. Where it is available, however, the individual's administrative law protection is limited by the original model from which it derives: the French Conseil d'Etat.

It took a long time for the Conseil d'Etat to offer some protection for the individual against state administrative encroachments, notably by way of a *recours pour excès de pouvoir*.[42] In more recent years, the French Conseil d'Etat, which operates, much like English courts, on a self-sustaining set of precedents, has accepted the inclusion of issues arising under the *principes généraux du droit* within its purview.[43] But the administrative court is not a human rights court, and

---

[41] '*Mahkamat al-jinayat al-kuwaitiyya tuhil 'Ali al-Khalifa 'alal-mahkama al-khassa* (Assize court of Kuwait transfers 'Ali Khalifa to the special court)', *al-Hayat*, 22 November 1995.

[42] Concept introduced by the French Conseil d'Etat in its decision of 21 December 1906, *Syndicat des propriétaires et contribuables du quartier Croix-de-Seguey-Tivoli*.

[43] Precedent established by the Conseil d'Etat in its decision *Syndicat général des ingénieurs-conseils*, 26 June 1959.

police activities remain, even in France, under the judicial control of ordinary jurisdictions.

Nonetheless, administrative law provides practical protection against state excesses in some cases. One such instance is 'the passport case' in Morocco.

A request for a passport was put to the relevant authorities in Tangiers— represented by the city governor—by a Mr Echemlal, a Moroccan national, by profession manager of a company. This was in 1979. Several months later, he had not heard back from the governor, whom he petitioned again in writing, and then by paying him a personal visit. This being to no avail, he petitioned the courts. Six years later, the Supreme Court of Morocco issued a judgment in his favour.

The reasoning of the Court, which takes a similar form to administrative decisions taken in France, lies in two distinct and brief parts. First, all relevant facts are cited. In this case, they include the status of the plaintiff, the particulars of the repeated requests made to the authorities, the fact 'that the governor has kept silent' throughout and thus implicitly issued a negative answer. Then the legal reasoning is spelled out. The court explained that 'the freedom to circulate in the whole world is a man's natural right' and that the petitioner had fulfilled all the administrative requirements which the law relating to the delivery of passports to Moroccan citizens required. The Court proceeded to annul the decision of the lower court, again in the format established by the French Conseil d'Etat:

Considering Art.9 of the Constitution which consecrates the freedom of circulation and asserts that any limitation to such freedom must be governed by legislation;

Considering that any citizen has the right to obtain a passport; that he cannot be denied this right except if a text of law expressly curtails it;

Considering that by refusing to renew the passport of the plaintiff or issuing him a new one, in the absence of a legal prohibition to that effect, the Governor of Tangiers had violated the law and that his decision is consequently vitiated by 'excès de pouvoir'.[44]

This decision is typical of the rule of law in the Middle East as developed by administrative courts where they exist: that a court should spend six years on a matter so evident as the right to a passport is indicative of the slow judicial operation in most Middle East jurisdictions, but the decision also shows some avenues of redress available to the wronged, persistent citizen.

Apostasy in Unified Yemen

During the three years of civil peace and institution-building in the unified Yemen (1990–3), the courts tried to ensure a more effective protection of the rule of law against overwhelming odds of extreme illiteracy and poverty. That the democratic

---

[44] *Echemlal* case, 11 July 1985, in *Revue Juridique, Politique et Economique du Maroc*, 20, 1988, 42–3, and comment by Amine Ben Abdallah, 'La délivrance du passeport en droit marocain', 29–41.

experience was unable to prevent the civil war in 1994 should not belittle the efforts of those who worked hard on the building of law-rooted state institutions. Constitutional review,[45] together with elections and a relatively active Parliament, are achievements which mark the recent history of the Yemen. The emergence of judicial review *lato sensu* is another such achievement, which some judges have tried to build up painstakingly in the face of obstacles difficult to imagine for the outsider. Until 1990, all judgments in San'a had remained hand-written. That year, the introduction of a typewriter in the Court marked a watershed, and this tardiness offers an indication of the reluctance of the executive, by design or ignorance, to grant courts the professional respect and budgetary support they need to develop as an independent power. In the absence of organized law reports, important decisions remain unknown, like the 'apostasy case' which was handed down by the Criminal Division of the Yemeni Supreme Court in 1992.[46]

In this case, the Criminal Chamber of the Supreme Court was considering a decision by a lower San'a court, which had stripped a university lecturer of his post and requested him to atone for what it considered blasphemous writings. The Supreme Court did not find sufficient evidence to consider the appellant an apostate, and reversed the decision. The argument is terse and brief, and comes after an exposition of the *ratio* of the first instance court and the rebuttal of the defendant: 'After taking notice of the file of the case and various expert reports and rebuttals, the Criminal and Military Division [of the Supreme Court] rules that the accused is innocent, who denied all allegations and asserted his attachment and pride in Islam from the beginning of his statements to the prosecution'.[47]

This is a tangible success for the criminal judge in the Yemen in the protection of free speech. But one needs to look at the fine print. Yemen's recent judicial record reveals judicial and constitutional failings which beset the Middle East at large.

Despite the heavy legacy of wars and general economic backwardness in the country, unified Yemen gave way to an innovative Constitution which has formally espoused two basic principles of the rule of law: an independent judiciary and a Supreme Court with a constitutional writ. A full book of the Yemeni Constitution regulates judicial and constitutional power. It attaches special care to the independence of the judiciary: 'The judiciary is an independent power ... and the judges are independent. There is no power over them other than the law. It is forbidden for any party to intervene in any way in cases or issues pertaining to justice. Such an intervention is considered a crime punished by law. Such crime knows no prescription' (Art. 120/147).[48] It is hard to conceive of stronger language. Further rules to

---

[45] Above Chapter 5.

[46] *Al-'Udi* case, 118/98, Supreme Court of the Yemen, Criminal and Military Division, decided 7 May 1992. Full Arab text reported in Mallat, 'Three recent decisions from the Yemen Supreme Court', *Islamic Law and Society*, 2, 1995, 71–90, at 87–91.   [47] ibid., at 90.

[48] For the dual numbering of articles in the Constitution of unified Yemen, see Chapter 5 n. 32.

ensure the proclaimed independence are then listed in the text: publicity of trials, an independent supreme judicial council to regulate and discipline the profession, and no removal of a judge from office without his express agreement. The concern in the Constitution for a totally independent judiciary is such that one would expect the Supreme Court to exercise to the full its constitutional competence under Article 124/151,[49] especially over basic human rights like freedom of expression. This competence is bolstered by Article 26/41, which opens Book 2 of the Constitution by listing the 'basic rights and duties of the citizen' and stipulates that 'the state guarantees the freedom of thought and the freedom to express one's opinion in speech, writing or photography [i.e. television] within the limits of law'.

The overall picture is more complex. Despite the possibility for the citizen to resort to the Court in order to solicit its constitutional protection, it is telling that the issue of freedom of expression came up in such a delicate matter as apostasy before the Criminal Chamber of the Supreme Court rather than before the Constitutional Chamber. In addition, the reversal of the apostasy charge was made by the Court on grounds of repentance, turning the matter into one of evidence related to the charge of apostasy, rather than on freedom of expression as such.

The pattern of constraints encountered in the last provision of Article 26/41 of the Constitution of Yemen, which limits basic rights by referring to their exercise 'within the limits of law (or of the *shari'a*)' is typical of Arab constitutions. As in the examples of Kuwait and Yemen (and in Israel under the label of 'security'), constitutionally protected basic human rights and freedoms are constrained by reference to 'the limits of law', that is to subsequent statutes which water down constitutional rights under the pretext of providing more detailed arrangements. These limits are generally included in special legislation or in clauses introduced in criminal or media codes, and render available constitutional protection irrelevant.

In the context of the Yemeni judiciary, judges have found it difficult to balance constitutional basic rights and the limitations introduced by ordinary laws, despite that lone decision on apostasy which may be correct morally though constitutionally weak in the absence of an open reference to freedom of speech. The need is obvious: if constitutional rights stipulated in the founding text are to see any concrete application, it is important to establish them clearly over and above any qualifying legislation. This problem of the confusion between ordinary courts and constitutional courts—to which can be added a motley of special courts—remains a major impediment to the rule of law coming of age in the Middle East.

The case of Yemen may appear more striking than those of Kuwait and Morocco, but judicial experiments are fragile and uncertain across the region. The example of the 'safe haven' experiment in Iraq offers a final example of this fragility.

---

[49] Text of Art.124/151 in Chapter 5, text at n. 32.

Judicial Review in a War-Torn Country: Courts in the Kurdish 'Safe Haven' of Northern Iraq

From the vantage point of the search for stability in other Middle Eastern countries, the brief judicial experience of Iraqi Kurdistan in 1994 shows the many pitfalls accompanying the complicated and arduous process of the search for the rule of law in a war-ridden region.[50]

In many ways, the situation in Northern Iraq was atypical for over a decade. Iraq is a country which has been subjected to severe dictatorship and an especially perverse use of 'law' over a quarter of a century. Two major wars were started by the Iraqi leadership, but the system was still in place two decades after the first war against Iran in 1980, and three decades after the coup which brought the Ba'th Party to the helm in 1968. When the second Gulf War led to the collapse of the army and a major rebellion—the Iraqi *intifada*—across the country in March 1991, special international circumstances brought into being what became known as the Kurdish 'safe haven', consisting of a region in the north which was protected internationally from central power, and where the writ of the central government in Baghdad stopped being enforced.

Elections were carried out in May 1992 within the safe haven, resulting in a Parliament which started legislating soon afterwards. Because the 'safe haven' was temporary and no formal secession announced, the new legislation was considered residuary. The use of Iraqi, as opposed to new Kurdish, laws continued as a matter of course. The result was a high dose of eclecticism. In family law, as well as in civil and criminal law, the Iraqi national codes continued to operate, with two exceptions: Ba'thist laws which were unacceptable politically were discarded, and new Kurdish laws took precedence over older Iraqi legislation. The general uncertainty resulting from the ill-defined nature of the safe haven, and the regional and international dimensions of the Iraqi crisis as a whole, underline the uniqueness of the experience, even in a Middle Eastern context.

And yet, the experience is also typical of a distinguishable trend in the region of the difficult search for the rule of law by way of the judiciary.

How far has the Kurdish judiciary operated for the protection of the citizen since the end of the former Iraqi ruler's reign of terror in the north in the summer of 1991? The answer to this question can be sketched in the light of a number of cases which were decided at the level of the highest court in the province—a court operating within the formal structure of the Iraqi state—the Court of Cassation.[51]

---

[50] On the Iraqi context at the time see my *The Middle East into the 21st century* (Reading, 1996), 71–126, and the literature cited therein.

[51] Called in Iraq *mahkamat al-tamyiz*. The structure is generally as follows: in penal law, there are regional courts of assizes (*jinayat*) for serious crimes, with a right of appeal to the Court of Cassation (criminal chamber). In civil law and personal status matters, there are courts of first instance, with an appeal to regional courts of appeal (*isti'naf*). From there lay further appeal on points of law to the Court of Cassation.

I have received, from Kurdish Iraq, a sample of decisions of the Court of Cassation, all rendered within a period of five months (January–May 1994), and dealing with three subject areas defined by the chamber ruling on the matter: personal status, civil, and criminal.[52]

Decision 7/18.1.1994 (Civil) examined a claim against a debtor which had been granted to the claimant by the first instance court and the appeal court. The Court of Cassation reversed that decision on the basis of the poor strength of the evidence of the debt, which had been written on the reverse side of a small flyer, and on the error of the lower court in discarding a plea of compensation which was pending before another first instance court.

In Decision 11/24.1.1994 (Civil) the Court of Cassation confirmed the lower court decision in a property dispute in the Zakho area. In a short judgment, the Court held that the copy of the land register was sufficient evidence of the plaintiff's original claim.

Among the six criminal decisions, two addressed relatively insignificant cases of theft by youngsters. Decision 10/12.2.1994 (Criminal—Minors), where the minors' section of the criminal chamber issued the judgment, simply reaffirmed the lower court's relatively lenient decision in a case of theft without violence. The judgment is interesting in view of the nature of the appeal. The lower court, and not the plaintiff or the public prosecutor, asked for the assessment of the Court of Cassation, and the Court duly obliged.

Decision 1/17.1.1994 (Criminal—Minors) was also a case of theft by a youngster. The lawyer of the accused had filed the appeal on the basis of the disregard by the lower court of the law on minors and too long a sentence of confinement. The decision was upheld by the Court of Cassation.

Decision 108/10.4.1994 (Criminal) dealt with manslaughter. The facts were not in dispute. The accused had been playing with his gun with mock threats to a friend, and an accidental shot killed the victim on the spot. The Court of Assizes in Irbil sentenced him to three years in prison. On appeal to the Court of Cassation, a plea was made on the basis of the killer's youth and clean record, as well as on the withdrawal of the complaint by the victim's family. The Court of Cassation confirmed the decision but reduced the jail term to two years.

Decision 86/28.3.1994 (Criminal) was a judgment on due process. The Court of Cassation reversed a decision of the lower criminal court which sentenced for violent action three participants in a terrorist cell, without proper respect for the rules enunciated in the Penal Code and in the Code of Criminal Procedure.[53]

The Court was held in full *banc*[54] in the two last cases under examination. This, as in France, takes place when a decision examined a first time by a chamber of the

---

[52] Eleven unpublished judgments kindly provided by Professor Nuri Talibani. Three deal with personal status, two with civil law, and six with criminal law. Personal status cases are discussed in Chapter 10.

[53] Although it is not possible to assess exactly how due process was violated in the absence of the full text of the articles cited, the Court of Cassation reversed because of a wrong interpretation of legislation.   [54] As in the French equivalent to *al-hay'a al-'amma, Assemblée Plénière*.

Court of Cassation is reversed, sent back down to the lower court to be re-examined in the light of the Cassation decision, but gets reaffirmed by the lower court. Then, upon appeal to the Court of Cassation a second time, the decision is held in the presence of all the judges.

In Decision 11/26.2.1994, the full court had to assess the decision of the Court of Assizes of Suleymaniyya not to abide by a former Cassation decision in a case of murder with criminal intent. The facts concerned a policeman and others involved in the shooting of two women who had fled the family home to join their lovers. The lower court had seemingly given lenient sentences in a poorly drafted judgment, and they were reversed a first time and sent down for reconsideration in the light of the Cassation decision. This again was not done properly, and the Suleymaniyya Court of Assizes reaffirmed its own previous judgment. Again the full Court of Cassation reversed.

The last decision under consideration was also issued by the full Court of Cassation. Decision 9/21.2.1994 is unusual because of its application of laws which were passed by the Kurdish Parliament after the establishment of the safe haven, in that case a statute specifically condemning actions taken against foreign workers. The two killers of an Australian aid worker, who also wounded three other persons working with him for the humanitarian organization Care, faced three charges which carried various sentences, including capital punishment. The capital sentence decided by the criminal court of Kirkuk was upheld by a unanimous Court of Cassation. After explaining the validity of the procedure leading to their arrest and condemnation, the Court affirmed

the decisions in their three branches and their validity under the law. As for the penalty imposed which is hanging until death in the case of the murder of Stuart Cameron, it is appropriate and corresponds adequately to the crime, in so far as the deep motive for the commitment of this crime and its ugly object call for the extirpation of those sentenced from society, so that it be rid of their mischief ... The decision was issued unanimously on 21.02.1994.

Here then is a sample of the Iraqi Kurdish judiciary in action in an unusual setting, and trying to protect basic rights as enunciated in 'normal' laws, that is in laws dealing with personal status, rights of property, sanctity of contract, and of course criminal issues and the right to life. Several features may be noted:

(1) The Court of Cassation was clearly keen to discipline lower courts not operating with due process and the proper reference to legislation. Several decisions were reversed with an evident keenness to 'educate' lower courts.

(2) The time separating the sentence of the highest court and the first judicial proceedings suggests a smooth functioning of the judiciary. Serious crimes were dealt with within one or two years. Civil and personal status matters were solved in a few months. This is unusually fast in the Middle East.

(3) The rationale for the decisions is carefully worked out, and there is a clear concern for a self-sustaining and coherent body of rules. As in Iraq and many Middle Eastern countries that follow the French model, the decisions of the Court of Cassation deal normally only in law—and not in fact—and tend to be short, although an expanded competence of the Court of Cassation with regard to assessing facts should be noted in our sample. Ten out the eleven judgments vary between two to four pages each; all offer a convincing and thoughtful legal pattern.

Despite the encouraging assessment, the experiment of the Iraqi Kurdish judiciary presented in the cases above was not solid enough to prevent the large-scale violence which erupted in May 1994.[55] How the disturbances broke out show *a contrario* the importance of an independent judiciary as well as its limitations in preventing violence or quelling it once it has set out to tear the fabric of society.

The conflict erupted in early May 1994 over land rights in the region of Qal'at Desai in the north-east of Iraq which were claimed by one middle-level leader of a faction close to the Kurdish Democratic Party (KDP).[56] The persons in control of the disputed plot were close to the rival Patriotic Union of Kurdistan (PUK). When the local KDP leader arrived with a group of armed followers to force the eviction from the land of the PUK locals, the conflict degenerated into a violent confrontation which left him and several others dead in its wake. A full civil war ensued until 1996, in the course of which with some 5,000 Kurds were killed.

In a situation like the dispute over land, the only recourse for the two parties should have been the courts, as indeed in the property case in the region of Zakho in which the Court of Cassation solved the dispute over the title to land.[57] Any of the cases adjudicated by the Court of Cassation which were presented in this section could have been the occasion of violent clashes between the litigants, if political parties had been involved in open armed support for one or the other party. Why they did so in the property case of Qal'at Desai may appear a moot point set against the general economic collapse and the political deadlock in the region; the important fact remains that despite the limitations faced by courts in this troubled and impoverished area of the Middle East, the horizon for the rule of law in daily life can only be the independent judge. The alternative is Somalia and Afghanistan under the Taliban, with chaos reigning supreme; or Syria, Iraq, at least until 2003, or Libya as the worst cases of government officials commiting crimes in total impunity, and a Middle East where the meaning of law is profoundly perverted.

[55] A report by British lawyer Adam Stapleton on 24 August 1994, regarding the possible establishment of a Commission of Inquiry into the factional fighting in Iraqi Kurdistan notes that 'the Minister of Justice [Kadir 'Aziz Jabbary]—the only post that is not party shared 50:50—complained that the two main parties not only interfered in the justice system, but simply by-passed it'. Report, para. 8. No such inquiry was ever established.
[56] The two main parties in Iraqi Kurdistan are the Kurdish Democratic Party (KDP) and the Patriotic Union of Kurdistan (PUK), which exclusively shared representation in Parliament following the elections in May 1992.　　[57] Decision 11/24.1.1994/Civil, cited at 231 above.

Epilogue: The Sisyphus Rock of Judicial Review

So much for examples of the rule of law/judicial review in the administrative and criminal fields. Multiple examples can be plucked from so many jurisdictions; the resulting picture is not encouraging. True, stories of courageous judges, lawyers, and litigants should also be told, but there remains much to be desired for the protection of basic rights in the traditional sense by the judiciary across the region. Nor is the rule of law better protected when constitutional courts and councils are set up to stand up to the rights embodied in the various constitutions. Public law in the Middle East is a field of great frustration for lawyers, judges, and the litigant. This is compounded by the various ways in which judges are constrained by executive power.

Examination of the modern court system suggests a deeply contradictory operation of the rule of law for the citizen. In a region which has been submitted to repeated and violent turmoil in the twentieth century, demand for justice is immense, but the rule of law has time and again been undermined by the judiciary's lack of independence and authority. In the field of constitutional and criminal law, whenever the slightest political overtone appears in a case—that is, prisoners of conscience, operations of the police and security services, review of electoral laws and elections, detention of political opponents under seditious acts, etc., the legal professions (private lawyers as well as prosecutors and judges) find themselves struggling in a generally adverse environment. In areas of public life which are considered eminently 'political', regardless of whether people toil under traditional monarchies or revolutionary potentates, executive power has been reluctant to allow any serious review of state power.

In the economic realm, transactions (especially international transactions) have tended to be more easily upheld, both as a business ethic and as the subject of adjudication by the courts. But the lack of authority of the courts in the constitutional field indirectly affects the less controversial arena of commercial law, as does the general system of patronage which is rampant in the Middle East. This leads to attempted flights away from judicial adjudication and the consequent rise of arbitration. Arbitration has found fashionable favour domestically and regionally, as it seems to offer obvious speed and simplicity in comparison with the uncertain and costly court system. The reality is more complex. As law merchant, commercial law concerns only a limited number of transactions—despite their larger monetary significance. This does not prevent the wide business demand for the rule of law across the spectrum. Only a strong and respected judiciary can ensure the effective sway of arbitration in commercial law.[58]

The rule of law is effective in the Middle East most remarkably in 'civil law', which is the general field of obligations arising under contract or tort between

---

[58] For an analysis and critique of arbitration, see section on arbitration in Chapter 9.

ordinary citizens. Middle East civil codes have succeeded in offering an unusual haven of legal stability. By building on comprehensive codes which remained untouched for several decades, obligations and contracts have turned into a rare and all the more precious repository of more solid legal rules. In contrast to constitutional texts, civil codes are the subject of a profound and original debate both for their genesis and their judicial interpretation. They remain monument-like staples of stability and anchors of reference for courts and litigants alike. To the less turbulent world of private law we now turn.

PART III
PRIVATE LAW

7

Introduction: From the Age of Codification
to the Age of Case-Law

An early text suggests that Caliph al-Mansur (r. 754–75) categorically rejected the codification of Islamic law which ibn al-Muqaffaʻ (d. 139/756) and other advisors were suggesting to him.[1] The account does not explain the lack of codification beyond the early period, but it is a fact that we do not find any trace of formal state-sponsored codes until the sixteenth century, when the first Ottoman *qanun-nameh*s were edicted. Considering the depth of the tradition since Eshnuna's laws and Hammurabi's Code, through to the Syro-Roman book in the fifth century CE, it is not clear why codification was interrupted for so long. A simple explanation may be that codes require state centralization, and that a central caliphate did not last long enough for state institutions to produce binding legislation, disseminate it, and induce judges to apply it. This left the business of law chiefly in the hands of classical jurists, who produced treatises that are closest in style to legislation first in the form of summaries, then in the *Ashbah wa nazaʼer* genre.[2]

This may be too simple. As with other negative questions, the explanation of why a particular legal genre did *not* emerge is naturally elusive. The fact is that no significant codification emerged in the Middle East before the 'reception' of European private law in the form of codes, ordinances, and statutes. This is why codification is correctly associated with the colonization process in the nineteenth century: thence my characterization of that new period as 'the age of codification' in the history of Islamic law.

Unlike most other legal systems which were subject to European colonization, Middle Eastern countries did not necessarily conform to the legal pattern of colonization, with the English common law being received in British colonies, and French (and Roman-Dutch) law being received in French or Dutch colonies.[3] Apart from Israel, where the system is a complex combination of indigenous

---

[1] Ibn al-Muqaffaʻ, *Risala fil-sahaba*, in *Athar* (Works) (Beirut, 1966) 354.

[2] See Chapter 2 on the pre-Islamic codes, and on the suggested periodization of Islamic law. On related aspects of codification, Chapter 2, *in fine*. On the *Ashbah* genre and its impact on modern codification, see Chapter 9.

[3] See generally K. Zweigert and H. Kötz, *An Introduction to comparative law* (Oxford 1998) chapters on 'the reception of the Code Civil', 98–118 and on 'the spread of the Common Law throughout the world', 218–37.

Jewish and Islamic-Ottoman law,[4] in addition to the English common law, countries which were under British domination did not squarely espouse the case-law format of English law. This is due to several factors, not least the late arrival of formal British colonization to the Middle East. It is only in the wake of the First World War that the British set foot in Iraq, Jordan, and Palestine. Elsewhere, British political sway was significant mostly in Egypt and in the Sudan, but Egypt adopted civil codes before English influence became dominant. The system of courts itself was more directly inspired by the French legal system. As a consequence, the English common law tradition remained of a residual nature in the Arab Middle East.

The dominance of civil law reception over the reception of the common law tradition is not absolute. In the Sudan for example—known as the Anglo-Egyptian Sudan before its independence in 1956,[5] the sway of English law remained significant, with the principle of 'justice, equity and good conscience', which also prevailed in Pakistan. Until the beginning of the 1980s, Anglo-Sudanese law developed into a mixture of local customs, of principles derived from the *shariʿa* and embodied in 'judicial circulars', and a system of courts which followed essentially English patterns.[6] Also, in Southern and Western Arabia, in particular Aden in former South Yemen and the 'Trucial States', the relatively earlier British colonization of the eighteenth and nineteenth centuries left significant marks on the legal systems of these countries after their independence in the 1960s and 1970s.[7]

These former British colonies notwithstanding, tradition in the Middle East is essentially one of civil law, with the Civil Code at the heart of the legal system. A distinction can be drawn here between countries with direct French or civil law-based traditions, and countries where domination was British, but where the civil law tradition prevailed regardless. For the former, the French impact can be

[4] For Islamic law in Israel, see Robert Eisenman, *Islamic law in Palestine and Israel: a history of the survival of tanzimat and shariʿa in the British Mandate and the Jewish state* (Leiden, 1978); Aharon Layish, *Women and Islamic law in a non-Muslim state: a study based on decisions of the shariʿa courts in Israel* (New York 1975). For the accumulation of legal layers in Israel, see Ronen Shamir, *The colonies of law: colonialism, Zionism and law in early Mandate Palestine* (Cambridge, 2000).

[5] See Zaki Mustapha, *Common law in the Sudan, an account of the 'justice, equity and good conscience provision'* (Oxford, 1971) cited by Anderson, *Law reform in the Muslim world* (London, 1976) 27.

[6] See e.g. Carolyn Fluehr-Lobban, 'Judicial circulars of the shariʿa courts in the Sudan 1902–1979', *Journal of African Law*, 27, 1983, 79–140.

[7] There is little scholarship on the development of law in South Yemen during colonization, and the information here is based on accounts by judge Nagib al-Shammiri, former Chief Justice in the Republic. See his 'The judicial system in democratic Yemen', in B. Pridham, ed., *Contemporary Yemen: politics and historical background* (London, 1984); and Herbert Liebesny, 'Administration and legal development in Arabia: Aden colony and protectorate', *Middle East Journal*, 9, 1955, 385–96. Some law reports are available for the early twentieth century in the Aden region. For North Yemen and the several voices of 'law', see the anthropological works of Brinkley Messick, e.g. *The calligraphic state: textual domination and history in a Muslim society* (Berkeley, 1993); and on criminal law, 'Prosecution in Yemen: the introduction of the niyaba', *International Journal of Middle East Studies*, 15, 1983, 507–18. On law in the Trucial States (the current United Arab Emirates) and the English-dominated Gulf countries, see Husain al-Baharna, *The Arabian Gulf states* (Beirut, 1975 (orig. Manchester, 1968)) xxi–lxii and 5–22.

described as massive and wholesale. For the latter, there were more nuances in the introduction of French-style codes. There, the amalgamation of several traditions, including the *shari'a*, offers a richer and more complex legal picture.[8] The difference, however, is more of degree than in nature.

The group of countries belonging to the category under direct French influence includes three states in the Maghreb—Morocco, Algeria, and Tunisia—and Lebanon and Syria in the Levant. Under civil law *lato sensu*, it also includes Libya under Italian domination, and Mauritania and the Western Sahara, which fell under Spanish rule. The second category of countries, formally or *de facto* British colonies, 'received' civil law nonetheless. They include Egypt, Iraq, Jordan, and Palestine-Israel.

Several factors may explain why the civil law tradition was adopted in preference to the common law in all these systems. Some of these factors are peculiar to a specific state formation, such as the role of French legal education in Lebanon and in Egypt, as well as the model the metropolis represented for law students in Algeria, Morocco, and Tunisia, where colonization came early and was massive in its determination to impose a French-style law.[9] In Lebanon, a special relationship had developed since the European Renaissance between Catholic France and some of the Christian Catholic sects which became politically dominant in the twentieth century. In Egypt, where France was influential culturally in the nineteenth century after the engineering feat of the Suez canal, British domination came at a time when a local judiciary and legal structure were already in place. Two French-inspired Civil Codes were introduced in Egypt in 1876 and 1883, and British domination did not find it convenient or beneficial to disrupt the system already in place.[10] Modern research suggests an accident of history as one reason for the Frenchness of the Egyptian legal system. The stronger power, Britain, wilfully surrendered in the early 1880s the projection of its own system of courts and legislation onto French judicial and legal influence in Egypt in return for political control.[11]

---

[8] For the teaching of Islamic law, as opposed to 'modern' law, in the twentieth-century Middle East, see generally M. Flory and J. R. Henry, eds., *L'enseignement du droit musulman* (Paris, 1989).

[9] For the adaptation of French law in civil law countries, see the survey of Bernard Botiveau, 'L'adaptation d'un modèle français d'enseignement du droit au Proche-Orient', in ibid. 229–52. For one of the oldest French schools of law in the area, see Jean Ducruet, *Faculté de droit, de sciences politiques et économiques. Livre d'or 1913–1993* (Beirut, 1995). See also Chapter 4, n. 5 on law curricula.

[10] Not surprisingly, there is an extensive literature on law in Egypt, which was at its most vital in the first half of the twentieth century. Among the best works in European languages, Jasper Yeates Brinton, *The mixed courts of Egypt*, rev. edn. (New Haven, 1968 (orig. edn, 1930)), Byron Cannon, *Politics of law and the courts in nineteenth-century Egypt* (Salt Lake City, 1988); Farhat Ziadeh, *Lawyers, the rule of law, and liberalism in modern Egypt* (Palo Alto, Calif., 1968); Nathan Brown, *The rule of law in the Arab world* (Cambridge, 1997 (reviewed in *Yearbook of Islamic and Middle Eastern Law*, iii, 1996, 543–44)), Bernard Botiveau, *Loi islamique et droit dans les sociétés arabes* (Paris, 1993) (also on Syria), and the works of Enid Hill on the penal system, *Mahkama! Studies in the Egyptian legal system* (London, 1979) and on 'Abd al-Razzaq al-Sanhuri, *Al-Sanhuri and Islamic law* (Cairo, 1987) (reviewed in *Maghreb-Machrek*, 117, 1987, 107–8).

[11] Barbara Allen Roberson, 'The emergence of the modern judiciary in the Middle East', in C. Mallat ed., *Islam and public law* (London 1993) 102–39.

Legal education and patterns of colonization notwithstanding, the reception of civil law was facilitated by two underlying currents: first, the comparative ease of reaching twentieth-century standards by the short-cut of comprehensive codes in the French tradition, as opposed to the slow build-up of the common law through court cases. This made passing statutes easier and more palatable than relying on a troubled judiciary for the development of case-law. Like Japan under the Meiji, there was a need for clear, simple and comprehensive codes that would regulate the most current legal transactions, and the Napoleonic Codes offered the required model.

The second factor was the nineteenth-century codification of Islamic law in important parts of the Middle East under Ottoman rule. This is the famous Ottoman Majalla (*Majallat al-ahkam al-'adliyya*, literally the journal of judicial rules), a compendium of civil law regulating duties and obligations in consonance with the Hanafi school of law. The imprimatur of the Majalla as an Islamic Civil Code on the French model and its success over time also offered the basis for a significant body of case-law in several Middle Eastern countries. But this was 'jurisprudence' in the French tradition, case-law which did not carry the weight of precedents in English common law. The relatively long life of the Majalla—between thirty and seventy or more years depending on the country—ensured that reception would favour the civil law over the common law tradition.[12]

There remained countries in the Middle East that knew neither direct European domination nor consistent Ottoman rule. This is essentially the case for central Arabia, where apart from some Ottoman forays in the eighteenth and nineteenth centuries, the region was in the hands of nomadic tribes which would be unified into the Saudi state by King 'Abdul 'Aziz ibn Sa'ud only in the mid-1920s. Understandably, Saudi Arabia offers no classical case of reception. To date, the operation of the law cannot be said to be unified, as the centres of legal tender get superimposed in a motley system of administrative regulations, code-like decrees, specialized tribunals and half-institutionalized dispensation of legal judgments and arbitration, alongside firmly established unwritten customs.[13]

The case of Iran is also special, in so far as colonization has been the exception rather than the rule, with England and Russia trying to establish, with only relative success, their formal domination over the country at the beginning of the century. Similarly, the Republic of Turkey, the successor of the dismembered Ottoman Empire on the north-east side of the Mediterranean, followed a specific legal course in which the Islamic tradition, including language and vocabulary, was until recently all but rejected in favour of a secular continental-style system of courts and codes.[14]

---

[12] On the Majalla and its world, see Chapter 8.

[13] On contemporary Saudi law, legal studies are rare and rarely comprehensive. But see Frank Vogel, *Islamic law and legal system: studies of Saudi Arabia* (Leiden, 2000).

[14] Erhan Adal, *Fundamentals of Turkish private law*, rev. 3rd. edn. (Istanbul, 1991); Tugrul Ansay and Don Wallace, eds., *Introduction to Turkish law*, 4th edn. (The Hague, 1996); June Starr, *Law as*

The domination of codes is not restricted to private law. By the twenty-first century, constitutions and criminal codes have become the norm across the Middle East, even in Saudi Arabia, Israel, Pakistan, and the Sudan, where Britain held sway.[15] It is in private law that codes are most readily found, particularly in the law of obligations. Here the Islamic law tradition is at its strongest, because of the centrality of the contract of sale in the edifice of classical *fiqh*. Commercial law and family law also followed suit. Codes and ordinances are common in both fields, with the minor exception of Saudi Arabia where a family law code is absent. Codification is the pivot of civil, commercial, and family law, but laws on the books, in the Middle East as elsewhere, find their fuller reality in the way they are applied in the courtroom. This last feature, that of French 'jurisprudence' or English 'case-law' or 'precedent', has so far been generally ignored in the study of contemporary Middle Eastern law, as it was in the treatment of classical Islamic law. Work on court registers marks a qualitative breakthrough in the scholarship of Islamic and Middle Eastern law, and is destined to shape a new and more scientific understanding of law in the Middle East. Reliance on court decisions is increasingly important in the modern age. Codes defined the emergence of the 'age of codification,' but private law in the Middle East, as elsewhere, cannot be understood outside the application of the law in court.

In the study of civil, commercial, and family law in Part III of the book, a new age is forming before our eyes, 'the age of jurisprudence' in the French sense of the term. In the age of jurisprudence, which is 'new' to the extent that scholarship is increasingly giving case-law the central attention it deserves in the proper study of any legal system, courts and their production of justice are key. In Arabic, the French concept of jurisprudence is commonly translated as *ijtihad*, and the case-law of the courts as *ijtihad al-mahakem*. Considering the heavy polysemy of *ijtihad*, my choice of the word is deliberate.

Private law is a privileged field in the search for a Middle Eastern legal family, and the style and substance of the law of obligations in several countries central to the analysis because of the wealth of the documentation available. Private law tends to be less clouded by political overtones than public law. Legal discussion pursues a steadier scientific course in private law disciplines. But scholarly distance does not mean that the debate over the *shari'a* and its role in private law has remained aloof from politics. Quite the contrary, although distance here is salutary.

metaphor: from Islamic courts to the Palace of Justice (Albany, NY, 1992). We lack a good introduction to the Iranian legal system, but see the successive entries in the country survey sections of *Yearbook of Islamic and Middle Eastern Law*, i, ii, iii (1994–7), by M. A. Ansari-Pour.

[15] See Part II, especially Chapter 4 on constitutions and Chapter 6 on criminal law.

8

Civil Law: Style and Substance

I assure you that we did not leave a single sound provision of the *shari'a* which we could have included in this legislation without so doing.

Sanhuri

As with public law issues, which are often raised in the context of the relationship between Islam and the modern state, the development of civil and commercial transactions could not escape the shadow cast by the age-old legacy of classical law, *fiqh*. The impact of *fiqh* on everyday transactions renders distinct the place of Middle Eastern law among the great legal systems of the world.

Fiqh as the common backbone of the contemporary Middle Eastern law of obligations is an uncertain and controversial hypothesis. The precise influence of the Islamic legal tradition on civil and commercial matters has been the subject of a century-long debate which goes back to the first codifications in the Ottoman Empire. Like the multi-headed hydra, this persistent question gets repeatedly raised, and the end of long and tortuous analyses on the different forms of application—or lack therof—of Islamic law to transactions in the Middle East is not in sight. Although the influence of the tradition on the contemporary scene may be debated, the prime place of civil law in the Islamic legal order cannot be doubted: the law of obligations, which has developed notably around the contract of sale, is one of the most sophisticated areas in classical Islamic law.[1]

Several approaches help clarify the dialectics between the classical tradition and modern law for daily actions and transactions.

A first approach dwells on the statutes enacted during the colonial era, when whole codes were copied from the West. During the legal *aggiornamento* which started in the mid-nineteenth century, several codes inspired by the civil law system were enacted in the Mashreq and in North Africa. In the Ottoman Levant (now Turkey, Syria, Lebanon, Israel-Palestine, Iraq, and Jordan), a code of commercial procedure was introduced in 1861, followed by a maritime code (1863), in addition to several statutes on commercial law which had been introduced wholesale in the previous decade. Most remarkable was the enactment of the

---

[1] For centrality of the law of sale in a classical context, see Chapter 2, section on *fiqh*. For its importance in commercial and economic law, see Chapter 9, section on the classical tradition.

French commercial code in the Ottoman Empire in 1850, which was also adopted in Egypt until its replacement by new laws in the twentieth century. French-style commercial codes were also introduced in most Middle Eastern countries.

Between such outright plagiarism, and the hanging onto the classical system in the absence of any major codification in states like the soon-to-become Kingdom of Saudi Arabia, a qualitative breakthrough took place in the shape of the Ottoman Majalla. Its success was immediate, and its enactment (official title: in Ottoman *Mecelle-yi ahkam-ı adliye, Majallat al-ahkam al-ʿadliyya* in Arabic) led to numerous Ottoman and Arab editions, and to several commentaries.[2] As the Ottoman legislator remained loyal to the spirit of *fiqh*, classical law was both strengthened and radically transformed in the process.

In his reference treatise on Islamic law, Linant de Bellefonds speaks of modern family codes in terms of 'legislative monuments'.[3] This expression describes even more aptly many compendia of the law of obligations which suceeded the Majalla across the Middle East.[4]

The Majalla is over 125 years old. It held sway in Palestine, Jordan, Iraq, Syria, Lebanon, and Turkey until the adoption of more recent codes. In Israel, a special statute abolished the Majalla in 1984,[5] after it had remained in force for a long time as a central reference for many contracts and transactions.[6] The Majalla still governs certain jurisdictions in the Middle East as a residual code, notably in the Occupied Territories. But it is in Jordan, where it stayed in force until the enactment of the Jordanian Civil Code in 1976, that the mark of the Majalla as institutional continuum is the most remarkable.[7] The spirit of the Majalla has permeated the entire Middle East ever since its enactment, which represented a major formal break with the taboo of codification in the millennium-long Islamic legal tradition.[8] The Majalla works as the archetype for all codified Middle Eastern civil law and marks the necessary starting point for the analysis of contemporary civil codes.

Before reviewing the law of obligations in the Middle East since the Majalla, some methodological perspectives inspired by contemporary research in comparative law may be useful.

---

[2] ʿAli Haydar (d. 1918), *Durar al-hukkam fi sharh Majallat al-ahkam*, also translated into Arabic by Fahmi al-Husaini, 4 vols. (Beirut edn., 1991) (the first volume of *Durer ul-hukkam, serh-i mecellet ul-ahkam* was published in Istanbul in 1881); Salim Rustom Baz (d. 1920), *Sharh al-Majalla*, 3rd edn. (Beirut, 1923 (orig. 1889)).

[3] Yvon Linant de Bellefonds, *Traité de droit musulman comparé* (Paris, 1965) vol. i, 42.

[4] An Egyptian lawyer expressly speaks of 'monument législatif' for the Egyptian Civil Code, see Chavagat, in *Travaux de la semaine internationale de droit, Paris, 1950- L'influence du Code Civil dans le monde* (Paris, 1954) 905.

[5] 38 Laws of the State of Israel 212, cited in Shimon Shetreet, *Justice in Israel: a study of the Israeli judiciary* (Dordrecht, 1994) 45. In Jordan, which formally controlled the territories west of the Jordan river until their occupation by Israel in 1967, the Majalla was replaced by the Jordanian Civil Code of 1976.

[6] Y. Meron, 'The Mejelle tested by its application', *Israel Law Journal*, 5, 1970, 203–15.

[7] In the Occupied Territories, the new Jordanian Code was never enacted, and so the Majalla remains law, with particular complications resulting from Israeli occupation, and the treaties following the Oslo Agreement in 1993.

[8] On this aspect of Islamic law, see Chapter 2 n. 490, Chapter 7 n. 1 and accompanying texts.

The work of Konrad Zweigert and Hein Kötz offers a useful model for the comparative law of obligations in the Middle East. For the German comparativists, the question is more about 'styles' than about rules or compilations. For this purpose, they have listed a number of criteria in the first volume of their *Introduction to comparative law*, notably '(1) the historical background [of a system] and its development; (2) [its] privileged and dominant method of legal thinking; (3) [its] distinct and specific institutions; (4) its identification of legal sources and their use; (5) its ideology'.[9]

To the list should be added vocabulary, which is particularly idiosyncratic in the law of obligations within each important legal family of the world.

Without dwelling at length on each of these criteria, the question is whether one common denominator that links them can be identified as Middle Eastern 'style'. My answer is positive: the specificity of Middle Eastern classical history, its more recent struggle against colonialism against a background of transnational Arab and Islamic influences, the importance of *fiqh*, the Qur'an and Sunna as legal reference points, all form a common background to the characteristic institutions which give a particularly familiar quality to Middle Eastern civil law.[10] This family air suffuses civil law in the two original Majallas of the Maghreb and the Mashreq, the Tunisian and the Ottoman, in the formation of which specific legislative goals of the drafters converge, together with their open drawing upon common doctrinal sources like the sixteenth-century Levantine Hanafi jurist, Ibn Nujaym (d. 970/ 1563).[11] A particular reference to the central role of custom illustrates this convergence: 'The *shari'a* was not content with merely taking into account custom, that is modern practices, but it also looked for them as they change. The general rule, according to Ibn Farhun, Ibn Nujaym and others, is that any law built on a practice or a tradition changes when the practice is altered.' This passage appears in the Introduction to the Tunisian Majalla of 1906.[12] Use of Ibn Nujaym is even more pervasive in the Ottoman Majalla, where his 'rules' were incorporated as 'general principles' and acquired immense authority as legal maxims in the Arab-speaking

---

[9] Konrad Zweigert and Hein Kötz, *An introduction to comparative law*, 3rd edn. (Oxford, 1998) 68.

[10] e.g. *shuf'a* (pre-emption) and *waqf* in land law, *hasr al-irth* (judicial inventory of the estate) in the law of succession, *majlis al-'aqd* (contractual session) in the law of contracts, *daman*, strict liability in the law of torts. More on these two key legal categories in the present chapter.

[11] Ibn Nujaym (d. 970/1563), *Al-Ashbah wal-naza'er*, Zakariyya 'Umairat ed., (Beirut, 1999). The genre (lit. similarities, also known as *qawa'ed*, rules) has not been well studied despite its importance as prototype 'private restatement'. The two most famous *Ashbah* authors are the Hanafi Ibn Nujaym and the earlier Hanbali Ibn Rajab (d. 795/1393), *al-Qawa'ed*, ed. Taha Sa'd, 2nd edn. (Beirut, 1988). An excellent update of the literature is by Wolfhart Heinrichs, '*Qawa'id* as a genre of legal literature', in Bernard Weiss, ed., *Studies in Islamic legal theory* (Leiden, 2002) 365–84. See also the discussion of the *Ashbah* genre in a historical context, above Chapter 2 *in fine*, and Chapter 7.

[12] David Santillana, rapporteur of the Committee for the Tunisian civil codification which was established in 1896, '*Ta'rib kalimat al-ustadh Santillana muqarrir al-lajna allati ta'allafat li-i'dad mashari' al-qawanin al-tunisiyya*', preface to *Majallat al-iltizamat wal-'uqud al-tunisiyya* (Tunisian Code of obligations and contracts), Mahmud ibn al-Shaykh ed. (Tunis, 1984) 16. Ibn Farhun (d. 799/1397) is an author from the Maliki school, which is dominant in North Africa, and the author of *Tabsirat al-hukkam*.

Middle East. The two best-known maxims state that 'legal rules change with time'[13] and that 'custom binds like a contract'.[14] They can be found within a set of principles that favour custom and practice (Arts. 37 to 45 of the Ottoman Majalla), including the importance of commercial practice for the determination of the law;[15] or, in a more prosaic vein, the example given by Article 40 in support of the principle that 'practice prevails':[16] 'That is to say, a person mandated to buy something for breakfast must buy what is usually required for that purpose, and not all the food for sale [in the store]'.[17] Likewise, the Tunisian Majalla refers to the supremacy of custom in some twenty articles. In discussing the obligations of the vendor, for instance, Article 603 explains that all the rules adduced must give way to 'local practice and the obligations of the parties'.[18] Custom is law also for obligations generally (Art. 516 Tunisian Majalla), sale (Art. 610), brokerage fees (Art. 604), credit sale (Art. 677), and agent's compensation (Art. 1144).

In Middle Eastern countries today, the practising jurist pays little attention to the Ottoman Majalla, having usually encountered it briefly in a course on the history of the institutions or in an introduction to civil law. Legislation has a poor memory, which shamelessly erases its predecessors, and a new civil code renders the old civil code immediately obsolete. An old code may remain in the habits of a profession—lawyers or magistrates whose entrenched habits render novelty disturbing—it immediately disappears in application. This disappearance itself is governed by law. In the Tunisian Majalla, the order of 15 December 1906 enacting the new law laconically stipulates in clause 3 that 'the rules of this Majalla must [henceforth] be applied in our Tunisian tribunals'.[19] Preceding laws are invariably superseded, save for the limited cases of conflict of laws in time. While preserving a residual role for the Majalla,[20] the Lebanese Code of Obligations and Contracts of 1932 bluntly repealed previous legislation: 'All the provisions of the Majalla and other previous legislation which are contrary to the present Code

[13] *la yunkar taghayyur al-ahkam bi-taghayyur al-azman* (Art. 39 Majalla).

[14] *al-ma'ruf 'urfan kal-mashrut shartan*, Art. 43 (lit. 'what is known as a custom is like what is known as a condition[al clause]').

[15] *al-ma'ruf bayna al-tujjar kal-mashrut baynahum*, Art. 44 (lit. 'what is known amongst merchants is like what is contracted between them').

[16] *al-haqiqa tutrak bi-dalalat al-'ada*, Art. 40 (lit. 'truth is left behind by custom').

[17] *ya'ni law wakkalta insanan bi-shira' ta'am walima la tashtari illa al-ta'am al-mu'tad fi mithliha la kull ma yu'kal*, comment on Art. 40 by 'Ali Haydar, *Durar al-hukkam*.

[18] The Tunisian Majalla was reproduced in calque by the Moroccan Code of 1913 (*Qanun al-iltizamat wal-'uqud*, code of obligations and contracts), and Art. 603 of the Tunisian Majalla was adopted verbatim in Art. 509 of the Moroccan Code. The corresponding articles are as follows: Art. 516 Tunisian Majalla = Art. 463 Moroccan Code, on the importance of custom in obligations generally; Art. 610 Tunisian Majalla = Art. 516 Moroccan Code on sale generally; Art. 604 Tunisian Majalla = Art. 510 Moroccan Code on brokerage fees; Art. 677 Tunisian Majalla = Art. 578 Moroccan Code on credit sale; Art. 1144 Tunisian Majalla = Art. 916 Moroccan Code on attorney's compensation.

[19] Decree in Tunisian Majalla, 23.

[20] *Bunasar v. Holikian*, Cassation Court (5th Chamber), 26 September 2000, reverts to Art. 945 of the Majalla for a case of incapacity ('*uth*), *Baz Reporter* (*Khulasat al-qararat al-sadira 'an mahkamat al-tamyiz al-madaniyya* 2000) (Beirut, 2001) 860.

of Obligations and Contracts or which cannot be reconciled with its terms are hereby repealed.' (Art. 1106). Other Arab codes have also followed this principle, typically reproducing an express provision of the Egyptian Code of 1949 which provides that any preceding text is repealed by the new law.[21]

In its break with the past, law works like the postulate of Saussurian linguistics, favouring the self-standing nature of language as a synchronic system. For Saussure, words may have roots, a history, and an etymology, but the language as a functioning whole is self-sufficient in time. Language functions like a closed system, the rules of which are internal and ahistorical. This is also the case with codes. The life of the code as an institution begins once the codification debate is over, that is when the legislative decree is passed by the competent executive authority, or the law enacted by parliament. As a rule, the previous law disappears. As language and style, however, if not in substantive law, it remains alive. In the case of civil law, the game of memory lost and regained takes place over several historical layers.

This chapter focuses on the codes governing the law of obligations in the Middle East as an institutional reference. Compared with the musical chairs' patterns of constitutions, codes make a firm impression on the field of daily obligations, and enjoy remarkable stability over time. Except for recent attempts to give effect to constitutions through constitutional courts and councils, constitutional texts tend to be ignored in practice, especially in the articles on human rights which are made ineffective by the executive power's arbitrary use of violence.[22] In contrast, Middle Eastern codes represent a solid basis for the daily application of civil transactions by ordinary courts, in part because everyday transactions take place away from the echelons of power. There may be a more compelling reason: in the quality of legal work that accompanied the modernization of civil law, notably in the Ottoman and Tunisian Majallas for the first generation and the 'Sanhuri codes' for the second, civil codes are the product of substantial analysis in the public sphere and result from an important debate between experts. In contrast with constitutions which often emerge, collapse, or get frozen though the whimsical attitude of the powers that be, civil codes do not get subjected to easy modifications or set aside for expeditious reasons. Although they erase their predecessors in principle, the civil law monuments take into account preceding texts, if only to better distinguish themselves.

When new civil codes were enacted in the Mashreq, they erased Ottoman legislation. A similar erasure affected *fiqh* when it was seized by the Majalla. For those who drafted the Majalla, Ahmad Jawdat, Sayf al-Din, al-Sayyed Khalil, Ahmad Khalusi, the main goal was eminently practical: 'Transactions cover in *fiqh*', they explained in their introductory Report, 'what goes by the name of civil law'.[23] The

---

[21] Law 131, 1948, Art. 1, repealing the Egyptian Civil Codes of 1875 and 1883. Decree-law 84, 18 May 1949 in Syria, repealing the Majalla and the statutes of the French Mandate period.

[22] Conclusion of Chapter 5, above.

[23] Ottoman Majalla, Reporters' introduction, Muharram 1286/Avril 1869, in Baz, *Sharh*, 9; civil law, *qanun madani*.

particular wealth in the field, especially in Hanafi law, they added, is well-known:[24] 'The hope is to offer a work on legal transactions which is precise, easily accessible, free of contradictions, includes chosen legal maxims, and is easy to read. Such a book would be of immense interest to all legal officers and members of secular tribunals, . . . thereby allowing reconciliation of trials and religious law'.[25]

So emerged a practical treatise, enacted between 1869 and 1876, which was inspired exclusively by Hanafi law, to govern the area of 'civil law'. While the field understood in the Majalla as 'civil law' does not conform exactly with the issues addressed by its illustrious French predecessor, the Ottoman Civil Code proved in certain aspects to be more logical and better thought out than the Napoleonic Code, as appears in its structure and its durability.

The Majalla: Structure

The Majalla consists of an introduction and sixteen books. The sixteen books that follow its long foundational Preamble have adopted the classical language and turn of phrase in various fields of contract, tort, and civil procedure, drawing heavily on the age-old riches of Middle Eastern Islamic law. Together, these fields form the non-ritualistic part of the law which, in contrast to the strictly religious world of worship,[26] constitutes the world of 'transactions'[27] in the *summa divisio* established by classical Islamic law.

Neither in classical law nor in the Majalla is there a general theory of contracts. 'General principles' adumbrate an overall architecture, but they remain too broad to bring comfort to lawyers. To balance a blurred picture, the Majalla, following the example of *fiqh* treatises, gives particular importance to a model contract at the heart of the system, the contract of sale. Sale is the subject of the Majalla's first book, and comprises over 300 articles (Arts. 101 to 403). The book is followed by the treatment of lease[28] (Book II), guarantee[29] (Book III), transfer[30] (Book IV), pledge[31] (Book V), deposit[32] (Book VI), gift[33] (Book VII), violation[34] (Book VIII), interdiction, duress, pre-emption[35] (Book IX), companies[36] (Book X), agency[37] (Book XI), settlement and release[38] (Book XII), admission[39] (Book XIII), action[40] (Book XIV), evidence and oath[41] (Book XV), and a final book on the judiciary[42]

---

[24] ibid. 10.

[25] Baz, *Sharh*, 11: legal transactions, *mu'amalat fiqhiyya*; law, *shar'*; secular tribunals, *mahakim nizamiyya*; trials, *da'awi*; religious law, *al-shar' al-sharif*.   [26] *'ibadat.*

[27] *mu'amalat.* A thought-provoking article by James Whitman, 'Long live the hatred of Roman law!', *Rechtsgeschichte*, 2, 2003, 40–57, suggests a *summa divisio* between families of law based on those that embrace rituals as part of the law, like Islamic law, and those that don't, like Roman law. To make sense of the law of rituals in the Islamic tradition, see Marion Katz, *Body of text: the emergence of the Sunni law of ritual purity* (Albany, NY, 2002).   [28] *ijara.*

[29] *kafala.*   [30] *hawala.*   [31] *rahn.*   [32] *amana.*   [33] *hiba.*   [34] *ghasb.*
[35] *hajr, ikrah, shuf'a.*   [36] *sharikat.*   [37] *wikala.*   [38] *sulh, ibra'.*   [39] *iqrar.*
[40] *da'wa.*   [41] *bayyinat, tahlif.*   [42] *qada'.*

(Book XVI), which ends with Article 1851 of the Ottoman Civil Code.[43] The subjects governed by the Majalla are wide-ranging, and include both substance and procedure. One also finds themes that appear surprising at first, for instance water law, which is developed in the book on companies and which includes irrigation rights and rights to drinkable water (Arts. 1262 ff), the regulation of wells (Arts. 1281 ff), water courses and their maintenance (Arts. 1321 ff), next to rules governing land division and civil and commercial companies (Book X on companies, Arts. 1045–448). Here, common property in its various legal applications explains the logic of the Majalla. A good lawyer with some knowledge of the tradition can find the relevant articles for his case without much trouble.

As in the Napoleonic Code, the Majalla provides rules on torts. While keeping to general principles in accordance with classical *fiqh*, tort rules are distributed between the Preamble and Book VIII dealing with 'violation'. In the Preamble, the best-known principles are found in Articles 19 and 20. Article 19 is rooted in the *hadith* establishing a general principle of strict liability, which is couched in poetical *hadith* terms.[44] The principle is confirmed in the next maxim, which demands that 'any harm be repaired' (Art. 20).[45] These articles are part of a *fiqh* corpus which stands in sharp contrast to the theory of responsibility in modern Western law.[46]

Excluded from the Majalla are two fields which a French civilist would find in a civil code: ownership, especially ownership of land (with the exception of water law), and family law. A conjunction of factors and the logic of *fiqh* explains why the Ottoman legislator avoided this subject. Land ownership had been regulated in separate legislation before the Majalla was compiled because of the urgency felt by the Ottoman state to clarify a complicated and unruly field.[47] Land reform was pressing and the state interests forced a different rhythm on land regulations. Family law, in contrast, did not present much urgency, and was codified much later, just before the collapse of the Ottoman Empire in 1917.

The most famous text of the Majalla is the Preamble, which is eminently didactic. Its first article offers a definition of the 'science of law': '*Fiqh* is the science of practical legal questions'.[48] The definition is followed by ninety-nine articles making up the best-known part of the Majalla. They are described as 'general

---

[43] Compare structure of classical texts by Sarakhsi and Kasani, Chapter 2, and the Egyptian Civil Code below.

[44] '*la darar wa la dirar*', an alliterative but redundant aphorism, originally a *hadith*, which Art. 19 of the Majalla reproduces verbatim, see Subhi Mahmasani, *Al-Nazariyya al-'amma lil-mujibat wal-'uqud fil-shari'a al-islamiyya* (General theory of obligations and contracts in Islamic law), 2 vols (Beirut, 1948) i, 214–15.   [45] Art. 20 Majalla, *al-darar yuzal.*

[46] Details below in section on torts.

[47] Law of 1858, which has given way to a significant literature of a mostly socio-historical nature. On land property in the Middle East, see e.g. Roger Owen, ed., *New perspectives on property and land in the Middle East* (Cambridge, Mass., 2001); Ann Elizabeth Mayer, ed., *Property, social structure and law in the modern Middle East* (New York 1985), and my review in the *American Journal of Comparative Law*, 35, 1987, 408–13; Farhat Ziadeh, *Property law in the Arab world* (Leiden, 1979).

[48] *Al-fiqh 'ilm bil-masa'el al-shar'iyya al-'amaliyya.*

principles',[49] and take the form of a series of succinct legal statements, some of which are committed to memory by many a Middle Eastern jurist to this day. Many form a common cultural reference point for Arab lawyers: 'In contractual matters, intent and meaning take precedence over wording and syntax';[50] 'acts are judged by intent';[51] 'the presumption is that things remain as they are';[52] 'harm must be repaired';[53] 'harm cannot be old',[54] 'the absence of debt is presumed'.[55]

There are several reasons why these statements are so well-known. In addition to being concise, they command legal consequences which, without always being easy to understand or apply, have generated an important exegesis which has considerably enriched the legal debate. One example is Article 2, *al-umur bi-maqasidiha*. My translation, 'things are judged by intent', gives a subjective interpretation of the *shari'a*, where intent commands interpretation. An early commentator illustrates the maxim as follows: 'If a man finds an object lost in the street and takes it with the intention of returning it to its owner, the object remains in his possession. If subsequently the object perishes, he would not be responsible. If however he has taken the object with the intention of keeping it, he will be held responsible for the loss of the object even in the absence of fault or of negligence on his part'.[56] Risk for the loss of the object depends on the finder's intention to keep it for himself, or to return it to its original owner. In the latter case, the finder in possession of the object is no longer responsible for its loss. This illustration is adopted in Article 769 of the Majalla regarding finders' possession of a lost object.

This maxim in Article 2, 'things are judged by the intent' of their author, like the article that follows it, 'the criteria for contract rests on intent not on expression',[57] derive from a well-known *hadith*: 'An act is judged upon intent'.[58] It consecrates, at first glance, the subjective nature of Islamic law. But if the last term in Article 2, *maqased*, were to be translated literally as 'objects' or 'objectives', we would be faced with a diametrically opposed view of the Majalla and, by extension, of Islamic law. This vision of the objective nature of Islamic law is strongly defended by 'Abd al-Razzaq al-Sanhuri:

Our presentation can be summarized [as follows:] the most important principle in matters of contractual interpretation in Islamic law is that the word is understood in its clear meaning, and that it is not feasible to stray from this meaning on the pretence of interpreting the

---

[49] *al-qawa'ed al-kulliyya*.
[50] Al-'ibra fil-'uqud lil-maqased wal-ma'ani, la lil-alfaz wal-mabani (Art. 3).
[51] *al-umur bi-maqasidiha* (Art. 2).   [52] *al-asl baqa' ma kan 'ala ma kan* (Art. 5).
[53] *al-darar yuzal* (Art. 20).   [54] *al-darar la yakun qadiman* (Art. 7).
[55] *al-asl bara'at al-dhimma* (Art. 8).   [56] Baz, *Sharh*, comment on Art. 2.
[57] Majalla, Art. 3, '*al-'ibra fil-'uqud lil-maqased wal-ma'ani, la lil-alfaz wal-mabani*'. Compare the French translation of the Majalla by Rota and Adamides, 'Code Civil Ottoman', in George Young, ed., *Corps de droit ottoman* (Oxford, 1906) vol. vi: 'Dans les conventions il faut considérer l'intention des parties et non le sens littéral des mots et des phrases employés'.
[58] *innama al-a'mal bil-niyyat*, a famous aphorism which can be found for instance in *Mukhtasar sahih Muslim*, Mustafa al-Bagha ed. (Damascus, 1990) 319; *Sahih al-Bukhari*, Muhammad and Nizar

intention of the parties. In this respect, Islamic law is in agreement with Western law. Islamic law, in contrast with Roman law, goes no further than the intention as expressed, and is not preoccupied with internal motive. If it becomes necessary to interpret the intention of the parties, the main source for interpretation is to be found in the expressions and statements that the parties used in the contract.[59]

There is no agreement on the objective or subjective nature of unilateral or bilateral contracts in Islamic law. It is impossible to square Articles 2 and 3 of the Majalla, which favour intention, with Sanhuri's analysis, which favours outward expression. In the absence of a decisive answer, one must be content with a compromise which is unclear in law, but which forces us to show some scepticism towards 'grand' principles resulting from a corpus that cannot be summarized easily. Sanhuri's reference to objectivity finds support, for instance, in the need for a formulation in the past of the deed of sale.[60] At the opposite end of the scale, Article 769 of the Majalla that governs the status of the lost and found object which perishes in the hands of its finder depends expressly on the finder's intention.

Some of the introductory articles themselves seem to negate the subjective nature suggested by Articles 2 and 3. Article 6,[61] a variation on the preceding article which deals with things remaining as they are,[62] can be read in conjunction with other maxims as an illustration of the objective theory of expressed declaration. If, for instance, a drainpipe in a house has been leaking over a neighbour's property for a long time, the owner of the house will not be held responsible. Article 13 states that 'deduction is not permitted where facts are clear',[63] and this principle of objective interpretation is reinforced by the maxims 'no interpretation in presence of a text',[64] and 'words are presumed true'.[65] Such literal construction is complicated by the fact that custom has precedence over literal understanding: 'The literal meaning of a word can be altered by custom'.[66]

There is therefore uncertainty over this issue, if not plain incoherence. Regardless of the details given in the Ottoman Majalla, notably in the introductory book, the intellectual pedigree of these general principles is doubly established.

Tamim eds. (Beirut, 1995) 11. In the large index of Sunni *hadith* of A. J. Wensinck (completed by J. P. Mensing), *Concordance et indices de la tradition musulmane: les Six Livres, le Musnad d'al-Darimi, le Muwatta' de Malik, le Musnad de Ahmad ibn Hanbal*, 2nd edn. (Leiden, 1992) (8 vols in 4, orig. edn. pub. between 1936 and 1988), one finds the *hadith* in Abu Dawud, Tirmidhi, Nisa'i, ibn Maja and Ahmad ibn Hanbal, vol. vii, 55.

[59] 'Abd al-Razzaq al-Sanhuri, *Masader al-haqq fil-fiqh al-islami* (Sources of law in Muslim *fiqh*), 6 vols. (Cairo, 1954–9) vol. vi, 35.

[60] The formula *bi't*, I sold, is considered as a firm offer, by contrast with the verbal mode *abi'*, I sell, which is not decisive in Muslim law for the formation of a contract. Kasani (d. 587/1191) is more nuanced on the question in *Bada'e' al-sana'e'*, v, 133; see discussion in Chapter 3, section on *fiqh*.

[61] *al-qadim yutrak 'ala qidamih*, lit. 'the old is left to its old status'.

[62] Art. 5 Majalla: '*al-asl baqa' ma kan 'ala ma kan*, presumption is for things to remain as they are'.

[63] *la 'ibra lil-dalala fi muqabalat al-tasrih*.   [64] Art. 14, *la masagh lil-ijtihad fi mawrid al-nass*.

[65] Art.12, *al-asl fil-kalam al-haqiqa*.

[66] As per the French translation of Art. 40, *al-haqiqa tutrak bi-dalalat al-'ada*, by Rota and Adamides, above n. 57. I simplified the translation into 'practice prevails' above, text at n. 16.

In their original aspect, some of these principles repeat maxims which hail from the tradition ascribed to the Prophet. Article 76 is a case in point, which states that 'proof is incumbent upon the plaintiff and oath upon the defendant',[67] a maxim borrowed straight from the *hadith*.[68] Similarly, Article 85 is a *hadith* that establishes that risk for loss of an object falls upon the person who was receiving benefit from that object.[69]

The other sources, although less prestigious, are no less solidly rooted in *fiqh*. They come from the great classical treatises, from the early period through to the anthologies of 'Indian fatwas',[70] in addition to the *Ashbah* genre,[71] notably the treatise of Ibn Nujaym, who also inspired the Tunisian Majalla as acknowledged in its introductory report.[72] There are numerous examples of Ibn Nujaym's direct influence on the Majalla. The maxim 'he who remains silent consents to nothing'[73] in Article 67 of the Ottoman Majalla appears in Ibn Nujaym's original text with the following explanation:

If a man sees another selling his property and stays silent, he is not bound by his silence; if a judge sees a minor or a legally incapable person or their slaves buying and selling and he remains silent, this does not constitute a permission to sell; and if a guarantor sees the person he has guaranteed ceding the guarantee and remains silent, the guarantee remains valid.[74]

To this text and its applications, Ibn Nujaym added thirty-seven exceptions.[75] One of the main exceptions is also incorporated into Article 67 of the Majalla. After establishing the legal neutrality of silence as principle, Article 67 adds a reservation: 'In a case of necessity, silence is evidence'[76] of the formation of contract.

The Spread of the Majalla

In the Middle East, the Majalla's legal influence should never be underestimated. This influence is obvious where it remained in force until replaced by completely redrafted codes. In Lebanon, it was repealed in 1932 by the Code on Obligations and Contracts, but it governed civil law in Syria until 1949, in Iraq until 1953, in Kuwait until 1960. In each of these countries, the Majalla remained the original fundamental legislative monument, against a background of shifting constitutional and penal laws dominated by the various mandates and protectorates. Even in Turkey, where it was abrogated by a Swiss Civil Code introduced by the

---

[67] *al-bayyina lil-mudda'i wal-yamin lil-munkir.*

[68] Wensinck, i, 258 (references to Bukhari, Tirmidhi, ibn Maja).

[69] *al-kharaj bil-daman,* Art. 85, Wensick, ii, 23 (references to Abu Dawud, Tirmidhi, Nisa'i, ibn Maja, Ahmad ibn Hanbal). See also Art. 87, *al-ghurm bil-ghunum,* which has the same meaning.

[70] *Al-fatawa al-'alamgiriyya* and *Al-fatawa al-tatarkhaniyya;* Baz, *Sharh,* 11. These fatwas are in reality *fiqh* books, and not fatwa compilations, as the title would otherwise suggest.

[71] Above n. 11.   [72] Cited above n. 12.   [73] *la yunsab ila sakitin qawl.*

[74] Ibn Nujaym, *al-Ashbah wal-naza'er,* 129.   [75] ibid. 129–31.

[76] *lakinna al-sukut fi ma'rad al-haja bayan.*

helvetophile minister for justice,[77] one should recall that the Majalla dominated the Ottoman then Turkish judicial world for half a century. Half a century of case-law is not insignificant, and the decisions can be read in the Ottoman language in law journals published at the time, while others were rendered in Arabic, some well after Istanbul had lost its power over the region.[78] Contrary to some constitutional texts dating back to that era, civil law was never suspended. And in contrast to constitutional laws, which courts have started implementing only exceptionally since the 1980s, civil law has been interpreted and reinterpreted by Middle Eastern courts for over a century.

The success of the Majalla can also be seen in the qualitative comments it elicited. The two most renowned comments were elaborated by Salim Rustom Baz and 'Ali Haidar, whose *Durar al-Hukkam* became a classic in this field. The *Durar*, published in four large volumes, constitutes a fine, detailed, exegesis. Unfortunately, it does not include Ottoman or Arabic case-law, but it offers sophisticated explanations and a valuable system of classical references.[79]

The Majalla's influence spread far beyond the Levant. In Egypt, as a model for codification, it paved the way for the first private restatements that followed the Western-style Codes of 1876 and 1883. It also inspired the masterly works of Muhammad Qadri Basha, the Egyptian Minister of Justice at a key juncture of legislative enactments.[80] In the Maghreb, similar attempts could be found in the Code Morand (Algeria, 1916, abolished by the Civil Code of 1976), and the Santillana restatement (Preliminary report on the Tunisian and Moroccan Codes), both more attentive to the Maliki doctrine which is dominant in North Africa. These attempts gave way to the current civil legal monuments: the Tunisian Majalla

---

[77] Zweigert and Kötz, *An Introduction to comparative law*, 178, on the adoption of the Swiss Civil Code in Turkey being attributed to coincidence, the Turkish Minister of Justice at the time having studied in Switzerland. Another explanation is suggested by Ismail Kemal Kabir: 'The reasons which have made Turkey prefer the Swiss Civil Code to all other European codes are the following: it is better and simpler than all other codes; it has a social and popular character, and it is easy to understand. One should also add its elasticity, which gives the judge a large power of appreciation.' *Travaux de la semaine internationale de droit*, above n. 4, 881.

[78] *Ceride-yi mahakim*, Ottoman journal of courts, first issue published by the Ottoman Ministry of Justice, 1879. Collection indexed in *Rahbar-i qavanin laheqe-si* (Istanbul 1301/1888–). For Arabic decisions, see Tamer Mallat (d. 1914), *Ahkam* (Judgments), facsimile edn. of decisions dated 1898–9, which I published in Beirut in 1999. *Huquq*, a bilingual Turkish-Arabic law journal and reporter, was started in Istanbul in 1307/1890.

[79] Above n. 2 for Haydar and Baz. The entry 'Medjelle' by J. H. Kramers in the *Enclycopaedia of Islam*'s 1st edn. (Leiden, 1936), cites other Ottoman commentaries by H. M. Diya' al-Din, and by 'Atif bey. The English translation by C. H. Hooper, *The Civil law of Palestine and Transjordan* (Jerusalem, 2 vols. 1933, 1936), also provides extensive comments. Later Arab authors have written commentaries, most remarkably the Iraqi jurist Muhammad Husayn Kashif al-Ghata', below n. 94.

[80] According to Enid Hill, *Sanhuri and Islamic law* (Cairo, 1987) 16, who follows Farhat Ziadeh, himself quoting Muhammad Husayn Haykal, the biographer of Muhammad Qadri Basha, Minister of Justice between 1879 and 1882. According to Byron Cannon, *Politics of law and the courts in nineteenth-century Egypt* (Salt Lake City, 1988) 130, Qadri Basha was appointed Justice Minister in 1881. He died in 1889. See further below, n. 117 and accompanying text.

of Obligations and Contracts in 1906, and its calque in the Moroccan Code of Obligations and Contracts, which was promulgated by Sultan Moulay Youssef in 1913. These codes, still current, have since been considerably enriched by text-books and case-law. More technical than the Ottoman Majalla, the Tunisian and Moroccan Codes are divided into two books, the first dealing with obligations in general, the second with special contracts (*contrats nommés*: sale, exchange, deposit and sequestration, agency, partnership).[81]

How much of the Majalla and its calques was Islamic law, and how much was received European law?[82] While it is undeniable that the Ottoman Majalla encouraged regional capitals to follow suit, and served as a model across the region, the evasive nature of comparative law inevitably limits any conclusions. At some abstract level, the codification of the law of obligations should be considered as a phenomenon directly inspired by Europe, where Napoleon's Code was imposed through imperial conquest. Such 'reception' of the Civil Code can be rejected or refined variously in the case of the Ottoman Empire, in so far as the codification was essentially that of Islamic, and more precisely Hanafi, law. In North Africa, prima-facie affinities between the Moroccan and Tunisian Codes and the preparatory works of scholars like Santillana and Morand with Islamic law are more striking than their resemblance to the French Civil Code.

Despite the interest in the French Code as the dominant doctrine in France and even in North Africa, a more attentive reading of Santillana and the draft Tunisian Code for which he was responsible reveals the importance of its debt to Islamic law by way of the Ottoman Majalla. The preliminary report elaborated by Santillana, just like that of the Ottoman rapporteurs, shows the delicate balance between 'the law of Europe'[83] and the law of Islam:

> The [legislative] Commission relied generally on the Maliki school, which is followed by the majority of Tunisians. However, it did not hesitate to adopt Hanafi doctrine every time it found that Hanafi rules complied, more than the Maliki ones, with the general system of the [Ottoman] Majalla and the principles of European law. In this project, nothing contradicts the holdings of the most famous jurists in Islam. The Commission was determined to establish rules only in the language of their jurists.[84]

This legal philosophy, expressed in a similar way by the authors of the Ottoman Majalla, can also be found later, when Sanhuri put together the Egyptian Civil Code (ECC). Before examining that other legislative monument, we must investigate the radical change introduced by the Majalla in other comprehensive restatements of the law of obligations in the Middle East which are less known, though no less important.

---

[81] In the Tunisian Majalla, the title of Book 1 refers to 'patrimoine in absolute' (*fima ta'mur bihi al-dhimma mutlaqan*.) The Moroccan Code entitles this part, 'obligations in general'.

[82] For the use of John Wansbrough's calques as concept for historical and comparative law, see Chapter 2.   [83] Santillana, in Tunisian Majalla, 11.

[84] ibid. 19.

Majalla Calques: Iran, Iraq, Saudi Arabia

Outside the Maghreb, the Majalla reached the non-Hanafi world via three routes. The most important calque to date was enacted in Shi'i Persia, which became Iran in 1934. As in the Ottoman Empire, legal reforms started in the late nineteenth century, but it wasn't until the third decade of the twentieth century that the Iranian Civil Code was completed. The Code uses very different sources from the Majalla's. It follows the Ja'fari school of Twelver Shi'ism which was and remains dominant in Iran. The structure of the Iranian Civil Code also differs from the Majalla's. The Code is divided into three books abstractly designed: Book I, promulgated in 1928, deals with property (Arts. 1–955). Book II covers persons (Arts. 956–1256) and Book III evidence (Arts. 1257–335); the latter two books were enacted into law in 1934–5. Contrary to the Majalla, land and family law are governed extensively by the Code. Marriage and divorce are regulated in Section 8 of Book II (Arts. 1534 ff), including the temporary marriage contract known as *sigheh* (Persian) or *mut'a* (Arabic) (Arts. 1577–9), which is only recognized by Shi'i law. The Code also governs succession law, which is included in Book I on property (*ab intestat* succession, Arts. 861–955; wills, Arts. 825–60). Torts, like sales, are governed in the Iranian Code under categories generally drawn from Shi'i *fiqh*. As for torts in the Majalla, the principle of responsibility without fault is the norm, and the occurrence of harm is sufficient to trigger compensation (Art. 328). A law in 1960 sought to mitigate this responsibility, but the 1979 Revolution went back to classical principles.[85] In sales, addressed under the title of nominate contracts,[86] the Iranian legislator combined French classification and *fiqh* terminology, the latter apparent in a long series of articles on options.[87] Interest on loans was tolerated in an indirect manner, no doubt in deference to common practice: 'The debtor may give mandate to the creditor, in a compulsory manner that allows the creditor to acquire, before the loan matures, a specific quantity of goods' (Art. 653).[88] The roundabout language shows the unease of the legislator, who did not wish to openly flout the injunction forbidding *riba* (interest), and resorted to elliptical syntax leading to the same result: to allow fixed interest on current loans ('a specific quantity of goods'). The article did not survive the Islamic Revolution.[89] The current editions of the Iranian Civil Code refer simply to the abrogation of this article.[90]

---

[85] Torts are addressed in Book I as 'obligations that arise without a contract, *dar elzamatike be-dun qarardad hasel mi-shavad*' (Arts. 301–37), and are divided, following the classical categories of the Islamic law of torts (Art. 307). See section on torts below.

[86] *mu'ayyan*, French 'nommés'.

[87] Options, *khiyarat*, Arts. 396–457. See section on options below.

[88] Loan, *qard*, Arts. 648–53.

[89] M. A. Ansari-Pour, 'Prohibition of interest under the Iranian legal system since the Revolution', in Hilary Lewis-Ruttley and Chibli Mallat, eds., *Commercial law in the Middle East* (London, 1995) 180.

[90] *hadhf shodeh*.

The spirit of the Ottoman Majalla is evident in the Iranian Civil Code, which remains the central piece of civil legislation in Iran. Unfortunately, the preparatory works of the Code do not seem to have survived. They were produced by 'a commission established in haste...under the directions of Mr. Davar, a distinguished statesman'.[91] The Commission, which was 'composed of jurisconsults in Muslim law and experienced magistrates', elaborated 'the first part of the Iranian Civil Code...taking into account the basic principles of Islamic law and legal ideas of modern law'.[92] Here again appear the essential components that the Ottoman Majalla gathered into a model, with the difference that legal sources are here Ja'fari rather than Hanafi.

Another similar work to the Iranian Civil Code, and perhaps more important from an intellectual point of view, is the outstanding book achieved by Muhammad Husayn Kashif al-Ghata', a Shi'i scholar from Najaf. Kashif al-Ghata''s political and intellectual contributions in the first half of this century are remarkable, though little known.[93] In the legal field, Kashif al-Ghata' published in the 1940s a detailed article by article commentary on the Majalla from a Shi'i critical point of view.[94] At that time, the Majalla was still law in Iraq, but Kashif al-Ghata''s book remained peripheral, despite its clear importance in a country with an important Shi'i constituency. The multi-volume work coincided with the onset of the Second World War, and was also probably marginalized by the dominant Sunni Iraqi leaders who were more interested in the pan-Arab trend at the time represented in law by 'Abd al-Razzaq al-Sanhuri. Sanhuri had a brief foray in Baghdad as a consultant for the establishment of a new Iraqi civil code.

The outstanding contribution to civil law by Muhammad Husayn Kashif al-Ghata' was never seriously considered, but it is also true that the Iraqi Civil Code of 1953 is not an exact copy of the Egyptian Code, as was the case in that period with the civil codes of Syria and Libya. The legislator in Iraq deferred to the important legacy of the Ottoman Majalla, which had been studied and applied by

---

[91] Ibrahim Docteur-Zadeh, *De la validité des contrats sous la chose d'autrui en droit positif iranien* (Paris, 1939) 57. Main current textbooks on Iranian civil law are by Naser Katuzian, *Huquq-i madani: Qawa'id-i 'umumi-yi qarardadha*, 5 vols. also by Katuzian, *Huquq-i madani: 'Uqud-i mu'ayyan* (Special contracts), 3 vols. and by Husayn Safa'i, *Huquq-i madani*, 2 vols. many of which are updated regularly. On Ali-Akbar Davar (d. 1937), see the entry in Ehsan Yarshater, ed., *Encyclopedica Iranica*, online at <http.www.iranica.com/newsite>.

[92] Djalal Abdoh, 'Aperçu général sur le droit civil de l'Iran', in R. Aghabian, ed., *Législation iranienne actuelle* (Tehran, 1939) 173.

[93] Few works have been published on Kashif al-Ghata' (1877–1954) despite his importance both scholarly and political, until some more recent attention in very different registers by Jawdat al-Qazwini and Silvia Naef. Qazwini published several manuscript texts of Kashif al-Ghata', including *Al-'abaqat al-'anbariyya fil-tabaqat al-ja'fariyya* (Beirut, 1998). Naef discusses his contributions to modern Iraq in several articles, including 'Communisme athée ou démocratie impérialiste? Le choix difficile d'un 'alim chiite dans les premières années de la guerre froide', in *Proceedings of the 17th Congress of the UEAI* (St Petersburg, 1997) 134–45; 'Un réformiste chiite—Muhammad Husayn Al-Kashif al-Ghata' ', *Die Welt des Orients*, 27, 1996, 51–86. No study has yet been carried out, to my knowledge, on his work as a civil law scholar.

[94] Muhammad Husayn Kashif al-Ghata', *Tahrir al-Majalla*, 5 parts in 4 vols. (Najaf, 1940–3).

Iraqi judges and lawyers for over three-quarters of a century. The new Iraqi composite code was attentive to classical terminology, even if some parts were almost entirely copied from Sanhuri's model. In the absence of more thorough research, it is difficult to conclude whether the work of Kashif al-Ghata' was the source of attention to classical Islamic law in the current Iraqi code. This forgotten treatise by one of the foremost jurists of the Najaf school and its relation to the new Iraqi Civil Code deserve a more detailed examination than is possible here. A systematic comparative exercise on the basis of that work would also provide a more precise assessment of the *aggiornamento* of classical Sunni and Shi'i law in the Middle Eastern law of obligations.

Beyond Persia and Mesopotamia, a third calque of the Majalla emerged in Hanbali Saudi Arabia. The Majalla had been enacted in the western part of the Arabian Peninsula under Ottoman control until the First World War, and was law in the holy cities of Mecca and Medina for half a century. The Hijaz, which was predominantly Shafi'i, saw the application of the Hanafi Majalla for several decades, but the history of law in that region of the world is poorly known, especially after Ibn Sa'ud's conquest and the unification of Arabia under a Wahhabi legal regime. A decree issued in 1928 established the Hanbali school, the legal offshoot of political Wahhabism, as the main, if not exclusive, school of law in the kingdom.[95] Hence Hanbalism in the 'Saudi Majalla', another legislative monument in the process of the Middle Eastern codification of civil law. As in the case of *Murshid al-hayran*, the restatement compiled in Egypt at the end of the nineteenth century by Muhammad Qadri Basha, and the Majalla's critical Shi'i edition by the Iraqi Kashif al-Ghata', this codification was an individual, private, endeavour. There remains an important difference between the Saudi calque and the private restatements carried out in Iraq or Egypt: because of the absence of a Saudi civil code, the Hanbali Majalla acquired, in time, a special importance which is difficult to assess in the absence of Saudi law reports, but which the daily practice of Saudi lawyers suggests has grown considerably since its publication in 1980.[96]

The author of the Hanbali Majalla is, curiously, a Hanafi judge, Ahmad ibn 'Abdallah al-Qari. Born into a learned legal family in 1309/1891, Qari studied in a renowned traditional school of Mecca, *al-madrasa al-saltiyya*. This school had been established twenty years earlier by Sheikh Muhammad Rahmatallah al-'Uthmani, who had left his Indian home country to escape British colonialism, and founded the school with the financial support of an Indian philantropist called Sawlat al-Nisa'.[97] This is where young Ahmad al-Qari studied Hanafi *fiqh*, 'which he mastered so well that he was sought for his science by all kinds of

---

[95] According to Schacht, *Introduction to Islamic law*, 101; but a rapid survey of the press in the Hijaz at the time, which I carried out in the Library of Congress in 2002, suggests more nuances than a straightforward imposition of Hanbali law. See also citation below at n. 103.

[96] Ahmad ibn 'Abdallah al-Qari, *Majallat al-ahkam al-shar'iyya*, 'Abdelwahab Ibrahim Abu Suleiman and Muhammad Ibrahim Ahmad 'Ali eds. (Djeddah, 1981). Information on the importance of that work from colleagues in Saudi Arabia.   [97] Hence the school's name. Qari, Majalla, 60.

people'.[98] After the fall of the Hijaz under Saudi control, Qari was appointed judge in Djeddah in 1345/1926, and rose in the hierarchy to become a member of the *Majlis al-shura* (top administrative tribunal) in 1349/1930, and then president of the *Mahkama shar'iyya kubra* of Mecca, probably the equivalent of the supreme civil court at the time. In 1357/1958, he was appointed by royal decree as head of the judiciary,[99] a position he kept until his death in 1359/1940.[100] This is a remarkable feat for a Hanafi:

Among the forgotten pages in the history of the Kingdom of Saudi Arabia, one should recall the decision of King 'Abd al-'Aziz to establish a legal committee[101] to draft a restatement like the Ottoman *Majallat al-ahkam*. This information appears in the official journal *[Umm] al-Qura*, issue number 141.[102] Effectively, the establishment of a committee composed of the best legal experts was envisaged [to draft a code] from the books of all four [Hanafi] schools. Such Majalla would be similar to *Majallat al-ahkam*, which the Ottoman government had enacted in 1293/1876. But it would differ in many respects, especially in its refusal to exclude a particular school. Any rule would be chosen by the committee on the ground of what is most adequate and beneficial to Muslims from all schools, in agreement with the Qur'an and Sunna.[103]

The task of bringing together the four schools must have been cumbersome. Instead of such a synthesis, a list of the six most authoritative books in Hanbali law was adopted to facilitate the work of judges.[104] These books remain to date the major points of reference for Saudi civil law. They were at the origin of Qari's compilation,[105] a compilation that was never published in his lifetime, even if it was probably completed in its first form towards the end of the 1930s. The edition we have is a major contribution to contemporary Hanbali Saudi law. It is remarkable for a set of detailed notes and a proficient introduction put together by two Saudi scholars, 'Abd al-Wahhab Ibrahim Abu Suleiman and Muhammad Ibrahim Ahmad 'Ali.

The structure of the Hanbali Majalla, which was considerably improved by the two editors in comparison to its original incomplete state, is similar to the Ottoman Majalla in its subdivision into books, but it follows the Hanbali approach in certain details of classification. The work contains 2,382 articles divided into 21 books.[106] The Saudi Majalla is therefore significantly longer than its Ottoman predecessor. Like the Ottoman Code, it does not regulate family law or property, and includes procedural aspects, arbitration, evidence, and the 'book of judges'.

---

[98] ibid. 66.   [99] *ri'asat al-qudat, hay'at tamyiz al-ahkam al-'aliya.*

[100] Al-Zarakli, *al-A'lam*, vol. 1, 156, cited in Qari, Majalla, 38.   [101] *lajna fiqhiyya.*

[102] 28 Safar 1347, 26 August 1927.   [103] Qari, Majalla, 29. School, *madhhab.*

[104] Fu'ad Hamza, *Al-Bilad al-'arabiyya al-sa'udiyya* (Arab Saudi country) (Mecca, 1355/1935), 189.

[105] Qari, Majalla, 29. The six Hanbali books are the following: Muwaffaq al-Din ibn Qudama (d. 620/1223), *Al-mughni*; Shams al-Din ibn Qudama (d. 682/1284), *Al-sharh al-kabir*; Musa al-Hijawi (d. 968/1580), *Al-iqna'*; Taqi al-Din Muhammad ibn Ahmad al-Futuhi, a.k.a. ibn al-Najjar (d. 972/1584), *Muntaha al-iradat*; Mansur Bahuti (d. 1051/1641), *Kashshaf al-qina' 'an matn al-iqna'* (gloss of Hijawi); *Sharh muntaha al-iradat* (gloss of Futuhi).

[106] For a useful comparison of the general structure with other restatements and codes, see the introduction to Qari, Majalla, 31–9.

In contrast with the Ottoman Majalla, Qari's compilation does not feature a 'general principles' preamble. The modern editors found in the judge's papers some indications of his intent to complete the work with a general preamble based on the *précis* drafted by the Hanbali jurist Ibn Rajab.[107] The planned preamble was never completed, and they edited these notes in the form of Majalla-style rules. The effort was not carried through systematically. Some 160 preliminary articles were reconstructed, but they cannot be considered maxims like their Ottoman counterparts, for they are neither accurate nor particularly concise.

The first article deals, for instance, with a marginal issue from ritual law, and is couched in the form of a question: 'Is running water similar to stagnant water?' Following ibn Rajab,[108] Qari must have been tempted to include ritual law, which often starts in *fiqh* works with principles dealing with water ablutions, but he did not pursue that line in the compilation. Most other introductory articles also fail as general principles, although some of them retain qualities reminiscent of the Ottoman Majalla's preamble. This is the case with Article 85: 'Rights are five: right to property, like the master's right over the money of [two types of slaves],[109] right to ownership, like the father's right over his son's money, usufruct, like the right of putting wooden piles[?] against the neighbour's wall, right to exclusivity such as lawful profits, and accessory rights that fulfil other rights, like the right over the mortgage of a mortgagor.[110] Details.'[111] Other articles on property rights are also conceived to operate like the Majalla's didactic maxims: 'Property types are four: property of an object and its usufruct, property of an object without its usufruct, property of usufruct without the object, and the property of the use (*usus*) without the profit (*fructus*).'[112] Article 89 on responsibility is in a similar vein: 'Responsibility has three causes: contract, possession [literally "hand"] and damage'.[113]

The unfinished character of the introductory book is also noticeable in its sudden mention of marriage and divorce (Arts. 145 ff), which is not taken up again. The rest of Qari's Majalla is far more precise, and its legal abstraction as well as the accuracy of its structure and syntax are enhanced by a didactic concern. Every book, and every section in each book, starts with a series of legal definitions.[114]

Of the codes and restatements in the age of codification, there only remain officially in force the Iranian Civil Code of the 1930s and the Ottoman Majalla in the Occupied Territories. The Majalla rules are commonly used as a persuasive authority in the Arab Levant, and Qari's Hanbali Majalla provides an increasingly authoritative text in an otherwise uncodified field. Irrespective of formal enforcement, a new legal world has come of age, which the Majalla, mixing the format of the Napoleonic Code with classical Islamic law, has firmly rooted in the Middle

---

[107] Ibn Rajab, *al-Qawa'ed*, above n. 11. [108] Ibn Rajab, *al-Qawa'ed*, 3, rule 1.

[109] *Al-mukatab* and *al-qinn*. [110] *haqq al-murtahin bil-rahn.*

[111] This article, as suggested by this final mention of details, *tafsil* (meaning that details will follow), shows the incomplete nature of the work.

[112] Art. 86: '*al-milk arba'at anwa': milk 'ayn wa manfa'a, wa milk 'ayn bila manfa'a, wa milk manfa'a bila 'ayn, wa milk intifa' min ghayr milk manfa'a.*'

[113] Art. 89: '*asbab al-daman thalathat, 'aqd wa yad wa itlaf.*' [114] *mustalahat fiqhiyya.*

Eastern law of obligations. The rediscovery of the Majalla is not a mere historical exercise, even if the historical enquiry is particularly enriching in and of itself. As was shown by Méliné Topakian, in a then innovative study of the comparative law of sales that included the Majalla alongside other Civil Codes and the project that would in time become the Vienna Convention on the Sale of Goods (1980),[115] the logic and substance of positive law in the Middle East, from Morocco to Iran, cannot be well understood without a detour into the Majalla, an impressive legislative monument of a period too little appreciated considering the exceptional quality of its jurists and lawmakers.

The 'Sanhuri Codes'[116]

From an institutional perspective, the Majalla as legislative monument marked a break with the tradition in two ways: it showed that codification was possible, even necessary; and that codification may, nay should, be composite. It was no longer obligatory to follow the exact rhythm of the classical model, but the classification by books following various contracts was preferred to the abstract subdivisions that the French authors of the late eighteenth century had injected into the architecture of the Napoleonic Code, abstractions which were carried in the German Civil Code (Bürgerlisćhes Gesetzbuch, BGB) to a degree sometimes criticized. Through such a compromise, the Ottoman compilers achieved both intellectual and practical success. The Majalla remains a remarkable success to date in legal history.

By introducing these two characteristics into civil law—codification and mixture—the Ottoman Majalla remains the dean of Middle Eastern civil codes, which is followed in calques from Morocco to Iran. In so far as the legal tradition in Egypt was also particularly rich, it could not lag behind. Egypt was lucky, in its effort to codify the law of obligations, to count amongst its jurists the celebrated 'Abd al-Razzaq al-Sanhuri.

The Majalla was never enacted in Egypt, by then largely independent from the Ottoman Porte. Before Sanhuri, we saw how a private codification of Islamic law had been carried out by Muhammad Qadri Basha. His many achievements include restatements on land ownership and civil law (*Murshid al-hayran*, 1890),[117] *waqf* (*Qanun al-'adl wal-insaf lil-qada' 'ala mushkilat al-awqaf,* 1893), as well as

---

[115] Méliné Topakian, 'Notes sommaires sur le contrat de vente dans les codes proche-orientaux', *Proche-Orient Etudes Juridiques* (Beirut, 1965) 251–69. See now Fatima Akaddaf, 'Application of the United Nations Convention on contracts for the International Sale of Goods (CISG) to Arab Islamic countries: Is the CISG compatible with Islamic law principles?', *Pace International Law Review*, 13, 2001, 1–57.

[116] Felicitous word by Nabil Saleh, 'Civil codes of Arab countries: the Sanhuri Codes', *Arab Law Quarterly*, 8, 1993, 161–7.

[117] Muhammad Qadri, *Kitab murshid al-hayran ila ma'rifat ahwal al-insan fil-mu'amalat al-shar'iyya 'ala madhhab al-Imam al-a'zam Abi Hanifa al-Nu'man mula'iman li-'urf al-diyar al-misriyya*

family law, which he had compiled into a restatement as early as 1875 (*Al-ahkam al-shar'iyya fil-ahwal al-shakhsiyya*). Qadri Basha also inspired other private compilations in North Africa, examples being Santillana in his Avant-projet à la Majalla Tunisienne (1899), and Marcel Morand in Algeria (1916). One finds this concern with codification also in Iraq before the major compilation carried out by Kashif al-Ghata', with an early private initiative to codify Shi'i family law.[118] In Egypt, two sets of very similar codes governed mixed courts whose jurisdiction applied to disputes where one party was not an Egyptian national (Code of 1875) and national courts (Code of 1883). These codes, together with Qadri Basha's compilation, are strongly reflected in Sanhuri's preparatory work for the Egyptian Civil Code. In turn, the Egyptian effort was extremely important in the codification of civil law in the rest of the Arab world.[119]

Born in 1895, 'Abd al-Razzaq al-Sanhuri remains the most famous Arab jurist of the twentieth century. Following studies in Cairo, then in France, where he wrote two theses, the first a comparative study on English law,[120] the other on classical Muslim public law,[121] he returned to Cairo to teach, then head, the main law school—called at the time King Fuad, now Cairo University. By 1936, he had already published important books on contracts,[122] and the government entrusted him with the chairmanship of the Commission responsible for redrafting the Civil Code. The work lasted for over ten years. After several revisions, the bill was enacted into law in 1949.

Throughout the four decades separating Sanhuri's first reflections and his very last pages of the tenth and last volume of his *Wasit*,[123] one is struck by his attention to comparative law.

---

wa-sa'ir al-umam al-islamiyya (The guide to the perplexed about the individual's status in legal transactions according to the school of Abu Hanifa and corresponding to the customs of Egypt and other Islamic nations) (Cairo, 1890).

[118] 'Abd al-Karim al-Hilli, *Al-ahkam al-ja'fariyya fil-ahwal al-shakhsiyya* (Personal status Ja'fari-Shi'i rules) (Baghdad, 1923).

[119] A fine mapping of the civil codes in the region can be found in Gian Maria Piccinelli, *La Società di persone nei paesi arabi* (Rome, 1990) 247, as well as a useful list of the main civil and commercial codes at 267–78.

[120] *Les Restrictions contractuelles à la liberté individuelle du travail dans la jurisprudence anglaise* (Paris, 1925).   [121] *Le Califat* (Paris, 1926).

[122] Notably *Nazariyyat al-'aqd* (Theory of contract) (Cairo, 1934).

[123] *Al-Wasit fi sharh al-qanun al-madani al-jadid* (Medium [but in reality extensive] commentary on the new Civil Code), 10 books in 12 large volumes (Cairo 1952–70). Sanhuri's *Wasit* is the standard reference on civil law for all lawyers in the Arab world. As with the great French civilists' major treatises, the *Wasit* is now updated by successors of Sanhuri ('Abd al-Basit al-Fiqi and 'Abd al-Baset Jami'i). Here I use the original edition. The literature on Arab-Middle Eastern civil law is vast, and I have restricted citations to the most important or most original references, including the recent article by Kilian Bälz, 'Europäisches Privaterecht jenseits von Europa? Zum fünfzigjährigen Jubiläum des ägyptischen Zivilgesetzbuch (1948)', *Zeitschrift für Europäisches Privatrecht*, 2000, 51–76. A useful bibliography in European languages is available in Valentina Donni, 'La responsabilità contrattuale nei codici di Tunisia, Egitto ed Emirati Arabi Uniti', in F. Castro, ed., *Questioni di integrazione giuridica nel mondo arabo e nel mediterraneo* (Rome, 2001) 3–68, at 60–8.

In 1954, the first volume of this magisterial treatise on Egyptian civil law summarized the main traits of Sanhuri's comparative method, already adumbrated in 1934 in a *Theory of contract*:

We should first egyptianize *fiqh*, and turn it into a pure Egyptian *fiqh* that meets our national character, and makes us feel the weight of our own reasoning. Until now, our law has been invaded by foreign influence, and foreign here means French. This occupation is not lighter, nor less inconsequential, than any other invasion. Egyptian law still seeks its guidance from French law; it fails to detach itself from French horizons, or to depart from its course. It lives in its shadow, and follows it faithfully. If we manage to make our law independent, to reproduce it in an Egyptian environment, to build it on Egyptian foundations so that it evolves of its own free will, we need to take that last step, and break out from the national circle to accede to the universal, so that we pay due tribute to humanity to advance law in the world: this is what scholarship agrees to call comparative law.[124]

Here surface the two poles of Sanhuri's method: on the one hand, the legacy of the French model in the precedents it spawned in Egyptian courts, on the other the need for Egyptianization, including its Islamic law component.

Egyptianization developed both in form and substance. In form, Sanhuri's own work provides the key to understanding Egyptian codification in the many stages of his research and commentary on the Code in draft and after its enactment. There is constant reference to the law as applied by Egyptian courts since 1880, and the jurisprudence of the so-called mixed courts,[125] which were also a very Egyptian phenomenon despite the clear influence of French law: 'Egyptian case-law has made a long journey over seventy-five years. It has the right now to its independence.'[126]

As for substance, the concern with legal Egyptianization is expressed by Sanhuri in candid terms:

There are three legislative sources: the first and foremost emanates from old civil codes, after they were refined and enriched by Egyptian case-law during the seventy years through which the courts interpreted and applied these codes. The texts of the current Code which get their inspiration from these sources, constitute approximately three quarters of the new legislation.[127]

The new Code 'naturally' incorporated old legislation, so that 'this Code does not provoke a revolution in civil transactions'.[128] Its articles reiterate the established theories of 'fault, cause, third party stipulation, and unjust enrichment',[129] which

---

[124] Sanhuri, *Wasit*, i, *ha'* [page 'e' or 5 in Arab lettering], reproducing a passage which appeared in his 1934 *Nazariyyat al-'aqd*.
[125] On mixed tribunals, for a time presided over by judge Jasper Brinton, see his *The mixed courts of Egypt* (New Haven, 1930 rev. edn. 1968); Byron Cannon, *Politics of law and the courts in nineteenth-century Egypt*, above n. 80; Mark Hoyle, *Mixed courts of Egypt* (London, 1991).
[126] Sanhuri, *Wasit*, i, *jim* [page c or 3].   [127] Sanhuri, *Wasit*, i, 34.   [128] ibid.
[129] Unjust enrichment for French *gestion d'affaires*, Arabic *al-fadala*.

had been adopted in the previous Codes, as well as matters of details concerning 'prescription, sale during terminal illness,[130] and mistake in transactions'.[131]

Modern notions established by Egyptian case-law are also confirmed, in particular 'abuse of right, formation of contract, fraud, *force majeure*, natural obligation, summons, fictive acts, joint property, legal acts in situations of terminal illness, acts of alienation',[132] as well as other more detailed matters such as 'judicial action for the recovery of interest, liquidated damages, automatic renewal of current accounts, prescription in *waqf* matters, corporate survival despite minority status, lessor's responsibility for hidden defects and for loss of the object leased, neighbourhood rights, and security for joint property'.[133]

Sanhuri provides several examples of the way he followed established Egyptian statutes and case-law. One example is the notion of 'exploitation' or 'disproportionate harm' which Egyptian courts had introduced to contain the effects of some abusive action, like an old man falling under the sway of a woman much younger, who succeeds in getting him to repudiate his first wife and to disinherit his children in her favour, or a woman who forces her husband to repudiate her by deliberately dilapidating his fortune. Article 129 of the Civil Code reflects Egyptian case-law:

If the obligations of one of the parties do not correspond in any way to the advantages he acquired by virtue of the contract or in consideration of the other contractor's obligations, and if it turns out that the injured party concluded the contract after the other party took advantage of a manifest inattention or overwhelming passion,[134] the judge may, upon request of the injured party, cancel the contract or mitigate its resulting obligations.[135]

Another example showing how the old Code was improved upon in the decisions of Egyptian judges concerns the stipulation for a third party beneficiary (Art. 136/ 198, Codes of 1876 and 1883). This allowed the creation of a more precise regime regarding the conditions for stipulation (Art. 154, new Egyptian Civil Code), the rights of the contracting parties, as well as the protection of the third party beneficiary.

Injunctions for payment (French *astreintes*) and liquidated damages also derive from modern Egyptian case-law. In the case of *astreinte*, Articles 213 and 214 ECC grant the judge extensive powers which were not provided for in the old Codes but which were developed by the courts.[136] The regime of liquidated damages was adopted *against* the previous Codes (Art. 123/181), which did not allow the judge to reduce the damage stipulated in the clause. Following Egyptian case-law, which overrode these texts, Article 224 of the Egyptian Civil Code enables the judge 'to reduce compensation [established by the liquidated

---

[130] Terminal illness, *marad al-mawt*.   [131] *al-ghalat fi 'aqd al-sulh*. Sanhuri, *Wasit*, i, 35.
[132] ibid.   [133] ibid.   [134] *istaghalla fihi tayshan bayyinan aw hawan jamihan*.
[135] Art. 129 ECC. The following two paragraphs of Art. 129 establish the conditions for the intervention of the judge, and summarize the principles established by Egyptian case-law between the two world wars.   [136] Sanhuri, *Wasit*, i, 41–2.

damages clause] if the debtor proves that the initial estimate [of the injury] was greatly exaggerated'.[137]

The confirmation of existing Egyptian law was evidently a priority for Sanhuri. In his major treatise, he insisted time and again on the continuity established by the Civil Code, and cited a long list of areas where this occurs.[138] This attention to 'national' law, he explained, has also been enriched by comparative law as an important secondary source. The new Egyptian Civil Code relied on foreign Codes 'to benefit as much as possible from any progress achieved by modern codification, in technical style and in legislative writing'.[139] From a substantive point of view, he explained, the new legislation draws on comparative law in matters of 'companies, the cession of debt, insolvency, liability for lack of discernment, liability for machinery, texts relating to *force majeure*, joint ownership in buildings, family property and agency in joint ownership of co-owners'.[140]

Sanhuri thought that the influence of modern non-Islamic and non-Egyptian legislation should remain limited, in contrast with provisions of national or Islamic inspiration. He did not wish the Egyptian judge to examine the original texts of foreign law: 'Legislative texts that find their sources in foreign codification must be completely severed from their source. It will not be permissible to turn to them for the purpose of application or interpretation.'[141] Throughout the Travaux Préparatoires (TP) foreign law is treated as a complementary source, unlike texts hailing from Egyptian case-law or the *shari'a* which require, in case of doubt, a return to the original texts. So what about the *shari'a* in this vast field? 'I assure you that we did not leave a single sound provision of the *shari'a* which we could have included in this legislation without so doing... We adopted from the *shari'a* all that we could adopt, having regard to sound principles of modern legislation.'[142]

This statement by Sanhuri is often quoted. It is not isolated. When describing the sources for 'his' Code, Sanhuri always insists on the privileged place of Islamic law. Next to local Egyptian law—the first and most important source—and comparative law—the third source—Sanhuri explains at the beginning of his *Summa* on civil law that 'the second source is Islamic law. The new codification kept what the former Egyptian codification had retained from Islamic law, and added new elements.'[143] The Preparatory Works for the Civil Code show how delicate and important the issue was to the Egyptian legislator: 'We have all said that the exclusion of Islamic law will lead to much unease in people's minds'.[144]

The discussion continued for years between the main participants in the Preparatory Works. It has not abated to date.[145] Whether in Parliament, in the

---

[137] ibid. 42–3.   [138] ibid. 70–3.   [139] ibid. 50–1.   [140] ibid. 51.
[141] ibid. 52.
[142] Ministry of Justice (Egypt), *Al-Qanun al-madani, Majmu'at al-a'mal al-tahdiriyya* (Travaux Préparatoires of the Civil Code), 7 vols. (Cairo, 1949) i, 85, hereinafter TP Egypt, passage cited for instance by Norman Anderson, *Law reform in the Muslim world* (London, 1976) 83–4.
[143] Sanhuri, *Wasit*, i, 34.   [144] *hiaj kabir fil-afkar*, Session president, in TP Egypt, i, 92.
[145] See good discussion in Bernard Botiveau, on the basis of a 1982 'Project for the codification of Islamic *shari'a* (civil law)', in *Loi islamique et droit dans les sociétés arabes* (Paris, 1993) 271–302. The

press or in the courts,[146] the debate shows clearly the two features of the Egyptian codification process: an interest in national case-law, even if based on articles copied from a code in France; and a wide-ranging comparative effort, with a special focus on the Islamic legacy.

Often in his writings on the Egyptian Civil Code, Sanhuri appears apologetic when he defends his use of *fiqh*. The accusation of ignoring Islamic law never surfaced in the case of the Majalla. Since Sanhuri was the author of one of the most important modern treatises in Islamic law,[147] one rightly wonders why the Islamic dimension of the Egyptian Civil Code continues to be subjected to so much questioning.

The difference between the Egyptian scene in the twentieth century, and the Ottoman scene in the late nineteenth century informs the levels of interaction between law and society, and reflects the persistent theme of 'Islam and the state' across the region. The re-emergence of the century-old debate since the 1980s bears the evident political characteristics of the Islamic law agenda introduced into the Middle East by the Iranian Revolution. The controversy will not be over soon, being is steeped in a much larger struggle that will not come to rest before a less violent balance is found within the troubled region. For the comparative lawyer, meanwhile, the Majalla and the Egyptian Civil Code offer two archetypal models for the role of Islamic law in the field of obligations. Egypt's codification, in turn, provides a model replicated in many countries of the region, in the same way as the Majalla operated as a model for the codification of civil law in the earlier period, from the Tunisian and Moroccan codes until the Iranian Civil Code through to the restatements of Morand, Qadri Basha, Qari, and Kashif al-Ghata'. In both archetypal cases, the Ottoman Majalla and the Egyptian Civil Code, the structure of the code and its terminology are the key indicators for the distinct style that characterizes the Middle Eastern law of obligations, leading in turn to questions of substance about the rules governing contracts and torts.

Part of the answer comes in the peculiarly European feel of the ECC's structure. The Egyptian Civil Code has a structure typical of the civilist doctrine, aiming at the

---

main articles of the Project are provided in an annex to the book, 327–56, together with a comment. I have discussed a particular aspect of the debate on the prohibition of *riba* (interest) in Egyptian civil law, in 'The debate on *riba* and interest in twentieth-century jurisprudence', in Mallat, ed., *Islamic law and finance* (London, 1988) 69–88, and in the unpublished chapter 5 of my Ph.D. thesis, 'The Renaissance of Islamic law' (London, 1990) 279–331.

[146] As discussed in Chapter 5, the Supreme Constitutional Court of Egypt (SCC) has systematically avoided examining the conformity with the Islamic tradition of legislation enacted prior to 1980, when the amendment to Article 2 of the 1971 Constitution came into force. This time-sensitive interpretation of Article 2 of the Constitution (*shari'a* considered as an obligatory source for Egyptian law) has kept the Civil Code outside the purview of constitutional review, but later occasional amendments were again subjected to the SCC review. This was the case for instance with the SCC decision of 22 February 1997 that confirmed the 'Islamic' constitutionality of Art. 609 as amended by a law of 1979 (extending the right to commercial lease to the lessee's heirs considered constitutional), SCC, *Al-ahkam allati asdaratha al-mahkama min awwal julio 1996 hatta akhir junio 1998* (Decisions of the Court from 1 July 1996 to end June 1998), vol. 8 (Cairo, 2000) 390–410, at 405.

[147] Sanhuri, *Masader al-haqq*, above n. 59.

projection of an overall coherence and systematicity of the law of obligations. It is composed of an introduction containing general principles, followed by two large parts: obligations or personal rights (Part One); and property rights (Part Two).

The introduction contains two chapters.

- The first chapter includes sources of law and their hierarchy, and the rules on the application of the Code in time and space.

- The second chapter deals with persons in general, physical and moral, including associations and foundations.[148] An overview of the different categories of property is also included in this chapter.

Part One on personal rights contains two books.

Book 1 deals with 'obligations in general' in five sections:

- Section 1 introduces sources (chapter 1: the contract; chapter 2: unilateral will; chapter 3: illegal acts, which cover liability in tort, chapter 4: unjust enrichment; chapter 5: law as a source of obligations).

- Section 2 of Book 1 deals with the effects of obligations (chapter 1: performance in nature; chapter 2: compensation; chapter 3: creditors' guarantees).

- Section 3 tackles the effects of obligations (chapter 1: conditions and terms; chapter 2: plurality of objects; chapter 3: plurality of parties).

- Section 4 is about 'assignment of the obligation' (chapter 1: transfer of debt; chapter 2: debt recovery).

- Section 5 deals with 'the extinction of the obligation' (chapter 1: performance; chapter 2: extinction of obligation by performance; chapter 3: extinction of the obligation without performance).

- Section 6 deals with evidence (chapter 1: written evidence; chapter 2: testimony; chapter 3: presumptions; chapter 4: confession; chapter 5: oath).[149]

Book 2 deals with 'named contracts' in five sections:

- Section 1 introduces the contracts affecting property (chapter 1: sale; chapter 2: exchange; chapter 3: donation; chapter 4: partnership; chapter 5: loan and rent; chapter 6: transaction).

- Section 2 of Book 2 deals with contracts affecting the use of property (chapter 1: lease; chapter 2: free loan[150]).

- Section 3 deals with services (chapter 1: construction contract; chapter 2: hire; chapter 3: agency; chapter 4: deposit; chapter 5: attachment).

- Section 4 is entitled 'aleatory contracts' (chapter 1: gambling and bets; chapter 2: life annuity; chapter 3: insurance contract).

- Section 5 deals with 'guarantees' (chapter 1: grounds; chapter 2: effects).

---

[148] *jam'yyat* and *mu'assassat* (lit. establishments, institutions), Arts. 54–80, abrogated in 1956.
[149] Section 6 (Arts. 389–417) was abrogated in 1968.
[150] *'ariya*, free loan, as opposed to *qard*, generally for interest.

Part Two on property rights is also divided into two books.

Book 3 deals with 'principal property rights' in two sections:

- Section 1 on 'the right of property' (chapter 1: property rights in general; chapter 2: acquisition of property, including occupancy, acquisition upon death, and derivative rights amongst the living).

- Section 2 deals with other rights that derive from property (chapter 1: *usus*, *fructus*, and lodging; chapter 2: possession; chapter 3: servitudes).

Book 4 deals with 'accessory property rights' in four sections:

- Section 1 deals with mortgages (chapter 1: constitution; chapter 2: effects; chapter 3: extinction).

- Section 2 deals with attachments (chapter 1, constitution; chapter 2, effects, removal, and extinction).

- Section 3 is about pledges (chapter 1: constitution; chapter 2, effects; chapter 3: extinction; chapter 4: various pledge types).

- Section 4 deals with categories of debt (chapter 1: general principles; chapter 2: categories of privileges), and concludes the Civil Code at Art. 1149.

This structure, though logical and systematic, is radically different from the 'books' of the tradition as adopted by the Majalla and its calques. Sanhuri did not even preserve the fundamental book on sale as model contract. Sale is part of a number of named contracts within Book 2 in the first Part. It is covered in only sixty-three articles (Arts. 386–449) and does not receive any particular prominence in the general system of obligations. This difference in treatment of a central contract by many civil codes of the contemporary Middle East, compared with the extensive treatment in classical Islamic doctrine and the Majalla's 300 articles on the sale contract, was noted.[151] Codification naturally includes an element of selection, but it is not surprising to see why Sanhuri's detractors feel uneasy about the unfamiliar structure of his Code. The ECC's division into four books may have sacrificed too much in favour of an aesthetic balance which is at times excessive: witness Book 4 wholly devoted to accessory property rights, a marginal field in both theory and practice, and the uneasy inclusion of a section 4 related to 'categories of debt' within that book.

Contracts

To better understand the interaction between the classical and modern law of obligations in the Middle East in terms of substance, let me conjure up the lively debate that took place in Cairo during the elaboration of the Civil Code.

Against those, who already in the 1930s were criticizing him for abandoning or ignoring the tradition, Sanhuri defended his position on several occasions, always

---

[151] Topakian, 'Notes sommaires sur le contrat de vente', above n. 115, 262–5 and annex, comparing the Lebanese, Egyptian, and Ottoman Civil Codes.

with the rigour associated with his reputation. In the public debates which were minuted in the Travaux Préparatoires, the question of the *shari'a* was the subject of a heated exchange between 'Sanhuri Basha' and a senator who was accusing him of ignoring it. The discussion resulted in the following statement by Sanhuri:

> Evidence is that the theory of contract, which is the theory brought up by Sadeq bey [the senator] to illustrate his argument that the *shari'a* was bypassed, can be summarised in three stages: how a valid contract is formed, how its effects are determined, and how the contract is terminated. Sadeq bey's example, you see, is only based on the modern classification for the three stages, a classification which is very distant from the rules under Islamic law.[152]

Let's examine in the rest of this section on contracts the place of Islamic law against the three 'modern stages of contract theory' that Sanhuri discussed actively in the Preparatory Works: formation, effects, termination.

Contracts—Formation

'Formation' constitutes the first stage in the life of the contract, and Article 89 of the ECC stipulates that 'the contract is formed by the exchange of consent between two parties expressing their common will, together with additional elements that the law may require'.

According to Sanhuri, modern Egyptian law follows an 'objective' theory which stands at the intersection of Islamic and Germanic law. I have mentioned Sanhuri's view on the objective nature of classical Islamic law, which he also expressed in his *Masader al-haqq*.[153] This is taken up again in his *Wasit*:

> With regard to Islamic law, although intent is the prevailing rule,[154] i.e. the real will of the contracting parties, jurists often stop at the apparent meaning of the words used by the parties, and do not reach beyond to get to the hidden meaning expressing the intention.[155] No doubt, this explains their detailed analysis of some expressions and words, and their long reflection on the significance of some expressions, and on what any difference in expression entails for the change in the rule that applies. In our opinion, it is not a matter of sticking to any given word, but rather about apparent will prevailing over real will.[156]

We saw earlier how the Majalla oscillates between the two tendencies, objective and subjective. Against Sanhuri, classical law as understood by the Majalla sounds subjective in the pledged sale,[157] which is assimilated to a pledge[158] rather than to a sale. Never mind that the contract is entitled sale, it does not have for its central object the delivery of the good to the buyer, for it mainly constitutes a guarantee on his debt.[159]

---

[152] TP Egypt, i, 86, see also in the *Wasit* the reference to the robust discussion, *hiwar 'anif*, within the Commission, Sanhuri, *Wasit*, i, 48.

[153] Sanhuri, *Masader al-haqq*, i, 77, 84 ff; See above, n. 59 and accompanying text. For my criticism of Sanhuri's reading of the classical doctrine, see Chapter 2, section on *fiqh*.

[154] *al-'ibra lil-ma'ani*, as per Majalla, Art. 2.   [155] *sarira*, lit. soul.

[156] Sanhuri, *Wasit*, i, 181.   [157] *al-bay' bil-wafa*, a form of credit sale.   [158] *rahn*.

[159] See Arts. 3, 118 and 396 ff of the Majalla, and the comments of Baz and 'Ali Haydar.

An application of the objective principle finds similar force in the Majalla's introductory articles, especially Article 13: 'derivative interpretation will not be admitted when the expression is clear'.[160] An additional example of this objective trend is provided in the chapter on donations, where Article 843 of the Majalla stipulates that 'the donor's offer is presumed in the case of delivery of the object, even though his express authorization consists in saying, if the money is available at the time of donation, here take this money, I have donated it to you.'[161] The validity of the donation can therefore be equally established in an 'objective' manner, this time by the act of delivery.

Writing and 'objectivity'. Ambivalence can also be found in the use of writing as evidence. *Fiqh* does not usually give much weight to writing as evidence. In the textbooks of the great classical jurists, as well as in court decisions, writing was second to oral testimony.[162] A Hanafi manual by an author from the nineteenth century shows the dilemma that obtains in an unwritten sale of land.[163] If oral testimony remains the departing principle, the ultimate evidence takes a written form, either in a private deed,[164] or, in the last instance, in a document registered in court.[165]

I was asked: if a person sells land[166] and does not resort to witnesses, is this sale binding? The answer is that he must be bound by it, as this is the right of the buyer. But he must admit it in the presence of two witnesses. If he refuses, the case is taken to the judge. If he confesses before the judge, the sale is written down in the court register . . . If the buyer asks for a copy of the deed, the seller must deliver it to him.[167]

How do the Majalla and the Sanhuri codes deal with the 'objective' nature of writing as evidence? The Majalla underlines the priority of oral testimony, but weakens it in two ways: Article 69 establishes first 'the equality of written and oral evidence'.[168] Writing is then taken up in the chapter on admission,[169] which starts by ruling that an admission in writing is just like an oral one,[170] then favours written over oral evidence.

In his comment on this chapter, Baz mentions the merchant's records to be sufficient evidence: 'There is no need for any other proof' (Art. 1608), since it has been customary for writings in merchants' books to be 'preferred by many over usual deeds'.[171]

The increased importance given to writing shows the difficult balance in the Majalla between the objective tendency—writing preferred as evidence—and the

---

[160] *la 'ibra lil-dalala fi muqabalat al-tasrih.*   [161] donated it to you, *wahabtuka iyyah.*

[162] See however Chapter 2 above on the importance of writing in daily life, and in the practice of notary-publics and courts.

[163] Muhammad Kamel ibn Mustafa ibn Mahmud al-Trabulsi, *al-Fatawa al-kamiliyya fil-hawadeth al-trabulsiyya*, completed in 1313/1895, publisher and date of publication unknown.

[164] *sakk.*   [165] *sijill.* On *sijills*, see Chapter 2, section on courts.   [166] *'iqar.*

[167] al-Trabulsi, *al-Fatawa al-kamiliyya fil-hawadeth al-trabulsiyya*, above n. 164, 69. We find here the long practice of courts as repositories of transactions.   [168] *al-kitab kal-khitab.*

[169] *al-iqrar*, confession, Arts. 1606–12.   [170] *al-iqrar bil-kitaba kal-iqrar bil-lisan.*

[171] Baz, *Sharh*, under Art. 1608.

principle of subjective will—oral testimony here being privileged. The Egyptian Civil Code takes up this theme by trying to follow Sanhuri while remaining consistent: it is the outside expression of the will which Articles 89 ff ECC retain, while considering it as the extension of internal will.[172] Intent can be established 'orally, in writing, or by the usual sign, it could also be established in cases that leave no doubt about the real intention' (Art. 90 ECC).

As confirmation of a trend which was true the world over, the passage to writing as the preferred type of evidence in Egypt can be found in all the Sanhuri codes, and follows the distinction established by Articles 1317 and 1318 of the French Civil Code between official and private deeds. The classification is incorporated in Article 390 of the Egyptian Civil Code, in Syria (Art. 5 of the Code of Procedure), in Iraq (Art. 450 of the Civil Code), in Libya (Art. 377 of the Libyan CC). All admit a gradual strength in evidence, with the official, notarized, 'authentic' deed coming first,[173] and in case of any formal defect, downgraded to 'private deed'.[174] Unless the notarized deed is challenged as a forgery,[175] it serves as evidence 'that has far reaching effects, for contracting as well as third parties'.[176] In this case, only an equivalent written form, or a confession in court, can be brought up against the deed.[177]

Private deeds are assimilated to authentic acts when the party recognizes his signature on the deed (Art. 394 ECC). The deed then becomes decisive evidence among the parties. Evidence is more limited towards third parties, because the date of the private deed must be confirmed before it becomes evidence against them (Art. 395 ECC).[178]

Testimony is relegated to a lower level as evidence, and the judge has a large power of appreciation. Written evidence holds in any case absolute authority over non-written evidence: 'Evidence by oral testimony cannot be provided, even when the dispute is for less than ten [Egyptian] pounds, in contradiction with, or in addition to, what is established in written evidence'.[179]

The superiority of writing over all evidence (except confession) forms an evident trend in the Majalla and its commentaries.[180] It is well established in the civil legislations of the Middle East, and in practice. Paradoxically, it appears as a modern vindication of the Qur'anic injunction on the need to see obligations strengthened in writing,[181] an elusive reality due to illiteracy, and could be detected in late authors' *fiqh* treatises.

The contractual session

A central role in the formation of the contract is played, in all legal systems, by offer and acceptance. Offer and acceptance in Islamic law are discussed within 'the contractual session', literally 'contractual sitting', *majlis al-'aqd*.

---

[172] Sanhuri, *Wasit*, i, 182.   [173] *al-waraqa al-rasmiyya*.   [174] *waraqa 'urfiyya*.
[175] *tazwir*.   [176] Sanhuri, *Wasit*, ii, 144.   [177] ibid. 151.
[178] For details, ibid. 108–10.   [179] Details in ibid. 394 ff.
[180] See Baz and Haydar under Arts. 1609–10. Both consider writing to be equivalent to oral admission.   [181] 'If you contract an obligation, write it down', Qur'an ii: 282.

During the formation of a contract, a particularity found in several Middle Eastern codes relates to the *majlis al-'aqd*. This concept is rooted in an old legal tradition, which found its way to the Majalla as well as to the second generation constituted by the Sanhuri Codes. The Egyptian Civil Code mentions the contractual session in Article 94:

1—If the offer is made during the contractual session, without an agreement about the exact moment when acceptance takes place, the offeror is freed from the offer if the acceptance is not expressed immediately. The same applies if the offer is made by a person to another over the phone or by any other similar means.

2—However, a contract is formed, even if the acceptance is not expressed immediately, when there is no indication that the offeror has changed his mind during the period separating offer from acceptance, and when acceptance was expressed before the end of the session.

One should note at the outset that this case emerges when both parties are in presence of each another. Problems arising from correspondence between offeror and offeree, various forms of agency, and specific contracts involving more than one party, such as auctions, elicit situations outside the definition of the contractual session.

The contractual session, as defined by the Egyptian law, 'does not cover the regular meaning of a session (or the location) but rather the period during which both parties are actively committed in contracting business without being affected by an outside event'.[182]

This view of the contractual session is firmly anchored in Hanafi law. Sanhuri mentions here his debt to Kasani:

We have adopted here the Hanafi system, which is the school from which the new Code chose its inspiration in this matter ... We reproduce here the analysis in the *Bada'e* [of Kasani]: 'As for the place of the contract, it is one. It is the unified nature of the session which matters, in that both offer and acceptance take place in the same session. If the session breaks, such as when the vendor offers to sell and the other party stands up and leaves the session before it is over, or when the offeree embarks on another activity suggesting that the session is over, and then he accepts, the contract is not concluded.' Let us stop at this marvellous analysis.[183]

The idea behind the contractual session is simple: the instantaneous nature of the session allows for certainty of terms that physical and temporal distance put at risk.[184] Offer and acceptance must take place immediately, otherwise the late response of the offeree is changed into a new offer. In a pre-modern world where communication is rarely immediate in the absence of the parties' physical presence

---

[182] Sanhuri, *Wasit*, i, 214.

[183] ibid. 215 n., citing Kasani, *Bada'e*, v, 137. School, *madhhab*.

[184] On the leitmotif of *fiqh* regarding the necessity for transactions 'not to lead to dispute', especially in commercial law, see Chapter 10.

together, this rule allowed for security in transacting. The Majalla incorporated the main principles in three articles in the book on sale:

Art.181: The contractual session is the meeting between the parties for the purpose of the sale.

Art. 182: Both parties have an option until the end of the session. For example, if one of the contracting parties makes an offer by saying, I buy or sell this object, and the other contracting party does not immediately reply by saying, I buy or sell, but gives his reply at the end of the session, the sale is concluded regardless of the lag [between offer and acceptance.]

Art. 183: If, after the offer is made and before the acceptance is expressed, an expression or a gesture is made indicating a change, the offer lapses and the acceptance is no longer valid. For example, if one of the contracting parties says, I sell or buy, and the other party, before accepting, does something else or engages in a conversation that has nothing to do with the sale, the offer lapses and the acceptance is no longer valid, even if it is expressed before the session is over.

While keeping the principle of the unity of the contractual session, the Egyptian Civil Code introduced some nuances, by considering for instance that a telephone call (or other similar 'sessions') is considered instantaneous. The nuances remain nonetheless within the line of classical Hanafi law and the Majalla.

Three questions persist, both in the writings of the classical jurists and in modern textbooks.

The first is about the contract by correspondence. In classical law, where the unity of the session is the departing point because of the insistence of the jurists on clarity and certainty in commercial transactions, correspondence is assimilated to session. This means adopting the theory of emission ('déclaration' in the French terminology).[185] It is sufficient for the offeree to declare his acceptance of the offer for the contract to be formed. Traditionally, offer is sent by the absent offeror with an emissary who represents him, and the meeting between the emissary and the offeree is assimilated to a contractual session. In the physical absence of the emissary-agent, 'the letter is considered as an oral expression',[186] and the acceptance by the offeree when he receives the offer concludes the contract: 'It is as if the offeror is present physically', writes Kasani.[187]

The second question relates to movement. How is the contractual session defined, in its physical dimension, when there is movement? For instance, the commentators suggest, when offeror and offeree are each riding a donkey, or sitting in a boat. Will the contractual session be continuous in this case? Kasani

---

[185] Generally on French terminology of offer and acceptance, see e.g. François Terré, *Droit civil: les obligations*, 6th edn. (Paris, 1996) 133–4, nn. 162 and 163.

[186] *Al-kitab kal-khitab*, Art. 69 of the Majalla, already cited; also Art. 173 confirming the principle in the case of sale, and Art. 436 for hire. See Mahmasani, *Al-Nazariyya al-'amma*, ii, 63.

[187] Kasani, *Bada'e'*, v, 138: *fa-ka'annahu hadara bi-nafsih*, in the case of an agent, a formula which is also used a few lines further down the page.

contrasts the two situations, by explaining that the movement of the boat, contrary to donkey riding, is independent of the will of parties. In the case of the boat, the contractual session continues *de facto* and *de jure*. In the case of parties walking or riding a donkey, the session is arguably interrupted by a voluntary movement of one of the riders. Sanhuri does not follow Kasani here. He interprets this passage of the *Bada'e'* to mean that the normal meeting of the parties' will is sufficient.[188] For him, both cases are the same in practice.[189]

This convergence shows the importance of a contractual session and its characteristics. Beyond details that a judge must assess, the session requires a unity in space and time on the one hand, and a particular, unifying spirit on the other. The disruption of the spirit in the contractual session is illustrated in Article 183 of the Majalla when a party engages in a different activity or conversation than the one inspired by the contract. In Egyptian law, the presumption is reversed. The contractual session remains, 'unless there is a clear indication that the offeror has gone back on his offer' (Art. 94 EEC).[190]

More fundamentally, the nature of the contractual session has caused problems to classical jurists because of diverging interpretations of the relevant *hadith*: 'Parties preserve their option as long as they are not separated'.[191] The question is whether it is possible to go back on a contract after the meeting during which the offer and acceptance were made so long as the contractual session continues. Jurists are divided on this point. In one interpretation, 'the sale is [first and foremost] a given word. As soon as contracting parties give their word, the sale is concluded.'[192]

The opposite position is followed if the contractual session is considered as a discrete and autonomous event defined by the physical presence of parties. In this interpretation, if the parties come to an agreement and the session continues, both the offeror and the offeree are at liberty to change their mind and go back on their commitment before the session ends.[193]

---

[188] *yakfi al-ittihad al-hukmi.*   [189] Kasani, *Bada'e'*, v, 137; Sanhuri, *Wasit*, i, 216.

[190] I confess having had a problem with the text of Art. 94 ECC ever since I tried to explain it to my students several years ago. Each of the two paragraphs in the article is coherent if taken on its own. In the first paragraph, the principle is that the offer or is freed from his offer if acceptance is not expressed immediately. The session is therefore interrupted by a time lag, or a change in conversation, or an intervening event. In the second paragraph, the principle is that the contract is concluded even if acceptance is not expressed at once, if the general context suggests that the offer remained standing. Taken together, the situation gets confused between a general context and a specific action. The confusion does not get dispelled by the long explanations of Sanhuri in *Wasit*, i, 213–15.

[191] See for the sources of this *hadith*, Mahmasani, *Al-Nazariyya al-'amma*, ii, 43. On the right of option in the context of the contractual session, see below n. 212 and accompanying text.

[192] ibid. ii, 43–4. Position attributed to Abu Hanifa, Shaybani, Malik and Ibrahim Nakha'i: once offer and acceptance meet, the contract is formed. Supporting this position is a citation by Malik on the basis of the practice of the people of Madina (in the *Mudawwana* of Sahnun, vol. x, 20, cited by Mahmasani, *Al-Nazariyya al-'amma*, ii, 44 n.1).

[193] Position taken by Shafi'i, Tabari, Abu Yusuf, and the Zahiris, ibid. Note the division beyond the schools' framework, with Abu Yusuf and Abu Hanifa representing the Hanafis on both sides of the interpretation.

This last solution is not the one accepted in modern law. Once the minds have met, the contractual session no longer affects the contract (Art. 183 Majalla, Art. 94 ECC). Common sense prevails,[194] and is enhanced by two considerations: acceptance of the *essential* points of the contract for it to be validly formed (Art. 95 ECC) and the theory of options, which revives a rich legal tradition in the *fiqh* on the life of the contract and its effects.[195]

In the phase of their formation, and beyond some refinements introduced by the tradition such as contractual session and options, the guiding principle remains that the meeting of wills is sufficient for the contract to be valid. This is the central thesis for contractual obligations in Islamic law, and is recognized by all the authors.[196] The Majalla conforms with this thesis by ruling that the meeting of offer and acceptance is sufficient for the formation of the contract: 'The contract is an obligation for the parties and their commitment to fulfil it. It is the expression of the meeting between offer and acceptance.'[197]

Following on from the definition of offer and acceptance, and the two parties' consent to form the contract, various codes develop a variety of specific contracts: for example, the restaurant owner or the merchant who put themselves in the position of offerors towards clients whose presumed acceptance they cannot reject (e.g. Art. 181 of the Lebanese Code on Obligations and Contracts). Some codes also provide conditions for offer and acceptance, such as the Majalla stipulating that a renewed offer to sell, but with a different price, constitutes a new offer (Art. 185 of the Majalla), and that acceptance is not valid if it introduces changes to the offer. The same article adds that 'acceptance must fully correspond to the offer. It cannot relate to only part of the merchandise or the price.' The Ottoman legislator gives the following illustrations:

For example, when the seller tells the buyer, I sell you this costume for 100 piastres, and the buyer accepts these terms, he takes the entire costume for the whole 100 piastres and may not take part of the costume for 50 piastres. Likewise, if the seller says, I sell you these two horses for three thousand piastres, and the buyer accepts, he must take both horses and pay the three thousand piastres. He cannot take one horse and pay one thousand five hundred piastres.[198]

Practical variations over the principle of consensualism could be extended ad infinitum across the civil codes in the Middle East, but the basic meeting between offer and acceptance constitutes the basis of any such variations. The judge ultimately decides on the validity of the meeting of minds. Arab case-law offers several illustrations of the principle. The Jordanian Court of Cassation has, for instance, considered a liquidated damages clause to govern the contract between the parties,

---

[194] Mahmasani, *Al-Nazariyya al-'amma*, ii, 44.
[195] Cf. below, section on the effects of the contract.
[196] Good summary in Mahmasani, *Al-Nazariyya al-'amma*, ii, 37–45.
[197] Art. 103 Majalla, for which I provide a more literal translation below, text accompanying n. 299. See also Art. 89 of the Egyptian Code, below text accompanying n. 300.
[198] Art. 185 Majalla; see also Art. 93 ECC, Sanhuri, *Wasit*, i, 209 ff.

despite the provision under the Jordanian Civil Code that allows varying the clause depending on the extent of damage resulting from contractual breach (Art. 364 of the Jordanian Civil Code). The party requesting the judge's intervention to lower the amount stipulated by the clause must prove that the damage incurred is less than the one stipulated in the clause.[199] Consensualism is also reflected in several other decisions, for example in the United Arab Emirates, where the Federal Supreme Court held in the case of an unregistered mortgage that 'the agreement of the parties on its essential elements is sufficient for the contract to be formed'.[200]

Contracts—Effects

Contractual effects are discussed in the textbooks of the best civilists like Sanhuri[201] and Sulayman Morcos[202] following the distinction made in the Egyptian Civil Code between the effects of contracts and the effects of obligations: 'The effect of contract is the constitution of an obligation, because contract is one of the sources of the obligation. However, the effect of an obligation is the binding need to execute it.'[203] In the Egyptian Civil Code, contractual effects are treated in the first book, chapter 1: the contract, section 1 (Arts. 145–56), whereas the full section 2 of Book 1 deals with the effects of an obligation. (chapter 1: specific performance; chapter 2: damages; chapter 3: creditors' rights, Arts. 199–264). With regard to contractual effects narrowly defined, the themes addressed by the Code include the definition of parties and their successors (Arts. 145, 146), the principles of contractual interpretation (Arts. 148–51), and contracts for the benefit of third parties, the French *stipulation pour autrui* (Arts. 153–6). On some of these important subjects and their relation to Islamic law, it is remarkable to see the limited attention Sanhuri gives to classical texts, despite the tangible possibilities available to the Egyptian legislator in this field.

On parties and successors, Sanhuri refers to universal creditors and to the Islamic tradition that puts heirs centre-stage, but these references are limited and overall secondary.

On contractual interpretation, Sanhuri could have relied on discussions he had himself developed about the 'objective' nature of Islamic law. True, interpretation

---

[199] Jordanian Cassation Court, Decision of 16 June 1997, *al-Majalla al-'arabiyya lil fiqh wal-qada'* (MAFQ), 7, 1988, 261.

[200] Supreme Federal Court, United Arab Emirates, Decision of 24 June 1987, MAFQ, 7 1988, 265, citation at 267. The judge nonetheless took into account the need to have the registration carried out under the strict rules of the official land register.

[201] Sanhuri, *Wasit*, i, 540–652 (*Aathar al-'aqd*, effects of the contract), ii, 715–1252 (*Aathar al-ilitizam*, effects of the obligation).

[202] Sulaiman Morcos, *Sharh al-qanun al-madani* (commentary on civil law), vol. i, *al-Madkhal lil-'ulum al-qanuniyya* (general introduction to legal sciences) (Cairo, new ed. 1967) 481–4 (*ahkam al-'aqd*, rules governing contracts); vol. ii, *Fil-iltizamat* (obligations) (Cairo 1964), 209–67 (*fi aathar al-'aqd*, effects of the contract), 535–729. Morcos is the other great Egyptian civilist of the twentieth century writing in Arabic. Chafic Chehata also left an important mark, but he wrote mostly in French.   [203] Sanhuri, *Wasit*, ii, 717.

operates here after the acceptance of the declared intention, that is, once the contract is formed. But Sanhuri does not refer at all to classical law in this part of his *Wasit*, despite elements of close concordance with the interpretation principles adopted in the Code, especially with regard to the centrality of what the parties intended. Such reluctance may have resulted from the consequence of applying classical *fiqh* categories as he understood them: Sanhuri would have contradicted his own objectivist interpretation.

Other principles correlate with *fiqh*, such as the principle of Article 148.2 ECC on 'the inclusion in the contract of what normally agrees with law, custom and justice, in accordance with the nature of the obligation'.[204] In his book on conditions, which are the classical law notary-public's standard contractual clauses, the great jurist Shamseddin al-Sarakhsi (d. *c.* 1090) had given several examples of 'all which the sale contract entails'.[205] The Ottoman Majalla had included similar principles, preferring intent over formula, and expressed its preference not to depart from clear expression. Sanhuri does not mention these precedents, and his principles of interpretation are developed in the Code on the basis of Egyptian and comparative case-law. Both in the ECC and in the *Wasit* commentary, there is little trace of *fiqh* in Sanhuri's legacy on this particular score.[206] This was not necessary, and in *Masader al-Haqq*, his famous lectures in Cairo in the early 1950s, Sanhuri explained that from the point of view of substance, the principle of consensualism (Majalla, Arts. 103 and 104), the need for good faith (Majalla, Art. 2), the refusal to ignore declared intent when the expression is clear (Majalla, Arts. 12 and 13), the search for common intention of the parties in case of ambiguity (Majalla, Art. 3), even the principle of interpretation in favour of the debtor in case of doubt, all these principles were systematically introduced into the Iraqi Civil Code's chapter on the interpretation of the contract, where the relevant Majalla maxims can be found verbatim (Arts. 155–66).[207] In the search for a coherence that does not ignore the classical tradition, it turns out that the Iraqi Code succeeds remarkably where the former Sanhuri codes had failed.

Effects on third parties

On contract as it affects third parties, in contrast, Sanhuri clearly opted to *oppose* the tradition. This is the case with *stipulation pour autrui*, 'which the Islamic *shari'a* does not allow',[208] except in limited fields like *waqf.* Sanhuri himself admits that contracts for the benefit of third parties represent for Egyptian law a revolutionary innovation: 'How was the Egyptian legislator able to accomplish

---

[204] *lakin yatanawal aydan ma huwa min mustalzamatihi wifqan lil-qanun wal-'urf wal-'adala bi-hasab tabi'at al-iltizam.*

[205] Sarakhsi, *Mabsut*, vol. 30, 172, *kitab al-shurut*, book of conditions/stipulations: *'fa-inna dhalik kullahu mimma yahtamil al-bay''.*   [206] Sanhuri, *Wasit*, i, 591–622.

[207] Sanhuri, *Masader al-haqq*, vi, 41–2.

[208] Mahmasani, *Al-Nazariyya al-'amma*, ii, 229. Confirmed by Sanhuri, *Masader al-haqq*, v, 161.

this revolution, in the old and new codes, against traditional rules? and how could it have allowed the contract to establish a right in favour of a third party?'[209]

Sanhuri's response is chiefly historical, and rests on the Roman law *stipulatio* as incorporated in the Napoleonic Code and developed in case-law. The principle has carried universal importance since the development of insurance, which is the typical contract that stipulates in favour of a third party who is foreign to the contract. In the detailed explanations that Sanhuri ventures, partly on the basis of Egyptian precedents, there is no trace of Islamic law. Sanhuri talks of *stipulation pour autrui* as a new, *sui generis*, category, which he would have liked to develop beyond the Civil Code text[210] to include the creation by the contract of both rights and obligations for third parties, if of course the third party agrees to honour the contractual obligation.[211]

Here the eclectic method makes the Egyptian Civil Code, in the acknowledgment of its main rapporteur, take a real and conscious step towards the classical tradition. One could suggest that later *fiqh* texts, such as a famous passage of the great Hanafi author Ibn 'Abidin on insurance,[212] offered a precedent for *stipulation pour autrui*, and that the Egyptian Civil Code could have found inspiration in that precedent. Regardless, Sanhuri's perfectly honourable acknowledgment that he at least did not know of any such precedent in Islamic law, and that contracts for third parties could not therefore be drawn from the *fiqh* corpus, has given rise to unfair criticism. This superficial criticism of Sanhuri seizes on occasional lapses to conclude that the Civil Code of modern Egypt has nothing to do with Islamic law.

Be that as it may, let us dwell further on 'the effects of the contract' in a comparative perspective, and appreciate the profound difference between the logic of *fiqh* and the logic of Western law in a field known to the classical legal tradition of Islam under the category of 'options'.

Options

In Western books on the law of obligations, whether Anglo-American or civilist, effects of the contract do not represent a category of their own. Once the contract has been formed, parties need to perform their respective obligations. The life of the contract fuses with the contract, with a few nuances about interpretation that bear only marginally on effects between the parties, or towards third party beneficiaries. As for defects of consent, French *vices du consentement*, they differ little between Islamic and Western law, in spirit or even in detail. The logic that underlines them in all legal systems is similar. What undermines parties' consent,

---

[209] Sanhuri, *Wasit*, i, 565.

[210] Art. 152 ECC: '*La yurattib al-'aqd iltizaman fi dhimmat al-ghayr, wa lakin yajuz an yuksibahu haqqan*' (The contract does not create an obligation towards a third party, but it can establish a right in his favour). [211] See Sanhuri's elegant discussion, *Wasit*, i, 581 n. 1.

[212] Ibn 'Abidin (d. 1252/1836), *Radd al-muhtar 'ala al-durr al-mukhtar* (Cairo 1272/1856) 5 vols., iii, 273–4), discussed in Carlo Nallino, 'Delle assicurazioni in diritto musulmano hanafita', in Nallino, *Raccolta di scritti editi e inediti* (Rome, 1942) vol. 4, 61–84. See Chapter 2, section on custom.

consequently the meeting of their minds, renders the contract void *ab initio*. Defects of consent do not warrant particular treatment in comparative perspective.[213]

But Islamic law includes a special category known as 'options'. This category gives the contract a life beyond the mere performance by the parties of their contractual obligations. Noel Coulson summarized it well:

In Western systems the contract itself is sacrosanct because all the necessary investigations and calculations are made, or are deemed to have been made, prior to its conclusion. In the Islamic system the procedure is virtually reversed. The first essential is to get the contract off the ground, to create the legal tie or *'aqd*, by mutual agreement. Then follows the time for reflection to ascertain whether or not the proper expectations of the parties are to be realized, and if they are not, to exercise the option to break the tie or rescind the contract. At this stage the Islamic *'aqd* [contract] is, comparatively, little more than a declaration of intent. Only when the wide-ranging and elaborate system of options is exhausted does the contractual commitment become fully imperative and legally binding.[214]

There is therefore life between the formation of the contract and its consensual or forced end. This life corresponds to particular rights for the parties which operate in the Islamic law of options as 'time out' on the contract, a time for reassessment.

In classical law, there are four[215] main options identified by Kasani, which he divides into two categories: 'conventional' and 'legal'. The option of selection[216] and the option of condition[217] are conventional.[218] The option of vision[219] and the option of defect[220] are legal.

Conventional options. The two conventional options, selection and condition, are in fact conditions tacitly accepted by the parties.

The option of selection, as its name suggests, allows the buyer a choice between two or more goods. He must exercise his option in a reasonable time, usually three days. The contract is therefore non-binding until the exercise of the option.[221] In case the goods perish before payment of the price and/or the option is exercised, risk (and liability) varies according to the type of goods and the exact moment they were lost. The buyer's choice, which is considered as inherently confirmed by the agreement of the parties, derives from common usage.[222]

---

[213] A section on defects of consent can be found in all the major books on civil law. Cf. Sanhuri, *Wasit*, i, 287–374; *Masader al-haqq*, ii, 97–215; Morcos, *Sharh al-qanun al-madani*, ii, 152–83. Mahmasani, *Al-Nazariyya al-'amma*, ii, 164–90. A more detailed book on the subject was published by the Iraqi jurist Muhammad Bahr al-'Ulum, *'Uyub al-irada fil-fiqh al-islami* (Vices of consent in Islamic law) (Beirut, 1984).

[214] Noel Coulson, *Commercial law in the Gulf states* (London, 1984) 73–4.

[215] Kasani provides the clearest discussion of options amongst the classical jurists of the Hanafi school, *Bada'e'*, v, 261–306.   [216] *khiyar al-ta'yin*. Kasani, *Bada'e'*, v, 261–3.

[217] *khiyar al-shart*. Kasani, *Bada'e'*, v, 263–8.

[218] Kasani, *Bada'e'*, v, 261: *Amma al-khiyar al-thabit bil-shart fa-naw'an, ahaduhuma yusamma khiyar al-ta'yin wal-thani khiyar al-shart*.   [219] *khiyar al-ru'ya*. Kasani, *Bada'e'*, v, 268–73.

[220] *khiyar al-'ayb*. Kasani, *Bada'e'*, v, 273–84.   [221] Non-binding, *ghayr lazim*.

[222] *Jawaz hadha al-naw' min al-bay' innama yathbut bi-ta'amul al-nas li-hajatihim ila dhalik. Bada'e'*, v, 261, bottom of page. For Kasani, *Bada'e'*, v, 263, the choice being a conventional one, it can

The option of condition may be considered, in comparative perspective, as a condition for the validity of the contract, making it binding on the parties because they are considered to have agreed to it. It is a suspensive time condition, with the two parties agreeing on either, or both, completing the contract within a given time. This option, according to Kasani, allows injustice to be removed, by giving the protected party the possibility of extricating itself from an agreement contracted under duress. Duress in that case is presumed and need not be proved.[223]

Legal options. There are two such options for Kasani. The option of vision, and the option of (hidden) defect. The option of vision operates when it does not fall within the power of the parties to examine the goods traded.[224] It is an option that law grants the buyer the right to exercise within a reasonable time-frame. In so far as it is triggered automatically, it becomes similar to the option for hidden defect,[225] as it presupposes that the buyer or the tenant can void the contract if the good to be sold or the property to be leased, once seen, does not correspond to what they agreed upon with the seller or the landlord. We are here at the heart of 'a time of reflection' granted the weaker party, when the object of the contract does not objectively correspond to his intention. Options operate in this case as a withdrawal clause, and the contract is considered never to have existed.

In his discussion of this category of legal options, contemporary Syrian jurist Zuhayli adds two further types:[226] the option of session,[227] and the option of payment.[228] We have met the first in the 'contractual session'. The right of option that derives from it is therefore a mere variation, which the Majalla formula explains in Article 182: 'The two parties have a right of option until the end of the meeting'.[229] It is a simple right to accept the offer within the contractual session, and is also known as 'the option of acceptance'.[230]

The payment option is a minor form of legal option, which supposes that either the parties have agreed tacitly to postpone payment and allow the debtor to reconsider his commitment within a time limit, usually set at three days; or the parties agreed, also tacitly, for the seller (or the creditor generally) to return the money to the buyer within that time and void the contract. Although this option

also be an option for the seller, who decides in exercising it which of two or several goods he will eventually sell.

[223] *Lil-haja ila daf' al-ghubn.* Kasani, *Bada'e'*, v, 264, bottom of page.

[224] *khiyar al-ru'ya.* Kasani, *Bada'e'*, v, 261–3; 293–7. We also find variations on the option of vision in the so-called option of description, *khiyar al-wasf.* In the major work of Syrian contemporary jurist Wahbeh al-Zuhayli, *Al-fiqh al-islami wa adillatuhu* (Islamic law and its reasons) (Damascus, 1984) 8 vols. the discussion of options is remarkably clear, vol. iv, 3103–32. For *khiyar al-wasf* and *khiyar al-ru'ya,* see Zuhayli, *Al-fiqh al-islami,* iv, 3123–31.

[225] *khiyar al-'ayb.* Kasani, *Bada'e'*, v, 273–84, 297–303. Zuhayli, *Al-fiqh al-islami,* iv, 3116–23.

[226] Zuhayli discusses six options, but notes that one finds up to seventeen categories in classical law, ibid. 3104.   [227] *khiyar al-majlis,* Zuhayli, *Al-fiqh al-islami,* iv, 3104–6.

[228] *khiyar al-naqd,* Zuhayli, *Al-fiqh al-islami,* iv, 3131–2. Majalla, Arts. 313–15.

[229] *Al-mutabayi'an* (the seller and the buyer) *bil-khiyar ba'd al-ijab ila akhir al-majlis.*

[230] *khiyar al-qubul,* cf. Baz, *Sharh,* under Art. 182 of the Majalla.

is part of a condition which is not expressed openly, the payment option is in fact a consensual option governed by the uses of commerce.

The field of options is elusive in the modern law of the Middle East. The confusion comes from the difference from its Western counterpart in the way the logic of contract operates, typically the contract of sale in Islamic law, as underlined by Noel Coulson's comment. In the Ottoman Majalla, options are discussed in detail in the book of sale.[231] They also appear prominently in the Iranian Civil Code, in Jordan, and in the Yemen.[232] But they are not treated separately in the Sanhuri Codes or in Iraq, and appear in a weak form in the Majallas of North Africa, where classical options are included under the category of suspensive conditions in the contract of sale in the Moroccan Code, and as 'sale options' in the Tunisian Majalla.[233] The Yemen Code, and the Code of the Emirates, which are the latest legislative monuments, treat options in a pedagogically meaningful way as 'characteristics that modify the effects of contract'. The section that deals with options in the Yemen Civil Code precedes the chapter on contractual conditions and time limits, and is limited to four main categories. It does not mention the option of selection, but includes three legal options: the option of session, which 'stops when parties separate' (Art. 225 YCC); the option of defect, which 'is necessary when [a defect] appears in the contract that diminishes its value and undermines its object' (Art. 238 YCC); and the option of vision, which operates when the object of the contract was not seen when the parties entered into the contract (Art. 35 YCC). The only conventional option which the Yemen Code mentions is the option of condition, which lasts three days if the option is mentioned in the contract without the exact time being defined (Arts. 227 and 228 YCC). By combining a mixture of common sense and logic, the Code succeeds in placing options in the context of being potential 'modifiers' of some contractual effects, and corresponds to their rather secondary place in the contractual practice that prevails in the modern law of obligations.

Case-law allows us to see, in a series of decisions that can be followed *a contrario*, how rarely options appear in court practice. In a large series of decisions in civil and commercial law over the two last decades in various Arab countries, just five are related to options, and this only under a very general sense of the term.

The first decision concerned a land transaction in Bahrain, which was considered by the Supreme Court to be dependent on a condition which was stipulated in the sale. By quashing a decision of the Court of Appeals, the Supreme Court decided that the statute of limitations ran only when the condition was fulfilled, and not from the time the sale contract was signed.[234] The second decision comes

---

[231] Majalla, Arts. 300–9, option of condition; Arts. 310–12, option of payment, Arts. 313–15, option of description; Arts. 316–19, option of selection; Arts. 320–35, option of vision; Arts. 336–55, option for hidden defect. The option of meeting is linked (correctly) to the contractual session, Art. 182.

[232] Iranian Civil Code, Arts. 396–457; JCC, Arts. 177–98; Yemen Civil Code, Arts. 223–53.

[233] Arts. 601–12, Moroccan Code; Arts. 700–11, Tunisian Majalla.

[234] Cassation Court of Bahrain, Decision of 25 March 1979, MAFQ 1, 1984, 135: 'The sale is held up by a suspensive condition, *al-bayʿ muʿallaq ʿala shart mawquf*'.

from Sudan, where the Court mentions the English principle of merchantibility when referring to an option of defect touching upon the sale of goods.[235] Guarantee against hidden defect in the French civil tradition is consecrated by the Algerian Supreme Court in the third decision.[236] In all three decisions that consider the contract not to be effective, there is no mention of options from the perspective of Islamic law.

The option granted to the buyer in the classical tradition is recognized expressly in the two other decisions. In Morocco, it surfaced in a promise to sell a flat, which the Court considered binding sixty days after the transaction was signed, in accordance with the disposition of the Code. The right to rescind the contract is allowed the buyer as a matter of principle, but the Court based its rationale on the terms of the Code rather than on classical law.[237] Only in Bahrain can one find a solid application of the *fiqh* tradition, when the Court considered that the buyer's option operates in his favour 'under Islamic law' because the object of the sale proved defective. The case is interesting because the litigious good was a plot of land which had been expropriated in part, and the Court confirmed the appellate decision which had given the buyer the option to rescind the contract, or to confirm his purchase whilst receiving some compensation for the difference in the property value.[238]

Within a series of several dozen civil law decisions, three decisions out of five show how the Western categories of 'condition' and '*terme*' took over the category of options in modern Arab case-law. Only the two last decisions use the language of classical law, of which just one does so in an open manner. Options as known in classical Islamic law are an exception in the contemporary law of the Middle East as applied by the courts, despite their formal presence in several civil codes.

Contracts—termination

In the absence of *force majeure*, act of God, or similar exceptional circumstances, a party is entitled to compensation when the other party breaches her contractual obligations. Basic principles are the same in all legal systems which recognise the individual as the subject of rights, and the contract as the consequent emanation of her free will: the obligation is to fulfil the terms of the contract, otherwise compensation is owed. The famous articles of the French Civil Code stating 'that legally formed contracts are considered law to the contracting parties . . . and must be performed in good faith',[239] and that 'any obligation which is not performed by

[235] Appeals Court of North Sudan region, Decision rendered in April 1983, MAFQ 4, 1988, 413, at 414–15.

[236] *Majlis a'la* (Supreme Council = Cassation Court) of Algeria, Decision of 29 February 1989, MAFQ 15, 1994, 263.

[237] Appeals Court of Casablanca, Decision of 22 May 1984, MAFQ 3, 1986, 417.

[238] Cassation Court of Bahrain, Decision of 26 January 1992, MAFQ 16, 1994, 262, Islamic law citation at 264.

[239] Art. 1134 French Civil Code: 'Les Conventions légalement formées tiennent lieu de loi à ceux qui les ont faites . . . et doivent être exécutées de bonne foi'.

the debtor gives rise to compensation',[240] are restated by all the Civil Codes of the region. Details of these restatements and their application in case-law in each jurisdiction are many, but the Sanhuri Codes all have in common a formulation and logic close to French law.[241]

In his *Masader al-haqq*, Sanhuri had explained that the rescission of the contract in classical law was an exception that Islamic law did not accept as a matter of course. Only in certain exceptional cases can the creditor fall back on the extinction of the contractual object, and consequently of the contract itself, so as not to perform her part of the bargain. Otherwise, the party who is harmed by the non-performance of the contract is not allowed in principle to rescind it. She must either request performance, or compensation. The principle is that 'the contract cannot be rescinded if a party does not perform his obligations'.[242] While I have not come across a definitive position on the priority of either specific performance or compensation in classical law, the *fiqh* books sound closer to the common law in their preference for financial compensation rather than forcing the performance of the defaulting party. This needs more research, and will remain too general and abstract in the absence of systematic evidence from court practice in the classical age.

In addition to seeking compensation or specific performance, the harmed party can raise an exception of non-performance to force an end to the contract. This solution was reached on the basis of some classical writings by the Civil Code of Iraq, which is strongly inspired by the Majalla and the *fiqh* tradition.[243] Iraqi law reached a middle position by focusing on the seller's right to withhold performance, and Article 280 of the Iraq Civil Code states that 'the seller can retain the sold good until the buyer pays him the totality of the agreed price'. By raising this solution as a principle which is valid for all synallagmatic contracts, withholding performance becomes an additional solution for the harmed creditor. This is how the Iraqi legislator viewed it: 'In all synallagmatic contracts, each of the parties to the contract can retain the good in his possession until receiving the agreed price'.

This last example shows a pragmatic fusion between ending the contract and withholding performance. A more evident aspect of contract termination in terms accepted by *fiqh* appears in the parties agreeing on a conventional resolution of the contract.[244] This category has no place in the Egyptian Civil Code, despite the

[240] Art. 1142 French Civil Code: 'Toute obligation ... se résout en dommages et intérêts en cas d'inexécution du débiteur'.

[241] Arts. 157–61 ECC. For a general list of corresponding articles in the Arab codes, see Sulaiman Morcos, *al-Mas'uliyya al-madaniyya fi taqninat al-bilad al-'arabiyya* (Civil liability in the legislation of Arab countries), vol. 1 (Cairo, 1971) 108–25.

[242] Sanhuri, *Masader al-haqq*, vi, 215–44, citation at 230.

[243] Corresponding texts in the part dealing with the right to retain the good in sale contracts, Arts. 278–84 Majalla, and in the part dealing with the right of retention in obligations generally, Arts. 246–8 ECC. Unfortunately, the dictatorship which has prevailed in Iraq since the 1958 Revolution, and which became even more severe from 1968 to the beginning of the twenty-first century, has precluded the healthy build-up of case-law on a remarkable legislative monument. Legal impoverishment is found to various degrees across the Arab world, but it is notorious in societies with oppressive dictatorial systems for almost half a century.   [244] *iqala.*

importance it finds in classical treatises.[245] The Iraqi Code includes it, following the tradition, if the subject-matter of the contract is still live and relevant.[246]

With Sanhuri this form of contractual ending was discontinued. He may have been right. Conventional termination is by nature the result of a new agreement between the parties, and does not pose a problem as such in practice. If the two parties agree one day to modify the contract, or end it, then there is no dispute outstanding. The contract is rearranged by *novation*, which simply replaces the previous contractual arrangements.

Unforeseen circumstances

A fundamental problem in ending a contract arises upon the alteration of obligations because of unforeseen or exceptional circumstances. The line here between contractual effect and the end of the contract is blurred. This uncertainty is manifest, in contemporary Arab law, in the difficulties raised by the narrow margin separating unforeseen circumstances and *force majeure* or act of God.

As in the celebrated formula of the French Civil Code, the principle is that 'the contract is the law of the parties'.[247] This formula, which is taken up in Article 147.1 of the Egyptian Civil Code, is balanced by *imprévision* for unforeseeable circumstances, which is mentioned as an exception in the following paragraph: 'In case of generalised exceptional circumstances, which it was impossible to foresee, and the occurrence of which makes the performance of the contractual obligation, even though it may remain possible, so onerous on the debtor that it threatens him with considerable loss, the judge may, depending on the circumstances and after having weighed both parties' interests, bring back the obligation under a reasonable ceiling. Any contrary clause is void' (ECC Art. 147.2).

These dispositions about *imprévision*, which expressly adopt the administrative case-law of the French Conseil d'Etat and its Polish and Italian applications in civil law countries,[248] meet the theory of *force majeure*, which is also close in its Egyptian formulation to the French 'impossibility for the debtor to perform his obligation for a reason which is foreign to him'.[249] The difference between *imprévision* and *force*

---

[245] See Kasani, *Bada'e'*, v, 306–10. The ECC uses instead the French category of *novation* (*tajdid*, Arts. 352–61). [246] Art. 182, Iraqi Civil Code.

[247] *al-'aqd shari'at al-muta'aqidin*. (Art. 147, para. 1 ECC, in calque of Art. 1134 of the French Code Civil, cf. Sanhuri, *Wasit*, i, 624–5). This is true of all legislation, classical or modern, but the Egyptian and French Civil Codes expressly mention contracts as 'the law of the contracting parties'. The Napoleonic Code owes the famous formula 'les conventions légalement formées tiennent lieu de loi à ceux qui les ont faites' to Jean Domat (d. 1696). Domat, *Lois civiles*, (Paris, 1756), liv.1, t. 1, s. 2, Art. 7.

[248] Jurisprudence (Case-law precedent) *Gaz de Bordeaux*, Conseil d'Etat, 30 March 1916. Egyptian case-law was uncertain before the Second World War. The Egyptian Court of Appeals had accepted in 1931 the idea of the judge revising the contract of an importer of goods who was forced to sell at a much lower price because of high taxes imposed by the direction of customs. But the Cassation Court overturned the decision (Decision of 14 January 1932, cited by Morcos, *Sharh al-qanun al-madani*, ii, 231–32) and reconfirmed the 'conservative' position of the courts until the adoption of the Civil Code in 1948.

[249] Art. 373 Egyptian Civil Code, *yanqadi al-iltizam idha athbata al-madin anna al-wafa' bihi asbaha mustahilan*; calque of Art. 1147 French CC, non-performance resulting from a cause that cannot be linked to the debtor.

majeure is that the judge may intervene in the case of *imprévision* to allow the contract to survive by modifying some of its terms. *Force majeure* in contrast renders impossible the performance of the contract and brings the parties back to where they were before its formation.

Fiqh does not know the distinction between *imprévision* and *force majeure*. Instead, it recognizes circumstances that destroy the contract outside the parties' will. The category is closer to *force majeure*, and closer indeed to the English term 'act of God'. It is described as 'the misery that descends from the heavens'.[250] There is no general theory, but the classical texts offer various instances in which the contract could not be performed because of catastrophes that destroy the harvest or ruin seasonal fruit.

What are the consequences for contract of the misery that descends from the heavens? Classical jurists are divided on this point over the standard contract of sale. For some the vendor is liable, for others the buyer. For fruit in particular, the division arises from two contradictory *hadith*s.[251] One then gets into complex disputes between the schools, and within each school. Malikis and Hanbalis, for example, seem to reject possession of the sold good as the criterion of responsibility, and distinguish between fungible and non-fungible goods. If the good that perishes is fungible, the seller is liable because it remains his property until delivery. If the object is non-fungible, the buyer assumes the risk.[252] Hanafis and Shafi'is hold a different view, which is chiefly based on possession. The party who holds the sold good when misery hits is liable. The position of classical law in the law of sale is fluid. It is less so in some categories of unforeseen circumstances which Kasani relates to lease, and which he allows to lapse[253] for more precise reasons relative to the leased object, the lessor, or the lessee.[254]

Modern Egyptian law did not try to incorporate the nuances found in *fiqh*.[255] The legislator explicitly rejected some of the solutions offered in the tradition in favour of an equitable type of solution fashioned after French administrative case-law and European codification and restatements in between the two world wars.

One could have imagined the adoption of a better rooted system drawn after *fiqh*, which the dean of Arab law does not fail to mention in later texts.[256] The great nineteenth-century jurist Ibn 'Abidin, for instance, offers a coherent overall principle: 'In the performance of an obligation, if an impossibility led to harm to the debtor physically or in his property, he has the right to ask for a revision of the

---

[250] *al-afa al-samawiyya*, Mahmasani, *Al-Nazariyya al-'amma*, ii, 243, refers the concept to the *Mughni* of ibn Qudama. One also finds in the classical texts the word *al-ja'iha*.
[251] Details of the two *hadith*s in Mahmasani, *Al-Nazariyya al-'amma*, ii, 244.
[252] ibid., 244–5.   [253] The debtor has an excuse, *'udhr*.
[254] Kasani, *Bada'e'*, iv, 197–201.
[255] Contrary to the Majalla, which allows excuse in the case of hire (but does not mention it in its general principles part), cf. Art. 443 Majalla: '*law hadatha 'udhr mani' li-ijra' mujab al-'aqd tanfasikh al-ijara* (lit., in case of excuse preventing the performance of the obligation of the contract, the contract of hire is voided)'.   [256] Sanhuri, *Wasit*, i, 633 n. 2, *Masader al-haqq*, vi, 90–110.

contract'.[257] This text, which Sanhuri cites,[258] may have been excluded by him for its great elasticity, and for the confusion which this classical theory 'considers as excuse in what modern theory sees as *force majeure* or exceptional circumstances, and which is beneath both theories'.[259] Non-performance is evidently considered exceptional, and cannot be understood to be other than a restriction on a more fundamental principle to honour one's obligations, as underlined by the Qur'an;[260] a principle which a classical author put in verse, and which can be translated as follows: 'It is not allowed to repudiate a transaction which has been concluded. The parties must agree or be forced to void it. They must be forced to respect its clauses.'[261]

The difficult balance between respecting one's engagement and the right to see the contract modified when the balance is broken for reasons outside the parties' control, stands at the heart of unforeseen circumstances, a category which has a long life in an unstable Middle East. It would be useful to see how courts adapt the textual dispositions to the hardships on contracts constantly threatened by the collapse of currency and by war. Unfortunately, we do not have a consistent series of judgments in the field across Arab jurisdictions.[262]

We do have, however, a decision from the Saudi Diwan al-Mazalim dated 6/2/1398 (17 January 1978) in a construction case.[263] A building had been started for a ministry under the terms of the contract. When the land needed to be excavated, the hard type of rock being dug halted the works, leading to the subcontractors demanding an increase in price from the contracting builder. To pursue the work, the builder-contractor requested a revision of the price by the ministry, and the two parties agreed to appoint a commission which, after a topographic and comparative study of other buildings, concluded there was a need to increase the price to an extent close to the request of the builder—4 million dinars—in

---

[257] Ibn 'Abidin, *Radd al-Muhtar*, v, 76.   [258] Sanhuri, *Wasit*, i, 634 n.   [259] ibid.

[260] Qur'an v: 1 and Qur'an xvii: 34: 'Honour your contracts'.

[261] Ibn 'Asem al-Malik (d. 829/1426), *Tuhfat al-hukkam fi niqat al-'uqud wal-ahkam* (The best decisions on the delicate points of contracts and judgments), text and translation Léon Bercher (Algiers, 1958) 51: *wa la yajuzu naqdu sulhin ubrima/wa in taradiyan wa jabran ulzima*.

[262] In Lebanon, the long civil war (1975–90) triggered a collapse of the national currency towards the end of the 1980s, and spiralling inflation. Many contracts were gravely undermined in the process, but the legislator did not address the imbalance, except to a small extent in the law concerning long-contracted rents. At the end of the war, more general legislation affecting all obligations was carefully introduced, mainly freezing statutes of limitation to allow some order in troubled contracts. The law included an Article 5 which appeared prima facie to give leeway to the judge to correct any contractual imbalance. But the courts systematically refused to apply it, and solemnly declared on one occasion that the law 'had not established a general rule which affected the Code of obligations and contracts by allowing us to vary the terms of a contract under the pretext of economic fluctuations, especially over the price agreed by the parties'. Decision of the Mount Lebanon Appeals Court, Civil Chamber, 12 March 1993, *Recueil Hatem* 211, 1994, 578–9. For the details of the law, see my 'Country survey: Lebanon', in Cotran and Mallat, eds., *Yearbook of Islamic and Middle Eastern Law*, 1994, 204–24, at 209. For the Egyptian equivalent, where courts also seem to have systematically rejected any judicial intervention in the contract, see Bälz, 'Europäisches Privatrecht', above n. 123, 67.

[263] Diwan al-Mazalim, Kingdom of Saudi Arabia, Decision of 6/2/1398 AH (17 January 1978), MAFQ 11, 1992, 291–7.

addition to the 3 million dinars originally asked for, plus 20 per cent for all the subcontracting. The ministry rejected the request on the basis that the law on procurements[264] requires the builder to study the nature of the terrain before presenting his estimate for the project. The Court rejected the ministry's position. It found in the case a typical example of *imprévision*:

This case raises what is known in the doctrine, in case-law generally, and in administrative case-law in particular as the theory of unforeseen material difficulties. The theory can be summarised as follows: 'If the party faces at the time of performance of his obligations material difficulties that have a purely exceptional character, and could not be in any way foreseen at the time the contract was concluded, it is possible for him to ask for total compensation for the harm done to him because of these difficulties.'[265]

The Court developed the principle by insisting on the exceptional nature of the circumstances. Otherwise, 'with due attention to good faith in the performance of contracts, and the party's responsibility towards reasonable obstacles which are evident for the prudent man',[266] he is held to his initial obligations. Since the judge is ultimately in charge of weighing these factors, the Saudi court saw in the particulars of the case enough reason to vindicate the harmed constructor and increase his dues, especially in the light of the slowness of the ministry to study the terrain and to appoint the official legally assigned to the conciliation committee.

How is the amount of damages to be calculated? The building company had requested an increase of some 4 million dinars to meet the new costs. It was granted the increase in full, but the Court held that the work had to be completed. The constructor had asked for an additional 25 per cent to compensate for harm resulting from the cessation of the work, but the commission saw the figure of 20 per cent to be more reasonable. As the conflict was getting worse, the constructor had asked for an increase of 100 per cent to meet his obligations. While considering 'that the basic principle in this type of cases was to assess harm on the day it occurred, and not on the day the court decides upon the compensation, as the judgment declares law and does not enounce it',[267] the court granted 10 per cent additional payment over the original 3 million dinars stipulated by the contract.[268]

All the elements of *imprévision* come together in the decision: unforeseeable and exceptional circumstances, defined less strictly than in the case of *force majeure* as occurrences which could not be foreseen in the contract, liability of the debtor, the ministry in that case, assessment of damage on the day it occurred, active intervention of the judge in redefining the terms of the contract. One can see the full adoption of 'modern' reasoning, including in the title of the category governing compensation. The *force majeure* in classical *fiqh*, which could have been included more forcefully in terms of both wording and substance, was not conspicuous in the Saudi Court's language.

---

[264] *munaqasa*.

[265] MAFQ 11, 1992, 295. The Saudi court used the word *fiqh* for 'doctrine', a neologism taken from French legal vocabulary.　　　　　　　　　　　　　　　　　　　　　[266] ibid.

[267] ibid. 296.　　　[268] ibid. 297.

Torts

A separate concept of tortious liability simply does not exist in classical law. The modern concept of *mas'uliyya taqsiriyya*—literally liability for shortcoming or negligence—is a straight translation from French law. The neologism underlines the structural difficulty in the passage from classical Islamic law to contemporary codification of the law of obligations. Transposing classical law in the field of torts elicits structural unease. The main reason is the absence of the concept of *faute* in the establishment of tortious liability, as we saw in the introductory principles of the Ottoman Majalla: they were drawn directly from the general *hadith* on the illegality of doing harm, and the need to repair harm done irrespective of provenance, fault, negligence, or intent by the author of the harm.[269] This characteristic is the more remarkable since it introduces an important distinction between the law of civil liability and criminal law. In Islamic criminal law, intent is central to the difference between murder[270] and involuntary manslaughter.

There is no *summa divisio* in *fiqh*, as prevails in modern law, between contractual and tortious liability. The great classical texts deal with liability in contract in the archetypal model developed in the book of sale. Compensation varies as a function of the various activities and transactions that may result in harm, including failure to honour the terms of the contract. Specialization does occur in tortious liability in some of the great classical jurists' works, most famous amongst which is Baghdadi's *Liabilities Compendium*,[271] but the themes they deal with remain heavily indebted to the generic category of *daman*, liability/reparation, including breach of contract. One finds in Baghdadi's *Compendium* several chapters on reparation for defective sale,[272] interrupted lease, agricultural contracts, as well as harm resulting from pilgrimage arrangements, for instance when a person asks for another person to go to Mecca in his stead, and a conflict arises over disbursements; or when heirs deny that the deceased had asked the agent to perform the pilgrimage. In the first case, additional expenses are borne by the pilgrim. In the second, 'presumption is in favour of the pilgrim'.[273]

One sees how contractual liability cannot be readily severed from tortious liability in Islamic law. It seems to me that the main reason finds its roots in the absence of a theory of *faute* or negligence as understood by the contemporary law of torts. The logic that the concept of *faute* imposes on the notion of responsibility in Western law is not the same logic which presides over *fiqh*. 'Instead of hanging on to the fact that motivates responsibility, [Islamic lawyers] use the legal consequence of the fact, which is reparation.'[274] This is correct: the logic followed in

---

269 *la darar wa la dirar; al-darar yuzal* etc., Articles of the Majalla cited above, nn. 54–5.

270 *al-qatl al 'amad*, voluntary homicide.

271 Abu Muhammad al-Baghdadi (17th century?), *Majma' al-damanat* (Beirut, 1987).

272 Baghdadi, *Majma'*, 213–43 (sale), 12–55 (hire).

273 Baghdadi, *Majma'*, 9: '*qala hajajtu 'an al-mayt wa ankarahu al-waratha fal-qawlu lahu*'.

274 Emile Tyan, *Le système de responsabilité délictuelle en droit musulman* (Beirut, 1926) 151.

fiqh derives from the absence of *faute* at the heart of the system, but it is wrong to try, like Tyan in his classical thesis, or Sanhuri in his mature work, to compensate for this absence with justifications like 'unlawfulness' for Tyan,[275] or with the introduction of the concept of fault in the field of torts like Sanhuri.[276]

There results a profoundly different structure for liability in torts as well as in contracts. Liability in Islamic law rests on a unifying theory which is based on the concept of harm, and results in the censorship of the harmful act regardless of fault, negligence, or illegality. Once harm is proved, lawyers look for exceptions, and justifications to lift it or attenuate it. Criminal law meets with the law of torts when the intention is criminal, but the general principle of compensation across the board remains throughout. The author of harm must repair it, with the defaulting party in a contract as one sub-application. Variations, exceptions, and nuances are all departures from the legal consequence, which is reparation for damage inflicted.

I am making the argument that the meeting of liability in contract and in tort over the concept of reparation—*daman*—is a unifying abstraction, but one would search in vain for a coherent theoretical explanation in the classical texts. Still, it is hard to resist the appeal of synthesis that derives from a general theory of liability. Some contemporary authors, like Zuhayli and Mahmasani, and Tyan in French,[277] tried to probe its traits. The codes themselves were confronted willy-nilly by the need for order in a complex field.

This is how Qari's Saudi Majalla deals with the subject. Book 12 of the Hanbali Majalla considers injury under its generic qualification as violation. Qari starts out by distinguishing three forms of violation causing injury: violation generically, corporal harm, and destruction of property.[278] The book is then divided into two sections, violation-seizure, and violation-destruction.[279] Qari then adds a section on criminal liability[280] which develops collective compensation under

---

[275] 'The general term which all jurisconsults use to express the notion which we call *faute* is *ta'addi*, ... [which] is the fact of carrying out an action without heeding the law, it is the very idea of unlawfulness' ('le fait d'accomplir un acte sans droit. C'est l'idée même d'illicéité'), Tyan, ibid. 173–4. Further: 'We see therefore in these solutions the Muslim jurists retaining responsibility where the right is not exercised, and rejecting it when the act is unlawful. The justice of the action is their criterion. They do not look to see whether there was negligence, or carelessness, or if the harm-doer has committed the incriminated act outside or beyond the limits which would have been respected by a person of average behaviour and intelligence. In a word, the notion of fault remains to date totally foreign to *ta'addi*.' (ibid. 176.)

[276] Sanhuri, *Wasit*, i, 776 ss, fault, *khata'*. In the passage on tortious liability in his great treatise, 743–75, Sanhuri doesn't make any reference to Islamic law.

[277] Tyan, *Le système de responsabilité délictuelle*; Wahbeh Zuhayli, *Nazariyyat al-daman fil-fiqh al-islami* (Theory of responsibility in Islamic law) (Damascus, 1970); Sanhoury (Sanhuri), 'La responsabilité civile et pénale en droit musulman', *Revue al-Qanun wal-Iqtisad* (Cairo, 15, 1945) 1–26; Jacques Hakim, *Le dommage de source délictuelle en droit musulman* (Paris, 1964). Jordanian judge Ghayth Mismar wrote an interesting thesis on the Islamic law of torts in the Jordanian context at London University at the end of the 1990s.

[278] *ghasb*, *arsh* and *itlaf* (violation, corporal harm, destruction, Arts. 1375–7).

[279] Seizure, *ghasb* (1378–422); destruction, *itlaf* (1423–56). Note the dual use of the concept of violation as generic term; and as 'seizure' by contrast with 'destruction'. [280] crime, *jinaya*.

tribal rules and underlines the difference between criminal responsibility and tort liability.[281] In crime defined as murder or the infliction of bodily harm, Qari makes the classical distinction between compensation resulting from a criminal act leading to death, and the lesser compensation for injury.[282]

Violation in the form of destruction of property[283] includes five chapters which cover 'direct harm': this is when the property of another person is destroyed. Here is the classic case of strict liability, which is presumed except in case of legitimate self-defence against a wild animal (Art. 1424), or the destruction of property with the consent of its owner (Art. 1425). Liability is strict and stops at the tortfeasor: 'The author is liable, and not the instigator'.[284] The example given in Article 1426 is that of a person who gives the key of his house to a thief. Only the thief, as direct author, is liable, but the following article allows for an exception in case it is impossible to punish the author or in case the instigator forced the author's hand in committing the tort. The Hanbali Majalla rejects responsibility if the good is not 'human' and concludes that compensation for the property destroyed[285] is similar to compensation for a good seized by force.[286] 'Compensation for destroyed property is the same as compensation for seized goods in terms of the nature of compensation if the object is not fungible, and in terms of value if it is fungible, estimated on the day when violation occurs.' (Art. 1427).

Strict liability is developed in the four subsequent chapters. Causal link is discussed extensively in chapter 2, then Qari turns to 'what happens on public thoroughfares' (chapter 3), liability for animals (chapter 4), and the rules for accidents (chapter 5). Here also, reparation is owed 'regardless of intent' (Art. 1423),[287] and Qari considers 'equal harm resting on fault and harm resting on intent'. He gives as an example a person who mistreats a mule, leading to the mule destroying some property. This person is liable whether or not she knew that the mule could react in this fashion (Art. 1433).[288]

Exceptions to strict liability are numerous. If a person is the instigator[289] rather than the author of harm, attention is given to the nature of the link and its immediacy,[290] and Qari introduces here the concept of reasonableness, which raises the question of a person's excessive use of her right.[291] If she irrigates his land while falling asleep, and the neighbour's land is harmed, or if she lights a fire 'which is large and does not conform to usage' (Art. 1431),[292] there is excess leading to liability.

---

[281] Art. 1407: *daman al-ghaseb ghayr daman al-jinaya*, the liability of the tortfeasor is different from the liability for a crime.

[282] *diyya* or *arsh*, the former monetary compensation for death (here *diyya*), the latter monetary compensation for bodily injury not resulting in death. If the liability is for *diyya*, the author of the tort must pay full compensation.   [283] *itlaf.*

[284] *al-mubashir awla bi-ihalat al-hukm ilayh min al-mutasabbib.*   [285] *mutlaf*, de *itlaf.*

[286] *maghsub*, de *ghasb.*   [287] *bi-qasd aw ghayri qasd.*

[288] *al-itlaf yastawi fih al-khata' wal-'amd.*   [289] *tasabbub.*   [290] *mubashara.*

[291] *tafrit.*

[292] *nar kathira tata'adda 'adatan aw bi-ta'jijiha fi rih shadida aw bi-tarkiha mu'ajjaja.*

Proximate cause is distinguished from distant cause. 'If a person lets an animal loose, and another person incites the animal to cause harm, liability falls on the one who incited the animal.' The principle behind this article is formulated as follows: 'If two causes meet, and one is more specific than the other, liability falls on the author of the more specific cause' (Art. 1432).[293] Temperance of strict liability appears here in the 'reasonableness' expressed in Article 1434, and allows a mule to go on the thoroughfare, even when heavily laden, 'on condition that harm be avoided'.[294] Reparation is owed again if the person who suffers harm from that animal is 'blind, minor or mentally impaired, or if she does not have the means to avoid the animal and was not forewarned' (Art. 1434). Reparation is also owed 'if a person builds a wall which leans on the road or on the neighbour's house. If the wall collapses, the person is strictly liable. If the wall is properly built, then leans and falls [for no fault of the builder], she is not responsible' (Art. 1445). 'If two post-men [on horseback] or horses collide, each postman is liable for the loss or harm in nature or in property occasioned to the other.'[295] Full liability stops in case of accident if a joint responsibility can be established: for instance two ships colliding because of excesses[296] committed by their captains.[297] One can imagine, the com-piler of the Saudi Majalla goes on to explain, that only one of the two captains has committed an excess. In that case, he would bear responsibility on his own. But if the accident is due to unexpected circumstances, such as a strong wind which ren-ders impossible control of the ship, then the Hanbali Majalla is ready to accept the captain's oath[298] to prove lack of responsibility (Art. 1454). The chapter on liability ends on a note of presumption of responsibility for the owner of a thing which causes harm because the thing is poorly equipped. 'There is excess in case the person in charge is not ready to assemble accessory or workmanship tools needed usually for the thing not to cause harm, same as if the person falls asleep while keep-ing the thing running' (Art. 1454).[299]

Treatment of tortious liability in the Saudi restatement may appear somewhat confused, but all five central principles identifiable in classical law can be found in the text: strict liability as principle, excess as mitigating factor, distinction between author and instigator, levels of causality depending on proximate causation, and likelihood in case of plurality of authors of contributory negligence.

Article 92 of the The Ottoman Majalla also establishes the principle of strict liability: 'Anyone is responsible for the damage he has caused another directly, even though unintentionally'.[300]

The principle, which is part of the general principles of the Majalla, is detailed in Book vii, which includes some 80 articles (Arts. 881–941). The articles are

---

[293] *idha ijtam'a sababan ahaduhuma akhass, ikhtassa al-daman bi-sahibih.*

[294] *al-darar alladhi yuhtaraz bih.*

[295] Art. 1452: *damana kullun minhuma ma fat 'alal-akhar min nafs wa mal.* In nature here means bodily harm.   [296] excess, *tafrit.*

[297] Captains as wardens, *al-qayyimin.*   [298] *yamin.*

[299] *'adam isti'dad al-qayyim bi-jam' al-alat al-lazima 'adatan min adawat wa 'ummal tafrit, wa kadha nawmuh ma'tarkiha sa'ira.*   [300] *al-mubashir damin wa in lam yata'ammad.*

better arranged than in the Saudi compilation, and clearer. One finds the same distinction between violation-seizure and violation-destruction. In the easier case of violation-seizure, the Majalla's authors simplify the classical law's complexities in a series of coherent articles. The violation is defined as 'taking over a person's property and keeping it without her consent' (Art. 881). The perpetrator must therefore return the property, otherwise he owes reparation. The rule is established in Article 890, and developed in the next article: 'The author of the violation-seizure must compensate the owner if he uses the property, whether the property perishes or gets lost, and whether the loss is his fault or not' (Art. 891). Details follow with variations which do not call for any particular comment (Arts. 892–911).

In the case of violation-destruction, the rule is also simple: 'Owes reparation whoever harms a person's property, whether the property is in his hands or in the hands of a person to whom he gave it, deliberately or not' (Art. 912). Here also, strict liability is the departing point. It then gets tempered by the distinction of classical Islamic law between direct author and instigator, which the Majalla also adopts.

The rule is that the direct author owes reparation, but that the reparation owed by the instigator requires his intent to bring injury or the illegality of the act.

In the Saudi and Ottoman Majallas, much order is brought to an elusive field in classical texts. Of the two restatements, the Ottoman text is more coherent, and one needs to study the century-long case-law of the Majalla's survival in various jurisdictions to see how it applied in the field of torts, in a research which requires considerable innovative work. Meanwhile, we can follow the application of the *fiqh* rules in modern tort law in Jordan, where the debt to the Majalla is conspicuous. After several attempts, the Jordanian Civil Code (JCC) was finally enacted in 1976, with two large volumes of Explanatory Memoranda drawn from the work of the legislative commission that prepared it.[301] These extensive Memoranda allow the examination of tortious liability with a particularly rich documentation, and Jordanian law reporters provide a useful follow up of its interpretation by the courts.

Strict liability is established in Article 256 of the JCC: 'Any harmful act engages the responsibility of its author to repair it, even in the absence of discernment'.[302] The Explanatory Memoranda dicuss the article within the general chapter of harmful act as source of obligation: 'The rules on liability for harmful act form in part what the Muslim jurists express under the concept of *daman*, which is for them either compensation for contract, or compensation for seizure, or compensation

---

[301] Naqabat al-muhamin (Bar Association), *Al-mudhakkirat al-idahiyya lil-qanun al-madani al-urduni* (Explanatory Memoranda of the Jordanian Civil Code), Ibrahim Aburahmeh ed., 2 vols. 3rd edn. (Amman, 1992).

[302] The formulation follows closely the Majalla's Art. 92, above n. 300. The principle is the same in the United Arab Emirates Civil Code of 1985 (*Qanun al-mu'amalat al-madaniyya li-dawlat al-imarat al-'arabiyya al-muttahida*), Art. 282: '*Kullu idrar bil-ghayr yulzim fa'ilahu wa law ghayr mumayyiz bi-daman al-darar*'.

for destruction'.[303] Compensating for contract is not the same as liability for breach of contract, because the first type of compensation concerns property which perished for reasons beyond the reach of the parties. 'Compensation for contract is not the same as contractual liability', the comment argues: 'Compensation for contractual liability does not concern a good that perished, but represents compensation for the failure of the debtor to honour his obligation under the contract. Contractual liability, in contrast, means that the contract requires one of the two parties to bear responsibility for the lost good.'[304]

Neither in the long section that follows (Arts. 256–92 JCC), nor in the extensive comments of the Explanatory Memoranda, does the distinction between liablity for the fact of a contract and contractual liability get developed further. After this problematic distinction, we are back in the field of torts as known and practised in the West. The comment briefly mentions compensation for seizure of a good that perished when in the possession of a third party, then develops compensation for destruction as the classic figure of harm done to another. This is the subject of a long treatment of the basic liability principles in Islamic law, concluding that 'the liability of a person that does a harm to another is monetary. It does not rest on fault'.[305]

Despite its best efforts, the Jordanian legislator was unable to extricate the field of torts from the dualist Western logic, and remained unable to keep to the unifying tradition of classical Islamic law under the concept of harmful act. In Jordan, as in modern legislation elsewhere, only the law of contract governs liability that derives from the consent between the parties, and its basic corollary principles: right of the creditor to ask for performance upon the breach by the debtor, and/or monetary compensation to bring back the parties to the *status quo ante*, including lost profits and interest (Arts. 246–9 JCC). *Mutatis mutandis*, all other Middle Eastern codes confirm the division on the premise that the breach of a contractual obligation is qualitatively different from compensation for tort.

One therefore finds two kinds of codes: those which tacitly recognize that liability in tort is fundamentally different from contractual liability, and in a concomitant *fiqh* logic, that fault is not a central element in tort. These codes try to remain faithful to the letter of the *shari'a* by keeping the unifying vocable *daman* and by openly rejecting fault as an intervening factor. Such is the case in Jordan, the UAE, and Iran. On the other side are the systems which openly adopted the *summa divisio* between tortious liability and contractual liability, and integrated fault as a formative element in tort: these are the codes of North Africa, Sanhuri's Egyptian Code, and its calques in Syria (1949), Libya (1954), Kuwait (1960, replaced in 1980), Somalia (1973), and Algeria (1975); the Lebanese Code of

---

[303] *Daman 'aqd*, compensation (lit. guarantee) for contract; *daman yad*, compensation for seizure (lit. guarantee for hand); *daman itlaf*, compensation for destruction. EM Jordan, i, 272–3.

[304] EM Jordan, i, 272.

[305] EM Jordan, i, 279, also citing the Ottoman Majalla's Arts. 916 and 960 on the absence of a condition of discernment to establish responsibility.

Obligations and Contracts of 1932; also in this particular case figures the Civil Code of North Yemen, which has applied in the unified Yemen since 1990.

Case-law

In court practice, and to a lesser extent in legislation, the 'Western' system has finally overtaken 'tradition', and the Jordanian case shows the tortuous ways of systems with opposed logics. From the legislator's point of view, we have just seen how Jordan's official Explanatory Memoranda make a sharp distinction between liability in tort and liability in contract which does not correspond to the three-way division which they seem to derive from Islamic law (compensation for breach of contract, compensation for unlawful seizure, and compensation for destruction). This contradiction suggests that their theoretical construct has somewhat lost its bearings, but the distinction is equally apparent in case-law: 'The way the Court of Appeals dealt with the case on the grounds of tort liability, even if it was introduced on the grounds of liability for harmful act, contradicts the causes and object of the action'.[306] In the particulars of this decision, a restaurant had been destroyed by a municipal expropriation committee without due process, and compensation was sought by the plaintiff. In its estimate of the harm, the Court of Cassation reversed the Court of Appeals' decision because it confused liability in tort and contractual liability. It refused to calculate compensation on the tortious principle of extent of harm done and lost profit. 'Compensation of loss should only result from harmful act.'[307] The restaurant was the property of the municipality, and the Court of Cassation reversed by basing compensation on the benefits of the operation from the beginning of demolition works to the end of the lease. Do not enter into consideration contractual considerations like goodwill (which applies only in non-municipal leases) or payment to the restaurant employees. Harm in tort, the Court concluded, does not apply in contract.

The Court followed a similar formal distinction in the case of road accidents, admitting three types of liability: contractual liability of the insurance company towards the harmed party, liability of the car owner, which operates in tort and is governed by the Driving Code, and the liability in tort of the driver which is governed by Article 256 of the JCC. There is no need to confuse them in law, the Court concluded.[308] One finds several similar decisions which emphasize the uniqueness of contractual responsibility, whether in the scrutiny of a liquidated damages clause,[309] the notice required in case of breach,[310] the operation of the

---

[306] Jordanian Cassation Court, Decision of 15 September 1987, in Naqabat al-muhamin (Amman Bar Association), *al-Mabade' al-qanuniyya li-mahkamat al-tamyiz, mundhu bidayat sanat 1989 hatta nihayat sanat 1991* (Legal principles of the Cassation Court, from the beginning of 1989 to end), n.d, vol. 7, ii, 1007. All the decisions which are cited were handed down by the Cassation Court.

[307] ibid. 1008.

[308] Jordanian Cassation Court, Decision of 7 February 1988, *Mabade'*, Jordan, 7, ii, 1013.

[309] ibid. 1001, 992 bottom of page, 1010 bottom of page. Art. 256, cited above text at n. 282.

[310] ibid. 1013–14.

statute of limitations,[311] or simply the rejection of contractual responsibility when 'the contract itself rejects such liability'.[312]

Even clearer in its rejection of classical tradition is the explicit survival of the concept of fault at the heart of the Jordanian Court of Cassation's decisions. In a thematic index covering three years of recent civil cases totalling about a hundred tort decisions, fault emerges as the central pillar of tort liability for the Jordanian Supreme Court.[313] Contrary to the express text of the Code and to *fiqh* principles, the Jordanian Court of Cassation did not hesitate to adopt the basic French tort philosophy: 'Art. 256 of the Civil Code specifies that any harm inflicted upon a person engages the responsibility of its author, even in the absence of discernment. Liability in tort rests on three pillars: fault, harm and the causal relation between fault and harm.'[314] In that particular case, the Court rejected the liability of a laboratory director working with customs by considering that he did not commit any fault under the uses of expertise in his profession when he wrongly estimated the value of the merchandise which he was examining.

The Jordanian Supreme Court therefore did not hesitate to establish fault as a defining element of tortious liability. The application is consistent, and can be found in some fifteen cases, together with the expected variations depending on the behaviour of the average person,[315] or that of a professional.[316] From time to time the word *daman* reappears,[317] but the principles and terminology of the Jordanian Civil Code, let alone of *fiqh*, remained behind.

Conclusion: On Style and Substance

The debate over the influence of *fiqh* on contemporary law can be extended or reduced at will. As in the Ottoman and Egyptian codifications which provide the two great models on which were grafted, in most Middle Eastern countries, attempts to fuse the classical and modern law of obligations, comparison must be carried out in both historical and lateral fashion. Historical: the Ottomans drew on classical law, and Sanhuri drew on Egyptian case-law. Lateral: the Majalla calques drew both on the Majalla and on its sources. Sanhuri was attentive to European and Islamic law, while no Arab legislation after Sanhuri could ignore his

---

[311] Three years after the discovery of the harmful act according to Art. 272 JCC, and for unjust enrichment under Art. 311, different time limitations for contracts depending on the type of contract, examples in *Mabade'*, Jordan, i, 538, 541, 548. The section on prescription includes brief reports on some sixty decisions, *Mabade'*, Jordan, i, 528–54.   [312] *Mabade'*, Jordan, 7, ii, 1036.

[313] Under the category 'damage' (*'utl wa darar*, a modern appellation), ninety-three decisions are reported in *Mabade'*, Jordan, 7, ii, 991–1038, to which should be added fourteen decisions listed under 'compensation' (*ta'wid*, also a modern appellation).

[314] *Mabade'*, Jordan, 7, ii, 1017 (Cassation, Decision of 28 May 1988). Similar formulation in a decision of 16 May 1987, ibid. 1000.   [315] *al-shakhs al-'adi*, ibid. 1007.

[316] The keeper of mechanical tools is held to a higher standard. Ibid., 991.

[317] e.g. Decision of 26 May 1997, *Mabade'*, Jordan, 7, ii, 1001; Decision of 12 November 1988, ibid. 1020–1.

formidable legacy. The debate on influence can never be closed, and comparative law is more an exercise in style than in mathematical rigour. The result of the exercise depends a lot on the size of the comparative lens used. Whether in the formation of contract, its effects, or its termination, or in the responsibility for tort, one will find in the legislative momuments a confluence of laws operating as so many different layers. The picture gets even more complicated when it comes to the codification that has taken place since the Iraqi Civil Code of 1953, the first clear mixture between the Majalla and the Sanhuri Codes. This characteristically hybrid system was followed by several countries, notably Jordan in 1976, the United Arab Emirates in 1985, and more recently in North, then unified, Yemen (1990).

Beyond substance and structure, the text of the Egyptian Civil Code includes an elusive dimension which brought much grist to the mill of Sanhuri's critics. The ECC seems estranged from Islamic law. We know from Sanhuri's two major works, *al-Wasit* and *Masader al-haqq*, as well as from private papers published in the late 1980s,[318] that he was deeply attached to his faith, and that he exerted strenuous scholary efforts to achieve convergence with the Islamic legal tradition.

Style and language, rather than substance, may be at the core of the debate over the modern law of obligations. In the list of criteria underlined by comparative law, the issue of style is the most elusive, because it is hard to compare codes on the basis of their respective styles. It is also the most central, because the large gap is clearest in the specific terminology which is naturally carried by the respective languages. To make progress on this score, some conclusions in the research carried out in this chapter should be set out in terms of vocabulary, syntax, and architectonics.

An important part of style is the choice of words. Words do not necessarily affect the result of the legal rule, but style, spirit, and context are directly engaged in vocabulary.

Liability is a good illustration. Use of the word *mas'uliyya* instead of *daman* does not necessarily change the substance of the law of contracts and torts. It is nonetheless *daman*, and not *mas'uliyya*, which one finds in the books of *fiqh* and in the Majalla, and *mas'uliyya* in the works of Sanhuri and the Arab Codes he compiled. Another illustration is in the field of contractual 'options'. Islamic law options have been reduced considerably in later Majalla-style codes, and are all but absent in the Sanhuri codes. Courts seem to ignore options even in countries where the codes have included them. Also absent in the overall system of contractual obligations is the archetypal role of sale in the great classical texts, in favour of a more abstract and central role for the concept of obligation itself. And in the civil law of torts, the dominant use of the word *khata'* for *faute* sheds light, by contrast, on the characteristic absence of classical categories like *ghasb* and *itlaf* in the Codes inspired by Sanhuri or the French tradition.

---

[318] Nadia al-Sanhuri and Tawfiq al-Shawi, *'Abd al-Razzaq al-Sanhuri min khilal awraqih al-shakhsiyya* (Sanhuri through his private papers) (Cairo, 1988).

One can go further in comparing syles by dwelling on syntax rather than on vocabulary. Consider the definition of contract in the Majalla, then in the Egyptian Civil Code: 'Contract is an obligation of the parties on an object and their commitment to it, and is the expression of the connection between offer and acceptance', says Article 103 of the Majalla.[319] The corresponding Sanhuri text is Article 89 of the ECC, which states: 'The contract is concluded by the mere exchange by the two parties of corresponding intents, with due attention to specific issues which the law may require additionally for the formation of the contract'.[320] For the reader of the translation into a Western language, the difference between the two texts is limited, even if Sanhuri's formulation appears more familiar, and far clearer. For the Arab jurist however,[321] the syntactic arrangement of the Majalla renders it immediately closer to the classical Islamic model, while the corresponding Egyptian sentence draws an immediate parallel with the French civil law model.

Analysing the structure of the sentence further yields more clues on the radical difference in style. In the case of the Majalla, the noun[322] introduces the phrase, and there is no verb. This is a common feature in classical language use. In the ECC in contrast, the verb introduces the phrase, a characteristic of translation from the corresponding European formulations. The language of the Majalla is far more elegant, but it is also less precise than the ECC's.[323] Finally, the Majalla's formulation is far more concise, with twelve words against twenty-two for the Egyptian Code (note this isn't the case in translation); such concision is typical of many other articles in the Code, especially in the ninety-nine introductory principles of the Majalla's first Book.

The stylistic difference between the Majalla calques and the Sanhuri Codes are reminiscent in comparative law of French and German styles in their is respective Civil Codes. In contrast to the German BGB, one finds in the French Civil Code lapidary formulas which tend to sacrifice legal precision to the profit of a literary, mnemonic style.[324] The similarly literary tone of the Majalla is obvious, leading to

---

[319] *'al-'aqd iltizam al-muta'aqidayn amran wa ta'ahhuduhuma bihi wa huwa 'ibara 'an irtibat al-ijab bil-qubul.*

[320] *yatumm al-'aqd bi-mujarrad an yatabadal tarafan al-ta'bir 'an iradatayn mutatabiqatayn, ma' mura'at ma yuqarriruh al-qanun fawqa dhalik min awda' mu'ayyana lin'iqad al-'aqd.*

[321] Arabic, one should recall, forms the linguistic matrix for legal Persian and Ottoman.

[322] Nominative, *al-mubtada'.*

[323] In the above-mentioned Article 103 of the Majalla, the mention of 'obligation towards an object' is superfluous, and the word connection (*irtibat*) between offer and acceptance is less appropriate than the concept of meeting, despite the existence of a verbatim equivalent to meeting in Arabic (*liqa', iltiqa'*).

[324] Zweigert and Kötz, *An introduction to comparative law,* 91–2, (comparing the principle *Pacta sunt servanda* to the formulae of the Napoleonic Code, Art. 1134, and of the German BGB, para. 241), and 145 (comparing the dual place for the treatment of sale in the BGB, paras 929 ff in the book on property about the transmision of legal title in sold merchandise, and paras 433 ff of the book on obligations regarding the moment when the creditor can ask that the merchandise be delivered to him, whereas the two problems are actually fused in the Anglo-Saxon tradition).

repetitions that weaken juridical rigour, but are more accessible to the literate non-lawyer.

In terms of references, contrary to the mixture of legal traditions we find in the ECC, the spirit of *fiqh* dominates the Majalla, from its adoption of *hadith* to the formulas of Ibn Nujaym and Ibn 'Abidin. Characteristic of the Ottoman Majalla style also are the curious illustrations that the compilers borrowed from Islamic casuistry when they added concrete examples to articles of the codes. This combination of a literary legal style and of practical illustrations within the text of an article is also typical of the private civil law restatements adopted as calques of the Majalla. The combination is nowhere to be found in the Sanhuri Codes. While the substance may be the same, the style is profoundly different. Lost is the concise, almost poetical *fiqh* formula which is characteristic of the Majalla, in exchange for additional clarity in the Sanhuri style. But it is also a loss of a millennium-old language against the conscious or unconscious following of Western models.

It is also true that the 'Sanhuri monument' which the ECC represents must be appreciated in a specific Egyptian context. The Majalla was never introduced into the laws of Egypt, where the Mixed Tribunals' case-law, and that of the national tribunals, developed over half a century on the basis of a law of obligations which is an undeniable import from the West, and an equally undeniable ignorance of classical Islamic law. One can only be surprised by the remarkable effort of Sanhuri to integrate Islamic classical law rules in an Egyptian legal milieu which was no longer used to them. In turn, as commentaries of great learning in the civil law of the twentieth-century Middle East, Sanhuri's *Wasit* and *Masader* have enriched comparative work well beyond Egypt.

The debate over the *shari'a* and the Egyptian Civil Code, and the Code's successors, will never end.[325] In the light of the findings of this chapter, the issue is better addressed in less black and white terms, and attention shifted from substance to style. The Syrian legislator, upon adopting the Sanhuri model to create more uniformity between the civil codes of the Arab world, put the issue succinctly: 'The Ottoman Majalla is distant in its redaction from modern legal style, and is closer to the language of *fiqh* than to the language of *qanun*'.[326]

To summarize, legal style is profoundly different in three identifiable areas: (1) in the Islamic legal tradition, the general architectonic is that of a number of books, at the centre of which stands the book of sale. The structure of modern codes tends to be more abstract, and presents categories and chapters which are

---

[325] Interesting reflections on the cumulation of references can be found in Bälz, 'Europäisches Privatrecht', above n. 123, section entitled 'Sanhuri's Kodifikation: Französisch, islamisch, ägyptisch?'

[326] '*wa hiya (al-majalla) fi siyaghatiha ba'ida 'an al-siyagha al-qanuniyya bima warada fi mawaddiha min al-itala wal-ishab wa dhikr al-amthila wal-asbab fa-kanat fi siyaghatiha ila lughat al-fiqh aqrab minha ila lughat al-qanun.' Al-mudhakkara al-idahiyya, al-qanun al madani al-suri* (Introductory explanatory report, Syrian Civil Code), Nuri ed. (Damascus, n.d.) 1.

closer to the Napoleonic model in their abstraction. (2) In terms of syntax, the turn of phrase in Islamic law has its own slightly *passé* noun-based form, which tends to be far more eloquent and arguably less precise than the verb-based sentence which is common to modern Arabic and French. (3) Finally, the choice of words may differ significantly, as in the concept of liability, which is at the heart of any law of obligations.

Beyond style, there may be a more substantive difference, and I have argued in this chapter that two competing logics are at work in the contemporary Middle Eastern law of obligations. In contrast to Western law, the classical Islamic legal tradition conceived of liability as compensation for harm: there is no *summa divisio* between contractual liability and liability in tort. Within the law of torts, there is no place for fault or negligence. The point of departure for liability is vested in its legal consequence as harm. Once harm is established, liability ensues, no matter whether in contract or in tort. This is not the way Western law operates. Torts and contracts are intrinsically different, and liability is profoundly different in each of the two major fields. Within torts, liability cannot be conceived outside *faute* and negligence. The whole Islamic system of torts should indeed be understood as a denial of French *faute* or common law negligence. In the Majalla and in other codes which are directly inspired by it, like the Jordanian Civil Code of 1976, this principle reveals a central difference in the field of obligations between Western and Middle Eastern law, and within the Middle East, between countries that adopt strict liability following the Majalla, like Jordan and many Gulf countries, and those which consider fault to be a constitutive characteristic in the law of tort, as in the Maghreb countries and the Levant.

From this overall perspective, it seems difficult to see how the two contrastive logics can ever meet in theory. This leads in practice to a disjunctive treatment, which is apparent both in Middle Eastern court cases and in the understanding of the field of obligations by modern commentators. A fascinating challenge for comparative law, it's a particularly difficult one for Middle Eastern civilists, law teachers and practitioners alike.

9

Commercial Law: Globalization
and Tradition

What matters in all things is custom.

Sarakhsi

In the contemporary civil law of obligations, a 'Middle Eastern style' was identified as a patchwork of European and local traditions with a language and a terminology sometimes derived from classical Islamic law, *fiqh*.[1] This is not the case for commercial law. Whether from an institutional and technical perspective, or whether in the language proper, Middle Eastern commercial law as found in legislation or court cases reads for both practitioners and scholars as a direct transposition of European law. The long-standing tradition of a civilization closely associated with trade seems irrelevant for the present commercial law of the area.

A brief presentation of commercial law decisions across the Arab world is sufficient to show the dominance of Western principles in the field, and the direct translation of Western terminology and rules for local transactions.[2] The decisions have been regrouped in categories which are familiar to the commercial lawyer, and offer ample illustration of the large-scale borrowing from Western commercial law.

Judgments

Syria. Quality of merchant. The Court of Cassation in Syria upheld a decision of the Bar of Lattaquie (north-west Syria) to debar a lawyer who was carrying on commercial activities whilst registered as a lawyer in contradiction with the Bar Association regulations. It held that the excuse of continuing his father's commercial practice was not relevant and that his registration in the commercial registry

[1] See Chapter 8.
[2] The following survey of court decisions is selected from some 100 commercial law reports from the Arab world, published between 1984 and 1997 in *al-Majalla al-'arabiyya lil-fiqh wal-qada'* (MAFQ).

was evidence which he did not rebut, and which, following previous decisions by the same Court of Cassation, established him as a merchant before the law.[3]

Bahrain. Quality of merchant. The quality of merchant, and hence the possibility of declaring bankruptcy, was conferred by the Bahraini Higher Court of Appeal on an Indian resident of Bahrain, who was not entitled as a foreigner to enlist in the register of commerce, but who was considered nonetheless a merchant in view of his trading activities. The Court reversed a Court of Appeal decision which considered that the person in question was a *prête-nom* for other companies, and as such was not entitled to benefit from the regime accorded to merchants. The Higher Court of Appeal stated:

The fact that the appellant [the Indian resident] was not of Bahraini citizenship and thus forbidden from practising commerce in Bahrain, and that subsequently he was not able to register in the commercial register does not prevent him being considered a merchant if the legal elements necessary [to establish the quality of merchant] are present. Article 9 of the Bahraini Code of Commerce considers a merchant any person having the capacity of merchant and taking as a matter of trade a commercial operation in his name and for his own benefit.

Even if he operated in some cases for the actual benefit of others,

this does not affect his quality as merchant, which he acquired by effectively engaging in commerce in his name. According to Art.18/2 of the Code of Commerce, the quality of merchant is established for whomever practises trade under a *prête-nom* or hides behind another person, in addition to his establishment [as merchant] on a personal basis.[4]

Kuwait. Quality of merchant. The High Court of Appeal of Kuwait examined in a long decision the problems relating to the acts of commerce and the quality of merchant. The case involved several legal principles established by the court, some of which were *obiter*. The facts of the case are complicated, and the decision not very clear. It brings together three commercial appeals over a dispute between heirs to a large piece of land and contenders to at least part of the land because of an operation of sale to merchants with an apparent view to a quick profit after division of the estate and resale. The court rejected all three appeals, and confirmed the original owners in their ownership, also confirming compensation to the purchaser at the time the debt was owed, which the court equated with the time the original suit was brought up. With regard to the specific commercial dimension of the dispute, the Kuwaiti Court of Cassation also confirmed the lower court in its objective appreciation of the quality of merchant on the basis of the mercantile nature of the deal over the land: 'Appreciation of the quality of

[3] Al-Jumhuriyya al-ʿarabiyya al-suriyya (Syrian Arab Republic), Mahkamat al-naqd (Court of Cassation), 6 June 1985, MAFQ 12, 1992, 205.

[4] Dawlat al-Bahrain (State of Bahrain), Mahkamat al-istiʾnaf al-ʿulya (higher appeals court), 3 January 1987, MAFQ 11, 1992, 334, at 336.

merchant can be established by all types of legal evidence . . . The establishment of the mercantile nature of a transaction is of the exclusive competence of the court of fact and there is no control over it.'[5]

Jordan. Liability. Port Authority. A finely argued decision of the Jordanian Court of Cassation held that the liability of a port authority for the loss of merchandise was part of its duties as carrier of this merchandise within the precinct of the port and could not be removed by an argument of *force majeure* derived from its loss because of theft. An Iraqi cargo had unloaded six containers into the port of 'Aqaba. Two containers went missing, and a criminal inquiry was in progress. The Port Authority was asked by the first instance court and the Court of Appeal to compensate the cargo liner in full. The Port Authority appealed before the Court of Cassation on the ground that the transport of the goods in the containers into the silos of the Port was not part of the operation of transport. The Court demurred, on the basis of the unity of the operation. The appellant also argued the necessity to wait for the result of the enquiry as penal law ties civil and commercial law. The Court rejected the argument as the inquest's objective was to look for possible thieves, and considered that its result was irrelevant to the liability of the Port Authority. Indeed, either the thieves were employees of the port and the Port Authority was responsible for them following Article 288 of the Civil Code, or they were foreign to both parties, and liability for the safety of the merchandise was entirely incumbent on the Port Authority.[6]

Bahrain. Liability. Duty of care. This was a case of goods transported in a container which had been seriously damaged. The Court of Cassation upheld the decisions of the lower courts (in first instance, *al-mahkama al-sughra*, because of the small amount involved, *c.* 600 dinars, then the upper court, *al-mahkama al-kubra*). Lower courts had awarded the money to the plaintiff—an insurance company, which had paid the insured merchant for receiving the damaged goods, and substituted itself for his claim against the defendant—a maritime carrier. The courts all agreed that the Bahraini Maritime code does not absolve the carrier from his duty to look after the merchandise carried, notwithstanding any clause to the contrary in the contract of transportation. The Court of Cassation noted that 'the carton boxes had been seen inside the container in the normal and usual way in the commercial field', and that the argument of the carrier that the merchandise had delivered the container in good shape did not suffice to remove or mitigate his liability.[7]

---

[5] Dawlat al-Kuwait (State of Kuwait), Mahkamat al-isti'naf al-'ulya, da'irat al-tamyiz (higher appeals court, section of cassation), 26 March 1986, MAFQ 16, 1994, 314 at 324.

[6] Al-Mamlaka al-urduniyya al-hashimiyya (the Hashemite Kingdom of Jordan), Mahkamat al-tamyiz (Court of Cassation), 19 January 1987, MAFQ 11, 1992, 327.

[7] Dawlat al-Bahrain (State of Bahrain), Mahkamat al-tamyiz (Court of Cassation), 10 June 1990, MAFQ 12, 1992, 202 at 203, 204.

Tunisia. Liability. Damaged goods. A decision of the Tunisian Court of Cassation confirmed the responsibility of the carrier toward the buyer in case of damage to merchandise carried by sea on the basis of Article 146 of the Code of Maritime Commerce, which stipulates that 'any damage to the merchandise is supposed to have taken place between possession and delivery so long as the carrier does not provide evidence otherwise'. The carrier, said the Court, did not rebut the presumption, and the stevedore to whom the carrier was imputing responsibility is not liable 'so long as the maritime carrier did not prove that the merchandise was in good condition when delivered to the stevedore'.[8]

Syria. Liability. Air carrier. In a long decision, the Court of Cassation confirmed the judgment of the Court of Appeal establishing the responsibility of a German air carrier for refusing to fulfil its obligation to transport the petitioner, a sick man who was coming back from New York to Damascus. The passenger had boarded the plane with a medic and a special bed, and was summoned by the captain to unboard. He died a few days later. Several legal aspects were addressed by the court which fall outside the commercial field proper: in the law of obligations, the remoteness of damage, in the law of conflict, the competence of the Syrian court on the basis of French precedents, and in the law of evidence and procedure, expert reports and the review of the evidence produced by the lower court. In the commercial field, the responsibility of the air carrier was established under the 1929 Warsaw Convention. The airline, the Court concluded, did not fulfil its obligations under the transport contract notwithstanding internal directives of the company allowing the captain of the plane to refuse boarding to a seriously ill passenger.[9]

Kuwait. Liability. Air carrier. The Warsaw Convention was also the main reference in a decision of the Kuwaiti Court of Cassation which established the responsibility of an air carrier for goods perishing in the custody of customs at the airport. The Court confirmed that liability started from receipt and ended only upon delivery. This did not prevent the judges from rejecting contributory negligence and from allowing liability to extend jointly and severally to the customs' office, so long as evidence did not exonerate that office from its responsibility. Solidarity between co-debtors, here the customs office and the air carrier, was total, and the victim could sue either for the totality of the debt.[10]

---

[8] Al-Jumhuriyya al-tunisiyya (Tunisian Republic), mahkamat al-taʿqib (Court of Cassation), 3 May 1982, MAFQ 11, 1992, 337 at 339.

[9] Al-Jumhuriyya al-ʿarabiyya al-suriyya (Syrian Arab Republic), Mahkamat al-naqd (Court of Cassation), 3 March 1987, MAFQ 11, 1992, 340–6.

[10] Dawlat al-Kuwait (State of Kuwait), Mahkamat al-istiʾnaf al-ʿulya, daʾirat al-tamyiz (higher appeals court, section of cassation), 13 February 1985, MAFQ 11, 1992, 349–53. For another decision in this field, translated in English in full, and mainly based on the Warsaw Convention, see *Dr Najeeb Al-Nuaimi v. Gulf Air*, decided by the court of Appeal of Doha, 9 June 1993, in E. Cotran and C. Mallat, eds., *Yearbook of Islamic and Middle Eastern law*, i, 1994, 558–64. (In a case

United Arab Emirates. Commercial instruments. Documentary letter of credit. In a procedurally complex decision,[11] the Supreme Federal Court of the United Arab Emirates established joint responsibility for a documentary letter of credit opened at a bank *in solidum*, even though one of the parties may have established a different relationship with the other debtor in the contract of partnership.

The bank was not party to the contract between the partners. Its knowledge of the contents and conditions of the partnership contract or the contract leading to its dissolution does not affect the obligation *in solidum* of the appellant and the other appellee since the opening of the documentary credit took place after the contract establishing the partnership.

There was no obligation on the part of the bank

so long as the bank did not accept absolving the joint debtor from the obligation contracted *in solidum* with his partner. The silence of the bank towards these letters is in reality a rejection of these arguments, especially since the appellant did not ask the bank for a remittance of the debt and the full discharging of the liability for the documentary credit to remain with [his partner].[12]

Jordan. Commercial instruments. Endorsement. In a brief decision, the Jordanian Court of Cassation rejected the appeal of an endorser who had issued an endorsement carrying on the bill the mention 'value of guarantee', and held that the Code of Commerce did not make any difference between the original debtor and the guarantor in this respect: This was a guarantee endorsement, said the Court, 'which like the usual endorsement, establishes transfer of property ... The person to whom endorsement was made can ask for the full value of the bill when due.'[13]

United Arab Emirates. Commercial instruments. Cheque.[14] The National Bank of Abu Dhabi had brought action against a client for unpaid debts, and received a judgment in its favour in first instance and on appeal. The defendant brought in the meantime another action against the bank for withholding twenty-two cheques made to his order, the value of which (some 2,623,000 dirhams; 1 US\$ 1995 = 3.7 UAE dirhams) amounted to a sum far beyond the compensation granted in the previous judgment. The bank argued that final decision had already been made by the other court, but the second court carried on and delivered judgment against the client. On appeal, the Court of Appeal of Abu Dhabi

---

of overbooked flights, the court awarded 'full compensation', set at 150,000 riyals (1 US\$ = 3.6 Qatari riyals in 1995), by air carrier to a first class passenger and his family, who were unable to board the plane, for 'loss of gain or the result of loss, and moral and material damage', at 564).

   [11] Dawlat al-imarat al-'arabiyya al-muttahida (United Arab Emirates), Al-mahkama al-ittihadiyya al-'ulya (Federal Supreme Court), 9 December 1987, MAFQ 11, 1992, at 331.

   [12] ibid. at 333.

   [13] Al-Mamlaka al-urduniyya al-hashimiyya (the Hashemite Kingdom of Jordan), Mahkamat al-tamyiz (Court of Cassation), 3 July 1991, MAFQ 14, 1993, 253, at 254.

   [14] Dawlat al-imarat al-'arabiyya al-muttahida (United Arab Emirates), al-mahkama al-ittihadiyya al-'ulya (Federal Supreme Court), MAFQ 14, 1993, 256–62.

held that the cheques were considered as a guarantee up to the value of the client's debt. It also appointed an expert to see whether the withholding by the bank of the cheques was acceptable 'under the customs of banking'.[15] The expert concluded as to the irregularity of the bank's practice in the case, as it should have carried on processing the cheques, even if it knew that there was no adequate provision, but the Court of Appeal decided nonetheless for the bank on the ground that 'the bank has two qualities: first, it is an agent for the purposes of cashing the cheques deposited with it, and, secondly, it is a pledged creditor benefiting from the cheque as security'.[16] The bank was therefore not liable for refusing to cash the cheque as it knew, notwithstanding the report of the expert, that there was no provision for the cheques deposited.

The defendant appealed in cassation before the Supreme Federal Court, which brought together the various actions and procedural incidents. At issue, the Court held, were five pleas from the appellant. It proceeded by rejecting four of them, while reversing the decision on one count.

The first argument was the wrong appreciation by the lower courts of the nature of the cheques and the expert's report. The Supreme Court saw that the practice of the bank was not irregular, that it was natural that the bank would credit the client's account upon receipt of the cheques, and that it would proceed back and debit them if it turned out there were insufficient funds. The cheque was to be considered therefore as prima-facie security.

The legal qualification of the cheque provided two additional arguments for the appellant, who claimed that no security could be made to affect a cheque under Article 1449 of the Law on Civil Transactions, which requires that the object of security must be capable of being sold in auction. Again, the court rejected the argument, holding that nothing prevents cheques from being considered as possessory pledges with a bank. The appellant claimed further that there were contradictions between the qualification of the decisions of the various appeal courts. The Supreme Court saw otherwise, explaining that the bank was operating in various capacities, but that they were all premised on the concept of cheque as security for the client's debt.

A fourth plea of the appellant in cassation to the effect of a contradiction between the decisions of the Court of Appeal as to the qualification of the cheque deposited with the bank was also rejected. 'It is not necessary for the pledgee bank', the Federal Supreme Court held, 'to return some of the cheques and to hold on only to the amount of the debt, since the money deposited as security must be considered one complete unit to guarantee the debt and is often superior to that debt'.[17]

However, the Court held for the client on one count. It held the bank liable for not carrying the procedure for bad cheques to its judicial end, notably for two out of the twenty-two cheques deposited, and considered that the two cheques, with a value of 150,000 dirhams (*c.* $40,000), 'were not a trivial sum' as argued by the

---

[15] ibid. at 258, '*hasb al-'urf al-masrifi*'.   [16] ibid. at 259.

[17] ibid. at 262. Argument based on comparative laws, '*hasb al-qawanin al-muqarana*'.

bank.[18] The responsibility of the bank was therefore established to that limited extent and the decision remanded down to the Court of Appeal for revision.

Iraq. Commercial instruments. Cheque endorsement. In a short decision, the Court of Cassation reversed a lower decision which had annulled a cheque because of the absence of mention in it of the place of its issuing. It based its decision on Article 185 of the new Iraqi Code of Commerce of 1984, which did not stipulate the place of issuing as one of the conditions of the cheque's validity.[19]

Iraq. Commercial instruments. Notarization of bill. Prescription. Also in a short decision, taken by majority, the Iraqi Court of Cassation held that a commercial bill retained its commercial nature even after notarization, and was therefore subject to the period of limitation under the Commercial Code.[20]

United Arab Emirates. Commercial instruments. Debtors' obligation in solidum.[21] The Federal Supreme Court of Cassation sitting in Abu Dhabi confirmed the decision of the Federal Court of Appeal sitting in the Emirate of Sharjah and rejected two pleas by the appellants: the first was a plea to disregard joint liability for a commercial bill. The second plea demanded the suppression of interest on late payment of the debt. On the first plea, the Supreme Court held that even if the law did not expressly acknowledge solidarity for a bill, the practice of commerce considered such papers to be commercial, and all obligors on the paper were jointly liable for discharging them. The Court cited the draft Code of Commercial Transactions (which was adopted in 1993, two years after the decision was handed down[22]) as further argument, even though a bill as such was not included among the commercial papers cited in the Code for joint liability. On the issue of interest, the Court explained that late payment, under the principle 'delay by the rich is harm',[23] requires compensation to the injured party, and that interest on late payment of the debt, which had been imposed by the lower courts as compensation, was warranted and legal.

Morocco. Commercial debt. Prescription. Reversing a decision by the Court of Appeal of Fes, the Supreme Court of Morocco held that the specific time limitation governing a commercial debt is to be found in the Commercial Code, Article 189 of

[18] ibid.

[19] Jumhuriyyat al-'iraq (Iraqi Republic), Mahkamat al-tamyiz (Court of Cassation), 28 January 1988, MAFQ 11, 1992, 347–8.

[20] Jumhuriyyat al-'iraq (Iraqi Republic), Mahkamat al-tamyiz (Court of Cassation), 28 January 1988, 31 July 1990, MAFQ 14, 1993, 268.

[21] Dawlat al-imarat al-'arabiyya al-muttahida (United Arab Emirates), Al-mahkama al-ittihadiyya al-'ulya (Federal Supreme Court), 23 December 1992, MAFQ 15, 1994, 299.

[22] Federal law 18 of 1993, which came into force 20 December 1993. For an overview of the Code, see Richard Price, 'United Arab Emirates', *Yearbook of Islamic and Middle Eastern Law*, i, 1994, 307–29.   [23] '*Matl al-ghaniyy zulm*' (*hadith*), in UAE decision above n. 21 at 302.

which 'holds all cases resulting from a commercial invoice against the accepting drawee, to be subject to a period of three-year time limitation', but that partial payment brings an end to the issue of limitation under Article 152 of the Code. The dispositions of the Civil Code were considered irrelevant.[24]

Algeria. Pre-emption in commerce. In a poorly worded decision, the Supreme Court of Algeria reversed a Court of Appeal judgment which had allowed the exercise of pre-emption over the transfer of commercial property—*fonds de commerce*. The contract between the new owner of the *fonds de commerce* and the original merchant was considered void by the Court of Appeal because the transfer had been made in the absence of the owner of the building where the commerce was located, who was allegedly denied his right to exercise pre-emption. The Supreme Court reversed by affirming the lack of relevance of the right of pre-emption in commercial sales.[25]

Libya. Bankruptcy. Directors' responsibility. In a confusing decision over a case which seems to have dragged on since before 1969, the Supreme Court rejected the applicability of the personal liability of directors, as mentioned in Article 555 of the Commercial Code, and the necessity to restrict liability to the assets of a bankrupt company. The facts seem to support a clear operation of fraud, in which directors of an import company received huge sums for material to be imported into Libya, which they put in their private bank accounts. The company went bankrupt, and the plaintiffs obdurately requested the examination of the personal responsibility of the directors beyond their ownership of shares in the company. While the decision of the Court did not appear too convincing in law in view of the evidence of fraud, it might be explained by 'a letter of the defendant to the president of the revolutionary council', which clearly acknowledged the fraud, but which might have acted to deter the Supreme Court judges from punishing the rogue directors who turned out to have strong connections in high places. Articles 554 and 555 of the Commercial Code, which hold directors responsible on their own fortune for fraud to the company, were set aside by the Court on the basis of the bankruptcy process which prevented debtors from pursuing directors outside the strict bankruptcy procedure.[26]

Bahrain. Bankruptcy. Date of appreciation. In a brief decision, the Court of Cassation in Bahrain refused to be drawn on the subject of assessing the effective

---

[24] Al-Mamlaka al-maghribiyya (Kingdom of Morocco), al-majlis al-aʻla (Supreme Court), 7 December 1988, MAFQ 11, 1992, 359–60 at 360.

[25] Al-Jumhuriyya al-jazaʼiryya al-dimuqratiyya al-shaʻbiyya (Democratic Popular Republic of Algeria), al-majlis al-aʻla (Supreme Court), 21 January 1984, MAFQ 16, 1994, 311.

[26] Al-Jamahariyya al-ʻarabiyya al-libyya al-shaʻbiyya al-ishtirakiyya al-ʻuzma (the Great Popular Socialist Arab Libyan Jamahiriyya), al-majlis al-aʻla (Supreme Court), 29 October 1984, MAFQ 11, 1992, 354–8. Letter to Muʻammar al-Qadhdhafi mentioned at 356 and 360.

date of bankruptcy of a merchant, leaving such assessment to the lower courts as an issue of fact.[27]

Kuwait. Bankruptcy. Liquidation of limited liability company. A plethora of suits and counter-suits had resulted from a dispute between a Kuwaiti 51 per cent shareholder in a limited liability company and his Syrian partner for 49 per cent of the shares, and the High Court of Appeal joined all claims in its judgment. The Court held that in case of disagreement which prevents the continuation of a limited liability company, and in the absence of regulations under the company articles of association, the rules under the Commercial Companies Law of 1960 require the appointment of a liquidator, who is in charge of assessing the dissolved company and of distributing the proceeds of the liquidation accordingly. The Court reversed a ruling of the lower court which had allowed the distribution of the assets on the basis of a balance dated at the start of litigation, and requested the newly appointed liquidator to proceed with the allocation of the remaining credit to the partners at the date of liquidation.[28]

There is little in these examples which a commercial lawyer trained in the West will not be comfortable with. Occasionally, as in the 1992 decision of the Federal Supreme Court of the United Arab Emirates on the joint liability of debtors whose signature appears on a commercial instrument, the issue of *riba*, 'interest', re-emerges. With the possible exception of Saudi Arabia, and recently of Iran, interest is invariably upheld.[29]

Variations will naturally occur in matters of detail, but the language is one which reads as a straight translation from a Western commercial code. Plagiarism—or borrowing—runs the whole gamut of the field of commercial law, from the objective quality of merchant to the mechanisms of bankruptcy, and typically includes technical rules on commercial papers, transport liability, and company law. The local commercial statutes, and the courts which apply them, adopt terminology and categories which are taken straight from Western practice. The executive, acting as legislator, will also ratify and incorporate Western-made international conventions in which Middle Eastern input is negligible, if not nil. The style of commercial law in the region is decisively Western.

The Classical Tradition

The direct bearing of foreign models may have not been necessary to that comprehensive extent. It is possible to detect in the misprepared and impoverished

---

[27] Dawlat al-Bahrain (State of Bahrain), Mahkamat al-tamyiz? (Court of Cassation), 28 June 1992, MAFQ 15, 1994, 303. Note the French terms of the Code of Bankruptcy and of Concordat Préventif, '*qanun al-iflas wal-sulh al-wiqa'i*'.

[28] Dawlat al-Kuwait (State of Kuwait), Mahkamat al-isti'naf al-'ulya (Higher Appeals Court), 10 January 1986, MAFQ 14, 1993, 270.   [29] See further section on Islamic banking below.

genesis of Middle Eastern commercial law, the symptoms of unease towards a forgotten tradition.

From time to time, it's as if the tradition seeks compensation for this disregard, sometimes in a deliberately provocative manner. This is most apparent in the recent manifestation of two phenomena which, this chapter will argue, operate as *fuite-en-avant*: arbitration, and 'Islamic banking'.

Before examining the purported unease, a flashback is necessary to see what commercial law might have meant in Middle Eastern history, and to wonder about the possible reasons for the chasm between the textual tradition and present legislation. The gap is perplexing because of the importance of commerce in the region, both as reality and as mental social construct, since at least the advent of Islam in the sixth century, and the persistence of its importance through the classical age.

Already a hundred years ago an orientalist scholar noted how the domination of commercial terms of the art operates in the Qur'an, in tune with what one would expect in a Meccan society whose Prophet was a trader by profession.[30]

Although a little studied field, what we know of classical commercial law requires, over the extensive span covered by Islamic law, the distillation of certain characteristics which offer some perspective on the present-day relationship between Islam and business.[31]

The list of references to commerce in the Qur'an is long: it includes contracts, the necessity of their certainty, the central importance of ethics, the strict requirements of honouring one's obligations, of putting them in writing, the importance of trade, in addition to the famous sentence in the second chapter explaining how trade has been allowed by God, but *riba* (interest, usury) forbidden.[32]

Apart form the *riba* question—and even then there is little which is qualitatively different from other Biblical religions—[33] the general ethical system cannot

---

[30] C. C. Torrey, *The commercial-theological terms in the Koran* (Leiden, 1892). See also in that early vein, Richard Grasshof, *Wechselrecht der Araber* (Berlin, 1899) who includes a refreshing note on the varieties of Islamic law, at 11–12: 'Daher gibt es in Islam so viele originale Rechtsysteme als es originale Juristen gibt; und diese sind nicht nur die Gründer der vier orthodoxen Schulen neben der Shi'a.'

[31] There is a large literature on the subject of classical trade in the Mediterranean (that is between Europe and the Orient), partly reviewed by Jean-Claude Garcin, 'Le JESHO et la recherche sur l'histoire économique et sociale des pays musulmans', *Journal of the Economic History of the Orient*, 36, 1993, 139–53. The most remarkable archival work was achieved by Samuel Goitein and his disciples, from Abraham Udovitch to Mark Cohen. One should also examine works which are less Mediterranean-centred such as, in Braudelian fashion, the books of K. N. Chaudhury on *Trade civilisation in the Indian Ocean: an economic history from the rise of Islam to 1750* (Cambridge, 1985); *Asia before Europe* (Cambridge, 1993). In a different, but no less encyclopaedic mode, see the trade tradition in South East Asia as portrayed in Denys Lombard, *Le carrefour javanais: essai d'histoire globale*, 3 vols. (Paris, 1990) especially vol. 2. The identification in the common law of Islam of trade patterns, which the French historian Fernand Braudel calls long wave or long structure (*longue durée*), might help understand how fourteen centuries have come to bear on the world of business in Islam. For this purpose, the law of trade is a useful indicator.

[32] 'Honour your contracts', v: 1, xvii: 34; 'put your debts in writing', ii: 282, 'woe to the fraudsters', lxxxiii: 1; 'God has allowed commerce and prohibited *riba*', ii: 275.

[33] There is understandably a large literature on the subject of 'the prohibited *riba*'. For an extensive discussion in twentieth-century Egypt, see my 'The debate on *riba* and interest in twentieth century

be labelled as exclusively Islamic. Most Qur'anic features are shared by world religions with regard to business and the necessity of ethics in the transactional relations of human beings. These are important for the survival of the business sanctity of contracts in any society. In the face of such trite facts, and to the extent that it is possible to discover a different slant in the documents borne by Islamic law, is there a *specificity* of business in Islam?

In a long-term perspective, specifically 'Islamic' intellectual and practical products can perhaps be summarized in a number of propositions adduced from classical *fiqh* texts.

The central role of trade. The first element is the centrality of trade, the universal respect it carries in Muslim civilization, and the importance of commerce as the nerve-centre of the city and of regional or international exchange. The free movement of goods is a key element in the intellectual structure of early Islam through to the present period. The fact that the Prophet Muhammad started his career as a caravan merchant is unique to the Islamic Prophecy; the other great monotheistic figures, Moses, Abraham, and Jesus, do not acknowledge the centrality of trade and commerce in any similar way. In the case of Jesus, the episode of the Temple merchants even points in the opposite direction, with the mercantile pursuit of wealth depicted in a derogatory manner.[34] In contrast, the original textual tradition of Islam and of Islamic law acknowledges the importance of commerce, including the security of long-distance trade and market sanctity, on both the ethical and the practical level. Whatever the reality of emporia in the early Islamic Hijaz,[35] the tradition of an Islamic Prophet-merchant is firmly received and developed across the centuries. Neither classical Christianity nor Judaism seem to have extolled 'the virtues of commerce' in such a detailed or enthusiastic way for 'the commercial professions' as did Dimashqi (eleventh century CE) in his *Mahasin al-tijara*.[36] Nor is

jurisprudence', in C. Mallat, ed., *Islamic law and finance* (London, 1988) 69–88; 'Tantawi on banking operations in Egypt', in M. Masud, B. Messick, and D. Powers. eds., *Islamic legal interpretation: muftis and their fatwas* (Cambridge, Mass., 1996) 286–96, and the references cited therein. John Noonan has written the standard treatise on the subject in canon law, *The scholastic analysis of usury* (Cambridge, Mass., 1957).

[34] Matthew xxi: 12; Mark xi: 15; Luke xix: 45; John ii: 13. See generally J. D. M. Derrett, *Law in the New Testament* (London, 1970) pp. xxiii, 278.

[35] In *Meccan trade and the rise of Islam* (Cambridge, 1987), Patricia Crone casts serious doubts on the centrality of trade in South Western Arabia as portrayed in such classical theses as Henri Lammens, *La cité de Taif à la veille de l'Hégire* (Beirut 1922); *La Mecque à la veille de l'Hégire* (Beirut, 1924). A typical Lammens portrayal is summed up in his *L'Islam* (Beirut, 1944) 21–2: '[Looking at Mecca at the time of the Prophet], on croit surprendre comme le bourdonnement d'une ruche humaine, se trouver aux abords de nos Bourses modernes ... La Mecque devient le paradis des caravaniers, des courtiers, des entremetteurs, des banquiers avec leurs prêts d'argent, placés à des taux usuraires ou paraissant tels à qui refuse de tenir compte des risques énormes du capital à cette époque et dans ce milieu de nomades insaisissables ... Au dire de Strabon, tous les Arabes sont courtiers ou commerçants ... A la Mecque, "on ne professait d'estime que pour les marchands", *man lam yakun tajiran falaysa 'indahum bi-shay'* [those who are not merchants are nothing to the Meccans].'

[36] *Mahasin al-tijara* (The virtues of commerce), published in Cairo, 1318/1900, and discussed at length in S. D. Goitein, *A Mediterranean society*, 5 vols. (Berkeley, 1967–88) in vol. 1; and in Claude

the display of legal cogency as remarkable in any pre-modern literature as that one found in the classical jurists' treatment of the contract of sale, which is, since early Islam, the measuring rod for all its 'contractual sisters'.[37]

Sale as paragon transaction. The contract of sale is the model contract in Islamic law, along the lines of which other contracts are constructed. Although there is neither theory of contract in classical Islamic law, nor any general theory of obligations such as for late Roman or French law, one does find an elaborate structure of Islamic law texts around the book of sales. Here is a typical formulation:

The basis of sale is the exchange of a desired commodity against another desired commodity.
This can be done by word or by deed.
As for word, this is known as offer and acceptance in the tradition of the jurists.
Treatment of offer and acceptance is twofold: first the mode of the offer and acceptance and second the nature of the offer and acceptance.
First the mode: offer and acceptance, we say—and God helps us to success—could be made in the present or in the past mode.
If in the past mode, then the seller would say 'I have sold' and the buyer 'I have bought'. The basis is then complete since this mode, albeit formulated in the past, constitutes an immediate offer in the language of lexicologists and jurists. Custom is decisive in this regard.[38]

This is how Kasani opens up the book of sale in his encyclopaedic legal treatise in the twelfth century. Strict legal logic then develops with the formulation of sale in the past tense, and the reason why use of the past tense is considered better: each of these formulae 'gives the meaning of sale, which is exchange: importance is in the meaning not in the expression'.[39]

This only makes sense in comparison with the alternative modes: formulation in the present tense. If the formulation of offer and acceptance is in the present tense, the contract is also concluded according to Kasani, but this is because the intention to sell and buy is ready and clear for both parties. Kasani is willing to consider both common practice and the parties' intention, which concur in this case. In contrast, he continues, an offer made in the form of a question, or in the imperative mode, is not acceptable in law, even though it may have been valid for the earlier jurist Shafi'i (d. 820), who used the contract of marriage as analogy. Why is that?

For Kasani, the rejection of the analogy with marriage is based on the specificity of the marriage contract, 'in which bargaining is unusual'. Kasani explains that one could follow in the contract of sale the possibility of accepting the conclusion of

Cahen, 'A propos et autour d' "ein arabisches Handbuch der Handelswissenschaft"', *Oriens*, 15, 1962, 160–71.

[37] Kasani (d. 1191), *Bada'e' al-Sana'e'*, Beirut, n.d., v, 167: '*wal-bay' wa akhawatuhu tubtiluha al-shurut al-fasida*' (contract and its sisters are annulled by void conditions).
[38] Kasani, v, 133: '*fi 'urf ahl al-lugha wal-shar' . . . al-'urf qadin 'alal-wad*''.
[39] '*Al-'ibra lil-ma'na la lil-sura.*' *ibid.*

marriage if the formula is, for the guardian of a woman, in the imperative (future) form, 'as when someone tells the other, "marry my daughter" and the addressee says "I have", or if one says "marry your daughter to me" and the addressee says "I have"'.[40] For Shafi'i, this should be equally valid for a formula in the imperative in the case of a sale, on the basis of analogy.

Kasani explains the reason why 'analogy has been abandoned' in this instance, despite the fact that there is no text to support such a departure. This, he says, is because of the process of bargaining which is inherent in sale, whereas bargaining would cause embarrassment in the case of marriage. In the case of a marriage, therefore, acceptance might be issued in the future imperative form, or in the form of an acquiescence to a question because it would not be right to involve bargaining in the process. The fact that the element of bargaining is inherent in sale provides enough of a contrast to sharply distinguish it from the marriage contract. It is possible to consider offer and acceptance in the form of a question and answer, in the imperative mode, for the conclusion of marriage. Such a tight mode is not allowed in the conclusion of a contract in the case of sale, because it would undermine the bargaining process which is of the essence in commerce.[41]

While it is not my purpose to present the details of the Islamic law of sale, three premises can be said to underlie the system of trade in classical law: certainty, flexibility, and pragmatism.

As to certainty, it is remarkable that, in one single page, Kasani repeats five times the need to avoid, in the terms of the contract, 'any oversight which may be conducive to litigation'.[42] Through certainty is consecrated the fulfilment of the exact intention of the parties as also manifested in the meeting of minds in the bargaining session.

Flexibility is offered through an elaborate system of options, perhaps one of the most complex areas of Islamic law, which is dominant and crucial for the study of the sale contract. The contract of sale is not binding unless 'it is clear from four options: the option of selection, the option of condition, the option against defects, and the option of vision'.[43] These are conventional or presumed clauses in the contract, and allow for contractual variations within an overall regulatory framework for their 'exercise'.[44]

Pragmatism is the third element. We have seen it in the very definition of sale. Pragmatism is a key component of the Islamic law merchant through the importance accorded by the jurists to custom as a central source and element in the system. Examples can be multiplied of striking formulae in which Kasani, like other jurists, is prepared to abandon strict rules in favour of the merchants' customs.

---

[40] ibid., at 133 bottom.　　　[41] ibid., at 134 top.

[42] *'Jahala mufdiya ila niza'*, 209. See also the formula elsewhere in the book, e.g. at 198, 207.

[43] *'An yakun al-'aqd khaliyan 'an khiyarat arba'at, khiyar al-ta'yin, wa khiyar al-shart, wa khiyar al-'ayb wa khiyar al-ru'ya, fala yalzam ma'a ahadin min hadhih al-khiyarat'*, 228.

[44] For a detailed discussion of options, see above Chapter 8.

The importance of custom. A characteristic of the long-term patterns of the Islamic law merchant is indeed custom, which plays a vital and controversial role, in that it is not generally associated with Islamic law, despite its importance for appreciating the long-term structure of Islamic business. According to the received understanding of 'the sources of Islamic law', custom does not feature among the usual sources.[45] But in the law of sale, custom is 'decisive', says Kasani. Nor is that an isolated rendering. A jurist like Sarakhsi (d. *c.* 1095) is no less emphatic:

> If a vendor buys a cloth, he is authorised to include in the price what was spent for sewing and transport, but he must say, 'This is what it cost me' and not 'I have bought it at such a price', because the latter formula would be wrong. The profit in that partnership contract, and the custom of the merchants, are taken into account. What customary practice authorises in addition to the buying price can be added on by the merchant. What practice excludes must be excluded.[46]

Custom is decisive in the law merchant, and one will find in Sarakhsi's *Mabsut* and many other texts that deal with the book of sales and with other contracts in Islamic law a systematic reference to trade customs, including *'adat al-tujjar*—the use of merchants and their practice—*ta'amul al-nas*, that is, the way people deal amongst themselves; *ta'aruf bayn al-nas*, the interaction between people; as well as the notion of *wajh al-tijara* or the direction of commerce. These are recurring concepts which provide an overall framework according to which Islamic law subjects the legality of commercial transactions in the city to the practice of merchants and people.[47]

Sometimes a contradiction arises over the clash between the necessity of certainty in the contract, and usage. In one instance of such a clash, Sarakhsi explicitly says that the law ultimately chooses what will facilitate people's lives.[48] In another example, which shows how the Islamic law merchant relies on custom, the departing point is that if one is selling something that does not yet exist, then certainty in the contract is undermined. In a long text, Sarakhsi explains that this is the theory. In practice, when you ask someone to sew a cloth or to build a house for you, it is not possible to know exactly how it will turn out. Would that render the contract void? The answer in strict, classical Islamic law, should be yes. In fact, the opposite practice was and remains widely used.[49] To repeat a formula Sarakhsi ascribes to one of two masters of the Hanafi school, Abu Yusuf (d. 798): 'What matters in all things is custom, *'urf*'.[50]

Kasani has equally striking formulae, one of which will be included, several centuries later, as one of the Ottoman Majalla's ninety-nine opening principles: in matters of sale, 'what is known by custom is equal to what is agreed upon as a clause'.[51]

---

[45] Further discussion of custom as source of law in Chapter 3.
[46] Sarakhsi, *al-Mabsut*, xiii, 80, discussed in A. Udovitch, 'Les échanges de marché dans l'Islam médiéval: Théorie du droit et savoir local', *Studia Islamica*, 65, 1987, 5–30, at 17. *Murabaha*, profit, *'urf*, custom. [47] Udovitch, 'Echanges de marché', 21.
[48] Sarakhsi, *al-Mabsut*, xiii, 115 ('*taysiran 'alal-nas*'). [49] ibid. 138. [50] ibid. 142.
[51] '*Al-ma'ruf bil-'urf kal-mashrut bil-shart*', Kasani, v, 167; the exact wording was adopted as Art. 43 of the Ottoman Majalla ('*Al-ma'ruf 'urfan kal-mashrut shartan*'), see also Art. 40: '*Al-haqiqa tutrak*

'This is what is cost me'. With certainty, flexibility, and pragmatism, a fourth element should perhaps be underlined in the Islamic law merchant. This appears in a text of Sarakhsi mentioned earlier as 'this is what it cost me':[52] in other words, the 'extras' that come into the price of a commodity are important as they imply that the law merchant is open to factors that are not strictly legal but are essential in the practice of trade.

A practical illustration is documented in sixteenth- and seventeenth-century Iraqi trade in Basra. Merchants had to allow for charges in what may be termed as protection costs, that is, 'the price merchants had to pay in taxes, tolls, fees, and bribes, to ensure the flow of their commodities'.[53] This was part and parcel of the cost of trade. The protection cost, it is acknowledged, 'was just as important as a camel'.[54]

In these testimonies, the notion of protection is introduced as an element of what one could nowadays describe as 'overhead'. Protection costs play a significant role in the determination of the ultimate price of the commodity. This is common usage, and a practice one naturally finds in dealing with the Middle East.[55] This overhead will inevitably come into the price of not how much one buys the commodity for, nor at what manufacturing cost it is produced, but how much it will ultimately cost in order for the trader to make a profit.

As in the realistic opening lines of Sarakhsi's book of sales, the benefit of a sale contract should be appreciated in its wider perspective: 'God has made money the reason for people benefiting from the world and enjoying it'.[56]

A Contemporary Echo: The Economics of the Law Merchant

Ten centuries after Dimashqi, Sarakhsi, and Kasani, the relevance of trade as an economic 'given' of an Islamic theory of 'economics' can be found in the works of Muhammad Baqer al-Sadr (d. 1980).

Sadr is important in the field of Islamic commerce for several reasons. First, his 800-page book on the Islamic economic system, *Iqtisaduna* (Our Economic

---

bi dalalat al-'ada, truth is left for custom'. Also on custom as *'ada* (usage), Majalla, Art. 36: *'Al-'ada muhkama,* usage is decisive'; Art. 41: *'Innama tu'tad al-'ada idha ittaradat wa ghalabat,* usage is followed if persistent'. Above, Chapter 8.

[52] Above, text accompanying n. 46.

[53] Dina Rizk Khoury, 'Merchants and trade in early modern Iraq', *New Perspectives on Turkey,* 5–6, 1991, 53–86, at 54.

[54] ibid., quoting N. Steensgaard, *Carracks, caravans and companies* (Copenhagen, 1973) 111.

[55] 'Protection' understood from a positive side is important in whatever business is being undertaken in Middle Eastern countries, and the concept of 'sponsorship' in Saudi Arabia is obviously the most eloquent example of how vital it is to secure financially the attention and the participation of the local important people who would facilitate this trade.

[56] Sarakhsi, *al-Mabsut,* xii, 108. Reason, *sabab.*

System),[57] and his views on the *Interest-free bank in Islam*[58] are two landmarks in twentieth-century Muslim reflection on the subject. Secondly, the originality of the work results from Sadr's heavy use of classical Islamic law. In an archetypal search for *longue durée*, one cannot rely on systematic series of data, which may or not be available for a relatively limited period of time. Sadr was aware of this constraint in his search for an Islamic theory of economics. In contrast, the legal tradition is rich and sustained, and Sadr's reliance on *fiqh* to expound the core principles of his system shows the way for trade patterns modelled on legal principles.

Sadr does not question, as did Marxist socialism which was the main object of *Iqtisaduna*'s criticism, the importance of free trade. For him, unimpeded commerce is a given, and the centrality of trade surfaces in the book through Sadr's use of the concept of 'distribution'. Distribution informs the two economic 'phases' in which the book is divided: distribution before production, and distribution after production.

Generally, the 'apparatus of distribution' is discussed by Muhammad Baqer al-Sadr by way of the two concepts which underpin it, need and labour. 'Two essential tools constitute the apparatus of distribution in Islam: labour, and need.'[59] In this perspective, property becomes 'a secondary element of distribution',[60] and is always limited by a set of moral values and social interests established by moral principles defined by religion. The three elements forming the basis of the distributive apparatus of Islam are summarized by Sadr as follows:

Labour is a primary tool of distribution from the standpoint of ownership. The person who works in nature reaps the fruit of his work and possesses it.

Need is a primary tool of distribution as the expression of a human right which is essential in life. Islamic society recognises and supplies essential needs.

Property is a secondary tool of distribution, by way of commercial activity which Islam permits within special conditions which do not conflict with the Islamic principles of social justice.[61]

From there, Sadr follows up the role of distribution in two phases which distinguish 'the general theory of distribution before production' from 'distribution in the post-production phase'. Acknowledging that the division is artificial, since 'the two studies [of distribution before and after production] are intertwined', he chooses a new angle to address 'the sources of production', which he had identified in the pre-production phase as 'land, raw materials, and the tools necessary for production'. Legal rules of distribution after production, in contrast, are concerned with 'productive wealth, which is the goods made by labour as exercised

---

[57] See *Iqtisaduna* (Our economic system), Najaf and Beirut, published in 2 vols, 1959–61, then in one. The book is discussed in Chibli Mallat, *The renewal of Islamic law* (Cambridge, 1993) chapter 4.
[58] *Al-bank al-la ribawi fil-Islam* (Interest-free bank in Islam) (Kuwait, 1969).
[59] *Iqtisaduna*, 308: apparatus of distribution, *jihaz at-tawzi'*; labour, *'amal*; need, *haja*.
[60] ibid. 321.   [61] ibid. 322.

over nature, and results from a combination between these material sources of production'.[62]

The legal framework regulating distribution in the second phase—the productive process—includes the importance of reviving and exploiting the land in its ownership,[63] the prohibition of *riba*,[64] the encouragement of commerce as productive activity and not as intermediation.[65]

It is clear that *exchange* in its material sense is one of the forms of production. The transportation of wealth from a place to another creates in many instances a new benefit and is considered an enhancement of the commodity's value for human need, whether the transportation is vertical—as in extractive industries, in which production operates an operation of transport of raw material from the depth of the earth to its surface—or horizontal, as in the transportation of products to the areas close to consumers, and readying them for customer use. This type of transportation enhances human needs.[66]

Sadr carries on with the legal scheme he derives from commerce, by adducing, as he does in the rest of the book, a number of legal texts from the classical tradition by various scholars belonging to all schools.[67] When this is done, the conclusion is the protection of commerce so long as it 'has a productive content'.[68] Intermediation is favoured when it is 'a branch of production'. From a famous letter of 'Ali, the fourth Caliph and first Shi'i Imam, to Malik al-Ashtar, his governor of Egypt, Sadr derives the importance of 'good' commerce:

It is clear from this text that merchants as a group are brought into one with the people of industry,[69] that is the manufacturers,[70] and they were all portrayed as the providers of benefits. The merchant creates a benefit in the same way as the manufacturer. ['Ali] followed on by explaining the benefits which the merchants create, and the operations that they accomplish, in securing wealth from far away places, from areas where people [i.e. buyers] do not naturally gather, and where they do not go.[71]

So commerce is for Sadr an unquestionable premise for his new 'economic theory', even if the legal texts used in *Iqtisaduna* are not typically those relating to commerce. Sadr's main concern in that seminal book was ownership of land, and of strategic resources like oil. Nonetheless, he found it important to emphasize the centrality of commerce as a productive branch of modern Islamic economic theory, which finds its main sources in the books of *fiqh*.

In the modern law of commerce, in contrast, not much of a remarkable tradition is acknowledged.

[62] ibid. 387–8, see also at 524.   [63] ibid. 590.   [64] ibid. 591–2.
[65] ibid. 621–2.   [66] ibid. 615. Emphasis added.
[67] '*al-nusus al-madhhabiyya*', ibid. 618–20, from Shi'i jurists like al-Saduq (d. 381/991), al-Shahid al-Thani (d. 966/1559), and al-Hurr al-'Amili (d. 1110/1699); Hanafis, like Ibrahim al-Halabi (d. 956/1549) and al-Marghinani (d .593/1197); Hanbalis like Ibn Qudama (d. 620/1223), as well as Malik (d. 179/195) and Shafi'i (d. 204/820).   [68] *Iqtisaduna*, 622.
[69] *dhawi al-sina'at*.   [70] producers, *muntijin*.   [71] *Iqtisaduna*, 618.

The Break: The Ottoman Commercial Code (1850)

Any familiarity with commercial law in the contemporary Middle East shows the lexical and structural chasm between the classical system and the modern codes. Commercial codes are strictly modelled after the civil law tradition in most countries, or, as in Israel, Jordan, and Pakistan, occasionally follow the common law tradition. The time-honoured lexicon of classical trade has fallen into disuse.

Nor can the Islamic law merchant be readily transposed into the modern world of commerce, but the dimensions just outlined offer a useful background for the practitioner: distribution comes, as an archetypal concern, before production, trade constitutes the nerve of the Middle Eastern city, sale is the model contract, custom is crucial to appreciating the operation of exchange and profit in real life, and the 'real cost' of the transaction, including the hidden costs of protection and intermediation, is the bottom line of any trade operation.

None of this seems crucial in modern statutory and court law, as seen in the survey of recent commercial law decisions presented in the first part of the chapter.

In many areas, ignorance of the tradition is not surprising. Notwithstanding the likely emergence of commercial papers in the Middle East where the *suftaja* seems to have been a long-established model of a letter of credit or even a 'cheque',[72] the complexities of commercial papers developed decisively only in the twentieth century, and it would have been very hard—though not theoretically impossible—to merge the sophisticated instruments of a rapidly changing commercial world scene with the remnants of a pre-capitalist medieval system.

How did that break come about formally?

A clear separation between *fiqh* and *qanun* can be traced to the Ottoman legislator's introduction, in the middle of the nineteenth century, of a commercial code which was a direct transposition from the French tradition.

Unlike for the Majalla, where a real effort was introduced, in terms of both rules and legal categories, to produce a code inspired by the Islamic legal tradition, there was clearly no regard for the tradition by the Ottoman legislator when dealing with commercial law.

---

[72] See e.g. Goitein, *A Mediterranean society*, i, 242. Also, Abraham Udovitch, 'Merchants and *amirs*: government and trade in eleventh century Egypt', *Asian and African Studies*, 22, 1988, 52–72, at 66: 'Islamic commercial law and practice recognized numerous forms and instruments of credit. For the transfer of an obligation from one place to the other and for its speedy redemption into cash, none was more effective or more efficient than the *suftaja*.' A papyrus dated *c.* 900 CE mentions the word in the plural, see Albert Dietrich, *Arabische Briefe aud der Papyrussammlung der Hamburger Staats- und Universitäts- Bibliothek* (Hamburg 1955) 15: '*wa qabilu minna al-safatij*' (and they accepted our 'promissory notes'). Dietrich also suggests translating it as 'cheque', at 22. Joseph Schacht translates *suftaja* as 'bill of exchange' (*An introduction to Islamic law* (Oxford, 1964) 78), and Udovitch, in an earlier work, as 'letter of credit' (Abraham Udovitch, *Partnership and profit in medieval Islam* (Princeton, 1970) 80).

Nor did the Ottoman legislator pay attention to the local conditions long acknowledged by the *shari'a*. Plagiarism was so widespread that the Ottoman borrower did not realize that the dispositions of the French system were totally inadequate in an Islamic society where the wife's property is by definition separate from her husband's in the absence of a regime of matrimonial property. This was noted by an early commentator:

The fourth section of the [Ottoman Commercial] Code relating to the rights of women and the articles that compose it are completely useless, and have not the least practical application in case of the husband's insolvency. Indeed for Ottoman civil law, marriage is nothing else than the legitimate union of man and woman for the exclusive perpetuation of the human race, and excludes any idea of association that would seek mutual help for bearing the expenses of life and family, uniting goods as well as individuals, or improving together, through the separate contribution of matrimonial goods, their lot and sharing it. This joint association between the spouses is neither arranged nor regulated, and this association does not actually exist.[73]

Piat further underlined the inadequacy of the Ottoman Code's extensive regulation (Arts. 264–70) of the matrimonial regime of joint property: 'In fact as well as in law, there is always separation, never community of goods between the spouses; the wife keeps the entire and exclusive administration and use of its movable and immovable property, which she disposes of entirely and freely, and which she can sell at any time without seeking authorisation from the husband, and in case he disagrees, from the civil tribunal'.[74] The French model was in this particular case alien and superfetatory.

Blind replication is also true for commercial partnerships, the mainstay of modern capitalist societies.

Classical commercial law of Islam does not know that form of partnership without which the present capitalist world cannot be understood: the limited company. One is then immediately faced with a problem, which derives from the long-term structure which the Islamic law of contract has imposed on the strict individuality of the commercial transaction. But for arguable exceptions (*waqf*, or trusts, and the *bayt al-mal*, the public treasury),[75] partnerships in Islamic law were never recognized as corporate entities which would be separate from the partners undertaking the trade. There is no corporate person in classical Islamic law, partly a consequence of the concern for certainty in that system. Islamic law, even with commercial ventures, deals primarily with the individual as bearer of commercial duties and rights, whose word and personal commitment are essential. The corporate entity, in contrast, is by definition more diffuse. Since commercial codes were

---

[73] Théophile Piat, *Code de commerce ottoman expliqué* (in Arabic and in French) (Beirut, 1293/1876) 809–10. [74] ibid., at 810.

[75] Literature on *waqf* in Chapter 2, n. 371. The legal concept of *bayt al-mal* is elusive. I discussed it in 'Report on the budget in classical and contemporary law', London, 1996 (unpublished), on the occasion of the dispute between the ruler of Qatar and his deposed father before the High Court in London. The classical text on budgetary 'rules' is by Ibn Mammati (d. 606/1209), *Kitab qawanin al-dawawin* (Rules of the ministries) (Cairo, 1943) (ed. A. 'Atiyya).

introduced in the Middle East in the 1850s, the field of company law has been torn between the necessity for a faceless legal dimension which is represented by the independent legal personality of a company, and the recognition of known and fully liable individuals in the effective running of trade.

Here borrowing from the West occurred on a large scale across the region. Already the first commercial codification of law in the Middle East appears at loggerheads with any attempt to adopt Islamic rules. The Ottoman Commercial Code of 1850 was a simple replica of the French Commercial Code introduced by Napoleon.

As in the case of matrimonial property, plagiarism was such that in the course of the first Middle Eastern commercial borrowing, the Ottoman legislator forgot that it was in the French Civil Code, and not in the Commercial Code, that the main regulations of commercial companies are to be found. Hence a skeletal chapter of ten articles on the *société anonyme*, which had by then become the most financially important vehicle in company law in France.

In the chapter entitled 'the third type [of companies, after the société en nom collectif and the société en commandite]: société anonyme', the Code prescribes under Article 20 that 'the company (which does not have a name) and which we call "anonyme" ... must not be designated under any of the partners' names'. It is necessarily 'qualified by the designation of the object of the enterprise' (Art. 21). Piat explains that 'the mere name of the company, or société anonyme, is sufficient to make known the special object which it deals with; it must be confined to it'.[76] The reason for this, another Ottoman commentator of the time explained, is the necessary dissociation between the company on the one hand, and, on the other hand, 'the shareholders and the managers who are not accountable for the expenses and the losses of the company beyond the shares in capital which they paid up and for which they are liable'.[77]

Only two articles in the Ottoman Code deal with the management of the *société anonyme*: 'The société anonyme is administered by time-bound agents who are revocable. They may be shareholders or not, and they may or not earn a wage' (Art. 22), and 'the administrators are liable only for the execution of the mandate they have received; they do not incur, because of their management, any personal or joint liability for the company's engagements' (Art. 23).

This is all one finds about the administration of the *société anonyme*. Rules dealing with shares and shareholders are equally succinct. Article 24 defines the scope of responsibility of the shareholders, who 'are liable only to the extent of their interests in the company', and the Code deals then with capital and shares: 'The capital of the société anonyme is divided in shares, and even in fractions of shares of equal value' (Art. 25). In principle, only bearer shares are admitted: 'The

---

[76] Piat, *Code de commerce*, 60; 'which does not have a name, *al-ghayr musammat*'.

[77] *Sharh qanun al-tijara, lihadrat 'utufatlu Wahan Efandi* (Wahan Effendi, commentary on the Commercial Code), Arabic translation by Nuqula Naqqash, Beirut, 1297/1880, in Ibrahim Sader, ed., *Majmu'at al-qawanin al-'adliyya* (Collection of civil laws) (Beirut, n.d.) 34.

share is established in the form of a bearer's entitlements (*titre au porteur*); in this case, cession operates by the transfer of title' (Art. 26) But the following article recognized, without naming it, nominal titles: 'The ownership of shares is established by their inscription in the books of the company. Cession operates by a declaration of transfer from the company, which is written in the margin of the title, and which will be registered in the company's books' (Art. 27). Registration of the ownership of shares allows minimal control over the issuance and transfer of shares, even if, as noted then, the Ottoman Code poorly adapted the French model which lists the formalities required for transfer: declaration written in the books, and the signature of the transferor or his representative.[78]

These short articles on the most important commercial company were supplemented by the necessity to seek an imperial decree authorizing the company's establishment (Art. 28) and the registration of the articles of association 'before the Tribunal of commerce' (Art. 31). In comparison with the two other types of company mentioned in the Code, the *société anonyme* looks like the least favoured object of legislative care. This brevity is compounded by the scant attention to companies overall, whilst other commercial matters were regulated thoroughly, such as the bill of exchange (Title 6, Arts. 70–146) and bankruptcy (the whole of Book 2, Arts. 147–288 for insolvency, Arts. 288–315 on bankruptcy). The legislator realized soon afterwards that such an important commercial institution required more elaborate treatment, which was introduced in a separate law a decade later.

With all its shortcomings, the first Commercial Code in the area offers a model one finds across the Middle East. All the codes are attentive to the detailed treatment of such areas as bankruptcy, commercial papers, the qualifications of the profession of trader, in a relatively straightforward translation of the Western models. This has been achieved through the wholesale introduction of comprehensive codes, or through separate laws on commercial establishments (*fonds de commerce*), offshore companies, commercial procedure, juxtaposed over the years in the field. To this legislation one must add international and regional conventions in fields such as maritime and air law, or commercial arbitration.

A list of commercial codes and their contents would be fastidious. These texts are more or less sophisticated. They may have been introduced wholesale, from the earliest, the Ottoman Code of 1850, to the most recent such Code, the Commercial Transactions Law of the United Arab Emirates (December 1993).[79] Specific commercial statutes may also have been introduced gradually. This was the case in Saudi Arabia from the 1930s onwards.[80]

---

[78] Piat, *Code de commerce*, 74.   [79] See Price, 'United Arab Emirates', cited above n. 22.

[80] The most important Saudi code is that known as *Nazam al-mahkama al-tijariyya*, passed more than sixty years ago, in 1350/1931. It regulates the profession of merchants (Arts. 1–10), including agents, commissioners (Arts. 18–41), companies (Arts. 11–17), commercial papers (Arts. 42–102); bankruptcy (Arts. 103–49); maritime commerce (full section 2, Arts. 150–430); the regulation of commercial proceedings, as well as various related taxes and fees (sections 3 and 4, respectively Arts 432–587 and 588–633).

Despite the straight reception of French law in the first Ottoman codification, it is not possible to read these statutes as complete and absolute replicas of Western counterparts, and the local practitioner will remain attentive to home-grown specificities, regardless of wholesale borrowing from the West. Indeed, some commercial statutes are particularly important for their specific Middle Eastern flavour, even if they are not necessarily inspired by the *shari'a*.

One area where the Middle East may have developed an institution which is typical, whilst not rooted in an older tradition, is agency law. Here, specific statutes, which have no Islamic pedigree, rule the field. While foreign antecedents can be found, their Middle East application was so autonomous that the statutes, with the help of courts, developed a life of their own.

Agency is in this regard a wide concept, and covers most contracts between foreign manufacturers and local importers. Considering that, outside the oil industry, trade is the nerve-centre of economic activity in the region, the importance of commercial agency cannot be overestimated.

I shall examine now some of the most characteristic legal traits in those countries where free trade is still the rule. Other countries which have espoused a more rigid 'socialist' framework, like Libya, Egypt, Syria, and Iraq before 2003, may share some of the commercial agency special rules which are under discussion, but the overall economic system remains centred on the state. While trade in other countries of the Gulf, the Levant, and North Africa are not free from burdensome constraints, the principle is based on an overall 'free' capitalist system. There, the rules on commercial agency go to the heart of commercial law in the private sector.

The Middle East is in this respect full of surprises.

Commercial Agency

A major element of surprise for the foreign manufacturer tends to arise over a dispute with his local commercial agent. The agent/distributor might have faithfully represented him over a period of years in a 'sole agency' contract which, for one reason or the other, the foreign principal would like to discontinue. For the Japanese manufacturer, the common law practitioner, or the European trader who is used to the protection of the European Communities' original Articles 85 and 86 regulating competition, the snare of the Middle Eastern agency/distributorship is the more surprising in view of the compensation owed by the foreign principal to the agent/distributor: 'In common law jurisdictions the principle of autonomy of contract applies with particular vigour to commercial agency. There is no special statutory regime governing commercial agents, no requirement for registration, no principle of compensation to the agent following lawful termination of the agency agreement.'[81] In contrast, the typical statutory legislation will run in the Middle East as follows:

> No person shall engage in the business of commercial agencies in the state unless his name has been entered in the Register of Commercial Agents prepared for this purpose in the Ministry. *A Commercial Agency which is not recorded in this Register shall not be recognised,* nor shall any claim be heard with regard thereto. (Art. 3)
>
> *An agent shall be entitled to commission* on transactions which the principal concludes himself or through another person in the agent's territory, *even if such transactions are not concluded as a result of the efforts of the agent.* (Art. 7)
>
> A principal shall not terminate the agency agreement in the absence of any reason to justify such action. An agency may not be re-registered in the Register of Commercial Agents in the name of another agent, *even if the previous agency is limited to a fixed term.* (Art. 8)
>
> If an agency is withdrawn at an inopportune time for any reason not attributable to the agent, the principal may be required to provide compensation for any losses and loss of anticipated profits. In the absence of proof that the agent committed a wrong justifying non-renewal, *the principal's refusal to renew an agent's contract after the expiry of its original term shall constitute an abusive exercise of rights entailing appropriate compensation...* (Art. 9)

Thus Federal Law No. 18 of 1981 regulating commercial agencies in the United Arab Emirates.[82] Such legislation is typical of the Arab Middle East, where a principal is forced to retain an agent—in the absence of a major fault—even if the agency agreement comes to an end. Breach of the agreement or failure to renew it will invariably lead the agent to claim compensation, and both the courts and the administrative agencies will play a large role in ensuring that the system is centralized and so tightly protected that any new agent would be either barred or deterred from carrying on the agency until full compensation is paid to the previous agent.

The discontinuation of the relationship, leading as a matter of principle to compensation for the agent regardless of the terms or length of the contract at the origins of this relationship, constitutes a first element of surprise for the foreign observer.

At the legislative origin of such exorbitant constraints on the principal, generally a foreign manufacturer or supplier, lies Lebanese Decree-law No. 34, issued on 5 August 1967 (amended 1975).[83] Decree-law 34 is the first such law to be passed in the Arab Middle East and represents the prototype for a plethora of agency/ distributorship legislative regulations in the UAE, the Gulf, and elsewhere, all featuring the same 'exorbitant' character as the original:

> A commercial representation contract shall be deemed to be made for the mutual benefit of the contracting parties. Therefore, in the event of its termination by the principal without

---

[81] Roy Goode, 'Preface', in Samir Saleh, *Commercial agency and distributorship in the Arab Middle East* (The Hague, 1995) p. xix. See generally on the subject my 'Comparative models of freedom of trade: the hurdle of Lebanese sole agency', in W. Shahin and K. Shehadi, eds., *Pathways to integration: Lebanon and the Euro-mediterranean partnership* (Beirut, 1997) 209–27.

[82] As amended by Federal Law No. 14 of 1988. Text reproduced in Saleh, *Commercial agency*, ibid., 11–37. Emphasis added.   [83] ibid., at 3–41.

any fault on the part of the agent or without any other lawful cause, the agent shall, *notwith-standing any agreement to the contrary*, be entitled to claim compensation equivalent to any damage he may have sustained or to *any profits he may have lost.* (Art. 4 § 2)

In addition,

The commercial representative shall also be entitled, *even in the event of termination of the contract by the expiry of its term and notwithstanding any agreement to the contrary*, to claim compensation to be determined by the court, when the efforts of the commercial representative have led to manifest success in the promotion of the trade mark of his principal or have resulted in an increase in the number of his customers and *the refusal of the principal to renew the agency agreement* has prevented the representative from reaping the profits of his success. (Art. 4 § 1)

Thus the first 'excessive' dimension: compensation for termination of agency as a matter of principle, regardless of its length or terms.

A corollary 'exorbitant' dimension arises in relation to the stringent application of the laws on agency/import by the judicial and administrative set-up within the country. These regulations are encountered with few variations across the Arab Middle East, and vest in the judicial and administrative apparatus which enforces the protection of the agent/distributor in an exclusive contract.

The judicial apparatus tends to be involved in the award of compensation, which it often sets, in order to take into account 'lost profits', at two, three, and up to five times the amount of the net annual average profits in the last few years of the agency.[84]

The administrative apparatus ensures that, once the agency is breached or not renewed, a subsequent agent would be held jointly liable with the foreign principal for the amount of compensation decreed by the Court. In some Gulf countries, the Ministry of Trade or a specialized committee will refuse the registration of a new agent so long as the termination of the previous agency has not been fully settled.[85]

In practice, this allows the impounding of goods and the involving of any new agent/importer as a joint debtor *in solidum* with the foreign principal/exporter to the agent/trader whose contract is terminated or not renewed. The necessity of registering the agency, and the explicit or implicit assimilation of distributorship and agency, are also common features in the area.

Thus arises the second element of dismay: the easy assimilation in the Middle East of the 'commercial agent' and the importer/distributor/trader: 'A trader who

---

[84] e.g. for Lebanon, various decisions reported in E. Abu 'Id, *Al-tamthil al-tijari* (Commercial agency), 2 vols. (Beirut, 1991). An early application appears in a Court of Cassation decision of 15 March 1973, upholding the plea of the petitioner that 'compensation is equivalent to lost profit for three years at least and five years at the most, calculated on the average profit of the three last years', *Hatem* (Lebanese law reporter), 142, 1973, 22, at 23. See also generally M. Mahmassani, *La représentation commerciale en droit positif libanais* (Beirut, 1972) 408–9.

[85] Centralization is crucial to the system: a decision of the Bahrain Court of Cassation rejected any compensation because the registration of the agency as required by Law 23 of 175 relating to commercial agencies and their organization had not been effected. Dawlat al-Bahrain, Mahkamat al-tamyiz, 10 November 1991, MAFQ 14, 1993, 263–7 at 266–7.

sells on his own behalf what he purchases in accordance with a contract which grants him the capacity of representative or exclusive distributor, shall be deemed to be the same as a commercial representative'.[86]

A distributor is therefore assimilated in the region to a commercial agent, and benefits from the exclusive clause even if he buys and sells on his own behalf.[87] Agent and distributor are amalgamated by Arab statutes, whereas they tend to be radically distinguished for purposes of competition in Europe (Arts. 85 ff of the original Treaty of Rome) and the United States (the Anti-trust laws). This appears to be the crux of the difference between the legal regime of distribution in the Middle East and its Western counterparts, and the one characteristic which seems to be conducive to foreign manufacturers shouting blue murder every time an Arab importer claims compensation for the termination of an agreement.

The vast impact on commerce of these regulations explains why, next to corporate work, representation and distributorship offer the commercial practitioner in the Arab Middle East the major anchor point in daily activity. In a region where commerce and banking have so far constituted the nerve-centre of wealth, Lebanese Decree-law 34 and its 1975 Amendment, as well as its Arab followers, are a central staple of commercial litigation.[88]

The special philosophy behind commercial agency Middle-Eastern style is illustrated in a decision of the Supreme Federal Court in the United Arab Emirates, which even conferred constitutional status on the laws of agency.[89]

The facts of the case are typical, and concern an exclusive agent selling computers in the country, who had the goods of a parallel importer impounded. A constitutional plea was brought to the Federal Court by the parallel importer, who argued against the constitutionality of Laws 1981 and 1988 on the basis that the *shari'a*, as the supreme law of the land, did not accept such abuse of the market, and that these laws were therefore conducive to hoarding.

The Court demurred, by explaining that if indeed hoarding was illegal under Islamic law,[90]

it appears from reading and analysing the text of the aforementioned law that it leads in no way to the prevention of commercial deals which are the object of commercial agency or the increase in price. These texts only regulate the relationship resulting from the contract

[86] Lebanon, Decree-law 34, 1967, amended 1975, Art. 1 § 2.

[87] In the UAE legislation noted above, there is no such explicit assimilation, but the necessity to register 'the agency' leads in practice to the assimilation of agent and importing trader. See generally Saleh, *Commercial agency*, above n. 81, chapters 1 and 11; and my book review in *Yearbook of Islamic and Middle Eastern law*, ii, 1995, 635–7.

[88] See for a Kuwaiti illustration within a comparative setting, the extensive analysis of Ahmad 'Abd al-Rahman al-Milhim, '*Mada taqyid 'aqd al-qusr lil-munafasa al-ra'siyya* (Restrictions on exclusive contracts by vertical competition rules)', *Majallat al-huquq* (Kuwait), 20, 1996, 13–108.

[89] UAE, Federal Supreme Court (Constitutional Chamber), 14 April 1993, MAFQ 16, October 1994, 109.

[90] Quoting the *hadith*, '*al-jalib marzuq wal-muhtakir mal'un*, the provider will be rewarded and the monopolist chastised', at 112.

of commercial agency between the commercial agent and between the manufacturer or supplier inside or outside the country, or the exporter and the exclusive distributor adopted by the producer. The legislator considers this contract to arise for the benefit of both contracting parties. The legislator did not prohibit its termination or its renewal as the appellant alleges, but allowed, under Art. 8 of the law, the termination of the agency contract by the principal and its non-renewal if there were reasons to do so. The legislator did prohibit the importation of merchandise or products or manufactured items or other goods that are subject to an official registration with the government with a view to circumvent the agent. It also authorised the principal to use one sole agent in the state considered as one unit or in each Emirate or in a number of Emirates, and it required commercial agents to provide spare parts, items and appendages which are necessary and sufficient for maintenance of the imported goods. This helps the flow of merchandise and facilitates commercial loans, bringing them to everyone's reach in various areas of great proximity. It leads to preventing increase in price.[91]

The Court went on to explain that this competitive reality

is not affected by the last section of Art. 5 of the Law on the exclusivity of the distribution of merchandise and services which are the object of the agency to the commercial agent within his territory, since the object of the agent is always to sell these products and trade them in order to get his commission. This encourages him to lower the price as much as possible, and to accept a small profit in order to reach this aim and stand on a par with other companies which produce goods with the same object and put them on offer in a competitive set-up with low prices. In addition, a failure in distribution or an attempt to hoard these goods to increase their price could be a reason that his principal might use to terminate the agency or to refuse its renewal.[92]

In conclusion, the Court said, 'the rules of this law do not encourage the hoarding which is prohibited by the *shar'* and do not lead to it. There is nothing in it which violates the rules of Islamic law, and consequently constitutional provisions. The appeal lacks base and should be rejected.'[93]

One can see in the Court's explanation a sophisticated battery of arguments in support of the agency/import laws of the UAE, some of which are textual (the *hadith*), some of which economic (prevention of monopoly, encouragement of inter-brand competition), some legal (mutually beneficial contracts). All in all, the constraining statutes are upheld in the name of a hazy, but real, commercial public order.

These explanations can be supplemented by the remarks of Lebanese commercial judges in an early case: for the Beirut commercial court, only an *exclusive* distributorship would be entitled to the protection of Decree-law 34, and the seller could come to an agreement with others at any time in the absence of the exclusivity clause.[94]

---

[91] ibid. at 110–11.   [92] ibid.   [93] ibid. at 111.

[94] Mahkamat bidayat beirut al-tijariyya (Commercial Court of Beirut, first instance), 23 December 1969, reported in Abu 'Id, *Al-tamthil al-tijari*, above n. 84, i, 55.

'Irrespective and notwithstanding all the aforementioned,' the Court held,

it is impossible, either from the point of view of social justice, or from an economic point of view, and in view of Lebanon's relations with the outside, to expand the interpretation of Article 1 section 2 of Decree-law 34, which does constitute a statutory exception undermining general principles and contradicting all established known legal rules and all usual practice in commerce, so that it is necessary to interpret the decision in a limited way, which restricts its application to commercial representatives who possess the quality of exclusive representatives or distributors, and who are harmed in absolute from the rescission of the contract binding them to their principal with regard to distributing a specific type of merchandise.[95]

Thus there is a further rationale for why the statute must be narrowly interpreted because both agent and principal are limited to 'specific types of merchandise' (usually excluding foodstuffs and medical drugs), and because the distributor will not benefit from the protection of the law so long as his contract is not explicitly 'exclusive'. Once it is so labelled, it is surmised, there is no reason why the supplier should not be held to the contract he wilfully signed.

The laws on commercial agency are well established in most open markets in the region, even if, under the new conventions with powerful economic actors like the European Union, the excessive protection of exclusive agents-distributors is targeted in the name of free competition and consumer protection. The return to 'freedom of trade', which is translated in this case as the illegality of exclusive agencies, has been put forward in countries like Jordan, Tunisia, and Lebanon by treaties passed or to be passed with the European Union. The rationale behind such conditions, from the EU drafters' perspective, is that consumers are the main victims of such segmented and exclusive arrangements.[96]

In the overall philosophy of commercial law, laws on commercial agency have a strange and inconclusive pedigree.

From an Islamic law perspective, principled opposition to the restrictions appears in the plaintiff's arguments in the UAE case: agency contracts are freely revocable under classical law, and forcing the principal to compensate an agent upon revocation of agency is beyond the contemplation of the straightforward doctrine as found in the *fiqh* books. The principle is that an agency is revocable at any time, and that no compensation is owed: 'agency is a non-binding contract, ... and a separate judgment cannot be entered thereupon ... The principal may terminate the agency whenever he wishes, on condition of informing the agent.'[97]

---

[95] ibid., at 60.

[96] For details of the EU treaties and practice and their implication for the Middle East, see my 'Comparative models', above n. 81, 223–37.

[97] '*Al-wikala min al-'uqud ghayr al-lazima ... wa la yasuhh al-hukm biha maqsudan ... fakan lil-muwakkil al-'azl mata sha'a bi-shart 'ilm al-wakil.*' Ibn Nujaym (d. 970/1563), *Al-bahr al-ra'eq fi sharh kanz al-daqa'iq*, with the commentary of Ibn 'Abidin (d. 1252/1836), 8 vols. (Cairo, 1311/1893), vii, 204.

Agency is, in regard to the *shari'a*, close to its equivalent under the common law. The Arab rules on commercial agency appear, in contrast, as typical illustrations of the prohibited practice of 'restraint of trade'. Regulation and compensation as discussed would not pass muster in a common law court, although a more nuanced conclusion may be warranted as soon as the agency becomes more specifically regulated. This would be the case in the increasingly complex variations taken by the new 'distribution networks', which include franchises and what English courts call 'solus agreements'.[98]

Whilst not rooted in the *shari'a*, Middle East agency law might have another historical pedigree which is French. The Lebanese statute of 1967 (modified and reinforced in 1975), which is the model for most Gulf legislation, owes much of its formulation to a French statute passed in 1958.[99] Unlike that French precedent, however, which remained limited in scope to a narrow category of commercial agents in France, the expansive concept of exclusive agency is a home-grown Middle Eastern product, which has adapted the logic of importation for the benefit of powerful merchants in the countries concerned. One can read many interpretations into the dominance of these statutes from their birth in the 1960s to date: they may be the local adaptation of French law, which was reinforced by a pattern of trade based on imports of manufactured European or Japanese goods. They may, if projected further into the past, be the commercial distribution equivalent of foreign concessions on trade, especially concessions on oil; or even concessions on large projects like the digging and operating of the Suez Canal. If so, there is an example here of the transformation of previous colonial patterns of dominance by the local elite for its own benefit. It may also be that the larger merchants have forced these statutes to protect themselves from the diktat of foreign agents, or from interference by local competitors: '[I]t would be a dangerous thing if one citizen started corrupting the relationship of other citizens with foreign companies and worked for the termination of their agreements', a Saudi court explained.[100] It may be, more prosaically, that big merchants are defending their turf against local competition by smaller merchants, or indeed dividing markets up.

Whatever the explanation, commercial agency in the Middle East is a typically local phenomenon, which dominates the patterns of trade in the region. As a specific regional manifestation, it may simply obey the universal rule that *lex mercatoria* is primarily the law of merchants, and Middle East merchants will not be constrained in their choice of law by other interests than the ones that suit them.

---

[98] See e.g. *Esso Petroleum Co. Ltd. v. Harper's Garage Stourport Ltd.*, 1968 [AC] 269, per Lord Wilberforce for the difficult distinctions made by the Lords. Also G. Treitel, *The law of contract* (London, 1991) 418.

[99] The origins of the Lebanese law lay in French Decree 58, passed on 23 December 1958, to protect the category of commercial agents. The French law is discussed in J. Hémard, 'Les agents commerciaux', *Revue Trimestrielle de Droit Commercial*, 1959, 573–624. The law was amended significantly by European directives. For further references, see Mallat, 'Comparative models', above n. 81, 217–20.

[100] Decision by the Saudi Board of Grievances in 1995 (no precise date), reported in *Middle East Commercial Law Review* (MECLR) 1, 1995, 23, with a comment by Nabil Saleh.

'Beware' is the practical advice to any foreign manufacturer who seeks distribution of its products in the region. Compensation for appointing a new agent without having settled with the previous one can be costly.[101]

Company Law

Commercial agency rules may offer a specificity that is typical of trade networks and practice as developed in the modern Middle East. A similar argument, but one which may have a deeper legal pedigree, can now be pursued in the area of company law.

Having noted the absence of a developed concept of 'company/corporation/ *société'* in the Ottoman Commercial Code of 1850, an easy explanation could be put forward. Why should one be surprised, that argument goes, not to find elaborate 'limited liability companies', especially in the form of 'public corporations' or 'sociétés anonymes', when such corporations were themselves in their infancy in the Western legal world of the nineteenth century? There is no reason to suppose that the Ottoman Empire, or Egypt, would resist the adoption of limited liability companies because of an absence of such legal entities in the Islamic law tradition. It would be merely sufficient, the argument continues, to note that the early codes are contemporaneous with a legal system which, in the West, is much less sophisticated than at present.[102]

There may be more to the matter than the appropriate historical dating of the emergence of codes, and the argument about resisting the limited liability of shareholders should be examined more closely in the context of an absent tradition of 'corporate personality' and of 'limited liability' in a Middle Eastern context.

As aptly expressed in a recent judgment in an English commercial court, Middle Eastern companies are often the vehicles of individual entrepreneurship: 'The plaintiffs are a company registered in Nassau and the defendants are a company registered in London, but the real protagonists in the dispute are individuals ... The evidence that I have heard suggests to me that the two companies are no more than convenient corporate vehicles for the business activities of their principal shareholders.'[103]

---

[101] In a 1996 case from Saudi Arabia, a German principal with an agency established in 1985 and terminated less than a decade later had to pay about US$2 million in compensation to the agent, MECLR, 3, 1996, A-42. This was calculated in commission fees over a period of two and a half years.

[102] A helpful work on companies in the Arab world can be found in Gian Maria Piccinelli, *La società di persone nei paesi arabi* (Rome, 1990). Although focused on partnerships, it offers a comprehensive guide to relevant company codes and literature. See charts at 247–51, and index of codes, 267–78. For the standard comparative work on company law in the West, see Alfred Conard, *Corporations*, 1st edn. (Mineola, NY, 1976, repr. 1991).

[103] Justice Phillips in *Lemenda Trading Co. Ltd. v. African Middle East Petroleum Co. Ltd.*, Queen's Bench Division, [1988] 1 All ER 413.

The sore point relative to company law and the lack of a separate corporate personality can be seen in operation in three major fields: limited liability, capital markets, and Islamic, as opposed to Western-style banking.

Limited liability

All Middle Eastern countries have adopted equivalents of the French system of *société à responsabilité limitée* and of *société anonyme*, which make a strict separation between the assets of a company and the individual assets of shareholders and directors.

One will find several decisions in which the limitation of liability is firmly entrenched. The standard principles can be found as early as the Ottoman Code of Commerce.[104] They are repeated in the first formulation of the Saudi commercial law, which defines the *'inan* company[105] as 'a company between two or more persons, with a specific capital in which each of the partners has a limited share, and in which the partner does not suffer a prejudice or a loss beyond his share in the capital'.[106] The principles of limited liability are repeated elsewhere in the codes, and a case from Kuwait sums them up:

> The principle in the limited liability company [the French-style SARL, *société à responsabilité limitée*] is the liability of each shareholder to the extent of his share … [This] liability is limited to the extent of his shares in the capital of the company, which is the main characteristic of this company, and from which it derives its appellation [as *'limitée'*].[107]

Yet neither law nor the business world has fully digested the separation, and some courts are reluctant to stop at the company's assets in case of unpaid debt.

This phenomenon is difficult to document in the absence of systematic law reporting, particularly in the Gulf states, where the size and importance of the companies in the era of oil is evident. Legal practice, as far as can be ascertained from lawyers and businessmen, confirms the difficulty, in countries where the persona of the directors and major shareholders of companies is paramount, in limiting liability to the capital and assets of the company, without touching upon the personal property of the decisive actors in such business ventures.

The example of BCCI, whose major shareholder in the person of the ruler of Abu Dhabi was called upon to foot the bill beyond the bank's assets and who obliged the bank's creditors beyond what the law of limited liability should have exacted, is a prime example of this *intuitu personae* of company practice in the Middle East.[108]

---

[104] Art. 24, quoted above, in the section on the Ottoman Commercial Code.

[105] 'One of the branches of which is constituted by the limited liability company', *Nazam al-mahkama al-tijariyya*, above n. 80, Art. 14. The limited liability company mentioned here is the French *société anonyme, sharikat musahama* in the original Arabic.   [106] Art. 13.

[107] Dawlat al-Kuwait, Da'irat al-tamyiz fi mahkamat al-isti'naf al-'ulya (High Court of Appeal), 2 May 1984, MAFQ 9, 1989, 336–8, at 337.

[108] See the remarks of Rashid Safa, 'Perspectives on bank failures in the Middle East', in H. Lewis Ruttley and C. Mallat, eds., *Commercial law in the Middle East* (London, 1995) 155–65, at 160:

While the problem seems to have arisen in similar terms from Saudi Arabia to Morocco,[109] three fully reported decisions from the United Arab Emirates and Bahrain illustrate the difficulty for courts to accept limitation on liability. Although the rulings do not altogether dismiss the principle of limited liability, the dilemma facing the judges is evident in the argumentation. Thus in Bahrain:[110]

Even if the established principle is, in the limited liability company (SARL), limitation to the extent of [the shareholders'] shares in the company and the impossibility for the company's creditors to ask them [for the company's debts] or execute [the debt] against their property; nevertheless, if the direction of the company is entrusted to one of the shareholders, on his own or with others, then he is subject to the rule of Art. 235 of the Law on Commercial Companies, which establishes the joint liability of directors towards the company, the shareholders and third parties for contravening the legal rules or the company statutes or for fault in the management in accordance to the rules of the joint-stock [*société anonyme*] companies. The creditors of the company, as third parties, can therefore attach the directors' *private* monies for damage resulting from their wrongful management.[111]

Allowing creditors to go after the private assets of the directors/shareholders was made possible here by a swift amalgamation of legal rules by the Bahraini Court of Cassation. It is also found applicable in the case of bankruptcy. 'This personal liability remains', the Court continued,

even after the dissolution of the company and its liquidation, so long as the directors remain in management and are considered liquidators before the appointment of an [official] liquidator under the terms of Art. 258 of the Law. This is the case regardless whether the behaviour of the directors leading to compensation is considered a crime under the terms of the Criminal Code or under the Law on Commercial Companies.[112]

To further assert the possibility of going after the personal property of the directors, possibly because the creditors were unable to execute a judgment in their favour ten years earlier 'due to the company's lack of a legal presence in Bahrain at the time of enforcement',[113] the Court did not stop at one director. It made all directors (typically also the main shareholders) jointly liable on their personal

'A striking feature of the BCCI failure is the aggressiveness with which the banking regulatory agencies in the major countries in which BCCI was operating had been soliciting contributions by the majority shareholders of BCCI, particularly from the Abu Dhabi Investment Agency. The contributions were to offset the losses incurred by the bank, which amounted to a staggering $11 billion by the time BCCI closed down. These agencies presented a strong moral, *though not legal*, case by capitalising on the public outcry, the widespread extent of the fraud committed by the managers of the bank, and the unprecedented amount of BCCI's losses. This "moral" case forced the Sheikhdom of Abu Dhabi to make substantial payments to compensate depositors' (Emphasis added). On BCCI generally, see Ibrahim Warde, *BCCI: perspectives from North and South* (Berkeley, 1991).

109 A similar dilemma in Morocco was presented in a communication of Abdellatif Mechbal, 'Le rôle unificateur de la cour de cassation marocaine en matière commerciale' (read in Arabic at a conference on 'Les cours judiciaires suprêmes dans le monde arabe'), Beirut, 15 May 1999.

110 Dawlat al-Bahrain, Mahkamat al-tamyiz (Court of Cassation), 8 March 1992, MAFQ 16, 1994, 307–10.   111 ibid., at 308. Emphasis added.

112 ibid. 310.   113 *li-'adam wujud kiyan laha fil-Bahrain waqt al-tanfidh*, at 309.

wealth in the process: 'If more than one director is responsible for the wrong, they are all liable jointly'.[114]

Another recent decision, from the UAE, faced a similar dilemma between limited liability and personal assets. Notwithstanding the results in the case, which are not very clear, the language used by the judges runs against the most basic principles of the restriction of shareholders' responsibility to the limited extent of their investment.[115]

The case is a complex one procedurally, and dovetails with a previous judgment. In the earlier decision, the Court of First Instance had decided a sum of money, together with interest, for the plaintiff, a bank which had advanced funds to the company in which the defendant and others were shareholders. On appeal, the defendant alleged that he was responsible 'only to the extent of his shares in the profits of the company, which are 27.5%'.[116]

It is not clear, in the decision of the Court, what the ultimate result was. The ruling was that the owner of the 27.5 per cent of shares should pay that proportion of the company's debt from his own private assets. So the Court accepted the appeal in part, concluding that the decision in first instance be 'varied, by annulling the judgment in its ruling about debt solidarity between the appellant, the first defendant company, and the rest of the shareholders, and about interest, and the rejection of the remainder of the pleas in appeal. The appellant must pay the costs for the appeal.'[117]

More importantly, the Court's reasoning exposes the dilemma faced by the interface of classical Islamic law rules and modern company liability:

It is usual under Islamic law (*shar'*) that in case there is no clause of solidarity in the statutes of the company, and if the company owes money related to its object and the company's assets are not sufficient to pay back the debt, the shareholders are liable *in their own assets* for payment of the debt to the extent of the share of each in the losses of the company (Art. 671 of the bill on civil transactions). The result is the liability of the company for its debts on all its assets, in addition to the responsibility of the shareholders/partners who are not bound *in solidum*, to the extent of the share of each one of them in the company's capital.[118]

One can see in this text the difficulty of reconciling the two principles of unlimited and limited liability of partners/shareholders.

More generally, these cases illustrate the competition between the two laws: the positive limited liability law, and the classical law in which persons are responsible on their personal assets. On the one hand, 'the first thing which needs to be taken into account is the emergence of a corporate personality of the company and assets

---

[114] ibid. 310. Wrongful and fraudulent management by directors, leading onto joint civil liability *in solidum* for all, can also be found in legislation outside the Middle East. But the wide reach of the above decisions should be noted.

[115] Al-imarat al-'arabiyya al-muttahida (UAE), Mahkamat isti'naf Abu Dhabi (Abu Dhabi Court of Appeal), 30 May 1984, MAFQ 5, 1987, 305–13.   [116] ibid., at 308.

[117] ibid., at 313.   [118] ibid., at 312. Emphasis added. Shareholders, partners, *shuraka'*.

which are independent from the wealth of the shareholders, as appears in the legislator's acknowledgment of the rules of the project of a Code of civil transactions, which is near completion . . .'.[119]

On the other hand, the larger picture is governed by the principles of the *shari'a*, which the Court mentions extensively *obiter*.[120] It results, as cited above, in the conclusion that 'the shareholders are liable *in their own assets* for payment of the debt'.

The Abu Dhabi Court of Cassation, in a more recent decision, also upheld a decision in appeal in which 'partners . . . will be jointly liable even if the company was a limited liability company'.[121] The Court, however, based its ruling on the fact that the shareholders in the company in question could not avail themselves of the limitation to their liability because the company had not been properly registered.

Capital markets

While all these borderline cases illustrate the dilemma caused by the fact that the classical legal system did not know any limitation on liability, a second derivation of the classical system's legacy may be illustrated in the difficulty of finding effective stock exchanges in the Middle Eastern Muslim world.

As a general pattern, most trading in commercial papers or otherwise occurs in discreet, private, environments. On occasion, secondary market places appear as *de facto* stock exchanges, but there is much to achieve in terms of volume and of business practices before a solid stock exchange starts to function in the region, a fact confirmed by the noted absence of a value-added oil derivatives market in the Gulf.[122] Where a stock market briefly developed, as in Kuwait, the collapse was prompt. In Suk al-Manakh, an informal financial market rose in the 1970s, but the whole structure collapsed with the circularity of inflated commercial paper trading in 1982.[123] A similar collapse took place in the Tel-Aviv stock exchange in October 1983, but stricter regulations have since been introduced.[124]

An indication of the difficulty faced by stock exchanges can be found in the dearth of good research on the subject in the Arab world. To my knowledge, no serious publications are available in Arabic, despite a number of well-attended Arab capital markets conferences.

---

[119] At 311.   [120] Full text at 311.

[121] [1995] 1 MELCR 26, report of Essam Al Tamimi.

[122] Fadel Chalabi, '*Mustaqbal al-naft fil-sharq al-awsat* (The future of oil in the Middle East)', in *Al-muqawwimat al-fikriyya wal-qanuniyya li-nizam sharq-awsati jadid* (The intellectual and legal frameworks for a new Middle East), conference held at SOAS, London, 19–20 December 1994, *Proceedings*, 7.

[123] Fadwa Adel Darwiche, *The Gulf stock exchange crash: the rise and fall of the Souq Al-Manakh* (London, 1986). The loss was evaluated at $40 billion.

[124] On the early experience of the Israeli 'emerging market', see Abdo Kadifa and Chibli Mallat, *The third stage of Zionism: high technology in Israel*, Centre of Near and Middle Eastern Studies (SOAS, University of London), occasional paper 1, May 1988.

Two exceptions—in English—will confirm the rule: one is an ESCWA regional report, which notes that 'most of the stock markets in the Economic and Social Commission for Western Asia (ESCWA) region are still in their infancy, lacking experience and with a relatively underdeveloped status, particularly in terms of laws, regulations and accounting systems'.[125] 'In terms of performance', the report explains, 'most stock markets in the ESCWA region are highly speculative and thus volatile. This imperfection stems partly from their status as underdeveloped, as lack of data and economic information in public shareholding companies give room to speculation and anticipation.'[126]

In terms of 'legal, regulatory and institutional frameworks', the report divides the countries under study into three groups. One group is that of the wealthy oil states with 'capital surplus', and includes countries like Kuwait, Oman, and Bahrain which are in the process of 'developing the necessary institutional and regulatory structures, starting with the stock exchange'. At the time of the report, Qatar and the UAE were still considering the establishment of stock markets, but Qatar has since adopted a law[127] and opened up the Doha stock exchange in May 1997. Among the capital surplus countries, Saudi Arabia has 'opted for a screen-based floorless securities trading mechanism managed by a specialized department in the Saudi Arabia Monetary Agency', which is the equivalent of a central bank. Beyond the formal institutions, one is still hard pressed to find the premises of a really independent stock exchange in operation in any Middle East country.

Nor is the situation, one should conclude from the report, much more hopeful in the rest of the jurisdictions surveyed: countries like Syria, Libya, and Iraq under the Ba'th do not have the minimal basis of free trade that would allow a stock exchange to operate. The establishment in Baghdad of a stock exchange in 1992 is a particularly cruel example of façade modernism in a country which was as closed upon itself economically as it was isolated internationally.

A more hopeful experience may be found in the third group identified by the report. This includes Jordan, Egypt, and Lebanon (and, outside the ESCWA remit, Tunisia and Morocco). In these countries, the search for stock exchanges is premised on their opening up to foreign capital and the prevailing sense within the authorities that domestic stock markets have a key role to play in financing economic growth. When one looks at the figures of market capitalization, however, and those of listed companies and their growth, the experiment remains paltry even in comparison to developing markets in neighbouring Pakistan and India, or further afield in South East Asia: 'The ESCWA region's stock markets represented in 1993 only 0.6 per cent of the total capitalization of the world's stock markets, while the region's GDP represented about 1.3 per cent of the world's

---

[125] ESCWA, *Stock markets in the ESCWA region* (New York, 1995) 1. (United Nations, E/ESCWA/ED/1995/3/Add.1, 4 December 1995, hereinafter ESCWA report). The ESCWA countries are Bahrain, Egypt, Iraq, Jordan, Kuwait, Lebanon, Oman, Palestine, Qatar, Saudi Arabia, Syrian Arab Republic, United Arab Emirates, and Yemen. [126] ibid. 1.
[127] Reference in Najeeb al-Nauimi, 'Qatar', in *Yearbook of Islamic and Middle Eastern Law*, iv, 1997–8, 371–3.

total'.[128] As for listings on the stock exchanges, there were 1,204 listed companies in the stock markets of the region in 1993, which 'represented only 8.2 % of that of the emerging markets and 6.8 % of the developed markets'. Interpretation of these figures must take account of the fact that very few companies listed are active. In most Arab countries with a stock exchange, the listing of seriously active companies rarely reaches the two-digit figure. Even then, only a small fraction of the companies' shares is on offer.

Among the countries described by the ESCWA report as closer to an operational stock exchange, we have a comprehensive policy study explaining the pitfalls facing both private and public efforts to establish an effective framework for the development of Lebanon's capital markets.[129] It is useful to examine some of its conclusions as a potential guide for the rest of the region.

In Lebanon, both the central bank and the stock exchange are heavily dependent on governmental regulations, as they would be in any other country; but they are more top-heavy due to the overbearing intervention of the government in the institutional framework of the Central Bank and the Beirut Stock Exchange (hereinafter, after its French appellation, 'the Bourse'). For all intents and purposes, the Bourse exists only on paper. The Central Bank is a sprawling and powerful institution.

The main problems of the stock exchange are clearly underlined in the report. The Bourse was created in 1920 and, after several amendments through to 1985, the

> development in the legislative framework did not improve the Bourse perspectives which remained very narrow and marginal thus unable to channel short-term capitals into medium and long-term credits via stocks and bonds ... In fact statistics show that since the early 60s and till the mid-70s at the outbreak of the war, the yearly volume of transactions in the Bourse did not exceed 0,70 % at best of the total volume of deposits in the banking sector. In most cases, this ratio stood at less than 0,60 %.[130]

As a result, the Bourse suspended its activities in 1983, with only forty-six firms being quoted, and, in effect, trading remaining concentrated in a mere fifteen companies.

For this ineffectiveness, the authors of the report mention several reasons, to which they suggest legal and financial correctives: one problem is the closed system of companies 'owned either by a very small number of persons or at best by families', who have few problems raising money with the commercial banking sector, itself—one may add—aflush with oil money in the 1970s, and itself sharing its directors and executives with the larger Lebanese industrial firms.

As for the Commercial Code, which was promulgated in the early 1940s, it is not sufficiently developed to accommodate the emergence of new and more sophisticated tools in financial markets across the world. In addition, the authors

---

[128] ESCWA report, 8.
[129] Nasser Saidi and Samir Nasr, *The development of Lebanon's capital markets* (Beirut, 1995) hereinafter cited as *Lebanon's capital markets*.   [130] ibid. 285.

note 'the absence of an effective supervisory authority', although when one looks at the structure of the Bourse, governmental input through the Ministry of Finance and the 'committee in charge of the Bourse' would indicate that the government has actually stifled the system through a bureaucratic network of controls. More pointed is the remark that 'shareholding companies have not respected the principle of transparency in their accounting practices and financial statements'.[131]

What are the suggested reforms? In part, the authors may be enlarging governmental meddling by suggesting, inter alia, the creation of a control commission whose main mission would be to guard, protect, and control the safety and regularity of operations. They also advise the government to 'enlarge the Exchange Committee by including people with financial and economic expertise in it', to 'amend the Beirut Exchange Laws and enact the necessary laws in the Code of Commerce to improve the role of public joint-stock companies at the expense of personal or family-owned ones'.

This is easier said than done, and the multiplication of laws and by-laws as well as the appointment of more bureaucrats 'with financial and economic expertise' will not necessarily decrease the overbearing control of the Ministry of Finance.[132] But mostly, 'personal or family owned' companies make up the basic social structure of capital ownership in Lebanon. The close and increasing intertwining of family politics, clientelism, and power, makes it difficult to see closely family-controlled companies giving way to the anonymous dynamic of a stock exchange. As for the creation of fiscal incentives to open up such companies to professional accounting, which has already been undertaken with a vast overhaul of company taxation law, and the lowering of rates across the board to 10 per cent of company profits and 5 per cent of dividends,[133] it will take some time for them to filter down the system in order to effect the company transparency hoped for by the authors. That is, if low taxation of companies remains.

A more important hurdle in Lebanon is the sacrosanct banking secrecy law, which remains beyond the contemplation of legislative reform. In the absence of the government being able to investigate the financial system under the secrecy law, one is hard put to find a solution to the multi-layered hurdles facing anonymous capital, and to secure the transparency needed for any stock exchange to flourish.

The survey of Lebanon's prospects for serious capital markets shows the continued limitations which face the Middle Eastern legislator in this field. Despite the hopes expressed in the policy report, which was finalized the mid-1990s, it is hard to find any determined follow-up to the wide range of measures therein suggested:

The authorities will be proposing legislation to enact a comprehensive Capital Markets Law. A Beirut Capital Markets Board (BCMB), set up as an independent authority under the capital markets law, would have overall responsibility for the organisation, regulation,

---

[131] ibid. 286–7; on government custody and organization of the Bourse, see also 292–5.
[132] *Lebanon's capital markets*, 299–300.
[133] See Mallat, 'Lebanon', in *Yearbook of Islamic and Middle Eastern Law*, i, 1994, 216–17.

supervision and control of markets, participants and securities. The BCMB would have a large degree of autonomy and independence in setting policy for the financial markets and their development, similar to the 'Banque du Liban' in determining monetary policy. Its governing board would have the equivalent of ministerial status. This independence from government is important for ensuring long-term financial market stability. An independent Beirut Capital Markets Commission (BCMC)—accountable to the BCMB—would act as the supervisory authority and industry 'watchdog'. Broadly, there will be three organizations: the Beirut Stock Exchange (BSE), the Beirut Money Market (BMM) and a central depository and clearing organisation.[134]

Of these, only the Bourse had started again, in 1995, after considerable infighting between its would-be directors, and its activity was dwarfed by the secondary market until the listing of the shares of the country's largest company on the Bourse.[135] But even then, the close association of the company with a narrow political circle of government officials has kept the ties between market and political clout dangerously intertwined. Regardless of the fate of one company, one thing is certain: so long as the most serious sector in the economy of Middle Eastern countries, that of banking and big industry, remains outside the structure of the stock exchange or of secondary markets, it is unlikely that capital markets will in turn appear serious.

This is not for lack of some financial circles wanting the development of these markets across the region, and needing a more fluid capitalization of the economy. For private foreign investment, the absence of a stock exchange prevents an exit strategy, and deters large-scale financing.

Nor, considering petrodollars, is the absence of mature stock exchanges simply a matter of available liquidities.

One of the possible explanations may be the profound individualism in the tradition of Islamic law, which is manifest in the difficulty of finding in the classical age anonymous shareholders' partnerships. Since the model partnership includes only two parties as in the partnership for profit and loss,[136] which typically engages them in a single transaction, no limited liabilities companies have emerged in the classical age.

This, however, must be a guarded conclusion. Without more careful research, the absence of effective stock exchanges cannot simply be put down to a Weberian-like explanation involving the dominance of legal 'individualism' in business in the Muslim world. While, as noted by the two available studies on stock markets, a

---

[134] *Lebanon's capital markets*, 22–3.

[135] Solidere, which is the 1991-established Lebanese Company for the Development and Reconstuction of Beirut Central District, with a capital of almost US$ 1.9 billion. It traded in secondary markets until 1996, when it was formally listed on the Bourse. See Mallat, 'Lebanon', 216, above nn. 214, 216; see also G. Mahmassani, 'Law and reconstruction in Lebanon', in Lewis Ruttley and Mallat, eds., *Commercial law in the Middle East*, 39–73, at 50–5.

[136] On companies in classical Islam, the standard work is by Udovitch, *Partnership and profit in medieval Islam*, above n. 72.

healthy and diversified listing of companies with minimal transparency is required, one may rightly wonder whether the legacy of a Middle Eastern legal calque which does not accept anonymity or limited liability may not constitute the larger hurdle to the emergence of a successful stock exchange.

Another factor in contemporary societies is the statist tradition in most 'socialist' countries of the post-independence era, like Naser's Egypt, and Syria and Iraq under the Ba'th. In historical terms, the oldest stock exchange organization was in Egypt, which never developed in any significant manner beyond the commercial market represented by the cotton industry in Alexandria.[137] That experience did not outlast the Naser period, and it is no coincidence that talk of a stock exchange happened only with the so-called economic opening up—the *infitah*—which timidly started in the 1980s.[138] Nor are the Gulf states less statist-oriented, in their own way, as rentier-type oil economies slow down the creation of independent and diversified markets.

Whatever the reasons, it is significant that all attempts to organize stock exchanges have remained constrained by both the volume of transactions and the narrow base of private shareholders even in large companies. The trend has changed slightly in the Gulf countries owing to the large surplus of financial liquidity after the upsurge in oil prices, but the World Bank remains sceptical about the trend. In a comprehensive report on 'Financial markets in a new age of oil',[139] it underlined 'the seeming disconnect between the financial sector and the real private economy'.[140] While equity markets remain concentrated in the Gulf, 'liquidity remains low in absolute terms and relative to the size of the local economy, resulting in constant excess demand for issuance and bonds that are tightly held once issued'.[141] In large part, the report explains, the reason why the 'business climate [is] not conducive to lending' is because of the 'inadequa[cy] … of the rule of law across much of the region' and the incapacity 'of the judicial system and the specific design of collateral and bankruptcy laws'.[142]

This did not prevent many bourses from finding their way onto the statute books across the Middle East. Buildings have even been dedicated to the purpose, but the stock exchanges have not yet outgrown their vacuous shells, while speculation remains rife in secondary money markets.

[137] The oldest organized 'market'/commercial exchange in the region was set up in Alexandria in 1861, and directed towards the sale of cotton and related manufacturing and transport industries. By 1927, there were two cotton-related commercial exchange sites in Alexandria, one in Khartoum, and a stock exchange in Cairo. None is significant presently. For the early regulation of stock exchanges in Egypt, see Muhammad Amin Kamel Malash, *Sharh qanun al-tijara* (Commentary on the commercial law), 2 vols. (Cairo, *c.* 1928) ii, 171–215.

[138] On which Enid Hill, 'Laws of investment, privatization and labour in Egypt', in Lewis Ruttley and Mallat, eds., *Commercial law in the Middle East*, 115–51; Alan Richards and John Waterbury, *A political economy of the Middle East* (Cairo, 1990) 238–62: 'The emergence of *infitah*'.

[139] World Bank, Middle East and North Africa, *Economic developments and prospects 2006, Financial markets in a new age of oil* (Washington, 2006). [140] ibid. p. vi.

[141] ibid. [142] ibid. 69.

Islamic banking

Formally within company law, banking is at the heart of modern economic life, in the Middle East and elsewhere. Western-style banking, meant here in its capitalist and socialist-nationalized versions, dominates the region, where the main division operates between a nationalized banking system such as in Iran, Egypt, Algeria, Syria, Libya, and a mixed or private sector as in the Gulf states, Israel, Lebanon, Morocco, or Tunisia.

This section does not intend to examine banking law in its dominant, Western dimension, which generally follows the rules and regulations of older, well-established, Western counterparts. Rather, attention is directed to the so-called phenomenon of 'Islamic banking', which emerged idiosyncratically in the early 1960s in rural Egypt, but which has expanded significantly since the mid-1980s, whilst continuing to account for a mere fraction of Western-style commercial transactions: 'As of early 1999, Islamic financial institutions, including banks and non-banks (securities firms, mutual funds, insurance companies, etc.) were present in more than 70 countries. Their assets exceeded the 200 billion dollars mark.'[143]

There is, considering this expansion, an understandably large literature on the subject, and several books have appeared in the past few years, some more felicitous than others. Of concern to this overview is Islamic banking as a third 'derivative' product of the classical system in its contrast and competition with Western commercial law. Unlike the problem of limited liability and the difficult emergence of stock exchanges, the Islamic banking phenomenon appears in a positive form: the search for new institutions which incorporate a real or hypostatized Islamic financial tradition.

The flight into Islamic banking is arguably one direct means which society has adopted to revive an abandoned commercial tradition. The advocacy is a clear one, and runs along the following lines: let's go back to the tradition in its pure form, get rid of interest, and establish a *riba*-free Islamic banking system. With such an ambitious challenge, immediate problems were bound to arise, both at governmental level and in private ventures.

There is no dearth of hurdles on the path to Islamic banking. The root problem is anchored in the famous prohibition of *riba*, translated variably as interest or usury, which offers the more spectacular side of unease between the classical and the modern traditions. Once *riba* is defined as 'interest', any modern banking transaction runs the risk of contravening Qur'anic prescriptions. This undermines the very basis of modern banking. A second problem is related to the structure of a limited company in the form of a bank, and the difficulties resulting from banking transactions which this company is destined to carry out or facilitate.

It is in this context that both private institutions and governments have been grappling with the Islamic prohibition on *riba*. The prohibition on *riba* still

---

[143] From Ibrahim Warde, *Islamic finance in the global economy* (Edinburgh, 2000), section 'about statistics and performance assessments', 6–9. Hereinafter Warde, *Islamic finance*.

dominates the entire field, and is illustrated in a seminal 1991 decision of the Pakistan Federal Shariat court.[144] On that occasion, which was understandably crucial for the whole economic system of a country basing its *raison d'être* on the 'purest' respect for the *shari'a*, a questionnaire was circulated by the court 'to distinguished 'ulama, scholars, economists and bankers of the country and abroad' (§ 18). It consisted of some sixteen questions, which are regrouped here under thirteen headings:

1. What is the definition of *riba* according to the Holy Qur'an and Sunnah of the Holy Prophet (p.b.u.h. [peace be upon him]). Does it cover the simple and compound interest existing in present-day financial transactions?

2. If banking is based on interest-free transactions, what would be its basic practical shape in conformity with the Injunctions of Islam?

3. (i) Does the interest on loans floated by the Government meet the national requirements prohibiting *riba*?
   (ii) What alternatives can be suggested for the banks in case they grant loans without interest for various requirements?

4. Can, in the light of the Injunctions of Islam, any differentiation be made between private and public banking in respect of charging of interest on banking facilities for various services rendered?

5. (i) Can the capital, according to the Injunctions of Islam, be regarded as an agent of production thus requiring remuneration for its use?
   (ii) Does devaluation of the currency affect the payment of loans taken before such devaluation?
   (iii) Can inflation causing rise in the cost/value of gold and consumer goods in term of currency have any effect on the sum borrowed?

6. What would be the alternatives in the context of present-day economic conditions to carry on domestic and foreign trade efficiently without availing of banking facilities based on interest?

7. Is interest permissible or otherwise on the transactions between two Muslim States or a Muslim and non-Muslim State?

8. Is it possible to carry on insurance business otherwise than on the basis of interest?

9. Does interest accruing to the Provident Fund come under *riba*?

10. Can the payment of prize money on Prize Bond of Saving Bank Account or other similar Schemes be regarded as *riba*?

11. Would it be lawful under Islamic Law to differentiate between business loans on which interest may be charged and consumption loans which should be free of interest?

12. If interest is fully abolished, what would be the inducements in an Islamic Economic System to provide incentives for saving and for economizing the use of capital?

13. Can an Islamic State impose any tax on its subjects other than Zakat and Ushr?

---

[144] *Mahmood-ur-Rahman Faisal v. Secretary, Ministry of Law*, PLD 1992 FSC 1, also published as a separate book, *Federal Shariat Court judgment on interest (riba)* (Lahore, 1992), including the decision (1–188) and Appendices (1–159).

The answers to the questionnaire were reproduced in a full book-length appendix of some 143 pages,[145] and were extensively used by the court itself to consider non-Islamic no fewer than twenty major Pakistani statutes, ranging from the Interest Act of 1839 to the Banking Ordinance of 1979. It is no surprise that the decision was frozen on appeal as it put in jeopardy a large number of legislative acts and risked undermining the whole banking system. Nor was this measure totally surprising in view of the fact that one of the strongest advocates of full Islamization, the late General Zia-ul-Haq, had himself agreed to postpone the overhauling of the financial system several times. As the Court explained, 'the question of interest was to remain outside the jurisdiction of the Federal Shari'at Court up to 25th June, 1983 ... [T]he bar [was] to continue till 25th June, 1990. The said period having expired the bar stood removed and the jurisdiction with regard to examining any provision of any fiscal law or any law relating to the levy and collection of taxes and fees or banking, insurance practice and procedure, now vests in this Court' (§ 63).

The long court decision, written by Chief Justice Dr Tanzil-ul-Rahman, did not strictly follow, or answer, all the questions it raised with the various experts. But the decision was premised throughout on a strict understanding of the prohibition of *riba* as equivalent to the prohibition of interest in whatever forms it may manifest itself.

The reasoning proceeds in several phases: it starts with an explanation of the stakes in the case, the procedure of the Court, including the call for expert witnesses and the aforementioned questionnaire, and the history of the prohibition of *riba* since the 1956 Constitution of Pakistan through to the final empowerment of the Federal Shariat Court to review the matter in June 1990.

Next is examined the definition of *riba* (§§ 65 ff). There is little original in the long section.[146] The Court covers the instances in which the word appears in the Qur'an and in the *hadith*, noting however that '*riba al-fadl* is outside the scope of the present discussion' (§ 71). The analysis culminates in the rejection of the alleged distinction between interest in consumer transactions, for which *riba* would be strictly forbidden, and interest on productive loans, where it could be tolerated: '[W]hen the Holy Qur'an prohibited interest, it applied to the interest on commercial loans for productive purposes as well as to the interest on consumptional loans' (§ 45).

Examining further the issue of *riba*, the Court went through various techniques associated with the interpretation of Islamic law, including the consideration of consensus (*ijma'*, §§ 125 ff) and 'weal' (*maslaha*, §§ 140 ff). It concluded on the

---

[145] ibid., Appendix A, 1–143.

[146] On the discussion of *riba*, see Warde, *Islamic finance*, 55–72; Abdullah Saeed, *Islamic banking and interest: a study of the prohibition of riba and its contemporary interpretation* (Leiden, 1997); Nabil Saleh, *Unlawful gain and legitimate profit in Islamic law* (Cambridge, 1986, 2nd edn., London, 1992); and the two articles mentioned above n. 33.

latter that 'the rule of Maslaha can't be invoked in aid to permissibility of "Bank Interest" ' (§ 152), and on the former that:

§ 137. As it has been explained in the earlier part of the judgment there are two types of *Riba*: (1) *Riba al-Nasiah* and (2) *Riba al-Fadal*. Presently in these petitions we are concerned with *Riba al-Nasiah* i.e., the interest charged on the money lent or in other words the addition over and above the principal sum advanced on loan. It includes all kinds of interest irrespective of the fact whether the rate stipulated is high or low and whether the interest is or is not added to the principal sum after fixed periods and whether the sum lent is for production or consumption purposes. So far as this kind of *Riba* is concerned we have not come across any difference of opinion regarding its prohibition. There is no Commentator of the Holy Qur'an, no narrator of *Ahadith*, and no Jurist of Islamic *Fiqh* worth the name who has even expressed or even mentioned any doubt regarding any obscurity or ambiguity in its meaning. The difference of opinion whatever is found is regarding *'Riba al-fadal'* and that is out of discussion in the context of Bank interest which is under our consideration.

The most interesting section in the decision concerns the last two items which the Court discussed before proceeding to invalidate the Pakistani statutes concerned with the prohibition of interest. One argument which it paid particular attention to was inflation and/or indexation as a possible exception to the strict application of the *riba* rule. If money depreciates, according to holders of a lenient view of banking which the court opposes, or if, alternatively, indexation is possible by contract or by state regulation, then why should the value of the money lent, rather than the fixed quantity, not be taken into account?

Several legal and policy matters are examined to refute the argument, most prominently the need to avoid manifest injustice by allowing creditors to be abused by debtors if they are repaid with the original monetary value of the loan even if it is worth several times less than its original value. In answer to that argument, the Court resorted to general principles of tort law, including the principle that 'the usurper will not be required to indemnify the loss caused to the value of the property or money as a result of a fall in its price' (§ 196), and to more general equity ('an evil ... should not be redressed by a similar or a bigger evil', § 176) and policy considerations:[147] 'Why should a lender be protected against inflation while the borrower is not similarly protected against deflation?'[148]

In the rich, albeit sometimes repetitive, argumentation, the most interesting passages occur when the Court is at odds with recent Pakistani case-law:

§231 For the above discussion, we would approve the three decisions reported as Messrs Bank of Oman Ltd. v. Messrs East Trading Co. Ltd. and others, Irshad H. Khan v. Mrs. Parveen Ajaz and Habib Bank Ltd. v. Muhammad Hussain and others (P L D 1987

---

[147] Even though it asserts the prevalence of Islamic law over any economic theories: 'The arguments given in support of indexation are mostly based on some economic principles and do not relate to Shari'ah' (*Mahmood-ur-Rahman*, § 177).

[148] ibid., § 228, quoting an article by Munawar Iqbal, presented at a seminar held in Pakistan in 1987.

Kar. 404, 466 and 612) and respectfully dissent with the above-cited judgment reported as
Aijaz Haroon v. Imam Durrani (P L D 1989 Kar. 304) as also adopted by the learned Judge
in Tyeb v. Messr Alph Insurance Co. Ltd. and others (1990 C L C 428) to the extent of
allowing an additional amount on loan based on indexation on account of inflation.

The views of Justice Wajihuddin Ahmed, the author of *Tyeb v. Messr Alph
Insurance Co. Ltd. and others*, are rejected in detail by the Federal Shariat Court.
In his decision, the Karachi judge relied on the nineteenth-century treatise of the
Hanafi jurist Ibn 'Abidin, who appears to argue the need to repay the lender with
'the real worth of the currency, which was the subject-matter of or for which the
contract was concluded'.[149]

The original text of the Levantine Ibn 'Abidin is not without a dose of uncertainty, which the great nineteenth-century jurist acknowledges in an attempt, at
the end of his short treatise, to find a middle way between a buyer and a seller who
agree on a currency worth less when payment is due than its real value at the time
of the contract.[150] All the arguments in between the acknowledgment of inflation
and the risk of endangering the certainty of contracts, together with a detour into
the habits of merchants, can be found in that treatise. They were reflected in the
opposing views of the Pakistani courts.

Nor was the saga over. At least two other important decisions followed, and
the debate continues in court and outside, with an ever extended injunction by the
court for the government to change the laws in accordance with its findings. In line
with this injunction, a decision was issued by the Shariat Appellate Bench of
the Supreme Court on 23 December 1999.[151] It was even longer than the *Mahmood*
decision, and confirmed the need to overhaul the economic and financial structure
of Pakistani legislation to conform with Islamic law within a year. As the pressure
mounted, the bench was changed, and a further appeal was lodged by one of the
banks aggrieved by the threat to its business. This time, the same Supreme Court of
Pakistan, ruling again on 24 June 2002 as 'Shariat review jurisdiction', reversed.[152]
The decision was much shorter, and the Court essentially dismissed the previous
judgments as misinformed, following several submissions to this effect by attorneys
acting on behalf of the federal government (especially Riazul Hasan Gilani, §§ 8, 9).
According to these statements, 'lack of information' or 'misinterpretation' seemed
to have contributed to the dismissal by the previous judges of a number of authorities like Sanhuri and other Egyptian leading jurists, and successive muftis from
Muhammad 'Abduh to Muhammad Tantawi. It was also intimated in the submissions that there had been a lack of appreciation of Shi'i law (§ 8) and of dealings
with non-Muslims (§ 13). Mostly, the Court responded positively to the peti-
tioning bank's general 'chaos' argument: '[I]n case the [challenged] judgment is

---

[149] Cited § 59 in the original decision, reproduced in *Mahmood-ur-Rahman*, § 210.
[150] Ibn 'Abidin, *Majmu'at rasa'el* (Collected treatises), 2 vols. (Beirut, n.d.) 57–67.
[151] *M. Aslam Khaki v. Syed Mohammad Hashim*, PLD 2000 SC 225.
[152] *United Bank Limited v. Farooq Brothers and others*, PLD 2002 SC 800. The bench consisted of
five judges and was presided over by Chief Justice S. Riaz Ahmed.

implemented, it would lead to chaos and anarchy in the country and a duty is cast on an Islamic state to take all steps which are necessary in the public interest and the welfare of the people and avoid chaos and anarchy' (§ 14). The Court allowed the appeal and sent the decision for review again to the Federal Shariat Court (§ 19).

Many of the problems associated with Islamic banks have been highlighted—though hardly solved—in the 1991 Federal Shariat Court decision. While the decision was never implemented, the number of private Islamic banks has increased dramatically over two decades, and their assets are real. Even Western banks operating in the Middle East have quickly re-adjusted with the establishment of 'Islamic portfolios'.

Islamic banks have mushroomed in the past twenty years, but the picture is still patchy. In some cases, as in some such enterprises in Egypt, failure has befallen the banks and given rise to the intervention of the government to offer protection to the small depositors who lost all their savings.[153]

In other countries, more success has been forthcoming, although the essential operations of the banks tend to be directed towards short-term financing of international trading.

For private institutions (and individuals), the challenge is to set up a system of banking which does not acknowledge any form of fixed fee on any transaction. A deposit or a loan of, say, 9 per cent yield per annum would be illegal. To replace it, and yet to retain the basic function of banking, the alternative generally proposed is for a financial institution to pay its depositors a share of its annual profit in a way which is akin to a distribution of dividends to the shareholders of a company. Under that 'first tier' of the *mudaraba* contract (the Roman *commenda*, known also as 'partnership for profit and loss'), the depositors would in effect be shareholders, and the return on the money deposited with the bank would not be previously fixed, so as to prevent the deposit from being tainted with the illegal *riba*. Similarly, in the loan extended by the bank to borrowers, the profit of the bank would be a function of the success of the project. The bank would enter into a contract of *mudaraba* with the borrower-entrepreneur, and would share in the success or failure of the project for which funds were extended. Hence the concept of a 'two-tier *mudaraba*'.[154]

The *mudaraba* is seen by the theoreticians of Islamic banks, following the Egyptian mufti Muhammad 'Abduh at the turn of the century,[155] through to

---

[153] On the experience of the so-called *sharikat tawzif al-amwal* ('Islamic' investment companies) in Egypt, see Warde, *Islamic finance*, 'new forms of Islamic finance', 80–4, and literature cited therein.

[154] Frank Vogel and Samuel Hayes, *Islamic law and finance. Religion, risk and return* (London, 1998) 130–1: 'A first-tier *mudaraba* is created when investors (we shall call them "depositors") place their capital with an Islamic bank, fund, or other financial institution, which here acts as the *mudarib* or working partner. The financial institution or *mudarib* in turn invests these funds with entrepreneurs (the equivalent of a conventional bank's borrowers) by means of second-tier *mudarabas*, in which the Islamic financial institution now has the role of capital investor ... The institution's profits then come not from interest income but from a percentage of the profits from the second-tier *mudarabas*.'

[155] On which Mallat, 'The debate on *riba*', above n. 33, 69–74.

Muhammad Baqer al-Sadr in 1969,[156] as mediating the basic relationship in an Islamic bank between depositors, the borrowers, and the bank.

The organization of a dual system of *mudaraba* contracts as a basic model for the Islamic bank appears straightforward enough under this scheme.[157] Things are not so simple, however, and one of the basic difficulties at the confluence of Islamic and contemporary banking is the idea of the bank itself. The reason why Islamic banking has been so unpalatable to the Western model is precisely because a depositor is normally not entitled to receive a return on his deposit whilst protecting his capital—his initial deposit. A loss incurred by the bank will eat up the depositor's capital, the mere existence of which cannot be guaranteed under the scheme of *mudaraba*. In addition to the complication of a classical Islamic system in which 'the concept of corporate personality' was not available, the agent in the traditional contractual arrangement 'was not liable for any part of the investment in case of loss'.[158] Since that agent in the classical contract is none other than the bank in a modern Islamic set-up, the initial worries of the governor of the Bank of England, who rejected the mere idea of an Islamic 'bank' in Britain, are understandable.[159] In another early appreciation of the basics of the system, an American regulatory official clearly showed the limitations of the system under US law:

The principle of operating as a partner, in which profits and losses of enterprises are shared, appears sufficiently at odds with U.S. practise and regulations as to make it unlikely that the Islamic financial institutions can operate here as commercial banks or thrift institutions. In addition, the prohibition of interest, while itself occasioning little or no regulatory objection, would appear to represent a substantial competitive disadvantage for such institutions.[160]

On the practical level, another significant problem arises from the marginal place of *mudaraba* in self-styled Islamic banks. Under the most optimistic accounts,

---

[156] Cited above n. 58. The banking contributions of Sadr are discussed in Mallat, *The renewal of Islamic law*, 169–87.

[157] This 'two-tier *mudaraba* system' is the dominant alternative scheme in theory. One should note, however, that a more elaborate system was presented by Muhammad Baqer al-Sadr in his early treatise on the Islamic-free bank. Sadr suggests a one-tier system in which the depositor and the entrepreneur would be the two parties to the contract, with the bank acting only as intermediary. See my discussion in *The renewal of Islamic law*, 169–73.

[158] Udovitch, *Partnership and profit*, above n. 72, 239, citing several authorities.

[159] For Robin Leigh-Pemberton, then governor of the Bank of England, Islamic banking is 'a perfectly acceptable mode of investment, but it does not fall within the long-established and well understood definition of what constitutes banking in this country'. Quoted in Warde, *Islamic finance*, 194 after the *Financial Times*, 28 November 1995. The original statement was given in late 1985. Al-Baraka, the only 'Islamic bank' allowed for a while in Britain, was eventually shut down in 1993. Another attempt is mentioned in more recent literature: 'During September 2004, the "revolutionary" concept of interest-free commercial banking became a reality in the United Kingdom when the Islamic Bank of Britain opened for business in London'. Michael Taylor, 'Islamic commercial banking—moving into the mainstream?', *The Transnational Lawyer*, 18, 2005, 417–29, at 417.

[160] Charles Schotta, then 'deputy assistant secretary of the treasury for Arabian Peninsula affairs'. 'Islamic banking and the U.S. regulatory climate', in Islamic banking and finance conference, *Proceedings*, Washington, DC, 25–6 September 1986, 1.

mudaraba schemes represent less than 10 per cent of banking operations.[161] Instead, the main vehicle or 'product' of Islamic banks is the so-called *murabaha*, which is none other than a facilitation by the bank of short-term loans, mostly in commercial export–import operations, for their most trusted clients.[162] While various exotic appellations are bestowed upon a basic scheme facilitating short-term sale, the legal vehicle is hardly original, or revolutionary. More seriously, for a financial system that prides itself on offering 'full' banking facilities from an Islamic perspective, it does not correspond to any particularly original scheme. *Mutatis mutandis*, other 'Islamic commercial vehicles', labelled *sukuk* in fashionable literature, have mushroomed in the past two decades to provide superficially 'Islamic' accommodations of Western equivalents.

Finally, and at the level of government, some countries have attempted to cleanse the macroeconomic banking system of *riba*. *Riba*-free legislation was passed, but the picture is also uncertain, especially with regard to the fact that the whole banking system is often under public ownership control. The still unimplemented decision of the Pakistan Federal Shariat Court shows the difficulty facing any modern Middle Eastern legislation in that central economic field.[163] The saga continues.

Islamic banking is a recent phenomenon, which indicates the importance of the *shari'a* in the most basic set-up of the banking system in the private as well as public sectors. Although the experiment is not sufficiently developed for an assessment of its durability, it is fair to say that it has countered Western banking with an unusual intellectual challenge. In the overall commercial field, however, the ultimate dominance of Western-style law still prevails, despite what a rich—though patchy—Islamic tradition of classical commercial law seems to offer.

Arbitration

If Islamic banking is to be partly perceived as the revenge of classical law from the point of view of substance, the tradition's revenge may also be taking another form, procedurally, in arbitration. Here, the focus has been to get back at the state and the slowness of its judicial system rather than the revival of classical concepts.

---

[161] e.g. Vogel and Hayes, *Islamic law and finance*, above n. 154, 135.

[162] '"Mark-up" transactions account for 80 to 95% of all investments by Islamic financial institutions. The best-known mark-up instrument is the *murabaha*, a cost-plus contract in which a client wishing to purchase equipment or goods requests the financial provider to purchase the items and sell them to him at cost plus a declared profit. It is thus a financing-cum-sale transaction: the bank purchases the required goods directly and sells them on the basis of a fixed mark-up profit, agreeing to defer the receipt of the value of the goods (although the goods can be delivered immediately)' Warde, *Islamic finance*, 133.

[163] For a masterful survey of the various countries, see ibid. 112–30; for the regulatory challenges under the new 'global' system of banking, see ibid. 180–204.

This is an area which is obviously not confined to commercial cases, but interest in arbitration has primarily been by commercial lawyers in the past few years, and institutional anchors on a national and regional level are primarily sought by merchants and law practitioners.

An appreciation of the arbitration process in the Middle East requires a return to basics. The basics here are Weberian: it is the state which has the exclusive right to exercise coercion, including violence. It is judicial power which wields, through the rule of law, the most sophisticated manifestation of state coercion. There is no rule of law without state monopoly of violence.

This stands in sharp contrast to the philosophy of arbitration, which is a consensual process by nature, at all levels of the process. The arbitration process does not in theory require coercion. By submitting to it rather than to the judge, the parties accept in principle the result of the award. Here, however, matters become particularly complicated in a Middle Eastern Arab context, and the whole Weberian theory comes to the fore with a vengeance. Arbitration remains an exception, in the settlement of intractable disputes, to the judicial process. Like any exception, it does not operate outside the framework of reference imposed by the main rule, which is judge-made decisions.

Weber's conclusions on state coercion offer the general background to the first part of my proposition in this epilogue on commercial law: so long as the judicial process in the Middle East does not develop to the extent needed to justify state monopoly over violence, its substitute in the form of arbitration will remain faulty. This is true of domestic as well as international arbitration, of which the commercial dimension is the most important.

The second part of the proposition is that the flight into arbitration will remain, despite all its shortcomings, the haven of merchants in search of a speedy settlement.

Why do commercial litigants wish to resort to arbitration rather than courts? The simple answer is their wish to avoid the judicial system. Reasons may vary: the process in court may be too slow, too unpredictable, too open, too unreliable, or too expensive.

Too slow: recourse to arbitration is the way to ensure, in theory, greater speed, as the informality of the arbitration procedure and the availability of the arbitrators appear to be far superior than any court would be able to sustain.

Too unpredictable: arbitration may offer greater predictability, or more assurance or comfort for the parties, who are able to choose, rather than an unknown judge, at least one arbitrator to each party's liking. Presumably the parties choose persons of higher integrity and dedication than might be forced upon them by a wobbly judicial system.

Too open: the arbitral process's closed or half-closed doors ensure improved discretion, which is particularly useful for business transactions. The award normally remains the property of the two parties, who might wish to keep it out of the public eye, for reasons connected or not with taxation or their preference to keep a low profile in business on litigation issues.

Too unreliable: arbitration may offer, in terms of control over the process, increased reliability, which dovetails with speed and predictability. Arbitration is a one-instance process, whereas the three-stages of normal procedure, all the way to the supreme court, means decisions which can be overturned, quashed, or weakened by dissent at various levels.

Too expensive: arbitration can result in lower costs for the litigants. Whilst high in International Chamber of Commerce cases, costs compare well in relative terms in less high-profile arbitral fora. A national or regional arbitral tribunal would normally be cheaper to go to than in the protracted process of local courts. While lawyers are usually needed in the arbitration of big commercial cases, the time factor of a quicker process brings overall costs down.[164]

Each of these reasons, which are universal, applies more or less accurately in the Middle East, where the reliability of justice suggests contradictory manifestations of the rule of law. In a region which has been subjected to repeated and violent turmoil in the twentieth century, economic transactions (especially international transactions) have tended to be more equitably upheld than human rights law, the penal process, or environmental grievances, both as a business ethic and as the subject of adjudication by the courts. This is not to say that the lack of authority of the courts in the constitutional field has not affected the less controversial arena of commercial law: the general system of patronage is rampant in the region.

For all these reasons, the Middle East has watched over the past decades a flight away from judicial adjudication and the consequent rise of arbitration. Arbitration has found great favour domestically and regionally, as it appears to offer obvious speed and simplicity in comparison with the uncertain and costly court system. As law merchant, however, it is plagued at all levels by the diffidence of the judiciary. This diffidence must be understood against the frustrated background of judicial office in most of the Middle East.

Judges in the region suffer from a combination of executive meddling, overwork, and low salaries. As a result, the judge, who should in theory be relieved by the advent of arbitrators to take on some of his or her work, finds a glittering chunk of commercial law, typically involving commercial transactions with a large monetary significance, being diverted to wealthy lawyers, or worse, to retired or former judges. When some of the fees of the arbitrators are known, and the most

---

[164] For the marshalling of these basic arguments on the virtues of arbitration in the regional context, see the explanatory memorandum (*mudhakkara idahiyya*) of the new Kuwaiti law on arbitration, Law 11, 1995, e.g. in *al-Majalla al-lubnaniyya lil-tahkim al-'arabi wal-dawli* (The Lebanese Review of Arab and International Arbitration), 1:1, 1996, 135–7.

basic comparison made in the judge's mind with his own fixed remuneration, the result can only be frustration.

So unless the salaries of judges are increased to match that of an arbitrator in commercial transactions, the result is what we have in the region: an increased interest in arbitration, especially in commercial circles, to avoid the courts, and a proportionate and rising frustration on the part of judges. This is compounded by the state's natural propensity to frown upon matters of importance adjudicated outside its control, and the loss of its natural Weberian monopoly of power.

How is this diffidence illustrated in the legislation and court cases of the Arab Middle East?

Legislation

Ever since the famous Aramco award, which pitted the government of Saudi Arabia against the powerful American oil company,[165] one lesson has been learnt by the wealthiest government in the Arab world: no administrative contract, that is a contract involving the state or one of its branches, will, by law, include an arbitration clause without express permission from the Council of Ministers.[166] Considering the importance of construction and other public contracts in the Kingdom, this brings arbitration beyond the pale of the most significant commercial transactions.

Whilst the Saudi case may be extreme, legislation tends to create all kinds of typically procedural problems to arbitration. This is done either for special contracts of some commercial significance, like those related to agency and distribution, or in a more general manner.

I have already discussed agency as a special area of commercial law, which dominates the rules and patterns of trade, and has led to special legislation designed to protect local importers by means of judicial compensation, in case of non-renewal of the contract, and administrative constraints to the appointment of a new agent by a foreign manufacturer.

Within commercial agency law, the exceptional—or excessive—rules are reinforced procedurally, to avoid agreements which bypass restrictive legislation.

---

[165] The proceedings of the Aramco case leading to the award against Saudi Arabia were published in ten volumes, *Arbitration between Government of Saudi Arabia and Arabian American Oil Company*, 1956. The award upheld Aramco's position against the Saudi government by confirming the rights of the company to the exclusive transportation of Saudi oil.

[166] Decree 58 of 25 June 1963, discussed e.g. in A. Ahdab, *Arbitration in the Arab countries*, (Deventer, 1990) 602. Also Statute on Arbitration, Royal Decree M/46 of 12.07.1403 H., corresponding to 25 April 1983, Art. 3: 'Government agencies are not allowed to resort to arbitration for settlement of their disputes with third parties except after having obtained the consent of the president of the Council of Ministers', and Implementation Rules, decree of the Council of Ministers 71, 2021/11, 8 September 1405, corresponding to 27 May 1985, Art. 8: 'Where a government agency is a party to a dispute which it deems appropriate to refer to arbitration, [it must draft a memorandum which] must be approved by the president of the Council of Ministers'.

Lebanon, which introduced the paragon commercial agency statute in the Arab world under Decree-law 34/67, also ensured that arbitration is kept at bay from adjudicating agency disputes:

Notwithstanding any agreement to the contrary, the courts of the place of business of the commercial representative shall be deemed to be competent to consider any disputes arising from the commercial representation contract.[167]

It was left to commentators to try to wriggle out of the prohibition on resorting to arbitration by suggesting that arbitration could be initiated in Lebanon *after* the dispute had arisen.[168] This public policy dimension, which is clearly averse to arbitration superseding the Lebanese law of commercial agency, has travelled in one way or another to the Gulf along with the initial statute. In the Gulf, an arbitration arrangement can hardly be effective, in case of breach, when the administrative agencies themselves (typically the Minister of Economy) are entitled to stop a new importer/dealer/agent from carrying out the agency so long as the conflict pending between the former agent and the foreign principal has not been settled. Whether rejected openly by legislation or hampered by administrative means, the uselessness in Lebanon of an arbitration clause in the initial agency contract is true of Bahrain, the UAE, Jordan, and Oman. This list is not comprehensive. As illustrated in a recent decision of the Court of Cassation in Kuwait allowing an arbitration clause to stand, against an opposite conclusion in a similar case by the Lebanese Court of Appeal, the situation of 'international arbitration and public order' is in a state of flux.[169]

There is another, more general form, of the aversion of national systems to commercial arbitration, especially when espousing an international form. This takes the shape of the difficulty of enforcing an arbitration award, whether a domestic or an international one, in an Arab jurisdiction. Various agreements and treaties, including the Amman Convention of 1987, or the New York Convention of 1958, to which several jurisdictions have adhered, have tried to circumvent the problem on paper.

Invariably, these treaties are undermined by 'public policy' considerations which the courts are all too prone to implement, and which the party that is dissatisfied with the award can put forward. Ways to do so are variously premised on public policy considerations, due process, the compulsory personal presence of both parties before the judges, and other constraining devices. These essentially procedural devices often result in the conflict getting carefully perused, if not effectively re-tried, by the local jurisdiction.

---

[167] Art. 5, Decree-law 34/67.

[168] See e.g. S. Saleh, *Commercial agency*, above n. 81, 3–39 to 3–41.

[169] The Kuwaiti decision is dated 6 February 1999, and is unreported. It allowed the arbitration clause between a foreign airfreight company and a local agent to stand, despite the fact that the arbitration was to be held in Beirut, not in Kuwait. In contrast, the Lebanese Court of Appeal rejected the application of an arbitration clause between a foreign company and its agent in Lebanon, ruling that

In addition, there is a long string of statutes setting aside arbitration awards granted internationally, by freezing them, subjecting them to various appeals, or simply ignoring them. Some of the most recent such legislation can be found in Algeria,[170] the UAE,[171] Kuwait,[172] Egypt,[173] and Tunisia.[174] The pattern of restrictions is clear.

Case-law

Statutes are not the only problem. A comment on UAE practice shows some of the problems facing the enforcement of foreign arbitration awards by the local courts:

The UAE court [before which enforcement of the arbitral award is sought] will still review the process of serving summons and notifying the party, especially if the arbitration award is challenged by the opponent party when an application is made to uphold the arbitration award by the UAE court. Further, a recent judgment delivered in the appeal of Indian Overseas Bank v. Ibrahim al Shirawi and others by the Dubai Court of Cassation in a matter relating to enforcement of a foreign judgment has thrown considerable doubt on whether a foreign arbitration award will be enforceable in the UAE.[175]

This is also true in Saudi Arabia, where foreign judgments are frowned upon and tend to be set aside by courts.[176] In a similar vein, a British barrister who has

the Lebanese courts were competent to adjudicate such disputes under the doctrine of public order, decision of 2 February 1999, reported in the daily *al-Diyar*, 23 May 1999, 24.

[170] Legislative decree no. 93/09 of 25 April 1993, section iii, included in the civil code under Arts. 442 and 458 bis (limitations under new Art. 442 of matters generally under public policy, and matters of 'legal persons governed by public law', general limitations under 458 bis 43). Text in MECLR, 1, 1995, 33–6 (in English).

[171] Arts. 203–18 of the Federal Law of Civil Procedure, e.g. Art. 235 considering the enforcement of foreign judgments and awards possible if 'state courts have no jurisdiction in the dispute'. See the strict application in a decision reported in MELCR 1:2, 1995, 73–4 and in *Indian Overseas Bank v. Ibrahim Mohammed al-Shirawi*, Cassation 117/1993 dated 20 November 1993. But see contra the upholding of a foreign arbitration clause, *Basamah Marketing Establishment v. Aldaulia Marketing*, Cassation 61/94, discussed in R. Price, 'United Arab Emirates', *Yearbook of Islamic and Middle Eastern Law*, ii, 1995, at 207–8.

[172] Law 11, 1995, making the whole process of the arbitration tribunal particularly complicated, despite arguments to the contrary by the aforementioned Explanatory Memorandum and the presentation by the representative of the Ministry of Justice in the proceedings of the Beirut Euro-arbitration seminar, December 1996, published as Muhammad Naser Nasrallah, '*Tarikh al-tahkim bi-dawlat al-Kuwait wa anwa'uh* (History and types of arbitration in the state of Kuwait)', *al-Majalla al-lubnaniyya lil-tahkim al-'arabi wal-dawli*, 3, 1996, 22–8 at 25–6.

[173] Law 27, 1994, vide Art. 58 on the inquisitive role of the courts as to parties and public policy. Text in English in *Yearbook of Islamic and Middle Eastern Law*, i, 1994, 500–17; in Arabic e.g. in *al-Majalla al-lubnaniyya lil-tahkim al-'arabi wal-dawli*, 1:1, 1995, 127–32.

[174] Law 42, 1993, vide Art. 81. Arabic text e.g. in *al-Majalla al-lubnaniyya lil-tahkim*, 1:1, 1996, 142–51 (but note the restriction of public policy to the concept understood 'under private international law').

[175] Esam al-Temimi's comment on *Indian Overseas Bank v. Ibrahim Mohammed al-Shirawi*, cited above n. 171, in MECLR, 3, 1996, 85; also discussed in R. Price, 'United Arab Emirates', in *Yearbook of Islamic and Middle Eastern Law*, i, 1994, at 330.

[176] Judgment of Diwan al-Mazalim reproduced in Lewis-Ruttley and Mallat, eds., *Commercial law in the Middle East*, 304–21.

practised in Oman noted how 'the status of foreign arbitral awards in Oman has been unclear, and, since the commercial judicature was constituted in its current form, more than ten years ago, there has been no case where direct enforcement of a foreign arbitral award has been granted'.[177]

A 1990 Court of Cassation case in Jordan will also serve as an illustration, *a contrario*, of domestic courts' resistance to arbitration, even in internal matters. In that decision, the highest Jordanian Court confirmed the Court of Appeal's decision to reverse the Court of First Instance in a case of arbitration between the municipality of the city of Basira and a public works company. The company had undertaken the building of a road which was not deemed to conform to the speci-fications of the original contract. When the conflict arose in 1981 on the fulfil-ment of contractual specifications, the two parties concluded an arbitration agreement, which resulted in 1986 in an award in favour of the municipality. The award was attacked before the Court of First Instance on several grounds, notably for lack of competence of the head of the municipality in entering into an arbitra-tion process, and, subsidiarily, because the arbitrators had overstepped the role given to them in the arbitration agreement. The Court of Cassation refused to be drawn into matters of fact which it considered lower judges solely competent to look into. By a majority of two (out of three), it held on the second argument that 'the court of appeal as court of fact, and following its competence in assessing evi-dence according to Articles 1/33 and 1/34 of the law of evidence, had concluded that the Council of the city of Basira had agreed on arbitration'. It further held that the Arbitration law of 1953 prevents the court from undermining an arbitral award except in specific and narrow cases, as when 'the award had been issued on the basis of a void arbitral agreement, or if the award had overstepped the time limit specified in the agreement, or if the award had fallen outside the limits of the agreement'. This assessment, the majority concluded, was a prerogative of the Court of Appeal as court of fact.[178]

The dissenting judge approved this last conclusion, but considered that the head of the Basira municipality did not have the right, in view of the Jordanian civil law and the law of municipalities, to enter into an arbitration agreement without an express authorization from the municipality's Council.[179]

One can see the resistance to a clear law, on a matter of domestic arbitration, both in the first instance court and from the dissenting judge. Of note, however, is the most important element in the process: time. Whilst the conflict arose in 1981, it took five years for an award to be granted, and a further four years to reach final approval in the judicial system. All five elements mentioned at the outset of this section were, in the process, defeated, and Weberian monopoly of law and power returned, in the process, to the state through its judges.

[177] Alastair Hirst, 'Court decisions on commercial arbitration in the Sultanate of Oman', MECLR, 2, 1995, 77–9, at 77.

[178] Al-Mamlaka al-urduniyya al-hashimiyya (the Hashemite Kingdom of Jordan), Mahkamat al-tamyiz (Court of Cassation), 8 March 1990, MAFQ 12, 1992, 197–200, at 199.

[179] ibid., at 200.

Another documented example from Jordan illustrates the time and speed factor involved in challenges to the arbitral award. In that case, the Court of Cassation had to streamline a procedurally complicated issue which arose from the stay of bankruptcy proceedings by a lower court following a decision of an arbitrator to dissolve a partnership. Two partners had started the original suit in 1977 against their fellow partner, and they asked the Court to appoint a guardian of the partnership, which it did. But the three partners came to an agreement in court for the amicable dissolution of the partnership under the supervision of an arbitrator, who duly took on his task, and attached some of the land belonging to one of the plaintiffs to cover the liabilities of the partnership. A decision to stay the attachment proceedings was granted, leading to the freezing of the whole dissolution process, with, as a result, the dragging on of the liquidation process for a decade. After various cross-appeals, the Court of Cassation brought some order into the process, explaining that the arbitration issue had been long decided upon by the courts, which had confirmed the liabilities of each of the parties in the partnership. The original plaintiff therefore had no business undermining the decision of the arbitrator, which had been confirmed by the Court, and the arbitrator's task was to continue unimpeded until full settlement of all the liabilities.[180]

Here also, the dilatory procedural manoeuvres of the party dissatisfied with the arbitration are clear, and the extensive time needed for the Court to force the implementation of the award clearly defeats the primary purpose of the arbitral effort: speed.

Considering the bottlenecks in legislation and case-law, one is entitled to some scepticism on the future of effective arbitration in the absence of a more solid rule of law across the system. The proliferation of legislation, protocols, arbitration courts and centres, all vying for a place in the sun, if not supremacy, in the Arab world, may be a sign of weakness rather than of strength. The absence of any serious reported arbitration in Rabat, despite a genuine attempt in the Amman Convention of 1987 to set it up as a major centre for arbitral awards, is one example of this pervasive reluctance. The move of the Court from Rabat to Cairo in 1994 gave brief hope for the beginning of a different, perhaps more successful, re-centring. The structural problems remain, for court practice is not encouraging. Both the state generally and the judge, in particular, will try to reclaim control over the arbitral process.

One way to avoid the shortcomings of arbitration includes the 'new' field of alternative dispute resolution (ADR). The difference with arbitration is known: the person who presides over an ADR procedure will not issue an award. His or her goal is an agreement between the parties in conflict. This is the only way to avoid the pitfalls of implementation, since the parties who have just agreed on a compromise will also want it to be effective. There is no loser in ADR. Such an

---

[180] Al-Mamlaka al-urduniyya al-hashimiyya (the Hashemite Kingdom of Jordan), Mahkamat al-tamyiz (Court of Cassation), 29 August 1992, MAFQ 16, 1994, 301.

agreement being naturally binding, the whole dimension of the judicial or arbitral process is left behind.

But then, is there a legal process at all? In theory, such resolution as may result from ADR is nothing more than a good old gentlemen's agreement. In practice, a combination of ADR, arbitration, and judicial process might offer ways out of the present deadlock between judges and arbitrators in the Arab world.

For lawyers in daily practice, the Catch-22 situation is the more dramatic since it imposes business rhythms which make arbitration a dramatic need, helping to avoid the long and painful route imposed by the judicial process. But arbitration is constantly undermined: whilst the idea of pushing the arbitral process forward seems naturally compelling, it is difficult to imagine either state or judge getting enthusiastic about it.

The more serious way out would be to bolster the judiciary. The more effective and comfortable the judiciary, the more a natural ally for the arbitrators, who take a lot of weight off the judges' back. But for arbitration to find its rightful place in the legal system, the financial and social balance cannot remain as dramatic as it is today. Frustrated judges will not readily give precedence to successful arbitrators. This is true of commercial arbitration, but no less true of any sort of informal process for the settlement of disputes.

Conclusion: On the Universality of the Law Merchant

Commercial law is a field with the greatest propensity to elude synthesis. This is because the law of merchants is intrinsically attached, if it wishes to be successful, to the day-to-day practice of its strongest bearers and defenders, the merchants themselves. In a famous dictum of Lord Mansfield, the universality of law merchant was asserted in a case of admiralty: 'The maritime law is not the law of a particular country but the general law of nations: "non erit alia lex Romae, alia Athenis; alia nunc, alia posthac; sed et apud omnes gentes et omni tempore, una eadem lex obtinebit" '.[181]

If the dictum is true, at some abstract level, for all law as interpreted and adjudicated by human beings, as in the original passage which Lord Mansfield borrowed from a reflection by Cicero on public law,[182] the universality of law merchant is particularly true in an epoch of unprecedented globalization of trade. While generalizing models are possible at different times in history, and trade patterns as crystallized into law detectable from Babylonian times, through to the classical

---

[181] *Luke v. Lyde*, 97 Eng. Rep. 787 (1759), at 617: 'It will not be the law of Rome, or the law of Athens; not one law now, one law hereafter; but one and the same law, for all people and for all times'. Quoted in my 'Un comparatiste anglais au XVIIIème siècle. Influences françaises sur la common law dans l'oeuvre de Lord Mansfield', *Revue Historique de Droit Français et Etranger*, 72, 1994, 383–400, at 392; and in conclusion to Roy Goode, *Commercial law* (London, new edn., 1995) 1212.

[182] Full passage in Cicero, *De Republica*, iii, 22.

age of Islam, the emergence of capitalist Europe, and the establishment of the World Trade Organization, some dilemmas have remained, as exciting and response-less as they were from the outset: the question of interest, excessive or otherwise, is one example. Another is the search for rapid solutions in business, through the court system, and if that fails, through a process of arbitration. A third is a characteristic 'dilemma of liability: the dilemma which most persistently launches judges into speculation on the meaning of corporate entity is related to the liability of corporate members for obligations—contractual or tortious—that arise from corporate activities. This is the question that springs first to most lawyers' minds when "corporate entity" is mentioned.'[183]

For the lawyer indeed, geared as she is to problem-solving, the maze of commercial regulations may appear daunting against the mixture of systems and institutions. Fortunately, the guiding force for problem-solving remains the businessman's sense of expediency and achievement, and the protection which Arab merchants have imposed on their 'agencies', against both the classical system and the dominant patterns in Europe, is a case in point. That instinct to cut through the law in search of solutions, or, what amounts to a close equivalent, profit, is eminently practical. In business, it is universal and overwhelming.

[183] Conard, *Corporations*, above n. 102, 424.

10

Family Law: The Search for Equality

The gradual development of the principle of equality is, therefore, a providential fact. It has all the chief characteristics of such a fact: it is universal, it is lasting, it constantly eludes all human interference, and all events as well as all men contribute to its progress.

Tocqueville[1]

In the opening pages of *Democracy in America* (1835), Alexis de Tocqueville explained his awareness of the acute necessity for a novel theory in the society which was emerging in the New World. In the new age, 'the equality of conditions is the fundamental fact from which all others seem to be derived and the central point at which all my observations constantly terminated'.[2]

Tocqueville would not have suspected how accurate these remarks would still be, on the other side of the planet, two centuries later. Not only do the requirements carried by 'the age of equality' extend to other societies than those spawned by the European or North American industrial revolution, but they can also prove of great analytical importance in the depiction of the logic of family law reform in the Muslim world of the twentieth century. In the Tocquevillian axioms of the age of equality—gradual, universal, and irreversible—can be found the fundamental principle against which developed the codification of family law in countries with a significant population of Muslim citizens: the equality of women and men before the law.

The premise of this chapter is that Middle Eastern legislators and judges in the twentieth century operate with an expressed or muted awareness of the legal equality between two individuals across the gender divide of the nuclear family: primarily of course husband and wife, but also daughter and son, brother and sister, father and mother. This premise is simple enough. In the age of Tocquevillian

---

[1] 'Le développement graduel de l'égalité des conditions est donc un fait providentiel, il en a les principaux caractères: il est universel, il est durable, il échappe chaque jour à la puissance humaine, tous les événements, comme tous les hommes, servent à son développement.' Alexis de Tocqueville, *Démocratie en Amérique* (Paris, 1951) i, 5–6.

[2] 'Je voyais de plus en plus, dans l'égalité des conditions, le fait générateur dont chaque fait particulier semblait descendre, et je le retrouvais sans cesse devant moi comme un point central où toutes mes observations devaient aboutir.' ibid. 2–3.

equality, the parties on both gender sides of the family fence are treated in the same way as a matter of principle: they share the same rights, duties, and obligations, and benefit from the equal treatment of the law.

In the classical Muslim world, which came of age long before the Tocquevillian era of equality, that premise was different, and the legal framework of family life was governed by values that had no place for the concept of equality between male and female: Kasani (d. 1191), one of the most remarkable and systematic jurists of the classical age, devised a special, seven-fold, classification for women,[3] who are 'usually known for their mental shortcomings'.[4] Accordingly, gender equality is a concept which cannot be projected backwards without serious risks of anachronism.[5] As a result, when an egalitarian prism is used for the assessment of gender-based rights, it stands in sharp contrast to an overall framework of classical law which is indifferent to gender equality. In the light of this contrast between modern Tocquevillian equality and a classical age which did not recognize it as part of its mental framework, the chapter examines some of the key categories in family life as currently regulated. In the contemporary Middle East, the field is also known as 'personal status law'.[6] This covers marriage, separation, maintenance and alimony, custody over children, wills and *ab intestat* inheritance in the law of succession.

The Classical Paradigm

In the received view of the classical Islamic world, the unequal legal appreciation of the two parties is well-known in its general traits and can be summarized in a number of 'acid tests':[7]

Marriage. Only a woman who has reached majority and has already been married (i.e. divorced or widowed) can get married without referring first to her guardian.

---

[3] In the book on *istihsan*, 'preference', for the purpose of regulating social interaction between men and women, Kasani classifies women into seven legal categories: 'Those married, those owned, those forbidden because of blood kinship, those forbidden for other reasons (suckling or *musahara*, in-law kinship), those owned by others, those foreign and free, and those who are related (to the man) but whose marriage (with him) is not forbidden'. Kasani, *Bada'e' al-sana'e' fi tartib al-shara'e'* (Cairo edn., 1910) v, 118–19. There follow several pages dealing with each category, 119–23; on Kasani, see index s.v.   [4] Kasani, v, 155: *lakin laysa laha kamal al-ra'i li-qusur 'aql al-nisa' 'adatan.*
[5] This is a concept borrowed from the French historian Lucien Febvre, *Le problème de l'incroyance au 16ème siècle* (Paris, 1947). See below n. 30.   [6] *Qanun al-ahwal al-shakhsiyya.*
[7] There is a significant literature on the subject. The best-known legal authorities include Y. Linant de Bellefonds and Maurice Borrmans (in French), Norman Anderson and Noel Coulson, more recently David Pearl, Doreen Hinchcliffe, Jamal Nasir, Lucy Carroll, Taher Mahmood, and Dawud Alami (in English). Writers on the subject in Arabic include Muhammad Abn Zahra in Egypt, Muhammad Jawad Mughniyya in Lebanon, Muhammad Bahr al-'Ulum in Iraq, A. Khamlishi (in Arabic) and Moulay Rachid (in French) in Morocco. Iranian authors include M. J. Ja'fari-Langarudi and Murtaza Mutahhari (in Persian).

In most other cases, the male guardian chooses for her, and may overcome her resistance.

The husband can take up to four wives. The Muslim husband can marry a non-Muslim woman belonging to the other world religions, the Muslim wife can only marry or be married to one Muslim man.

During married life, the wife owes obedience to the husband, from which derive a number of constraints, which, if infringed, put her in the penalized position of disobedience, *nushuz*. *Nushuz* is exclusively associated with women.

Termination of marriage. In the law of separation, repudiation, *talaq*, is the prerogative of the husband. This is a unilateral right which is not granted to the wife.

Upon termination of marriage, classical Islamic law does not recognize 'alimony' or 'ancillary relief' as an entitlement of the repudiated or divorced wife. The end of marriage stops in classical law any payment of maintenance to the wife by the husband in the absence of children. When there are children, any money which the husband may pay to his divorced wife is directly connected to her status as caretaker of the broken marriage's children. Although the right to 'ancillary relief' does not strictly pertain to the sphere of equality, it is an important acid test in contemporary Muslim societies.

Custody. Custody of the child is entrusted to either mother or father, depending on age and sex. The younger child tends to go to the mother's care, and the father takes on custody when the child reaches a given age. The father has an overall right to guide the child's education in any case, as he is considered 'the head' of the family and its ultimate guardian, even after divorce. There is therefore a difference between custody and guardianship,[8] and the father is invariably the guardian of the child after separation, even if the mother is granted the more effective right to custody up to a certain age, after which even custody reverts to the father.[9]

---

[8] The separation in Islamic law between custody (*hadana*) and guardianship (*wilaya*) offers a useful indication of the universal impossibility of finding a Gordian knot solution to conflicting parental claims. For application in Tunisia, see Mounira Charrad, 'Repudiation versus divorce: responses to state policy in Tunisia', in E. Chow and C. Berheide, eds., *Women, the family and policy: a global perspective* (Albany, NY 1994) 60: 'Laws on child custody have been among the most effective in improving women's position and family experiences, and judges overwhelmingly have interpreted the new laws in favor of women. Lawyers report that this has been the case even in rural areas .... The legal distinction between custody and guardianship has caused difficulties, however. The law gives guardianship (or legal responsibility for the child) to the father, while the mother has custody—and therefore the day to day care. In everyday life, the lines between guardianship and custody become blurred, giving rise to conflict between the two parents.'

[9] In one modern authoritative compendium which compares the four Sunni Schools, the mother's right to the child's custody is said to be for (1) Hanafis: boy until 7 years of age, girls: 9, or until puberty; (2) Malikis: boy until majority, girl until marriage, and her marriage must have been consummated; (3) Shafi'is: boy until 'he can differentiate between his father and his mother, and he is made to choose ... ', and the case is similar for girls with some nuances; (4) Hanbalis: 7 for both boy and girl. Al-Jaziri, *Al-fiqh 'ala al-madhahib al-arba'a (Fiqh according to the four schools)*, 5 vols. (Beirut, repr. 1990) iv, 523–4, quote at 524, original published in the 1930s. The 'established' differences

Succession. The law of succession is determined by a few cardinal principles. *Ab intestat* inheritance is strictly regulated, in a refined and complex system of arithmetic equations. Here, the acid test of gender equality is determined by the principle of the woman—essentially the wife, mother, and daughter—receiving half of the prescribed share for the corresponding male in the family structure: husband, father, and son. The formula is repeated twice in the Qur'an: 'To the male twice the share of the female'.[10]

Upon the death of the husband, in the simplest figures, the surviving wife receives a quarter of the estate if there are no children, one-eighth if there are any children. Upon the death of the wife, the husband receives half and a quarter in the corresponding scheme. In the presence of her brother, the daughter never receives more than half of his share. The share of father and mother is more complicated, but the mother never receives more than her husband's share in Sunni law, even if there are cases where she might inherit the same as him.[11]

The second principle, 'no will for more than one third of the estate',[12] means that *ab intestat* inheritance is dominant for at least two-thirds of the deceased's property.

between the schools may be less rigid than books like Jaziri's might suggest. For Twelver Shi'is, a modern author puts the age at 2 for boys and 7 for girls 'for the majority of the *muta'akhkhirin* (the late scholars)', but a wide divergence is noted between them. Muhammad Bahr al-'Ulum, *Adwa' 'ala qanun al-ahwal al-shakhsiyya al-'iraqi* (Lights on the Iraqi personal status law) (Najaf, 1963) 151–4, quote at 154. On this important book, see my 'Shi'ism and Sunnism in Iraq: revisiting the codes', in C. Mallat and J. Connors, eds., *Islamic family law* (London, 1990) 71–91.

[10] *Wa lidh-dhakar mithlu hazz al-unthayayn,* Qur'an iv: 11; iv: 176. The fusion of different rules of succession in the classical age persists in this case to the present as a typical Middle Eastern law paradigm. In Egypt, for instance, the rule is still law for both Christian and Muslim Egyptians, as it also is in Iraq. On this legal Middle Eastern *calque*, see Chapter 2, especially the discussion of the remarkable 'appendix' of the Italian scholar Nallino on a copyist's addendum to an early Christian code including the formula, at n. 49. For a different type of innovative research in the Islamic law of succession, see D. Powers, *Studies in Qur'an and hadith: the formation of the Islamic law of inheritance* (Berkeley, 1986) (arguing that there was a proto-Islamic law of inheritance between Qur'anic revelation and the Islamic law of succession as known in the classical age); M. Mundy, 'The family, inheritance and Islam: a re-examination of the sociology of *fara'id* law', in A. al-Azmeh, ed., *Islamic law: social and historical contexts* (London, 1988) 1–123 (on the social transformation of inheritance law across the ages).

[11] In the case of a person who dies leaving a father, a mother, and a son, they receive respectively 1/6, 1/6, and 2/3. If a person dies leaving a mother and a father only, the mother receives 1/3 against 2/3 for the father. These two cases are true for both Shi'is and Sunnis. There is one sole instance, which occurs in Shi'i law, where the mother receives more than the father. This is when a woman dies leaving behind her a husband, a father, and a mother. For the Shi'is, the husband gets 1/2, the father 1/6, and the mother 1/3, following the letter of the Qur'an iv: 11. The Sunnis would give the husband 1/2, 1/3 to the father, and 1/6 to the mother following an elaborate interpretive scheme stemming from the difficulty of allowing the mother to inherit more than the father. The case is known as *al-'umariyyatan*, in reference to the Caliph 'Umar ibn al-Khattab, to whom the interpretation is attributed, or *al-gharawiyya* (in reference to the fame associated with it in some reports). See for instance 'Umar 'Abdallah, *Ahkam al-mawarith fil-shari'a al-islamiyya* (Succession rules in Islamic law), 4th edn. (Cairo, 1965) 142–6; Wahbeh al-Zuhayli, *Al-fiqh al-islami wa adillatuhu* (Islamic law and its reasons), (Damascus, 1984) x, 7787–9. A clear English exposition of the basic inheritance rules can be found in David Pearl, *A textbook on Muslim personal law* (London, 1979, 2nd edn., 1987) 138–88.

[12] *'Al-wasiyya bith-thulth, wal-thulth kathir* (and the third is too much)'. Bukhari (d. 870), *Sahih*, 9 vols. (Cairo, 1376 AH) iv, 4, with cross-references to Kirmani, 'Asqalani, 'Ayni, Qastalani.

The third cardinal principle, which is restricted to Sunnis, is the prohibition of a will in favour of an heir receiving a share in the estate under the following *ab intestat* rule: 'No bequest in favour of an heir'.[13] The combination of these limitations on free wills and the rigid system of *ab intestat* rules[14] makes variations on the so-called Qur'anic rules of succession extremely limited.[15]

At this very general level, Shi'i law includes an important variation on the Sunni system, because of the importance of *'asaba*, or male agnates, in the Sunni law of succession. This concept, which I have argued is a calque from the fifth century CE Syro-Roman Code,[16] establishes the entitlement of the male kin, however distant from the deceased, to such part of the estate as might not have been distributed under the Qur'anic shares. This portion can be significant,[17] and is crucial for the inheritance scheme viewed under the equality scheme. The Sunni principle of 'the remainder to the agnates' is bluntly rejected in Shi'i law by the rule of 'nothing to the agnates', following the *hadith* ascribed to the Shi'i Imam Ja'far al-Sadeq (d.765): 'As for the *'asaba* (the agnates), dust in their teeth'.[18] The practical consequences may be important, as the Shi'i system turns out to be much more favourable to a daughter than the Sunni system in the following common configuration: in a family where the deceased father leaves one daughter and no son, the Sunni system restricts the share of the daughter to the portion established

---

[13] *La wasiyya li-warith.* ibid.

[14] In one famous *hadith*, the Prophet enjoins people to learn the Qur'an and the rules of succession, to avoid endless disputes between heirs. The *hadith* on 'the knowledge (or science) of succession (*'ilm al-fara'ed*) as half of all science' is also common. See for citations and discussion e.g. 'Abdallah, *Ahkam al-mawarith*, above n. 11, 14.

[15] Note that the two principles relating to wills are Prophetic *hadith*, and that the Shi'is do not accept the later, *la wasiyya li-wareth*. Relative freedom of *inter vivos* gifts, and rules of *waqf* (trusts) may in practice alleviate the rules of *ab intestat* succession. There is a large literature on *waqf*, less on the law of gifts.

[16] Above Chapter 2, which develops the following argument: the concept of *'asaba* does not appear in the Qur'an. It is known in Sunni *hadith* as the saying which Ibn Tawus heard from the Prophet: *'Alhiqu al-fara'ed bi-ahliha fama baqiya li-awla rajul dhakar*, give the shares [of the estate] to those to whom it belongs [under the rules of the Qur'an], and what remains to the closest male'. The formula appears four times in Bukhari's book of *fara'ed* (viii, 124–31, at 126, 127 twice, 128). Curiously, the word *'asaba* appears only once in Bukhari, in a different context relating to a rare case of succession in which a woman dies in labour, with the consequence that the foetus also dies. The *hadith* in this case gives her estate to her sons and husband, but leaves '*al-'aql 'ala 'asabatiha*, reason to her *'asaba*' (at 128). The rule is unclear, and relates to the law of *diyya*. It is also remarkable that the word *'asaba* does not appear in one of the earliest extant treatises on the law of succession, Sufyan al-Thawri's (d. 778) *Kitab al-fara'ed*. However, the aforementioned *hadith* appears in the following form: *'Alhiqu al-mal bil-farayed, fa-idha turikat al-farayed, fa-awla rajul dhakar*, give the money according to the [Qur'anic] shares, but if the shares are left [i.e. exhausted], then to the closest male'. Hans-Peter Raddatz, 'Frühislamisches Erbrecht nach dem *Kitab al-Fara'id* des Sufyan at-Thawri, Edition und Kommentar', *Die Welt des Islams*, 13, 1971, 26–78, *hadith* at 35.

[17] In an extreme instance, a man dies leaving his wife and a distant cousin on the male side of the family. The widow gets 1/4 and the cousin the remaining 3/4.

[18] See Chapter 2 n. 106. This Shi'i saying is related for instance in the major compendium of Shi'i legal *hadith* by al-Hurr al-'Amili (d. 1693), *Wasa'el al-shi'a*, xxvi, 85 (*al-mal lil-aqrab wal-'asaba fi fihi al-turab*, property to the closest relative, and dust in the mouth of the agnates). It is also related in other books, such as Kulayni (d. 941), *al-Kafi*, 8 vols. (Tehran, 1978–) vii, 75; and Tusi (d. 1067) *al-Tahdhib*, 10 vols. (Tehran, 1997) ix, 276. Details kindly provided by Khaled 'Atiyyah.

in the Qur'an: one-half. The remainder goes to the nearest male kin. If the deceased is survived by an agnatic uncle or cousin, however distant, the remaining half goes in its entirety to him. There is no way for the father to increase his daughter's share by will because of the two principles just mentioned (no bequest to an heir, and no bequest for more than a third). To avoid this result, the Sunni father would convert to Shi'ism, ensuring that his sole daughter, because she is the closest kin, receives under Shi'i law his entire legacy. The difference between the two systems has prompted a number of *causes célèbres* of prominent twentieth-century Muslim personalities who changed their allegiance from Sunni to Shi'i law in order to take advantage of a system of inheritance which is more favourable to their sole daughters.

Thus appears a noteworthy specificity of Shi'i law, which gives precedence to a daughter over her male next-of-kin. But in the overall context of gender equality, the case is marginal in so far as the daughter's larger share operates only in the absence of a son. Whether in Sunni or in Shi'i law, if the daughter has a brother, the Qur'anic rule of half the share applies, and she gets half of what her brother inherits. Both in Shi'i and Sunni law, the woman—daughter, sister, wife, or mother—tends to receive less than her counterpart on the male side of the family.

Variations in family law can establish further institutional inequalities, most notably in the *mut'a* or temporary marriage for the Shi'is, and slave law in the classical age, which introduces other elements of unequal treatment between the slave male and the slave female. If slavery as legal category has all but disappeared in the twentieth century, temporary marriage *(mut'a)*, which is an institution open to men only, is still known in a large country like Shi'i Iran. It allows a married or single man to contract *mut'a* for a stipulated amount of time—it could be several years or a few minutes—with any number of women he may wish. Once the 'contractual time' has lapsed, the *mut'a* marriage is automatically dissolved. A married woman cannot contract *mut'a*, and, in theory, a virgin woman who is single is also barred from contracting *mut'a*.[19]

Overall, the woman is clearly the disadvantaged party at law. For a full picture, one ought to mention that the absence of equality also works positively for the woman in some circumstances, essentially with regard to the payment of the dower on or after marriage, and with the provision of maintenance and non-monetary forms of protection during marriage. The *mahr*—the sum of money paid by the bridegroom to his wife upon marriage, and which is sometimes translated as dowry to distinguish it from the Western dower—is owed by the husband to his wife.[20] In return, there is no dower owed by the wife to the husband. As a monetary debt of the husband, it is supplemented throughout married life by the necessity to cater

---

[19] Recent works on the marriage of *mut'a* include Shahla Haeri, *The law of desire: temporary marriage in Shi'i Iran* (London, 1989). An early twentieth-century account of *mut'a* was published in Iraq by Tawfiq al-Fukaiki. A large classical literature on *mut'a* appears in traditional Shi'i law books.

[20] To lessen confusion, *mahr* is translated as dower in this chapter.

for the wife's usual expenses as well as for the household as a whole. Upon separation, the wife as mother is entitled to the continued payment by her former husband of expenses incurred by the marriage children if they live with her. Even if the wife is of considerable means, the classical age did not impose on her any reciprocal treatment towards her husband. This is another illustration of the different mental mould governing the classical and modern outlooks, which contemporary projections backward cannot account for satisfactorily.

Other variations of inequality in classical *fiqh* which work to the advantage of women include the notion of the wife's stipulations in the contract. For many schools, marriage, like any other contract, should allow inclusion by the parties of specific stipulations or conditions to the wife's advantage.[21] These conditions are well illustrated in Hanbali *fiqh*. *Al-Mughni*, a lengthy treatise which was written by the Hanbali jurist Ibn Qudama (d. 1223) and which is still used in Saudi courts (where family law has not yet been codified), makes a distinction between three types of such stipulations.

The first type is constituted by conditions that render marriage void *ab initio*.[22] This is for Ibn Qudama the case of *mut'a* or temporary marriage (which, as previously mentioned, is unacceptable for Sunnis), and of marriage which requires the acceptance of a third party (e.g. the mother of the bride, who cannot usually be her guardian), or a marriage which specifies a moment in time when the husband is set to repudiate his wife. In the presence of such stipulations, the whole contract of marriage is null and void.

The second type of condition leaves marriage intact, for only the illegal condition is considered void. Such are the clauses, writes Ibn Qudama, 'which stipulate non-payment of dower or of marital maintenance'.[23] All these clauses are simply made ineffective because they contradict the normal effects of marriage, but the marriage contract stands.

The third type of condition offers the most distinctive feature generally associated with Hanbali *fiqh*, and opens the possibility for the wife to include stipulations in her favour: 'For instance, if the husband accepts not to make her leave the house which she owns, or her country, or accepts not to force her to travel, ... or (even) if he was ready not to take another wife. [He would then have to respect these stipulations], and if he did not, she could get the marriage dissolved'.[24]

On the strength of this testimony of Ibn Qudama, the question is whether a clause requesting a change in some of the typical features of the usual matrimonial regime would be valid. The full picture on the divergence from the traditional dominant system by way of these stipulations in the classical age is not known. In one notary-public contract formulary in twelfth-century Spain, the marriage contract stipulates 'the express mention of the wife's seven conditions ... whose

---

[21] Conditions, stipulations: *shurut*.
[22] *Yubtil al-nikah min aslih*. Ibn Qudama, *Al-Mughni*, vii, 448.
[23] Ibn Qudama, *al-Mughni*, vii, 450–2. Maintenance: *nafaqa*.
[24] Ibn Qudama, *al-Mughni*, vii, 448.

disregard by the husband commands divorce'.[25] In the modern age, stipulations that permit a wife to free herself of the marriage contract in the event her husband takes another wife have become a current legislative provision in many Muslim countries. The practice itself is not uncommon. It is known as 'the retention by the wife of her freedom to divorce'. The woman can therefore stipulate in her marriage contract that 'she has her freedom in her hand'.[26] Such stipulations, along with education clauses (i.e. pursuing further education), the request to have a separate home from her husbands' parents (or other wives), as well as clauses on the amount of deferred dower, have become usual practice in a number of contracts of marriage across the Muslim world.

Among the second type of stipulations, which leave the contract of marriage standing, but which are void in themselves, Ibn Qudama includes 'the case where the husband demands that the wife pays for his maintenance or gives him any money'.[27] These stipulations are void in themselves because they contradict the substance of marriage and because 'they include the negation of rights which are [normally] required in the contract'.[28] Other texts in the tradition indicate the possibility of the woman asking for a reduction in maintenance in case she fears repudiation. But the system of stipulations is clearly designed to offer protection to the wife, as is stated by the Hanbali Bahuti (d. 1641) in his *Kashshaf al-Qina*': 'The other type of valid stipulation in marriage is one which brings benefit to the wife in ways that do not contradict [the essence] of the contract, such as an increase in her dower or in her maintenance, or a request that the husband does not move her out of her house or town ... All these stipulations are valid and binding [for the benefit] of the wife.'[29] Here we have another instance of inequality, which operates expressly in favour of the wife, and allows some perspective on the system as a whole. Inequality between genders is structural in classical Islamic law. The two parties were not equal, and could not actually be conceived as equal. Gender equality was beyond the mental horizon of the classical age.[30]

---

[25] Abu Ishaq al-Gharnati (d. 1183), *Al-watha'eq al-mukhtasara* (Summary of forms) (Rabat, 1988) 17: '*wa tudhkar al-shurut al-sab'a 'ala al-taww, wa hiya: al-tazwij, wal-tasarri wa ittikhadh umm al-walad wal-maghib wal-idrar wal-rahla wal-ziyara wa 'aqd dhalik bi-yamin aw tamlik, aw talaq in fa'ala shay'an min dhalik bi-ghayr idhniha*'. The book of formularies in Sarakhsi's eleventh-century *Mabsut* (vol. 30, 167–209) does not deal in any detail with marriage contracts, nor do the three contracts from the Geniza, dating from the eleventh and twelfth centuries, and published in Geoffrey Khan, *Arabic legal and administrative documents in the Cambridge Genizah collection* (Cambridge, 1993) 193–9. A more extensive examination of *fiqh* books and of formularies would shed important light on both the practice and theory of Islamic law across the ages. On Gharnati see above Chapter 2, section on formulae.

[26] *Al-'isma* (here in the meaning of freedom from the marital bond) *bi yadiha* is the popular formula.

[27] *Sharata 'ala al-mar'a an tunfiqa 'alayh aw tu'tiyahu shay'an*. Ibn Qudama, *al-Mughni*, vii, 448.

[28] ibid.   [29] Bahuti, *Kashshaf al-qina*' (Beirut edn., 1987) iv, 82.

[30] Avoidance of the 'sin of sins, anachronism' thoroughly distinguishes the historian from the lawyer, who will look in the past for 'precedents' to support the arguments of the party he defends, even if those precedents could be taken out of context. Lucien Febvre has powerful lines against such an attitude: 'Pour l'historien ... le problème est d'arrêter avec exactitude la série des précautions à prendre, des prescriptions à observer pour éviter le péché des péchés—le péché entre tous, irrémissible: l'anachronisme'. *Le problème de l'incroyance*, above n. 5, 6. On the other hand, 'all history is

Schools of law know many variations on these themes, but it is remarkable that modern legislation has included, across the board in the Arab and Muslim world, the validity of Hanbali-style stipulations. Similarly, several jurisdictions have accepted the more lax Maliki theory of *darar* (harm, injury), which facilitates a woman's right to request a divorce and is the closest equivalent to the no-fault divorce of the contemporary Western world.

I mentioned harm to the wife and forms of evidence proving it in some of the formulae literature of Moroccan and Spanish classical Islamic law, notably 'the demand by the wife to get her right to divorce because of her husband's mistreatment'.[31]

The feature of the Maliki divorce for mistreatment, and, even more remarkably, for 'harm', is the basis of a significant number of modern reforms in the law of divorce. The possibility for the wife to rest her case for separation under the general concept of 'harm' has been taken up in several modern codes. Its earliest enactment in statutory law was adopted in the Sudan:

Chronologically, it is the Sudanese circular no 17 of 1916 (arts. 14 and 15) which, by incorporating the preparatory works of the Egyptian law 25 of 1929, has first introduced to a country regulated by Hanafi law, the conception, unknown outside countries of Maliki obedience, which was founded simply on the disagreement between spouses, and to say it all, on the incompatiblity of character.[32]

The variations which can be found in classical law, such as the wife's divorce stipulations in her marriage in the Hanbali school, and her right to divorce for harm in the Maliki texts, show how some aspects of the tradition support an enhanced position for the woman. They sound like an anticipation of the Tocquevillian concept of the age of equality. Notwithstanding their allure, these dispositions were exceptions in a male-dominated legal world. More accurately, modern gender equality was not within the compass of classical law. It is against this 'unequal' background that modern codification has taken place.

Legislative eclecticism. The pressure for equality between the genders was clear in the mind of 'modernist' legislators, across the board. The frame of reference for legislative policy is the same as predicted by Tocqueville for America and the West as the cardinal characteristics of 'the age of equality': 'universal, lasting and relentless'. At the same time, received Qur'anic injunctions, or perhaps the sheer weight of the tradition, historic and sociological, have rendered total equality difficult to

contemporary', in the famous aphorism of Benedetto Croce. Nor is the inequality between genders, of course, unique to classical Islam, as is evident in Medieval Europe and Japan.

[31] Above Chapter 2, text at nn. 454–6.

[32] Y. Linant de Bellefonds, *Traité de droit musulman comparé* (Paris, 1965) ii, 478. See also de Bellefonds's extensive treatment of the subject at ibid. 477–9, for the various countries which followed the Maliki precedent, and at 461–3, for the references and rationale in Maliki classical argumentation.

implement in the law. This is when eclecticism came to the rescue. It is known in Arabic as *takhayyur*.

Eclecticism informed by the allure of the egalitarian gender model is the way the modern Middle East has reformed family law. Both statute and court law were shaped by the requirements imposed by the age of equality, in contrast to a classical family law system in which gender equality had no room. Reform could not provide equality outright by a stroke of the legislative pen,[33] yet the legislator managed through various eclectic measures to address the gender divide in a context informed by the egalitarian yearning of the Tocquevillian paradigm.

The plateau reached by eclectic innovation created a watershed not only for the substance of family rights, with the clear objective of improving the lot of the traditionally weaker female party. It also signalled stability inside the state with the emergence of a unified family law, and/or of a judiciary which was unified under the concept of one competent jurisdiction for all. In most Middle Eastern countries, the family judge became firmly entrenched in the national judicial structure, albeit a specialist. This was the time of national unification, and few countries escaped the centralizing mould of the nation-state.

The process of jurisdictional unification relegated the family law judge to a section of the first instance court, with appeals all the way to the Court of Cassation/ Supreme Court deciding the correctness of lower decisions on points of law. The matter of judicial competence was therefore simplified within each country, although the picture for non-Muslim minorities remains blurred by the inevitable autonomy required for such matters as the celebration of marriage, its validity or termination, and 'personal status' judges, recognized and sometimes paid by the state.[34]

Of the Middle East countries, only Lebanon and Israel avoided the unifying pattern, despite some unsuccessful attempts in Lebanon, in accordance with the trend in other Arab jurisdictions, to pass a unified inheritance law, while keeping marriage regulations as a prerogative of the separate community courts.[35] Both the family law systems of Israel and Lebanon have run to date with separate jurisdictions for Christians, Muslims, and Jews, and within each large denominational

---

[33] On the difficulties of 'Western secular' marriage in Kemalist Turkey, see e.g. Hifzu Timur, 'Civil marriage in Turkey: difficulties, causes and remedies', *International Social Sciences Bulletin*, 9, 1957, 34–6, reprinted in Herbert J. Liebesny, *The law of the Near and Middle East* (Albany, NY, 1975) 167–70 (but see the nuances introduced by Antony Allott, *The limits of law* (London, 1980) 222–4). In Iraq, a radical egalitarian reform of *ab intestat* succession in 1959 was an outright failure, and the law was changed in 1963. Mallat, 'Shi'ism and Sunnism', above n. 9, 72, 90; Norman Anderson, 'Changes in the law of personal status in Iraq', *International and Comparative Law Quarterly*, 1963, 1026–31.

[34] Egypt is the most remarkable example, because of the large Christian Coptic community. For a general treatment of the subject, see e.g. Maurice Sadeq, *Al-ahwal al-shakhsiyya li-ghayr al-muslimin fi misr* (Law of personal status for non-Muslims in Egypt) (Cairo, 1987); Ramadan Abul-Su'ud, *Al-wasit fi sharh ahkam al-ahwal al-shakhsiyya li-ghayr al-muslimin: dirasa muqarana fil-qanun al-misri wal-lubnani* (Treatise on the law of personal status for non-Muslims, a comparative study of Egyptian and Lebanese law) (Beirut, 1986).

[35] See Marie-Claude Najm, *Principes directeurs de droit international privé et conflit de civilisations, relations entre systèmes laïques et systèmes religieux* (Paris, 2005).

community, between sects and sub-sects. Each community has its own separate law, and its own separate judge. But even there, some nuances should be introduced for the complex 'conflict' cases, in which parties share neither nationality nor religion.[36] The jurisdictional dimension is equally blurred: in Lebanon, for instance, all Lebanese 'non-Muslims' are subject to the same law of inheritance, passed in 1959, and any case arising between non-Muslims gets decided by national courts, on which sit judges from all confessional denominations.[37] This allows Muslim judges on the bench to adjudicate disputes over wills and other succession conflicts between Lebanese Christians. Since exclusively Muslim-staffed courts adjudicate corresponding disputes which arise between Muslims, an imbalance results. Conversely, in case of conflicts of jurisdiction between Muslim courts, the national-secular jurisdictions become competent, even if all the litigants are Muslim. The national court may even be headed by a Christian judge, ruling on a question of Islamic law arising between Muslim litigants. This is a complex area, with subtle, almost intractable, details.[38] It is also the place of idiosyncratic procedural rules which are fascinating, but remain the stuff of exceptional cases. Substantive family law in the region is predominantly Islamic, the central subject of this chapter.

[36] The following decision of the Lebanese Court of Cassation shows some of the complications involved, which work both in a Muslim/non-Muslim context and within a Muslim one between Muslims of various denominations. In that decision, the Lebanese court sitting at the apex of the main judicial order (civil, commercial, and criminal) affirmed the validity of a Muslim contract of marriage decided by the Ja'fari (Shi'i) Court of Appeal. One of the sons of a first marriage celebrated before the Sunni court attacked the validity of a subsequent marriage before the Ja'fari Shi'i court, in order to exclude his father's second wife from inheriting. Several points were raised, notably that adjudication by the Shi'i court was in contradiction with public order, and that that lower religious court had not justified its decision legally. The Court of Cassation, which includes judges from all religious denominations, noted that both the adjudication and the justification of the lower judgment were valid: 'The marriage took place in accordance with Islamic law. Marriage is a contract based on agreement in which legally capable husband and wife express their accord. Delay in the registration of the change of confession [*madhhab*, from Sunni to Shi'i] before the *ifta* [office of the Mufti] administration of the state, and the delay in registering this change, do not affect the validity of the contract from the point of view of Islamic law'. Al-jumhuriyya al-lubnaniyya (Lebanese republic), Mahkamat al-tamyiz (Court of Cassation), 91/159, decision of 27 August 1991, *hay'a 'amma* (court *en banc*, *Assemblée Plénière* president and six judges). First instance decision on 7/1/91, reversal on appeal 20/3/91, reported in *Al-Majalla al-'arabiyya lil-fiqh wal-qada'* (MAFQ) 13, 1993, 163 at 166.

[37] On the law of 1959, see the classic treatments by Emile Tyan, *Notes sommaires sur le nouveau régime successoral au Liban* (Paris, 1960); and Ibrahim Najjar, *Droit matrimonial—successions* (Beirut, 2nd edn., 1997 (1st edn., 1983)).

[38] Examples: for Christian Catholic marriages in Lebanon, a dispute over marriage or divorce which is adjudicated in a Catholic court can go all the way to Rome, where the Vatican Rota court is competent under Lebanese law. In Islamic law, the question over 'who is a Jew', and the resulting competence of laws and tribunals, has still not found a decisive answer. In Egypt, Christians may be ruled for marriage and divorce by their own laws and the judges in their own community, but any discrepancy or rejection of the law by the two parties brings in the national courts and the application of the 'law of the land', which is Islamic, see Abul-Su'ud, *Al-wasit*, above n. 34, 223 ff. This also opens up the whole field of private international law, with a significant literature on the subject. Early accounts on the application of Islamic law in the USA and in the UK can be found, respectively, in D. Forte, 'Islamic law in American courts', *Suffolk Transnational Law Journal*, 1983, 1–33 (but not on family); and B. Berkovits, 'Transnational divorces: the Fatima decision', *Law Quarterly Review*, 104, 1988, 60–93. The literature has grown substantially since, particularly in view of the expansion of Muslim communities in Europe and America.

Before examining family law in its exclusively Islamic form in the context of the Tocquevillian egalitarian paradigm, one should note the usefulness of the comparative terrain in a world in which Muslims communities are increasingly 'globalized'.

In mixed countries, Islamic law assumes a dual function, first by revealing by contrast how non-Islamic law operates, secondly by offering its own grey zones, so numerous these days in case-law. To use Deleuzian categories in the first function,[39] the 'grey' zone operates at the intersection of community laws—Christian/Western and Muslim, but also, as in Israel, Jewish and Muslim. Islamic law also offers its own grey zones—and so many of them at every juncture—from fatwas on the legitimacy of the US occupation of Iraq to genetic engineering. In this context, family law is the most remarkable place for intersection, with a significant body of case-law in the Middle East, and an increasing one in the West. With the emergence of Islam as a central new concern in European societies, and, as the cliché goes, as the fastest growing religion in the USA, the new face of private international law is also Muslim, or Islamic, and this is where the convenient theory of public policy/*ordre public* is revived most readily.[40]

It is in fact mostly in family disputes that clashes with Islamic law rules are encountered in court: the better known illustrations are in polygamy, male repudiation, and rules of no compensation for the divorced female, male inheritance double the share of the female, enjoined wills and succession; cross-marriage, adoption, and custody and guardianship, with issues of transnational custody a recurrent feature of tormented litigation. When these rules arise in Western courts, they get systematically struck down under established public order theories.

The Legislative Search for Equality

On substance, the details of the Tocquevillian paradigm must be followed in each of these 'acid tests'. The premise is the *de facto* legal subservience of women which was typical of the classical age, against the complex variations bringing redress to her situation in the different Middle Eastern jurisdictions. I propose to look more closely at some of these common areas, particularly marriage and divorce, against the test of gender equality.

---

[39] Towards the end of his life, French philosopher Gilles Deleuze got interested in 'what Primo Levi calls the grey zone (*la zone grise*) ... What creates law is not codes or declarations, it is case-law (*jurisprudence*). Case-law is philosophy of law, and proceeds by singularity, and prolongation of singularities.' Gilles Deleuze, *Pourparlers* (Paris, 1990) quotes at 233, 209–10.

[40] Sample literature recently published: Ann Laquer Estin, 'Embracing tradition: pluralism in American family law', *Maryland Law Review*, 2004, 540–603 (growing accommodation in US courts but persistent 'core values'); Lindsey E. Blenkhorn, 'Islamic marriage contracts in American courts: interpreting *mahr* agreements as pre-nuptials and their effect on Muslim women', *Southern California Law Review*, 2002, 189–233; 'Table-ronde: Répudiations de droit musulman', *Revue Internationale de Droit Comparé*, 2006, 5–116 (articles by Hugues Fulchiron, Marie-Laure Niboyet, Fatan Sarehane, Ali Mezghani, Nahas Mahieddin, Léna Gannagé).

The 1986 Arab Family Law Project: restatement of the eclectic period

Contemporary Middle Eastern family law codes, aptly described as 'legislative monuments', belong in the main to the late decolonization period and the early days of independence.[41] The Code of 1953 in Syria, the Code of 1959 in Iraq; in North Africa, the 1957–8 Moroccan Mudawwana and the 1956 Code of Tunisia with its unique ban on polygamy; in Pakistan, the Muslim Family Law Ordinances of 1961, all these codes belong to a period which can be described as one of *takhayyur*, eclecticism.[42]

The model of the eclectic period can be seen at work in the attempt to produce a unified code for the entirety of the Arab world. This is the 'restatement' of family law carried out by Arab ministries of justice in the late 1970s and early 1980s under the name of the Unified Arab Code of Personal Status.[43] The search for one common legal restatement of family law was facilitated by the establishment for some years of family law codes in most Middle Eastern jurisdictions, such as those which followed independence, but legislative precedents started as early as the Ottoman Family Code of 1917. When the draft text of the Arab Family Law Project was produced in 1986, it harked back to the days of those jurists who were looking to consolidate the innovative experience by a systematic and explicit effort at eclecticism. The Arab Family Law Project was constructed under the same method adopted earlier in the century, when the first reformists and codifiers were looking into classical texts to find precedents which would provide textual support for improvements in the status of women, an effort adumbrated in Qasem Amin's celebrated book on the liberation of women.[44] In this book, the outlook of which is illustrative of Tocqueville's age of equality, Amin insisted on the need to bring women back into the civil fold as equal to men. While the essay mostly focused on educational means, the legal realm of gender equality was opened up in the process.

The eclectic method of legislative reform with a view to equality is simple though learned. It consists of choosing from amongst the various schools of law, as well as from jurists from all walks of classical *fiqh*, the one interpretation which

---

[41] The concept of 'monuments législatifs' is often used by Linant de Bellefonds in his *Traité*. See also my use of the term for civil codes, Chapter 8.

[42] A collection of Arab family law statutes on marriage and divorce is now available in English. Dawoud Sudqi El Alami and Doreen Hinchcliffe, *Islamic marriage and divorce laws in the Arab world* (London, 1996). A previous useful compendium is by Tahir Mahmood, *Family law reform in the Muslim world* (Bombay, 1972).

[43] The Unified Arab Code of Personal Status, *Mashru' qanun 'arabi muwahhad lil-ahwal al-shakhsiyya* [hereinafter the Arab Family Law Project], 'agreed' in final form in 1986, was some ten years in the making. It appears, together with a detailed commentary in the form of preparatory works, in MAFQ 2, 1985, 11–43 (for the text), 43–263 (preparatory works). It also appears as a publication of the Arab Lawyers' Union, Cairo, n.d., with five brief commentaries. An English translation can be found in the appendix to J. Nasir, *The Islamic law of personal status* (London 1986, new edn., 1990).

[44] *Tahrir al-mar'a* (Cairo, 1899).

seemed most appropriate for codification in a given area. Hence *takhayyur*, choice or eclecticism, akin, in modern legal parlance, to legislative forum shopping.

This had become current in post-colonial countries, so much so that, by the time of the Arab Family Law Project, eclecticism had become derivative. Contemporary Arab jurists who produced the Project exercised their selectivity at one further remove, by amalgamating legislative texts which were already in place, and which were themselves the product of the first stage of eclecticism accomplished in the early part of the twentieth century.

The model which resulted in the Arab Family Law Project crowns the eclectic period, and offers a striking paradigm of the family codes which belong to the twentieth century. To this extent, and in contrast to the new concerns and possibly the new paradigms which are aired at the start of the new millennium,[45] the model of the eclectic period across the Muslim world over the past hundred years can be typically described through the treatment of marriage and divorce as provided in the text of the Arab Family Law Project.

Marriage. The first chapter of the Project is devoted to a brief description of betrothal, which either the man or the woman may cancel, with presents returned if one party is clearly responsible for backing out, and the possibility of compensation in case of injury. However, presents offered or exchanged are not normally returned (Arts. 1–3, 3b, 4).

Marriage, which is defined as a contract,[46] gives rise in the Arab Family Law Project to a number of principles of equality between husband and wife, whether in terms of the capacity to enter into it, the conditions for its validity, or the obligations that result from the contract or its termination.

Examples of the egalitarian nature of marriage appear in the possibility for both parties to introduce Hanbali-style conditions which, if disregarded, lead to dissolution: 'The injured party can, upon the infringement of the condition, ask for the rescission of the contract, or for judicial divorce' (Art. 6d).

Capacity is fulfilled for both parties upon attaining their eighteenth birthday (Art. 8). It is forbidden to marry a minor, whether male or female, before the age of 15, except under special circumstances which the judge must assess. The traditional right of the male guardian of the female minor to marry her against her will is replaced by the possibility for the judge to overcome the opposition of the guardian of a minor of either sex, after giving him (or her) a reasonable period to put forward the reasons for persisting. If the minor persists in his or her wish to get married, the judge may ignore the guardian's opposition.

Polygamy is allowed by the Project, but temperance is applied to protect first or subsequent wives following traditional eclecticism devices: the Qur'anic fear of

---

[45] The new paradigms operate along lines concerned, worldwide, with the effective empowerment of women regardless of their legal status. It is difficult to predict how the law will respond, but quotas for women MPs in parliament (in Iraq for instance) are harbingers of this trend.

[46] *Mithaq, 'aqd.*

likely unfairness to several wives[47] is given legal substance by the necessity for the judge to grant permission to the husband only after the fulfilment of several conditions, notably assurances about the husband's financial ability to provide for more than one family, informing the new wife that he is already married, and informing the present wife or wives that the husband is about to marry again (Art. 31).

Provisions related to dower and maintenance and to the rights and duties of husband and wife are traditional: the wife has the right to adequate maintenance by her husband, the right to keep her maiden name, and the right to retain her financial autonomy and her personal assets, including the dower, against the husband's possible intrusion. To the husband is owed 'the wife's care, her obedience to him in his capacity as head of the family'.[48] But she 'supervises' domestic life within the house and organizes it (Arts. 42.1 and 42.2).

To the eclectic paradigm belong rights within married life. This is the case of maintenance for the wife and children, which normally falls on the husband, except in the case of the wayward wife. The classical term *nashiz* or *nushuz* is not used in the Arab Family Law Project, but the wife loses the right to maintenance if she leaves the marital home without legal excuse, if she prohibits the husband from entering the marital home, or if she works outside the house without his permission, so long as his prohibiting her from working is not unreasonable (Art. 57). A specific maintenance provision stipulated in Article 61 bars the husband from forcing several wives to live in the same house. Any wife may refuse at any time such an arrangement (Art. 62). But, as in classical law, maintenance stops when marriage ends. Except for the nominal and discretionary compensation known as *mut'a* (not to be confused with the Shi'i temporary marriage also known as *mut'a*), there is no provision for alimony to the wife in Islamic law.

The Arab Family Law Project goes on to address maintenance for children and family. Some improvements are introduced into the text, such as the necessity for the mother, if the father can't pay for the children and if she has independent means of wealth, to cater for them until they come of age. For the girl, this is when she gets married. For the boy, this is when 'he reaches an age where his peers are used to earn their living, after the age of sixteen, except if he is a student who pursues his studies with adequate success' (Art. 63).

Termination of Marriage. Divorce and separation constitute the other important section of the Arab Family Law Project. Here, the panoply of procedures for separation is laid out in some detail. They include, side by side, formulaic procedures which have long fallen out of use such as *zihar*—this is a formula uttered by the husband, equating his wife with his mother, and leading to divorce (a practice however frowned upon in Qur'an lviii: 2–4); and *ila'* (Qur'an ii: 226), which is

---

[47] This appears on two occasions in the Qur'an iv: 3 and iv: 129: 'Marry women as you like—two or three or four. But if you fear that you will not be just, then only one'; and 'You will not be able to be just with [your] women, even if you try'.

[48] *Al-'inaya bihi, wa ta'atuhu bil-ma'ruf, bi-i'tibarihi rabb al-usra.*

explained in the Arab Family Law Project as the wife's right to demand judicial separation if 'her husband swears to not having had intercourse with her for more than four months',[49] along with a definition of *mukhala'a* to mean the termination of married life by agreement between husband and wife (Arts. 100–3), presumably on the wife's initiative. She might in this case have to pay compensation to the husband.

The more eclectic dimensions of the Project appear in the section on judicial separation, and in some of the articles regarding repudiation.

Repudiation, which is the unilateral right of the man known as *talaq*, is constrained by several methods which can be found in various Arab codes, such as the rejection of a *talaq* conditioned on specific actions or omissions.

There are two types of *talaq* in classical law, revocable and irrevocable, with a subdivision affecting the irrevocable type.

The irrevocable *talaq* is one where the husband has uttered a formula effecting repudiation three times, with repudiation becoming irrevocable upon the completion of the third utterance. This is the 'major' mode. The irrevocable character of the *talaq* can also occur by the lapse of the period of 'recall' or 'return'. When the 'recall' period is over, even if the husband has not uttered the fatidic third utterance, *talaq* becomes irrevocable in the 'minor' mode.

In the revocable *talaq*,[50] the husband can 'recall' his wife during the period of the waiting period, or *'idda* (three menstrual periods/lunar months). So the period for 'recall' could be shortened by the issuance of the notorious third repudiation, which immediately terminates marriage in an irrevocable, major, way. If conduct, for example sexual intercourse, shows the husband's willingness to resume marital life during the waiting period, any previous *talaq* pronouncement becomes void. Hence the qualification of the repudiation as 'revocable'. If marital life resumes, any utterance of repudiation would count as 'new'. If, however, the waiting period lapses and the wife is not recalled either expressly or by conduct, the revocable *talaq* becomes irrevocable, that is, final. But this type of irrevocable *talaq* is considered of a 'minor' nature, to be distinguished from the irrevocable *talaq* in a 'major' mode, which takes place upon instant or successive 'triple repudiation'.

The major difference between minor irrevocable *talaq* and major irrevocable *talaq* appears in their respective consequences: while both formally end marital life, in the case of the minor irrevocable *talaq* former husband and wife can get married again by observing the basic conditions for any marriage, notably the payment of a new dower. In case of major irrevocable *talaq* (i.e. the instant or successive pronouncement of three repudiation formulae), a new marriage will be

---

[49] For *zihar and ila'*, see Arts. 121 and 122 of the Arab Family Law Project, which tie the classical and obsolete formulae of the husband to a four-month period. In this type of formulaic law, one should also mention *li'an*, with divorce resulting from the husband swearing that his wife has committed unchastity, but there is no mention of *li'an* in the Arab Family Law Project. See also in a historical context, Chapter 2 n. 17.

[50] *Raj'i.* For statutory definitions of the various forms of *talaq*, see below nn. 97–9 and the citations of the Yemeni codes.

possible only after the fulfilment of four conditions: (a) the divorced wife enters into marriage with another man; (b) the marriage is consummated; (c) the marriage is ended by repudiation or death of the husband; (d) a waiting period[51] is observed. These safeguards are designed to offer some protection for the wife against the idiosyncratic husband.

The revocable *talaq* is obviously less harsh than the irrevocable one. It is considered in the Arab Family Law Project as the 'normal' one,[52] and the return to marital life[53] is encouraged by the Arab legislators (Art. 99).[54] In reality, the difference is one of degree rather than nature. Repudiation as husband's prerogative is the bottom line.

Modern legislation has introduced key procedural elements to put constraints on the *talaq* of the classical age. Following several Middle Eastern jurisdictions, and for obvious reasons relating to the protection of the wife against her husband's idiosyncrasies, the Arab Family Law Project considers the *talaq*, unlike in classical law, to 'occur by a declaration before the judge, and the judge must, before accepting it, try to mend between the spouses' (Art. 95). This is an important procedural device introduced by the majority of Middle Eastern codes to constrain the originally unfettered husband's power. Here the procedural requirement is used to temper the unilateral and extra-judicial nature of the *talaq*.[55] But even in the age of equality, the words chosen in the Arab Family Law Project are timid. It is clear from the text that the court does not technically 'issue' the right, which remains the prerogative of the husband. The judge may ultimately constrain *talaq* or condone it, but the pronouncement of *talaq* remains firmly the husband's right to the exclusion of wife or judge.

The power of the husband to terminate marriage at will is balanced in the Project by the increased ways in which marriage can be terminated at the wife's behest, even in the absence of conditions introduced in the initial marriage contract. This comes

---

[51] *'Idda*. There are two calculations for *'idda*, three menstruations before a divorced wife can get married again, and four (lunar) months and ten days for the widow. The origin of the difference can be found in Qur'an iv: 229 and iii: 334, respectively.

[52] i.e. in case of ambiguity, the *talaq* is presumed to be of the revocable type.

[53] Return: *raj'a*.

[54] Several Middle Eastern jurisdictions have tried to limit the threefold repudiation formula by requiring that each pronouncement take place in a moment in time clearly distinct from the preceding one. This presumably tempers the nefarious repetition of the *talaq* in one angry session. The contrived device is illustrative of the difficulty to find egalitarian variations on the classical age rights. One should note here that there is no ultimate iron rule in reform, as a woman will not necessarily benefit from tempering *talaq* provisions by reducing the forms of repudiation to the revocable type. It is sometimes to her advantage that the husband be forced to break the knot, so as to remove the sword of Damocles hanging over her head with his exercise of his right to recall her.

[55] Although cynics might also ascribe it to the state wanting to know exactly what the marital situation of its citizens is at any given time. The argument of state interventionism is not decisive so long as state control or centralization could be done without requiring an appearance before the judge. The law could just force the husband to register his final (or even revocable) *talaq* with the administration within a certain period of time of its utterance, without the administration being allowed to interfere with it. Appearing before the judge, however, presents a real constraint on an erratic or ill-willed husband who wishes to repudiate his wife only 'privately'.

under the heading *tatliq* (from *talaq*), or judicial separation, which the wife can exercise, according to the Project, on a number of grounds. One ground allows the wife to request the termination of marriage if intercourse has not taken place, or if the husband has not paid her dower as promised. Another ground for separation is the prolonged absence of the husband, or his refusal to pay maintenance. More useful than these exceptional cases is judicial separation on the ground of harm: 'Each of the two spouses can demand separation because of harm (*darar*) which prevents the continuation of common life' (Art. 108). This is clearly the most important accommodation of the original Maliki concept corresponding to 'the irretrievable breakdown of marriage'. The judge should in that case try his best to bring the parties to some understanding, but he must grant the separation if all efforts to repair the rift fail. Then marital life will have proved 'unsustainable', with marriage having irretrievably broken down.

That the wife could initiate the process is the most important feature of the search for egalitarianism. There one can see how the classical inequality in the terms of separation has been tempered by procedural constraints imposed on the husband by forcing him to carry the repudiation in court, and by the extension of the right to the wife to initiate court proceedings with a view to forcing separation in case of harm. When construed as the unsustainability of marital life, it becomes close to the no-fault divorce of Western law.

Custody. A third important area also covered by the Arab Family Law Project is children's custody. Here, the classical distinction between guardianship and custody proper is reinforced with much more clarity, so that custody tends to become the primary prerogative of the mother, whilst guardianship remains firmly within the father's rights.

The Arab Family Law Project devotes two separate chapters to parental responsibility. In Articles 133 ff, custody is defined as 'the protection of the child, its education and teaching, and its supervision in so far as supervision does not contradict the right of the guardian over the child'. In the section on guardianship, the Arab legislators entrust the father with the guardianship of the minor's property and person. 'Guardianship over the minor's person goes to the father' (Art. 166), as does guardianship over the minor's property, which 'is the exclusive right of the father' (Art. 167). Then follow some details on the father's guardianship over the minor's property, and the possibility for the judge to control the process if it appears that the father is not exercising due care. But the Project does not develop the father's guardianship over the child's person any further. This is a good illustration of modern efforts to use the relatively innocuous separation between guardianship and custody in order to enhance the mother's supervision by way of 'custody' while waxing lyrical about a relatively empty 'right of the father to guardianship'.

In contrast to the father's guardianship of the minor's person, the custody of the mother is far reaching and detailed: first, the Project ensures that the married mother has the right of custody for the son until he is 14, and for the daughter until she marries (Art. 137). In case of divorce, this right goes automatically to her, all within the control of the judge 'in the best interest of the child' (Art. 138). Outside the age limitation, the mother's custody ceases only if she decides to live in a country which makes it 'hard for the guardian to carry on his responsibilities towards the child' or if she remarries (Art. 143.2), but the judge may decide otherwise 'for the benefit of the child' (Art. 135). The Project goes to great lengths to keep the possibility of a non-Muslim divorced mother retaining custody, against the automatic termination of custody for difference of religion in classical law. In that case, 'the mother's custody will continue so long as her abusing her position to raise the child in other than its father's faith is not proven' (Art. 136).

In all these instances, the judge arbitrates any conflict, but the egalitarian trend weighing in favour of the mother is evident.[56]

'Feminist' criticism of reforms

It would be presumptuous to think of the Arab Family Law Project as 'the end of history' in personal status reform. For a strict egalitarian test, many elements do not pass muster, despite approximations to the model which are achieved in substance (e.g. best interest of the child in custody), or in procedure (e.g. the constraints on the man's right of repudiation).

Rather than applying such a strict test, it may be helpful to pursue the analysis of the Arab Family Law Project as eclectic paradigm by examining the attitude of two women who have dealt with the legal questions arising from the main areas of egalitarian reform in the Project. Their articulate reaction offers a lively appreciaion of the paradigmatic dimension of eclectic codification in the light of the pressures brought about by the age of equality.

The first illustration is provided by Bint al-Huda, an Iraqi woman who had a significant influence in Islamic circles in the contemporary Shiʿi world until her execution by the Iraqi government in 1980. The second voice can be heard in the extensive comments directly made on the Arab Family Law Project by a female lawyer, Fathiyya Shalabi, who belongs to the Egyptian Bar Association as well as to the Women Committee of the Arab Lawyers' Union.[57] Unlike Shalabi's commentary, Bint al-Huda's writings predate the Arab Family Law Project, but they are directly relevant to several acid tests of equality with which that codification, as indeed most other personal status codes—and courts—in the Arab and Muslim world have been concerned throughout the twentieth century.

Bint al-Huda's Islamic feminism provides an altogether different point of departure. Albeit not a jurist, the Iraqi female militant offers a model of the modern

---

[56] There is no decisive change in the system of *ab intestat* inheritance under the Project, and the rules on succession trigger little debate.

[57] Fathiyya Shalabi's commentary appears on pp. 97–106 of the Arab Family Law Project, as published by the Arab Lawyers' Union (hereinafter Shalabi, followed by the page). The commentary is competent, but not scholarly.

Muslim woman which can be usefully compared and contrasted to the Arab Project key issues.

Bint al-Huda was born Amina al-Sadr in 1937 and grew up in the city of Najaf in Southern Iraq. There is little information on her life, but we know she was extremely active in the Islamic renewal which developed around the traditional law colleges in the city from the 1960s until the all-out repression of the Ba'th system in the late 1970s. The two most prominent Iraqi victims of the repression were Bint al-Huda and her famed brother Muhammad Baqer al-Sadr. Both disappeared and are believed to have been killed on 8 April 1980.[58]

Bint al-Huda was a novelist who devoted most of her writings to depicting the ideal model of the 'Islamic' woman. For her, the premise was that women and men were totally equal, even if each one's place in society is distinct from the other. The main thrust of her thesis runs along a traditional 'separate but equal' argument, and one can question its egalitarian or 'feminist' label. Yet, in those sections of her work where she discusses women's legal rights, the results are in many ways similar to those of other celebrated 'feminist' voices in the later twentieth century. They can be summed up, from a legal angle, under three headings:

(1) *Separation of property*. The wife has exclusive control over her assets, and can dispose of them as she sees fit: 'The Muslim woman has total right over her personal property. She can, at all stages of her life, dispose in absolute freedom of her movable or immovable goods, whether she is a daughter, a wife or a mother, with due regard to public order. The Muslim husband does not have the right to dispose of the property of his wife or to touch it without his wife's consent.'[59] This, for Bint al-Huda, justifies the fact that she might get half the share of her brother or her husband if the succession is *ab intestat*.

This fits well with the Arab Family Law Project, as both admit the principle of the woman inheriting half the man's share, whilst giving particular importance to the financial autonomy of the wife and the need to preserve it.

(2) *Right to choose the husband*. On marriage, Bint al-Huda's guidelines also fit well with the Project. She insists on the right of the woman to choose her husband, and invokes a *hadith* from Imam Musa Ibn Ja'far. Marriage, in a quote attributed to the eighth-century Shi'i imam, 'will take place in accordance with the woman's wish, for she has the right over her person'.[60]

---

[58] Mallat, 'Le féminisme islamique de Bint al-Houda', *Maghreb-Machrek*, 116, 1987, 45–58; For first-hand recollections of Bint al-Huda in her last years in Iraq, Muhammad Rida al-Nu'mani, *Al-shahid al-sadr, sanawat al-mihna wa ayyam al-hisar* (Martyr al-Sadr, the tragic years and the days under siege) (Tehran, 2nd edn., 1996) 216–27 (her stand againt the Iraqi authorities), 327 (her death).

[59] Bint al-Huda's works were collected in three volumes and entitled *Al-Majmu'a al-qasasiyya al-kamila* (Collected novels) (Beirut, n.d. (early 1980s)). For a description of this collection, which also includes her non-fiction works, Mallat, 'Le féminisme', previous note at 56 n.7. The quote here is from her article, '*Al-mar'a wal-milkiyya* (Woman and property)', in *Al-Majmu'a*, iii, 327.

[60] '*Ra'i al-mar'a fil-zawaj* (The opinion of the wife regarding her marriage)', *Al-Majmu'a*, iii, 158. Musa ibn Ja'far (d. 799) is the seventh imam of the Twelver tradition, which is the dominant branch of Shi'ism.

(3) *Right to divorce*. On divorce, equality is also advocated by the Iraqi writer: 'In the same way that Islam permits the husband to pronounce the repudiation in case of necessity, Islam has also granted [the right to divorce] to the wife in special circumstances, if she brings a complaint before the judge and the judge admits her grievance. Islam has also allowed her to include in her marriage contract a clause imposing the divorce on her husband when she so decides.'[61] This is familiar terrain, which belongs to the realm of the Arab Family Law Project, and to the law in many Middle Eastern jurisdictions. The woman's right to insert stipulations in the contract and the possibility of her calling for separation before the judge do not put into question the husband's unilateral right of *talaq*. This is indicative of the limits of the legislative response to the full egalitarian spirit of the age.

On this score, perhaps the more interesting aspect is the convergence of the views of Bint al-Huda, whose point of reference is her brother's and Najaf's world-view, which inspired the Iranian Revolution, and those of the more mundane Egyptian representative of women in the Arab Bar Association, Fathiyya Shalabi. As the following comments will show, both find themselves, with slight nuances, within the limitations established by the Arab Family Law Project.[62] Together, Bint al-Huda's 'classical' arguments and Fathiyya Shalabi's lawyerly criticism confirm that a consensual 'feminist' form characterizes the approach to the codes and their entrenchment in the system in the age of equality.

Fathiyya Shalabi's text is brief, and deals with only 17 articles of the total 293 articles of the Project. But the Egyptian lawyer's choice is typical, and often takes the form of legislative counter-proposals.

Shalabi's approach is expressly governed by a search for more egalitarian principles. She makes a clear even if perfunctory attempt to systematic treatment, with proposals for closer and more equal collaboration between husband and wife 'in contributing to family expenses if the wife works or if she has a personal income'.[63] The working or wealthy wife's contribution is requested with even more emphasis as a comment on Article 52, which 'allows the wife who has a personal income to contribute to family expenses'. Shalabi proposes to transform the possibility into a legal requirement.[64] Similarly, the obligation of the wealthy or working wife to contribute to the children's maintenance after the dissolution of marriage is introduced as a comment on Articles 132 to 145, following the guiding principle adopted by the commentator that 'the education of children and their maintenance are the shared responsibility of mother and father'.[65]

---

[61] '*Al-talaq fi nazar al-islam* (Divorce from Islam's perspective)', *Al-Majmu'a*, iii, 192.

[62] It may be also worth noting that Bint al-Huda in her numerous writings on the 'equality' of women never mentions polygamy or the *mut'a*. To that extent, her silence is more eloquent than the explicit acceptance of polygamy in Fathiyya Shalabi's commentary on the Code. Shalabi, 98.

[63] Shalabi, commentary on Art. 42 of Arab Family Law Project, 99.

[64] Shalabi, 99, under Art. 52.   [65] ibid. 102.

The provision in the Arab Family Law Project allowing the request for separation in the event married life cannot be continued because of a mental or physical defect, is supplemented accordingly by the possibility of compensation, paid by whichever spouse finds him- or herself in a markedly better financial position after the separation.[66]

An egalitarian solution was naturally sought in those few articles which the commentator found too vague or uncertain. Most attention is accorded to undermining, wherever possible, the superior position of the husband in an institution whose parties should be considered equal. Shalabi suggested deleting a mild reference to the supervision of the husband in Article 5,[67] and replacing it with confirmation of the social importance of family cohesion. The possibility of maintenance for the wife being stopped by the husband if 'she works outside the house without the agreement of the husband, in so far as his opposition is not excessive' (Art. 57.4), was rendered innocuous by the commentator's insistence that the wife be required, in her proposed amendment, to cater equally for the family if she is wealthy or if she works.[68]

Three areas which the Arab Family Law Project had ignored were the focus of suggestions made by the commentator to improve upon the drafters' restatement.

The first requirement is procedural. It is significant because in actual practice this is an area in which the weaker bargaining position of a woman tends to be taken advantage of. The Project demands 'official evidence as proof of marriage' (Art. 7). In her comment, Shalabi proposes a more binding arrangement. 'We suggest that the contract include a number of conditions put by each party to the other, which the registrar of marriage should explain to the two parties, such as the woman's right to retain her freedom to divorce,[69] and her right to request that the husband does not marry another ... in order to enlighten the woman about her rights. Specifying these conditions in the contract solves several problems.'[70] Other procedural demands include details which the contract must stipulate, such as the status of the husband, notably his financial situation, whether he is already married, and the place of residence of his other wife or wives, so that they be informed by the registrar of the new intended marriage.

These conditions and procedures, which are not required by the Project, but which are not prohibited either, go to the heart of modern practice.[71] Their request

---

[66] ibid. 101.

[67] Art. 5, Arab Family Law Project: 'Marriage is a legal contract between a man and a woman the objective of which is the establishment of a stable family under the supervision (*ri'aya*) of the husband ...'.   [68] Shalabi, 97.

[69] *'isma*. Above n. 26, and accompanying text.   [70] Shalabi, 98.

[71] Constraints on procedure are of the essence in modern legislation and court attempts to increase the protection of women against abusive use of *talaq*. In a decision by the Kurdish Court of Cassation in Northern Iraq's 'safe haven', the Court reversed the judgment of first instance when it did not follow the proper rules of procedure relating to divorce. The Court of Cassation noted that the lower court had not paid attention to the conflicting arguments of the testimonies and held that the pronouncement in the same session of three *talaqs* was equivalent to only one pronouncement,

by the commentator sheds some light on the resilience of traditional uses which allow a man to marry several wives. It also underlines the ignorance on the part of many women of the possibility open to them to improve their marital situation by including in the marriage contract their right to automatic separation should their husband later decide to take another wife.

In connection with this last subject, the Egyptian commentator suggested an important second amendment to the Project: add a provision which makes available to the wife the right to seek a judicial divorce (in case no conditions are included to that effect in the contract) on the sole basis of 'psychological dejection'. [72]

The third suggestion addresses the need to provide adequate maintenance to the wife after divorce.

Admittedly, feminist criticism and the Arab Family Law Project are merely indicative. In fact they fall within the search for gender equality across the Middle East. As law operates in real life, how are these discussions reflected in Middle Eastern statutes and court decisions?

The Egalitarian Paradigm in Post-independence Reforms

The Arab Family Law Project, which was completed in 1986, drew on a well-established record of family law reforms in the Middle East. Codes had been, in the main, completed soon after independence in most Middle Eastern countries. In each country that passed a family code, the social and ideological background behind the amendments to the codes was obviously different, and reforms took place at varying paces, with Egypt introducing piecemeal legislation from the 1920s through to the present. Some Gulf countries have never codified family law.[73] In most other cases, as in Syria, Tunisia, Morocco, or Iraq, law reform was comprehensive, and resulted in full codes, respectively in 1953, 1956, 1958, and 1959. Among the latest examples of full codification before the Arab Family Law Project stands the 1976 Jordanian legislation which replaced the former 1953 code. Similarly, in Algeria, Libya, and Kuwait, comprehensive family law codes were passed in 1984. On all these occasions, the philosophy of eclecticism,

---

and that the payment of the *mahr mu'ajjal* (remainder of dower, to be paid in case of divorce) was due irrespective of the alleged settlement out of court. 'The court should look again into the matter and proceed on the right track with the present reversal in mind and due attention to any new facts which may arise', the Court finally held. Court of Cassation, Kurdistan, Iraq, unpublished decision, 23.1.1994. These and other unpublished decisions of the Court of Cassation of Kurdistan (Northern Iraq) (see Chapter 6) are on file with the author.

[72] *Nufur nafsi.*

[73] Arab countries without a codified family law are Saudi Arabia, the United Arab Emirates, Qatar, and Bahrain. In the Gulf, Kuwait enacted a Code in 1984, and a Royal Decree established a personal status law in Oman in 1997; see David Wilson and Richie Alder, 'Oman', in E. Cotran and C. Mallat, eds., *Yearbook of Islamic and Middle Eastern Law*, iv, 1997–8, 385.

takhayyur, was evident. All codes have adopted strong features of the age of equality as opposed to the classical tradition.[74]

Some of the most telling illustrations of the legislative search for gender equality can be found in the most recent attempts to introduce limited legislative changes to already existing codes. Whilst these piecemeal interventions illustrate the lure of the egalitarian paradigm, they also show the difficulty faced by the legislator who envisages breaking fully with the limitations imposed by classical law. Different as the experiments and the countries can be—Syria in 1975, Iraq in 1978, and Egypt in 1979 through to 1985—the similarities in the texts adopted by each country underline the appeal of gender equality.

In Syria, important changes were brought about by the legislator in a 1975 reform, by way of procedural changes limiting the husband's prerogatives established in the 1953 text. As in the Arab Family Law Project, procedural requirements were tightened for both the registration of marriage and divorce (Arts. 45.3 and 88). To further protect the wife against polygamy, the original version of Article 17 allowed the judge to refuse marriage to a second wife if it is clear that the husband cannot support both of them. In the amended text, he must produce in addition 'a legal reason'[75] to take a second wife.

Other measures on the road to equality appear in the rights over custody for the divorced woman, and the protection of her right to the dower to avoid the risk that her relatives lay their hand on it.

In Iraq, there were more frequent attempts to improve the position of women, even if, as in Syria, reform was limited to specific issues. In some cases, the changes in the law were tied to the idiosyncrasies of the long Iran–Iraq War (1980–8) and the political whims of the day, such as when restrictions were put on the woman's custody over her children if she married a non-Iraqi;[76] the notorious legal encouragement to repudiate Iranian spouses; or the addition of the husband's sodomy as a legitimate ground for the wife's demand for separation.[77]

---

[74] See detailed studies on the Algerian and Jordanian family codes in the 1970s and early 1980s by Maurice Borrmans, 'Le nouveau code algérien de la famille dans l'ensemble des codes musulmans de statut personnel, principalement dans les pays arabes', *Revue Internationale de Droit Comparé*, 1986, 133–9; and Lynn Welchman, 'The development of Islamic family law in the legal system of Jordan', *International and Comparative Law Quarterly*, 37, 1988, 868–86, respectively.

[75] *Musawwegh shar'i*.   [76] Law 106 of 1987.

[77] Law 125 of 1981. Ludicrous interventions of the legislator—in this case the Revolutionary Command Council with the signature of Saddam Hussein—have produced such curious texts as: 'The following clause shall be added at the end of para (a) of Article 40 of the Personal Status Law: "There shall be considered a matrimonial faithlessness [and hence a ground for separation as a woman's right] when the husband practices the act of sodomy in any way whatsoever"' (Art. 1 of Law 125 of 1981, Seventh Amendment to the Law of Personal Status 188 of 1959, in *al-Waqa'e'* *al-'Iraqiyya*, English version, 10.2.1982, 5). Another bizarre instance of legislative drafting, this time with the signature of Ahmad Hasan al-Bakr, came in a 1979 amendment. This is the extended doctrine of *tanzil*, which allows an otherwise excluded grandchild from inheriting because of the primacy of closer male kinship after the death of his or her father or mother. The official English formulation of the Iraqi text appears verbatim as follows: 'Article 1: The following Article shall substitute Article 74 (as annulled) of the No 188 of 1959 for personal Status. Article 74–1. If a son, whether he is male or female[!], dies before the death of his father or mother, he shall be considered as living when one of

But the mainstay of the reformist wave appears in the extensive 1978 Iraqi amendment to the 1959 family code. The amendment includes the prohibition of forced marriages, penalties for marriage without judicial notification, wider grounds for the woman to demand separation, and the strengthened right of a mother to custody over her minor children. This is in the same vein as developments in Egypt between 1979 and 1985. The case of Egypt is well documented.[78] There, the features of the model are most evident, including the fact that egalitarian attempts never come easy. In Egypt, the enhanced status for women was brought about by apparently minor changes to previous legislation by the so-called Jihan Bill of 1979, but the changes were forceful enough to elicit a barrage of opposition which raised family law to constitutional status. The new law triggered strong opposition in the country, especially after it was held unconstitutional by the Supreme Constitutional Court on the grounds that it was passed by President Sadat in 1979 under emergency regulation powers, whilst the nature of the law did not require urgent executive enactment. The law was eventually passed by normal legislation, in roughly its original form, after heated debates in Parliament.[79]

The reformist dispositions of the 1979 Jihan Bill follow a pattern which should by now be familiar: more stringent duties of disclosure upon marriage (number of wives, place of residence, Art. 11 bis, para. 1), coupled with severe penalties if not respected (Art. 23 bis); duty to register the repudiation (Art. 5 bis); better controlled process of judicial separation, with due apportionment of blame to the party whom the judge holds responsible for the breakdown (Arts. 7–10); the right of a wife whose husband marries another to ask for divorce 'even if she did not stipulate in the initial marriage contract that he should not marry another woman' (Art. 11 bis, § 2).

What about the three more radical measures suggested in the comments of Fathiyya Shalabi to improve on the Arab Family Law Project's treatment of women's rights: (a) compulsory conditions benefiting the wife in the marriage contract; (b) psychological dejection as sufficient reason for her to initiate divorce proceedings; and (c) payment of alimony after divorce?

(a) None of the Arab countries has made stipulations obligatory, but they have expressed their lawfulness openly.[80] In one significant case, the Egyptian lawyer's

---

them dies and his entitlement of inheritance shall be transferred to his sons, males or females according to the Shar' provisions as regarded binding will be provided that it must not exceeding one Third of the inheritance.' Law 72 of 1979, Third Amendment to the Law of Personal Status of 1959. *Al-Waqa'e' al-'Iraqiyya*, English version, 26.9.1979, 5.

[78] Hoda Fahmy, *Divorcer en Egypte. Etude de l'application des lois du statut personnel* (Cairo, 1986). Bernard Botiveau, *Loi islamique et droit dans les sociétés arabes* (Paris, 1993) 191–231.

[79] See Chapter 5, section on the Supreme Constitutional Court of Egypt.

[80] e.g. Art. 19, Law 84–11 of 1984 in Algeria: 'The two spouses may stipulate in the marriage contract any conditions which they consider beneficial provided that these conditions do not conflict with the provisions of this law'. Iraq, Law 188, 1959, Art. 6.3; Kuwait, Law 51, 1984, Arts. 40–2; Morocco, Mudawwana of 1958, Art. 3.

suggestion of a compulsory type of 'explanation by the registrar' to the contracting wife of her rights to include sundry conditions in the contract has flourished in practice. This was conspicuous in post-revolutionay Iran, where the marriage contract increasingly appears in the form of a standard document, in which some twelve conditions are included to enhance the rights of the wife. It is reported that, at least in the richer circles of society, the standard contract has become a *sine qua non* for the protection of the wife's rights upon her marriage.[81]

(b) The second proposal equating harm and 'psychological dejection' has found its way to modern Arab or Muslim codes indirectly. 'Psychological dejection' as grounds for separation had always been possible under the form of *mukhalaʿa* divorce.[82] There, the wife and husband can agree on separation, but she might be requested to pay some compensation to him since divorce takes place in this case on terms which the two parties agree upon privately. As for the possibility of the wife initiating separation or divorce proceedings regardless of the husband's acquiescence, it may be available, in the closest case to 'psychological dejection', under the Arab Family Law Project's general heading of 'harm which makes common life impossible to continue' (Art. 108). A number of Arab jurisdictions have incorporated a wide concept of 'harm' which is typically formulated in Kuwaiti law: 'Either spouse shall have the right before or after consummation to petition for judicial divorce on grounds of *darar* (harm) caused to him or her by the other by word or deed of a kind which makes it impossible for persons such as them to continue living together. The court shall be required to do everything in its power to reconcile the couple but if this is not feasible it shall appoint two arbitrators either to reconcile them or divorce them' (Arts. 126, 127). The arbitrators ultimately weigh the degree of 'harm' leading to the breakdown of marriage, and apportion the blame, with the consequent compensation (including the return of the dower in case the wife is at fault) to be paid to the 'injured party'.[83]

(c) The third suggestion emerged as one of the most controversial measures behind the family law debate in Egypt from 1979 through the 1990s. The Arab Family Law Project itself stipulates under Article 97b that 'the repudiated woman can ask for compensation if the husband has abused his right of repudiation, and the judge may assess compensation up to a maximum of three years of maintenance [calculated at the time of repudiation]'.

While supporting the measure, Fathiyya Shalabi called for the judge to have a more extensive role of in redressing the balance without reference to any multiple

---

[81] For a list of the conditions, and the practice in post-revolutionary Iran, Ziba Mir-Hosseini, *Marriage on trial. A study of Islamic family law* (London, 1993) 57–8, summarized below nn. 104–5 and accompanying text. Conversely, it is reported that these stipulations are fought by men in the higher circles of Saudi society despite their prima-facie conformity with the dominant Hanbali tradition. Mai Yamani, 'Some observations on women in Saudi Arabia', in Mai Yamani, ed., *Feminism and Islam* (London, 1996) 263–82, at 275.   [82] Or *khulʿ*.
[83] Similar provisions can be found in several other jurisdictions, e.g. Jordan, Law 61, 1976, 'Judicial divorce on grounds of dispute and discord', Arts. 132 ff.

of maintenance level, 'in accordance with the longevity of marriage and what the wife has contributed during her shared marital life'.[84] Western influence clearly surfaces in this suggestion. This, again, is reflected in several legislations, in the form of the extension of alimony in recent Iraqi, Syrian, and Egyptian amendments to their respective codes.

In Syria, the most noteworthy aspect of the 1975 reform is the change in compensation given to the wife who was divorced 'in an excessive manner'. The limit on alimony was raised to a sum equivalent to three years of annual maintenance (instead of one year previously, Art. 117). In Iraq also, the most significant amendment came in Law 77 of 1983, which stipulated the right to the conjugal flat for a wife who gets repudiated. This was further reinforced five years later by the law extending her right to the flat 'even if her husband has offered to a third party the house or flat which he owns before he repudiated her'.[85]

Egypt, adopting Syrian terminology, raised alimony in case of 'excessive' repudiation, to the equivalent value of two years' annual maintenance (Art. 18 ter of the 1985 law). As in Iraq, the more revolutionary measure came in Egypt with regard to the conjugal home: 'The husband who repudiates his wife must arrange for his children from the repudiated wife and their custodian an independent lodging. If he does not do that during the *'idda*, they can remain in the rented conjugal flat without him throughout custody' (Art. 18 ter). Since the likelihood of custody falling on the repudiated wife is high, this meant that the husband was ejected from the conjugal home until the end of custody, even if it was originally his rented property. The curious mention of rental (as opposed to ownership of the conjugal flat) must be understood in the context of the severe housing crisis in Egypt and the large number of houses subject to rent-control legislation.

The alimony episode as a focus of both constitutional and family law provides a good example of the entrenchment of the eclectic paradigm. It also means a deeper legal transformation of the status of family law in the system, from the classical law precinct of conservative quiescence to an ideological background for which family law becomes a key constitutional issue. In Egypt, the acrimonious debate turned the private law sphere of personal status into a public law battleground for opposing philosophies at the highest level in the system.[86]

There are numerous examples of partial reforms in the Middle East, including in Morocco, Iran, and Pakistan, which, in the main, clearly belong to the quest for

---

[84] Shalabi, 100.

[85] Law 27, 1988 (one article). *Al-Waqa'e' al-'Iraqiyya*, Arabic version, 22.2.1988, 170.

[86] Decisions on gender brought on constitutional grounds before the Supreme Constitutional Court (SCC) of Egypt show an activist court for women's rights. Among recent reported decisions, the SCC struck down a law prohibiting members of the Council of State from marrying non-Egyptian women (18 March 1995, SCC vi, 567–96); confirmed the right of a woman to ask for divorce in case of harm, when the husband got married again without her consent (14 August 1994, SCC vi, 331–57); imposed the financial obligation incumbent on the father to pay for the upkeep of the child from the time such payment was discontinued, and not from the time of the court decision imposing that obligation (14 August 1994, SCC vi, 231–56).

equality under the Tocquevillian pradigm. Some of these reforms came before the Arab Family Law Project of 1986, some after. In all cases, the philosophy was much the same. Among the most recent egalitarian amendments, the family law of unified Yemen offers a further illustration of this philosophy of eclecticism in the search for enhanced gender equality, this time in a comprehensive code.

Yemen's 1992 Family Laws: Egalitarian Eclecticism in a Comprehensive Code

Legislative efforts in Iraq, Syria, and Egypt are examples of the dominance of the notion of gender equality in the debate over the issue of women's rights in Middle Eastern societies. This issue is naturally reinforced by the prominence of a similar debate worldwide in the twentieth century,[87] and the controversy has tended to develop in every single case where women's rights in Muslim societies are involved, with political overtones which invariably render the issue controversial.

Much of the Arab Family Law Project found its way to the statute books in at least one Arab jurisdiction. Soon after the coming together of the two Yemens in 1990, a systematic effort towards unifying the divergent legislations of the Democratic and Popular Republic of Yemen (South Yemen, Law 1, 1974) and the Arab Republic of Yemen (North Yemen, Law 3, 1978) was successful in a number of areas, notably in family law. Law 10 on Personal Status was promulgated in the unified Republic of Yemen on 29 March 1992.[88] It includes 351 articles, some of which are taken verbatim from the Arab Family Law Project, as in the first few articles on betrothal, which reproduce the corresponding text word by word. After that, the provisions get more selective, as the allegiance of the legislator to the Arab restatement is tempered by the wish to incorporate the statutes of the two previous Yemens, with a clear preference given to the 1978 North Yemeni compilation.

It is generally recognized that the two systems were at opposed philosophical and political poles, with North Yemen appearing respectful of the tradition embodied by classical law, and South Yemen emerging as the most radical socialist state in the Middle East. By comparing the three texts (in the former South Yemen, the former

---

[87] Jane Connors, 'The women's convention in the Muslim world', in Yamani, ed., *Feminism and Islam*, above n. 81, 351–72.

[88] The three codes are available respectively in: (a) *Al-mulhaq al-qanuni lil-jarida al-rasmiyya raqm 9*, dated 28 February 1974 (former South Yemen, hereinafter referred to as SY after the cited article of the law); (b) *Tashri'at al-jumhuriyya al-'arabiyya al-yamaniyya, min 1/1/1978 hatta 31/12/1978* (former North Yemen, hereinafter NY); and (c) *Al-jumhuriyya al-yamaniyya, wizarat al-shu'un al-qanuniyya, al-qarar al-jumhuri bil-qanun raqm 20 li-sanat 1992 bi-sha'n al-ahwal al-shakhsiyya* (hereinafter Y). This last statute is the one currently in force across the Yemen. For an interesting book on South Yemen family laws by the former Chief Justice of the Republic, see Nagib al-Shammiri, *Huquq al-mar'a fi tashri'at al-yaman al-dimuqrati* (The rights of women in the laws of Democratic Yemen) (Aden, 1984). The book includes useful statistics, which are rare in the field despite their importance for an appreciation of the real impact of legislation.

North Yemen, and in the unified Yemen), however, both aspects of the paradigm—eclecticism and the search for gender equality—are apparent despite the disparities in the declared ideological allegiances of the formerly opposed halves. In fact, eclecticism has dominated family legislation in both North and South Yemen since the 1970s. Both countries drew on various reforms in the field across the region. It is therefore not surprising that the 1992 family code of unified Yemen replicates the eclectic paradigm common in the contemporary Middle East.

The paradigm provided by the Arab Family Law Project, South Yemen 'socialist' law, and North Yemen 'traditionalist' law can now be illustrated in their impact on current Yemeni law.

Marriage. The Family Code of unified Yemen establishes the right of choice in the marriage contract: 'A contract which rests on duress exercised upon the husband or the wife is void' (Art. 10 Y). A special chapter on guardianship over women (Arts. 15–23 Y) explains the conditions under which duress against the woman upon marriage may be inferred, and the principle is formulated in Article 23 Y: 'The acceptance of the wife is necessary. The virgin's acceptance may be her silence. The acceptance of the non-virgin must be expressed.' Despite the apparent acknowledgment of the absolute right of the woman to marry a man of her choice, other prerogatives remain with her guardian. Notwithstanding the prohibition to marry a male or female minor, with majority set at 15 (Art. 15 Y), the guardian's prerogatives over his female ward remain significant. He is entitled for instance to marry his ward out (Art. 21 Y). However, his behaviour will be considered unreasonable, and he may be overruled by the judge, if he refuses to marry his ward against her will 'when she is major, sane, and accepts a [spouse] of equal social standing' (Art. 19 Y).[89] The only exception, the Article continues, is the refusal by the guardian to accept the suitor until he has checked on his standing and social mores, but he does not have more than one month for his investigation.

The result is a complex combination: the Yemeni legislator has incorporated the institution of male guardianship over the adult woman, but limited it by postulating the woman's right to choose her husband, and by allowing the judge to intervene against the 'unreasonable' guardian.

The situation was not different in previous legislation. In the Northern Yemen law of 1978, similar articles were enacted, but a further safeguard for the minor woman was included:

Acceptance by the wife is necessary. The virgin's acceptance may be her silence. The acceptance of the non-virgin must be expressed.

---

[89] *Kuf'*, of equal social standing. The concept of *kafa'a*, equality in status, can be found in the classical law books, and is important as social practice. It has found its way into some modern legislation, but is not really a justiciable issue in practice. For classical law, see Mona Siddiqui, 'Law and desire for social control: an insight into the Hanafi concept of *kafa'a* with reference to the *Fatawa 'Alamgiri* (1664–1672)', in Yamani, ed., *Feminism and Islam*, above n. 81, 49–68; see also Farhat Ziadeh, 'Equality (*Kafa'ah*) in the Muslim Law of Marriage', *American Journal of Comparative Law*, 6, 1957, 503–17.

Marriage contracted by the guardian for an adult female will not be effective without her consent.

Marriage contracted for a minor female is valid on condition that she accepts it at the marriage ceremony.[90] The meeting between an unmarried woman and a man without a third person being present,[91] the marriage ceremony, or sexual intercourse[92] will not be allowed before she is sixteen years of age and capable of sexual intercourse.

Any person who contradicts the rules stipulated in the present article will be imprisoned for a period of no less than a year and not exceeding three years, in addition to compensation[93] resulting from the crime[94] and the consequent penalty.[95] (Art. 20 NY)

The article is more favourable to women than its counterpart in the South Yemen Code. In South Yemen, no minimum prison sentence was stipulated for individuals who violated family law regulations. While a maximum penalty of two years was established in Article 49 SY, there was no minimum sentence. It is true that gender equality was, unlike any other legislation, stipulated in the definition of marriage by the legislator: 'Marriage is a contract between a man and a woman who are equal in rights and obligations, on the basis of mutual understanding and respect, with a view to establishing a stable family which is the main cement of society'[96] (Art. 2 SY). The details of the 'socialist' South Yemeni family law, despite the legislator's best efforts, made the application of the principle of equality harder to achieve than in the 'backward' North.

Guardianship of the would-be wife was not mentioned at all in the South Yemeni text, but was entertained indirectly in two articles. Article 8 SY stipulates that 'marriage is valid only in the presence of two major and sane individuals', and Article 10 SY makes 'delegation ... possible in marriage'. This opens the door to the guardian marrying the female ward, even if, as in North Yemen, she must agree to the marriage (Art. 5 SY). Other constraints (minimum age, Art. 7 SY; difference of age not exceeding twenty years for women under 35 years of age, Art. 9 SY) are variations on familiar themes, including compulsory marriage registration.

This is common procedural ground in all three Yemeni legislations. In the current family law of unified Yemen, registration of marriage is stringent. The drafter of the contract of marriage, as well as the guardian and the husband, must inform the authorities within a week of the conclusion of marriage. The registration paper must include the age of the parties, as well as other details such as the amount of the advanced and deferred dowers (Art. 14 Y). The 1992 Yemen text is taken verbatim from Article 11 of the North Yemen 1978 law. The Code of South Yemen was also careful to reject the effectiveness of marriage without 'registering it before the competent official' (Art. 6 SY), but the safeguards in unified Yemen have incorporated the need, underlined in the Arab Family Law Project, to protect women against abusive marriages by express statutory regulations.

In contrast, marriage stipulations which are important to Bint al-Huda and to Fathiyya Shalabi are not mentioned in the unified Yemen Code, except that 'any

---

[90] *Zafaf.*   [91] *Khulwa.*   [92] *Dukhul* (lit. penetration, i.e. sexual intercourse).
[93] *Arsh.*   [94] *Jinaya.*   [95] *Gharama.*   [96] *Al-lubna al-asasiyya lil-mujtama'.*

condition which does not fulfil a purpose [i.e. consideration] for [at least] one of the spouses will not stand' (Art. 7 Y). The possibility of including conditions to protect the wife is left open, subject to this very lax criterion. In effect, nothing prevents the inclusion of several conditions for the protection of the wife in the marriage contract. Again, the legislator has followed the precedents established by North Yemen (Art. 4 NY) and the Arab Family Law Project. In South Yemeni legislation, there was no mention of marriage stipulations.

Polygamy is also allowed, and the Unified Yemen legislator adopted the suggestions of the Arab Family Law Project faithfully: financial capacity of the husband is required, in addition to the need to inform a first wife of the intention to marry another, as well as informing the wife to be that the husband is already married (Art. 12 Y). No such requirements appear in the legislation of North Yemen, but the corresponding articles in South Yemen offer the closest approximation to the requirements of the age of equality in polygamy's delicate domain. Provisions limiting polygamy appeared as follows in South Yemen:

It is forbidden to take a second wife without written permission of the competent tribunal, which will grant it only upon evidence for one of the following:

1) the wife's sterility established medically, if sterility was unknown to the husband before marriage.
2) the wife's permanent or contagious illness, with no hope of cure, established medically. (Art. 11 SY)

These are clearly stringent conditions on the husband wishing to have more than one wife, and the first wife can demand judicial separation if her husband marries again (Art. 29.2 SY). With Tunisia, South Yemen came closest to the effective legal ban of polygamy in the Muslim Middle East.

South Yemen is also unique in not mentioning a bar to the marriage of a Muslim woman to a non-Muslim man. In contrast, the prohibition is reaffirmed, in blunt terms, in the North Yemeni law (Art. 29 NY) and in the Unified Yemen Code (Art. 26 Y): 'A Muslim woman cannot marry a non-Muslim man'.

There is a long chapter in current Yemeni law on marital life: the right to obedience is mentioned, and defined 'in so far as it benefits the interest of the family, and in particular' such duties for the wife as readiness for sexual intercourse, not going out from the marital home without the husband's permission, albeit 'in accordance with custom'. The text also requires her to live with him in the house unless she has stipulated differently in the marriage contract (Art. 40 Y). The husband, in turn, must grant maintenance, provide the conjugal home, respect her financial autonomy, and treat co-wives equally (Art. 41 Y). The husband cannot force his wife to live with another of his wives 'unless she agrees, and she may go back on her acceptance whenever she likes' (Art. 42.2 Y). This is similar to the Arab Family Law Project and to the law of North Yemen. While many provisions are taken from the North Yemen precedent, it is noteworthy to see the derogatory word *nashiz* for the 'wayward, disobedient' wife disappear in the more recent Yemeni text, as it did in the Arab Family Law Project. Similarly, allowing wives to refuse cohabitation is an addendum which the new text clearly owes to the Project, rather than to Yemeni legislative precedents. This is eclecticism at its best.

Termination of marriage. In 'socialist' South Yemen, the laconic equalization of man and woman prevented the legislator from going into the details of cohabitation between several wives, and the concept of obedience is altogether ignored by the 1974 Code. However, the acid test of *talaq* resurfaced in a telling fashion. The principle is stated peremptorily in Article 25a SY: 'Unilateral *talaq* is forbidden'. But the Code goes on to regulate *talaq*, and there is little doubt that, with all the efforts of the legislator, the two parties are not quite equal with respect to separation: the husband's *talaq*, as it turns out, is not forbidden, but it is constrained, as in the eclectic paradigm, by the necessity of a judicial procedure (complicated by the meddling of South Yemen's peculiar 'popular committees', Art. 25b SY). The two types of *talaq* (revocable and irrevocable) are also acknowledged (Arts. 26 to 28 SY). Only then does the South Yemen legislator move to judicial separation and the headings under which both husband and wife can demand it (Art. 29 SY). If the husband is found guilty of the marriage breakdown, alimony is limited to a maximum equivalent to a year's maintenance. South Yemen was behind other Arab jurisdictions in that respect.

Former North Yemen offers the clearest definition of the various types of *talaq* and their legal consequences in Articles 66, 67, and 68, and these dispositions are reproduced verbatim in the unified code of 1992. Under Article 66 NY (Art. 67 Y),

repudiation is revocable after effective intercourse when there is no compensation agreed and when it has not been pronounced three times. If the *'idda* period has lapsed and the husband had not called for his wife to return to him, the repudiation becomes irrevocable. This is the case of the irrevocable *talaq* of the minor type.[97] If the repudiation is uttered three times, the *talaq* would be an irrevocable *talaq* of the major type.[98]

The Code explains these nuances further by stipulating that 'the revocable repudiation does not end marriage, and the husband can call his wife back during *'idda*; but if the period of *'idda* lapses and he hasn't called her back, then the repudiation becomes an irrevocable *talaq* of the minor type' (Art. 67 NY, Art. 68 Y). The difference between minor and major irrevocable *talaq*s is explained in Article 68 NY (Art. 69 Y):

The irrevocable *talaq* ends marriage immediately. If it is of the minor type, it will not prevent the husband from marrying his wife with a new contract and a new dower during the *'idda* or after. If the irrevocable *talaq* is of the major type with three utterances of repudiation having been completed, then the woman cannot go back to the man without having been married to another inbetween, with effective intercourse and a subsequent completed divorce. Only then can the previous husband marry her, with a new contract and a new dower.

---

[97] *Baynuna sughra*, above nn. 50–3 and accompanying text.   [98] *Baynuna kubra*.

How is the repudiation as unhindered privilege of the husband tempered by the requirements of the age of equality? In the North Yemen Code of 1978, the legislator added an elaborate scheme of evidence which weakens the unilateral dimension of *talaq* as follows:

If the two spouses agree that *talaq* has taken place and differ on its being revocable or irrevocable, the [last] word is of the spouse who denies irrevocability, unless the husband insists that the triple *talaq* has taken place. In that case, the [last] word is his.

If the wife continues to deny the legality [of marriage], and fails to offer the evidence, and if she persists in her refusal [to act as a married wife], she is considered *nashiza* [wayward].

If the two spouses differ on the fact of *talaq* in the past, the [last] word is to the one who denies it. But if the difference concerns the present or the future, then the husband's word is absolute whether he denies *talaq* or confirms it.

If the two spouses differ as to the conditions affecting *talaq* in timing or in substance,[99] the [last] word is to the one who denies conditionality.

If they differ over the fulfilment of the condition, the word is to the one who denies fulfilment ... (Art. 69 NY)

This is an elaborate—almost Kafkaesque—system, but it denotes the importance of procedure in divorce. In a situation where the wife is on the receiving side of unilateral repudiation, the complex procedure of Article 69 NY works, once unravelled, to her advantage, even if the principle of the husband's unilateral right to repudiate his wife arguably receives only marginal dents.

The way this procedure was simplified in the law of unified Yemen is a good example of the variations in the eclectic paradigm to the advantage of the wife:

If the two spouses agree that *talaq* has taken place and differ on it being revocable or irrevocable, the [last] word is of the spouse who denies irrevocability, unless the husband insists that the triple *talaq* has taken place. In that case, the [last] word is his.

If the two spouses differ on the fact of *talaq* in the past, the [last] word is of the spouse who denies it. (Art. 70 Y)

Here the simplification over the previous law is clearly to the wife's advantage, in the common situation in which she is the weaker party on the receiving end of a unilateral act. But the article is couched in language underlining the legislator's dislike for divorce, independently of the fact that the husband only can initiate it as *talaq*. This fits well with the aphorism ascribed to the Prophet, in which 'of all things allowed, the most distasteful to God is *talaq*'.[100] However, it operates, in the current Yemeni law, to the disadvantage of the wife when it comes to her right to

---

[99] For instance, the exact moment when the last repudiation was uttered, or any conditions for it to take effect, such as 'I repudiate you if you leave the house'.

[100] *Abghad al-halal ila allah ʿazz wa jall al-talaq*, reported e.g. in Shawkani's compilation of traditions, *Nayl al-awtar* (Beirut edn., n.d) vi, 220, with a variant: '*Ma khlalaqa allah shayʾan abghad ilayh min al-talaq*, God has not created something he dislikes more than *talaq*'.

ask for judicial separation on the grounds of 'harm'. The new Yemeni law ties harm to the refusal of the husband to pay maintenance during marriage (Art. 122 Y).

In contrast, the alimony in the event of abusive *talaq* is regulated by Article 71 of the Law of 1992 in the unified Yemen:

If a man repudiates his wife and it becomes apparent to the judge that the husband has divorced her arbitrarily without any reasonable cause and that this will cause her distress and hardship, the judge may rule, with due regard to the husband's means, that he pay her compensation not exceeding the amount of one year's maintenance for a woman of her status in addition to the maintenance of the waiting period. The judge may make payment of this compensation a lump sum or a monthly allowance. (Art. 71Y)

While the principle of compensation is admitted in an improvement on classical law, the Yemeni legislator stuck to the lower end of compensation amongst Middle Eastern legislators.

Custody. It remains, in the case of Yemen, to briefly mention the law of custody. The law of South Yemen dealt with the subject perfunctorily: custody goes to the mother, for the boy until the age of 10, for the girl until the age of 15, 'even if the mother gets married'. In all cases, 'the court will appreciate ... in the light of the elements involved in the case with the support of social research',[101] (Art. 46.1 SY) 'in the interest of the child' (Art. 46.2 SY). One limitation upon the custodian is 'the prohibition to take the child out of the Republic ... except by permission of the court' (Art. 48 SY). Recourse to the court would presumably be needed even if both parents agreed privately that the child could go abroad.

In contrast, the regulations of the North Yemen law, and those of the 1992 Code, are more specific. The 1992 legislation (Arts. 138–147 Y) is copied almost entirely from the 1978 North Yemen text (Arts. 130–9), with a slight difference in the ages until which the mother has a right to custody of the child. The North Yemen legislator did not make a distinction between boy or girl. The age is 7 for both, but the judge can raise it to 10 (Art. 131 NY). In the unified Code, the boy is under the mother's custody until age 9, and the girl until she is 12, but the judge can decide otherwise 'in the interest of the child' (Art. 139 Y).

All these examples support the idea that legislators in the twentieth-century Middle East were driven by a concern for gender equality that enhances the position of women in personal status laws. They did not succeed in all the tests, and the almost total absence of reform in succession laws to the benefit of mothers, wives, and daughters, is a reminder of the difficulty of overcoming social practices bolstered by clear Qur'anic injunctions. What is true of *ab intestat* succession laws is also true of polygamy.

---

[101] *'Ala daw' waqa'e' al-qadiyya al-mud'ama bi-bahth ijtima'i.* The terminology is typical of socialist jargon, and highly unusual in Middle Eastern family legislation.

The classical system has also remained well entrenched with regard to the prevention of Muslim women marrying Christian men, whereas the reverse case is allowed: a Muslim man may marry non-Muslim women at will. The way round the system, especially in countries like Egypt and Lebanon where sizeable non-Muslim groups exist, is the acceptance of marriage between a Muslim woman and a non-Muslim man conducted outside the country, the effects of which are recognized in the wake of its subsequent registration in the consulate of the country concerned. Registration of a 'secular' marriage contracted abroad is therefore possible, even if there is no room for such marriage within the jurisdiction proper.[102]

In other personal status areas, moves towards gender equality have been achieved by a mixture of substantive laws and elaborate procedures. These legislative measures limit the husband's classical right of unfettered repudiation; increase the autonomy of women with regard to the choice of their spouse; put limitations of equal treatment and judicial control over polygamy; and open up the possibility for the wife to request a divorce from the judge on the basis of harm. In addition, a hitherto unknown concept of alimony was introduced for abusive repudiation, and some of the original advantages for the wife were enhanced, such as the forced payment of dower and the priority of its settlement over any other debt the husband may have. All in all, the reforms were all based on eclecticism of a first degree (choosing from the schools of law elements and interpretations which enhance the woman's position) and of a second degree, deriving from other Muslim countries' reformist legislation, all the way from the Indian Ocean to the Atlantic.

But as in all other fields, the real test of any statute lay in its application. What is the reality of court practice?

Courts and the Egalitarian Test

It is not possible to follow through all the acid tests and see how they are operating in the judgments of Middle Eastern courts. In part, there is no complete set of decisions in any one jurisdiction which would be upheld consistently and regularly so as to allow a sustained examination of law and court practice. Additionally, whereas it is possible to examine every piece of legislation (where there is one) and appreciate the degree of eclecticism in the acid tests and the modern legislator's concern for equality, judicial decisions remain difficult to fathom because family law disputes are particularly prone to out-of-court settlements.

Often litigation ends at first instance level, and does not proceed on appeal. First instance decisions are rarely reported, and settlements outside the court require a

---

[102] I had an occasion to examine the practical details of such mixed marriages in Lebanese law, and some reflections were published in the law page of the Beirut *Daily Star*, 24 April 1997, together with a case about custody in a mixed marriage in the United Arab Emirates, also published in Cotran and Mallat, eds., *Yearbook*, iii, 1996, 513–14. See also below section on custody, text at nn. 115 ff.

special type of investigation which has been undertaken only recently, and documented more fully by political scientists and by anthropologists than by lawyers and law reporters.[103] In order to assess the pertinence of the egalitarian paradigm pursued here, it is important to widen the net of investigation. The remainder of this study pursues court law through some of the higher court decisions available, as well as in the emerging field covered by Middle East anthropologists and political scientists, in some of the acid tests presented earlier, namely marriage and separation, and custody.

Marriage and separation Litigation over issues related to the conclusion of marriage is rare, as the nature of the disputes does not generally lend itself to judicial adjudication, for instance whether a broken betrothal would lead to compensation, or whether the dower has been effectively paid upon marriage. Other subjects which do not usually lead to reported cases include the registration of marriage, informing second wives of previous or current marital commitments, as well as the use of stipulations in the marriage contract. In contrast to divorce, these issues do not usually lead to litigation, and only field investigations of a sociological or anthropological type can indicate to what extent procedural devices in favour of the wife are effectively implemented. Practice differs widely from country to country, and would naturally differ within a country following location (rural versus urban) and class differences. It was noted that stipulations are not current in marriage contracts in wealthier milieux in the Saudi Hijaz, even if Hanbali law tends to be particularly developed in terms of conditions in favour of the wife. In contrast, it seems that the 'Islamic feminism' of the Iranian Revolution has encouraged the widescale adoption of standard contracts of marriage, which include a long list of stipulations. These safeguards, which are not mandatory, but 'are now printed in every marriage contract' in Iran, offer a vivid illustration of the egalitarian paradigm in the context of Islamic family law:

The marriage contracts of [women married after 1982, the year when post-revolutionary standard marriage contracts were issued], contain two main stipulations to which the husband consents by signing. The first requires the husband to pay his wife, upon divorce, up

---

[103] Among many books in a growing field, see for the twentieth-century Middle East: Enid Hill, *Mahkama! Studies in the Egyptian legal system* (London, 1979) (on Egypt); Allan Christelow, *Muslim law courts and the French colonial state in Algeria* (Princeton, 1985); Laurence Rosen, *The anthropology of justice: law as culture in an Islamic society* (Cambridge, 1989) (on Morocco in colonial times); also by Rosen, *The justice of Islam*, Oxford, 2000; Ron Shaham, *Family and the courts in modern Egypt. A study based on decisions by the shari'a courts 1900–1955* (Leiden, 1993); Shahla Haeri, *The law of desire* (on contemporary Iran), above n. 19; Ziba Mir-Hosseini, *Marriage on trial* (on contemporary Morocco and Iran), above n. 81. Earlier authors include Jean-Paul Charnay, *La vie musulmane en Algérie d'après la jurisprudence de la première moitié du XXème siècle* (Paris, 1965) (on colonial Algeria), and, further afield, Daniel Lev, *Islamic courts in Indonesia* (Berkeley, 1972); Donald Horowitz, 'The Qur'an and the Common Law: Islamic law reform and the theory of legal change', *American Journal of Comparative Law*, in two parts, 42, 1994, 233–93, 543–80.

to half of the wealth he has acquired during that marriage, provided that the divorce has not been initiated or caused by any fault of the wife. The court decides whether or not the fault of the divorce lies with the wife. The second stipulation gives the wife the delegated right to divorce herself after recourse to the court where she must establish one of the conditions which have been inserted in her marriage contract, namely . . .[104]

Here follows a long list of standard clauses barring or penalizing the husband's failure to support the wife, mistreatment, conviction for various offences, desertion, as well as 'the husband's second marriage without the consent of the first wife or his failure to treat co-wives equally'.[105]

While observation of pre-trial and court negotiations would provide better documentation on the quest for equality and the practical way by which the wife's position gets strengthened, one still finds from time to time judicial traces of the egalitarian paradigm in matters which are not usually litigated. This is the case with a recent report from the Kuwait Court of Cassation in which *khulwa*, which is the privacy between husband and wife, was deemed complete or 'correct' so long as there was no third person present at the meeting. Once the *khulwa* was considered complete by the Court, it became equivalent to sexual intercourse, and the husband had to pay the dower in full because the marriage was considered consummated.[106]

Also in this register of rarely litigated issues, an unusual Moroccan decision throws light on the formal elements needed for the validity of the marriage contract and their importance for modern courts. The case arose over a dispute in Morocco between the heirs of a man and a woman who presented herself as his wife and who asked for her share of the succession. The question was whether marriage had to be proved in a formal way, with all the paraphernalia of witnessing, registration etc., or whether testimonial evidence was sufficient. In a contemporary context, the issue would not arise, as the conditions for a valid marriage according to the Moroccan *Mudawwana* (the family code of 1958) are stringent,[107] but the woman argued that her marriage was contracted before the law was passed. This was held insufficient to establish marriage by the court, which quoted a number of *fiqh* passages from the Maliki scholar Khalil (d. 1374) and his commentators. The would-be wife and heiress lost her plea, and the court underlined its rejection of her arguments with a number of classical texts which were provided in support of the convergence between classical conditions and modern requirements for the solemnization of marriages.[108]

---

[104] Mir-Hosseini, *Marriage on trial*, above n. 81, 58, 57.   [105] ibid. 57.

[106] The husband was seemingly arguing that there hadn't been full privacy, and that there would consequently be no reason for him to pay the full dower. One can see how the judges are keen to intepret an antiquated concept like *khulwa* in a way which serves the wife's interest. Dawlat al-Kuwait, Mahkamat al-isti'naf al-'ulya, da'irat al-tamyiz, 17 March 1986, MAFQ 16, 1994, 133–7 (Kuwaiti Court of Cassation).

[107] Arts. 41–3 include witnesses, registration, and a list of detailed documents.

[108] Al-mamlaka al-maghribiyya, al-majlis al-a'la, 28 January 1986, MAFQ 8, 1988, 141–44 (Moroccan Supreme Court).

This case suggests that courts in modern Morocco do not easily entertain a common law type of marriage which is not properly registered and documented.[109] There are no hard-and-fast rules here, and one can see the fluctuation of the courts in the rare cases where such issues reach full-fledged adjudication. The Moroccan Supreme Court refused to entertain the appeal of a man who was denying having been married with a wife (and having had a daughter with her) in order to avoid the payment of maintenance. The Court held that any type of evidence of marriage could, both under classical law and under the *Mudawwana* (Art. 5.3), be produced in exceptional circumstances when witnesses were not present, and the marriage certificate not properly registered.[110] In a similar area, the Iraqi Court of Cassation asserted the possibility for the wife to prove marriage by producing any type of evidence in a case where the husband had been killed on the Iran–Iraq front. For reasons which are unclear, the wife, who was acting as 'the martyr's heiress', was unable to produce evidence, and the Court of Appeal held nonetheless for her. The Court of Cassation reversed reluctantly, suggesting that, in the absence of any evidence which the wife could produce, she should have at least resorted to the affidavit of the parents of the deceased husband.[111]

In contrast to the conditions for the conclusion of marriage, separation is widely documented in Middle Eastern law reports. The constraints brought about by various legislation on the husband's right to unilateral repudiation have been noted: the main legislative tools consist of judicial steps to formalize divorce; of limited alimony or compensation to the repudiated wife; of indirect impediments restricting the father's right to custody over the children; and most importantly, of the wife's right to terminate marriage through the concept of injury or harm (*darar*), which is the classical near equivalent to Western no-fault divorce. Many reported higher court decisions reinforce the legislator's egalitarian efforts to confirm in practice the eclecticism-based novelties adopted in contemporary statutes.

---

[109] Another lurid case in Morocco arose in a dispute over a wife's faithfulness to her husband. The couple were married in May. A month later, a doctor's evidence established her as being seven and a half months pregnant. The child was born in August, and the husband refused to recognize paternity. Lower courts, on the basis of an unclear argumentation of classical law allowing presumption of paternity if the child is born between six months and a year after marriage, held for the wife. The husband appealed to the Supreme Court, who supported his plea for divorce and his rejection of paternity on a simple computation of birth and marriage dates. Al-mamlaka al-maghribiyya, al-majlis al-a'la, 2 March 1987, MAFQ 7, 1988, 132–4 (Moroccan Supreme Court). See a similar case in Jordan, in which the Court of Appeal rejected the plea for full dower to the wife who had given birth shortly after being married to another man. The Court rejected the request by the wife to be paid her dower by the second husband by noting the short period separating her giving birth and the second marriage, but it rested the case on classical arguments relating to her violation of the need to observe the *'idda* period. The decision is a typical adaptation of antiquated rules under classical law to modern scientific reality. Al mamlaka al-urduniyya, Mahkamat isti'naf 'amman al-shar'iyya, 2 February 1985, MAFQ 5, 1987, 89–91 (Jordanian Court of Appeal, *shar'*). Note that, in both cases, the courts ultimately held for the husband.

[110] Al-mamlaka al-maghribiyya, Al-majlis al-a'la, 13 June 1983, MAFQ 4, 1986, 103–6 (Moroccan Supreme Court).

[111] Al-jumhuriyya al-'iraqiyya, Mahkamat al-tamyiz, 29 July 1984, MAFQ 3, 1986, 71–2 (Iraqi Court of Cassation).

One example is the Kuwait Court of Cassation upholding in 1986 a Court of Appeal ruling which had granted separation to the wife on the basis of harm. The issue was complex procedurally, as the husband had also tried to bring a suit for non-obedience of the wife, which the Court of Cassation also rejected. It was clear that the principle of harm would apply on terms defined by the wife, as her main contention was that she had married her husband in 1978, that the husband had chosen not to have intercourse with her for six months after marriage, leading her to move out of the household. Four years hence she brought an action on the basis of harm, and the court of first instance ordered an investigation. On the basis of the investigation, it rejected the wife's demand, who lodged an appeal. The Court of Appeal, on the wife's request, asked the husband to swear an oath confirming his contention that intercourse was made impossible by the wife. He took the oath, upon which the Court of Appeal ordered arbitration. The two appointed arbitrators held respectively in favour of the wife and the husband, and a third arbitrator was appointed by the court, whose conclusions were favourable to the wife; upon which basis the Court of Appeal granted her separation for harm. The Court of Cassation confirmed the procedure, explaining that under classical Maliki law as integrated in Articles 127 to 132 of the Family Code of 1984, arbitration was indeed the proper way forward in case the wife is unable to effectively prove harm was done to her.[112]

The Kuwaiti Court of Cassation also upheld lower court decisions granting divorce to the wife whose husband had not had intercourse with her for several years, and who did not provide a conjugal home for her to live in. All substantive attempts to prove otherwise were rejected by the judges, on the basis that the Court of Cassation was not prepared to entertain issues of fact; also rejected were procedural pleas on various grounds of allegedly faulty evidence of witnesses and arbitrators.[113]

Whilst it has become usual to pronounce judicial separation in cases where the request for divorce emanates from the wife, generally on the ground of harm, the judges have in several instances insisted on improving the lot of the wife through forcing the husband to secure for her, as the custodian of the children, the conjugal home (or a home of similar standard). Thus, the Libyan Supreme Court reversed a decision of the Court of Appeal which did not grant the wife, following Article 70 of Law 10/1984, the right to an adequate residence so long as her right to custody remained. The substitute financial grant decided by the Court of Appeal, the Supreme Court held, would simply not do.[114]

---

[112] Dawlat al-Kuwait, Mahkamat al-isti'naf al-'ulya, da'irat al-tamyiz, 6 January 1986, MAFQ 14, 1993, 86–90 (Kuwaiti Court of Cassation).

[113] Dawlat al-kuwait, Mahkamat al-isti'naf al-'ulya, da'irat al-tamyiz, 27 January 1986, MAFQ 15, 1994, 159–62 (Kuwaiti Court of Cassation).

[114] Al-jamahiriyya al-'arabiyya al-libiyya al-sha'biyya al-ishtirakiyya al-'uzma, al-mahkama al-'ulya[?], 8 May 1991, MAFQ 15, 1994, 170–4 (Libyan Supreme Court).

One sees in these cases how the judge tends to interpret the law in favour of the wife by expanding flexible notions such as harm. One problem with regard to classical law, however, is that it may in certain circumstances be helpful to the wife if such notions are interpreted in a strict manner.

This was the case of a woman in the United Arab Emirates, who put forward a literalist interpretation of classical law in order to end her marriage, by invoking an obscure sentence from Malik's (d.795) *Mudawwana* so that the repudiation of the husband be made irrevocable. We have here a situation in which the wife, for whom the lower courts had granted a comfortable pension, was keen to see the divorce confirmed in absolute, whilst the husband was trying to have the decree rescinded. The case went up to the Family Division of the Supreme Court after the husband was considered in first instance and on appeal to have completed the triple repudiation of the major mode, and lost the case for keeping the marriage. He then went to some *'ulama* for support, and they pronounced fatwas in his favour by affirming that the two first utterances of repudiation by the husband should count as threats and not as first and second utterances of the triple repudiation. The Supreme Court, on the authority of Malik, held

that the plea of the petitioner was rejected, since it is well known that the school of Malik, which must be followed in the country for personal status issues, holds that if a husband tells his wife 'you are forbidden to me', then she is divorced irrevocably, as mentioned in the *Mudawwana*, vol.2, p.393: 'I said, have you seen the man who says to his wife you are forbidden to me, would she ask for his intention [to repudiate her], or would she query him on any matter? He answered: he cannot be queried about anything according to Malik'. This [formula] constitutes a complete triple repudiation.

The argument, the Court continues, renders irrelevant the question whether the previous utterances were to be counted or not.[115]

Custody. The debate over custody has acquired in recent years a significant international dimension. Here, court decisions offer an illustration of the Tocquevillian egalitarian paradigm in a transnational perspective, typically in so-called mixed marriages. The classic form is a dispute over child custody between a Muslim husband from a Middle East country seeking to win guardianship of the child after divorcing his wife, a Western national who may or may not be Muslim herself. If this case appears before a Middle Eastern court, the statutes have, until recently, tended to operate according to distinctions of gender and age, of which the usual example, in Sunni law, is a statute which grants automatic right of guardianship of a minor to the mother, up to a certain age (e.g. 7 years for the boy, 9 years for the girl), whilst this right reverts to the father, also automatically, after this age.

In Shi'i law, there is no consensus in the works of the classical jurists on the daughter's age, but the Iranian civil code has retained the age of 7 as the point where

---

[115] Dawlat al-imarat al-'arabiyya al-muttahida, da'irat al-naqd al-shar'iyya, 20 March 1993, MAFQ 15, 1994, 147–52, at 152 (United Arab Emirates, Federal Court of Cassation, *shar'*).

custody passes to the father (Art. 1170). This is the overall principle derived from classical authors, even if some jurisdictions with strong Shi'i influence on the law, like Iraq, have developed their legislation to introduce formally, as in the Amendments of 1978 and 1987, a much more fluid concept of the child's interest: 'A mother has a better right to keep the custody of the child and to take care of him both during and after separation unless the child is harmed of that'.[116]

Variations in the age at which the daughter or the son stop being in the custody of their mother coincide in recent legislation with a novel examination of the particular circumstances of the two parents 'in the best interest of the child'. Such expressions are increasingly recurrent both in legislation and in the decisions of the courts. In the case of Iraq, the 1987 Amendment reads:

The (mother) custodian must be a trustworthy adult who is able to educate her ward and protect him. The absolute right of custody of the mother does not cease upon her remarriage, and the court decides in that case who from the father or the mother has a better entitlement to custody in the light of the interest of the ward.[117]

Even if classical sources have tended to favour the father as the head of the household, a significant change has taken place in the perception of custody by the legislator. The trend is also perceptible in court decisions.

The best interest of the child appears as the increasingly dominant factor in the judicial assessment of the right to custody. For instance, the Supreme Court of Tunis rendered a decision granting the right to guardianship to the maternal grandmother of the child, and not to his father. The mother had exercised guardianship over the child when he was 5, and she was killed in a traffic accident a year later. Under Tunisian law, custody would normally go to the surviving father, and the Court of Appeal asked for the transfer of custody from the maternal grandmother to the father. When the grandmother appealed to the Supreme Court, the Court reversed the appellate decision by noting that 'the main issue is who is better suited for the child' and 'that the interest of the child is what needs to be examined in the first place'.[118] In a similar vein in Sudan, the Court of Appeal entrusted custody to the maternal grandmother against the father, as she was perceived 'to be better suited' to exercise custody over the child than him.[119]

---

[116] Iraq, Law 21, 1978, *The Official Gazette*, English version, 19.4.1978, 5 (Art. 7.1 of Law 21, modifying Art. 57 of original Law 188 of 1959).

[117] *Fi daw' maslahat al-mahdun*. Law 106, 1987, *Al-waqe' al-'iraqiyya*, Arabic version, 16.11.1987, 830 (sole article, modifying Art. 57.2 of original Law 188 of 1959 and subsequent amendments).

[118] Al-jumhuriyya al-tunisiyya, Mahkamat al-ta'qib, 19 October 1981, MAFQ 10, 1989, 113–14. Citations at 114 (Tunisian Court of Cassation). '*Maslahat al-mahdun*' is also the formula adopted by the Egyptian SCC, 15 May 1993, v. 2, 260–90, at 285.

[119] Jumhuriyyat al-Sudan, Mahkamat al-isti'naf, Portsudan, 9/9/1987, MAFQ 10, 1989, 115 (Sudan, Court of Appeal). See also a Libyan judgment confirming a decision of the Court of Appeal in favour of the right to the custody of her six children, who had returned them to their father 'temporarily', that is until she could secure a house for them and herself to live together. Al-jamahiriyya al-'arabiyya al-libyya al-sha'biyya al-ishtirakiyya, al-mahkama al-'ulya, 30 May 1990, MAFQ 14, 1993, 105–8 (Libyan Supreme Court).

Two recent unpublished decisions from Iraqi Kurdistan show the care given by the court to circumstances of custody for the child's benefit (here in a dispute over who must pay maintenance), irrespective of parental gender. Decision 5/18.1.1994 (Personal Status) examined the appeal against the court of first instance which held for the wife who had asked for a divorce from her husband. The husband was mistreating her physically and the first instance court granted her two monthly alimonies, one for her and one for her guardianship of the child born in wedlock. The Court of Cassation reversed because of the obvious mistake of the expert appointed by the Court—an error over the gender of the child!—and noted that the lower court 'had submitted the evaluation of the maintenance by the expert before checking the resources available to the defendant [the husband] and the defendant's behaviour, to properly appreciate maintenance in the light of these revenues and the social and economic state of the two parties'.[120]

Decision 11/23.1.1994 (Personal Status)[121] also reversed the lower court ruling on the issue of the exact assessment of maintenance and the procedure for the appointment of the expert. There a widowed mother brought a case of maintenance against her father-in-law to pay for her custody over her two children. She was awarded an insignificant monthly pension by the lower court. The Court of Cassation reversed, noting that the normal evaluation of alimony had been disregarded along with rules appointing an expert and the assessment of his work.[122]

In a similar vein, the Supreme Court of Morocco reversed a decision of the Court of Appeals which had evicted a divorced woman from the flat in which she resided with her children, despite the fact that she had expressly renounced her right to the flat at the time of divorce.

Residence is included in the maintenance of children and is a right which belongs to them. The [mother], so long as she remains their guardian and lives with them as guardian, cannot renounce her rights of guardianship. By acknowledging the acceptance by the appellant of the amount of maintenance including the eviction, the Court has contradicted Art.127 [of the Personal Status Code].[123]

Also favouring the wife was a decision of the Federal Supreme Court of the United Arab Emirates, which refused to change visit arrangements for the father who was complaining that his wife remarrying meant that he had to travel extremely long distances so that he could comply with 'visitation rights' and allow the children to see their mother. A lower court had granted custody to the father over his five children, but rights of visit to the divorced mother were arranged so that he had to bring them to her once a week. She had remarried and was living in

---

[120] On file with the author.   [121] On file with the author.

[122] The Kurdish court noted in fine *obiter* the necessity 'for the lower court to point out in its judgment, in the usual style, clear [legal] considerations and this by using words and expressions which are clear and understandable, as well as unifying the different Kurdish dialects in the future'. The Court decision is however in Arabic.

[123] Residence, *sukna*. Al-mamlaka al-maghribiyya, Al-majlis al-aʻla, 23 July 1984, MAFQ 12, 1992, 123–4, at 124 (Moroccan Supreme Court).

a different city, and both the first instance court and the Court of Appeal confirmed the original arrangements regardless of distance. The Federal Supreme Court reaffirmed these decisions by noting that

even if the rule was that the requirement that the father should simply bring the children over to their mother, and that he did not need for that reason to suffer from long travel which might entail some danger [the father had explained that travelling back by night was dangerous because of poor lights and 'errant camels'], this was also true for the mother who would also be required to travel. The matter of the balance between the parties is left to the court of fact which decides what is less hazardous for the interest of the children.

Judgment for the mother.[124]

Despite these examples, which generally express the courts' sympathetic and 'modern' attitude to the child's best interests, the process cannot be viewed as a straightforward abandonment of classical rules in favour of a fully egalitarian concept. This caveat is also necessary for a country like Tunisia, which is widely known for its 'liberal' legislation in family law because of its ban on polygamy in the region (along with Turkey, which has adopted secular laws). Tunisian law retains the father's prerogatives in terms of

the distinction between custody and guardianship. Whereas custody involves day to day care, guardianship refers to legal responsibilities for the child such as authorizing a passport, signing official papers for school enrollment and the like. When the father is alive, the CPS [the 1956 Code of Personal Status and its amendments, principally in 1981] systematically makes him the child's guardian after divorce, even when the mother has custody and thus takes daily care of the child.[125]

Progress towards parental equality in terms of custody over the child is slow, but many reported cases of the higher courts in the Middle East prove that the egalitarian test has taken root in this field against classical rules, with the very practical interest of the child in mind.

Another acid test arises from the traditional rule that a mother who remarries loses her right to custody. It is immaterial that the father himself may have remarried, and he is entitled to exercise custody on the mere ground of his former wife having married 'a stranger'. In a tortured decision, the Moroccan Supreme Court reversed the ruling of the Court of Appeal which had held that the marriage of a divorced wife with a foreigner did not necessarily terminate her right to custody over the child. The facts of the case were complex, since it was actually the maternal grandmother of the child who was asserting custody on the basis that her husband was actually the guardian of his daughter until she married, that he was consequently not 'foreign' to the grandchild, and that she and her daughter could benefit from this fact to keep custody of the child. The Court of Appeal was swayed by the

---

[124] Dawlat al-imarat al-'arabiyya, al-mahkama al-ittihadiyya al-'ulya, 22 March 1992, MAFQ 13, 1993, 161 at 162 (UAE Federal Supreme Court).
[125] Charrad, 'Repudiation versus Divorce', above n. 8, 56.

argument, 'and the objective of the legislator is to do good and prevent harm'. But the Supreme Court noted that the articles of the Moroccan *Mudawwana* (Arts. 99 and 105) presented an extremely 'clear text stipulating that the marriage of a woman who has custody with a foreigner, the new husband being not kin to her, terminated her custody, thus preventing any interpretation otherwise'. By equating the grandfather and grandmother, who had paid for the upbringing of the child, the Supreme Court held that the Court of Appeal had contradicted a clear rule of the Code.[126]

Against the textual constraints which the Morrocan judge found difficult to ignore, the legislative trend in favour of 'the best interest of the child' approach is evident, even in cases where the mother marries a foreigner. The statutory trend was adopted by the Arab Family Law Project, which does not mention a different religion of the wife as bar to custody (Art. 143). The presumption in the Project is that a non-Muslim woman may be perfectly capable of catering for the Muslim education of her child. Evidence to the contrary must be proved. A decision of the Algerian Supreme Court illustrates this trend: 'What is looked at in custody is the interest of the child, and Islamic law has given precedence in this to females on the mother's side to the extent of the interest of the child'.[127]

In recent field work in Iran, it was observed that disputes over custody lead to negotiations in which the court plays an important part:

[T]his allows the court to modify the rigidity of the Shi'a custody rules; apart from divorce procedures, this is another legacy of the pre-revolutionary legal reform. Under the [previous law], the courts were given discretionary powers in dealing with questions of child custody at the expense of the Shi'a custody rules. If the couple failed to reach a satisfactory agreement, the court was empowered to grant custody to the parent whom it considered more suitable. It also had the power to determine the arrangement for paying the expenses involved in the maintenance of the child while in custody of either parent. At present, although a Special Civil Court hears custody cases in Iran, the judge's discretionary power is severely limited. He is bound to rule according to the articles of the Civil Code, derived from the Shi'a stance in which the right of women to child custody is decidedly restricted. Despite this restriction, the Islamic judge plays an important role in shaping the couple's agreement and in the process becomes the very agent through whom the law is modified.[128]

Conclusion: The Moroccan Reform and Beyond

In a Western context, issues such as adultery, cohabitation, remarriage, custody, are delicate and fluid relations where law and social habits interact in a complex way which is hard to assess for Middle Eastern countries in the absence of statistics and detailed field work. While these relations vary significantly depending on the

[126] Al-mamlaka al-maghribiyya, al-majlis al-aʿla, 26 March 1984, MAFQ 13, 1993, 168–9 (Moroccan Supreme Court).

[127] Al-jumhuriyya al-jazaʾiriyya al-dimuqratiyya al-shaʿbiyya, al-majlis al-aʿla, 9 January 1984, MAFQ 15, 1994, 153–5, at 154: interest of the child, *faʾidat al-mahdun* (Algerian Supreme Court).

[128] Mir-Hosseini, *Marriage on trial*, above n. 81, 154.

country and the social position of all actors concerned, the criteria against which Islamic family law institutions operate are specific. Recent scholarship has for instance shown how, in the particular case of temporary marriage (*mut'a*), the forms of behaviour are extremely complex and cannot be assessed simply either in terms of textbook law or in terms of generalized statements on the 'conservative' or 'liberal side'.[129] The recent work of anthropologists has constituted a remarkable complement to juristic assessments, as the dry approach of the jurists on the basis of apparently clear-cut texts is enriched with practical examples from the day-to-day life of Middle Eastern courts.

Nor is it possible to make a blanket statement about all the statutes in all the countries of the Middle East by suggesting that the legislator has invariably been moved by a wish to bridge the traditional legal gap between husband and wife, against a received tradition where such egalitarianism was not contemplated. For one thing, the whole of the law of succession has been unaffected by this trend. Where reform has taken place, concern was restricted to allowing orphaned grandchildren, male and female, to inherit in lieu of their predeceased parents. This was done either, as in Pakistan, by way of representation, which allowed the grandchildren 'to step into' their deceased parents' shoes and inherit in their place against a traditional interpretation which did not allow such substitution;[130] or by way of the 'obligatory bequest', as in Egypt, which introduced the notion that the orphaned grandchildren would automatically receive a third of the deceased's estate. This 'obligatory bequest takes precedence over other bequests'.[131] Still, the

---

[129] Shahla Haeri, *The law of desire*, above n. 19, chapter one.

[130] Article 4 of the Pakistan Muslim Family Law Ordinance, 1961: 'In the event of the death of any son or daughter of the propositus before the opening of succession, the children of such son or daughter, if any, living at the time the succession opens, shall *per stirpes* receive a share equivalent to the share which such son or daughter, as the case may be, would have received if alive'.

[131] Art. 78.1, Egyptian Law 71 of 24 June 1946. Art. 76 establishes the mechanisms of the obligatory bequest: 'If the propositus does not make a bequest for the descendants of a child who had predeceased him, has died at the same time, or has been presumed dead, equal to the portion of the estate of the propositus that would have been due to him had he survived, the descendants shall by right be entitled to a bequest equal to that portion up to one-third of the estate; provided that they are not legal heirs and that they have not received from the propositus under whatever title as a gift a portion equal to that which their forebear was entitled, they shall have the right to the remainder under the title of an obligatory bequest.

These bequests are due to the children of a daughter and the descendants of a son no matter what degree they belong to, provided they are linked to the propositus exclusively through the male line. In the latter case any ascendant excludes his own descendants, but not those of others. The portion of each ascendant shall be distributed among his descendants of whatever degree they may be in accordance with the rules concerning *ab intestat* succession in the same manner as if he or his ascendants who link him with the propositus had died after the death of the latter and as if the death of these ascendants had taken place in order of their lineage.' Note that the shares going to the orphaned grandchildren continue to be determined by the *ab intestat* rules despite the characterization of the scheme as 'a bequest'. In simple words, the deprived grandchild steps into his parent's shoe. For a classic treatment of a complex subject, see J. N. D. Anderson, 'Recent reforms in the Islamic law of inheritance', *International and Comparative Law Quarterly*, 14, 1965, 354–65; and his *Law reform in the Muslim world* (London, 1976) 155–6; also Coulson, *Succession in the Muslim Family*, 143–57. A good documentary source on inheritance law in English can be found in Liebesny, *The law of the Near and Middle East*, above n. 33, 174–209.

cardinal principal of two shares for the male to one share for the female remains well-entrenched for Muslims (and many Christians) across the whole Middle East, with the sole exception of Turkey, which had introduced the Swiss version of a civil code incorporating gender equality for the succession scheme.[132] In Iraq, the introduction of the principle of gender equality in the inheritance of sons and daughters in 1959 was a major element in the downfall of the government of 'Abd al-Karim Qasem in 1963. The first legislative measure taken by the new government was the repeal of this provision in the Family Code, and it is unlikely that the edifice which is half a century old will be much dented in post-Saddam Iraq.[133] It is significant that the whole field of succession was passed over in silence by Fathiyya Shalabi despite her otherwise extensive discussion of the law of marriage and divorce.[134]

Even outside succession law, the egalitarian search is not a hard-and-fast rule in Middle Eastern legislation. For instance, the consolidated law in the Yemen is less 'progressive' in some of its rules than the previous South Yemeni law; the Algerian Code of the Family of 1984 put limitations on previous advances towards gender equality in that country, despite the adoption of the main staples of Arab egalitarian measures.[135] A new Code re-established most of these measures in February 1995.[136] The see-saw movement followed a similar phenomenon in neighbouring Morocco, where reforms in 1992 followed a wide campaign for equality advocated by women, but stayed well within the average, commonly accepted ground.[137] Since then, a major reshaping of the family code has been adopted, alongside women's advocacy in the streets, for or against reform, turning family law reform into a fixture of the legislative debate.

Moroccan developments at the turn of the twenty-first century, which resulted in part from the mobilization of Moroccan women for their rights, offer a fitting

---

[132] 'Children inherit in equal parts', Art. 439.2, Turkish Civil Code.

[133] For the early debate on the Iraqi family law of 1959–63, see Mallat, above n. 9; for an early treatment of family law in post-invasion Iraq, Kristen Stilt, 'Islamic law and the making and remaking of the Iraqi legal system', *George Washington International Law Review*, 36, 2004, 695–755, esp. at 748–54 (on Governing Council Resolution 137, the controversial family law resolution introduced by the interim Iraqi government and repealed by the American administrator).

[134] There is in Shalabi's comments on the Arab Family Law Project only a small section on inheritance which suggests giving more prominence to the sole daughter (or daughters), whose inheritance rights are severely reduced by distant male relatives under the *'asaba* principle. Shalabi, 102.

[135] For instance, 'les obstacles mis à la polygamie sont donc moins stricts en 1984 qu'en 1981'. Hélène Vandevelde, 'Le code algérien de la famille', *Maghreb-Machrek*, 107, 1985, 52–64, at 54. See also her previous article, 'Où en est le problème du code de la famille en Algérie?', *Maghreb-Machrek*, 97, 1982, 39–54. In a bill introduced in 1981, the judge could allow polygamy under specific circumstances. This disappeared in Algeria's 1984 legislation, except that the other wives could ask for divorce if they did not agree to the husband taking a new wife. Similarly, the freedom of women outside the home was slightly curtailed in 1984.

[136] Kamel Saïdi, 'La réforme du droit algérien de la famille: pérennité et rénovation', *Revue Internationale de Droit Comparé*, 2006, 119–52.

[137] The 1992 statutory reform was limited to an increased role for the judge as controller of the abusive use of repudiation (revision of Art. 48 of the *Mudawwana*) and polygamy (revision of Art. 30). See the discussion of the Moroccan women's campaign, and the basic characteristics of the reform in M. al-Ahnaf, 'Maroc: le code du statut personnel', *Maghreb-Machreq*, 145, 1994, 3–26.

conclusion to the chapter. While the egalitarian trend remains the general norm, its further entrenchment will be a function of the real struggle, on the social and legal level, of the main party concerned, women. Even the Islamic revolution in Iran, which first abolished some of the reforms introduced by the Ancien Régime in the late 1960s and in 1975,[138] was back on an egalitarian course ten years into the revolution in the wake of women's self-mobilization.

Moroccan reform of family law, which entered into effect on 5 February 2004 in the form of an amended *Mudawwana*, bears all the characteristics of the trend towards egalitarianism identified in this chapter.[139] By adapting classical law to establish 'constitutional equality between men and women before the law',[140] and respect for international conventions and charters,[141] the Moroccan legislator reformed the main family law categories in line with the paradigm generally established across the region.

Marriage. Women and men are 'consecrated' as equal in the law, and the family is placed 'under the joint responsibility of the spouses' (Art. 4). The age of marriage was raised for women to 18 (Art. 19), which makes guardian control over her inapplicable. 'Obedience' is no longer required, so *nushuz* becomes irrelevant. Polygamy remains possible in theory, but so many procedural watchdogs are established that it becomes extremely difficult in practice. The first wife can make it a condition of her marriage that the husband does not marry another wife, and both the first and a subsequent wife must be informed about the polygamous situation, with their express assent needed for the husband to get married again. In addition, the judge oversees the capacity of the husband to be 'fair' to his wives and to the children from a subsequent bed, should the husband contract several marriages with the consent of all the wives. As a consequence, polygamy is both discouraged and controlled (Arts. 40–6).

Termination of marriage. Repudiation, *talaq*, gives way to the right to divorce for both spouses, and repudiation cannot be exercised unilaterally any longer (Title 3, Arts. 78–93). Repudiation can no longer be made verbally, and must operate under the control of the judge (Art. 79). Dissolution of marriage is made possible for both spouses, again under judicial control (Title 4, Arts 94–113).

Upon termination of marriage, the judge is asked to control the distribution of assets in a way that takes into account the rights of the divorced woman (Art. 84 in case of repudiation, Art. 97 in other cases). While 'alimony' is not a recognized

---

[138] Doreen Hinchcliffe, 'The Iranian Family Protection Act [of 1967]', *International and Comparative Law Quarterly*, 17, 1968, 516–21; Anderson, *Law reform in the Muslim world*, 119–24, 128–9.

[139] Text of the law in Arabic, French, and Dutch as appendix to Marie-Claire Roblets and Jean-Yves Carlier, *Le Code marocain de la famille* (Brussels, 2005) 145–387.

[140] 'Preamble (*dibaja*)', ibid. 382–7, at 386: '*al-takris al-dusturi lil-musawat amam al-qanun*'.

[141] ibid. 386: '*iltizam al-mamlaka bi-huquq al-insan kama huwa muta'araf 'alayha 'alamiyyan*, commitment by the Kingdom to human rights as universally recognized'.

right, the law grants the divorced wife and her children living with her the right to the marriage home (Art. 168), but she does not have an automatic right to the marital home if she doesn't have children (Art. 196). The separate regime for assets remains (Art. 49), which tends to protect the wife against the husband taking over her property, but assets acquired during marital life are subject to redistribution under the control of the judge, who may grant them in part or in totality to the divorced wife (Arts. 34, 84).

Custody. Custody of the child does not depend on age and sex any longer. The right to custody over the child is the mother's as a matter of principle, then the father's (Art. 171), until the child reaches the age of 15, whereupon he or she can choose their guardian (Art. 166). Although the father remains the 'guardian' as of right (*wali*, Art. 236), the difference in classical law between custody and guardianship is reduced. The wife does not lose her right to custody if she relocates within Morocco (Art. 178), but her custody could be challenged before the judge if she leaves the Kingdom (Art. 179). If she remarries, she retains her right to custody 'if the child is under 7 years of age, or if the child is harmed by separation' (Art. 175). With nuances, Morocco's new dispositions are typical of family law reform across the Muslim world.

These amendments to the laws of marriage, divorce, and custody offer a paradigmatic sample of family law reform across the Arab and Muslim world over the past half-century, and many similar egalitarian dispositions can be found in other jurisdictions. But the egalitarian or corrective trend remains almost inexistent in the case of succession, and the Moroccan amendments on that score are restricted to allowing grandchildren issuing from the deceased person's daughter to inherit in the same way as grandchildren issuing from the deceased person's son, without departing from the double share owed to males (Art. 319, together with obligatory bequest, Art. 372). Equality between men and women in succession law is not acknowledged in any Muslim jurisdiction.

The process is similar, overall, in the case of the supreme courts of the Middle East, as typically illustrated in recent decisions on custody. While the classical legacy is a weighty departure point for twentieth-century judges in terms of gender equality, one can see in the more enlightened decisions the strenuous efforts of judges and litigants to reinterpret the classical system to increase gender equality.

Whither, then, are we tending? No one can say, for terms of comparison already fail us. There is greater equality of condition among Christians at the present day than there has been at any previous time, in any part of the world, so that the magnitude of what already has been done prevents us from predicting what is yet to be accomplished.[142]

---

[142] 'Où allons-nous donc? Nul ne saurait le dire; car déjà les termes de la comparaison nous manquent: les conditions sont plus égales de nos jours parmi les chrétiens, qu'elles ne l'ont jamais été dans aucun temps ni dans aucun pays du monde: ainsi la grandeur de ce qui est déjà fait empêche de prévoir ce qui peut se faire encore.' Tocqueville, *Démocratie en Amérique*, i, 6.

PART IV
CONCLUSION

11

Epilogue: Justice and Lawyering in the Middle East

L'avenir dure longtemps.
Louis Althusser[1]

At the end of the journey, it wouldn't be amiss to consider the rule of law as practised by its main agents against the historical record that has reached us from the manuals of judges in the classical age. The legal profession, or the ensemble of professions which use law as a full-time bread-winning activity, offers a privileged way to assess the rule of law in society. On the contemporary side, practical experience trumps any available scholarly books, which are even less common in the Middle East than in European or American jurisdictions. While one occasionally finds memoirs written by the occasional lawyer or judge as a 'life in the law' genre, legal practice tends to be dwarfed in these memoirs by the more pronounced political imprint of the lawyer or judge writing his recollections.[2] On the classical side in contrast, a unique genre in the Islamic tradition, known as *adab al-qadi* (literally manners, or literature, of the judge), features manuals by judges on the way they view their job and exercise their responsibilities. One finds here an unusual paradox: pointed material on the 'real' life of the law exists in the classical age, while it remains scant in the modern world.

To ascertain patterns in the authority of law as it operated during the classical age in contrast to the way Middle East lawyers perceive it nowadays, I will refer again to the manual for judges of Ibn Abi al-Dam, a *qadi* of the thirteenth century, together with some material in and around the classical age as reflected in archival sources.

There is scant record on the judge himself, who lived in Syria from 583 to 642/1244, but his book on *adab al-qadi* contains some remarkable comments on the profession.[3] The manual is important in the light of the extraordinary

---

[1] Title of his posthumous autobiography (Paris, 1993).

[2] For two enticing books from prominent lawyers in Iraq and Lebanon respectively, see Sulaiman Faydi, *Mudhakkarat* (Memoirs), edited by son Basil (Beirut, 1998); Wajdi Mallat, *Mawaqef—Positions* (Beirut, 2005).

[3] Shihab al-Din Ibn Abi al-Dam, *Kitab adab al-qada'* (The book of the ways of judgeship), ed. Muhammad 'Ata (Beirut, 1987). See Chapter 2, section on *qadi* literature.

documentation it carries against the infamous image of *kadi-justiz* that remains associated with the idea of 'Oriental despotism' that dominates the Western perception of the Islamic 'Middle Ages'. In Karl Wittfogel's seminal book, 'Oriental despotism' describes societies where arbitrariness prevails because of a mode of economic production determined by the scarcity of water, and hence of a dominant role for the state, which destroys individual autonomy for the sake of organizing water resources.[4] Wittfogel extended the concept far beyond the Middle East, to encompass totalitarian states such as China and the then Soviet Union, but it is the Near Eastern original model of the 'hydraulic state' which stands at the core of his argument. Such absoluteness, steeped in the characteristic absence of the rule of law and the dominance of a behemoth state, mirrors the received image of the *qadi* dispensing arbitrary justice under the proverbial tree. Extant *qadi* manuals and recently researched archives of courts belie both negative images.

Ibn Abi al-Dam's manual is long and detailed. Designed to guide both judges and lawyers, it covers pretty much what a practitioner, on the bench or on the court floor, would need to know. This book, which is typical of the genre, offers a comprehensive portrait of the world of judges and litigants at the time. The exposé is eminently practical: 'What we have mentioned in this book is common in the court of the judges as between litigants . . .'.[5] Although some of the issues are elusive and may be somewhat complicated for a modern reader, it is clear that the book is intended as an aid to practising jurists. It is divided into six long chapters, which the author presents in the introduction to the work, interspersed and followed by models and case-studies covering the appointment of judges, court set-up, trials and procedures, testimonies, relations between different judges, and typical contracts and formularies. The outline of the book, presented in the introduction, is repeated at the end of Book 5:

> This then is the concluding word on the nature of judgeship, the rules and art of judges, what they must do, what they may do, what is forbidden to them and what is abhorred, the rules of trial and evidence, the trial sessions and the conduct of litigation between the parties, testimonies and the like, judicial referrals from the sitting *qadi* to other judges.[6]

In a large book of over 500 pages, the author remains modest:

> These issues, on the whole, despite their importance, are but a drop in the sea, selected from the relevant books in the school of our eponym *imam* Shafi'i. They are indispensable for whomever assumes judgeship among the people, and if a person is not competent in the details and principles of the law alike, knowledgeable about the school he follows, and well-versed in the opinions of his companions and their arguments, he should not take on this important, crucial and dangerous position.[7]

The opening of the book, traditional in the *adab al-qadi* genre, carries the argumentation on the nature of the profession generally. This is different from the arid

---

[4] Karl Wittfogel, *Oriental Despotism* (New Haven, 1957).
[5] Ibn Abi al-Dam, *Kitab adab al-qada'*, 365.   [6] ibid. 364–5.   [7] ibid.

collocation of stories in the works of Waki' (d. 330/941), the earliest writer extant on 'the stories of judges'.[8] The Qur'anic and *hadith* apparatus is taken for granted, and reliance on the differences between various Sunni jurists dominant. In line with the tradition, our Syrian jurist is inconclusive on the allure of the profession. He starts with an example drawn from traditional verses and reports on how fearful and difficult an exercise, and at the same time how important, is the task of the judge. After an extensive list of quotes, the debate ends inconclusively: 'These reports, on the whole, [are divergent], some alluring, some deterring ... [But] this is what the *imams* have said and done in the matter of judging. Some have taken up the post, and some have refused.'[9]

This section does provide a number of clues on the state of the judiciary at the time, notably the provision by the treasury of a salary sufficient to cater to a judge's dignity.[10] One also learns the attention which the judge should give to his predecessors,[11] including in the choice of professional witnesses and other aides to the court.[12] The judge must be careful, we are told, to avoid the court's clerk being bribed, as the clerk controls access to him. We also find a useful and relaxed discussion of the relationship between the schools of law: 'If a judge is a Shafi'i, and his opinion leads him to the school of Abu Hanifa in some dispute, he is entitled to adopt it in his judgment'.[13] Perhaps the most telling information about the state of justice and the responsibility of the judge for the authority of law is the detailed procedure suggested in the manual on the way a judge just appointed reviews all cases of detainees held in jail.[14]

The chapters that follow cover other tangible ground, including the conduct of the trial by the judge, and fairness towards litigants generally (book 2). Then evidence and trial sessions are discussed (book 3), followed by the deposition of witnesses and how to direct them during the trial (book 4), the relations between judgments issued by other *qadis* and their probatory value (book 5), and the art of court registers, standard formulae, and letters (book 6).

The author concludes the book with 'the reason why we have dealt with all these issues'. While the well-versed judge 'might not need much of the book', he modestly suggests, it will be most helpful to the 'lawyer who stands near the judge's courts, and rises up to plead'.[15]

With explanations offered on various 'common practical issues', the manual is 'especially intended for the lawyers who have set themselves out to defend their

---

[8] Waki', *Akhbar al-qudat* (Stories of judges), ed. 'Abdel 'Aziz Mustafa al-Maraghi, 3 vols, (Cairo, 1366–9/1947–50).

[9] *fahadhih al-ahadith bi-jumlatiha ba'duha murghib, wa ba'duha murhib*, Ibn Abi al-Dam, *Kitab adab al-qada'*, 24; *fahadha ma sar ilayhi al-a'imma qawlan wa fi'lan fi-taqlid al-qada' wal-imtina' 'anh*, ibid. 30.   [10] ibid. 58.

[11] ibid. 75.   [12] ibid. 59–66.

[13] *idha kana al-qadi shafi'iyyan fa-addahu ijtihaduhu ila madhhab Abi Hanifa fi haditha, jaza lahu al-hukmu biha*. Ibn Abi al-Dam, *Kitab adab al-qada'*, 54, citing Mawardi.

[14] Ibn Abi al-Dam, *Kitab adab al-qada'*, 71–4.

[15] All quotes in the paragraph in Ibn Abi al-Dam, *Kitab adab al-qada'*, 550: lawyer is *wakil*. Judge is *hakem*.

clients'.[16] This address is important. It shows that a specialization has occurred over the years, and that a 'profession' of legal counsels-representatives was alive and well at the time of Ibn Abi al-Dam. It also suggests that, at one point, lawyers did constitute 'a profession' in classical Islam—though not a recognized 'corporation'—while judgments from the eleventh/seventeenth-century Tripoli (Syria) court show that most litigation was carried out by the parties themselves or by family representatives, rather than by paid professional lawyers.[17] Absence of professional attorneys was also a feature of courtrooms in other parts of the Ottoman Empire, as substantiated by scholarship covering Turkish courts in the first part of the seventeenth century,[18] but not in the Syria-Egypt of Ibn Abi al-Dam's thirteenth century.

While this conclusion calls for the need to reassess the ebb and flow of the legal profession in Middle Eastern history, as well as the need not to over-idealize the past, perhaps the most remarkable discovery in Ibn Abi al-Dam's manual comes from the presentation of a standard format for judgments which corresponds in exacting detail to the practice of the seventeenth-century Tripoli court, four centuries apart: a perfect legal calque indeed.[19]

Ibn Abi al-Dam's manual is also important for the wealth of material it offers the practitioner both in terms of procedure and in terms of substance.

For substance, the 'nineteen common issues' which form the final chapter cover all types of private law, including sale, torts, mandate, marriage, *waqf* (trust). One learns for instance about the validity of the sale when carried out by the father in the name of his son, the sale of an object entrusted with the depositor, the capacity of the parties, the sale of an object which is not immediately available . . .[20]

In terms of procedure, typical questions include the way the register should be held,[21] or the way the case is reported: 'The writing should be done by the scribe, to preserve the dignity of the judge'.[22] One finds also detailed rules concerning absent parties,[23] testimony and evidence,[24] the letters/recommendations from

---

[16] ibid.   [17] Above, Chapter 2, section on courts and case-law.

[18] 'The number of cases in Kayseri in which both litigants in the case were represented by vekils [*wakil*, attorney] was exceedingly small, in no sicil [register] being as many as 1 % of cases . . . It seems very likely, then, that there was no professional class of vekils in Kayseri, nor in Amasya or Karaman . . . Between 1600 and 1625 Kayseri did not have a class of professional vekils, and most likely Amasya, Karaman, and even Trabzon did not either.' Ronald C. Jennings, 'The office of vekil (wakil) in 17th century Ottoman Sharia courts', *Studia Islamica*, 42, 1975, 147–69, quotes at 164 and 168.

[19] We learn for instance about the time limit to produce evidence: 'The defendant asks for a three-day notice to produce exhibits, and the judge grants him three days . . . in accordance with the law. *Fa-istamhala al-mudda'a 'alayhi al-hakem thalathan li-ihdar ma'ared fa-amhaluhu al-hakem . . . jawaz al-imhal fi dhalik thalathat ayyam shar'an.*' Ibn Abi al-Dam, *Kitab adab al-qada*', 436. See for a three-day example in seventeenth century Tripoli, 'The Franjiyyeh case', in 'Umar Tadmuri, Frederic Ma'tuq, and Khaled Ziadeh, eds., *Watha'eq al-mahkama al-shar'iyya bi-Tarablus* (Documents of the shar'i court of Tripoli, Lebanon, full facsimile of the 1666-7 register), Tripoli 1982, 153. Decision translated in full in Chapter 2.

[20] Ibn Abi al-Dam, *Kitab adab al-qada*', 463–550 for the common issues. The problems relating to sale are discussed extensively at 463–73.   [21] *mahadir wa sijillat*, ibid. 367 ff.

[22] *al-awla an yakun bi-khatt katibih, iqamatan li-ubbahat al-qadi*, ibid. at 348.

[23] Absent party, *al-da'wa 'alal-gha'eb*, Ibn Abi al-Dam, *Kitab adab al-qada*', 205–18.

[24] *Passim*, books 2 and 4, ibid. 79–126, 261–339.

one judge to another judge,[25] the conduct of the trial,[26] the use of fatwas,[27] and even a sense of hierarchy amongst judges.[28] Close correspondence between the manuals for judges and the operation of the courts centuries apart suggests a serious, if not obviously accomplished, operation of the rule of law. On all kinds of problems one encounters in court, from attempts to bribe judges and clerks, to the over-use of paper or deliberate lying, the judge tries to offer solutions.

So what about *qadi-justiz*[29] in the light of justice in the courtroom as described by a *qadi* in an age where people were convinced, with some legitimacy, that the rule and authority of the law was far superior in their world than in any other conceivable contemporaneous society? The answer requires some further investigation on the situation of judgeship in thirteenth-century China or India. Ibn Abi al-Dam did not give much thought to possible examples elsewhere on the planet of his time, which lay outside the boundaries of a rather closely knit Muslim world in terms of legal scholarship and interaction.

That, for sure, is not the world of present-day *qadi*s, whether they studied French law in Egypt, Morocco, or Lebanon, Egyptian or US law in the Gulf, or indeed just their traditional *fiqh* texts. Their societies have all come under the severe scrutiny of the rule of law as perceived under universal standards, and they themselves know perfectly well what judicial review and a truly independent judiciary mean. Unlike Ibn Abi al-Dam, however, contemporary judges are understandably defensive about their own authority. In the light of systematic adversity endured under authoritarian governments across the Muslim world since independence in the 1950s, a subdued profession of judges and lawyers keeps hauling the Sisyphus rock of the rule of law, while governments keep resisting accountability by fighting judicial review outright, stonewalling on its decisions, stacking the judicial system, or simply replacing rule of law with rule by law. It is telling that we do not have manuals such as Ibn Abi al-Dam's in the twentieth century. In the absence of such sophisticated deontological guidelines, I shall now illustrate the fight for justice on the contemporary scene from a practitioner's perspective.

In a wide-ranging volume on the rule of law from a comparative and multidisciplinary perspective, the editors concluded their introductory remarks by reflecting on '[t]he preconditions that make the rule of law possible'.[30] These, they note further, rest on 'a functioning, independent judicial system [as] a key element in the maintenance of civil society and the possibility of non-military settlement of disputes'.[31] Although one might lose sight of this underlying truth, the judge is the main repository of legal adjudication, hence the centrality of 'the judge as metaphor' for the stability and fairness of all contemporary societies.[32] While the

---

[25] Called *kitab hukmi*, ibid. 343–65. A full standard formula of the 'to whom it may concern' appears at 347.   [26] Suits, *da'awa*; and *majame' al-khusumat*, litigation sessions, ibid. 129 ff.

[27] e.g. at 469–74.   [28] See Chapter 6.

[29] Max Weber, *Economy and society* (Berkeley, 1968) iii, 976, passage cited in Chapter 2.

[30] Norman Dorsen and Prosser Gifford, eds., *Democracy and the Rule of Law* (Washington 2001) p.xv.

[31] ibid.

[32] Chibli Mallat, *Al-Dimuqratiyya fi Amirka* (Democracy in America) (Beirut, 2001) 147.

stability of some pre-modern societies does not necessarily conform to the centrality of that metaphor—for instance, judges and courts seem far less important in
pre-modern East Asia or Central Africa, at least in surviving records—this is not
the case in the classical Arab-Muslim world, where the importance of the judge,
and of the law in general, can hardly be doubted: classical manuals destined for
judges and attorneys offer an important contrast to the everyday life of their successors in the modern Arab world.

The judge, rather than the other legal professions that come to mind, is central
to the Arab-Islamic tradition. Amongst the many professions connected in some
way to the law—the main three being law teacher, lawyer, and judge—the
metaphor of the judge is the most compelling, in so far as decision-making over
matters of importance to parties in conflict rests with him:

> [T]he priority of the judicial form of dispute resolution is a function of the fact that it is
> judges who must ultimately define the authority that mediators, arbitrators, and special
> masters exercise—not the other way around—and so long as this remains true, judges and
> the work they do are bound to retain the position of dominant importance they have
> occupied in our [US] legal culture from the start.[33]

This is not unique to the American context. The judge as metaphor is a universal image, at least in civilizations where law is recognised as an important
discipline.

From an experience of the rule of law in the region which has straddled the best
part of the past two decades, I must draw sobering conclusions, in the face of so
many false starts and discouraged hopes, about the effectiveness of the judge and
the court over which he presides as a soothing human recourse for litigants.
Looking at the 'noblest' dimension of judgeship, constitutional review, one has
the worrying example of Egypt. For the first time in Egypt's history, a Supreme
Constitutional Court (SCC) started operating as an institution in 1980, with a
recognizable leadership, serious case-writing, and judicial censorship of executive
and legislative acts over a consistent number of years. In the work of the Court,
citizens were seeing some of their fundamental rights at last recognized and
defended.

A quarter of a century later, accumulated case-law is available, testimony to a
good day for the SCC, but the Court acts less and less as a deciding voice in the
Egyptian public arena.[34] In other countries in the region, the drive towards constitutional review has continued and expanded, but the experiment in Lebanon, the
latest country to try establishing seriously the principle of judicial review of laws
under the constitution, collapsed soon after it was started in the mid-1990s.

Constitutional review was also happening in Iran, and in Israel, but the results
are equally disappointing. In the least-known experiment, that of Iran, the proper

---

[33] Anthony Kronman, *The lost lawyer* (Cambridge, Mass, 1993) 317–18.
[34] On the SCC and other similar courts hereinafter, details in Chapter 5.

review of legislation and electoral processes, which had formally started in 1979, was scuppered by the members of the Council of Guardians, themselves over-stretching their power to prevent Parliament and a reformist president from carrying out the popular demand for freedom and participation.

The most recent victim of once high expectations is the Israeli Supreme Court, which not only proved incapable of responding to the legitimate demands for minimal protection by the non-Jewish minority in Israel, but has managed to con-secrate *in law* the authoritarian behaviour of the executive branch in ways that neither international standards nor natural law are able to condone. Against an embattled daily scene between Palestinians and Israelis over the past century, this collapse does not come as a surprise, and few would question the retreat of law in the face of open and sometimes systematic violence on both sides. But the phe-nomenon strikes root in ways that are not yet fully clear, and we must adjust our appreciation of the nature of government in Israel in the light of the failed rule of law for Jews and Muslims (as the largest non-Jewish minority) affected by the emergence of the Israeli state in 1948.

Similar results appear across the Middle East: in Algeria, the Constitutional Council, and the courts at large, are meaningless in the context of the ruthlessness exercised by both the military government and the Islamic extremist groups. In Yemen, the reliance on the judiciary collapsed after the civil war in 1994.

The name of the game has therefore been rule by law instead of rule of law, and the problem lies not merely in the way constitutional review was allowed then undermined. Lack of independent judicial review operates at all levels, but it is mainly a function of lack of free political representation. The disappointment is strongest for rule of law advocates who have become frustrated with their own call for democracy, a universal call which they were hoping to see extended to the region after the collapse of the Berlin Wall and the democratization achievements in many parts of the world. The Muslim Middle East (here including Israel as a country that rules over the lives of Muslims more numerous than its Jewish popu-lation) remains by and large a notable exception to the rise of democracy across the planet. Beyond the understandable dejection resulting from the collapsed legal and democratic process across the region, the loss of faith in the judiciary underlines the graver dimension of the trend downwards, not only as hopes were raised only to be betrayed, but also because executive power has learnt the game so well that it systematically and skilfully stacks the top judiciary with individuals of its own persuasion. This is not limited to public prosecutors—or their equivalents in the various jurisdictions as the criminal arm of the state—but extends to the supreme courts' judges within each jurisdiction, and sensitive judgeships further down the ladder. Reversing that process may take years; meanwhile the authority of the law is undermined in its most 'central and decisive [role] for the profession as a whole'.[35]

---

[35] Kronman, *The lost lawyer*, above n. 33, 318.

This has become so dramatically the norm that the whole legal profession is forced to reconsider its bread-winning daily dedication in an existential manner. While faith in the authority of the law and its fairness re-emerges with the sudden courage of one court or the occasional heroic judge—tiny consolations that the public takes refuge in—the reality of arbitrariness and executive fiat is daunting.

As a result, practitioners fight a disheartening (and so far losing) battle to protect the authority of the law, in the hope that one day, a John Marshall-like judicial Phoenix will rise through the safety nets devised by executive power, by stealth through the ruse of reason (in Hegel's *Philosophy of History*), or, also in a Hegelian metaphor, by the necessity of the 'rule of law-State' understood as the ultimate historical embodiment of the Spirit (in Hegel's *Philosophy of Law*).

Meanwhile, other soothing considerations operate to relativize daily disappointments. Some are professional, when the use of law is managed to enhance the lawyer's financial well-being with some crafty commercial settlements; others are geographical: loss of faith on the Egyptian scene, for example, is redeemed with a sudden opening in Bahrain, in Morocco, or even in Indonesia. This goes beyond the Muslim world. Since universal jurisdiction has developed on the European and other Western scenes, compensation can also be sought under unusual horizons, such as in the International Criminal Court and other instances of universal jurisdiction, in an experience which is halting yet hopeful. Others are domestic, and the judiciary offers occasional successes to individual human rights: the successful fight for the right to a passport in Morocco, the failure of blasphemy cases in Yemen and in Lebanon, the occasional check on the executive in Egypt, the first *Katzir* ruling in Israel, all show a picture which is not all dark judicially: in the first case, a plaintiff whose right to a passport had been stonewalled for years by the administration was vindicated by a decision of the Supreme Court.[36] In Yemen and in Lebanon, courts were able to undermine complaints against authors and singers accused of blasphemy: after years of harassment, the accused were deemed innocent of the grave accusation levelled against them.[37] In Egypt, the Court of Cassation eventually quashed the abusive jailing of the leading dissident Saadeddin Ibrahim, but only after he had spent two years in prison.[38] In Israel, the Supreme Court acknowledged the right of non-Jews to rent a flat in a compound owned, like most of the disposable land, by the Jewish Fund or the

[36] *Echemlal* case, Moroccan Supreme Court, 11 July 1985, reported in *Revue Juridique Politique et Economique du Maroc*, 20, 1988, 42–3, and discussed in Chapter 6.

[37] In Yemen, *al-'Udi* case, Supreme Court, Criminal and Military Division, 7 May 1992, discussed in Chapter 6; in Lebanon, the singer Marcel Khalifeh was acquitted on 14 December 1999 of blasphemy for using passages from the Qur'an in a song (but he was not arrested during the trial). Full report carried by the daily *al-Nahar* (Beirut), 15 December 1999.

[38] Decision of the Egyptian Court of Cassation, 18 March 2003, dismissing accusations of using foreign funds to 'discredit the reputation of Egypt'. A comment on the case before that final decision can be found in Curtis Doebbler, 'The rule of law v. staying in power: *The State of Egypt v. Saad Eddin Mohammed Ibrahim*', *Yearbook of Islamic and Middle Eastern Law*, 8, 2001–2, 353–63.

Israeli government.[39] Unfortunately, these cases rarely become benchmarks, and the rule of law lapses again soon enough to discourage the whole profession, and the public at large.

On a short timeline, the rule of law offers the scene of a 'two steps forward/one step backward' play, or, more often over the past half-century, a 'one step forward/two steps backward' scenario. Cycles being what they are, the critical mass might suddenly bring the rule of law firmly into being in a given jurisdiction. Alternatively, systematic degradation of the law unleashes violence, which is the result that flows from an ailing legal process. The spiral downwards can reach cataclysmic proportions, the harbingers of which one saw in Halabja, Iraq, on 16 March 1988, when some 5,000 villagers were gassed to death by their own government, and in New York on 11 September 2001, when militants claiming Islamic legitimacy killed 3,000 people in a blatant crime against humanity.

More optimistically, what might constitute for the legal profession a critical mass in favour of the rule of law, as yet reached nowhere in the region, but that would allow it to come of age? Beyond the overwhelming evidence of failed cases and failed states, how is it possible to deconstruct the dead-ends reached over the past two decades, so that one may be able to successfully navigate those critical junctures where the machine of justice regularly breaks down?

As a rule of thumb, the elusive answer can be expressed by comparison with jurisdictions where the rule of law functions reasonably well—for example, in the UK, Sweden or New Zealand. There the people lawyering *sense* that cases are conducted with a high degree of legal and judicial independence and fairness, say 80 to 90 per cent of the time, with the remaining cases subject to a number of uncontrolled factors, including 'politics' casting its disturbing shadow, luck, the quality of legal representation, or the length of the judge's leg—these factors are universal. In the Middle East, the picture is topsy-turvy, with law *stricto sensu* offering 20 per cent of the time the factors that tend towards a litigious case being decided fairly, the remaining 80 per cent being determined by a combination of will power, corruption, and executive intervention. When lawyers finally believe their case will be responded to with more law than politics, then the threshold that makes for confidence in the system might have been reached. We are far from that percentile, which is itself not particularly high: if British or French lawyers felt that half of the cases dealt with in court were regulated mostly by politics, they would not feel proud of their 'rule of law' or 'Etat de droit' societies.

Another way of looking at law's authority considers the judge less as a metaphor than as a professional recruit, with a focus on the judiciary's composition, education, and background. The experience varies widely in the Middle East. In most countries, the system follows the French model in which judgeship is a career

---

[39] HCJ 6698/95, *Qaadan v Minhal Mekarkai Israel*, HCJ 6 54(1) PD 258 (2000). Above Chapter 6 n. 28.

embarked on early in life when joining a special magistrates' school, between the ages of 25 and 30, slowly climbing the ladder until retirement at circa 65. Together with this system, one finds strong reliance on the traditional *'ulama* in three juris-dictions, Saudi Arabia, Iran, and Yemen, but the judiciary in all three countries is a mixture of the traditional and the 'modern'. Additionally, the ministries of justice tend to supplement the bench with appointees from outside the hierarchy, partly because of the lack of qualified personnel, more worryingly as a means of stacking the courts. For traditional and modern judges alike, the system remains structurally flawed: joining the profession is not prestigious enough, because the judiciary is perceived not to be independent enough from executive power. A crit-ical criterion will be met when the best lawyers in town start actively seeking judgeships, as they see themselves elevated to a fulfilling benchmark in their careers. Unlike Britain and the United States, where judicial positions appear as the crowning jewel in one's lawyerly life, few successful attorneys in the Arab-Muslim world are prepared to give up their legal practice for a position in the judiciary—save perhaps the very top posts, heads of cassation courts and constitu-tional councils as end-of-career honorific titles.

Alternatively, and until some more scientific indicators are developed, the rule of law can be gauged through the perception of the courts from outside, by the liti-gant and by the public at large. Ultimately, law produces a good, however intangi-ble, which is 'justice' from a macroeconomic viewpoint, and 'the fair and firm settlement of a dispute' in a microeconomic perspective. In both cases, the 'judi-cial product' is an alternative to violence in the public space for its consumers, social groups and individuals alike.

The performance of that function, producing justice and hence peace, is defect-ive across the Middle East. Hardly a family that owns a real estate property in Cairo does *not* have a case pending in some court, often for several years, and few expect either a fair result, or a rapid one: justice delayed is the rule. A recent survey shows a wide variation in the recovery of debt, from a week in Tunisia to two years in Lebanon.[40] One would want to look more closely at the first figure, lest hasty proceedings mask arbitrariness, but delay in payment is a pattern practitioners and litigants suffer from systematically. It is known in derogatory terms as 'the Saudi style (or disease)', and is typical of an oil-producing government whose budget falls on hard times, because of market downturn, mismanagement, and/or bad habits, and which, protected by its political and legal immunity, delays pay-ment with no possible recourse for the creditor. Justice delayed is most evident when private creditors in the Gulf countries struggle for their work to be paid for by the debtor, usually the government or one of its agencies, even when there is no dispute whatsoever that the performance has been completed and the contract honoured.

[40] Contribution by Cheryl Gray at the Middle East Institute/World Bank seventh annual confer-ence on 'Transparency and the rule of law', Washington, 12 June 1992.

Daily practice is especially hard for lawyers, who find their fees undermined by a similar process of bargaining with their clients upon completion of a case, but mostly because the obligation becomes so watered down that they have to admit to their clients from the outset that recovery cannot be complete even if their plea falls squarely on the side of the law. Rule of law here loses a crucial part of its authority, and the whole system gets undermined in the process: delay means that summary courts are summary only in name, recourse to criminal procedure is used to frighten the recalcitrant defendant because civil cases allow so much delay that justice gets systematically denied in civil and administrative courts. This is worse in criminal proceedings, and a classic means of humiliating the debtor (sometimes even the creditor) is to get her to bow to some forced deal by arresting her on the eve of the weekend. In this way a three-day stay in prison is secured, until the relevant prosecutor can be challenged—at the earliest the following week, as he is hard to get hold of over the weekend—by the lawyer of the person arrested, who will then be released from prison because there are no conceivable criminal charges that can stand scrutiny.

Mirrored in the metaphor of the ailing judge are the law school, legal education generally, and the bar: while some empirical work is needed to tally numbers, classes held in what was once the most prestigious law school in the Middle East— Cairo Law School, previously King Fuad School—are simply depressing. One finds several hundred students in the classroom, huddled in run-down buildings, listening to a lecturer reading typed notes which he has been giving for over two decades. The scene is reproduced in the vast majority of law schools in the region. This translates into the poor quality of legal literature, and of judgments. Law publications have become, with a few exceptions, unreadable. Cairo University's *Majallat al-Qanun wal-Iqtisad* (Journal of law and economics), which was from the 1930s until the early 1950s as prestigious as the best law journals in Paris and London, does not nowadays deserve to attract even average articles. Amongst the most distressing frustrations for legal scholarship is the unavailability across the Arab world of respected journals produced at law universities; while bar associations have become the hotbed of lawyers frustrated by both the collapse of the legal market under the weight of numbers and the humiliation of the rule of law by their own governments.

All the branches of the profession are subject to some form of degradation, which varies in intensity depending on the nature of the cases addressed. The more demanding expectations operate at the higher level, which may be called 'constitutional' for short. Here the typical cases concern freedom of expression, fairness of the electoral process, accountability for abuse of power, shielding the market from executive corruption (including confiscation of property and the forcing of commissions on state contracts), all the way to the accountability of top officials for war crimes and crimes against humanity. The gamut is wide, and several examples are displayed in the constitutional decisions to be found in various Middle Eastern countries. The conclusions reached by George Sfeir in a comprehensive survey of

Arab legal systems summarize the problem at hand: 'If . . . the essential quality of constitutionalism has been the legal limitation on government, the excessive authority of the Executive and the personality of power with which it is commonly identified represent, together with judicial review, the two main problems of constitutionalism in the Arab states'.[41] Worse, rule by law is increasingly the name of the game, that is, the deformation of 'due process' to advance a clearly illegitimate goal of government. Examples from real life go from the trivial—a note under the door of a hotel signed by 'the secret services (*mukhabarat*)', asking the host to vacate the room within two hours because it is needed for some high-level delegation visiting the country—to the revolting—the closing down of a television station in Lebanon on account of its having violated the rules on advertising in an electoral campaign fought six months earlier, concomitantly with a decision of the Constitutional Council appointing a candidate who received 2 per cent of the vote for the parliamentary seat under dispute.

Yet humans fight for their rights. They seek justice wherever they can, and short of domestic accountability, victims take their pleas to judges outside if they can. Nothing inflamed the hopes of people in the region like the so-called 'Sharon affair', when survivors of the Sabra and Shatila camps and relatives of hundreds who disappeared in September 1982 brought their grievances to the Belgian courts under the law of 'universal jurisdiction' in June 2001. The Belgian Court of Cassation confirmed their rights, but heavy pressure from US government officials forced the Belgian government to introduce retroactive legislation to stop the case.[42] Here also, justice continues to operate in fits and starts. Suleiman al-Adsani, the Kuwaiti national who had been tortured by Kuwaiti security services, brought his case to the English courts. After a long judicial battle, he failed to get redress and appealed his case to the European Court of Human Rights, where he lost by only a slim margin on account of the immunity of the State of Kuwait.[43] In 2005, the trial of Saddam Hussein and his aides started in Iraq, under a law heavily influenced by the pattern of tribunals dealing with mass murder across the globe. Also in 2005, the assassination of Rafiq Hariri, the former Prime Minister of Lebanon, and 22 other persons, including aides and passers-by led to the largest demonstrations in the history of the country asking for 'the truth'. This led to a UN criminal investigation which released grave reports on the assassination commandeers.[44]

---

[41] George N. Sfeir, *Modernization of the law in Arab states* (San Francisco, 1998) 227.

[42] On the Sharon case, see John Borneman, ed., *The case of Ariel Sharon and the fate of universal jurisdiction* (Princeton, 2004); 'Special Dossier on the "Sabra and Shatila" case in Belgium', *The Palestine Yearbook of International Law*, 12, 2002–3, 183–280.

[43] *Al-Adsani v. the United Kingdom*, 34 Eur. Ct. HR 29, (2001) Judgment of 21 November 2001. See Chapter 6, section on Kuwait.

[44] See e.g. my 'Preface', in Sélim Abou, *Freedoms: cultural roots of the Cedar Revolution* (Beirut, 2005) 4–14. Ongoing UN investigation with published reports by successive investigators Peter Fitzgerald, Detlev Mehlis, and Serge Brammertz.

In an ironic development, a region which has the deepest historical pedigree, stretching from the second millennium BCE, and possibly the richest uninterrupted recorded legal tradition in the planet for its laws' many Deleuzian *plateaux*, was resorting to outside help in making its wrongdoers accountable. Domestic flaws, surely, will in due course be reversed. People will continue to fight for their rights. Scholarship can help, and more work of a comparative and historic nature is needed to reclaim justice in ways that bring out the best in the style of that tradition, while achieving standards under universal rule. This book hopes to add a little adobe to a huge, sometimes heroic undertaking for decency by individuals and communities across the Middle East. Law as we have discovered it in this Middle East journey has the deepest pedigree in the planet. It perforce will have a future, for the future lasts even longer.

Bibliography

Only references mentioned in the book are included in this bibliography, which lists books, articles, chapters in books, and reports. Newspaper articles and book reviews are not referenced. Codes and restatements are generally included in the separate Table of Cases, Legislation, Verses, and *Hadiths*.

Important works, including those that are repeatedly used in this *Introduction*, are preceded with an asterisk.

Abbott, Nabia, *Studies in Arabic literary papyri*, 3 vols, Chicago, 1954–72.

Abdallah, Amine Ben, 'La délivrance du passeport en droit marocain', *Revue Juridique, Politique et Economique du Maroc*, 20, 1988.

'Abdallāh, 'Umar, *Aḥkām al-mawārīth fil-sharī 'a al-islāmiyya* (Succession rules in Islamic law), 4th edn, Cairo, 1965.

Abdoh, Djalal, 'Aperçu général sur le droit civil de l'Iran', in R. Aghabian, ed., *Législation iranienne actuelle*, Tehran, 1939.

*'Abidīn, ibn, *Majmū 'at rasā'el* (Collected treatises), 2 vols, Beirut, n.d.

—— *Radd al-muḥtār 'alā al-durr al-mukhtār*, 5 vols Cairo, 1327/1909.

Abul-Su'ūd, Ramaḍān, *Al-waṣīt fi sharḥ aḥkam al-aḥwāl al-shakhṣiyya li-ghayr al-muslimīn: dirāsa muqārana fil-qānūn al-miṣrī wal-lubnānī* (Treatise on the law of personal status for non-Muslims: a comparative study of Egyptian and Lebanese law), Beirut, 1986.

Abū 'īd, Eliās, *Al-tamthīl al-tijārī* (Commercial agency), 2 vols, Beirut, 1991.

Abū Zahra, Muḥammad, *Muḥāḍarāt fī maṣāder al-fiqh al-Islāmī: al-kitāb wal-sunna* (Lectures on the sources of law in Islamic law: the Book and the Sunna), Cairo, 1956.

—— *al-Aḥwāl al-shakhṣiyya* (Personal status law), 3rd edn, Cairo, 1957.

Ackerman, Bruce, 'The rise of world constitutionalism', *Virginia Law Review*, 83, 1997.

Adal, Erhan, *Fundamentals of Turkish private law*, 3rd edn, Istanbul 1991.

Ahdab, Abdelhamid, *Arbitration in the Arab countries*, Deventer, 1990.

Aḥmadī, 'Alī, *Majma'-e tashkhīṣ-e maṣlaḥat-e neẓām*, Tehran, 2005.

al-Ahnaf, Muhammad, 'Maroc: le code du statut personnel', *Maghreb-Machreq*, 145, 1994.

al-Ahrām, *Al-taqrīr al-istratījī 1989* (Strategic report 1989), Cairo, 1990.

Akaddaf, Fatima, 'Application of the United Nations Convention on contracts for the International Sale of Goods (CISG) to Arab Islamic countries: Is the CISG compatible with Islamic law principles?', *Pace International Law Review*, 13, 2001.

El-Alami, Dawoud Sudqi and Hinchcliffe, Doreen, *Islamic marriage and divorce laws in the Arab world*, London, 1996.

El-Alem, Mustafa, 'Libya', *Yearbook of Islamic and Middle Eastern law*, 1, 1994.

Algar, Hamid, 'Shi'ism and Iran in eighteenth-century Islamic history', in T. Naff and R. Owen, eds, *Studies in eighteenth century Islamic history*, Carbondale, III., 1977.

—— ed., *Islam and revolution*, Berkeley, 1981.

'Ali-Akbar Davar', entry in Ehsan Yarshater, ed., *Encyclopedica Iranica*, online at <http.www.iranica.com/newsite>.

Ali-Karamali, S. and Dunne, F., 'The *ijtihad* controversy', *Arab Law Quarterly*, 9, 1994.

Allott, Antony, *The limits of law*, London, 1980.

Alterman, Jon, *New media new politics: from satellite television to the internet in the Arab world*, Washington, 1998.

Amar, Emile. See Al-Wanscharisi.

al-'Āmilī, al-Ḥurr, *Wasā'el al-shī'a*, 30 vols, Beirut, n.d.

al-'Āmilī, Zayn al-Dīn, known as al-Shahīd al-Thānī, *al-Rawḍa al-bahiyya*, 10 vols, Qum, 1975.

Amīn, Aḥmad, *Fajr al-Islām*, *Ḍuḥā al-Islām*, and *Ẓuhr al-Islām*, 10 vols, Cairo, 1930–52.

Amīn, Qāsem, *Taḥrīr al-mar'a* (The liberation of women), Cairo, 1899.

Anderson, Norman, 'Changes in the law of personal status in Iraq', *International and Comparative Law Quarterly*, 1963.

——— 'Recent reforms in the Islamic law of inheritance', *International and Comparative Law Quarterly*, 14, 1965.

——— Law reform in the Muslim world, London, 1976.

Anis, Mona, 'The state we're in', *Al-Ahram weekly*, Cairo, 16–22 June 2005.

Ansari-Pour, M. A., 'Prohibition of interest under the Iranian legal system since the Revolution', in Hilary Lewis-Ruttley and Chibli Mallat, eds, *Commercial law in the Middle East*, London, 1995.

Ansay, Tugrul and Wallace, Don, eds, *Introduction to Turkish law*, 4th edn, The Hague, 1996.

'Aqīl, ibn, *al-Wāḍiḥ*, 2 vols, Beirut, 1996.

al-'Asalī, Kāmel, ed., *Wathā'eq maqdisiyya tarīkhiyya* (Historical Jerusalemite documents), 3 vols, Amman, 1983–9.

al-Asfahānī, Abu al-Faraj, *al-Aghānī*, 25 vols, Beirut, 1955.

al-'Assāl, ibn, *al-Majmū' al-safawī*, Jirjis Filothaus 'Awad ed., Cairo, 1908.

al-Athīr, ibn, *al-Kāmil fil-tārīkh*, 9 vols, Cairo, 1929.

al-'Aṭiyya, Khāled, *Mu'jam fiqh al-jawāher*, Beirut, 1996.

al-Azami, M. M., *On Schacht's Origins of Muhammadan Jurisprudence*, Riyadh, 1985.

al-Azmeh, Aziz, ed., *Islamic law: social and historical contexts*, London, 1988.

Bābawayh. See Ṣadūq.

Baderin, Mashood, *International human rights and Islamic law*, Oxford, 2003.

al-Baghdādī, Abū Muḥammad, *Majma' al-ḍamānāt*, Beirut, 1987.

al-Baharna, Husain, *The Arabian Gulf states*, Beirut, 1975.

Baḥr al-'Ulūm, Muḥammad, *Adwā' 'alā qānūn al-aḥwāl al-shakhṣiyya al-'irāqī* (Lights on the Iraqi personal status law), Najaf, 1963.

——— '*al-dirāsa wa tārīkhuhā fil-najaf* (Studies and the history of education in Najaf), in Ja'far al-Khalīlī, ed., *Mawsū'at al-'atabāt al-muqaddasa, qism al-najaf* (Encyclopaedia of the Shi'i holy places), Beirut, 1964.

——— '*Uyūb al-irāda fil-fiqh al-islāmī* (Vices of consent in Islamic law), Beirut, 1984.

Bahūtī Manṣūr, *Kashshāf al-qinā' 'an math al-iqua'* (Gloss of Hijāwī), 6 vols, 1983.

——— *Kashshāf al-qinā'*, Beirut, 1987.

——— *S'arḥ muntahā al-irādāt* (Gloss of Futūḥī), 5 vols, Mecca, 1997.

Bakhash, Shaul, *The reign of the Ayatollahs*, New York, 1984.

Bakhit, Muhammad Adnan, *The Ottoman province of Damascus in the sixteenth century*, Beirut, 1982.

Bälz, Kilian, 'Submitting faith to judicial scrutiny through the family trial: the Abu Zayd case', *Die Welt des Islams*, 37, 1997.

—— 'Europäisches Privaterecht jenseits von Europa? Zum fünfzigjährigen Jubiläum des ägyptischen Zivilgesetzbuch (1948)', *Zeitschrift für Europäisches Privatrecht*, 2000.

Bammel, E., Barrett, C. K., and Davies, W. D., eds, *Donum gentilicium: New Testament studies in honour of David Daube*, Oxford, 1978.

*al-Bannānī, Muḥammad ibn Muḥammad, known as Firʿawn, *al-Wathāʾeq al-Fāsiyya* (The Fes formulae), ʿAbd al-Karīm Masrūr ed., Rabat, 1988.

Barak, Aharon, 'Foreword: a judge on judging: the role of a supreme court in a democracy', *Harvard Law Review*, 116, 2002.

Barazi, Khaled, '*The Majlis Mebusan (Meclis-i Mebusan)*: The Ottoman Parliament', London Ph.D., 2002.

Barkan, Ömer Lûfti, *Contributions à l histoire économique et sociale de l'Empire ottoman*, Leuven, Belgium, 1983.

Batatu, Hanna, *The old social classes and the revolutionary movements of Iraq*, Princeton, 1978.

—— *Syria's peasantry, the descendants of its lesser rural notables, and their politics*, Princeton, 1999.

*Bāz, Salīm, *Sharḥ al-Majalla*, Beirut, 1923.

Beccaria, Cesare, *Dei deletti e delle pene*, Livorno, 1765.

*Bellefonds, Yvon Linant de, *Traité de droit musulman comparé*, 3 vols, Paris, 1965–73.

Berkovits, Bernard, 'Transnational divorces: the Fatima decision', *Law Quarterly Review*, 104, 1988.

Bernoussi, Nadia, 'Les méthodes constitutionnelles du juge marocain', in *Les aspects récents du droit constitutionnel*, Tunis, 2005.

Blaustein, Albert and Flanz, Gilbert, eds, *Constitutions of the countries of the world*, New York, 1971–.

Blenkhorn, Lindsey E., 'Islamic marriage contracts in American courts: interpreting *mahr* agreements as pre-nuptials and their effect on Muslim women', *Southern California Law Review*, 2002.

—— 'Table-ronde: Répudiations de droit musulman', *Revue Internationale de Droit Comparé*, 2006.

Bligh, Alexander, 'The Saudi religious elite (*ulama*) as participant in the political system of the Kingdom', *International Journal of Middle East Studies*, 1985.

Bligh-Abramski, Irit, 'The judiciary (*qadis*) as a governmental-administrative tool in early Islam', *Journal of the Economic and Social History of the Orient*, 35, 1992.

Borneman, John, ed., *The case of Ariel Sharon and the fate of universal jurisdiction*, Princeton, 2004.

Borrmans, Maurice, *Statut personnel et famille au Maghreb de 1940 à nos jours*, Paris, 1977.

—— 'Le nouveau code algérien de la famille dans l'ensemble des codes musulmans de statut personnel, principalement dans les pays arabes', *Revue Internationale de Droit Comparé*, 1986.

Botiveau, Bernard, *Loi islamique et droit dans les sociétés arabes: mutations des systèmes juridiques du Moyen-Orient*, Paris, 1993.

Bottéro, Jean, 'Le "Code" de Hammurabi', in Bottéro, Jean, *Mésopotamie: L'écriture, la raison et les dieux*, Paris, 1987.

—— *Babylone et la Bible*, Paris, 1994.

Boyle, Kevin and Sherif, Adel, eds, *Human rights and democracy: the role of the Supreme Constitutional Court of Egypt*, London, 1996.

Braudel, Fernand, *Les Mémoires de la Méditerranée*, Paris, 1998.

Brinner, W. M. and Ricks, S. D., eds, *Studies in Islamic and Judaic traditions*, 2 vols, Atlanta, 1986–9.

Brinton, Jasper Yeates, *The mixed courts of Egypt*, rev. edn, New Haven, 1968.

Browne, Edward G., *The Persian revolution of 1905–1909*, Cambridge, 1910.

Brown, Nathan, *Constitutions in a nonconstitutional world*, New York, 1991.

—— 'Arab administrative courts and judicial control of the bureaucracy,' February 1997, available online at <http.www.geocities.com/nathanbrown1/SOGpaper.html>.

—— *The rule of law in the Arab world: courts in Egypt and the Gulf*, Cambridge, 1997.

Brunschvig, Robert, 'Les *usul al-fiqh* imamites à leur stade ancien', in *Le Shi'isme imamite*, Paris, 1970.

—— 'Urbanisme médiéval et droit musulman', *Etudes d'islamologie*, 2 vols, Paris, 1976.

Burton, John, *The collection of the Qur'ān*, Cambridge, 1979.

al-Būṭī, Muhammad Sa'īd Ramaḍān, *Fiqh al-sīra*, 2 vols, Beirut, 1967.

Cahen, Claude, 'A propos et autour d' "ein arabisches Handbuch der Handelswissenschaft"', *Oriens*, 15, 1962.

*Calder, Norman, *Studies in early Muslim jurisprudence*, Oxford, 1993.

Canal-Forgues, Eric, ed., *Constitutions des pays arabes*, Beirut, 2000.

Cannon, Byron, *Politics of law and the courts in nineteenth-century Egypt*, Salt Lake City, 1988.

Cappelletti, Mauro, *The judicial process in comparative perspective*, Oxford, 1989.

Carlier, Jean-Yves and Verwilgen, Michel, eds, *Le statut personnel des musulmans: Droit comparé et droit international privé*, Brussels, 1992.

Carroll, Lucy, 'Qur'an 2:229: "A Charter Granted to the Wife"? Judicial *khul* Pakistan,' *Islamic Law and Society*, 3, 1996.

—— 'The Pakistan Federal Shariat Court, Section 4 of the Muslim Family Laws Ordinance, and the orphaned grandchild', *Islamic Law and Society*, 9, 2002.

Chalabī, Fāḍel, '*Mustaqbal al-nafṭ fil-sharq al-awsaṭ* (The future of oil in the Middle East)', in *Al-muqawwimāt al-fikriyya wal-qānūniyya li-niẓam sharq-awsaṭī jadīd* (The intellectual and legal frameworks for a new Middle East), London, 19–20 December 1994.

Chalmeta-Gendrón, P., 'Un formulaire notarial hispano-arabe du iv/x siècle: glanes économiques', *Revista del Instituto Egipcio de Estudios Islámicos en Madrid*, 23, 1985–6.

Chanbour, Issam, *La coutume et l'usage conventionnel en droit musulman*, Beirut, 1981.

Charnay, Jean-Paul, *La vie musulmane en Algérie d'après la jurisprudence de la première moitié du XXème siècle*, Paris, 1965.

Charrad, Mounira, 'Repudiation versus divorce: responses to state policy in Tunisia', in E. Chow and C. Berheide, eds, *Women, the family and policy: a global perspective*, Albany, NY, 1994.

Chaudhury, K. N., *Trade civilisation in the Indian Ocean: an economic history from the rise of Islam to 1750*, Cambridge, 1985.

—— *Asia before Europe*, Cambridge 1993.

Chehata, Chafik, *Etudes de droit musulman*, 2 vols, Paris, 1973.

Chodhosh, Hiram, 'Comparing comparisons: in search of methodology', *Iowa Law Review*, 84, 1999.

Christelow, Allan, *Muslim law courts and the French colonial state in Algeria*, Princeton, 1985.

Cobban, Helena, *The Palestinian Liberation Organization*, Cambridge, 1984.

Collinet, Paul, *Histoire de l'école de droit de Beyrouth*, Paris, 1925.

Conard, Alfred, *Corporations*, 1st edn, Mineola, NY, 1976, repr. 1991.

Connors, Jane, 'The women's convention in the Muslim world', in Mai Yamani, ed., *Feminism and Islam*, London, 1996.

Cook, Michael, *Early Muslim dogma: a source-critical study*, Cambridge, 1981.

—— *Muhammad*, Oxford, 1983.

—— and Crone, Patricia, *Hagarism: the making of the Islamic world*, Cambridge, 1977.

Corbin, Henry, *En Islam iranien*, 4 vols, Paris, 1971–2.

*Cotran, Eugene and Mallat, Chibli, eds, *Yearbook of Islamic and Middle Eastern law*, 1994–.

—— —— eds, *The Arab-Israeli accords: legal perspectives*, Leiden, 1996.

—— and Sherif, Adel Omar, eds, *The role of the judiciary in the protection of human rights*, London, 1997.

*Coulson, Noel, *A history of Islamic law*, Edinburgh, 1964.

—— *Succession in the Muslim family*, Cambridge, 1971.

—— *Commercial law in the Gulf states*, London, 1984.

Crone, Patricia, *Meccan trade and the rise of Islam*, Oxford, 1987.

—— *Roman, provincial and Islamic law: the origins of the Islamic patronate*, Cambridge, 1987.

—— 'Shura as an elective institution', *Quaderni di Studi Arabi*, 19, 2001, 3–39.

*al-Dam, ibn Abī, *Kitāb adab al-qadā'* (The book of the ways of judgeship), Beirut, 1987.

Dāmād Efendī = Shaykhzādeh, see Ḥaskafī.

Dardīr, Aḥmad, *al-Sharḥ al-kabīr li-Shams al-Din al-Shaykh Muḥammad 'Arafah al-Dasūqī 'alā al-sharḥ al-kabīr li-Abī al-Barakāt Aḥmad Dardīr*, 4 vols, Cairo [198–?]

Darwiche, Fadwa Adel, *The Gulf stock exchange crash: the rise and fall of the Souq Al-Manakh*, London, 1986.

Daube, David, *The New Testament and rabbinic Judaism*, New York, 1973 (repr. of London, 1959 edn).

Deleuze, Gilles, *Pourparlers*, Paris, 1990.

—— and Guattari, Félix, *Mille plateaux*, Paris, 1980.

Delong-Bas, Natana, *Wahhabi Islam: from revival and reform to global jihad*, London, 2004.

Derrett, J. D. M., *Law in the New Testament*, London, 1970.

Desportes, Frédéric, and Le Guhénec, Francis, *Le nouveau droit pénal*, i, *Droit pénal général*, Paris, 1994.

Deguilhem, Randi, *Le waqf dans l'espace islamique: outil de pouvoir socio-politique*, Damascus, 1995.

Dietrich, Albert, *Arabische Briefe aud der Papyrussammlung der Hamburger Staats- und Universitäts- Bibliothek*, Hamburg, 1955.

Docteur-Zadeh, Ibrahim, *De la validité des contrats sous la chose d'autrui en droit positif iranien*, Paris, 1939.

Doebbler, Curtis, 'The rule of law v. staying in power: *The State of Egypt v. Saad Eddin Mohammed Ibrahim*', *Yearbook of Islamic and Middle Eastern Law*, 8, 2001–2.

Domat, Jean, *Lois civiles*, Paris, 1756.

Donni, Valentina, 'La responsabilità contrattuale nei codici di Tunisia, Egitto ed Emirati Arabi Uniti', in F. Castro, ed., *Questioni di integrazione giuridica nel mondo arabo e nel mediterraneo*, Rome, 2001.

Donohue, John, 'The development of political and social institutions in Iraq under the Buwayhids, 334–403 H.: the fall and rise of the caliphate', Harvard Ph.D., 1966.

—— 'Individualisme, corporatisme et Etat: où se trouve la civilité dans la société civile au Moyen Orient?', *Travaux et Jours*, 65, 2000.

—— *The Buwayhid dynasty in Iraq 334 H./945 to 403 H./1012: shaping institutions for the future*, Leiden, 2003.

Dorsen, Norman and Gifford, Prosser, eds, *Democracy and the rule of law*, Washington, 2001.

Doumani, Beshara, *Rediscovering Palestine: merchants and peasants in Jabal Nablus, 1700–1900*, Berkeley, 1995.

Doumet-Serhal, Claude and Hélou-Nahas, Michèle, eds, *Michel Chiha 1891–1954*, Beirut, 2001.

*Driver, G. R., and Miles, John, eds, *The Babylonian laws*, Oxford, 1953.

Ducruet, Jean, *Livre d'or 1913–1993 de la Faculté de droit, de sciences politiques et économiques* Beirut, 1995.

Dumper, Michael, *Islam and Israel: Muslim religious endowments and the Jewish state*, Beirut, 1993.

Dutton, Yasin, *The origins of Islamic law*, London, 1999.

Ebied, R. Y., and Young, M. J. L., eds, *Some Arabic legal documents of the Ottoman period*, Leiden, 1975.

Eilts, Hermann, 'Traditionalism v. Modernism—a royal dilemma?', in P. Chelkowski and R. Pranger, eds, *Ideology and power in the Middle East*, Durham, NC, 1988.

Eisenman, Robert, *Islamic law in Palestine and Israel: a history of the survival of tanzimat and shari'a in the British Mandate and the Jewish state*, Leiden, 1978.

Ely, John Hart, *Democracy and distrust*, Cambridge, Mass., 1980.

Enayat, Hamed, *Modern Islamic political thought*, Austin, Tex., 1982.

Englard, Itzhak, *Jewish law in ancient and modern Israel: selected essays*, New York, 1971.

—— *Religious law in the Israel legal system*, Jerusalem, 1975.

Escovitz, Joseph, *The office of qadi al-qudat in Cairo under the Bahri Mamluks*, Berlin, 1984.

Esposito, John, ed., *The Oxford encyclopaedia of the modern Islamic world*, 4 vols, New York, 1995.

Estin, Ann Laquer, 'Embracing tradition: pluralism in American family law', *Maryland Law Review*, 2004.

El Fadl, Khaled Abou, *Rebellion and violence in Islamic law*, Cambridge, 2001.

al-Fahad, Abdulaziz, 'Ornamental constitutionalism: the Saudi Basic Law of governance', *The Yale Journal of International Law*, 2005.

Fahmy, Hoda, *Divorcer en Egypte. Etude de l'application des lois du statut personnel*, Cairo, 1986.

Farhūn, ibn, *Tabsirat al-ḥukkām fī uṣūl al-aqḍiya wa-manāhij al-aḥkām*, Cairo, 1885.

Al-Fatāwā al-'ālamgiriyya = al-Fatāwā al-hindiyya.

al-Fatāwā al-Ghiyāthīyya (by Dāwūd ibn Yūsuf al-Khafīb), Cairo, 1904.

al-Fatāwā al-hindiyya al-musammāt bil-fatawa al-'ālamgiriyya, Cairo, 1310.

al-Fatāwā al-hindiiyya (by al-Shaykh Nizām), *wa-bi-hāmishihi Fatāwā Qāḍīkhān wa-Fatāwā al-Bazzāzīyya*, 6 vols, Diyar Bakr, Turkey, 3rd edn, 1973.

al-Fatāwā al-tātārkhāniyya (by 'Ālim ibn al-'Alā' al-Anṣārī al-Andaraptī al-Dihlawī al-Hindī), Karachi, 1990.

Fayḍī, Sulaimān, *Mudhakkarāt* (Memoirs), Beirut, 1998.

Febvre, Lucien, *Le problème de l'incroyance au 16ème siècle*, Paris, 1947.

Feldman, Noah, *After Jihad: America and the struggle for Islamic democracy*, New York, 2003.

Finet, André, *Le Code de Hammurapi*, Paris, 1973.

Fiss, Owen, *Liberalism divided*, Boulder, Colo., 1996.

—— 'The war against terrorism and the rule of law', *Oxford Journal of Legal Studies*, 26, 2006, 235–56.

Flory, Maurice and Henry, J. R., eds, *L'enseignement du droit musulman*, Marseille, 1989.

—— and Mantran, Robert, eds, *Les régimes politiques arabes*, Paris, 1991.

Fluehr-Lobban, Carolyn, 'Judicial circulars of the *shari'a* courts in the Sudan 1902–1979', *Journal of African Law*, 27, 1983.

—— *Islamic law and society in the Sudan*, London, 1987.

Forte, David, 'Islamic law in American courts', *Suffolk Transnational Law Journal*, 1983.

Fossaert, Robert, *La Société*, 6 vols, Paris, 1977–83.

—— *Le Monde au 21ème siècle: une théorie des systèmes mondiaux*, Paris, 1991.

—— *L'Avenir du socialisme*, Paris, 1996.

—— *Civiliser les Etats-Unis*, Paris, 2003.

Frantz-Murphy, Gladys, 'A comparison of Arabic and earlier Egyptian contract formularies', *Journal of Near Eastern Studies*, 4 parts, 1981, 1985, 1988, 1988.

Fromkin, David, *A Peace to end all peace: the fall of the Ottoman empire and the creation of the modern Middle East 1914–1922*, New York, 1989.

Al-Fukaikī, *al-Mut'ah wa-ātharuhā fī al-iṣlāḥ al-ijtimāī* (Temporary marriage and its effects on social reform), Beirut, n.d.

al-Futuḥī, Taqī al-Dīn Muhammad ibn Aḥmad, a.k.a. ibn al-Najjār. See Bahūtī, Manṣūr, *Sharḥ muntahā al-irādāt*.

Garcin, Jean-Claude, 'Le JESHO et la recherche sur l'histoire économique et sociale des pays musulmans,' *Journal of the Economic History of the Orient*, 36, 1993.

Geller, M. J., 'Early christianity and the Dead Sea Scrolls', *Bulletin of the School of Oriental and African Studies*, 57, 1994.

Gerber, Haim, *State, society, and law in Islam: Ottoman law in comparative perspective*, Albany, NY, 1994.

—— *Islamic law and culture 1600–1840*, Leiden, 1999.

Gewirtz, Paul, ed., *Global constitutionalism: nationhood, same-sex marriage*, Yale Law School Global Constitutionalism Seminar, 21–4 September 2005.

*al-Gharnāṭī, Abū Isḥāq, *al-Wathā'eq al-mukhtaṣara* (Summary of forms), Rabat, 1988.

Goitein, Samuel, 'The birth-hour of Muslim law', *The Muslim World*, 50, 1960.

—— *Studies in Islamic history and institutions*, Leiden, 1966.

*—— *A Mediterranean society: the Jewish communities of the Arab world as portrayed in the documents of the Cairo Geniza*, 5 vols, Berkeley, 1967–88.

—— 'The interplay of Jewish and Islamic laws', in B. S. Jackson, ed., *Jewish law in legal history and the modern world*, Leiden, 1980.

Goldziher, Ignaz, *Die Zāhirīten: ihr Lehrsystem und ihre Geschichte*, Leipzig, 1884. Translated by Wolfgang Behn as *The Zahiris: their doctrine and their history*, Leiden, 1971.

—— *Introduction to Islamic law and theology*, A. Hamori tr., Princeton, 1981.

Goode, Roy, 'Preface', in Samir Saleh, *Commercial agency and distributorship in the Arab Middle East*, The Hague, 1995.

—— *Commercial law*, London, 1995.

Grabar, Oleg, *The illustrations of the maqamat*, Chicago, 1984.

Graëffly, Romain, 'Le conseil constitutionnel algérien. De la greffe institutionnelle à l'avènement d'un contentieux constitutionnel?', *Revue de Droit Public*, 5, 2005.

Graham, William, *Divine word and prophetic word in early Islam*, The Hague, 1977.

Grasshof, Richard, *Wechselrecht der Araber*, Berlin, 1899.

Gray, Cheryl, contribution at the Middle East Institute/World Bank seventh annual conference on 'Transparency and the rule of law', Washington, 12 June 1992.

Grohmann, Alfred, *Arabic papyri in the Egyptian museum*, 6 vols, Cairo, 1934–62.

Gronke, Monica, *Arabische und persische Privaturkunden des 12. und 13. Jahrhunderts aus Ardabil (Aserbaidschan)*, Berlin, 1982.

Guellil, Gabriela Linda, *Damaszener Akten des 8/14. Jahrhunderts nach at-Tarsusis Kitab al-I'lam, Eine Studie zum Arabischen Justizwesen*, Bamberg, 1985.

Haarman, Ulrich, 'Die Sphinx. Synkretistische Volksreligiosität im spätmittelalterlichen islamischen Ägypten', *Saeculum*, 29, 1978.

Haeri, Shahla, *The law of desire: temporary marriage in Shi'i Iran*, London, 1989.

—— 'Divorce in contemporary Iran: a male prerogative in self-will', in Chibli Mallat and Jane Connors, eds, *Islamic family law*, London, 1990.

Hairi, Abdul Hadi, *Shi'ism and constitutionalism in Iran*, Leiden, 1977.

Hakim, Basem, *Arabic-Islamic cities: building and planning principles*, London, 1986.

Hakim, Jacques, *Le dommage de source délictuelle en droit musulman*, Paris, 1964.

al-Ḥakīm, Muḥammad Taqī, *Al-uṣūl al-'āmma lil-fiqh al-muqāran* (General principles in comparative jurisprudence), Beirut, 1963.

al-Hakīm, Muḥsin, *Mustamsak al-'urwa al-wuthqā*, 14 vols, Qum, 4th edn, 1980.

—— *Minhāj al-ṣāliḥīn*, 2 vols, Qum, 1993.

Ḥalabī, Ibrāhīm. See Ḥaskafī.

Hale, William, *Turkish politics and the military*, London, 1994.

Hallaq, Wael, 'Was the gate of *ijtihad* closed?', *International Journal of Middle East Studies*, 16, 1984.

—— 'Was Shafi'i the master architect of Islamic jurisprudence?' *International Journal of Middle East Studies*, 25, 1993.

—— 'From *fatwas* to *furu'* growth and change in Islamic substantive law', *Islamic Law and Society*, 1, 1994.

—— *A history of Islamic legal theories: an introduction to Sunni usul al-fiqh*, Cambridge, 1997.

Hallo, William, 'A model court case concerning inheritance', in Tzvi, Abusch ed., *Riches hidden in secret places, ancient near eastern studies in memory of Thorkild Jacobsen*, Winona Lake, Indi. 2002.

al-Hamadhānī, Badī' al-Zamān, *Maqāmat*, Beirut, 1965.

Ḥamza, Fu'ād, *Al-Bilād al-'arabiyya al-sa'ūdiyya* (Arab Saudi country), Mecca, 1355/1935.

Hanf, Theodor, *Co-existence in wartime Lebanon—death of a state and birth of a nation*, Oxford, 1993.

al-Ḥarīrī, *Maqāmat*, Beirut, 1978.

Ḥaskafī, *Al-durr al-muntaqā*, (gloss of Dāmād Efendī, *Majma' al-anhur*, itself a gloss on Ḥalabī, Ibrāhīm, *Multaqā al-abhur*), 4 vols, Beirut, 1998.

Hawting, G., '*Ilā'* and *ẓihār* in Muslim law', *Bulletin of the School of Oriental and African Studies*, 57, 1994.

*Ḥaydar 'Alī, *Durar al-ḥukkām fī sharḥ Majallat al-aḥkām*, Fahmī al-Husainī tr., 4 vols, Beirut 1991 (original Ottoman: *Durer ul-hukkam, serh-i mecellet ul-ahkam*, Istanbul, 1881).

Haykel, Bernard, *Revival and reform in Islam: the legacy of Muhammad al-Shawkani*, Cambridge, 2003.

Ḥazm, ibn, *al-Muḥalla*, 12 vols, Beirut, 1988.

Heffening, W., '*Mutʿa*', *Encyclopaedia of Islam*, 1st edn, Leiden, 1916.

Hegel, G. W. F., *Vorlesungen über die Geschichte der Philosophie*, in *Werke*, Suhrkamp edn in 20 vols, 4th edn, Frankfurt, 2003, vol. xix.

Heinrichs, Wolfhart, '*Qawaʿid* as a genre of legal literature', in Bernard Weiss, ed., *Studies in Islamic legal theory*, Leiden, 2002.

Hejailan, Hussam Salah, 'Saudi Arabia', *Yearbook of Islamic and Middle Eastern law*, 7, 2000–1.

Hémard, Jean, 'Les agents commerciaux', *Revue Trimestrielle de Droit Commercial*, 1959.

Heyd, Uriel, *Studies in old Ottoman criminal law*, Ménage, V. L, ed., Oxford, 1973.

Hiba, Aḥmad, '*Taʿlīq ʿalā ijtihād ḥawla wilāyat al-maḥkama al-dustūriyya al-ʿulyā* (Comment on a case on the competence of the Supreme Constitutional Court)', *Al-Majalla al-ʿarabiyya lil-fiqh wal-qaḍāʾ*, 12, 1992.

al-Ḥijāwī, Mūsā. See Bahūtī, *Manṣūr, Kashshāf al-qināʿ ʿan matn al-iqnaʿ*.

Hill, Enid, *Mahkama! Studies in the Egyptian legal system*, London, 1979.

——*Al-Sanhuri and Islamic law*, Cairo Papers in Social Science, 10, 1987.

—— 'Majlis al-Dawla: the administrative courts of Egypt and administrative law', in Chibli Mallat, ed., *Islam and public law*, London, 1993.

—— 'Laws of investment, privatization and labour in Egypt', in Lewis Ruttley and Chibli Mallat, eds, *Commercial law in the Middle East*, London, 1995.

al-Ḥillī, ʿAbd al-Karīm, *Al-aḥkām al-jaʿfariyya fil-aḥwāl al-shakhṣiyya* (Personal status Jaʿfari-Shiʿi rules), Baghdad, 1923.

al-Ḥillī, al-Muḥaqqiq, *Sharāʾeʿ al-Islām*, 4 vols, Najaf, 1969.

Hinchcliffe, Doreen, 'The Iranian Family Protection Act [of 1967]', *International and Comparative Law Quarterly*, 17, 1968.

Hirst, Alastair, 'Court decisions on commercial arbitration in the Sultanate of Oman', *Middle East Commercial Law Review* (MECLR), 2, 1995.

Hjerrild, Bodil, 'Islamic law and Sasanian law', in Christopher Toll and Jakob Skovgaard-Petersen, eds, *Law and the Islamic world: past and present*, Copenhagen, 1995.

Hooper, C. H., *The Civil law of Palestine and Transjordan*, 2 vols, Jerusalem, 1933, 1936.

Horowitz, Donald, 'The Qurʾan and the Common Law: Islamic law reform and the theory of legal change', *American Journal of Comparative Law*, in 2 parts, 42, 1994.

Hourani, Albert, *Arabic thought in the liberal age 1789–1939*, Cambridge, 1983.

——*A history of the Arab peoples*, London, 1991.

Hoyle, Mark, *Mixed courts of Egypt*, London, 1991.

al-Hudā, Bint, *Al-Majmūʿa al-qaṣaṣiyya al-kāmila* (Collected novels), 3 vols, Beirut, n.d.

Hudson, Michael, *Arab politics—search for legitimacy*, New Haven, 1993.

*Humphreys, R. Stephen, *Islamic history*, Princeton, 1991.

Huntington, Samuel, *The clash of civilizations and the remaking of the world order*, New York, 1996.

Idris, Hady Roger, 'Le marriage en Occident musulman. Analyse de fatwas médiévales extraites du *Miʿyar* d'al-Wansharisi', *Revue de l'Occident Musulman et de la Méditerranée*, 12 1972; 17, 1974; 25, 1978.

al-Idrīsī, *Anwār ʿūlī al-ajrām fil-kashf ʿan asrār al-ahrām*, in Ulrich Haarman, ed., *Das Pyramidenbuch des Abu Jaʿfar al-Idrīsī*, Beirut, 1991.

Imber, Colin, *Ebu's-su'ud, the Islamic legal tradition*, Edinburgh, 1997.

Inalcik, Halil, *The Ottoman empire: the classical age, 1300–1600*, London, 1973.

Jackson, Sherman, *Islamic law and the state: the constitutional jurisprudence of Shihāb al-Dīn al-Qarāfī*, New York, 1996.

Jafri, S. H. M., *The origins and early development of Shi'a Islam*, London, 1979.

Jakobsen, Thorkild, 'An ancient Mesopotamian trial for homicide', in *Studia Biblica et Orientalia III: Oriens Antiquus*, Rome, 1959.

al-Jazīrī, *Al-fiqh 'alā al-madhāhib al-arba'a (Fiqh* according to the four schools), 5 vols, Beirut, repr. 1990.

Jennings, Ronald C., 'The office of vekil (wakil) in 17th century Ottoman Sharia courts', *Studia Islamica*, 42, 1975.

—— 'Kadi, court and legal procedure in 17th-century Ottoman Kayseri', *Studia Islamica*, 48, 1978.

—— 'Limitations of the judicial powers of the Kadi in 17th-century Ottoman Kayseri', *Studia Islamica*, 50, 1979.

—— 'Divorce in the Ottoman *shari'a* court of Cyprus, 1580–1640', *Studia Islamica*, 78, 1993.

—— *Studies on Ottoman social history in the sixteenth and seventeenth centuries*, Istanbul, 1999.

Johansen, Baber, *The Islamic law on land tax and rent*, London, 1988.

*—— *Contingency in a sacred law: legal and ethical norms in the Muslim fiqh*, Leiden, 1999.

Joubair, Antoine, *Kitāb al-hudā*, 2nd edn, Kaslik (Lebanon), 1991.

Junblāt, Kamāl, '*Risālatī ka-nā'eb* (My calling as parliamentarian)', in *Les Années Cénacle*, Beirut, 1997.

Juynboll, G. A., *Muslim tradition: studies in chronology, provenance and authorship of early hadith*, Cambridge, 1983.

Kadifa, Abdo and Mallat, Chibli, *The third stage of Zionism: high technology in Israel*, Centre of Near and Middle Eastern Studies (SOAS, University of London), May 1988.

Kamali, Muhammad Hashim, *Principles of Islamic jurisprudence*, Malaysia, 1989.

—— 'Appellate review and judicial independence in Islamic law', in C. Mallat, ed., *Islam and public law*, London, 1993.

Kant, Immanuel, *Treaty on perpetual peace*, original German: *Zum ewigen Frieden*, Königsberg, 1795.

Karam, Nicolas, ed., *Business laws of Kuwait*, Leiden, 1992.

*al-Kāsānī, 'Alā' al-Dīn, *Badā'e' al-ṣanā'e' fi tartīb al-sharā'e'*, 7 vols, Beirut, n.d.

Kāshif al-Ghaṭā', Muḥammad Ḥusayn, *Taḥrīr al-Majalla*, 4 vols, Najaf, 1940–3.

—— *Al-'abaqāt al-'anbariyya fil-ṭabaqāt al-ja'fariyya*, Jawdat al-Qazwīnī ed., Beirut, 1998.

Kasravī, Aḥmad, *Tarīkh-i mashrūṭah-i Īrān*, (History of the Iranian Constitution), Tehran, 1961.

Kātūziān, Nāṣir, *Huquq-i madani: Qawa'id-i 'umumi-yi qarardadha (Civil law, general rules)*, 5 vols, Tehran, 1975–.

—— *Huquq-i madani: 'Uqūd-i mu'ayyan* (Special contracts), 3 vols, Tehran, 1994.

Katz, Marion, *Body of text: the emergence of the Sunni law of ritual purity*, Albany, NY, 2002.

Kaufhold, Hubert, *Syrische Texte zum Islamischen Recht*, Munich, 1971.

—— 'Über die Entstehung der Syrischen Texte zum Islamischen Recht', *Oriens Christianus*, 69, 1985.

Kepel, Gilles, *Muslim extremism in Egypt: the Prophet and Pharaoh*, Berkeley, 2003.

Khadduri, Majid, *al-Risala fi usul al-fiqh: Treatise on the foundations of Islamic jurisprudence*, Baltimore, 1961, repr. Cambridge, 1987.

*Khaldūn, ibn, *al-Muqaddima*, Beirut edn, 1978. English translation by Franz Rosenthal in 3 vols, New York, 1958.

Khaled, Mansur, *Nimeiry and the revolution of dismay*, London, 1985.

Khalidi, Tarif, *Arabic historical thought in the classical period*, Cambridge, 1994.

Khallāf, 'Abd al-Wahhāb, *'Ilm uṣūl al-fiqh* (Jurisprudence), 7th edn, Cairo, 1956.

Khamlīshī, Aḥmad, *al-Ta'līq 'alā qānūn al-aḥwāl al-shakhṣīyya*, (Commentary on the personal status law), Rabat, 1984.

Khan, Geoffrey, *Arabic legal and administrative documents in the Cambridge Genizah collections*, Cambridge, 1993.

Khan, Saad, *Reasserting international Islam: a focus on the organization of the Islamic Conference and other Islamic institutions*, Oxford, 2001.

al-Khaṣṣāf, Abu Bakr, *Kitāb al-ḥiyal*, J. Schacht ed., Hanover, 1923.

Khomeyni [Khumainī], 'Fatwa on Salman Rushdie', *Summary of World Broadcasts* (Britain), 15 February 1989, ME/A2.

Khoury, Dina Rizk, 'Merchants and trade in early modern Iraq', *New Perspectives on Turkey*, 5–6, 1991.

al-Khū'ī, Abul-Qāsem, *Minhāj al-sāliḥīn*, 3 vols, Qum, 2000.

al-Khumainī, Rūḥullāh, *Taḥrīr al-wasīla*, 2 vols, Najaf, 1967.

—— *Al-ḥukūma al-islāmiyya* (The rule of the jurist), Najaf, 1971 (Persian: *velāyat-e faqīh*, various eds).

*Khūrī, Yūsif Quzma, ed., *Al-dasātīr fil-'ālam al-'arabī 1829–1987* (Constitutions in the Arab world 1829–1987), Beirut, 1988.

Kimmerling, Baruch, *Zionism and territory*, Berkeley, 1983.

—— *The invention and decline of Israeliness*, Berkeley, 2001.

Koschaker, Paul, *Hammurabi's Gesetz*, 6 vols, Leipzig, 1904–23.

—— *Rechtsvergleichende Studien zur Gesetzgebung Hammurabis: Königs von Babylon*, Leipzig, 1917.

Kramers, J. H, 'Medjelle', *Encyclopaedia of Islam*, 1st edn, Leiden, 1936.

—— 'Tanzimat', *Encyclopaedia of Islam*, 1st edn, Leiden, 1936.

Kretzmer, David, *The legal status of the Arabs in Israel*, Boulder, Colo., 1990.

—— *The occupation of justice: the Supreme Court of Israel and the Occupied Territories*, New York, 2002.

Kronman, Anthony, *The lost lawyer*, Cambridge, Mass., 1993.

Kulaynī, *al-Kāfī*, Tehran, 1978–.

Lammens, Henri, *La cité de Taif à la veille de l'Hégire*, Beirut, 1922.

—— *La Mecque à la veille de l'Hégire*, Beirut, 1924.

—— *L'Arabie occidentale avant l'hégire*, Beirut, 1928.

—— *L'Islam*, Beirut, 1944.

Lapidus, Ira, *A history of Islamic societies*, Cambridge, 1988.

Lau, Martin, 'Introduction to the Pakistani legal system, with special reference to the law of contract', *Yearbook of Islamic and Middle Eastern Law*, i, 1994.

Lawbook of 1000 decisions, part 1 edited by J. J. Modi, Poona, 1901; part 2 edited by T. D. Anklesaria, Bombay, 1913.

Layish, Aharon, *Women and Islamic law in a non-Muslim state: a study based on decisions of the shari'a courts in Israel*, New York, 1975.

Leeman, W. F., *Foreign trade in the Old Babylonian period*, Leiden, 1960.

Lev, Daniel, *Islamic courts in Indonesia*, Berkeley, 1972.

Lewis, Bernard, *The emergence of modern Turkey*, Oxford, 1961.

—— *The Middle East: a brief history of the last 2000 years*, New York, 1995.

Liebesny, Herbert, 'Administration and legal development in Arabia: Aden colony and protectorate', *Middle East Journal*, 9, 1955.

—— 'Administration and legal development in Arabia: the Persian Gulf principalities', *Middle East Journal*, 10, 1956.

*—— *The law of the Near and Middle East*, Albany, NY, 1975.

Lijphart, Arendt, 'Consociational democracy', in Gurpreet Mahajan, ed., *Democracy, difference and social justice*, Delhi, 1988.

Little, Donald, *A Catalogue of the Islamic documents from al-Haram al-Sharif in Jerusalem*, Beirut, 1984.

Lombard, Denys, *Le carrefour javanais: essai d'histoire globale*, 3 vols, Paris, 1990.

Lowry, Heath, *Studies in defterology: Ottoman society in the fifteenth and sixteenth centuries*, Istanbul, 1992.

Lutfi, Huda, 'A study of six fourteenth century *iqrars* from al-Quds relating to Muslim women', *Journal of the Economic and Social History of the Orient*, 26, 1983.

McChesney, R. D., *Waqf in Central Asia: four hundred years in the history of a Muslim shrine, 1480–1889*, Princeton, 1991.

McDermott, Martin, *The theology of al-Shaikh al-Mufīd (d. 413/1022)*, Beirut, 1978.

Macuch, Maria, 'Die Zeitehe im Sasanidischen Recht—ein Vorlaufer der shiʿitischen mutʿa-Ehe in Iran?', *Archaeologische Mitteilungen aus Iran*, Berlin, 18, 1985.

*Mahmaṣānī, Ṣubḥī, *Al-Naẓariyya al-ʿāmma lil-mūjibāt wal-ʿuqūd fil-sharīʿa al-islāmiyya* (General theory of obligations and contracts in Islamic law), 2 vols, Beirut, 1948.

—— *Muqaddima fī ihyāʾ ʿulūm al-sharīʿa* (Introduction to the revival of Islamic law studies), Beirut, 1962.

Mahmassani, Ghaleb, 'Law and Reconstruction in Lebanon', in Hilary Lewis Ruttley and Chibli Mallat, eds, *Commercial law in the Middle East*, London, 1995.

Mahmassani, Maher, *La représentation commerciale en droit positif libanais*, Beirut, 1972.

Mahmood, Tahir, *Family law reform in the Muslim world*, Bombay, 1972.

Maimūn, ibn [Maimonides], *Dalālat al-ḥāʾirīn*, Muḥammad Zāhed al-Kawtharī ed., Cairo, 1369/1949.

—— *Mishneh Torah*, New Haven, Yale Judaica Series, 1949–.

Makdisi, George, 'The significance of the Sunni schools of law in Islamic religious history', *International Journal of Middle East Studies*, 11, 1979.

—— *The rise of colleges*, Edinburgh, 1981.

—— 'L'islam hanbalisant', *Revue des Etudes Islamiques*, Paris, 1983.

—— *ibn ʿAqil*, Edinburgh, 1997.

Makdisi, John, 'Islamic law bibliography', *Law Library Journal*, 78, 1986.

Malash, Muḥammad Amīn Kāmel, *Sharḥ qānūn al-tijāra* (Commentary on the commercial law), 2 vols, Cairo, *ca.* 1928.

Mālik ibn Anas. See Saḥnūn.

al-Mālik, ibn ʿĀṣem, *Tuhfat al-ḥukkām fī niqāṭ al-ʿuqūd wal-ahkām* (The best decisions on the delicate points of contracts and judgments), text and translation Léon Bercher, Algiers, 1958.

Mallat, Chibli, 'Le féminisme islamique de Bint al-Houda', *Maghreb-Machrek*, 116, 1987.

—— 'The debate on *riba* and interest in twentieth century jurisprudence', in C. Mallat, ed., *Islamic law and finance*, London, 1988.

—— 'Religious militancy in contemporary Iraq: Muhammad Baqer as-Sadr and the Sunni-Shi'a paradigm', *Third World Quarterly*, spring 1988.

—— *Shi'i thought from the South of Lebanon*, Centre for Lebanese Studies, Oxford, 1988.

—— 'The Renaissance of Islamic law: Muhammad Baqer as-Sadr, Najaf and the Shi'i international', London Ph.D., 1990.

—— 'Introduction—Islamic family law; variations on state identity and community rights', in C. Mallat and J. Connors, eds, *Islamic family law*, London, 1990.

—— '*Madkhal ilal-adab al-ṣaghīr: al-mujtama' al-madanī, ḥuqūq al-aqalliyyāt wal-thaqāfa fil-mashriq* (Introduction to littérature mineure: civil society, minority rights and culture in the Mashreq)', *Al-ab'ād al-thaqāfiyya li-ḥuqūq al-insān fil-waṭan al-'arabī* (Cultural perspectives on human rights in the Arab world), Cairo, 1993.

—— 'Obstacles to democratization in Iraq: a reading of post-revolutionary Iraqi history through the Gulf War', *Rules and rights in the Middle East: democracy, law and society*, Seattle, 1993.

*—— *The renewal of Islamic law: Muhammad Baqer as-Sadr, Najaf and the Shi'i international*, Cambridge, 1993.

—— 'Law and the Nile river: emerging international rules and the *shari'a*', in J. A. Allan and P. Howell, eds, *The Nile: sharing a scarce resource*, Cambridge, 1994.

—— 'Readings of the Qur'an in Najaf and London: John Wansbrough and Muhammad Baqir al-Sadr', *Bulletin of the School of Oriental and African Studies*, 57:1, 1994.

—— 'Lebanon', in *Yearbook of Islamic and Middle Eastern Law*, i, 1994.

—— 'Un comparatiste anglais au XVIIIème siècle. Influences françaises sur la common law dans l'oeuvre de Lord Mansfield', *Revue Historique de Droit Français et Etranger*, 72, 1994.

—— 'Islamic law: reflections on the present state in Western research', *al-Abhath* (American University of Beirut), 43, 1995.

—— 'The quest for water use principles: reflections on *shari'a* and custom in the Middle East', in J. A. Allan and C. Mallat, eds, *Water in the Middle East: legal, political and commercial implications*, London, 1995.

—— 'Three recent decisions from the Yemen Supreme Court', *Islamic Law and Society*, 2, 1995.

—— 'Tantawi on banking operations in Egypt', in M. Masud, B. Messick, and D. Powers, eds, *Islamic legal interpretation: muftis and their fatwas*, Cambridge, Mass, 1996.

*—— *The Middle East into the 21st century*, Reading, 1996.

—— 'Comparative models of freedom of trade: the hurdle of Lebanese sole agency', in W. Shahin and K. Shehadi, eds, *Pathways to integration: Lebanon and the Euro-mediterranean partnership*, Beirut, 1997.

Mallat, Chibli, 'Joint ventures', in R. Naser and T. Kashishian, eds, *Lebanon and Europe: forging new partnerships*, Beirut, 1998.

—— *Tajdīd al-fiqh al-islāmī* (tr. of *The renewal of Islamic law*), Beirut, 1998.

—— 'The state of Islamic law research in the Middle East', *Asian Research Trends* (Tokyo), 8, 1998.

—— *Al-Dīmuqrāṭiyya fi Amīrka* (Democracy in America), Beirut, 2001.

—— 'Constitutionalism in Lebanon: continuities and discrepancies', Paper contributed to 'The Lebanese system: a critical reassessment', conference organized by the center for Behavioral Research (AUB and the Chiha Foundation, 18–19 May 2001.

—— 'The original sin: "terrorism" or "crime against humanity"?', *Case Western Journal of International Law*, 34, 2002.

—— 'Federalism in the Middle East and Europe', *Case Western Journal of International Law*, 35, 2003.

—— 'Renforcer la Société Civile contre l'Etat: Horizons du travail international au Proche et Moyen Orient,' commentaire sur le Rapport de la Banque Mondiale sur la Gouvernance au Proche et Moyen Orient (Etats PMO, MENA countries), Paris, 2003, 21 November 2003, <http.www.worldbank.org/europe>.

—— 'Constitutions for the 21st century: emerging patterns—the EU, Iraq, Afghanistan...', Herbert L. Bernstein Memorial Lecture in International and Comparative Law, Duke Law School, 28 September 2004.

—— 'Du fait religieux dans les institutions', in Chibli Mallat, ed., *L'Union Européenne et le Moyen-Orient: Etat des lieux*, Beirut, 2004.

—— 'La Nausée and Al-Nakba: rewriting 1948', *The Daily Star*, Beirut, 4 September 2004.

—— ed., *L'Union Européenne et le Moyen-Orient: Etat des lieux*, Beirut, 2004.

—— 'The need for a paradigm shift in American thinking: Middle Eastern responses to "what we are fighting for"', in John Borneman, ed., *The case of Ariel Sharon and the fate of universal jurisdiction*, Princeton, 2004.

—— *Awrāq ri'āsiyya* (Presidential papers), Beirut, 2005.

—— 'Islamic legal theory: introducing *usul al-fiqh*', in A. Peczenik, gen. ed., *Encyclopaedia of legal theory and philosophy of law*, <http://www.ivr-enc.info/en/article.php?id = 35>; also in *Islamic Law and Society*, 12, 2005.

—— 'Preface', in Sélim Abou, *Freedoms: cultural roots of the Cedar Revolution*, Beirut, 2005.

—— 'Comparative law and the Islamic (Middle Eastern) legal culture', in Mathias Reimann and Reinhard Zimmermann, eds, *The Oxford handbook of comparative law*, Oxford, 2006, 609–39.

—— 'On the philosophy of Islamic law', in Chibli Mallat and Leslie Tramontini, eds, *From Boston to Beirut via Baghdad, Festschrift for John Donohue*, Beirut, forthcoming.

—— 'Universalité de Michel Troper: du droit musulman', in Chibli Mallat, ed., 'Dossier—Philosophie du droit', *Travaux et Jours*, 2007.

—— and Connors, Jane, eds, *Islamic family law*, London, 1990.

Mallat, Tamer, *Aḥkām* (Judgments), Beirut, 1999.

Mallat, Wajdi, *Mawāqef—Positions*, Beirut, 2005.

Mammātī, ibn, *Kitāb qawānīn al-dawāwīn* (Rules of the ministries), Cairo, 1943.

Mandaville, Jon, 'Usurious piety: the cash *waqf* controversy in the Ottoman empire', *International Journal of Middle Eastern Studies*, 10, 1979.

Mango, Andrew, *The Turks today*, London, 2004.

Manẓūr, ibn, *Lisān al-'arab*, Beirut, 1959.

Maqrīzī, Ahmad ibn 'Alī, *Khitat*, 3 vols Beirut, 1959.

Marcus, Abraham, *The Middle East on the eve of modernity: Aleppo in the eighteenth century*, New York, 1989.

Marghīnānī, *al-Hidāya*, 4 vols, Beirut, 1999–.

Margoliouth, D.S., *The table-talk of a Mesopotamian judge: being the first part of the Nishwar al-muhadarah or Jami' al-tawarikh*, 2 vols, London, 1921–2.

Marx, Karl and Engels, Friedrich, *Sur la religion*, Paris, 1980.

Marwazī, al-*Kāfī*, Chester Beatty library, Dublin, ms. 4263.

al-Māwardī, *Adab al-qāḍī*, M. Sirḥān ed., 2 vols, Baghdad, 1971.

——— *al-Ḥāwī al-kabīr fī fiqh madhhab al-Imām al-Shāfiʿī radiya Allāh ʿanh: wa-huwa sharḥ Mukhtaṣar al-Muzanī*, 19 vols, Beirut, 1994.

Mayer, Ann Elizabeth, ed., *Property, social structure and law in the modern Middle East*, New York, 1985.

Al-Mays, Khalīl, *Fahāris kitāb al-mabsūṭ*, Beirut, 1978.

Mechbal, Abdellatif, 'Le rôle unificateur de la cour de cassation marocaine en matière commerciale' (read in Arabic at a conference on 'Les cours judiciaires suprêmes dans le monde arabe'), Beirut, 15 May 1999.

Melchert, Christopher, *The formation of the Sunni schools of law, 9th–10th centuries C.E.*, Leiden, 1997.

Meron, Yaakov, 'The Mejelle tested by its application', *Israel Law Journal*, 5, 1970.

Messarra, Antoine, *Théorie générale du système politique libanais*, Paris, 2004.

Messick, Brinkley, 'Prosecution in Yemen: the introduction of the *niyaba*', *International Journal of Middle East Studies*, 15, 1983.

——— *The calligraphic state: textual domination and history in a Muslim society*, Berkeley, 1993.

Mez, Adam, *The Renaissance of Islam*, London, 1937.

al-Milḥim, Aḥmad ʿAbd al-Raḥmān, '*Madā taqyīd ʿaqd al-quṣr lil-munāfasa al-raʾsiyya* (Restrictions on exclusive contracts by vertical competition rules)', *Majallat al-ḥuqūq* (Kuwait), 20, 1996.

Ministry of Justice (Egypt), *Al-Qānūn al-madanī, Majmūʿat al-aʿmāl al-taḥḍīriyya* (Travaux Préparatoires of the Civil Code), 7 vols, Cairo, 1949.

Mir-Hosseini, Ziba, *Marriage on trial. A study of Islamic family law*, London, 1993.

*Modarressi, Hossein, *An introduction to Shiʿi law*, London, 1984.

Modrzejewski, Joseph Mélèze, *Les juifs d'Egypte de Ramsès II à Hadrien*, Paris, 1997.

Montesquieu, *Pensées*, in *Oeuvres complètes*, Paris, 1964.

*Morcos [Murquṣ] Sulaimān, *Sharḥ al-qanūn al-madanī* (Commentary on civil law), 2 vols, Cairo, 1964, 1967.

——— *al-Masʾūliyya al-madaniyya fī taqnīnāt al-bilād al-ʿarabiyya* (Civil liability in the legislation of Arab countries), vol.1, Cairo, 1971.

Morris, Benny, *The birth of the Palestinian refugee problem revisited*, 2nd enlarged edn, Cambridge, 2004.

Mottahedeh, Roy, *The mantle of the prophet*, London, 1986.

——— 'Consultation and the political process in the Islamic Middle East of the 9th, 10th, and 11th Centuries', in Chibli Mallat ed., *Islam and public law*, London, 1993.

——— 'Some Islamic views of the pre-Islamic past', *Harvard Middle Eastern and Islamic Review*, 1, 1994.

Motzki, Harald, *Die Anfänge des Islamischen Jurisprudenz—Ihre Entwicklung in Mekka bis zur Mitte des 2./8. Jahrhunderts*, Stuttgart, 1991.

Moulay Rachid, Abderrazak, *La condition de la femme au Maroc*, Rabat, 1984.

al-mudhakkara al-īḍāḥiyya, al-qānūn al madanī al-sūrī (Introductory explanatory report, Syrian Civil Code), Nūrī ed., Damascus, n.d.

Muffs, Yochanan, *Studies in the Aramaic legal papyri from Elephantine*, Leiden, 2003.

Mughniyya, Muḥammad Jawād, *al-Aḥwāl al-shakhṣiyya* (Personal status law), Beirut, 1964.

Muḥammad, ʿAbd al-Raḥmān Fahmī, '*Wathāʾeq lil-taʿāqud min fajr al-islām* (Contractual documents from early Islam)', *Bulletin de l'Institut d'Egypte*, 53 and 54, 1971–2, 1972–3.

Mukhtaṣar ṣaḥīḥ Muslim, Muṣṭafā al-Bāgha ed., Damascus, 1990.

Mullā Khusraw, *Durar al-ḥukkām fī sharḥ Ghurar al-aḥkām*, 2 vols, Istanbul, 1844.

al-Muqaffaʿ, ibn, '*Risāla fil-ṣaḥāba*', in *Āthar* (Works), Beirut, 1966.

al-Murr, ʿAwad, 'The Supreme Constitutional Court of Egypt and the protection of human and political rights', in Chibli Mallat, ed., *Islam and public law*, London, 1993.

Mūsā, Ibrāhim ḥajj, *Al-tajriba al-dīmuqrāṭiyya wa taṭawwur naẓam al-ḥukm fil-Sūdān* (The democratic experiment and the development of the system of government in Sudan), Cairo, 1970.

Musā, ida, Jawdat, ed., *Al-qarārat al-ṣādira ʿan al-dīwān al-khāṣṣ fī tafsīr al-qawānīn wal-majlis al-ʿālī li-tafsīr al-dustūr min 1/1/1976 ilā 31/12/1991* (Decisions rendered by the Special Council for the Clarification of Legislation, and by the High Council for the Clarification of the Constitution from 1/1/1976 to 31/12/1991), ʿAmman, 1992.

Mustapha, Zaki, *Common law in the Sudan, an account of the 'justice, equity and good conscience provision'*, Oxford, 1971.

Mutahharī, Murtaḍā, *Nizām-i ḥuqūq-i zān dar Islām* (Legal rights of women in Islam), Qum, 1974.

Naef, Sylvia, 'Un réformiste chiite—Muhammad Husayn Al-Kashif al-Ghita', *Die Welt des Orients*, 27, 1996.

—— 'Communisme athée ou démocratie impérialiste? Le choix difficile d'un '*alim* chiite dans les premières années de la guerre froide', in *Proceedings of the 17th Congress of the UEAI*, St Petersburg, 1997.

Nahal, Galal, *The judicial administration of Ottoman Egypt in the seventeenth century*, Minneapolis, 1979.

an-Naʿim, Abdullahi Ahmad, *Toward an Islamic reformation: civil liberties, human rights and international law*, Syracuse, NY, 1990.

Nāʾīnī, Muḥammad Ḥusain, *Tanbīh al-umma wa tanzīh al-milla*, Najaf, 1906.

al-Najafī, Muḥammad Ḥasan, *Jawāhir al-kalām*, 15 vols, Beirut, 1992.

Najjar, Ibrahim, 'Le droit de la famille au Liban au xviiième et xixème siècles: Contribution à l'étude du droit des non-musulmans sous l'Empire Ottoman', *Proche-Orient Etudes Juridiques*, 40, Beirut, 1987.

—— *Droit matrimonial—successions*, 2nd edn, Beirut, 1997.

Najm, Marie-Claude, *Principes directeurs de droit international privé et conflit de civilisations, relations entre systèmes laïques et systèmes religieuxs*, Paris, 2005.

*Nallino, Carlo, *Raccolta di scritti editi e inediti*, vol. iv: *Diritto musulmano e diritti orientali cristiani*, Rome, 1942.

*Naqabat al-muḥāmīn (Bar association), Amman, *Al-mudhakkirāt al-īḍāḥiyya lil-qānūn al-madanī al-urdunī* (Explanatory Memoranda of the Jordanian Civil Code), Ibrāhīm Abūraḥmeh ed., 2 vols, 3rd edn, Amman, 1992.

al-Najafī, *Kanz al-daqaʾiq*, Zahan, Iran, 2003.

Nasir, Jamal, *The Islamic law of personal status*, London, 1986, new edn, 1990.

Naṣrallāh, Muḥammad Nāṣer, '*Tārīkh al-taḥkīm bi-dawlat al-Kuwait wa anwāʾuh* (History and types of arbitration in the state of Kuwait)', *al-Majalla al-lubnāniyya lil-taḥkīm al-ʿarabī wal-dawlī*, 3, 1996.

al-Nauimi, Najeeb, 'Qatar', in *Yearbook of Islamic and Middle Eastern Law*, iv, 1997–8.

Nawawī, M., Abū al-Faḍl Ibrāhīm, M., and Khafājī, M., 'Ṣaḥīḥ ibn ʿAbdallāh al-Bukhārī', in Bukhārī, *Ṣaḥīḥ*, Cairo, 1376/1956.

Noonan, John, *The scholastic analysis of usury*, Cambridge, Mass., 1957.

Nujaym, ibn, *Al-baḥr al-rā'eq fī sharḥ kanz al-daqā'iq*, with the supercommentary of ibn 'Ābidīn, 8 vols, Cairo, 1311.

*——— *Al-ashbāh wal-nazā'er*, Zakariyya 'Umairāt ed., Beirut, 1999.

al-Nu'mānī, Muḥammad Riḍā, *Al-shahīd al-ṣadr, sanawāt al-miḥna wa ayyām al-ḥiṣār* (Martyr al-Sadr, the tragic years and the days under siege), 2nd edn, Tehran, 1996.

al-Nuwaiḍī, 'Abdal-'Azīz, *Al-Majlis al-dustūrī bil-Maghreb* (The Moroccan constitutional court), Casablanca, 2001.

Ostrorog, Léon, *The Angora* [Ankara] *reform*, London, 1927.

Owen. Roger, ed., *New perspectives on property and land in the Middle East*, Cambridge, Mass., 2001.

——— *State, power and politics in the making of the modern Middle East*, 3rd edn, London, 2004.

Özel, Soli, 'Turkey at the polls: after the tsunami', *Journal of Democracy*, 14:2, April 2003.

Pascual, Jean-Paul, *Damas à la fin du XVIe siècle: d'après trois actes de waqf ottomans*, Damascus, 1983.

Patton, Walter, *Ahmed ibn Hanbal and the Mihna: a biography of the Imam including an account of the Mohammedan inquisition called the Mihna, 218–234 A.H.*, Leiden, 1897.

Pearl, David, *A textbook on Muslim personal law*, London, 1979, 2nd edn, 1987.

Peri, Yoram, *Between battles and ballots: Israeli military in politics*, Cambridge, 1983.

Perikhanian, Anait, 'Iranian society and law', *Cambridge History of Iran*, 3:2, *The Seleucid Parthian and Sasanian periods*, Cambridge, 1970.

Peters, Rudolph, '*Idjtihad* and *taqlid* in 18th and 19th century Islam', *Die Welt des Islams*, 20, 1980.

Piat, Théophile, *Code de commerce ottoman expliqué*, Beirut, 1293/1876.

Picard, Elisabeth, *Lebanon, a shattered country*, London, 1996.

Piccinelli, Gian Maria, *La società di persone nei paesi arabi*, Rome, 1990.

Playfair, Emma, ed., *International law and the administration of Occupied Territories*, Oxford, 1992.

*Postgate, J. N., *Early Mesopotamia: society and economy at the dawn of history*, London, 1992.

Pouzet, Louis, *Damas au VII/XIIIème siècle. Vie et structures religieuses dans une métropole islamique*, Beirut, 1988.

Powers, David, *Studies in Qur'an and hadith: the formation of the Islamic law of inheritance*, Berkeley, 1986.

——— 'A court case from fourteenth-century North Africa', *Journal of the American Oriental Society*, 110, 1990.

——— 'On judicial review in Islamic law', *Law and Society Review*, 26, 1992.

——— '*Futya* in medieval Spain and North Africa', in Chibli Mallat, ed., *Islam and public law*, london, 1993.

Price, Richard, 'United Arab Emirates', *Yearbook of Islamic and Middle Eastern Law*, ii, 1995.

——— and Al Tamimi, Essam, eds, *United Arab Emirates Court of Cassation judgments, 1989–1997*, The Hague, 1998.

—————— eds, *United Arab Emirates Court of Cassation judgments 1998–2003*, Leiden, 2005.

Pritchard, J. B. ed., *Ancient Near Eastern texts*, Princeton 3rd ed., 1969.

Qadrī, Muḥammad, *Kitāb murshid al-ḥayrān ilā ma'rifat aḥwāl al-insān fil-mu'āmalāt al-shar'iyya 'alā madhhab al-Imām al-a'ẓam Abī Ḥanīfa al-Nu'mān mulā'iman li-'urf al-diyār al-miṣriyya wa-sā'ir al-umam al-islāmiyya* (The guide to the perplexed about the individual's status in legal transactions according to the school of Abu Hanifa and corresponding to the customs of Egypt and other Islamic nations), Cairo, 1890.

al-Qalqashandī, Aḥmad ibn 'Abdallāh, *Subḥ al-a'shā*, Cairo, 14 vols, 1913–18.

Qarā'alī, 'Abdallāh, *Mukhtaṣar al-sharī'a*, Beirut, 1959.

*al-Qārī, Aḥmad ibn 'Abdallāh, *Majallat al-aḥkām al-shar'iyya*, 'Abdelwahāb Ibrāhīm Abū Suleimān and Muḥammad Ibrāhīm Aḥmad 'Alī eds, Djeddah, 1981.

Qattan, Najwa, 'The Damascene Jewish community in the latter decades of the eighteenth century: aspects of socio-economic life based on the registers of the sharia'a courts', in T. Philipp, ed., *The Syrian land in the eighteenth and nineteenth centuries: the common and the specfic in the historical experience*, Stuttgart, 1992.

Qudāmā, 'Abd Allāh ibn Aḥmad ibn, *al-Mughnī*, Beirut, 14 vols, 1984.

——— *al-Mughnī, wa-yalīh al-Sharḥ al-kabīr* (Gloss of Shams al-Dīn ibn Qudāma), 16 vols, Cario, 1996.

Qudāma, Shams al-Dīn ibn. See Qudāma, 'Abd Allāh ibn Aḥmad ibn, *al-Mughnī, wa-yalīh al-Sharḥ al- kabīr*.

Rabbath, Edmond, *Mahomet, prophète arabe et fondateur d'état*, Beirut, 1981.

Raddatz, Hans-Peter, 'Frühislamisches Erbrecht nach dem *Kitab al-Fara'id* des Sufyan at-Thawri, Edition und Kommentar', *Die Welt des Islams*, 13, 1971.

Rafeq, Abdul-Karim, 'Less registres des tribunaux', *Bulletin d'Etudes Orientales*, 1973.

——— 'The law-court registers of Damascus with special reference to craft-corporations during the first half of the eighteenth century', in J. Berque and Dominique Chevallier, eds, *Les Arabes par leurs archives XVIē–XXē siècles*, Paris, 1976.

——— 'The Islamic '*ulama*, Ottoman law and Islamic *sharī'a', Turcica*, 1994.

Raghib, Yusuf, *Marchands d'étoffes au Fayyoum au iii/ix siècle d'après leurs archives (actes et lettres). I, les actes des Banu Abd al-Mu'min*, Cairo, 1982.

Rajab, Ibn, *al-Qawā'ed*, ed. Ṭāha Sa'd, 2nd edn, Beirut, 1988.

Ramlī, Khayr al-Dīn, *al-Fatāwā al-khayriyya li naf' al-bariyya*, Beirut, 1974.

al-Rasheed, Madawi, *A history of Saudi Arabia*, Cambrige, 2002.

Rawls, John, *The law of peoples*, Cambridge, Mass, 1999.

Raymond, André, *Artisans et commerçants au Caire au xviiième siècle*, 2 vols, Damascus, 1973.

Reid, Donald Malcolm, *Cairo University and the making of modern Egypt*, Cambridge, 1990.

Repp, R. C., *The Müfti of Istanbul*, London, 1986.

Richards, Alan and Waterbury, John, *A political economy of the Middle East: state, class, and economic development*, Boulder, Colo., 1990, 2nd edn 1996.

al-Rifā'ī, Abdel Jabbār, ed., *Falsafat al-fiqh wa maqāṣed al-sharī'a* (Philosophy of law [*fiqh*] and meanings of law [*sharī'a*]), Beirut, 2001.

Roberson, Barbara Allen, 'The emergence of the modern judiciary in the Middle East', in C. Mallat, ed., *Islam and public law*, London, 1993, 102–39.

Roblets, Marie-Claire and Carlier, Jean-Yves, *Le Code marocain de la famille*, Brussels, 2005.

Rodinson, Maxime, *Mahomet*, Paris, 1961, new edn, 1968.

Rosen, Lawrence, *The anthropology of justice: law as culture in an Islamic society*, Cambridge, 1989.

Rosen, Lawrence, *The justicee of Islam*, Oxford, 2000.

Rosenthal, Franz, *The Muslim concept of freedom prior to the nineteenth century*, Leiden, 1960.

Rota and Adamides, 'Code Civil Ottoman', in George Young, ed., *Corps de droit ottoman*, vol. vi, Oxford, 1906.

Roth, Martha, 'The slave and the scoundrel CBS 10467, a Sumerian morality tale?', *Journal of the American Oriental Society*, 103, 1983.

Rowe, Peter, ed., *The Gulf War 1990–91 in international and English law*, London, 1993.

al-Ṣabbāgh, M., *Al-ḥadīth al-nabawī* (The Prophetic *ḥadīth*), 4th edn, Beirut, 1981.

Sádaba, F. J. Aguirre, 'Un documento de compraventa árabico-granadino', *Andalucía Islámica*, 1, 1980.

Ṣādeq, Maurice, *Al-aḥwāl al-shakhṣiyya li-ghayr al-muslimīn fī miṣr* (Law of personal status for non-Muslims in Egypt), Cairo, 1987.

al-Ṣadr, Muḥammad Bāqer, *Al-maʿālim al-jadīda fil-uṣūl* (The new configuration of *usul*), Beirut, 1964.

—— *Al-bank al-lā ribawī fil-Islām* (Interest-free bank in Islam), Kuwait, 1969.

—— *Iqtiṣādunā* (Our economic system), Beirut, 1977.

—— *Durūs fī ʿilm al-uṣūl* (Studies in jurisprudence), 4 vols, Beirut-Najaf, 1978–80.

al-Ṣadūq, al-Shaykh ibn Bābawayh al-Qummi, *al-Amālī*, Tehran, 1996.

Saeed, Abdullah, *Islamic banking and interest: a study of the prohibition of riba and its contemporary interpretation*, Leiden, 1997.

Safa, Rashid, 'Perspectives on bank failures in the Middle East', in H. Lewis Ruttley and C. Mallat, eds, *Commercial law in the Middle East*, London, 1995.

Safaʾi, Ḥusayn, *Ḥuqūq-i madanī* (Civil law), 2 vols, Tehran, 2003.

Ṣaḥīḥ al-Bukhārī, Muḥammad and Nizār Tamīm eds., Beirut 1995.

Saḥnūn, *al-Mudawwana al-kubrā* [li-Mālik ibn Anas], 16 vols, Cairo, 1906.

—— *al-Mudawwana al-kubrā*, 9 vols, Cairo, 1999.

Said, Edward, *Orientalism*, London, 1978.

al-Saʿīdī, ʿAbd al-Mitʿāl *al-Mujaddidūn fil-Islām, min al-qarn al-awwal ilal-rābiʿ ʿashar* (The reformers in Islam, from the 1first to the fourteenth centuries), Cairo, n.d.

Saïdi, Kamel, 'La réforme du droit algérien de la famille: pérennité et rénovation', *Revue Internationale de Droit Comparé*, 2006.

Saidi, Nasser and Nasr, Samir, *The development of Lebanon's capital markets*, Beirut, 1995.

al-Ṣalāḥ, ibn, *Muqadimma fī ʿulūm al-ḥadīth* (Introduction to the science of *hadith*), Damascus, 1984.

—— Adab al-muftī wal-mustaftī, Beirut, 1986.

Saleh, Nabil, *Unlawful gain and legitimate profit in Islamic law*, Cambridge, 1986, 2nd edn, London, 1992.

—— 'Civil codes of Arab countries: The Sanhuri Codes', *Arab Law Quarterly*, 8, 1993.

Ṣāliḥ Subḥī *Ulūm al-ḥadīth, wa-muṣṭalaḥuhu: ʿard wa-dirāsah* (Science and terminology of *hadith*: presentation and study), Damascus, 1959.

al-Sanʿānī, ʿAbd al-Razzāq, *al-Muṣannaf*, Ḥabīb al-Aʿẓamī ed., 11 vols, Beirut, 1970–2.

Sanhoury, A. A. [Sanhūrī], *Les Restrictions contractuelles à la liberté individuelle du travail dans la jurisprudence anglaise*, Paris, 1925.

—— *Le Califat*, Paris, 1926.

—— *Naẓariyyat al-ʿaqd* (Theory of contract), Cairo, 1934.

—— 'La responsabilité civile et pénale en droit musulman', *Revue al-Qanun wal-Iqtisad*, Cairo, 15, 1945.

* al-Sanhūrī, ʿAbd al-Razzāq, *Maṣadier al-ḥaqq fī al-fiqh al-islāmī* (Sources of law in Islamic law), 6 vols, Cairo, 1954–9.

——*Al-Wasīt fī sharḥ al-qānūn al-madanī al-jadīd* (Medium commentary on the new Civil Code), 12 vols, Cairo, 1952–70.

al-Sanhūrī, Nādiā and al-Shāwī, Tawfīq, *'Abd al-Razzāq al-Sanhūrī min khilāl awrāqih al-shakhṣiyya* (Sanhuri through his private papers), Cairo, 1988.

*Santillana, David, 'Preface' to *Majallat al-iltizāmāt wal-'uqūd al-tūnisiyya* (Tunisian Code of obligations and contracts), Maḥmūd ibn al-Shaykh ed., Tunis, 1984.

*al-Sarakhsī, Shams al-Dīn, *al-Mabsūṭ*, 30 vols, Cairo, 1909.

Sayigh, Yazid, *Armed struggle and the search for state: the Palestinian national movement, 1949–1993*, Oxford, 1997.

Schacht, Joseph, 'Foreign elements in ancient Islamic law', *Journal of Comparative Law*, 3–4, 1950.

—— *The origins of Muhammadan jurisprudence*, Oxford, 1950.

—— *An introduction to Islamic law*, Oxford, 1964.

—— 'Modernism and traditionalism in a history of Islamic law', *Middle Eastern Studies*, 1, 1965.

Schirazi, Asghar, *The Constitution of Iran*, London, 1997.

Schluchter, Wolfgang, ed., *Max Webers Sicht des Islams: Interpretation und Kritik*, Frankfurt, 1987.

Schotta, Charles, 'Islamic banking and the U.S. regulatory climate', in Islamic banking and finance conference, *Proceedings*, Washington, DC, 25–6 September 1986.

Schulze, Rheinhardt, *Islamischer Internationalismus im 20. Jahrhundert: Untersuchungen zur Geschichte der Islamischen Weltliga (Mekka)*, Leiden, 1990.

Selb, Walter and Kaufhold, Hubert, *Das Syrisch-Römische Rechtsbuch*, 3 vols, Vienna, 2002.

Sfeir, George N., *Modernization of the law in Arab states*, San Francisco, 1998.

Shaddād, ibn, *Tārīkh al-malik al-ẓāhir*, Beirut, 1983.

al-Shāfi'ī, *al-Umm*, 7 vols, Cairo, 1903–8.

*—— *al-Risāla*, Aḥmad Muḥammad Shāker ed., Cairo, 1939.

Shaham, Ron, *Family and the courts in modern Egypt. A study based on decisions by the shari'a courts 1900–1955*, Leiden, 1993.

Shalabī, Fathiyya, *Mashrū' qānūn 'arabī muwaḥḥad lil-aḥwal al-shakhṣiyya* (Arab Family Law Project), Cairo, n.d.

Shamir, Ronen, *The colonies of law: colonialism, Zionism and law in early Mandate Palestine*, Cambridge, 2000.

al-Shammīrī, Nagīb, *Ḥuqūq al-mar'a fī tashrī'at al-yaman al-dimūqratiyya* (The rights of women in the laws of Democratic Yemen), Aden, 1984.

—— 'The judicial system in democratic Yemen', in B. Pridham, ed., *Contemporary Yemen: politics and historical background*, London, 1984.

Shapiro, Martin, 'Islam and appeal', *California Law Review*, 68, 1980.

al-Shāṭibī, Ibrāhim ibn Mūsā, *al-Muwāfaqāt*, 'Abdallah Darāz ed., 4 vols, Beirut, 1975.

Shaw, Stanford, *History of the Ottoman empire and modern Turkey*, Cambridge, vol.1, 1976; vol. 2 (with Ezel Kural Shaq), 1977.

Shawkānī, *Nayl al-awṭār*, 10 vols, Beirut, n.d.

Shaybānī, *Kitāb al-Aṣl*, Shafiq Shiḥāta [= Chafic Chehata] ed., Cairo, 1954.

—— *Kitāb al-Aṣl*, Abul Wafā' al-Afghānī ed., Beirut, 1990 (orig. edn, Haydarabad, 1386/1966).

Shbārū, 'Iṣām, *Al-qaḍā' wal-quḍāt fil-islām* (The judiciary and judges in Islam), 2 vols, Beirut, 1982.

——— *Qāḍī al-quḍāt* (The chief justice), Beirut, 1986.

Shehadeh, Raja, *From occupation to interim accords: Israel and the Palestinian Territories*, London, 1997.

Shetreet, Shimon, *Justice in Israel: a study of the Israeli judiciary*, Dordrecht, 1994.

al-Shirāzī, Ṣadr al-Dīn (known as Mulla Ṣadrā), *Al-Ḥikma al-mutaʿāliya fil-asfār al-ʿaqliyya al-arbaʿa* (The four philosophical voyages), 9 vols, Qum, n.d.

Siddiqui, Mona, 'Law and desire for social control: an insight into the Hanafi concept of *kafāʾa* with reference to the *Fatawa ʿAlamgiri* (1664–1672)', in Mai Yamani, ed., *Feminism and Islam*, London, 1996.

Skovgaard-Petersen, J., *Defining Islam for the Egyptian state: muftis and fatwas of the dar al-iftā*, Leiden, 1997.

Slaughter, Anne-Marie and Ikenberry, John, eds, *Forging a world of liberty under law: US national security in the 21st Century*, Princeton, 2006.

Snouck-Hurgronje, C., 'Le droit musulman', in *Selected works*, Leiden, 1957.

Sontheimer, Gunther-Dietz and Aithal, Parameswara Kota, eds, *Indology and the law: studies in honour of Professor M. Derrett*, Wiesbaden, 1982.

Soroush, Abdolkarim = Surūsh, ʿAbd al-Karīm, *Qabz va baṣt-i tiūrīk-i sharī ʿat* (constriction and expansion of the theory of Islamic law), Tehran, 1991.

——— *Reason, freedom, and democracy in Islam: essential writings of Abdolkarim Soroush*, Mahmoud Sadri and Ahmad Sadri, trs. And eds., New York, 2000.

'Special Dossier on the "Sabra and Shatila" case in Belgium', *The Palestine Yearbook of International Law*, 12, 2002–3.

Starr, June, *Law as metaphor: from Islamic courts to the Palace of Justice*, Albany, NY, 1992.

Steensgaard, N., *Carracks, caravans and companies*, Copenhagen, 1973.

Steinkeller, Piotr, 'The renting of fields in early Mesopotamia and the development of the concept of "interest" in Sumerian', *Journal of the Economic and Social History of the Orient*, 24, 1981.

Stewart, F. H., 'Tribal law in the Arab world: a review of the literature', *International Journal of Middle East Studies*, 19, 1987.

Steyn, Johan, 'Guantanamo Bay: the legal black hole', *International and Comparative Law Quarterly*, 53, 2004.

Stilt, Kristen, 'Islamic law and the making and remaking of the Iraqi legal system', *George Washington International Law Review*, 36, 2004.

al-Subkī, Taqi al-Dīn, *Fatāwā*, 2 vols, Beirut, 1992.

al-Suyūṭī Jalāl al-Dīn, *Kitāb al-radd ʿalā man ukhlida ilal-arḍ wa jahila anna al-ijtihād fī kulli ʿasrin farḍ*, Khalīl al-Mays ed., Beirut, n.d.

Syrisch-Römisches Rechtsbuch aus dem fünften Jahrhundert, Karl Georg Bruns und Eduard Sachau eds, Aalen, 1961 (repr. of Leipzig, 1880).

Szlechter, Emile, *Les lois d'Esnuna*, Paris, 1954.

——— 'La "loi" dans la Mésopotamie Ancienne', *Revue Internationale des Droits de l'Antiquité*, 12, 1965.

Ṭabāṭabāʾī, Aḥmad, 'Al-Āthar al-qānūniyya al-mutarattiba ʿalā ḥukm al-maḥkama al-dustūriyya 1/1994 (Legal consequences deriving from the Constitutional Court's decision 1/1994)', *al-Muḥāmī* (Kuwait), 18, August–September 1994.

Tadmurī, ʿUmar, *Wathāʾeq nādira min sijillāt al-maḥkama al-sharʿiya bi-ṭarablus* (Rare documents from the records of the sharʿi court in Tripoli), Beirut, 2002.

*——Maʿtūq, Frederic, and Ziādeh, Khāled, eds, *Wathāʾeq al-maḥkama al-sharʿiyya bi-ṭarablus* (Documents of the sharʿi court of Tripoli), Tripoli, 1982.

Taghrībirdī, ibn, *al-Nujūm al-zāhira fī mulūk miṣr wal-qāhirah*, 16 vols, Cairo, 1963–71.

al-Tannūkhi, Muḥassin ibn ʿAlī, *Nishwar al-muhadarah*, ʿAbbūd al-Shālijī ed., 8 vols, Beirut, 1971–3.

——*al-Faraj baʿd al-shidda*, ʿAbbūd al-Shālijī ed., 5 vols, Beirut, 1978.

Tarazi, A. M., 'Saudi Arabia's new Basic Laws: the struggle for participatory Islamic government', *Harvard International Law Journal*, 34, 1993.

Taylor, Michael, 'Islamic commercial banking—moving into the mainstream?' *The Transnational Lawyer*, 18, 2005.

Terré, François, *Droit civil: les obligations*, 6th edn, Paris, 1996.

——ed., *L'américanisation du droit*, Paris, 2001.

Timur, Hifzu, 'Civil marriage in Turkey: difficulties, causes and remedies', *International Social Sciences Bulletin*, 9, 1957.

Tocqueville, Alexis de, *Démocratie en Amérique*, 2 vols, Paris, 1951.

Topakian, Méliné, 'Notes sommaires sur le contrat de vente dans les codes proche-orientaux', *Proche-Orient Etudes Juridiques*, 1965.

Torrey, C. C., *The commercial-theological terms in the Koran*, Leiden, 1892.

al-Ṭrābulsī, Muḥammad Kāmel ibn Muṣṭafā ibn Maḥmūd, *al-Fatāwā al-kāmiliyya fil-ḥawādeth al-ṭrābulsiyya*, n.d, n.p.

Travaux de la semaine internationale de droit, Paris 1950—L'influence du Code Civil dans le monde, Paris, 1954.

Treitel, Gunter, *The law of contract*, London, 1991.

Troper, Michel, *Philosophie du droit*, Paris, 2003.

Tucker, Judith, *In the house of the law: gender and Islamic law in ottoman Syria and Palestine*, Berkeley, 1998.

Tūsī, *Tahdhīb al-aḥkām*, 10 vols, Tehran, 1997.

Tyan, Emile, *Le système de responsabilité délictuelle en droit musulman*, Beirut, 1926.

——Histoire de l'organisation judiciaire en pays d'Islam, 2 vols, Paris, 1938–43. In one vol, Leiden, 1960.

——'Le notariat et le régime de la preuve par écrit dans la pratique du droit musulman', *Annales de la Faculté de Droit de Beyrouth*, 2, 1945.

——*Notes sommaires sur le nouveau régime successoral au Liban*, Paris, 1960.

*Udovitch, Abraham, *Partnership and profit in medieval Islam*, Princeton, 1970.

——'Les échanges de marché dans l'Islam médiéval: Théorie du droit et savoir local', *Studia Islamica*, 65, 1987.

——'Merchants and *amirs*: government and trade in eleventh century Egypt', *Asian and African Studies*, 22, 1988.

United States Commission on International Religious Freedom, *The Religion-state relationship and the right to freedom of religion or belief: A comparative textual analysis of the constitutions of predominantly Muslim countries*, Washington, 2005.

Vandevelde, Hélène, 'Où en est le problème du code de la famille en Algérie?', *Maghreb-Machrek*, 97, 1982.

——'Le code algérien de la famille', *Maghreb-Machrek*, 107, 1985.

Vermes, Geza, *The Dead Sea Scrolls in English*, 4th edn, London, 1995.

Vesey-Fitzgerald, S., *Muhammadan law*, London, 1931.

Vogel, Frank, *Islamic law and legal system: studies of Saudi Arabia*, Leiden, 2000.

—— and Hayes, Samuel, *Islamic law and finance. Religion, risk and return*, London, 1998.

Wāhan Effendī, *Sharḥ qānūn al-tijāra* (commentary on the commercial code), Arabic translation by Nuqūla Naqqāsh, Beirut 1297/1880, in Ibrāhīm Sāder, ed., *Majmū'at al-qawānīn al-'adliyya* (Collection of civil laws), Beirut, n.d.

Wakī', *Akhbār al-quḍāt* (Stories of judges), 3 vols, Cairo, 1366–9/1947–50.

Wakin, Jeannette, *The function of documents in Islamic law*, Albany, NY, 1972.

Wali, Fathi, *Qanun al-qada' al-madani al-kwaiti* (The Law of Kuwaiti civil judiciary), Kuwait, 1977.

Wansbrough, John, *Quranic studies: sources and methods of scriptural interpretation*, Oxford, 1977.

—— *The sectarian milieu: content and composition of Islamic salvation history*, Oxford, 1978.

—— *Lingua franca in the Mediterranean*, London, 1996.

al-Wanscharisi, Ahmad, *La pierre de touche des fétwas; choix de consultation juridiques des faqihs du Maghreb*, Émile Amar, tr. and ed., 2 vols, Paris, 1908–9.

—— *al-Mi'yār al-mughrib wal-jāmi' al-mu'rib 'an fatāwā ahl ifrīqiyā wal-andalus wal-maghrib*, 13 vols, Beirut, 1981–3.

Warde, Ibrahim, *BCCI: perspectives from North and South*, Berkeley, 1991.

*—— *Islamic finance in the global economy*, Edinburgh, 2000.

al-Wardī, 'Alī, '*Nāder Qalī wa mashrū' al-madhhab al-khāmes* (Nader Qali and the project of the fifth school)', in *Lamaḥāt ijtimā'iyya min tārīkh al-'irāq al-ḥadīth* (Social approaches to the history of modern Iraq), Baghdad, 1969–79.

Watt, Montgomery, *Muhammad at Mecca*, Oxford, 1953.

—— *Muhammad at Medina*, Oxford, 1956.

Weber, Max, *Economy and society*, 3 vols, Berkeley, 1968.

Weiss, Bernard, 'Interpretation in Islamic law: the theory of *ijtihad*', *American Journal of Comparative Law*, 26, 1978.

—— *The search for God's law: Islamic jurisprudence in the writings of Sayf al-Dīn al-Amidī*, Salt Lake City, 1992.

—— 'Introduction', in Bernard Weiss, ed., *Studies in Islamic legal theory*, Leiden, 2002.

Welchman, Lynn, 'The development of Islamic family law in the legal system of Jordan', *International and Comparative Law Quarterly*, 37, 1988.

*Wensinck, A. J. (completed by J. P. Mensing), *Concordance et indices de la tradition musulmane: les Six Livres, le Musnad d'al-Darimi, le Muwatta' de Malik, le Musnad de Ahmad ibn Hanbal*, 8 vols in 4, orig. edn. 1936–88, Leiden, 2nd edn, 1992.

Westbrook, Raymond, *Studies in Biblical and cuneiform laws*, Paris, 1988.

—— 'Biblical law', in N. S. Hecht, B. S. Jackson, S. M. Passamaneck, Daniela Piattelli, and Alfredo Rabello eds, *An Introduction to the history and sources of Jewish law*, Oxford, 1996.

Whitman, James, 'Long live the hatred of Roman law!', *Rechtsgeschichte*, 2, 2003.

Wiederhold, Lutz, 'Legal-religious elite, temporal authority, and the caliphate in Mamluk society: conclusions drawn from the examination of a "Zahiri revolt" in Damascus in 1386', *International Journal of Middle East Studies*, 31, 1999.

Wilson, David and Alder, Richie, 'Oman', *Yearbook of Islamic and Middle Eastern Law*, iv, 1997–8.

Wittfogel, Karl, *Oriental Despotism: a comparative study of total power*, New Haven, 1957.

World Bank, Middle East and North Africa, *Economic developments and prospects 2006, Financial markets in a new age of oil*, Washington, 2006.

Yamani, Mai, 'Some observations on women in Saudi Arabia', in Mai Yamani, ed., *Feminism and Islam*, London, 1996.

—— *The Hijaz and the quest for an Islamic identity*, London, 2004.

Yapp, Malcolm, *The Near East since the First World War: a history to 1995*, London, 1996.

Yaron, Reuven, *The laws of Eshnunna*, Jerusalem-Leiden, 1969, 2nd rev. edn, 1988.

Yergin, Daniel, *The Prize, the epic quest for oil, money, and power*, New York, 1991.

Zahlan, Rosemarie Said, *The Making of the modern Gulf states: Kuwait, Bahrain, Qatar, the United Arab Emirates and Oman*, London rev. edn, 1999, orig. 1978.

Zahū, Muḥammad Abū, *Makānat al-sunna fī al-islām* (The place of *sunna* in Islam), Cairo, 1984.

al-Zarqā, Muṣṭafā, *al-Fiqh al-islāmī fī thawbihi al-jadīd* (Islamic law in its new robe), Damascus c.1960.

Ziadeh, Farhat, 'Equality (*Kafa'ah*) in the Muslim Law of Marriage', *American Journal of Comparative Law*, 6, 1957.

—— *Lawyers, the rule of law, and liberalism in modern Egypt*, Palo Alto, Calif., 1968.

—— *Property law in the Arab world*, Leiden, 1979.

*Ziādeh, Khāled, *Al-ṣūra al-taqlīdiyya lil-mujtamaʿ al-madīnī* (The traditional image of urban society), Tripoli, 1983.

—— *Arkeolōgia al-muṣṭalaḥ al-wathāʾiqī* (The archeology of documentary terminology), Tripoli, 1986.

—— '*Hal al-ijtihād amr mumkin, qirāʾa fī malaff al-ijtihād wal-tajaddud* (is *ijtihad* possible? A reading in the dossier on legal interpretation and renewal)', *Al-Ijtihād*, 11–12, 1991.

al-Zubaydī, *Tāj al-ʿarūs*, Benghazi, n.d.

al-Zuḥaylī, Wahbeh, *Naẓariyyat al-ḍamān fil-fiqh al-islāmī* (Theory of responsibility in Islamic law), Damascus, 1970.

—— al-Fiqh al-islāmī wa-adillatuhu: al-shāmil lil-adilla al-sharʿiyya wal-āraʾ al-madhhabiyya (Islamic law and its reasons: compendium of legal arguments and school opinions), Damascus, 1984.

Zwaini, Leila and Peters, Rudolph, *A bibliography of Islamic law 1980–1993*, Leiden, 1994.

*Zweigert, Konrad and Kötz, Hein, *An introduction to comparative law*, Tony Weir tr., 3rd edn, Oxford, 1998.

Index